Poetry
for Students

Poetry for Students

**Presenting Analysis, Context and Criticism on
Commonly Studied Poetry**

Volume 8

Mary K. Ruby and
Ira Mark Milne,

Editors

Foreword by David Kelly, College of Lake County

GALE GROUP

Detroit
New York
San Francisco
London
Boston
Woodbridge, CT

Poetry for Students

Staff

Series Editors: Mary Ruby and Ira Mark Milne.

Managing Editor: Dwayne D. Hayes.

Research: Victoria B. Cariappa, *Research Team Manager.* Andy Malonis and Cheryl Warnock, *Research Specialist.* Corrine A. Boland, Tamara C. Nott, and Tracie A. Richardson, *Research Associates.* Timothy Lehnerer, Patricia Love, *Research Assistants.*

Permissions: Maria Franklin, *Permissions Manager.* Kelly Quin, *Permissions Associate.* Erin Bealmear, *Permissions Assistant.*

Production: Mary Beth Trimper, *Production Director.* Evi Seoud, *Assistant Production Manager.* Stacy Melson, *Production Assistant.*

Imaging and Multimedia Content Team: Randy Bassett, *Image Database Supervisor.* Robert Duncan and Michael Logusz, *Imaging Specialists.* Pamela A. Reed, *Imaging Coordinator.*

Product Design Team: Cynthia Baldwin, *Product Design Manager.* Cover Design: Michelle DiMercurio, *Art Director.* Page Design: Pamela A. E. Galbreath, *Senior Art Director.* Gary Leach, *Graphic Artist.*

Copyright Notice

National Advisory Board

Table of Contents

Just a Few Lines on a Page

I have often thought that poets have the easiest job in the world. A poem, after all, is just a few lines on a page, usually not even extending margin to margin—how long would that take to write, about five minutes? Maybe ten at the most, if you wanted it to rhyme or have a repeating meter. Why, I could start in the morning and produce a book of poetry by dinnertime. But we all know that it isn't that easy. Anyone can come up with enough words, but the poet's job is about writing the *right* ones. The right words will change lives, making people see the world somewhat differently than they saw it just a few minutes earlier. The right words can make a reader who relies on the dictionary for meanings take a greater responsibility for his or her own personal understanding. A poem that is put on the page correctly can bear any amount of analysis, probing, defining, explaining, and interrogating, and something about it will still feel new the next time you read it.

It would be fine with me if I could talk about poetry without using the word "magical," because that word is overused these days to imply "a really good time," often with a certain sweetness about it, and a lot of poetry is neither of these. But if you stop and think about magic—whether it brings to mind sorcery, witchcraft, or bunnies pulled from top hats—it always seems to involve stretching reality to produce a result greater than the sum of its parts and pulling unexpected results out of thin air. This book provides ample cases where a few simple words conjure up whole worlds. We do not ac-tually travel to different times and different cultures, but the poems get into our minds, they find what little we know about the places they are talking about, and then they make that little bit blossom into a bouquet of someone else's life. Poets make us think we are following simple, specific events, but then they leave ideas in our heads that cannot be found on the printed page. Abracadabra.

Sometimes when you finish a poem it doesn't feel as if it has left any supernatural effect on you, like it did not have any more to say beyond the actual words that it used. This happens to everybody, but most often to inexperienced readers: regardless of what is often said about young people's infinite capacity to be amazed, you have to understand what usually does happen, and what could have happened instead, if you are going to be moved by what someone has accomplished. In those cases in which you finish a poem with a "So what?" attitude, the information provided in *Poetry for Students* comes in handy. Readers can feel assured that the poems included here actually are potent magic, not just because a few (or a hundred or ten thousand) professors of literature say they are: they're significant because they can withstand close inspection and still amaze the very same people who have just finished taking them apart and seeing how they work. Turn them inside out, and they will still be able to come alive, again and again. *Poetry for Students* gives readers of any age good practice in feeling the ways poems relate to both the reality of the time and place the poet lived in and the reality of our emotions. Practice is just another word for being a student. The information given here helps you understand the way to read poetry; what to look for, what to expect.

With all of this in mind, I really don't think I would actually like to have a poet's job at all. There are too many skills involved, including precision, honesty, taste, courage, linguistics, passion, compassion, and the ability to keep all sorts of people entertained at once. And that is just what they do

with one hand, while the other hand pulls some sort of trick that most of us will never fully understand. I can't even pack all that I need for a weekend into one suitcase, so what would be my chances of stuffing so much life into a few lines? With all that *Poetry for Students* tells us about each poem, I am impressed that any poet can finish three or four poems a year. Read the inside stories of these poems, and you won't be able to approach any poem in the same way you did before.

David J. Kelly
College of Lake County

Introduction

Purpose of the Book

The purpose of *Poetry for Students* (*PfS*) is to provide readers with a guide to understanding, enjoying, and studying poems by giving them easy access to information about the work. Part of Gale's "For Students" Literature line, *PfS* is specifically designed to meet the curricular needs of high school and undergraduate college students and their teachers, as well as the interests of general readers and researchers considering specific poems. While each volume contains entries on "classic" poems frequently studied in classrooms, there are also entries containing hard-to-find information on contemporary poems, including works by multicultural, international, and women poets.

The information covered in each entry includes an introduction to the poem and the poem's author; the actual poem text; a poem summary, to help readers unravel and understand the meaning of the poem; analysis of important themes in the poem; and an explanation of important literary techniques and movements as they are demonstrated in the poem.

In addition to this material, which helps the readers analyze the poem itself, students are also provided with important information on the literary and historical background informing each work. This includes a historical context essay, a box comparing the time or place the poem was written to modern Western culture, a critical overview essay, and excerpts from critical essays on the

poem, when available. A unique feature of *PfS* is a specially commissioned overview essay on each poem by an academic expert, targeted toward the student reader.

To further aid the student in studying and enjoying each poem, information on media adaptations is provided when available, as well as reading suggestions for works of fiction and nonfiction on similar themes and topics. Classroom aids include ideas for research papers and lists of critical sources that provide additional material on the poem.

Selection Criteria

The titles for each volume of *PfS* were selected by surveying numerous sources on teaching literature and analyzing course curricula for various school districts. Some of the sources surveyed included: literature anthologies; *Reading Lists for College-Bound Students: The Books Most Recommended by America's Top Colleges;* textbooks on teaching the poem; a College Board survey of poems commonly studied in high schools; and a National Council of Teachers of English (NCTE) survey of poems commonly studied in high schools.

Input was also solicited from our expert advisory board, as well as educators from various areas. From these discussions, it was determined that each volume should have a mix of "classic" poems (those works commonly taught in literature classes) and contemporary poems for which information is often hard to find. Because of the interest in expanding the canon of literature, an emphasis was also placed on including works by international, multicultural, and women authors. Our advisory board members—current high school and college teachers—helped pare down the list for each volume. If a work was not selected for the present volume, it was often noted as a possibility for a future volume. As always, the editor welcomes suggestions for titles to be included in future volumes.

How Each Entry Is Organized

Each entry, or chapter, in *PfS* focuses on one poem. Each entry heading lists the full name of the poem, the author's name, and the date of the poem's publication. The following elements are contained in each entry:

- **Introduction:** a brief overview of the poem which provides information about its first appearance, its literary standing, any controversies surrounding the work, and major conflicts or themes within the work.

- **Author Biography:** this section includes basic facts about the poet's life, and focuses on events and times in the author's life that inspired the poem in question.

- **Poem Text:** when permission has been granted, the poem is reprinted, allowing for quick reference when reading the explication of the following section.

- **Poem Summary:** a description of the major events in the poem, with interpretation of how these events help articulate the poem's themes. Summaries are broken down with subheads that indicate the lines being discussed.

- **Themes:** a thorough overview of how the major topics, themes, and issues are addressed within the poem. Each theme discussed appears in a separate subhead and is easily accessed through the boldface entries in the Subject/Theme Index.

- **Style:** this section addresses important style elements of the poem, such as form, meter, and rhyme scheme; important literary devices used, such as imagery, foreshadowing, and symbolism; and, if applicable, genres to which the work might have belonged, such as Gothicism or Romanticism. Literary terms are explained within the entry, but can also be found in the Glossary.

- **Historical and Cultural Context:** This section outlines the social, political, and cultural climate *in which the author lived and the poem was created.* This section may include descriptions of related historical events, pertinent aspects of daily life in the culture, and the artistic and literary sensibilities of the time in which the work was written. If the poem is a historical work, information regarding the time in which the poem is set is also included. Each section is broken down with helpful subheads. (Works written after the late 1970s may not have this section.)

- **Critical Overview:** this section provides background on the critical reputation of the poem, including bannings or any other public controversies surrounding the work. For older works, this section includes a history of how poem was first received and how perceptions of it may have changed over the years; for more recent poems, direct quotes from early reviews may also be included.

- **Sources:** an alphabetical list of critical material quoted in the entry, with full bibliographical information.

- **For Further Study:** an alphabetical list of other critical sources which may prove useful for the student. Includes full bibliographical information and a brief annotation.

- **Criticism:** at least one essay commissioned by *PfS* which specifically deals with the poem and is written specifically for the student audience, as well as excerpts from previously published criticism on the work, when available.

In addition, most entries contains the following highlighted sections, set separately from the main text:

- **Media Adaptations:** a list of audio recordings as well as any film or television adaptations of the poem, including source information.

- **Compare and Contrast Box:** an "at-a-glance" comparison of the cultural and historical differences between the author's time and culture and late twentieth-century Western culture. This box includes pertinent parallels between the major scientific, political, and cultural movements of the time or place the poem was written, the time or place the poem was set (if a historical work), and modern Western culture. Works written after the mid-1970s may not have this box.

- **What Do I Read Next?:** a list of works that might complement the featured poem or serve as a contrast to it. This includes works by the same author and others, works of fiction and nonfiction, and works from various genres, cultures, and eras.

- **Study Questions:** a list of potential study questions or research topics dealing with the poem. This section includes questions related to other disciplines the student may be studying, such as American history, world history, science, math, government, business, geography, economics, psychology, etc.

Other Features

PfS includes a foreword by David J. Kelly, an instructor and cofounder of the creative writing periodical of Oakton Community College. This essay provides a straightforward, unpretentious explanation of why poetry should be marveled at and how *Poetry for Students* can help teachers show students how to enrich their own reading experiences.

A Cumulative Author/Title Index lists the authors and titles covered in each volume of the *PfS* series.

A Cumulative Nationality/Ethnicity Index breaks down the authors and titles covered in each volume of the *PfS* series by nationality and ethnicity.

A Subject/Theme Index, specific to each volume, provides easy reference for users who may be studying a particular subject or theme rather than a single work. Significant subjects from events to broad themes are included, and the entries pointing to the specific theme discussions in each entry are indicated in **boldface.**

Illustrations are included with entries when available, including photos of the author and other graphics related to the poem.

Citing Poetry for Students

When writing papers, students who quote directly from any volume of *Poetry for Students* may use the following general forms. These examples are based on MLA style; teachers may request that students adhere to a different style, so the following examples may be adapted as needed.

When citing text from *PfS* that is not attributed to a particular author (i.e., the Themes, Style,

Historical Context sections, etc.), the following format should be used in the bibliography section:

"Angle of Geese." *Poetry for Students.* Eds. Marie Napierkowski and Mary Ruby. Vol. 1. Detroit: Gale, 1997. 8–9.

When quoting the specially commissioned essay from *PfS* (usually the first piece under the "Criticism" subhead), the following format should be used:

Velie, Alan. Essay on "Angle of Geese."*Poetry for Students.* Eds. Marie Napierkowski and Mary Ruby. Vol. 1. Detroit: Gale, 1997. 8–9.

When quoting a journal or newspaper essay that is reprinted in a volume of *PfS,* the following form may be used:

Luscher, Robert M. "An Emersonian Context of Dickinson's 'The Soul Selects Her Own Society.' " *ESQ: A Journal of American Renaissance* 30, No. 2 (Second Quarterl, 1984), 111–16; excerpted and reprinted in *Poetry for Students,* Vol. 2, eds. Marie Napierkowski and Mary Ruby (Detroit: Gale, 1997), pp. 120–34.

When quoting material reprinted from a book that appears in a volume of *PfS,* the following form may be used:

Mootry, Maria K. " 'Tell It Slant': Disguise and Discovery as Revisionist Poetic Discourse in 'The Bean Eaters,' " in *A Life Distilled: Gwendolyn Brroks, Her Poetry and Fiction,* edited by Maria K. Mootry and Gary Smith (University of Illinois Press, 1987, 177–80; excerpted and reprinted in *Poetry for Students,* Vol. 1, Eds. Marie Napierkowski and Mary Ruby (Detroit: Gale, 1997), pp. 59–61.

We Welcome Your Suggestions

The editors of *Poetry for Students* welcome your comments and ideas. Readers who wish to suggest poems to appear in future volumes, or who have other suggestions, are cordially invited to contact the editor. You may write to the editor at:

Editor, *Poetry for Students*
Gale Group
27500 Drake Rd.
Farmington Hills, MI 48331–3535

Literary Chronology

c. 450–c. 1100: "The Seafarer" is the product of an anonymous poet during the period of Old English literature, and is found in the *Exeter Book*, a work containing the largest known collection of Old English poetry and kept at Exeter Cathedral, England.

700: *Beowulf* is composed at about this time.

1300–1699: Humanism as a philosophical view of the world is prevalent in this period.

1300–1699: The Renaissance begins in the fourteenth century and continues for the next 300 years.

1558–1603: The Elizabethan Age begins with the coronation in 1558 of Elizabeth I as Queen of England and continues until her death in 1603. Elizabethan literature is recognized as some of the finest in the English language.

1564: William Shakespeare is born in Stratford-upon-Avon.

1575–1799: The literary style known as Baroque arises in the late-sixteenth century and remains influential until the early-eighteenth century.

1600–1625: The Tribe of Ben, followers of Ben Jonson, were active in the early part of the seventeenth century.

1600–1799: The Enlightenment period in European social and cultural history begins in the seventeenth century and continues into the eighteenth century.

1600–1650: Metaphysical poetry becomes a prominent style of verse in the first half of the seventeenth century.

1603–1625: The Jacobean Age begins with the coronation in 1603 of James I of England and continues until his death in 1625.

1609: William Shakepeare's poem "Sonnet 29" is published in *Shakespeares Sonnets*.

1616: William Shakespeare dies in Stratford and is buried in the chancel of Trinity Church.

1625–1649: The Cavalier Poets, a group of writers that includes Robert Herrick, John Suckling, are active during the reign of Charles I of England (1625–1649).

1660–1688: The Restoration Period begins when Charles II regains the throne of England, and it continues through the reign of his successor, James II (1685–1688). Restoration literature includes the first well-developed English-language works in several forms of writing that would become widespread in the modern world, including the novel, biography, and travel literature.

1675–1799: Neoclassicism as the prevailing approach to literature begins late in the seventeenth century and continues through much of the eighteenth century.

1700–1799: The English Augustan Age (the name is borrowed from a brilliant period of literary creativity in ancient Rome) flourishes through-out much of the eighteenth century.

1700–1725: The Scottish Enlightenment, a period of great literary and philosophical activity, occurs in the early part of the eighteenth century.

1740–1775: Pre-Romanticism, a transitional literary movement between Neoclassicism and Romanticism, takes place in the middle part of the eighteenth century.

1740–1750: The Graveyard School, referring to poetry that focuses on death and grieving, emerges as a significant genre in the middle of the eighteenth century.

1750–1899: The Welsh Literary Renaissance, an effort to revive interest in Welsh language and literature, begins in the middle of the eighteenth century and continues into the following century.

1775–1850: Romanticism as a literary movement arises in the latter part of the eighteenth century and continues until the middle of the nineteenth century.

1794: Robert Burns's poem "A Red, Red Rose" is published in *A Selection of Scots Songs*, edited by Peter Urbani.

1800–1899: The Gaelic Revival, a renewal of interest in Irish literature and language, takes place throughout much of the nineteenth century.

1809–1865: The Knickerbocker School, a group of American writers determined to establish New York as a literary center, flourishes between 1809 and 1865.

1830–1860: The flowering of American literature known as the American Renaissance begins in the 1830s and continues through the Civil War period.

1830–1855: Transcendentalism, an American philosophical and literary movement, is at its height during this period.

1830: Emily Dickinson is born on December 10 in Amherst, Massachusetts.

1837–1901: The Victorian Age begins with the coronation of Victoria as Queen of England, and continues until her death in 1901.

1848–1858: The Pre-Raphaelites, an influential group of English painters, forms in 1848 and remains together for about ten years, during which time it has a significant impact on literature as well as the visual arts.

1850: The poets of the so-called Spasmodic School are active in the 1850s.

1874: Robert Frost is born in San Francisco, California.

1875–1899: Aestheticism becomes a significant artistic and literary philosophy in the latter part of the nineteenth century.

1875–1899: Decadence becomes an important poetic force late in the nineteenth century.

1875–1925: Expressionism is a significant artistic and literary influence through the late nineteenth century and the early twentieth century.

1875–1925: The Irish Literary Renaissance begins late in the nineteenth century and continues for the next several decades.

1875–1925: The Symbolist Movement flourishes in the closing decades of the nineteenth century and the opening years of the twentieth century.

1875–1950: Realism as an approach to literature gains importance in the nineteenth century and remains influential well into the twentieth century.

1890–1899: The decade of the 1890s, noted for the mood of weariness and pessimism in its art and literature, is known as the Fin de Siècle ("end of the century") period.

1896: Emily Dickinson's poem "My Life Closed Twice Before Its Close" is published posthumously in her third collection entitled *Poems by Emily Dickinson, third series*.

1900–1999: The philosophy of Existentialism and the literature it inspires are highly influential throughout much of the twentieth century.

1900–1950: Modernism remains a dominant literary force from the early part to the middle years of the twentieth century.

1907–1930: The Bloomsbury Group, a circle of English writers and artists, gathers regularly in the period from 1907 to around 1930.

1910–1920: Georgian poetry becomes a popular style of lyric verse during the reign of King George V of England.

1910–1930: New Humanism, a philosophy of literature, is influential for several decades, beginning around 1910.

1912–1925: The Chicago Literary Renaissance, a time of great literary activity, takes place from about 1912 to 1925.

1912–1922: Imagism as a philosophy of poetry is defined in 1912 and remains influential for the next decade.

1912–1922: Ezra Pound's poem "The River-Merchant's Wife" is published in his third collection of poetry entitled *Cathay: Translations.*

1919: The Scottish Renaissance in literature begins around 1919 and continues for about forty years.

1920: The Harlem Renaissance, a flowering of African American literary activity, takes place.

1920–1930: The label Lost Generation is applied to a generation of American writers working in the decades following World War I.

1920–1930: The Montreal Group, a circle of Canadian poets interested in dealing with complex metaphysical issues, begins in the late 1920s and flourishes for the next decade.

1920–1970: New Criticism as a philosophy of literature arises in the 1920s and continues to be a significant approach to writing for over fifty years.

1920–1960: Surrealism, an artistic and literary technique, arises in the 1920s and remains influential for the next half century.

1924: Robert Frost is awarded the Pulitzer Prize in poetry for his collection *New Hampshire.*

1965: Negritude emerges as a literary movement in the 1930s and continues until the early 1960s.

1930–1970: The New York Intellectuals, a group of literary critics, are active from the 1930s to the 1970s.

1931: Robert Frost is awarded the Pulitzer Prize in poetry for his *Collected Poems.*

1934: Dylan Thomas's "The Force That through the Green Fuse Drives the Flower" is published in his first collection of poetry entiltled *18 Poems.*

1935–1943: The Works Progress Administration (WPA) Federal Writers' Project provides federally funded jobs for unemployed writers during the Great Depression.

1937: Robert Frost is awarded the Pulitzer Prize in poetry for his collection *A Further Range.*

1940: The New Apocalypse Movement, founded by J. F. Hendry and Henry Treece, takes place in England in the 1940s.

1940: Postmodernism, referring to the various philosophies and practices of literature that challenge the dominance of Modernism, begins in the 1940s.

1942: "Vancouver Lights" is published in Birney's first collection of poems, *David and Other Poems.* The book received the Governor General's Award for Poetry, the most prestigious award given for poetry in Canada.

1943: Robert Frost is awarded the Pulitzer Prize in poetry for his collection *A Witness Tree.*

1950: The so-called Beat Movement writers begin publishing their work in the 1950s.

1950: The Black Mountain Poets, emphasizing the creative process, become an influential force in American literature in the 1950s.

1975: Structuralism emerges as an important movement in literary criticism in the middle of the twentieth century.

1953: "Drought Year" is published by Australian poet Judith Wright.

1957: Frank O'Hara's "Why I Am Not a Painter" is published in the *Evergreen Review.*

1958–1959: Robert Frost serves as Consultant in Poetry to the Library of Congress.

1960: William Stafford's poem "At the Bomb Testing Site" appears in his first collection of poetry entitled *West of Your City.*

1960–1970: The Black Aesthetic Movement, also known as the Black Arts Movement, takes place from the 1960s into the 1970s.

1999: Poststructuralism arises as a theory of literary criticism in the 1960s.

1963: "Autumn Begins in Martins Ferry, Ohio" is published in James Wright's third collection of poetry entitled *The Branch Will Not Break.*

1999: New Historicism, a school of literary analysis, originates in the 1970s.

1972: George MacBeth's poem "Bedtime Story" is published in his collection entitled *Collected Poems: 1958-1970.*

1975: Ted Kooser's poem "The Constellation Orion" is published in *Three Rivers Poetry Journal.*

1977: Donald Hall's poem "Names of Horses" is published in the *New Yorker.*

1979: Seamus Heaney's poem "A Drink of Water" is collected in the volume entitled *Field Work.*

1979: Mary Oliver's poem "Music Lessons" is published in her third volume of poetry entitled *Twelve Moons.*

1979: Philip Levine's poem "Starlight" first appeared in the journal *Inquirey* and is reprinted in *Ashes: Poems New and Old* in 1979, a collection that won both the National Book Critics Circle Award and the American Book Award.

1981: A. D. Hope's poem "Beware of Ruins" is published.

1981: Linda Pastan's poem "Ethics" is published in her sixth volume of poetry, *Waiting for My Life*.

1984: "To a Sad Daughter" is published in Michael Ondaatje's 11th collection of poetry entitled *Secular Love*.

Acknowledgments

The editors wish to thank the copyright holders of the excerpted criticism included in this volume and the permissions managers of many book and magazine publishing companies for assisting us in securing reproduction rights. We are also grateful to the staffs of the Detroit Public Library, the Library of Congress, the University of Detroit Mercy Library, Wayne State University Purdy/Kresge Library Complex, and the University of Michigan Libraries for making their resources available to us. Following is a list of the copyright holders who have granted us permission to reproduce material in this volume of *Poetry for Students (PFS)*. Every effort has been made to trace copyright, but if omissions have been made, please let us know.

COPYRIGHTED EXCERPTS IN *PFS*, VOLUME 8, WERE REPRODUCED FROM THE FOLLOWING BOOKS:

Birney, Earle. From "Vancouver Lights" in *Fall by Fury*. McClelland & Stewart, 1977. Reproduced by permission of McClelland & Stewart, Inc. The Canadian Publishers. Hall, Donald. From "Names of Horses" in *Old and New Poems*. Copyright © 1990 by Donald Hall. All rights reserved. Originally published in The New Yorker. Reproduced by permission of Houghton Mifflin Company. Heaney, Seamus. For "A Drink of Water" in *Field Work*. Faber & Faber, 1979. Copyright © 1976, 1979 by Seamus Heaney. Reprinted by permission of Faber & Faber Ltd. Hope, A. D. From "Beware of Ruins" in *Antechinus: Poems, 1975-1980*. Angus & Robertson, 1981. Reproduced by permission of author and Curtis Brown, Ltd. Kooser, Ted. From "The Constellation Orion" in *Sure Signs: New and Selected Poems*. University of Pittsburgh Press, 1980. Reproduced by permission. Levine, Philip. From "Starlight" in *New selected poems*. Alfred A. Knopf, Inc., 1991. Reproduced by permission. Macbeth, George. From "Bedtime Story" in *Collected Poems 1958-1970*. Atheneum, 1972. Reproduced by permission of Sheil Land Associates. O'Hara, Frank. From "Why I Am Not a Painter" in *The Collected Poems of Frank O'Hara*. Alfred A. Knopf, Inc., 1971. Copyright © 1971 by Maureen Granville-Smith, Administratix of the Estate of Frank O'Hara. Reproduced by permission. Oliver, Mary. From "Music Lessons" in *Twelve Moons*. Little, Brown and Company, 1979. Copyright © 1979. Reproduced by permission. Ondaatje, Michael. For "To a Sad Daughter" in *The Cinnamon Peeler*. Knopf, 1991. Copyright © 1991. Reproduced by permission of Random House, Inc. Pastan, Linda. From "Ethics" in *Waiting for My Life*. W.W. Norton & Company, Inc. Copyright © 1981 by Linda Pastan. Reproduced by permission of publisher and author. Stafford, William. For "At the Bomb Testing Site" in *Stories That Could Be True*. Harper & Row, 1960. Copyright © 1960 by William Stafford. Reproduced by permission. Thomas, Dylan. For "The Force That through the Green Fuse Drives the Flower" in *Collected Poems*. New Directions, 1953. Copyright 1939, 1946 by New Directions

Publishing Corp. Copyright 1952 by Dylan Thomas. Reprinted by permission of David Higham Associates Limited. Wright, James A. From "Autumn Begins at Martins Ferry, Ohio" in *The Branch Will Not Break: Poems*. Wesleyan University Press, 1963. Copyright © 1963 by James Wright. Reproduced by permission of University Press of New England. Wright, Judith. From "Drought Year" in *A Human Pattern: Selected Poems*. ETT Imprint, 1995. © Judith Wright, 1971. Reproduced by permission.

PHOTOGRAPHS AND ILLUSTRATIONS APPEARING IN *PFS*, VOLUME 8, WERE RECEIVED FROM THE FOLLOWING SOURCES:

Birney, Earle (full white beard, lined face), photograph by Erik Christensen. The Globe and Mail, Toronto. Reproduced by permission of The Globe and Mail.

Burns, Robert (wearing dark vest top opened to a small v), painting.

Dickinson, Emily, photograph of a painting. The Library of Congress.

Hall, Donald (dark suit, vest and tie, carnation on left lapel) photograph. The Library of Congress.

Heaney, Seamus (wearing a dark tweed sports coat, floral pattern tie), photograph by Jerry Bauer. Reproduced by permission.

Kooser, Ted (wearing button-down collar shirt outdoors, leaves in background), photograph. University of Pittsburgh Press. Reproduced by permission.

Levine, Philip (standing outside, mountains in background), photograph. Reproduced by permission.

O'Hara, Frank, photograph. AP/Wide World Photos. Reproduced by permission.

Oliver, Mary and Paul Monette, National Book Awards, New York, November 18, 1992, Photo by Mark Lennihan. AP/Wide World Photos. Reproduced by permission.

Ondaatje, Michael, photograph by Thomas Victor. Reproduced by permission of the Estate of Thomas Victor.

Pastan, Linda. Goodman/Van Riper. Reproduced by permission.

Pound, Ezra (in plaid shirt, V-neck vest, dark hair and beard), photograph. The Library of Congress.

Shakespeare, William, illustration. The Library of Congress.

Stafford, Dr. William E., photograph. AP/Wide World Photos. Reproduced by permission.

Thomas, Dylan (with cigar in right corner of mouth), photograph. The Library of Congress.

Wright, James, photograph by Ted Wright. Reproduced by permission of the Estate of James Wright.

Contributors

Emily Archer: Emily Archer holds a Ph.D. in English from Georgia State University, has taught literature and poetry at several colleges, and has published essays, reviews, interviews, and poetry in numerous literary journals. Entry on *Ethics*.

Jonathan N. Barron: Jonathan N. Barron is associate professor of English at the University of Southern Mississippi. He has written numerous articles and edited a number of books of essays on poetry, and is editor of *The Robert Frost Review*. Original essays on *At the Bomb Testing Site*, *The River Merchant's Wife*, *Starlight*.

David Caplan: David Caplan is a doctoral candidate at the University of Virginia. Entry on *A Drink of Water*. Original essays on *Autumn Begins in Martins Ferry, Ohio*, and *Why I Am Not a Painter*.

Heather Davis: Heather Davis has an M.A. in English literature and creative writing from Syracuse University and is an editor and freelance writer. Entry on *Why I Am Not a Painter*.

Jhan Hochman: Jhan Hochman holds a Ph.D. in English and an M.A. in cinema studies. His articles have appeared in *Democracy and Nature, Genre, ISLE,* and *Mosaic.* Entries on *Beware of Ruins*, *Drought Year*, and *Music Lessons*. Original essays on *Beware of Ruins*, *Drought Year*.

Jeannine Johnson: Jeannine Johnson received her Ph.D. from Yale University and is currently visiting assistant professor of English at Wake Forest University. Original essays on *Autumn Begins at Martin's Ferry, Ohio, Beware of Ruins, My Life Closed Twice before Its Close*.

David Kelly: David Kelly is an instructor of creative writing at several community colleges in Illinois, as well as a fiction writer and playwright. Entries on *My Life Closed Twice before Its Close*, and *A Red, Red Rose*, and *Sonnet 29*. Original essays on *My Life Closed Twice before Its Close*, and *A Red, Red Rose*, and *Sonnet 29*.

Aviya Kushner: Aviya Kushner, who is the poetry editor for *Neworld Renaissance* magazine, earned an M.A. in creative writing from Boston University. Original essay on *A Drink of water, The Force That Through the Green Fuse Drives the Flower, My Life Closed Twice before Its Close, Why I Am Not a Painter*.

Michael Lake: Michael Lake earned an M.A. in English from Eastern Illinois University and is a published poet. He currently teaches English at a Denver area community college. Entry on *The Seafarer*. Original essay on *The Seafarer*.

Mary Mahony: Mary Mahony earned an M.A. in English from the University of Detroit and a M.L.S. from Wayne State University. She is an instructor of English at Wayne County Community College in Detroit, Michigan. Entries on

Force That Through the Green Fuse Drives the Flower and *The River Merchant's Wife.*

Bruce Meyer: Bruce Meyer is director of the creative writing program at the University of Toronto's School of Continuing Studies. He is the author of 14 books, including the poetry collections *The Open Room, Radio Silence*, and *The Presence.* Original essays on *Autumn Begins in Martin's Ferry, Ohio, The Force That Through the Green Fuse Drives the Flower, A Red, Red, Rose, The Seafarer, Sonnet 29, To a Sad Daughter*, and *Vancouver Lights.*

Carolyn Meyer: Carolyn Meyer holds a Ph.D. in modern British and Irish literature and has taught contemporary literature at McMaster University, Mt. Allison University, and, most recently, the University of Toronto. She has presented papers internationally on the poetry of Seamus Heaney and John Montague. Her article "Orthodoxy, Independence, and Influence in Seamus Heaney's *Station Island*" has been reprinted in *Critical Essays on Seamus Heaney*, edited by Robert F. Garratt (1995). She is the coeditor of *Separate Islands: Contemporary Irish and British Poetry* and of a forthcoming college reader. Original essay on *A Drink of Water.*

Morton Rich: Morton Rich holds a Ph.D. from New York University and is a professor of contemporary American literature. He currently teaches at Montclair State University in New Jersey and publishes poetry and critical articles. Original essay on *Music Lessons* and *Why I Am Not a Painter.*

Cliff Saunders: Cliff Saunders teaches writing and literature in the Myrtle Beach, South Carolina, area and has published six chapbooks of verse. Entry on *Names of Horses*. Original essay on *The Constellation Orion.*

Chris Semansky: Chris Semansky holds a Ph.D. in English from Stony Brook University and teaches writing and literature at Portland Community College in Portland, Oregon. His collection of poems *Death, But at a Good Price* received the Nicholas Roerich Poetry Prize for 1991 and was published by Story Line Press and the Nicholas Roerich Museum. Semansky's most recent collection, *Blindsided,* has been published by 26 Books of Portland, Oregon. Entries on *Bedtime Story, The Constellation Orion, Starlight*, and *Vancouver Lights*. Original essays on *At the Bomb Testing Site, Bedtime Story, The Constellation Orion, Names of Horses, Starlight*, and *Vancouver Lights.*

Pamela Steed Hill: Pamela Steed Hill, the author of a collection of poetry titled *In Praise of Motels,* has had poems published in more than 90 journals and magazines and has twice been nominated for a Pushcart Prize. She has an M.A. in English from Marshall University and is an associate editor for university communications at Ohio State University. Entries on *Autumn Begins in Martin's Ferry, Ohio*, and *To a Sad Daughter*. Original essays on *The Constellation Orion* and *Starlight.*

Melissa Stein: Melissa Stein earned an M.A. in English from the University of California, Davis, and is a freelance writer and editor. She has had poems published in several periodicals, including American Poetry Review, and two anthologies. Entry on *At the Bomb Testing Site.*

Alice Van Wart: Alice Van Wart is a writer and teaches literature and writing in the Department of Continuing Education at the University of Toronto. She has published two books of poetry and has written articles on modern and contemporary literature. Original essays on *Ethics, The Force That Through the Green Fuse Drives the Flower, Music Lessons, Sonnet 29, Starlight*, and *To a Sad Daughter.*

At the Bomb Testing Site

William Stafford

1960

"At the Bomb Testing Site" is an unusual work: it is an antiwar poem that never directly mentions war. In a review in *Field,* Charles Simic called the poem "A political poem in which not a single political statement is made."

The poem appeared in *West of Your City,* William Stafford's first collection of poetry, which was published by a small press in 1960. One of Stafford's best known and most widely anthologized poems, "At the Bomb Testing Site" deals with the conflict between the natural environment and the artificial world that man has imposed upon it.

The title refers to the atomic bomb testing in the New Mexico and Nevada deserts that began in 1945. Although the poem implicitly refers to the horrors of war and the ravages of radiation fallout, it is anything but a "no-nukes" polemic. Instead, it focuses on the behavior of a lizard that is about to be destroyed in a test explosion, and it implies that humans will be destroyed as well by their obsession with technological progress and political domination. Like most of Stafford's work, this understated poem employs everyday, colloquial language and is steeped in a western landscape.

A conscientious objector to World War II, Stafford was forced to spend four years in a labor camp, and his antiwar stance was reinforced by this experience—but he published no poems that speak about it directly. Stafford often said that he didn't see himself as "a very political person"; there were just some issues on which one simply *had* to take

William Stafford

a stand. In an interview about "At the Bomb Testing Site," he revealed one of the main impulses of his writing: "Every poem I have ever written is a quiet protest poem."

Author Biography

William Stafford was born on January 17, 1914 in Hutchinson, Kansas, where he lived until his mid-teens. Hit hard by the Depression, Stafford's family moved many times as his father searched for work. Stafford earned a bachelor's degree from the University of Kansas, and had nearly completed a master's degree when World War II began in 1942. Registered as a conscientious objector, Stafford was incarcerated in public service camps, and spent the four years of the war cutting trails, fighting forest fires, and terracing eroding land in Arkansas, California, and Illinois. As a pacifist in a country that saw so many of its young men killed, he faced public scorn, suspicion, and enmity.

In the camps, Stafford began a routine of rising early to write every morning, a habit that lasted throughout his life and informed his style and philosophy of writing. In 1944, he married Dorothy Hope Frantz, with whom he had four children. As his master's thesis, Stafford wrote *Down in My*

Heart, an engaging account of life in the CO camps. The book was published in 1947.

In 1948, Stafford and his family moved to Portland, Oregon. Stafford taught at Lewis and Clark University until his retirement in 1980, with brief absences to earn a Ph.D. in creative writing at the University of Iowa (1950-52) and to teach at a number of colleges and universities across the United States. He was named the Oregon Poet Laureate in 1975.

Although his poems appeared in many literary magazines, Stafford didn't publish his first collection of poetry, *West of Your City,* until 1960, when he was 46. *Traveling through the Dark,* published in 1962, won the National Book Award for Poetry, and he was awarded National Endowment for the Arts and Guggenheim Foundation grants in 1966. His many volumes of poetry include *The Rescued Year* (1966), *Allegiances* (1970), *Stories That Could Be True* (1977), *A Glass Face in the Rain* (1982), and *An Oregon Message* (1987). He wrote several books about the art and craft of poetry, including *Writing the Australian Crawl* (1978) and *You Must Revise Your Life* (1986).

Since the 1970s, Stafford has been recognized as a major poet. Because of his poems' strong sense of place, Stafford is often referred to as a "Midwest" or a "Pacific Northwest" poet, and his work is included in a number of regional anthologies. However, Stafford resisted the label of regional poet, claiming that it was only natural for a poet to write about where he was, wherever that happened to be.

Stafford was also well known for his open, uncritical (and some say nonacademic) approach to writing. Because he wrote so often and so much, he hardly ever revised. "Poems to me are nothing special," he wrote in *You Must Revise Your Life.* "They are just the language without mistakes." Before his death in 1993, Stafford published an astonishing 400 poems—and doubtless wrote thousands that never made it to the printed page.

Poem Text

At noon in the desert a panting lizard
waited for history, its elbows tense,
watching the curve of a particular road
as if something might happen.

It was looking for something farther off   5
than people could see, an important scene
acted in stone for little selves
at the flute end of consequences.

There was just a continent without much on it
under a sky that never cared less.   10
Ready for a change, the elbows waited
The hands gripped hard on the desert.

Poem Summary

Lines 1-2:

These lines introduce the subject of the poem: a desert lizard. With just a few words, these lines convey great heat (the sun is highest in the sky at noon), great solitude (the desert is thought of as a desolate place in which creatures and plants must struggle for survival) and great urgency (the lizard is "panting" and "tense," implying exertion or a fight-or-flight reaction). From the poem's title, we know that the lizard lives in an area upon which a bomb is about to be dropped. Use of the word "elbows" instead of "legs" attributes human qualities to the lizard, inviting the reader to identify with this creature, and implying that the lizard's fate might be ours as well.

This tiny lizard in the midst of the vast desert is made to seem yet smaller by the use of the abstract word "history." Given the context, "history" can refer to the lizard's individual life in the desert, which is about to come to a close; human history, including the development of technology and weapons such as the atom bomb in the title; and collective human history, how mankind is destroying itself and its environment. This sort of multiple meaning recurs in many lines in this short poem, which makes the most of each word.

Lines 3-4:

Here we learn that the lizard is tense because "something might happen," which we already know involves history. The word "road" implies mankind's presence and intervention in this desert landscape, as the only roads in the desert are man-made. The lizard literally looks at the road, but, in a larger sense, is also watching what humanity is doing. If "something" happens, it will be brought about by man. The "particular road" can also be interpreted figuratively as the course of events of the lizard's life, which is about to be brought to an end by the actions of people. The word "curve" reinforces that what is about to happen can't be seen yet; it's just around the corner.

The quiet, casual, ordinary language of these lines—especially using the nondescript word "something" to refer to the enormity and violence of a bomb explosion—create a tension that strengthens the poem's emotional effect.

Lines 5-8:

This stanza attributes to the lizard an ability to perceive truths that human beings, in their myopic and self-important quest for power, cannot grasp. These lines express the paradox that the closer one is to the ground (i.e. to nature), the farther one can see. Line 4's "something might happen," which refers to the explosion, is now expanded to "something farther off," the larger consequences of nuclear weapons in particular and of war in general. The use of the word "selves" personifies the lizard (and other animals that are implied), giving it a consciousness. The word "little" is ironic, as this tiny creature has greater prescience and compassion than beings two hundred times its size, who are in reality the small-minded ones. "Little" also implies humble, in contrast to human greed. So the lizard, one of the "little selves" connected to the earth as part of nature, can see the backdrop of natural history, which existed before man imposed his own history by building cities and roads, dividing up the land into political territories, and fighting to defend them.

The "important scene" that these humble creatures witness is the slow, inevitable unfolding of natural history. This history is acted or performed by the stone of the earth itself, billions of years old. The creatures also watch the supposedly important (i.e. to humans) scene of the atomic age and the cold war, the human drama that may end up extinguishing all life on the planet. They know the plain truth that we destroy ourselves physically and spiritually by ignoring the essential unity of all things, and by mistreating our environment and each other.

We often hear the expressions "carved in stone" or "set in stone," which imply permanence, but Stafford chooses the word "acted" instead to convey the idea of history as a play or film. Human history is only an act put on for a short while—made even shorter by our destructive impulses. This idea echoes the well-known passage from Shakespeare's *As You Like It* (Act 2, Scene 7) that "All the world's a stage, / And all the men and women merely players: / They have their exits and their entrances; / And one man in his time plays many parts, / His acts being seven ages," as well as his depiction in *Macbeth* (Act 5, Scene 5) of life as a brief play: "Out, out, brief candle! / Life's but a walking shadow, a poor player / That struts and frets his hour upon the stage / And then is heard no more."

Media Adaptations

- You can listen to William Stafford reading "With Kit, Age 7, At the Beach" on the Academy of American Poets site http://www.poets.org/lit/listen.htm#S. This is an audio sample from a 1970 tape containing readings from a number of Stafford's poems, introduced by Frederick Morgan. You may order the tape on the site.

- William Stafford reads two poems on Volume Two of the CD set *In Their Own Voices: A Century of Recorded Poetry.*

- The Poetry Center at San Francisco State University (www.sfsu.edu/~newlit/archives.htm) has an archive of videotapes of poetry readings that are rentable by mail. William Stafford reads nearly 50 poems.

- William Stafford reads his children's poetry book *The Animal That Drank Up Sound,* accompanied by Matthew Smith's contemporary music, on an audiocassette published by Harcourt Brace & Company in 1993.

- *William Stafford and Robert Bly: A Literary Friendship* (Reiss Films, 1994) is a lively documentary about the friendship of these two American poets.

The last line of this stanza is a striking combination of the abstract and concrete, comparing the narrow opening of a wine glass or flower (as in "fluted") or the end of a slender musical instrument (a flute) with the end result of momentous actions. The line works in an impressionistic way: "flute" is a light and delicate word, as set against the weight of "consequences." Little selves like the lizard may seem to be unimportant and far away, at the narrow end of the spectrum, but are really a part of the big picture, and when changes are brought about in or by nature, they are affected too. They are harmed when the environment is harmed. Small creatures don't possess the power (or will) to destroy their own environment, but they do have the ability to perceive when the end is at hand.

Lines 9-10:

This sentence reinforces the statement in the previous stanza that a fundamental lack of harmony exists between man and nature. To many humans, nature is "not much." And to the natural world, in the larger sense humans are "not much" either. Although stated in the same simple declarative manner as the rest of the poem, these lines take a more extreme stance, reducing North America to "just a continent" of no interest to the sky. Saying that the sky does not care is an example of the poetic technique of *pathetic fallacy,* or attributing human traits or feelings to inanimate nature. The use of this technique enlarges a particular feeling ("The person who will detonate the bomb doesn't care about the lizard"), making it seem universal ("The sky doesn't care about any of us"). It also suggests that the sky and the earth have their own existence apart from human ambition and folly.

Humans who would explode a bomb just as a test, killing many lizards and other forms of life, clearly do not respect the environment from which they gain their very sustenance. And it seems that humans also think little of destroying the hundreds of thousands of human lives in the crowded cities upon which bombs will be dropped. Yet here there is also an intimation that works against the poem's pessimistic message: the sky may never care, but people—including the author of the poem—do at least have that capacity, whether they use it or not.

Lines 11-12:

The poem returns to the lizard, further describing its preparation for the blast. The repetition of the words "elbows" and "waited" from line 2 bring us back to the beginning of the poem, creating a sort of cycle. But here, the lizard that was an "it" in lines 2 and 5 is now referred to only in terms of its body parts: "the elbows," "the hands." This use of the undefined article "the" depersonalizes the lizard, making it a wider symbol of the natural world. Because these lines do not specify who or what these elbows and hands belong to, they also suggest that the hands and elbows might be numerous—that many creatures are facing annihilation—and that they could belong to humans as well (since lizards have feet, not hands). A third, figurative, sense of the poem's last line is that mankind has the desert in its grip, and one can imagine the huge hands of the bomb tearing up the sand and soil. This careful word choice again prompts the reader to identify with the lizard, and to experience the horror of the impending explosion. Using the words "a change" to describe a violent death continues the poem's understated style.

The last line changes the tone of the poem with its emphatic one-syllable words and its repetition of consonant sounds—"h" and "d" in "hands," "gripped," "hard," and "desert." These harsh, clipped sounds reinforce that something unimaginably violent and devastating is about to occur.

The lizard is not resting or lying on the desert surface, allowing itself to be blown into the air but braces itself by "gripping" the earth. This little life meets its own death head-on, with total awareness of what is about to happen. Though the lizard is apparently "ready," the poem fully conveys the terror and fear of facing an unnatural death, implying that no form of violence is acceptable—not toward the soil, not toward animals, and not toward humans.

Themes

Death

"At the Bomb Testing Site" makes a big point by focusing on something very small: a solitary desert lizard facing destruction. By describing something concrete, the poem addresses the unimaginable. It works by subtly enlarging our perceptions of nature, violence, and death. The poem is written in a quiet, casual tone that increases in intensity in the third stanza but never mentions the words "death" or "war." Instead we get that information from the title and infer the rest from the unfolding description of the lizard. The closest the poem comes to a direct comment is in line 11's "a change," which is a euphemism for "annihilation." In this context, the word "change" is chilling—how can we think of death this way? If we follow this reasoning, we must wonder how we can read the casualties of a bombing as just numbers on a page, or how a soldier can turn a key that will end up killing thousands.

Another sense of "a change" is scientific: the conversion of matter into another form, part of the natural process of death. But the lizard fixes upon natural history—"something farther off / than people could see"—while it faces a death that is anything *but* natural. The poem presents two conflicting messages about death: death is ordinary, a constant element of nature, and death is a horror both perpetrated and feared by humans. Thus, the poem reinforces death as a part of the natural order at the same time it depicts the tragic disorder of human violence.

Although this poem offers no graphic descriptions of radiation burns, the rubble of leveled buildings, or the ravages of cancer, it conveys the enormity of nuclear testing and nuclear war. The very absence of such graphic images allows each reader to fill in the blanks, tapping into the fears and premonitions of death that we all have. The poem conveys the vulnerability and helplessness of an individual against a power much larger than itself. It is dreamlike in its force: the reader is trapped by having a sense of wanting to stop the lizard's (our) death from happening, but also knowing that the bomb will drop (has already dropped) and that the lizard (we) will die. Specifically, the poem pulls forth associations with the fatal effects of nuclear weapons, such as the loss of life in Hiroshima and Nagasaki, and the threat of total annihilation if World War III were to begin.

Individuals vs. Nature

"At the Bomb Testing Site" offers a complicated view of our relationship to the natural world. Through its personification of the lizard ("elbows" and "hands"), the poem firmly reminds us that we are animals. At the same time, it conveys that nature is unfeeling and "other" ("a sky that never cared less").

The bomb testing is performed in the desert precisely because it is looked upon as "deserted." But this sentient lizard—nature's animate self—occupies this land, and destroying it (along with countless birds, plants, spiders…) with a manmade weapon shows that the natural and human worlds are out of alignment. At the base of this standoff is another great irony: humans belong to the earth—we arose from it—and now we are fashioning weapons from its raw materials in order to destroy ourselves. Even without direct human casualties, creation and testing of these weapons have poisoned the air, water, and earth, elements essential to sustaining life. These actions have moved us closer and closer to "a continent without much on it."

The lizard sees "acted in stone" that eventually the world will end, and possibly begin again, in the cycle of the universe. Nature will win out after the human "scene" has played out. In this lies the truth that humans came from nature and will return to it.

The lizard's fate is decidedly manmade—it is not the victim of a snake, or of thirst, or of the desert's great heat. In the political survival of the fittest, in the obsessive love of technology, human beings have upset the balance of nature. This poem makes clear that people lack the most important vision of all—how to live in harmony with each other and with their environment.

Topics for Further Study

- Investigate a scientific "advance" that has turned out to be harmful to humankind. What was the initial response to the scientific development? How was the truth discovered or revealed? What was the result?

- Imagine a room (or a landscape, or a place you know) in which something important has just happened. Write a poem describing the room itself without telling what has happened there.

- Compare and contrast the depictions of the threat of nuclear war in a recent movie and a film from the 1960s.

- Describe what makes a poem "political," giving examples from the work of one or more poets.

- Explore the controversy surrounding the dropping of the atomic bomb on Japan in 1945. Who supported this action? Who opposed it? What were the forces that led to the use of the bomb?

- Think of an abstract word—rage, ecstasy, loneliness, freedom, hope, etc.—and write down all of the concrete images that the word brings to mind. Then, write a poem using only concrete descriptions that convey or suggest the larger concept.

Choices and Consequences

This poem implicitly presents the reader with a choice: will humans continue to mistreat their environment and each other, moving along the "particular road" the lizard sees for us? Or will we be able to feel the weight of this poem, understand the consequences of our actions, and change our behavior?

That the poem is set before the bomb is dropped in the desert fills the reader with the horror of foreknowledge, giving and taking away the choice to stop what is about to happen. The phrase "as if something might happen" suggests that the violence about to take place may not *have* to happen; that there might be an alternative. The lizard readies himself and waits for death because it has no choice. But since humans willfully cause this destruction, they do have a choice.

America chose to develop, test, and employ the nuclear bomb—and to do these things secretly—which made an arms race among unfriendly countries inevitable. This poem, written in the midst of cold war hysteria, makes clear the irony of a country's building bombs to demonstrate its strength, just so it can prevent itself from being bombed.

By setting up a parallel between the death of the lizard and the death of the natural environment, including the death of human beings, this poem raises our consciousness that even seemingly little actions (killing one lizard) may have grand consequences (extinguishing the human race and perhaps all life on earth). By posing the question of how we will die, the poem asks us to consider and choose how we will live.

Style

"At the Bomb Testing Site" is a three-stanza poem written in free verse: the poet does not adhere to any particular pattern of rhyme or meter, as in a sonnet or villanelle. However, the poet pays very careful attention to patterns of imagery, figures of speech, line breaks, and the sounds of words. Stafford is well known for his "plain-style," or fairly straightforward, "talky" language, devoid of elaborate wordplay. (It has been said that in poetry readings, his audience often couldn't tell where his introduction left off and his poem began.) Yet even in his apparently simple language lie patterns that affect a reader intuitively and give the writing the quality of a legend or parable.

"At the Bomb Testing Site" begins and ends in a description of the lizard, a technique that entices the reader to reenter the poem after reading it. Abstractions such as "waited for history," "important scene," and "consequences" lend importance and a mythic quality to the poem, but the concrete images of the lizard's actions anchor them in the real world. The repetition of words—"waited," "elbows," and "something"—amplifies and slightly changes their meaning while unifying the poem.

One of the poem's subtle rhythmic techniques is the use of assonance, or repetition of vowel sounds within words. For example, the long "e" in "people could see, an important scene" implicitly links the people to what they cannot perceive. Similarly, the poem's last line "The hands gripped hard on the desert" repeats hard "h" and "d" sounds for an effect like a sharp jab. This intensifies the emotional force of the poem, leaving it to the reader to resolve the tension of the final line.

Of the five sentences that make up this poem, three appear in the last stanza. The longer sentences slow down reading and give a deliberate feel as the scene is being revealed bit by bit. With its short declarative sentences, the last stanza moves more quickly and ends with a hard impact, the way a falling object accelerates before it hits the ground.

Historical Context

In what some historians have called the single most important event of the twentieth century, the world's first atomic bomb was dropped in the desert near Alamogordo, New Mexico, in July of 1945. This bomb test, code-named "Trinity," ushered in the nuclear age. When the bomb exploded successfully, J. R. Oppenheimer, the theoretical physicist who directed the development of the bomb from its raw materials, said "I am become Death, shatterer of worlds," echoing a Hindu scripture. Kenneth Bainbridge, who was responsible for the bomb's detonation, exclaimed, "Now we are all sons of bitches." A War Department memo of July 18, 1945, describes the feelings of those who witnessed the blast: "The effects could well be called unprecedented, magnificent, beautiful, stupendous, and terrifying. No manmade phenomenon of such tremendous power had ever occurred before.... It was that beauty the great poets dream about but describe most poorly and inadequately.... [The] awesome roar ... warned of doomsday and made us feel that we puny things were blasphemous to dare tamper with the forces heretofore reserved to The Almighty."

In 1939 Hungarian scientists Leo Szilard and Eugene Wigner began to fear that the Germans would harness atomic technology and employ it in the impending war. They convinced Albert Einstein to write a letter to President Franklin D. Roosevelt encouraging immediate research and development of nuclear technology. In 1941, the "Manhattan Project" began. Four years and $2 billion later, the United States had secretly developed three weapons: one uranium and two plutonium bombs. The first plutonium bomb, tested in New Mexico, surpassed all expectations: it had the power of 18,600 tons of TNT (or dynamite), ten times what

was predicted, and an explosive force equal to all bombs dropped on London during the Blitz. According to the 1945 War Department memo, the blast destroyed all vegetation for 1,200 feet, melted the sand underneath into green glass, shattered windows for 120 miles, and blew radioactive material over an area of the same diameter. Even today, according to the *Seattle Times,* radioactivity at the Trinity site is ten times normal background levels. The government told local residents—some of whom lived only 20 miles from the test site—that an arsenal of ammunition had exploded.

At the time of the Trinity test, World War II had been raging for nearly six years, with more than 35 million people killed worldwide. While victory had been declared in Europe in May, the battle continued in Japan, and the Soviet Union pledged to enter the fight against the Japanese in August. At the end of July, the U.S. government issued an ultimatum that the Japanese homeland would face "prompt and utter destruction" unless it surrendered unconditionally—but this warning did not mention the bomb. On August 6, the warplane Enola Gay dropped a uranium atomic bomb on Hiroshima; three days later, the Soviet Union invaded Japan, and a plutonium atomic bomb was dropped on Nagasaki. The Japanese surrendered unofficially on August 14, ending World War II. The two bombs killed more than 100,000 people instantly, injured as many, and it is estimated that an equal number have died—and are still dying—from the effects, including cancer, birth defects, and other radiation-related illnesses.

The bombing of Japan was—and still is—hotly contested: the Japanese power was weakening, and many feel that the war would have ended soon, without extensive U.S. casualties. The theory holds that the Americans dropped the bomb on Japan to keep the Soviets from entering the war and gaining power. Whatever the case, the secrecy surrounding the development of the atomic bomb created enmity that launched the cold war and nuclear arms race, forever changing the face of world politics and culture. Cold war paranoia and nuclear hysteria became a part of daily life for Americans, especially in the 1950s.

Many nuclear tests followed internationally: the Soviet Union in 1949, Great Britain in 1952, France in 1960, China in 1964, and India in 1974. Tests have been conducted in the air, underground, and underwater. The United States carried out more than 1,000 bomb tests in Colorado, Alaska, Mississippi, New Mexico, and Nevada. In 1951, a test site the size of Rhode Island was established in the

Compare & Contrast

- **1945:** The United States has an arsenal of two bombs.

- **1961:** *Life Magazine* offers tips on building bomb shelters, which has been urged by President Kennedy.

- **1962:** Rachel Carson's *Silent Spring,* a book about how the use of DDT poisons the earth, is published. The resulting public outcry about pesticide use leads to changes in the laws affecting the air, land, and water, and launches the environmental movement as we know it today.

- **1963:** Preaching nonviolence, Dr. Martin Luther King delivers his "I Have a Dream" speech in Washington, D.C.

- **1986:** The Soviet nuclear reactor at Chernobyl melts down, releasing 10 times the radiation of the Hiroshima bombing. The Soviet Union's arsenal reaches 45,000.

- **1995:** A Gallup poll shows that 60 percent of Americans surveyed cannot name the president who ordered the 1945 bombing of Japan. 22 percent don't know that bombs were dropped at all.

- **1997:** A United Nations-sponsored conference on global warming is held in Kyoto, Japan to address the issue of how to reduce carbon dioxide emissions worldwide.

- **1998:** India carries out a series of nuclear bomb tests.

Nevada desert, even though prevailing winds blowing east would carry radioactivity across the country. By 1960, when "At the Bomb Testing Site" was published, nearly 90 tests had been carried out at the Nevada Test Site, and more than 900 by 1992, when a moratorium was established by President George Bush. Cumulatively, these tests exposed troops and downwind residents to 148 times the radiation released in the 1986 Chernobyl meltdown.

Downwind of the Nevada tests, where—before the danger of radioactivity was common knowledge—children played in the fallout dust as if it were snow, there developed an alarming increase in the incidence of leukemia, cancer, and other illnesses. While the Atomic Energy Commission repeatedly assured the public, "There is no danger," nuclear contamination spread as far as New England, poisoning sheep, milk, wheat, fish, and soil. In 1980, a Congressional investigation team concluded, "The greatest irony of our atmospheric nuclear testing program is that the only victims of United States nuclear arms since World War II have been our own people."

In 1963, The Limited Test Ban Treaty was signed by representatives of the United States, United Kingdom, and Soviet Union, prohibiting tests of nuclear weapons above ground, under water, and in space. After 2,046 tests worldwide and decades of protest and legal action by environmental and activist groups, the Comprehensive Test Ban Treaty was signed in September of 1996 by all five declared nuclear powers—the United States, Great Britain, France, China, and Russia, prohibiting all testing. India refused to sign, and carried out a test in 1998.

The Nuclear Regulatory Commission reported that as of 1967, nuclear testing killed between 35,000 and 85,000 people worldwide. The violent legacy of atomic testing continues today.

Critical Overview

In a 1961 review of *West of Your City* in the *Virginia Quarterly Review,* James Dickey called Stafford "a real poet, a born poet." At the same time, in the *Hudson Review,* Louis Simpson contended that "Stafford is one of the few poets who are able to use the landscape and to feel the mystery and imagination in American life." He cited "At the Bomb Testing Site" as an example of the strength and purpose of Stafford's voice, arguing that the poet deserved wider and more serious critical attention. Critic Peter Davison in the *Atlantic Monthly* compared the poem to Yeats's "The Second Coming," noting its prophetic power. Stafford's work has also been likened to that of Robert Frost and Walt Whitman.

Critics over the years have tended to disagree about Stafford's standing as a poet—some accuse his "plain-style" of being repetitive, dull, or preachy; others find truth and meaning in his depictions of midwestern life, Native American culture, and the natural environment. Many critics agree with Richard Hugo's assessment in the *Kansas Quarterly* that "Stafford's world may not be large, but his poems are big enough," while others like Richard Howard, that he is a minor poet because his work is limited, static: "The poems accumulate but they do not *grow;* they drift like snowflakes into a great and beautiful body of canceling work" *(Parnassus).* It has been said that Stafford's work did not change or develop significantly over his more than thirty-year poetic career. He has even been taken to task for simply publishing too much.

Despite this controversy, the critics seem to agree that at his best, Stafford is a poet of vision and substance. "At the Bomb Testing Site" is one of Stafford's most highly acclaimed poems and has helped to establish his place in the canon of twentieth-century American poetry. In the *New England Review,* Leonard Nathan praised this political poem for its understatement and lack of rhetoric and polemic, calling it "the poem about nuclear destruction I am most moved by." In an era that saw much grandiose, author-centered writing, he especially admired the poem's ability to "shift its subjectivity to another creature—a creature noted for its cold blood—and offer instinctual anticipation as a kind of measure for the unspeakable." Charles Simic in *Field* similarly lauded the poem's "extraordinary vision," exploring each line's layered meanings and intuitive associations and noted that "poems such as this one open the largest view of the earth, sky, mortals and their true and false gods."

Criticism

Jonathan Barron

Jonathan N. Barron is associate professor of English at the University of Southern Mississippi. He has written numerous articles and edited a number of books of essays on poetry, and is editor of The Robert Frost Review. *In this essay, Barron shows how Stafford uses the techniques of a poetic movement from the 1960s, Deep Image poetry, to meditate on the meaning of history.*

Ever since he published his first book in 1959, William Stafford has voiced the emotional commitment of a kind of poetic activism. More specifically, Stafford, a conscientious objector in World War II, regularly uses his poetry to reveal a deep animosity to militarism. But few of his poems before the publication of "At the Bomb Testing Site" (1966) join his anti-militaristic sentiments with the environmentalism one often associates with the Pacific Northwest. One of the best ways to approach Stafford's "At the Bomb Testing Site," then, is to read it as a particular expression of this twin political concern: pacifism and environmentalism.

Great themes, no matter how engaged or engaging, however, do not necessarily create great poetry. For that, craft and style must be taken into account. No matter how noble the twin themes in "At the Bomb Testing Site" may be, the poetry itself succeeds because of its skilled use of a poetic device, the Deep Image, that was new to American poetry in the 1960s. Born in the American Midwest, the Deep Image poetry movement rejected and revised conventional poetic approaches to description. Typically, poets render objects, gestures, and scenes as precisely as they can. The depiction of "the things of this world," to use the title of a famous poem by American poet Richard Wilbur, was standard practice for American poetry after World War Two. Such poetry asks readers to see clearly, almost as if each poem were an especially vivid photograph. The Deep Image, however, was a rebellion against such attention to the surface look of things. Poets sought the spiritual mystery at the heart of all matter through poetic images built out of nouns, that, when combined, reveal a surreal, surprising, and mystical truth.

According to the creators of the Deep Image movement—poets Robert Bly and James Wright— if ever there was a time for spiritual renewal, for the healing work of poetry, then it was in the traumatized period of the 1960s. Bly, in particular, through the vehicle of his own magazine (initially called *The Fifties* when it began publication in the late 1950s and then changed to *The Sixties* with the decade's change), urged American poets to make poetry function as such a healing force by turning their attention away from the surface concerns of the material world and looking instead at the spiritual, emotional world below. He famously

" *One of the best ways to approach Stafford's 'At the Bomb Testing Site,' then, is to read it as a particular expression of this twin political concern: pacifism and environmentalism.* "

made this case in an essay provocatively titled, "A Wrong Turning in American Poetry," where he lashed out at the early 20th-century Modernists for ignoring the deeper truths that were supposed to be the very life-blood of poetry. Bly argued that if poets would use Deep rather than literal or surface images then their poems would at last truly speak out of the depths of the unconscious mind, out of the profound emotions one usually associates with the soul, or the deepest psychological feelings. The Deep Image movement soon gained much prominence as such poets as Louis Simpson, Galway Kinnell, Mark Strand, and W. S. Merwin began to make use of its techniques in their work. By the mid-1970s, however, this sort of poetry no longer dominated the literary magazines as it once had, and, it is now a rare thing indeed. Nonetheless, the movement's demand that poetry not be so obsessed with surface pictures, and social events to the exclusion of deeper spiritual concerns continues to influence poets.

William Stafford is one of the many poets who, although not formally associated with him or his circle, found Bly's ideas compelling. And of the many poems in which Stafford makes use of the Deep Image technique, "At the Bomb Testing Site," is, perhaps, the most successful. This poem singles out a number of images: the desert, a lizard, and an empty road. What quickly becomes apparent is that these images are more than just literal references to "the things of this world." They are, as well, Deep Images conjuring up primordial feelings and beliefs.

The first such image is the desert, long a landscape familiar to the poetic imagination. To the poetic mind, wilderness of the sort one finds in the

American west typically conjures up images of danger and fear but also of freedom and limitless expansion. In this poem—thanks to the prominent role of two other images, lizard and road—the desert is not a typically poetic metaphor for these things. Instead, it belongs to the military imagination, where the vast stretches of uninhabited land refer only to ideal sites for target practice. By playing the conventionally poetic association of the desert (limitless if risky possibility) against the contemporary militaristic use of that desert (target practice), Stafford, in three quatrains, gives voice to what would soon be a fully formed environmental movement. "At the Bomb Testing Site" couples Stafford's own morally based stance against combat with a love for and concern for the natural landscape. Simply by playing three images— desert, road, and lizard—against one another Stafford is able to make them tell a far deeper story than the more conventional anti-militaristic poem might have told.

Rather than reducing opposition in the poem to simple cliches—saying how marvelous and pretty and free nature is, and how evil and sinister the bomb-loving military is, Stafford, instead, chooses a profoundly ugly, frightening, hardly loveable creature, the lizard, and his dangerous and equally frightening home, the desert, as his Deep Images or metaphors for nature's glory. By focusing on a lizard in the desert, Stafford refuses to traffic in cliches about the beauties, mysteries, and wonders of nature that need to be preserved. Instead, he returns his readers to the palpable fear of imminent warfare, of potential nuclear holocaust, by making that threat clear even to a lizard. The fear of nuclear war felt by so many Americans during the Cold War emerges in this poem through the image of a lizard staring at a distant road.

This first stanza is surprising, then, because of its focus on an animal that has no conventional poetic qualities. Typically, lizards do not evoke human sympathy; instead, they tend to be vessels of fear, loathing, disgust. What might it mean that this animal, so off-putting to humans, carries the focus of the poem? It means that this poem wishes to place the reader in the condition of the primeval, natural, non-human world: a world that cannot be made human and that is not subject to human ideals. When the desert and the road are viewed from the lizard's perspective they reverse their meaning. The road, a sign of life and escape to a human in the desert, is, to the lizard, an intrusive frightening mechanism that sends dangerous vehicles racing at enormous speed towards him. In other words,

What Do I Read Next?

- More than 100 poets, including Allen Ginsberg, Adrienne Rich, Sharon Olds, and Gary Snyder, offer their views of atomic politics in *Atomic Ghost: Poets Respond to the Nuclear Age,* published in 1995.

- *Learning to Live in the World: Earth Poems* is a 1994 collection of 50 poems by William Stafford about the relationship between humans and the natural world. *Traveling through the Dark* is Stafford's 1963 National Book Award-winning collection. *The Way it Is: New and Selected Poems* (1998), compiled by Robert Bly, Naomi Shihab Nye, and Kim Stafford, is a definitive collection of 400 poems, including more than 70 previously unpublished works—including a lyric the poet wrote on the day of his death. A *Library Journal* review says that the poems "reveal many of Stafford's themes—his affinity for Native Americans, love of nature, protest of war, and concern about the dangers of technology."

- *American Ground Zero: The Secret Nuclear War* (1993), photographed by Carole Gallagher, is a moving and often shocking photoessay book about the victims of radioactive fallout from bomb testing in Nevada. These "downwinders" tell their own stories, which reveal the American government's cover-up of the devastating effects of the tests.

- Richard L. Miller's 1986 book *Under The Cloud: The Decades of Nuclear Testing* is a compelling and comprehensive depiction of the nuclear testing saga, from the political intrigue of the arms race to the deadly effects of radiation fallout.

- Those who enjoy Stafford's casual, talky style and his deep sense of place may want to read Jo McDougall's 1991 poetry collection *Towns Facing Railroads,* which depicts small towns and ordinary lives with extraordinary eloquence and force.

- *Down in My Heart* (1947), Stafford's memoir of his four years in conscientious objector camps during World War II, is a stirring depiction of the fellowship among COs and the public's enmity toward them.

- *Hiroshima: Three Witnesses,* published in 1990, contains first-person accounts of the atomic holocaust by Japanese writers Hara Tamiki, Ota Yoko, and Toge Sankichi. In prose and poetry, these writers bear witness to the horrors of the 1945 bombing.

- *The Sleep of Grass* (www.newsfromnowhere .com/home.html) is a tribute to William Stafford, with poems by David Ignatow, Robert Bly, Linda Pastan, Kathleen Norris, and others.

- Intriguing War Department releases written by the generals involved in the 1945 Trinity bomb test are posted online on www.enviroweb.org/issues/nuketesting/trinity and www.dannen.com/decision.

Stafford's environmentalism is not at all naive or simple. If we are to claim to love nature, then, he suggests here, we had better be willing to love lizards and deserts not just kittens and daffodils. The lizard, after all, knows the desert as his home. Humans, the real threat, as represented by the road are particularly dangerous because on that road one finds "history." When Stafford uses the word, "history," he is reminding us that this concept of time—history as the inevitable "road to progress," as a march towards some better goal, is an entirely human idea.

Stafford uses the fear of this road, of this human idea of history evoked by the lizard to wonderful effect here. After all, most readers are most likely afraid of lizards or, at least, repelled by them. While most people cannot be sympathetic to this creature, then, the poem asks them, nonetheless, to understand its fear of us, of our history. History, here, is more than just an empty cliche, it is more than just the "road to progress." It is also quite specifically a bomb, an entirely human act of willful, deliberate change, an active intervention in the landscape, and, above all else, a process of destruction.

What does the lizard see? What is just down the road? Certainly, it must be the bomb test site, the place for explosions. But is this just any bomb? In 1960, the conjunction of the words desert, history, and bomb would refer to nuclear weaponry. Notice that rather than say that the lizard awaits the mushroom cloud of an exploding nuclear device, Stafford tells us instead that it awaits "history." In the context of this poem, "history" is also a metaphor for "the Bomb," a nuclear weapon. In other words, no other bomb but a nuclear one would invoke so grand a term as "history." Bombs, even in the 19th-century, were old news; but to readers in 1960, one bomb was continual news. It even had managed to colonize an entire noun. Merely by adding a capital "B" to the word (from "bomb" to "Bomb") one could invoke the specter of nuclear annihilation. After all, in 1960, nuclear weaponry was recent enough to have changed the very meaning of history. For the first time ever, humanity had found a way not only to destroy itself but other species as well. Who better then this ancient replica of pre-history, the lizard, to witness the end-result of human history, the nuclear bomb?

In the second stanza, the poem develops its condemnation of human history further. So far Stafford has established the lizard as an image of eternal, timeless, pre-historical nature. Then he has it become witness to history in the form of a nuclear weapon to be exploded just down the road. As the poem says, the lizard "was looking for something farther off / than people could see, an important scene / acted in stone for little selves / at the flute end of consequences." What is this scene? Who are these "little selves?" And what is "the flute end of consequences?" Each of these images is also "Deep." To ask these questions is to reveal their uncertain, mysterious status. (Stafford's metaphorical language, however, also suggests that this lizard is expecting something). "The flute end" as a narrow funnel reducing itself to a point not only describes the apex of a nuclear explosion but also, in geometric terms, the final point of vision. There, on the end of the horizon, this "little self," this lizard, will be made witness to a bizarre scene, a weird drama in stone: the explosion. The horror of this passage is that nature (the lizard), will learn from human history (the Bomb) the truth of total destruction.

The final stanza returns to the image of the lizard in order to prepare it and readers for the in-

evitable lesson: all life, all nature is expendable and the only stewards of history, humans, seem to care very little about it. It is significant to note here that the first two stanzas are each one sentence while the final stanza consists of three sentences. This final stanza already represents a fracturing of the atom of poetic form. Also, each four line stanza (or quatrain) contains a kind of split rhyme, an exploded couplet that still—albeit barely—works. In any four line stanza, readers inevitably look for some kind of rhyme scheme. In the first stanza of "At the Bomb Testing Site," "lizard" (line 1) might be said to (barely) rhyme with "road" (line 3) through the "d" sound, since even one end consonant is a connection. In the second stanza, similarly, "selves" rhymes with Aconsequences" insofar as they share the same two last letters. And in the third stanza, "it" (line 9) rhymes with "desert" (line 12). The point is that each stanza has, at least, the suggestion of a rhyme, of a couplet. But in the last stanza such rhymes vanish. All of this play with form underlines the destructive power of human craft, of human artfulness, of human history. If nature gave us rhymes, patterns, and music, we, as humans, have seen to it to destroy each and every one of those gifts.

In a final bizarre, even surreal image, the lizard, in the last two lines, metamorphoses into a human: it is now said to have elbows and hands. This metaphor, comparing the lizard to a human, brings the two worlds, human and natural, together. We are, says Stafford through this surreal Deep Image of the grasping lizard, all animals. When Stafford associates the primal and prehistoric reptile with the cultured and contemporary human, he tells us that, when it comes to the Bomb, both will have to grip hard and wait. By focusing on the lizard's perspective and invoking the strategies of the Deep Image movement, the poem quietly makes its pacifist case against warfare. It asks readers to consider the meaning of history itself and of the still common assumption that history always marches progressively forward towards a better future. In this poem, evolution from a lizard to a human with hands takes us only to one result: fear.

Source: Jonathan Barron, in an essay for *Poetry for Students,* Gale Group, 2000.

Chris Semansky

Chris Semansky's most recent collection of poems, Blindsided, *published by 26 Books of Portland, Oregon, has been nominated for an Oregon Book Award. In the following essay Semansky examines William Stafford's "At the Bomb Testing Site" as a political poem.*

At a time when literally thousands of love poems are written every day, and the poem of personal loss is the dominant flavor of lyric, William Stafford's poem, "At the Bomb Testing Site," asks us to reconsider the relationship of the personal to the political and to enlarge our sense of the public self to include the interests of creatures as well as human beings, to consider the consequences of universal loss, not just personal. However, he does not do this by clobbering us over the head with his ideology or by belaboring the obvious or ranting about the cause du jour; he does it indirectly and quietly by asking readers to bear witness to an unbearable event while in the skin of another. He does not employ the imperial "I" of so much political pronouncement poetry; he does not base his "position" on identity politics; he does not batter down open doors. He sketches the outline of fear, and he lets readers, with their knowledge of history, fill in the rest.

The poem begins with a reptile's eye view of a nuclear bomb testing site:

> At noon in the desert a panting lizard
> waited for history, its elbows tense,
> watching the curve of a particular road
> as if something might happen.

Stafford manages to create a sense of anxiety by attributing to the lizard a consciousness capable of "wait[ing] for history." Lizards are cold-blooded creatures and, Stafford implies, it takes cold blood to endure what history has to offer. The curve in the road parallels the curve of the lizard's elbows, suggesting something coiled, ready to spring, more snake than lizard-like. The lizard's "panting" and the fact that it is noon underscore the idea of imminence as well, and the image of a road as the animal's visual focus further prepares us for the "accident" looming just ahead, around the curve. The second stanza turns cryptic.

> It was looking at something farther off
> than people could see, an important scene
> acted in stone for little selves
> at the flute end of consequences.

The reptile, all instinctual knowing and geared for survival, has eyes for the future. The "important scene" here could be, as Charles Simic speculates in his *On William Stafford: The Worth of Local Things,* "the matchstick figure of the Indian humpbacked flute player ... surrounded by other matchstick figures ... enacting a scene, a sacred dance." Simic refers to Kokopelli, a Native American deity who has appeared as a petroglyph all over the American Southwest since A.D. 200. He is often shown with a hunched back and playing a

> *This is a poem of witness; it is also intensely personal in its depiction of the lizard, its attention to the nonhuman world, and its evocation of the dread that the possibility of nuclear annihilation engenders."*

flute. Historians theorize that his name may derive from the Hopi or Zuni name for a god, "Koko," and the word "pelli," an indian name for the Desert Robber Fly (his antennae give him a bug-like appearance). In Native American lore he is variously described as a trickster or a minor god who is also a harbinger of fertility, traveling the desert impregnating young women and bringing good fortune to farmers' crops. The music of his flute warns the villagers of his approach, and his hunched back may actually represent a trader's pack filled with beads and shells, ready to be traded for chunks of turquoise or other valuable stones. Kokopelli, then, can be seen as a trickster figure for human and nonhuman life. His music is leading the lizard, and all other living creatures, into a future of certain doom, impregnating the earth with death. Or, conversely, he can be seen as a symbol of fertility and life which are about to be lost to the ravages of a nuclear explosion.

This image suggests the ominous nature of Nature's, and humanity's, inability to stop its own potential destruction. Instead, the lizard, and humanity by extension, can only watch as the scene is enacted. Stafford's poem relies not on a moral but rather on the idea that evoking such a sense of dread will move readers to action. Morals are for survivors, this poem says. They require civilization. This bomb test site could be any one of the various sites which have been used throughout the world to test nuclear devices. However, the images depicted most closely resemble the Trinity site in the desert in central New Mexico. It was there that the Manhattan Project culminated with the detonation of the first nuclear device on July 16, 1945.

The site in the desert is called the "Jornada del Muerto" or "Walk of the Dead." The shock wave resulting from the blast broke windows 120 miles away and was felt 160 miles away. A flash of bright light from the blast was seen over the entire state of New Mexico and in parts of Arizona, Texas, and Mexico, and a mushroom cloud rose to over 38,000 feet. Less than a month later, "Little Boy" and "Fat Man," names given to the nuclear bombs dropped over Hiroshima and Nagasaki, Japan, exploded, wiping out hundreds of thousands of people. Since those explosions, there have been almost 2,000 more nuclear explosions around the world. But the lizard hadn't seen that yet. He waited, powerless.

> There was just a continent without much on it
> under a sky that never cared less.
> Ready for a change, the elbows waited.
> The hands gripped hard on the desert.

In this last stanza, Stafford evokes Naturalism, only here it isn't nature's indifference to humanity being described, the staple theme of Naturalistic literature, but humanity's indifference to nature. The "continent" is the desert itself, and Stafford's description of it as largely barren can be forgiven as he is fusing the lizard's perspective with his human one. His focus on the lizard's parts, its elbows and hands, humanizes the creature and asks us to look closer at the description, to imaginatively participate in the apprehension, the anticipation of a change that itself cannot be imagined.

This is a poem of witness; it is also intensely personal in its depiction of the lizard, its attention to the nonhuman world, and its evocation of the dread that the possibility of nuclear annihilation engenders. In *Against Forgetting: Twentieth-Century Poetry of Witness,* Carolyn Forche, has this to say about the increasingly blurred lines between the personal and the political:

> Poetry of witness presents the reader with an interesting interpretive problem. We are accustomed to rather easy categories: we distinguish between "personal" and "political" poems—the former calling to mind lyrics of love and emotional loss, the latter indicating a public partisanship that is considered divisive, even when necessary. The distinction between the personal and the political gives the political realm too much and too little scope; at the same time, it renders the personal too important and not important enough…. The celebration of the personal, however, can indicate a myopia, an inability to see how larger structures of the economy and the state circumscribe, if not determine, the fragile realm of individuality.

Stafford's poem avoids the pitfall of "partisanship" by making no pronouncements, letting the work of description speak for him. Critic John Gery

observes in *Nuclear Annihilation and Contemporary American Poetry: Ways of Nothingness* that the poem "speaks with an understated power, best evoked through obliquity, as it diminishes the global significance of atomic testing without trivializing it." Gery considers Stafford's poem an "apocalyptic lyric," a type of response to the nuclear age in which we live. Such lyrics embody a postmodern sensibility, Gery argues, which build on an acceptance of impending nuclear annihilation to imagine human continuity. Gery writes that apocalyptic lyrics "strive to shock us into recognizing the extreme violence of the nuclear threat (though not, in most cases, for gratuitous reasons), yet they do so in terms that by lyric conventions draw attention to our humanity…. these apocalyptic poets stretch (and sometimes strain) their metaphors so that, at their best, they deepen our sense of annihilation, particularly by the way they alter our sense of personal experience itself." The image of the desert is already an image of nothingness. Coupled with the "important scene / acted in stone" and an apathetic sky, Stafford's poem does indeed "deepen our sense of annihilation." But if all that we experience as readers is deeper dread, how is this a political poem? Leonard Nathan writes in *On William Stafford: The Worth of Local Things* that Stafford's poem, and other political poems of indirection, help us to "subtly shift the way we see … reality, keeping our imagination alive to possibilities. And perhaps—though this may be wishful thinking—spreading through a wider consciousness than that represented by the tiny audience for poetry." It may well be wishful thinking, but that, Stafford's poem suggests, is better than no thinking at all.

Source: Chris Semansky, in an essay for *Poetry for Students,* Gale Group, 2000.

Sources

Andrews, Tom, ed., *On William Stafford: The Worth of Local Things,* Ann Arbor, MI: University of Michigan Press, 1993.

Baker, Paul R., ed., *The Atomic Bomb: The Great Decision,* New York: Holt, Rinehart and Winston, 1968.

Carpenter, David A., *William Stafford,* Boise, ID: Boise State University, 1986.

Davison, Peter, "The New Poetry," *Atlantic Monthly* Vol. 210, November 1962, p. 88, excerpt reprinted in *On William Stafford: The Worth of Local Things,* Ann Arbor: The University of Michigan Press, 1993.

Des Pres, Terrence, *Praises and Dispraises: Poetry and Politics, the 20th Century,* New York: Viking Penguin, 1988.

Dickey, James, "William Stafford," *Virginia Quarterly Review* Vol. 37, No. 4, autumn 1961, p. 640, reprinted in *On William Stafford: The Worth of Local Things,* Ann Arbor: The University of Michigan Press, 1993.

Dietrich, Bill, "Fifty Years from Trinity," *The Seattle Times,* July 1995, online at WEBedition/Education: www.seattletimes.com/trinity.

Forche, Carolyn, ed., *Against Forgetting: Twentieth-Century Poetry of Witness,* New York: W.W. Norton, 1993.

Garrison, Steve, "William Stafford," *Dictionary of Literary Biography,* Vol. 5: *American Poets Since World War II,* Gale Research, 1980, pp. 292-99.

Gery, John, *Nuclear Annihilation and Contemporary American Poetry: Ways of Nothingness,* Tampa, FL: University Press of Florida, 1996.

Howard, Richard, "Someday, Maybe," *Parnassus* Vol. 2, No. 2, spring/summer 1974, p. 213-20.

Hugo, Richard, "Problems with Landscapes in Early Stafford Poems," *Kansas Quarterly* Vol. 2, No. 2, spring 1970, pp. 33-38.

Kitchen, Judith, *Understanding William Stafford,* Columbia: University of South Carolina Press, 1989.

Nathan, Leonard, "One Vote," *New England Review and Breadloaf Quarterly,* Vol. 5, 1983, pp. 521-24, excerpt reprinted in *On William Stafford: The Worth of Local Things,* edited by Tom Andrews, Ann Arbor: The University of Michigan Press, 1993.

Nordstrom, Lars, *Theodore Roethke, William Stafford, and Gary Snyder: The Ecological Metaphor as Transformed Regionalism,* Stockholm, Sweden: Uppsala, 1989.

Pinsker, Sanford, *Three Pacific Northwest Poets: William Stafford, Richard Hugo, and David Wagoner,* Boston: Twayne Publishers, 1987.

Simic, Charles, "At the Bomb Testing Site," *Field,* fall 1989, pp. 8-10, reprinted in *On William Stafford: The Worth of Local Things,* edited by Tom Andrews, Ann Arbor: The University of Michigan Press, 1993.

Simpson, Louis, "Important and Unimportant Poems," *Hudson Review* Vol. 14, No. 3, autumn 1961, pp. 461-70, excerpt reprinted in *On William Stafford: The Worth of Local Things,* Ann Arbor: The University of Michigan Press, 1993.

Stafford, William, *West of Your City,* Los Gatos, CA: The Talisman Press, 1960.

Stafford, William, *Writing the Australian Crawl: Views on the Writer's Vocation,* Ann Arbor: The University of Michigan Press, 1978.

Stafford, William, *You Must Revise Your Life,* Ann Arbor: The University of Michigan Press, 1986.

For Further Study

Andrews, Tom, ed., *On William Stafford: The Worth of Local Things,* Ann Arbor: The University of Michigan Press, 1993.

> The most comprehensive collection of Stafford criticism, this book contains excerpts or full texts of more than 50 book reviews, general essays, and essays about particular poems or articles. The lack of an index makes navigating the book somewhat difficult, but this is an excellent survey as well as a springboard for further research.

Gery, John, *Nuclear Annihilation and Contemporary American Poetry: Ways of Nothingness,* Tampa: University of Florida, 1995.

> An in-depth study of nuclear theory and American poetry, this book examines four distinct poetic approaches to nuclear culture—protest poetry, apocalyptic lyric poetry, psychohistorical poetry, and the poetry of uncertainty—and discusses the work of a range of poets, from Gertrude Stein to John Ashbery.

Holden, Jonathan, *The Mark To Turn: A Reading of William Stafford's Poetry,* Lawrence: University Press of Kansas, 1976.

> In this review of Stafford's first five books, Holden suggests that Stafford's poetry is far more sophisticated than commonly held, and identifies a pattern of interlocking metaphors that bring depth and vision to the work. He sets forth that Stafford's depiction of Nature's "otherness" is a source of his poems' imaginative energy.

Stafford, William, *Writing the Australian Crawl: Views on the Writer's Vocation,* Ann Arbor: The University of Michigan Press, 1978.

> In essays, poems, and interviews, Stafford provides insight into his poetic process and his views on the art of writing.

Autumn Begins in Martins Ferry, Ohio

James Wright

1963

Like many of James Wright's poems, "Autumn Begins in Martins Ferry, Ohio" is an autobiographical account of an occurrence in Wright's hometown in southeastern Ohio. It was published in the 1963 collection *The Branch Will Not Break,* a book which came to mark a turning point in the poet's writing style, moving him from formal, rhyming patterns to a more lyrical free verse. This poem highlights a subject consistent in Wright's work, namely the distressing and pitiable lives of many working class Americans who struggled through the Great Depression of the 1930s and whose descendants still struggle today.

The setting for "Autumn Begins" is a typical Friday night high school football game with most of the players' fathers watching from the stands. The narrator of the poem, presumably Wright himself, concentrates more on the men than on the game, depicting them as miserable factory workers who drink too much and can only dream of the heroes they will never be. Their wives are described as "starved pullets / Dying for love," essentially a comment on the husbands themselves who are incapable of or uninterested in intimacy. The brief mention of the boys playing football is also a reflection on the fathers. By watching the violent game, the men imagine that they too are virile and strong, but all the while, they must live their fantasy lives through the lives of their young sons.

This poem is both a portrayal of the way a depleted social environment can also diminish people's spirits and an illustration of the crudeness and

violence that Americans have come to think of as acceptable and normal. Throughout his life, James Wright experienced love-hate relationships with his hometown, his state, and his country. The poetry he wrote reflects heavily on those struggles, and "Autumn Begins in Martins Ferry, Ohio" captures a moment on the negative side.

Author Biography

James Wright was born in 1927 in Martins Ferry, Ohio, a small industrial town in the southeastern part of the state. Located just across the Ohio River from Wheeling, West Virginia, Martins Ferry shares with its bordering neighbor rows of factories and steel mills where most of the towns' men worked when Wright was growing up. His own father dropped out of school at an early age and spent fifty years at Hazel-Atlas Glass, a factory that would appear in several of Wright's poems. Wright loved his father but detested the life his father lived and vowed not to fall victim to it himself. He used education as a means to escape Martins Ferry, earning his bachelor's degree from Kenyon College in 1952 and his master's and doctorate degrees from the University of Washington in 1954 and 1957. At Kenyon, he studied under John Crowe Ransom, a well-known and highly respected poet regarded as one of the founding fathers of the New Criticism. Ransom's influence on Wright's style was evident in the young poet's early work, which was well crafted and usually formal in style like that of the New Critics. Before leaving Kenyon, Wright received the Robert Frost Poetry Prize. At the University of Washington, Wright studied under Theodore Roethke, also one of America's foremost poets at the time, and Roethke's work as well profoundly influenced Wright's own, sending it in a more casual, "loose" direction. Over the years, Wright's poetry and publications became as popular and highly regarded as those of his teachers, and he, in turn, would have his own students to influence. Wright taught at the University of Minnesota (1957-1963), Macalester College in St. Paul (1963-1964), and Hunter College in New York (1966-1980). Although he enjoyed much success with his poetry and his teaching, Wright also suffered bouts of depression and mania. During the worst times, he drank excessively and was denied tenure at the University of Minnesota because of his frequent drunkenness. His home life was nearly as traumatic. During the early 1960s, he and his first wife separated several times

James Wright

and eventually divorced, forcing Wright to give up custody of his two sons. In 1967, Wright remarried and would enjoy a more stable marriage with his second wife for thirteen years. Although Wright did manage to escape the desolate world of Martins Ferry, Ohio, the poverty and human suffering he witnessed there as a child were always with him in his writing, in his social commentary, and in his personal grief. Wright contracted cancer of the tongue and died in a New York City hospital in 1980.

Poem Text

In the Shreve High football stadium,
I think of Polacks nursing long beers in
    Tiltonsville,
And gray faces of Negroes in the blast furnace at
    Benwood,
And the ruptured night watchman of Wheeling
    Steel,
Dreaming of heroes.   5

All the proud fathers are ashamed to go home.
Their women cluck like starved pullets,
Dying for love.

Therefore,
Their sons grow suicidally beautiful   10
At the beginning of October,
And gallop terribly against each other's bodies.

Media Adaptations

- Hear James Wright read "Autumn Begins in Martins Ferry, Ohio" by clicking on the "Hear It!" icon at: www.poets.org/lit/poem/jwrigh01 .htm.

- A 47-minute cassette was recorded by James Wright in 1976-77 entitled "Poetry and Voice of James Wright." This tape includes 24 poems, but it is now out of print and very difficult to find.

Poem Summary

Line 1:

It is not unusual for Wright to begin his poems with simple statements indicating place or person so that the reader knows exactly where or who the speaker is. (His poem "At the Executed Murderer's Grave" begins: "My name is James Wright, and I was born / Twenty-five miles from this infected grave / In Martins Ferry, Ohio....") It is also not unusual for the poet to use real-life places and people in his more autobiographical poems, and that is the case here. In 1924, Martins Ferry High School was dedicated as the Charles R. Shreve School, and that was its name when Wright attended high school there in the early 1940s. The key to this opening line, however, is not just his mention of the school itself, but the football stadium in particular. As the rest of the poem will indicate, Wright sees football as a violent game that has become an American ritual—a much beloved one, at that—in spite of the barbarism and destructive nature it represents.

Lines 2-4:

These three lines imply two separate but equally important notions about the narrator's relationship to his surroundings. First, he sets himself up as a detached observer, someone who does not belong to the scene he is watching. What he observes is not the game on the field, but the people in the stands, the fathers who have come to watch their sons play. Secondly, Wright indicates his feelings about the local men and the lives they lead, using language that suggests both abhorrence and sympathy toward them. He thinks "of Polacks nursing long beers in Tiltonsville" (another nearby factory town), but the distasteful euphemism is not so much an ethnic slur as a recognition of the plight of so many immigrants who came to America. Whether their ancestors' immigration was by choice or by force ("And the gray faces of Negroes in the blast furnace at Benwood"), many ethnic groups found themselves struggling to make a living and a home for their families in the United States. The night watchman in line 4, also a factory worker, is "ruptured" in more ways than one. On the literal level, we may assume he has a medical problem, but he is also torn and broken in a spiritual or emotional way. Like these men, Wright's father worked hard for very little in return, and this is the life that the poet desperately avoided.

Line 5:

Wright ends the first stanza with three simple words that sum up the pathetic lives of the men he has described in the previous lines: they can only dream of what they have never been and will never be. The game of football, however, is a vehicle for their dreaming, and Wright will emphasize this point in the final stanza.

Lines 6-8:

In line 6, the fathers encounter two opposing feelings. They are both "proud" and "ashamed." This quick juxtaposition is indicative of the dual roles that Wright believes most of America's working class has been forced to play. On the outside, the men are nearly beaten down by poverty, frustration, and a hopeless future. On the inside, they take pride in the strength and endurance of their sons who fight so bravely on the field. But for all the comfort they receive from their children, their wives evoke just the opposite. The "women cluck like starved pullets," and this shames their husbands who feel at fault for "starving" them. The poet likens the wives to young hens clucking about the barnyard in search of food, painting a picture of lonely, fretful women who have no real communication, no real relationship with their husbands. But these wives are not starving for food—they are "Dying for love." These three words that make up line 8 are actually more indicative of the men's troubles than of the women's. The line reflects their impotence, perhaps literally, but more likely emotionally. They have no ability to change their lives, to better their environments, or to provide a generous lifestyle for their families. Rather than confront the reality of home life, they stay away as much as possible. They drink for hours in local bars or go to sporting events while their wives grow lonelier and feel more unloved.

Line 9:

This one-word line is the link between the first two stanzas and the closing and serves to turn the poem into a type of syllogism. In this form of deductive reasoning, we have two propositions and a conclusion, such as in: *All men are mortal; Socrates is a man; therefore, Socrates is mortal.* Wright's poem is not as simple and plain as this example, but "Therefore" does indicate a cause and effect relationship between what has been said before and what is to follow. The final three lines expose the "effect" of the rest of the poem.

Lines 10-12:

Wright has already established that the fathers see their sons as heroic and that they derive a dream-like pleasure from watching them play the game of football. We are not surprised, then, that the boys grow beautiful in line 10, but that they "grow suicidally beautiful" is somewhat of a shock. Interpretation of this adverb has generally fallen along two lines with critics over the years. On one hand, the sons are seen as victims of their fathers' dreams, having to play out the violent roles that make them "heroes." On the other hand, they are viewed as desperately willing to fight for their moment of glory even though it will be short-lived, if it comes about at all. In *James Wright: The Poetry of a Grown Man,* Kevin Stein notes that "Though the connection between the despair of the parents and the violent actions of the sons does not follow altogether logically, as the 'therefore' would suggest, still, the speaker's syllogism achieves seamless closure. Having seen the 'ruptured' dream of their fathers and mothers, the sons passionately partake of their own 'suicidally beautiful' ritual of competition, each hoping he, unlike his father before him, will achieve momentary glory...." Critic David Dougherty views the ritual in a different way. In *James Wright* he states that "The youths train and sacrifice to live out the frustrated dreams of their fathers.... Their athletic skills and developed bodies are sources of beauty, but the controlled violence on the field is suicidal.... Community rituals have degenerated to episodes of institutionalized violence in which the sons are victims of their fa-

thers' aspirations, and the implication is that they will sire sons who will in turn sacrifice for them."

Whether the boys are fighting for their own short-lived glory or simply playing the role of pawns for their fathers' imaginations, the last two lines of the poem tell us that when football season rolls around each year, the sons will "gallop" like stampeding horses and play with fearless abandon. The image of their throwing themselves "terribly" against each other goes hand-in-hand with Wright's overall portrait of desperate people helpless to exert any real control over their own lives.

Themes

American Dream

On a rather obvious level, "Autumn Begins in Martins Ferry, Ohio" is about the struggles of America's working class. Wright grew up during the Depression and spent his entire youth witnessing the effects of a society that glamorizes wealth and power on the poor and powerless. He uses this poem and many others to portray the way he views the barren lives of blue-collar men and women: they drink too much, they are lonely, they are ashamed, and they find their only comfort in dreaming of a better life. Most of Wright's work expresses the opinion that those dreams do not often come true.

The brief, simple descriptions of the men who sit in the stands at the football game ("Polacks nursing long beers," "Negroes in the blast furnace," "the ruptured night watchman of Wheeling Steel") actually reveal ample, complex problems in their day-to-day existence. These are not problems initiated by personal ineptness or any lack of intelligence or desire on their part. Rather, the poem alludes to the doleful, daily grind of their lives as what they have been handed by American society and the political agendas that keep the status quo intact. Wright often asserted disillusionment with the principals on which he believed his country operated: greed, indulgence, and necessary and accepted inequality. While men like the poet's own father and those in the poem go to work in factories, drink in bars at night, and avoid going home to their lonely wives, there are others who enjoy easy jobs, make lots of money, and live happy lives at home. Wright was not naive enough to believe that wealthy people are always content, but he did see a sharp dividing line between those who made it to the top and those who

Topics for Further Study

- Consider whether you enjoy more and understand better poems that are written in free verse or in a formal (rhymed, metered) style. Explain why you prefer one over the other and how one style may be more difficult to read than the other.

- Report on how your community views its local athletic teams and the effects that any suspected illegal acts (paying players, recruiting violations, etc.) has had or would likely have on the social climate surrounding local sports.

- Write an essay on how you think most immigrants to the United States felt upon their arrival and how those feelings may have changed over time.

- Pretend you have just retired from a factory where you worked for 50 years and write a letter to a grandchild telling him or her how you now feel.

had to "hold up the world" for them. Ironically, without factories, mills, and mines, the pleasures enjoyed by America's elite would not be possible. But this poem offers no consolation in that fact.

Alienation and Loneliness

The first two words of the second line in "Autumn Begins in Martins Ferry, Ohio" denote a subtle theme in the poem that becomes more visible as we read more of James Wright's work. Alienation from one's own environment appears often in his poems, usually taking the form of the narrator as an observer, not a participant, in the poem's action. The words "I think" at the beginning of the line set the narrator apart from his surroundings. He *thinks* of the factory and steel mill workers who sit around him watching their sons play football, but he is not one of them. He does not mention any personal connection to the game, nor is he one of the "proud fathers ... ashamed to go home." Instead, he very poignantly states, *"Their* women cluck ... "* and *"Their* sons grow suicidally beautiful...." But although the speaker is personally un-

attached to the situation, he is not without empathy for those directly involved.

The dismal scene portrayed in the poem would easily include Wright's own father who spent 50 years working in a glass factory. With fierce and desperate determination, the poet escaped the same fate by getting an education and moving away from Martins Ferry. He intentionally alienated himself from the environment of his childhood and that of his family. This estrangement is different from that felt by people who want to fit in, but, for whatever reason, sense that they do not. Wright's poem speaks to a self-inflicted separation, sometimes physical and always psychological. The narrator—Wright himself—has "been there," so the understanding, sympathy, and even grief he feels for the working men and their families are real. What is missing from the poem is the belief that the men sitting in the stadium "Dreaming of heroes" can do the same as he did: flee the working class life and start a new one with a rewarding career (both monetarily and intellectually) and a happy relationship with their wives and children. There is no rallying cry in the poem to suggest its characters have any control over their own environment or their fate within it. Rather, these men, women, and children greet each day with resignation and will one day leave their children and grandchildren behind to follow in the same dull footprints. Only the poet has securely alienated himself from this world.

Flesh vs. Spirit

Several of Wright's poems make mention of sports and most often the game is football. "Autumn Begins" is centered around this seasonal event—one that quickly grew in popularity and has become a very real part of American culture. But why football? Why do sports such as bowling, sailing, fencing, volleyball, or even baseball not elicit the same fervor and, often times, violence from people who go to see them? The answer may seem obvious: people prefer excitement and power in their sports more so than tedious strategy and finesse. In a 1979 interview with poet Dave Smith, Wright said of football and the people in his hometown: "The football season, then, was very intensely a communal activity, a communal occasion. Teams from the various towns along the Ohio River ... met and provided a point of focus in which the members of the distinct communities would see one another. Sometimes this meeting, this confrontation with the ritualized, formalized violence of those football teams, would inspire a peculiar kind of violence in the spectators too."

The men whose "sons grow suicidally beautiful" view their boys as heroes—strong, virile, fearless. These are adjectives they cannot apply to themselves and so they are content to sit and watch their sons "gallop terribly against each other's bodies." Other sports surely involve rough physical contact, but the game of football supports (in theory, if not always in practice) a *controlled* violence, "ritualized, formalized," in the poet's words. This makes it especially appealing to those who can only dream of being powerful and in control.

Style

"Autumn Begins in Martins Ferry, Ohio" is written in free verse, an open style that is non-syllabic and non-rhyming. If we count the poem's line syllables or even the number of lines themselves, there appears to be complete randomness in its construction: five lines in the first verse, three in the second, and four in the third and syllable totals for each line that amount to 9, 13, 15, 11, 5, 11, 8, 4, 2, 11, 9, and 13, respectively. If, though, traditional form does not hold the poem together, the imagery and the placement of particular words most surely provide its cohesion.

Prior to *The Branch Will Not Break*, the book in which "Autumn Begins" first appeared, James Wright wrote mostly in very stylized verse, patterning his work after the likes of Robert Frost and E.A. Robinson, as well as the crafted seventeenth-century poets Ben Johnson and John Donne. With his new book, however, Wright relaxed the form and sought to present his poetry—specifically, its *meaning*— through brief but powerful imagery. His credo became the "pure clear word," extracted from another of his poems ("Many of Our Waters: Variations on a Poem by a Black Child") in which he says, "The young poets of New York come to me with / Their mangled figures of speech, / But they have little pity / For the pure clear word."

"Autumn Begins" is filled with pure, clear words, making this rather short poem speak loudly and powerfully. The first verse describes the men in the poem, the second verse describes the women, and the third their sons. Each verse makes use of very descriptive adjectives, adverbs, and verbs to bring the images to life: "nursing long beers," "gray faces of Negroes," "ruptured night watchman," "cluck like starved pullets," and "gallop terribly against each other's bodies" all paint a very vivid picture of the scene, even that of the women who are not actually present in the football stadium. As seen earlier, even the otherwise generic word "Therefore" becomes crucial in this poem, and its placement on a line alone connotes the power it holds in forming a bridge between the first two verses and the third. Notice, also, how the last lines of verses one and two mirror each other in both structure and description. The men are "Dreaming of heroes" and the women are "Dying for love." The participles alone—"dreaming" and "dying"— present an unsettling juxtaposition of images and essentially sum up Wright's version of life in working class America.

Lines 10 and 12 also offer a striking comparison, along with a similar flow of syllabic sound. Pronounced slowly and deliberately, "grow su-i-ci-dal-ly beau-ti-ful" and "gal-lop ter-ri-bly a-gainst" ring hauntingly on the tongue and link the fate of the young football players to that of their dreaming fathers and dying mothers. After closely examining the poem's structure, we may find that the verse is not quite as "free" as first presumed. Truly there is no traditional form at work here, but Wright's careful selection of words and their placement in creating a short poem do reflect deliberate and particular attention to detail.

Historical Context

The 1950s and 1960s were tumultuous times in American history. Although the 1950s are often looked back upon with nostalgia and regarded as a decade of innocence, bobby socks, and souped-up cars, it was also the decade of McCarthyism and the Communist Control Act, atomic testing, air raid shelters, and a government-backed "Red Scare" to maintain public support for a large military budget. According to Howard Zinn's *A People's History of the United States,* during the period from 1944 to 1961, "The country was on a permanent war economy which had big pockets of poverty, but there were enough people at work, making enough money, to keep things quiet.... The lowest fifth of the families received 5 percent of all the income; the highest fifth received 45 percent of all the income." Also during this period, James Wright graduated from high school in Martins Ferry, earned his bachelor's degree, joined the army and was stationed in Japan during the American occupation, returned home to go to graduate school, and began writing poetry. By the early 1960s, he had won the Yale Series of Younger Poets Award and was

Compare & Contrast

- **1948:** Only 33 percent of all adults in the United States graduated from high school.

  1963: The high school graduation rate increases to 46 percent.

  Today: Eighty percent of U.S. adults hold high-school diplomas.

- **1929:** Pop Warner Little Scholars, a national youth football program, is founded in Philadelphia, Pennsylvania.

  1947: Pop Warner hosts its first National Championship event.

1998: Pop Warner has leagues in 38 U.S. states.

Today: Pop Warner is in 1,400 communities nationwide; the NFL Players' Association estimates that 60 to 79 percent of NFL players took part in Pop Warner football.

- **1970s-1990s:** Total participation in high-school football hovers around one million.

  Today: Football remains the largest male-participant, high-school sport in the United States.

---

working on his first free-verse collection which included "Autumn Begins in Martins Ferry, Ohio."

The state of the American economy played a major role in the poet's work, from the Great Depression of the 1930s in which he grew up to the post World War II war economy with its "big pockets of poverty" into which many of Wright's hometown acquaintances fell. Especially troubling to him were not just the debilitating effects of working hard for little money, but the fact that there was such a marked imbalance in the distribution of wealth in America. That the small percentage at the top of society acquired nearly half the income for the entire country was difficult for Wright to swallow. When given the chance, he spoke publicly about his outrage over injustice and inequality, but his most common venue for expressing disgust and cynicism (as well as sympathy and compassion) was his poetry. "Autumn Begins" paints a typical picture of life for the working class during the 1950s. The highlight of the week was a Friday night high school football game, which provided both a diversion from workday drudgery and an opportunity to fantasize about a more romantic, heroic existence.

Although this poem centers mostly on the feelings of the "proud fathers," the second verse is important in depicting the wives of the working class men. They are seen as ineffectual and helpless, simply waiting for their husbands to return home and make them happy. And they are uneducated. Compare the scenario in Wright's poem to a description of American women in the March 7, 1960, issue of *Time:* "The educated American woman has her brains, her good looks, her car, her freedom … freedom to choose a straight-from-Paris dress (original or copy), or to attend a class in ceramics or calculus; freedom to determine the timing of her next baby or who shall be the next President of the United States." This was the time of Jackie Kennedy who set the standard for dress and hairstyle for many years in America's female population. It was the time of an emerging women's movement and changing attitudes about traditional gender roles. And it was a time of a new spiritual and sexual freedom for women unlike anything imagined in previous decades. But in Wright's Martins Ferry, time had stood still. Most women there had not attended calculus or ceramics classes; they could not afford dresses from Paris and did not own their own cars; and they most certainly did not feel they had their "freedom." They were, in light of the poet's environment, mere "pullets."

In the 1979 interview with Dave Smith, Wright addressed the issue of what may be called the upper-class "attitude." He stated that, "The person who is born to privilege … [or has attained it], is often trying to show a common touch he does not really have. One of the most astonishing and, to me, fascinating examples of this is to be found in a photograph that appeared in a newspaper during the 1960 presidential election campaign." Wright goes on to relate the circumstances of the photo in which the wealthy, esteemed Henry Cabot Lodge, Richard Nixon's running mate, was visiting Coney Island. According to Wright, "Lodge knew that he was superb," in his beautiful, expensive white shirt. In order to fit in with the "common" people of Coney Island, though, Lodge had rolled up his sleeves and was not wearing a tie. He also held a hot dog in his hand, and this was the point of fascination for Wright. "The expression on his face revealed profound conflict," Wright said of Lodge. " … He looked at that hot dog as if it were an obscene object which he *had* to eat."

Clearly, a vivid contrast in one's own environment and that of a much more privileged world provides fuel for a creative mind to draw upon. Asked about his feelings on his hometown, Wright seemed both nostalgic and apologetic: "My feelings about it are complicated. People in that place have gotten angry with me for things I've written…. I haven't always written about Martins Ferry but I have tried sometimes to write about the life that I knew."

Critical Overview

As is common with many creative artists who change their style after acquiring a following of fans who like the "old" ways, criticism can be quick and harsh. Wright had his share of bad reviews after publishing his third book, *The Branch Will Not Break,* which marked a very vivid turning point in his poetry. In "The Work of James Wright," an article by fellow poet and friend Robert Bly, the writer describes the views of two particular critics who did not like Wright's new style: "Many reviewers watched this move with hostility," Bly said. "Larry Rubin, Jr., American scholar from Hollins College, … said of Wright: '… he has gone off on a tangent, it seems to me. He has completely abdicated the job of giving meaning to what he describes….' [Critic] Thom Gunn [stated]: 'In *The Branch Will Not Break,* Wright has pretty well reversed his attitude to style and content…. He is far from being interested in moral questions now, and there is a deliberate avoidance of anything resembling thought.'"

Despite these two similar reproofs, however, Wright's poetry in general—and *Branch* in partic-

ular—was, and still is, very highly regarded by writers, scholars, and the poetry-reading public. In Peter Stitt's article, "James Wright: The Quest Motif in *The Branch Will Not Break,*" the critic states that this book of poems "… is generally regarded as marking [Wright's] transformation into an important and path-breaking contemporary poet. It has been described by various critics as 'the real watershed in Wright's work,' 'one of the key books of the 1960s,' and as containing poetry 'unlike anything being written in America at the time.'" One of those poems "unlike anything being written" was the highly praised "Autumn Begins in Martins Ferry, Ohio," and it is likely the most anthologized poem from the collection.

Criticism

David Caplan

David Caplan is a doctoral candidate at the University of Virginia. In the following essay he considers the hopelessness that "Autumn Begins in Martins Ferry, Ohio" expresses.

Grammarians should love James Wright's poem, "Autumn Begins in Martins Ferry, Ohio." As many grammar textbooks lament, casual writers rarely take seriously transitional words such as "consequently," "so," and "therefore." As a consequence, these words are often used indiscriminately, tacked on to sentences that seem to be a little short or to lack sufficient rhetorical grandeur. Where these grammatical lapses occur, errors in logic frequently follow; for example, causation is implied where no causation exists.

"Therefore," however, is the most important word in "Autumn Begins in Martins Ferry, Ohio." It is only the word which warrants a complete line; three words comprise the next shortest line. Furthermore, "[t]herfore" is conspicuously placed at the start of the final stanza. There the entire poem turns on this seemingly modest word.

The first two stanzas describe the hardscrabble inhabitants of Wright's hometown. The "autumn" that "begins" in Martins Ferry, Ohio suggests a seasonal cycle; yet the poem's characters do not change so much as remain stuck in bitter unhappiness. In only five lines, the first stanza provides sketches of a variety of people, "Polacks nursing long beers," "Negroes" working on the floor of steel factories, and a plant's night watchman. These lines emphasize the economic causes of these men's mis-

What Do I Read Next?

- James Wright's first published collection of poems, *The Green Wall* (1957), and his second, *Saint Judas* (1959), make for interesting comparison to his third book, *The Branch Will Not Break* (1963), which includes "Autumn Begins in Martins Ferry, Ohio." After reading the first two and then the third, one can easily see his change in style and understand what sent many poetry critics to their opposing corners.

- *To a Blossoming Pear Tree* (1977) was Wright's last collection published before his death. The poems in it represent yet another departure from style, in the form of prose poems. Many of these brief "paragraphs" of descriptions were inspired by Wright's visits to Europe, particularly Italy, and their images portray his love of the countryside there, as well as its people. Never far from home in thought, though, the poet also included in this collection several poems that make mention of Ohio.

- Today, sports fans are not as naive as they may have been in the past when it comes to high school and college athletics and the corruption that sometimes permeates both. Rick Telander,

- former writer for *Sports Illustrated*, examines the myths that surround sports—college football in particular—in his *The Hundred Yard Lie* (1989). This is a tell-all account from a person who has spent much of his career dealing with the world of athletics in America.

- In 1963, President John F. Kennedy was assassinated in Dallas. Many say this act ended America's "age of innocence" that occurred in the 1950s. Michael L. Kurtz's *Crime of the Century: The Kennedy Assassination from a Historian's Perspective* (1982) offers an account of the crime that is free of sensationalism and the "yellow journalism" that has often permeated the hundreds of others books and articles on Kennedy's death.

- Teacher and former *Chicago Tribune* columnist Robert Wolf collects the writings of people seldom read or heard in *An American Mosaic: Prose and Poetry by Everyday Folk* (1999). This book includes writings by America's rural citizens whose lives have been determined by harsh economics, as well as poems and stories by homeless men and women.

---

ery. Stuck in grueling or desperately lonely jobs, they suffer from a sense of unrelenting sadness. Their lives are like the "faces of the Negroes,": "gray," bored, cheerless, and hopeless.

Calling them "Polacks" and "Negroes," "Autumn Begins in Martins Ferry, Ohio" emphasizes the men's ethnic identities. (Only the night watchman's race and/or national origin remains undefined). These racial and ethnic differences, though, give way to larger similarities. These characters' ethnic identities differ, but they live essentially similar lives and share the same dream. They spend their days working hard and "[d]reaming of heroes."

In the grim scenes that "Autumn Begins in Martins Ferry, Ohio" presents, economic reality trumps racial identity. For those familiar with Marxist thought, it easy to see how the poem echoes

some of Marxist cultural analysis. Alienated from their labor, workers such as the "ruptured night watchman" enjoy little power over their lives. While the poem sympathetically presents members of the lower class, lower-class life is depicted as dreary. In a manner similar to classic Marxist studies of working class labor in northern England, "Autumn Begins in Martins Ferry, Ohio" depicts individuals ground down by repressive economic forces.

Part of what's striking about the opening stanza is the wealth of regional detail it presents. Its references to "the Shreve High football stadium," "Tiltonsville," "the blast furnace at Bernwood," and "Wheeling Steel" establish Wright's interest in the particularity of local experience. The opening lines' frame structure implicitly raises this issue. Watching a highschool football game, the speaker, who soon disappears from the poem, wonders why the region so passionately competes at and follows this violent sport. As its title indicates, "Autumn Begins in Martins Ferry, Ohio" considers why certain people in a certain place live the way they do.

In the second stanza, the poem shifts from the workplace to the home. The difference between the grim reality the men endure and the fantasies they dream intensifies their sense of shame. While the first stanza suggests the economic roots of the men's misery, the second shows how this unhappiness moves into their home lives. "All the proud fathers are ashamed to go home"; ashamed of their lives, they do not want their wives and children to see them in their present condition. Instead of the "heroes" they dream of, the men see themselves as powerless. Their sense of embarrassment and disgrace makes them less capable of love, in both its physical and emotional manifestations. The result is a kind of death between husband and wife, father and mother.

As I suggested before, the poem turns on the word, "[t]herfore," which starts the third stanza. To see the importance of this otherwise unobtrusive word, it is helpful to consider how the last stanza would differ if it began with a word similar but not quite equivalent to "therefore." For example, "so" claims the same basic dictionary definition as "[t]herefore." However, "so" is much more conversational than "therefore"; a speaker who uses words such as "Polacks" and "blast furnace" would be much more likely to say "so" than "therefore." Furthermore, it is difficult to hear almost any speaker talking in a casual context say, "therefore." "So how can I help you?" a shopkeeper might ask a visitor to her store, not "Therefore, how can I help you?"

In short, "[t]herefore" is more elevated than the rather plain style that precedes. It signals a change to a grander diction which echoes a grander subject matter. In the opening stanza the men dream of heroes; in the final stanza their sons try to live these fantasies. The football game is modified with adverbs reminiscent of heroic struggle: "Their sons grow suicidally beautiful / … And gallop terribly against each other's bodies." The language is majestic. The sons are not highschool jocks wasting their time with a particularly brutish sport. Instead, they are closer to figures from a classical epic engaged in quests or characters from a Greek play doomed to act out deadly family dramas. The rhetoric inflates the football players to literally

> *In the grim scenes that "Autumn Begins in Martins Ferry, Ohio" presents, economic reality trumps racial identity."*

larger-than-life proportions. Horses, not people, "gallop."

"Therefore" also belongs to the language of a logical argument, whether a syllogism ("A=B and B=C. Therefore, A=C") or the rhetoric of a formal argument. According to convention "therefore" signals a conclusion. "Autumn Begins in Martins Ferry, Ohio" traces the effects of the men's unfulfilled dreams. Shamed by the work they do and the lives they lead, the men dream of heroes and the women of love. These dreams are passed to their sons, who pursue them perhaps unknowingly. "Therefore" signals how the children are propelled by forces beyond their control. Just as the economic forces oppress their parents, their parents' unachieved hopes motivate their desire for glory. Like the third part of a logical syllogism, the boys' lives are dictated by what precedes them: their fathers' shame and their mothers' lack of love. In the poem, the changing of the seasons seems to bring repetition of the past, not change. Similarly, the boys are fated to repeat their parents lives.

The final stanza shows how football enacts a ritual of eroticism and self-destructive violence. The lines I quoted in a previous paragraph combine the violent and the erotic: "Their sons grow suicidally beautiful / … And gallop terribly against each other's bodies." In the world the poem presents, the desire for love can only be expressed through violence; what is beautiful must be suicidally so. At the same time, the opposite seems true, as acts of violence become loving. The poem's last word emphasizes this point. The players not only "gallop terribly against each other" but "gallop terribly against each other's *bodies*" (my italics). "[B]odies" emphasizes the paradoxically tender violence of football. In gestures of suicidal beauty, the players don't seem to want to hurt each other so much as express an otherwise inarticulate beauty. They gallop like showhorses, luxuriating in the crowd's admiration and their own power.

In a famous line, Irish poet W. B. Yeats expressed his ambivalence about the Irish Easter Rebellion, "A terrible beauty is born." The final image in "Autumn Begins in Martins Ferry, Ohio" echoes this celebrated phrase. However, the players who "gallop terribly against each other's bodies" are not giving birth to a "terrible beauty" as Yeats despaired of the Irish Rebellion. Instead, they repeat the cycle they were born into, a pattern of unfulfilled dreams, love expressed through violence, and violence raised to the passion of love. At the start of autumn, another generation toils unhappily ever after.

Source: David Caplan, in an essay for *Poetry for Students,* Gale Group, 2000.

Jeannine Johnson

Jeannine Johnson currently teaches writing and literature at Harvard University. She has also taught at Yale, from which she received her Ph.D., and at Wake Forest University. Her most recent essay is on Adrienne Rich's "To a Poet," published in the Explicator. *In the following essay, Johnson considers Wright's use of memory and geography in "Autumn Begins in Martins Ferry, Ohio," arguing that his commitment to place prevents him from inappropriately idealizing his subject.*

In "Autumn Begins in Martins Ferry, Ohio," James Wright offers a stark but loving portrait of his postindustrial hometown. The human objects of Wright's attention are outsiders: they include "Polacks" and "Negroes," factory workers and neglected housewives, and an assortment of grown men living vicariously through teenage athletes. These are people who, by most social measures, have failed; or, if they succeed they do so only in their dreams and in their memories. While Wright's powers of observation are exceptionally sharp, he adopts as his poetic persona one who is not so much an observer of the scene he describes but a sympathizer within it. This poet sees too much to detach himself from these lives, and he carefully constructs his moral position as participant and artist. What might with another poet become unjust criticism is with Wright fair commentary. And while some poets might mourn for what these people and this place could never have become, Wright does not falsely idealize them. The poet does not sever the people of Martins Ferry, Ohio, from their memories and dreams nor from the harsh truths of their lives. For even though it is in the imagination—in theirs and in the poet's—that they become whole and beautiful, such visions are meaningless without their ties to reality.

Poet W. H. Auden chose Wright's first book of poems, *The Green Wall,* as the winner of the Yale Series of Younger Poets award for 1957. In his foreword to that book, Auden asserts that "in Mr. Wright's poems … the present is not unhappy but unreal, and it is memories, pleasant or unpleasant, which are celebrated for their own sake as the real past." While Wright composed "Martins Ferry" after completing *The Green Wall,* Auden's remarks illuminate the later poem as well as those in his early collection. Although the poet depicts fathers who are "ashamed," mothers who are "Dying for love," and sons who are "suicidally beautiful," the character of "Martins Ferry" tends much more toward the unreal than the unhappy. The inhabitants of this town are not so much disappointed with the present as resigned to it. The "Polacks nursing their long beers" and the "Negroes" whose faces are grayed by their shifts in front of the blast furnace do not rejoice in their fortunes, but neither do they complain about them.

There are several factors that lend an "unreal" quality to the world that Wright portrays. The "night watchman of Wheeling Steel"—a plant across the river from Martins Ferry in Wheeling, West Virginia—is "ruptured" because, instead of attending to the present, he is "Dreaming of heroes" while he performs his duties. The spectators at the football game also exist in a kind of limbo between past, present, and future: the fathers are reluctant to leave even after the game is finished because returning home means returning to the present, abandoning the realm of the imagination and the glories of the past. Temporality is confused even in the structure of the poem. In the first line of the poem, the poet announces his position "In the Shreve High football stadium." But in the next line, he mentally takes leave of the stadium in order to think about others in the town. In the second stanza, the poet returns to the football field, but only after the game is over. The poem ends in the third stanza at an intermediary moment, during the game itself, when the sons of Martins Ferry "grow suicidally beautiful" and "gallop terribly against each other's bodies." The simple present tense of the verbs "grow" and "gallop" suggests a kind of stasis, as if these actions have no beginning and no end. This is a situation that those in the stands might wish for: a never-ending game and an uninterrupted distraction from their lives. However, the verb tense implies not only continual motion but a repeated action, and it seems to signal that memory will never erase reality, and that the condition of this town and its inhabitants will never change.

Martins Ferry's spiritual condition will never change, despite the certainty of constant techno-logical progress (represented in the poem by the mills and factories). In his foreword to *The Green Wall,* Auden notes that Wright often confronts the fact that modern human "society ha[s] a self-made history while the rest of nature does not." In other words, our vocations and lives are no longer based in the rural but in the industrial-technological world, and thus we have lost our necessary link to nature and its particular kind of ahistorical cycles. "Autumn Begins in Martins Ferry" confirms this situation. The title of Wright's poem suggests an essential connection between the change of seasons and the people of this small Ohio town. However, the poem reveals that the natural seasons and hu-man lives develop independently of each other: technology will advance and the mechanization of modern life will continue, but not according to any calendar determined by nature. The people of Mar-tins Ferry attempt to reunite with the organic year through the seasons of sports. Through football, they achieve the reassurances of predictability and the comforts of a diversion from everyday activi-ties. Nevertheless, the reconciliation with nature is incomplete at best, and the violence of the game impairs its consolatory capacities.

The poem's subject is typical of Wright's ma-ture work, in which he frequently addresses themes of deficiency, estrangement, and alienation. It is also common for him to use as his setting the Mid-west, the place of his birth and the region where he spent the greater part of his life. He was born and raised in Ohio and attended Kenyon College. Later, Wright taught at the University of Minnesota and at Macalester College in St. Paul, and many of his poem titles mention such cities as Minneapolis, Chicago, Pine Island (Minnesota), and Fargo (North Dakota). But Wright seems most personally invested in his vision when he returns to his home state. In "Many of our Waters: Variations on a Poem by a Black Child" (1969), Wright addresses the Ohio River: "Oh my back-broken beloved Ohio. / I, too, was beautiful, once, / Just like you. / We were both still a little / Young, then. / Now, all I am is a poet, / Just like you." Here the poet revis-its the complicated relationship between the past and the present—between memory and reality— and he attests that poetry springs naturally from ge-ographical place. He also reiterates that beauty, though perhaps degraded, is never fully destroyed and can always be dredged up, even from a "back-

> *... [T]his poem marks a beginning (of autumn) as well as an end (of idealized youth), and though the poem's scene is somewhat bleak, its tone is not despairing."*

broken" river. In this poem as in "Martins Ferry," Wright refuses to correct imperfections and in so doing he defies the artificiality of nostalgia and false memory.

Throughout his life, Wright was affiliated with formal educational institutions, and he received many awards from established, high-brow sources. He received a Ph.D. from the University of Wash-ington, where he studied with the poet Theodore Roethke. The year after John Ashbery won the prestigious Yale Series award, Wright won the same prize. He spent much of his life teaching at colleges and universities, wrote reviews and criti-cism for scholarly journals, and won the Pulitzer Prize for his *Collected Poems* (1971).

However, though Wright moved easily in aca-demic circles, his poetry resists over-intellectual-ization. A poem such as "Autumn Begins in Mar-tins Ferry, Ohio," written relatively early in Wright's career, is especially accessible to a non-scholarly audience. He is frequently quoted as say-ing that he "wanted to make the poems say some-thing humanly important instead of just showing off with the language." His dedication to the hu-man element does not force him to compromise his facility with language, as he demonstrates in "Mar-tins Ferry": "All the proud fathers are ashamed to go home. / Their women cluck like starved pullets, / Dying for love." Here the poet compresses into two short sentences the reaction of the fans after they have witnessed their team lose a football game. The brevity of Wright's statements is in ten-sion with the expanse of emotional devastation that these people feel when their only release from the ordinary fails to satisfy them. The only unusual word in these lines is "pullets," a term Wright uses instead of "chickens" likely because it is more del-icate and supple. In addition, "pullets" is a term used to refer specifically to young chickens. By identifying the youthfulness of the women, Wright verifies that already their lives have become prematurely—and inevitably—routine.

Yet this poem marks a beginning (of autumn) as well as an end (of idealized youth), and though the poem's scene is somewhat bleak, its tone is not despairing. Rodney Phillips, a curator of English and American literature at the New York Public Library, has maintained that Wright's "voice became one of the sweetest of the age, his great subject the heart's passage to the deepest interior consciousness, to the moment of perfect awareness, of pure being and of pure enlightenment." But in Wright's poems one never achieves this purity of self-knowledge without first grounding oneself in a particular geographical place. Location is not merely an ornament in Wright's poetry but provides an integral part of its meaning, and poetry is not compensation for reality but is a means by which to unearth reality's rough beauty.

Source: Jeannine Johnson, in an essay for *Poetry for Students,* Gale Group, 2000.

Bruce Meyer

Bruce Meyer is the director of the creative writing program at the University of Toronto. He has taught at several Canadian universities and is the author of three collections of poetry. In the following essay, Meyer analyzes how Wright captures the "poetry" of the game of football in "Autumn Begins in Martins Ferry, Ohio."

Ubiquitous in the American landscape, in every city and small town, is the football stadium. As one flies over the nation on an autumn night, the eye is immediately drawn to the rectangles of light, the football fields of local high schools and colleges. Football is to the American consciousness what chivalry was to the Middle Ages. It is both a male code of behavior and a social ritual. Like the runner who was the pride of his town in A. E. Housman's "To An Athlete Dying Young," football is a means by which towns are united behind their champions. The poetry is in the game and the game is raw, brutal, and highly imagistic. The good catch, the hard tackle, the gleaming helmets of the offensive and defensive lines all bespeak a kind of gladiatorial splendor, a test of strength for the participants, and a beautiful spectacle of Aristotelian proportions for the beholder. In a 1979 conversation with Dave Smith in *American Poetry Review,* James Wright commented on his poem "Autumn Begins in Martins Ferry, Ohio," in which he de-

scribes the annual ritual of the football season and the impact it has on small American towns. For Wright, the game of football was a great, De Tocquevillian leveler of the classes, a world where, in the very Jeffersonian sense, men were not only created equal but made equal through their own abilities. "In my home town, Martin's Ferry, Ohio, people were quite strikingly separated from each other along class lines. It is difficult to talk about class in America because we have the powerful myth of the common man, the myth of the absence of any class distinction…. What a startling experience it is to be a young American conditioned, to a certain extent, to believe we have no class distinctions in American society, then suddenly to get into the army and realize, if you are an enlisted man, that an officer, even a second lieutenant, for all practical purposes and down to the smallest detail, is regarded—and you regard him—almost as a distinct species." For Wright, the game of football in his hometown of Martins Ferry, Ohio, as he recalls it in his poem, "Autumn Begins in Martins Ferry, Ohio," is a seasonal ritual where the value of an individual is measured in that most American of ways—through performance.

Wright commented in the same interview that he perceived the value of those games as "occasions for the expression of physical grace." Indeed, in the poem, there is something recognizably magnificent and tragically beautiful in the way the young men of the town "gallop terribly against each other's bodies" in the annual autumn ritual. It is that sense of poetry, an almost haiku-like precision and focus that borders on the ritualistic, that Wright attempts to capture in the poem.

As is the case with many of Wright's poems, the entire work is crafted around the application of sharp, focused images that carry the weight of a statement that borders on narrative. Almost a series of tableaux, "Autumn Begins in Martins Ferry, Ohio," presents several "scenes" of life in the town revolving around the game of football and the working classes for whom the game is the great social leveler: the "Polacks nursing long beers in Tiltonsville," the "gray faces of Negroes in the blast furnace at Benwood," the "ruptured night watchman of Wheeling Steel." They are all "dreaming of heroes." For them, the game is an alternative reality beyond the confines of their daily existence, and like a religion they perceive the actions of football as a ritual bordering on martyrdom.

What lies at the root of this "ritual" is, as Wright terms it, a kind of passion where the "sons grow suicidally beautiful / At the beginning of Oc-

tober." There is a sense, just as there is in Housman's poem, that the champions are martyrs and
that their sacrifice is reminiscent of the Adonis/
Tammuz myth where the protagonist must die to
ensure life and renewal for his society. The word
"gallop" in the final line seems to suggest that the
young men, the "sons," are like animals being led
to a slaughter, and the seasonal theme ties the "gal-
loping" and "suicidal beauty," to the autumnal rituals of the harvest and Samhain. What must be remembered is that the Celtic festival of Samhain,
the traditional root of the Halloween celebration,
was originally a slaughter festival when the fat-
tened and beautiful animals were ritualistically
killed for a feast in order to save the precious feed
grains for human consumption during the long winter months. At the root of Wright's rather elliptical
perceptions of the football ritual is a sense of a
bloodsport, or at least a blood ritual, where sacrifice and martyrdom lurk behind the images with a
eerie sense of unspoken presence. It is this 'presence,' this sense of haunting, that makes the poem
so intriguing—just as the game itself, its imaginative associations and poetic perceptions offer an alternative reality to both players and spectators
alike.

The middle stanza of the poem reinforces the
idea of football as an escape from reality. The first
stanza, in its rather documentary use of the images
of working class occupation, shows the dignity inherent in hard, physical labor. The second stanza,
however, underscores the difficulty and banality of
the working class life. The "proud fathers" are
"ashamed to go home," a strange statement that
suggests both the agony of defeat and the focused
elevation and esteem in which they venerate the
game. The suggestion here is that the difference between the banal reality of home life and the heightened reality of the game are absurdly distant for
those "proud fathers." The gap between the two realities is underscored further by the delightfully absurd image of the "women" who are "like starved
pullets / Dying for love." These hen-like creatures
are both delightful and absurd in that they express
the same sense of driving, passionate desire that the
fathers and sons express through their devotion to
the sport.

It is this sense of passion, of an unspoken undercurrent of desire, that is the most haunting element of the poem. True to Wright's vision of working-class virtues, what must be said cannot be said
in words but in the poetry of motion and performance, whether that performance takes place in the
reality of a daily job or in the playful, imaginative

> *Football is to the American consciousness what chivalry was to the Middle Ages. It is both a male code of behavior and a social ritual.*"

"sport" of the game of football. It is the power of
the imagination in raw, physical action that so at-
tracts and fascinates the poem's persona. After all,
the first line of the poem locates the entire work in
the imagination. As the persona sits in the "Shreve
High football stadium," he "thinks" of the reality
behind the game and forms a list of all those work-
men who toil at their various occupations. This
sense of physical dedication to a purpose is the poetry in the process of the poem. The images unfold
not as a poetic record of the passion and the pride
that the figures in the poem bring to both the game
and to life, but as a series of pointers that allude to
the depth of living and action that lie embedded in
every deed. The beauty of the "suicidal sons" is not
just in the downs and plays on the field, or in the
score on the board, but in the living and the imaginative aspirations that those of the world around
the game pour into the yards and downs. For
Wright, poetry is not just the images or the narrative but the meaning one brings to the structures
and ideas of a work—and it is this process, of bringing meaning to something one believes in that lies
at the core of our most profound and spiritually driven desires. Football is a religion, and as far as
Wright is concerned in this poem, so is poetry. Both
present the structures into which a huge amount of
experience can be read, and both leave the beholder
searching for more meaning, more interpretation
and more imaginative possibilities.

Source: Bruce Meyer, in an essay for *Poetry for Students*, Gale Group, 2000.

Sources

Bly, Robert, "The Work of James Wright," in *The Pure Clear Word,* edited by Dave Smith, Urbana: University of Illinois Press, 1982, pp. 78-98.

Dougherty, David C., *James Wright,* Boston: Twayne Publishers, 1987.

Hirsch, Jr., E.D. et. al., eds. *The Dictionary of Cultural Literacy,* Boston: Houghton Mifflin Co., 1993.

Smith, Dave, "James Wright: The Pure Clear Word: An Interview," in *American Poetry Review* Vol. 9, No 3, May/June 1980, reprinted in *The Pure Clear Word,* edited by Dave Smith, Urbana: University of Illinois Press, 1982, pp. 3-42.

Stein, Kevin, *James Wright: The Poetry of a Grown Man,* Athens: Ohio University Press, 1989.

Stitt, Peter, "James Wright: The Quest Motif in *The Branch Will Not Break,*" in *The Pure Clear Word,* edited by Dave Smith, Urbana: University of Illinois Press, 1982, pp. 65-77.

Zinn, Howard, *A People's History of the United States,* New York: Harper and Row, 1980.

For Further Study

Bly, Robert, *Remembering James Wright,* St. Paul: Ally Press, 1991.
    This is friend Robert Bly's long account of Wright's life. Although not an official "biography," it depicts both the poet's public and private life, including material about the painful break-up of his first marriage.

Morgan, Bruce, "In Ohio: A Town and the Bard Who Left It," *Time,* Oct. 19, 1987, pp. 9-10.
    Although only a brief article, it is interesting to read about Wright's reputation in his hometown of Martins Ferry. The article includes quotations from members of the poet's family.

Wright, James, *Above the River: The Complete Poems,* Middletown, Conn.: Wesleyan University Press, 1990.
    In addition to being a collection of Wright's entire published works, this book contains an exceptional introduction by contemporary poet Donald Hall. Hall was a close friend of James Wright, and he tells a compelling story of some of the poet's best days, some of his worst days, and the day of his death.

Bedtime Story

George MacBeth
1972

"Bedtime Story" appears in the third section of George MacBeth's *Collected Poems: 1958-1970*. It consists of thirteen free-verse quatrains told from a narrator whose point of view is inconsistent. In the Foreword to this collection MacBeth writes that the poems in this section are "written for those who (like myself) regard themselves as children." While that may be so, MacBeth is no ordinary child. Poems such as "House for a Child," and "A Child's Garden" are grouped with poems such as "When I Am Dead" and "Fourteen Ways of Touching the Peter." Regarding oneself as a child, for MacBeth, means engaging in poetic mischief. "Bedtime Story" is a parody of bedtime stories, in that it uses the form of such a story to poke fun at the idea of happy endings and to undercut the notion that human beings are essentially good, or have generaally benign intentions towards one another. One could imagine childrens' book author Maurice Sendak creating illustrations for the poem.

Speaking from a future, post-apocalyptic time, and recounting a story of the past, the poem's narrator describes an incident in the Congo between the "Mission Brigade" and its encounter with the "last man." MacBeth describes the incident in quasi-allegorical terms, implicitly criticizing the history of European colonialism and suggesting that human nature will never change: we will always trend towards self-destruction and remain blind to our own self-deception. The accidental death of the last human being parallels the deaths, both cultural and physical, of millions of Africans at the hands of colonial powers such as France and Great Britain. MacBeth seems to be saying that this has happened in the past and it will happen again. Although we put ourselves in the best possible light in the stories we tell about ourselves, the fact is that we deceive ourselves in doing so. The poem also echoes stories of the mythic wild child, that human being raised in the jungle away from the civilizing influences of society and his inevitable encounter with that society.

MacBeth's writing can be seen as postmodern. His mixing of poetic forms, his view of verse as disposable, and his use of experience as a stylistic rather than "content-laden" element all mark him as a writer more interested in the playfulness of language rather than its capacity to represent enduring human subjects and themes. In this sense MacBeth is less of a writer, more of a sculptor of words, concerned with the materiality of language and the ways in which it can be shaped.

George MacBeth died in 1992 of a motor neuron disease.

Author Biography

George MacBeth is a poet of trickery and wild contradictions who has made a career out of defying expectations for what constitutes "good" poetry. Born in 1932 to George MacBeth and Amelia Morton Mary Mann MacBeth in the small town of Shotts, Scotland, MacBeth was raised in Sheffield. His poetry, however, is marked with a big city, often world-weary consciousness. In 1955 he graduated from New College, Oxford with a degree in Classical Greats, and later produced shows on literature and the arts for the BBC. His poetry, however, often undermines the constraints, both thematic and stylistic, of Classical literature. Although his first collection of poems, *A Form of Words* (1954), was relatively in keeping with the conventions of mid-century British poetry, most of the poetry he published after is a macabre verse laden with black humor, which embraces various kinds of satire, parody, and often unidentifiable tones. MacBeth writes from a wide repertoire of formal poetic structures which include syllabics, acrostics, sonnets, and other kinds of given forms, to explore ideas of animal violence, cruelty, corpse loving, and other "unseemly" subjects. Critics have not always been kind to MacBeth, many of them claiming that he has been obsessed with form over content and has wasted his talents. Instead of sulking, MacBeth has appropriated such criticism, making it a part of his work. On the dust jacket of the *Collected Poems: 1958-1970,* he includes this blurb from an anonymous writer in *The Times Literary Supplement:* "Extraordinary gifts arrogantly wasted," along with others which similarly question his talent. MacBeth further emphasized his disdain for the judgements of literary critics when he edited *The Penguin Book of Sick Verse* (1963), which included sections on visions of doom, sick jokes, and subjects few other poets would touch.

Poem Text

Long long ago when the world was a wild place
Planted with bushes and people by apes, our
Mission Brigade was at work in the jungle.
    Hard by the Congo

Once, when a foraging detail was active   5
Scouting for green-fly, it came on a grey man, the
Last living man, in the branch of a baobab
    Stalking a monkey.

Earlier men had disposed of, for pleasure,
Creatures whose names we scarcely remember—   10
Zebra, rhinoceros, elephants, wart-hog,
    Lion, rats, deer. But

After the wars had extinguished the cities
Only the wild ones were left, half-naked
Near the Equator: and here was the last one,   15
    Starved for a monkey.

By then the Mission Brigade had encountered
Hundreds of such men: and their procedure,
History tells us, was only to feed them:
    Find them and feed them;   20

Those were the orders. And this was the last one.
Nobody knew that he was, but he was. Mud
Caked on his flat grey flanks. He was crouched,
    half-
    armed with a shaved spear

Glinting beneath broad leaves. When their jaws cut   25
Swathes through the bark and he saw fine teeth
    shine,
Round eyes roll round and forked arms waver
    Huge as the rough trunks.

Over his head, he was frightened. Our workers
Marched through the Congo before he was born,   30
    but
This was the first time perhaps that he'd seen one.
    Staring in hot still

Silence, he crouched there: then jumped. With a
    long swing
Down from his branch, he had angled his spear too
Quickly, before they could hold him, and hurled it   35
    Hard at the soldier

Leading the detail. How could he know Queen's
Orders were only to help him? The soldier
Winced when the tipped spear pricked him.
    Unsheathing his
Sting was a reflex.   40

Later the Queen was informed. There were no
    more
Men. An impetuous soldier had killed off,
Purely by chance, the penultimate primate.
    When she was certain.

Squadrons of workers were fanned through the   45
    Congo
Detailed to bring back the man's picked bones
    to be
Sealed in the archives in amber. I'm quite sure
    Nobody found them

After the most industrious search, though.
Where had the bones gone? Over the earth, dear,   50
Ground by the teeth of the termites, blown by the
    Wind, like the dodo's.

Poem Summary

Lines 1-8:

The title of this poem itself functions as a trap for the readers' expectations. Conventionally a bedtime story might involve a tale of adventure pitting good against evil with good winning out in the end. The child listens, rapt with attention, maybe cathartically purging his or her emotions and energies along with the characters, then, exhausted, falls asleep, knowing that all is safe with the world. MacBeth's version, however satirizes the idea of bedtime stories while parodying their form. Using a standard fairytale opening, the first stanza sets the scene. We understand that the present is a tame, and by implication more civilized, place because the past is described as "wild." The Mission Brigade is a military expedition force sent to search for green-fly, which are insects, primarily aphids, which feed by sucking sap from plants. Why they are scouting for geen-fly is left unstated, but it is the first clue that the speaker of the story and those of the Mission Brigade are possibly not human. The expedition is in the Congo, a central African country. The man they encounter is called "grey" possibly to emphasize his age. We also understand that he is uncivilized, at least in comparison to the Mission Brigade, because he is "stalking a monkey," most likely for food. The baobab tree is a large tree found in tropical Africa whose trunk sometimes reaches thirty feet in diameter. The tree bears hard-shelled fleshy fruit and large white flowers.

Lines 9-16:

These stanzas place the speaker firmly in some future mythical world from which our present world is described. By including relatively common animals such as deer and rats in a list with more exotic and rare animals such as lions and rhinoceros, the speaker is making a judgement about the contemporary world's separation from, even carelessness towards, nature. The "wars" can be read as mythical wars. Consider the nuclear conflagrations of *Mad Max,* or other futuristic, post-apocalyptic films and novels in which some human survivors live a kind of primitive existence cut off from those with more resources. In this case, only one of those survivors remain.

Lines 17-24:

These stanzas alert us to the speaker's view that the task of the brigade was humanitarian. The speaker's comments are informed by history. Although he knows while telling the story that the man found was the last, at the time the soldiers in the Mission Brigade did not. The description of the man crouching and with a spear underscores the man's primitive, almost animal-like nature, as does describing the man's sides as "flat grey flanks."

Lines 25-32:

The poem becomes confusing here, as the point of view changes, much as it might if this story were told in film. Now the speaker describes the encounter from the eyes of the last man, who, hiding, witnesses the soldiers cutting down trees and the "fine teeth" of the saws "shine." These descriptions might also be literal ones of the creatures of the Mission Brigade. The lines remain ambiguous. We now have a clearer sense how far in the future the speaker is, as he states that "Our workers / Marched through the Congo before he was born."

Lines 33-40:

The action in these stanzas, as in previous stanzas, is propelled forward by MacBeth's use of enjambment, a way of carrying over the syntactic unit from one line to the next. This technique allows MacBeth to couple our surprise as readers following the action with the last man's surprise at seeing the soldiers, and the soldiers at seeing and then being attacked by, the last man. The speaker uses rhetorical questions instead of direct statements to tell us that the man could not have possibly known that the soldiers' intentions were harmless, when he asks "How could he know Queen's / Orders were only to help him?" By referring to the soldiers' ac-

Media Adaptations

- This website on mass extinction provides charts, statistics, and scientific facts to buttress claims about the dwindling numbers of species left on earth. http://www.lassp.cornell.edu/newmme/science/extinction.html

- The WorldBook provides this website which contains essays and historical background on species' extinction, past and present: http://www.worldbook.com/fun/wbla/earth/html/ed12.htm

- For extensive information of Scottish history, consult the following website: http://members.tripod.com/cunninghamc/NationalHistory/NatScotHistory.html

- Professor George Landow of Brown University has compiled an extensive bibliography on the history of Colonial Africa: http://landow.stg.brown.edu/post/africa/histbibl.html

- Frank Marshall directed the film adaptation of Michael Crichton's novel, *Congo,* in 1995. The story details an expedition into deep, dark Africa that runs into an unknown race of killer apes.

---

tions as results of the Queen's orders, MacBeth uses metonymy, Metonymy is a kind of figurative language in which the literal term for one thing is applied to another with which it is associated. Here, "Queen's orders" refers to the soldiers' actions. The last few lines of stanza ten employ understatement to say that the soldier hit by the last man's spear killed him: "Unsheathing / his / Sting was a reflex." By this we are also to understand that it was an accident.

Lines 41-48:

The last man's death is not described. Again, the transition from scene to scene is filmic. We are only told that "the Queen was informed." Blaming the soldier by calling him "impetuous," the speaker then informs us that the last man, was also "the penultimate primate." Primates are an order of animals which include monkey, apes, and man. This statement can be read two ways: the first is that the

last primate is the monkey the man was stalking; the second way is to assume that the speaker and his species are a kind of trans-or posthuman primate. The poem does not clear up this point but leaves it open. By having soldiers search for the remains of a human being because humans are extinct and so they can be preserved, MacBeth reverses the order of things in which human beings often hunt species into extinction, then keep a few remaining specimens in zoos or, if all specimens are dead, preserve them in a museum.

Lines 49–52:

The poem's last image is another play on the idea of extinction. In this case, MacBeth compares the extinction of human beings with that of the Dodo, a large flightless bird of the island of Mauritius, which has been extinct since the 17th century. "Dodo" is also a form of slang for a stupid person or a simpleton, both of which would fit MacBeth's characterization of human beings.

Themes

Language and Meaning

"Bedtime Story" uses the form of a folktale to tell a story about the end of humanity and to pose a moral. Folktales are short narratives usually in prose form but sometimes in verse, which have been transmitted orally from generation to generation. Their original author is unknown, if there ever were an original author, and the tale itself changes over time as it is repeated and changed little by little. Myths and fables are two common forms of folk tales; both are attempts to explain natural phenomena and human behavior. MacBeth's poem takes on the features of a folktale in how it attempts to explain the past and the disappearance of human beings from the planet. The narrator tells us that it was humanity that was responsible for the extinction of animals, whose name the narrator and his ilk (a non-human, or post-human species) can "scarcely remember." Man himself, we are told, was almost eliminated "After the wars had extinguished the cities." The transmission of the story is foregrounded when the narrator says that "History tells us." The moral of the story—that humanity was responsible for its own demise and the demise of other species and that the current species in power had done everything it could to save human beings—is underscored in how the death of the last man is described, i.e., as an accident, and in how it attempted to preserve the memory of the last man by searching for its bones. When the speaker says that "I'm quite sure / Nobody found them" we are reminded once again of the story's tenuousness, of its "storiness," as opposed to fact or a first-person witnessing of experience.

Nature

MacBeth pits human nature against non-human Nature to emphasize (by predicting) the depths to which humanity will fall if it continues to ignore its responsibilities to the natural environment. This is most forcefully underscored by the fact that the story is told at a point in time when there are no more human beings in the world, the last one having being killed accidentally by a soldier from the Mission Brigade many years before. The theme of extinction crops up repeatedly. Not only have all human beings been destroyed, but all animals have been destroyed as well: "Zebra, rhinoceros, elephants, warthog, / Lion, rats, deer." The only living primates are monkeys, an appropriate animal that MacBeth uses for comic effect. Whatever species the narrator belongs to is equally guilty of wrecking havoc on nature, though seemingly unaware of it. In the seventh stanza we see these creatures destroying trees, "When their jaws cut / Swathes through the bark and ... [the last man] saw fine teeth shining." This difficult passage can be read two ways: the first is to see the description as metaphoric of the machines those in the Mission Brigade use to clear the jungle, the "Round eyes" standing for headlights, the "forked arms" for a fork lift or like machine. A second way of reading this passage is to see it as a description of the colonizing creatures themselves. After all, we know that they are not men because there is only one human being left in the world, and he is about to be killed. The irony is that whatever post-human species the narrator belongs to exhibits a very *human* nature in his recounting of the story and his own obliviousness to the gravity of his "people's" killing off the last man and (presumably) destroying much of the jungle as well. The last stanza highlights the utter oblivion that comes with extinction. Not even the bones of the last man can be found. All that is left is the stories of them.

Topics for Further Study

- Compare MacBeth's narrator in "Bedtime Story" with Craig Raine's in "A Martian Sends a Postcard Home." Discuss the similarities and differences and explain what they can tell us about human nature and being "other."

- Write your own bedtime story in the form of a folktale or fairytale about a pressing social topic.

- Re write MacBeth's poem from the point of view of the last man.

wards colonialism and humanity's relationship to the natural world.

Parodies imitate features of literary works or literary genres, often treating "lowlier" subjects than the work or genre they imitate. MacBeth signals a conventional bedtime story by beginning "Long long ago ...," but then launches into a story which can be read as an allegory of Britain's own colonial history. The "last man" is a type, representing the uncivilized "savage," whom European countries such as Britain and France felt they had to conquer before helping. MacBeth satirizes colonial attitudes towards its professed mission when he tells us that the Brigade's intention were only honorable—"to feed them." He similarly satirizes humanity's propensity for first hunting a species into extinction or near extinction and then preserving that species in natural history museums and zoos in the next to last stanza.

The poem itself is a narrative, related almost filmically. MacBeth shifts point of view and makes sometimes abrupt transitions in telling the story. His use of enjambment, or run-on lines, also helps propel the story forward, keeping readers interested in what happens next.

Style

A free-verse parody of a bedtime story, "Bedtime Story" is composed of thirteen quatrains of verse which allegorically satirize European attitudes to-

Historical Context

In the 1950s Britain witnessed a renewed interest in poetry, particularly in people who desired to

Compare & Contrast

- **1962:** Scotland-born Sean Connery appears in the first James Bond film, Dr. No.

  1995: Scotland's film and tourist industries receive a boost when *Braveheart,* Mel Gibson's film about William Wallace, wins five Oscars and makes the world aware, again, of Scotland's history.

  Today: Ireland-born Pierce Brosnan now plays James Bond.

- **1950:** Scottish Nationalists steal the "Stone of Destiny" from Westminster Abbey. This was Scotland's Coronation Stone, taken by the English in 1296. By tradition all British Monarchs have to be crowned while sitting on it. It was eventually recovered from Arbroath Abbey.

  1996: The Stone of Destiny is finally returned to Scotland permanently, 700 years after it was stolen by Edward I.

  1997: Scottish people voted yes for "Devolution" for Scotland, by a 75 percent majority. This would give Scotland it's own parliament, not tied to English parliamentary systems, for the first time in several centuries.

- **1958:** The most prominent political party of the Democratic Republic of Congo, Movement National Congolais (MNC), was founded in 1958 by Patrice Lumumba, a third-class clerk in the district revenue office of the postal service. Before that, another Congolese political party existed but only brought people together along ethnic lines.

  1960-65: Political turmoil engulfs the Democratic Republic of Congo. Lumumba is assassinated by forces loyal to Colonel Mobutu Sese Seko, who eventually takes over the government in 1965.

  1971: Seko renames the country the Republic of Zaire and asks Zairean citizens to change their names to African names.

  1997: Seko is overthrown by Laurent Kabila and Rwandan-backed rebels, who literally "rename" the country the Democratic Republic of Congo.

- **205 million B.C.:** At this time, many species of amphibians and reptiles became extinct. The extinction set the stage for the rise of the dinosaurs, which for a time became the world's dominant animals.

  65 million B.C.: The last living dinosaur species vanished from the Earth. Many other terrestrial species and many marine species also became extinct during this time. The extinctions led to the rise of mammals and marked the beginning of the Cenozoic Era, in which we live today.

  Today: Ecologists estimate that we have lost hundreds of thousands of species in the past 50 years. The experts predict that if present trends continue, we are likely to lose one-half of all living species within the next century.

---

move poetry foreword, or at least away from what some poets feared it was becoming. One phenomenon which received much attention then and which has gained a place in the literary history of England is a group of writers called The Movement. Consisting of Philip Larkin, Kinglsey Amis, John Wain, Thom Gunn, D. J. Enright, Donald Davie, John Holloway, Elizabeth Jennings, Robert Conquest, and a few others, The Movement stood for writing about real people and real events and in returning British poetry to a stricter versification, away from what they perceived as the growing sloppiness of free verse and other organic forms. In addition to opposing much of what was happening in American poetry, they opposed melodrama and hysteria, which they thought much of the poetry of World War II embodied, and (largely) thought of themselves as anti-romantic. Critics sometimes labeled them as conservative in their seeming resistance to experimentation and their desire to "forget" the war. The Movement's work is showcased in Conquest's anthologies, *New Lines,* and *New Lines 2,* published in 1956 and 1963 respectively. Some of the poets mentioned, however, claim that no such group existed, that it is largely a manufactured label for the convenience of literary critics, who need to lump and categorize to make sense of so many diverse approaches to poetry. In an interview with Jhan Hochman for *The Portland Review,* Thom Gunn, for example, notes "That kind of thing [artistic groupings] is really a wonderful example of the b—s— of literary categories. It strikes me as a more meaningless category than most, 'The Movement.'" Eight people were supposed to have been in The Movement, but everybody was writing like that. It wasn't just those eight people."

Yet another group of writers, curiously enough called The Group, which included Ted Hughes, Peter Redgrove, and MacBeth, arose in opposition to The Movement. It stood for poetic change and for experimenting with different forms and ways to present poetry, and was to a degree driven by critics as much as poets. The Group had more of an underground flavor to it, as almost anyone could secure an invitation to one of its gatherings. However, meetings took on the often stodgy tenor of workshops, during which poems were often discussed in light of practical criticism. Though Mac-Beth distanced himself from labels as much as possible, he often attended meetings of The Group, in large part because of its desire to renew poetry's function as an oratorical as much as a written art. MacBeth himself was an enthusiastic performer of his poetry and in general supportive of developing poetry as a performing art. MacBeth disliked The Movement, in part because of the seriousness with which its members approached poetry. In the *Dictionary of Literary Biography* Lawrence R. Ries quotes MacBeth as saying that "The Movement weren't prepared to churn out a bad poem about the most important experience of their lives. A willingness to do that seems to me the first essential of an important poet." MacBeth's own relentless stylistic playfulness and his willingness to write (and publish) many very bad poems underscore both his interest in poetry more as process than product.

Critical Overview

Writing for the *Dictionary of Literary Biography,* Lawrence Ries says of MacBeth's poetry that "The

critical response to the individual publications has been mixed: angry, admiring, frustrated, laudatory." Ries further observes the difficulty reviewers and literary historians have had in placing Mac-Beth in an established literary category, or movement, even though he was associated to some extent with The Group, a gathering of poets who attempted to rejuvenate poetry readings and gatherings, among other endeavors. Critic M. L. Rosenthal, writing in *The New Poets: American and British Poetry Since World War II,* describes (in 1967) MacBeth as "a lively, witty, young poet, [though] there is nothing in his work that could in any sense be called revolutionary." Perhaps the best way to understand MacBeth's relationship to his critics is to read the blurbs he includes on the dust jacket of his books. Because he did not hold that poetry necessarily had to be great, or even good, he did not attempt to curry the favor of critics, like many of his contemporaries. Critical judgements, for MacBeth, were a farce. The list of "endorsements" on the cover of his *Collected Poems: 1958-1970* include the following and illustrate his attitude towards those who would write, either ill or well, of him: "Extraordinary gifts arrogantly wasted." (—Anonymous writer in *The Times Literary Supplement*); "His poems are pretentiously exotic, encrusted with gimmickry .... Play is an important element in poetry, but it is one which can easily be abused. The games Macbeth is playing will not engage the reader." (Robert B. Shaw, *Poetry*); "He has a seminal intelligence which is perhaps the strongest in British poetry since Auden." (Peter Porter); "He is one of the more exciting and talented of the young British poets.... MacBeth, clearly an original poet, is developing considerable intellectual range with a remarkable metrical variety and skill." (*Choice*).

Criticism

Chris Semansky

Chris Semansky's most recent collection of poems, Blindsided, *has been published by 26 Books of Portland, Oregon. In the following essay Semansky explores the relationship between the actual and the imaginary in MacBeth's "Bedtime Story."*

George MacBeth made a career out of offending the literary tastes of critics and establishment poets. It was not only his treatment of lowly poetic subjects such as masturbation or necrophelia, but

What Do I Read Next?

- Hannah Arendt's 1968 study, *Imperialism: Part Two of the Origins of Totalitarianism,* provides a provocative exploration into the cultural and political underpinnings of Fascist ideologies.

- MacBeth's *Collected Poems: 1958-1970,* published in 1972 provides a rewarding look at MacBeth's genius as well as his silliness. This book is entertaining and provocative.

MacBeth also was not a believer in the idea that poetry should necessarily be enduring. "Bedtime Story" is a poem that will probably not endure, yet its very title alludes to kinds of expression which do endure, namely folktales. In this sense, MacBeth plays a trick on his audience, something he did often during his career as poet, novelist and television producer. In his relentless experimentation with language and his focus on the materiality of the word, MacBeth embodies the "spirit" of postmodern play, often leading readers to a place of seeming meaning only to then spring a trap door on them. An examination of "Bedtime Story" shows how his poetry often suggests various meanings without exhausting, or sometimes even developing, them. This can be confusing, even exasperating, and requires readers not to reach too hard for definitive meanings.

The poem begins with a common refrain often used to signal fairytales and folktales. This conforms to how we expect a bedtime story to begin, and we prepare ourselves for a tale about a mythic place. That place approximates our image of the earth itself, but the time period is unclear. It could be ten thousand years ago or it could be as recent as a few hundred, or even a hundred years ago. When we are then told that the "Mission Brigade was at work in the jungle / Hard by the Congo," we think of Africa in colonial times. The first Europeans to explore Central Africa, the Portugese, established a close commercial relationship with the Kongo Kingdom in the fifteenth century. By the nineteenth century, this region of the continent was broken up into tribal power centers, and in 1910 Middle Congo became part of French Equatorial Africa, which included Gabon, the Central African Republic, and Chad. Today, The Democratic Republic of Congo, formerly known as Zaire, is Africa's third-largest country, with a population estimated at 46,000,000. The country shares borders in the east with Burundi, Rwanda, Tanzania, and Uganda; in the west with the Congo Republic; in the north with the Central African Republic and Sudan; and in the south with Angola and Zambia. We do not know the time to which the narrator refers, but the Congo itself, today as in the past, evokes an image of lushness and wild primates, of untamed nature. The country is known for its game reserves and national parks sheltering animals, such as lions, monkeys, gorillas, zebras, antelope, elephants, and other rare animals like the Bonobo apes and the Okapi antelopes. But it is not the *actual* Congo to which the speaker refers. It is a Congo of the imagination which draws on our image of the real Congo. This image is developed in the second stanza when we are now presented with a baobab tree, a lush flowering fruit tree found in tropical Africa. But what is the Mission Brigade doing scouting for green-fly, a kind of insect that eats sap from trees? And who is this "last living man"? Insects such as termites, crickets, grasshoppers, and palm grubs form a staple of the Congolese diet, but the Mission Brigade is not Congolese. When we are told that there were wars which "extinguished the cities," we begin to reconfigure our sense of what kind of story we are being told and realize that quite possibly we are hearing the tale of someone who is not human, who somehow evolved out of human beings or from another species. After all, who is telling the tale if the "last living man" is what he is described as being?

The poem provides clues, but no answers. MacBeth plays with the idea of the last man as he plays with the idea of the Congo. The "last man" conjures images of the wild child, a type popularized in myths and movies (think of Tarzan or Truffaut's movie, *The Wild Child*), that human being born in the wilderness and raised by animals who encounters civilized human beings and is overwhelmed by their strangeness, their otherness. The last man also suggests a boogie man, that evil, mischievous character so prevalent in "darker" bedtime stories. In this case, the man could stand for a fear of nature itself, or at least the animal part of human nature, which the tale-teller is attempting to either mock or come to terms with. Another possibility is that MacBeth is satirizing the ways in which imperialist Europeans have behaved towards Africans. Hannah Arendt says this about the psychology of white racist thought in her study *The Origins of Totalitarianism:*

> What made [Africans] different from other human beings was not at all the color of their skin but the fact that they behaved like a part of nature, that they treated nature as their undisputed master, that they had not created a human world, a human reality, and that therefore nature had remained, in all its majesty, the only overwhelming reality—compared to which they appeared to be phantoms, unreal and ghostlike. They were, as it were, "natural" human beings who lacked the specifically human character, the specific human reality, so that when European men massacred them they somehow were not aware that they had committed murder.

The seventh stanza compounds our confusion as to who is doing the narrating. Now we see the brigade moving through the jungle from the point of view of the last man himself, or at least how the narrator himself thinks the last man saw the brigade, with his "shaved spear"

> Glinting beneath broad leaves. When their jaws cut
> Swathes through the bark and he saw fine teeth
>   shine,
> Round eyes roll round and forked arms waver
> Huge as the rough trunks

These lines are ambiguous at best, indeterminate at worst. On the one hand they can be metaphors for saws and other heavy equipment, but what would "forked arms ... Huge as the rough trunks" be doing above him? At this point, the description breaks down and we are left to make sense of imagery which does not seem to fit.

When the last man attacks one of the soldiers, we are told that "the tipped spear pricked him." Judging from the proximity of the man swinging down from the tree we would expect the spear to do more than simply "prick" the soldier. This provides more evidence that perhaps the narrator's "people" are not people. However, we are confused once again when the Queen is brought into the story. Because we know that MacBeth is Scottish and lived most of his life in Britain, the first queen that comes to our mind is the Queen Mother of the United Kingdom. However, MacBeth, it seems, is merely using the Queen as a type in order to echo a certain sense of noblesse oblige that the British Empire (and Empires in general) exhibited, or at least believed it exhibited, towards its colonized subjects. In the actual, historical Congo, European masters put the Congolese people to work in plantations and mining sectors. Little or no effort was

made to educate them with the exception of Catholic missionaries who sought converts. The Queen is used in this poem satirically, to suggest self-deception on the part of the narrator and his species in their attitude towards the last man. As readers we are meant to be shocked to learn that the brigade had orders to "bring back the man's picked bones to be / Sealed in the archives in amber."

Perhaps the most confusing and enigmatic statement made in "Bedtime Story" occurs in the eleventh stanza, when the speaker says that "the penultimate primate" has been killed off. If the last man is the next-to-the-last primate, who is the last? One possible answer is the monkey he had been stalking earlier in the poem. Another answer is the species (a post-primate human?) to which the narrator belongs. In either case, we are given no further information. The poem leaves the question unresolved. As if to mock the reader's (expected) confusion, MacBeth ends the poem with an image of another actually extinct animal, the dodo, a flightless bird whose name itself has become a label of derision. The answer to the riddle of this poem's actual meaning has too been "Ground by the teeth of the termites, blown by the / Wind ....

Source: Chris Semansky, in an essay for *Poetry for Students,* Gale Group, 2000.

Sources

Arendt, Hannah, *The Origins of Totalitarianism,* New York: Harcourt, Brace & World, 1968.

Hochman, Jhan, "An Interview with Thom Gunn," *Portland Review,* Vol. 28, No. 2, 1982, pp. 21-78.

MacBeth, George, *A Child of the War,* J. Cape, 1987.

MacBeth, George, *Collected Poems: 1958-1970,* New York: Atheneum, 1972.

MacBeth, George, *My Scotland: Fragments of a State of Mind*

Ries, Lawrence R., *Dictionary of Literary Biography,* Volume 40: *Poets of Great Britain and Ireland Since 1960,* edited by Vincent B. Sherry Jr., Detroit: Gale Research, 1985, pp. 327-337.

Rosenthal, M. L., *The New Poets: American and British Poetry Since World War II,* London: Oxford University Press, 1967.

Schmidt, Michael and Grevel Lindrop, eds., *British Poetry Since 1960,* Carcanet, 1972.

For Further Study

Acheson, James, and Romana Huk, eds., *Contemporary British Poetry: Essays in Theory and Criticism,* State University of New York Press, 1996.

Devoted to close readings of poets and their contexts from various postmodern perspectives, this book offers a wide-ranging look at the work of feminists and "post feminist" poets, working class poets, and poets of diverse cultural backgrounds, as well as provocative re-readings of such well-established and influential figures as Donald Davie, Ted Hughes, Geoffrey Hill, and Craig Raine.

Gregson, Ian, *Contemporary British Poetry and Postmodernism: Dialogue and Estrangement,* New York: St. Martins Press, 1997.

Gregorson examines how postmodern ideas such as intentionality, ideology, and indeterminacy have shaped contemporary British poetry. This is a sometimes rewarding, sometimes frustrating study.

Beware of Ruins

A. D. Hope
1981

A. D. Hope's "Beware of Ruins" (1981) is a poem about memory and imagination motivated to engage by viewing ruins from a Renaissance past. Seeking the world's past arouses the poet to find and reconstruct his own past of things read and experiences lived—the ruins being, themselves, a kind of materialized memory which inspires flights into memories of one's own cultural and personal experiences. The poem is also about aging, about how one would romantically and ideally reconstruct, through ruins, another's past, but with much more difficulty, reconstruct oneself in one's own past. In this latter sense, "Beware of Ruins" gestures toward an expression of how one is dead to the past and moving toward the death in the future.

"Beware of Ruins" has been chosen for inclusion in *The Norton Anthology of Modern Poetry* (1988), and in *A. D. Hope: Selected Poems* (1986). The poem appears, in terms of commentary, ignored. Perhaps the poem is thought to stand on its own without need of praise or blame, or, on the other hand, stand on its own in terms of self-sufficiency, needing neither notes nor interpretation. While the poem most assuredly stands alone in each of these senses, "Beware of Ruins" has been underappreciated and underanalyzed, at least in the United States.

Author Biography

The foremost poet of Australia, Alec Derwent Hope, was born in Cooma, New South Wales in 1907. He was the oldest of five children of a Presbyterian minister and a former teacher, and was educated at home in most subjects by his mother and in Latin by his father. In 1911, the family moved to Campbell Town, on the east side of Tasmania. Hope was lucky enough to have access to his parents ample library of classical, English, and religious literature, which ironically, did not contain a single volume of Australian fiction or poetry, work considered at that time undeveloped by "cultured" people. Hope remembers his first verses being written when he was eight, "a pious rhyme in fifty-two stanzas—one for each week in the year—composed for my mother's birthday and designed to encourage her in her Christian duty." Hope recalls that his mother "gently suggested that I might perhaps consider improving my own conduct rather than hers." Hope also received formal education at a Quaker school in Hobart until the family moved back to New South Wales in 1921. There he resumed secondary school and became enamored with a young painter who took Hope on as a kind of protege. She thought his poetry was imitative and overly passionate. She suggested he burn it all and begin again, this time drawing from his own experiences. Hope thought that was one of his best poetry lessons. Afterwards, Hope attended the University of Sydney. Though he wanted to study medicine, his talents in the humanities commanded attention and he studied literature, philosophy, and psychology. He also co-edited the university's Arts Journal. After graduating in 1928 with a University Medal in philosophy, Hope went to University College, Oxford on scholarship to read English. His career at the venerable institution was less than dazzling. In 1931, he graduated near the bottom of his class. The experience was invaluable in that Hope studied under such literary luminaries as C. L. Wrenn (translator of *Beowulf*), J. R. R. Tolkien, and C. S. Lewis.

Hope returned to Sydney ashamed of his Oxford performance. At that time, there was an economic depression. Hope could not find a job so he went off to camp on land owned by his father. There, he began teaching himself Russian and emending Christopher Marlowe's *Doctor Faustus*, a task that would end up taking him almost fifty years. In 1932, after his sabbatical, Hope trained at Sydney's Teacher's College, and became a tutor in the arts at St. Paul's College. Hope did not find this work fulfilling and suffered bouts of temporal schizophrenia. His condition was aggravated when Hope became a relief teacher in Sydney secondary schools. In 1936, Hope began research for the Department of Education and moved to Canberra to take charge of a trades school. By the time he returned to Sydney late in 1936 he was engaged. In 1937, Hope was next appointed a lecturer in education at the same school at which he had studied, Sydney Teacher's College. This appears to have been a dreadful experience, especially when he was assigned to teach statistics: he found he knew less than some of the students who eventually taught the class. He did however, meet James McAuley, a promising young poet who read Hope's work and told him what elements to discard. This was Hope's second most valuable poetry experience. Hope was next appointed to lecture in English at Sydney Teacher's College, a position which suited him better than his previous appointment. During this period Hope had three children.

Before he became known as a poet, Hope gained notoriety as a biting literary critic who denounced Jindyworobak, the name of a movement which tried to make poetry Australian by packing it with distinctly Australian objects and words. Hope also made a name as a radio personality, "Anthony Inkwell," who conducted children's poetry programs for the Australian Broadcasting Corporation. In 1945, Hope was appointed senior lecturer in English at the University of Melbourne and held that position until 1951 when he became professor of English at its Canberra satellite campus. The Canberra campus soon became the independent Australian National University where Hope became the new university's first professor of English. There, he taught Australia's first course in Australian literature.

When Hope's artist friend told him to burn his poems and begin again, Hope saw fire as a friend. Later it became his enemy. While moving to another residence, Hope stored most of his works at the university for safekeeping. Unfortunately, a fire broke out and burned almost all of it. What remained, he put into his first book, *The Wandering Islands* (1956), which was met with a chilly reception because the poems were thought to be not Australian enough, and too "learned, bookish, and cosmopolitan." The rest of Hope's biography is literary history: a string of publications in both poetry and criticism, and a list of numerous awards. Most of them were from Australia, but Hope was appointed special consultant in poetry at the Library of Congress in Washington D.C., and in 1972, received the Order of the British Empire for, among other things, his *Collected Poems* (1972). In 1979, Hope published *The New Cratylus,* in which his unrepentant views against modernism remained strong. His latest book of poems was *Orpheus*

(1991). As of the early 1990s Hope was still writing and translating.

Poem Text

Beware of ruins: they have a treacherous charm;
Insidious echoes lurk among their stones;
That scummy pool was where the fountain soared;
   The seated figure, whose white arm
Beckons you, is a mock-up of dry bones   5
And not, as you believe, your love restored.

The moonlight lends her grace, but have a care:
Behind her waits the fairy Melusine.
The sun those beams refract died years ago.
   The moat has a romantic air   10
But it is choked with nettles and obscene
And phallic fungi rot there as they grow.

Beware of ruins; the heart is apt to make
Monstrous assumptions on the unburied past;
Though cleverly restored, the Tudor tower   15
   Is spurious, the facade a fake
Whose new face is a death-mask of the last
Despairing effort before it all went sour.

There are ruins, too, of a less obvious kind;
I go back; cannot believe my eyes; the place   20
Is just as I recall; the fire is lit,
   The table laid, bed warmed; I find
My former world intact, but not, alas,
The man I was when I was part of it.

Poem Summary

Lines 1-3:

The poet as narrator cautions his reader about ruins, at this point, any ruins. Their "treacherous charm" might, at this point, remind one of a kind of cliché about women since Eve. The ruins' "insidious echoes" make them ghostly as a graveyard, and the "scummy pool" adds a tad of horror to the scene, especially with its echoes of a temporally distant fountain. This may evoke feelings of discomfort, but intrigues one to plunge farther into them, to reconstruct a past that beckons, allures one away from the present.

Lines 4-6:

Near the pool is a seated figure of white marble or plaster, white like bones are, white: the color of survival, the color of ghosts. The seated figure, like the ruins, beckons one as love once dead but come back, white like death in life, like a consumptive paleness sometimes considered beautiful. Perhaps the figure is a woman?

Media Adaptations

- A taped interview with Hope is conducted by Ruth Morse for Canto Carcanet in Broadbottom, Cheshire, 1988.

Lines 7-9:

Moonlight on the figure (now revealed as a woman) further associates her with love, but something lurks *behind* her appearance like a memory. Melusine is a mermaid creature from a story by Jean d'Arras written in 1387. Melusine looks human but every Sabbath turns into a kind of mermaid, more accurately, a snake from the waist down, a creature who cannot be seen by her husband lest it destroy their relationship. When he sees her in the bath one Sabbath, she runs off never to be seen again in human form. Thus Melusine is a creature of treacherous appearance, a bit evil, not to be trusted, at least from the waist down. Folded into this image is the masterful ninth line, which indicates that while moonlight might be the light of love, it lacks the warmth of the sunlight which lies "behind" it like a memory. In this way, moonlight is the ruins of sunlight, and therefore, a treacherous light.

Lines 10-12:

The moat is misleading. It is choked with irritating nettles and fungi growing in the rot-filled water. The "phallic" nature of the fungi makes the moat obscene, as if the moat were pornography filled up with images of the penis.

Lines 13-18:

In the scene of stones, pool, statue, and moat, appears a Tudor tower. Perhaps a reasonable interpretation of this stanza is that one is apt, through time, to feel that one's past—or oneself in the past—was better than it really was, good thoughts soothing the mind. Such thoughts are "monstrous assumptions," spins or interpretations of the "unburied past" made (dug up) in the present. Through interpreting the past in a good light, memory puts a kind of façade on the past (the Tudor tower). This façade is, perhaps, the last good instance one re-members, an instance the rememberer uses to cover what is and what was the crumbling tower (the past). In this stanza the past is represented by both a decaying tower and a corpse, a tower that will decay despite its facade and a corpse that decom-poses despite its death mask.

Lines 19-24:

The last stanza marks a reversal of images while still adhering to the subject of memory. Where the first three stanzas involved a present nar-rator walking into a ruined present with a statue, pool, moat, and tower, and from it reconstructing a favorable, standing past, here the narrator walks into a past scene—perhaps a sensual one—fully in-tact and as beckoning as the seated figure in the first stanza. But here the man is not who he once was, is older (this poem was written when the poet was 74). This time, it is not the past scene that is in ruins, but the narrator's present self, a man who has aged and is becoming himself a ruins. The nar-rator is unable to reconstruct himself as a young man in the way he might attempt to reconstruct the past of a ruined scene.

Themes

Memory and Reminiscence

The word "echoes" is the first indication that "Beware of Ruins" concerns memory. As ruins are a kind of echo of time past, an echo is a kind of ru-ins of time passing, an original sound decaying. The poem speaks to the problem that memory interprets the past as better than it was, perhaps because it is easier and more pleasurable for the mind. As eyes graze over ruins, trying to imagine them once again intact, so the memory (one's past eyes) grazes over one's past (ruins) and attempts to reconstruct it. What Hope finds is that while he accurately re-members a past scene he experienced, it is much more difficult to imagine himself as a younger man in the scene. Why? Because it is painful? Because he is ashamed of who he was in the past? These choices seem unlikely because of the word, "alas." It is more probable that the poet just cannot find a young self to place back in the past he has recon-structed so pleasantly, so invitingly. In other words he is unable to reconstruct the ruins of himself. At this juncture, it could be inferred that Hope's pre-sent self is too alive to be usurped by the past. If so, then, Hope gets this wrong and such a state is

not regrettable. For only if he were dying in the pre-sent might he be able to imagine himself as a vital young man, egregiously vital. This points to a func-tion of memory not usually made light of: that in order to remember the past the present is tem-porarily put on hold, paralyzed, or in decay. If the present cannot be stilled, it might be too fully alive and able, even self-satisfied. Rather than mourning lost youth with an "alas," perhaps Hope should have understood his unconscious satisfaction with an ag-ing self: there is no need to supplant it with a younger counterpart. This, by the way, could fit with Hope's biography, for while his first fifty years were full of doubt, displeasure and insecurity, his later years, in which he wrote "Beware of Ruins," were successful. But then one must also be wary of biography since it too is a ruins.

Truth and Falsehood

Ruins hearken back to a past one is apt to in-terpret as having been better, in the way that some people "cling" to the past as if it were one's par-ent, as if fearful or deeply dissatisfied of the pre-sent and future. For it has been said that those glancing far behind (or far ahead) of them are avoiding what is "right in front" of them or "be-fore" them (both, curiously enough, expressions of the present). Though appearing to occur in the pre-sent, moonlight is refracted light, issues from sun-light already past. The moon contributes its false light to romanticize the ruins; thus, in this sense, it is false.

Now then, people are said to "take refuge" in the past and "retreat" into a past they "re-collect" or "re-member." Such expressions point to the truth behind the falsehood of memory, a memory which reconstructs the past as better than the present. If people "take refuge" from the past, it must be that the present is *chasing* them; if we "retreat" to the past, then we must be *battling* the present and where it is headed—the future. But the problem is, the past is *scattered* so that we must "re-collect" it. And the past is *dismembered* so that to gain access we must "re-member" it. But such actions are re-constructions, and reconstructions are not originals. Hope is not admonishing us never to reconstruct the past, but more interestingly, to question such reconstructions, remain aware that while memory reconstructs, it does not duplicate. Moreover, the additions and subtractions made by memory are likely to be treacherous because they are made not only out of insufficient knowledge but, sometimes, from a need that points to a deficiency in the world (scummy pools, choked moats), in oneself, or both.

Death

This poem is not about literal death, but death in a figurative sense: the death of the past in the present and the present in the past. The narrator cautions us that while we might want to imaginatively follow the beckoning arm of the white-as-death statue into a "love restored," and imaginatively re-make the scummy pool into a beautiful fountain, we must be careful because the past is dead to us. And literal reconstruction is no better, even if based on the memories of many people, and thereby more accurate. The Tudor tower can never be duplicated since it is decayed and knowledge of it in the past is always insufficient, always *passed* knowledge. On the other hand, the poem speaks of the death of the present in the past. We cannot re-place ourselves in the past for we have been utterly changed by the present. "You can't go back": the reason being that one is as dead in the past as the past is dead in the present. What exists are ghosts, the flavor of once-was, the white present of absence. The poet has aged out of the past and, as much as he would like to, is unable to return. The best he can do is put himself as he is in a past that once was. This, however, is too much a lie to produce pleasure. He must content himself with the lesser evil of being dead to the past and alive in the present. The poet sadly reconciles himself to what is.

Style

"Beware of Ruins" consists of four six-lined stanzas, each with a rhyme scheme of *abcabc*. The meter is a fairly regular iambic pentameter except for the fourth line in every stanza which is a ragged iambic tetrameter. This is a conversational meter (iambs describing the usual topography of spoken English), as if the narrator is casually giving advice to his readers as we walk with him around the ruins. There is only one near rhyme: "place" with "alas," what appears to be this poem's acceptable flaw. Iambs are sometimes accompanied by other patterns. For example, lines 1, 14, 19, and 20:

> Be**ware** of **ru**ins: they **have** a **trea**cherous **charm**
> **Mon**strous a**sump**tions on the un**bur**ied **past**
> There are **ruins too** of a less ob**vious kind**
> I go **back** can**not** be**lieve** my **eyes** the **place**

These occasional trochees, anapests, dactyls, pyrrhics, and amphibrachs give the lines variation and interest, keep them from sounding too regular or too stiff. While the rhyme scheme of the poem is rather unusual, the meter is almost as old as po-

Topics for Further Study

- According to "Beware of Ruins," what is Hope's theory of memory? Do you agree with it? If not, where are its weaknesses?

- Discuss the color white in the context of death (don't forget Moby Dick!). Research cultures that employ white as the color of death. Can you make any generalizations about cultures that use white and those that use black?

- Discuss why the future and the present—as well as the past—might also be full of "treacherous charm."

- Do research on death masks. Find out for what purposes they were used and how they were made.

etry. It is as if Hope had placed a new façade (rhyme scheme) on an old structure (iambic pentameter), a structure which apparently he does not find ruined by extensive use. The meter marks Hope as partly classical, the rhyme scheme as partially innovative. Hope is a poet who doesn't move toward the future without a foundation in the past, the kind of past that still stands on its own feet.

Historical Context

Malcolm Fraser was the Liberal and National candidate for prime minister of Australia in 1975. He won. Despite the "liberal" in the party name, Fraser's administration cut every kind of social expenditure (for the poor, for science, the arts, and education) but contributed lavishly to the military, farms, and businesses. He also raised the salaries of government workers, and most controversially, Fraser vastly increased the apportionment to Australia's secret police, the ASIO. Despite or because of these measures, unemployment increased over one percentage point from 1975-77 while inflation somewhat decreased. In 1977, another election was called for the benefit of the incumbent parties and

Compare & Contrast

- **1980:** Chief Justice of Australia's High Court, Sir Garfield Barwick was, without declaring his interest, sitting in judgment on cases brought to his courtroom by wealthy corporations in which Barwick's own private family company, Mundroola Pty Ltd, owned shares. Most cases were decided in favor of those corporations in which the judge had interest.

  June, 1999: Prime Minister John Howard refuses to sack one of his front-bench team whose company, Cape York Concrete Pty Ltd, was awarded a $175,500 defense contract. Howard admitted that Parliamentary Secretary Warren Entsch breached ministerial code by failing to declare, as required by Mr. Howard's code, that he was director and company secretary of Cape York Concrete the company receiving the substantial government contract.

- **1981:** AIDS is first recognized as a distinct disease in the U.S. The earliest American cases were traced back to 1977.

  June, 1999: In the United States, the cumulative number of reported AIDS cases from the beginning of the epidemic in 1981 through June 1998, is 665,337.

- **1981:** At the Sequoyah nuclear plant, near Chattanooga, Tennessee, eight workers are exposed to radioactive water, as a core is nearly exposed; it is only one of a series of such accidents.

  1999: A leading US scientific organization comes up with new findings supporting Nevada's Yucca Mountain nuclear site as suitable for the long-term storage of spent nuclear fuel. The reason is that water is not expected-based on research into the geologic past of the site-to seep into the area.

- **1979:** Restoration of Leonardo da Vinci's "The Last Supper" begins in Milan.

  May, 1999: The 20-year restoration of Leonardo da Vinci's "The Last Supper" is completed and the controversial results are exposed to public display. The restoration has been lauded by the Italians and contested by the international community.

they won again, defeating Labor decisively. Again, in 1980, Fraser was elected. Why did the Liberal and National party continue to win elections despite their decreased social spending? Probably because by 1980 inflation had fallen five percentage points since 1975 when Fraser first took office. It is still a much debated historical point whether the decrease in government spending was responsible for the fall in inflation. A second reason for continued election of Fraser was that those who controlled the money put Fraser back in office for his increased development of export industries that both garnered the country money and pleased overseas investors. This enabled the paying down of foreign debt. Other reasons for Fraser's success was a rational foreign policy, that cemented relations with China, and denounced racism wherever it was seen, going to the point of being instrumental in ending white rule in Rhodesia and ushering in black rule for the transformed country renamed Zimbabwe.

Certain trends were apparent in Australia in the seventies and eighties. Immigration increased from 7.5 million in 1947 to 17 million in 1990. Whereas immigrants had previously been mostly white and European, the government increasingly allowed a more diverse panorama, especially those of Asian descent. The government also increasingly transformed itself, at least officially, from an agent of assimilation to one moving towards a program respecting a diversity of practices and peoples under one government. Women's rights also made strides during this period, especially when the native Australian, Germaine Greer, published her extremely influential book *The Female Eunuch* in 1970. During the postwar period, Australia grew further away from Britain and closer to the United States, supporting the United States with soldiers for the Vietnam War. For the sake of its economy, Australia also grew closer to Asia, especially Japan. The role of the central government, in terms of power, gradually overtook the state governments. Unionization also continued and to this day Australia remains one of the most unionized of Western countries. Finally, like most countries in the world since the 1980s, the economy has come to dominate politics and the interests of most Australians.

Critical Overview

While little or no criticism appears available on "Beware of Ruins," at least in the United States, what Ruth Morse writes about Hope's poetry in her introduction to *A. D. Hope: Selected Poems* (1986) applies: "The general effect [is] a kind of elevated conversational tone: the lines give the impression of a speaking voice, but are often more formal or complex than an actual speaker would be. While his syntax exploits normal English order, his adherence to formal metres gives him the added resources of a traditional rhythm and rhyme."

Writing in his work *A. D. Hope*, Kevin Hart argues that Hope is a visionary who longs "for an organic wholeness" and a "heightened sense of the primacy and irreducibility of poetry." But Hope's poetry is not visionary in the tradition of the French poet, Rimbaud who sought a disordering of all the senses during the Symbolist Movement. Instead, Hope gains "vision through a creative ordering of the senses, a vision which," Hart continues, "encourages the poet to remain in society, not to set oneself against it."

Finally, Robert Darling (1997) calls Hope "a poet of the imagination rather than the observed world," and utilizes a quote from Hope to clarify. Hope says that the poet's "licence ... is to create quite another nature than that in which he lives, though he must find his elements there." If Darling's and Hope's statements are used to analyze "Beware of Ruins," it can be said they both clarify and obscure the poem. The world in "Beware of Ruins" is a scene most likely fashioned from a site of ruins seen in the real world and, in addition, the ruins (memories) seen or read about in books, books being understood as both part of the world and apart from it. Hope creates the poem from the remembered fragments of things experienced in three dimensions (the world) and things that have

appeared on the dimensions of the page, canvas, or screen. This makes Hope a poet of the "observed world," a world which comes to the poet's memory as ruins, the simultaneity of preservation and destruction. The ruins, however, are given a new nature through the constructions of the imagination, specifically the poem.

Criticism

Jhan Hochman

Jhan Hochman is a writer and instructor at Portland Community College in Portland, Oregon. He is the author of Green Cultural Studies: Nature in Film, Novel, and Theory, *1998. In the following essay, Hochman attempts to flesh out and analyze A. D. Hope's notions of romantic reconstruction and romantic reliving of the past.*

In "Beware of Ruins" (1981) A. D. Hope cautions against attempts to process the past, to romanticize either it or one's place in it by recalling or recasting these in a favorable, even romantic light. In the first three stanzas of the poem, two kinds of romanticization are cautioned against: imaginative and literal reconstruction of actual ruins. In the final stanza, however, another kind of romanticization is addressed, one that attempts not so much to reconstruct or bring back the past, but imaginatively relive it, relive one's own past by reinserting oneself into one's past memories. Both processings of the past—romantic reconstruction and romantic reliving—are, according to Hope, either treacherous or impossible.

The ruins described by the first three stanzas are stones that were once a structure (probably a castle), a pool once a fountain, a statue, a moat, and another structure perhaps part of the same scene: a decaying Tudor tower with either a real or imagined facade. All of these elements inhabit the story of Melusine, mentioned in stanza two. In "The Noble Story of Melusine, or The Romance of Melusine in Prose" (1387) by Jean d'Arras, Elinas, King of Albania (another says Scotland), diverted his grief for causing the death of his wife in a hunting accident. One day he went to a fountain to drink. Approaching, he heard a woman singing, the beautiful fairy Presine. Eventually Presine agreed to wed Elinas on condition he never visit her during childbirth. But when the birth of his triplet daughters was announced, Elinas was so excited he forgot himself and burst in on the queen bathing their

What Do I Read Next?

- *Illuminations* (1968), by Walter Benjamin is a collection of essays from one of the most interesting and independent thinkers of the Frankfurt School. Especially apropos to "Beware of Ruins" is the essay "Theses on the Philosophy of History."

- Michel Foucault's *Language, Counter-Memory, Practice* (1977), is a collection of essays, and interviews with the author. See especially, "Nietzsche, Genealogy, History."

- *A Primer of Freudian Psychology* (1982) is a small introduction to Freud's thought and practice, of which memory and dreams comprise two indispensable constituents. Includes an index.

- *The Collected Poems of W. B. Yeats* (1996) contains many poems of aging, memory and death. See especially "Sailing to Byzantium," and "A Prayer for Old Age."

- "Gerontion" (1920) by T.S. Eliot is an excellent poem on aging.

---

daughters: Melusine, Melior, and Palatina. Presine cried out and disappeared with her daughters to Lost Island. There she reared them and daily took them to a mountain to view Albania. Presine told her daughters that their father's breach of promise banished them from Albania. Time passed. At fifteen, Melusine asked her mother of what her father was guilty. Angered, Melusine decided on revenge: with her sisters, Melusine set out for Albania where the three girls took the king and all his wealth, and, by a charm, enclosed him in a mountain. Presine found out and punished them, condemning Melusine to become, every Saturday, a serpent from the waist down. If, however, Melusine married a man that promised never to see her on Saturdays, she would be able to have a "normal" life. Melusine later met Raimondin, a man who had killed his uncle in a hunting accident. Raimondin was grieving and wandering in a forest and arrived at the Fountain of Thirst near a high rock. There he glimpsed,

by the light of the moon, three ladies, the principal being Melusine. Her beauty and amiability quickly won him. She soothed him, concealed the accidental killing of his uncle, and married him, making him promise to never see her on Saturdays. If he breached the oath she said she would leave him. With her great wealth, Melusine built him many castles, especially Lusignan. But Destiny—that would have Melusine single—was incensed against her: Destiny fashioned a characteristic deformity for each of Melusine's children. Even then, Raimondin's love for her remained unshaken, at least until Destiny renewed her attack: Raimondin's cousin made suggestions of Melusine having an affair. Raimondin peeked through a bathroom door one Saturday to find out and beheld Melusine alone splashing in a tub, her lower torso a snake. Melusine departed from him, and, in obedience to Destiny, roamed the earth as a suffering specter. Only when one of her descendants was to die at Lusignan would she become visible. Her words at parting were, "But one thing will I say unto thee before I part, that thou, and those who for more than a hundred years shall succeed thee, shall know that whenever I am seen to hover over the fair castle of Lusignan, then will it be certain that in that very year the castle will get a new lord; and though people may not perceive me in the air, yet they will see me by the Fountain of Thirst; and thus shall it be so long as the castle stand in honor and flourishing—especially on the Friday before the lord of the castle shall die." Immediately, with wailing and loud lamentation, she left the castle of Lusignan, and has ever since existed as a specter of the night. Robert Graves, in *The White Goddess* (1966), believes that the tradition of the mermaid or snake-torsoed female goes back to Aphrodite ("risen from sea-foam") who in Botticelli's *Birth of Venus* (1485-86) is blown in from the sea on a large scallop shell. Aphrodite has also been identified with the moon-goddess, Eurynome, whose statue at Arcadia was a wooden mermaid. And finally, in English ballads, the mermaid stands for the bittersweetness of love.

> This poem that began as a warning ends more like a lament for the irreversibility of one's own aging.

With such research or knowledge, Hope assembled his haunted ruins. The assemblage is incredibly adept, for in the poem, Melusine is identified with the moon, indicating romance, water (tides and reflecting pools, but fountains as well), femaleness (the sun being male), and a kind of undependability since Melusine is apt to regularly vary like the moon. Melusine is a changeling figure, one a man cannot love without regret. Since Melusine is a specter or fairy, love cannot be dependably restored, reconstruction of the castles she built cannot be faithfully executed, and one should avoid inserting one's own "love restored" in such a scene. Love is dead and ruins remain ruins despite imagination and restoration. Romanticization is exposed as artificial, a lie, and as such should cause one to lose the thirst for a past never to flow again. In addition to employing the specter of Melusine, Hope indicates these ruins are treacherous by refocusing our eyes from the romanticized past to the more dilapidated present, to the phallic fungi and nettles, to how moonlight is old, cold, and inhospitable to love, at least in comparison to the relatively fresh warmth of sunlight. Finally, that restored facade on a Tudor tower is a death mask which Hope sees most pessimistically, not as the tower fully intact, but the tower before it began to decay. A building facade cast as a death mask is a kind of personification, the kind of mask fashioned from a face contorted in despair at the onset of the body's decay or death. Hope, himself, puts the worst mask on the past, cautioning us against the devil of decay, lying and laying beneath the angel of appearance.

The second type of reprocessing the past occurs in the poem when an attempt is made by the narrator/poet to relive his past. This reprocessing differs from the kind in the first three stanzas where another's past was imaginatively or actually reconstructed in ruins, or the past of another served as the diorama in which to insert one's own past ("love restored"). In this final scenario, Hope claims that he is able to accurately reconstruct his past, itself a romanticized or romantic one, with its *mise en scene* of a fire lit, a "table laid," and a "bed warmed." The reason he cannot insert himself into this intact environment is not because of the scene, but because of himself, because he has aged. Whereas in the first three stanzas, the intact observer is able—even if imprudently—to insert himself into the reconstructed ruins, in the final stanza the recaller is himself a ruins unable to insert himself into the intact, remembered scene. This poem that began as a warning ends more like a lament for the irreversibility of one's own aging.

The two kinds of dioramas of the past into which one attempts to get into (in order to restore love), then, are the dioramas of some other past (ruins) and the dioramas of one's own past. What Hope seems to imply is that insertion of oneself into the diorama of some other past points up the deadness of the past to the present, while insertion

of oneself into the diorama of one's own past points to the deadness of the present in the past. Either way, for the Hope in "Beware of Ruins," the past is a diorama of death, an assembled still life in three dimensions, a *nature morte,* whose very lack of animation is what allows it to be "enlivened." And if the past seems "enlivened" it is not because the past can ever become alive but because the Imagination—that first and foremost lovesick desecrator of graves and exhumer of corpses—casts a bewitching spell to make it seem so.

Source: Jhan Hochman, in an essay for *Poetry for Students,* Gale Group, 2000.

Jeannine Johnson

Jeannine Johnson currently teaches writing and literature at Harvard University. She has also taught at Yale, from which she received her Ph.D., and at Wake Forest University. Her most recent essay is on Adrienne Rich's "To a Poet," published in the Explicator. *In the following essay, Johnson examines Hope's failed attempt, in "Beware of Ruins," to spare his readers from the pain of nostalgia.*

A. D. Hope's "Beware of Ruins" delivers a warning against nostalgia. In this poem, Hope cautions us not to romanticize the past, whether it be our own personal past or the history of previous generations. The poet fears our tendency to misremember the past as having been better than it was, and he questions our inclination to imagine our lost loves as having been restored amidst the wreckage of time. The title becomes a kind of refrain in the poem, repeated in the first and third stanzas and then revised in the final stanza. Hope repeats his warning, as if aware of our unwillingness to heed it. However, as the poem progresses, the poet shows himself to be just as susceptible to the kind of fantasies that he distrusts, revealing that he, too, is included among those to whom the poem is directed.

The past is represented by "ruins" in this poem not because it is corrupt or destroyed but because it can never be properly relived or accurately reconstructed. In the first three stanzas, the poet explores a site of literal ruins, the stone remains of an ancient castle or palace. He notes a "scummy pool," the broken sculpture of a "seated figure," a "moat," and a "Tudor tower." These are striking features, but the poet warns us about misinterpreting their significance. These ruins "have a treacherous charm; / Insidious echoes lurk among their stones…." It is one thing to recognize that the cur-

In this poem, Hope cautions us not to romanticize the past, whether it be our own personal past or the history of previous generations."

rent state of disrepair does not correspond to the castle's former condition, and that, for instance, the "scummy pool" marks the spot where once "a fountain soared." But it is another thing altogether to try to derive some personal meaning from this wreckage by imposing our own lives on it. The poet knows too well that "the heart is apt to make / Monstrous assumptions on the unburied past." He declares that the parts of our history which lie unburied are those that we are especially likely to idealize. He implies that our vision is untrustworthy, that it misleads our inner sight and causes our imaginations to stray into false memories.

Hope uses the poem's form to help him sound the alarm about idealizing the past. The fourth line in each stanza is indented and, since it contains eight rather than ten syllables, is shorter than the other five. This structural irregularity calls attention to the ideas and images in those fourth lines. In the first three stanzas, the objects in the fourth line are a seated figure, a moat, and a facade. All of these objects are enticing illusions, and the poet's language becomes progressively stronger in describing them as he tries to demonstrate just how deceptive they are. The seated figure "Beckons" us to project our dreams upon it, but it is finally revealed to be "a mock-up of dry bones / And not, as you believe, your love restored." The poet concedes that "The moat has a romantic air," but exposes that impression as false. In fact, the water around the ruins "is choked with nettles and obscene / And phallic fungi rot there as they grow." What might have been symbols of joyful sexuality transform, in the poet's unglorified view, into sinister "phallic fungi." This rotting form becomes something even more menacing in the third stanza: the facade is not only a "fake" but a "death-mask of the last / Despairing effort before it all went

sour." The poet makes it clear that when we apply a romanticized screen to the past, we do nothing more than create a plaster cast of a corpse, and that even this effort is knowingly futile.

In contrast with the suspicious facade, a table set for dinner and a warm bed appear in the truncated fourth line in the final stanza. In describing these objects, the poet declines to use the threatening language of the first three stanzas, suggesting how much greater is the danger of projecting false visions on these more familiar articles. Several other shifts also occur in the fourth stanza and further underscore the risks one takes in a different kind of visit to the past. In this stanza, the poet's voice changes from the second person to the first person, signalling that the scope of his concerns is becoming more exclusive. The site also changes from an impersonal, common relic to a more private preserve, a ruin "of a less obvious kind." This spot is unique to the poet, and his physical passage inside this room located in his "former world" symbolizes a retreat into the interior of his emotions: "I go back; cannot believe my eyes; the place / Is just as I recall…." Ironically, the poet doubts his own vision, which is what he urged us to do in the first three stanzas. His eyes are thoroughly reliable, but his imagination and self-perception still fail him. He reports that "I find / My former world intact, but not, alas, / The man I was when I was part of it." Now that he looks inward, Hope realizes that the most momentous changes have been the alterations within himself, not in the world around him.

Hope's poetic theory is conservative, and he steadfastly believes that the only legitimate poetry is formal poetry. He criticizes free verse, which is poetry written without rhyme, meter, or other regular formal patterns. In "Free Verse: A Post-Mortem," one of several essays included in the collection, *The Cave and the Spring,* Hope makes the following pronouncement: "The truth about free verse is that it is not free and it is not verse. It is not free because it has no discipline by which its freedom may be assessed. It is not verse because it has neither measure nor metre." Somewhat unfairly, Hope views free verse as inherently unrigorous, and he considers it to be more closely related to prose than to poetry. He asserts that since free verse does not develop according to a strict design, it cannot create the kind of tension and anticipation that formal poetry can. He continues to explain that "surprise comes from variations on the pattern that metre leads us to expect. Without expectation of one thing we cannot be surprised by another, which is why free verse in spite of its variety rarely gives us those shocks of delicious surprise that real poetry always affords." In other words, what shocks or makes an impression is not merely what is new or unusual but what is unexpected, and expectation is produced by establishing and adhering to some form of convention.

The kinds of surprises for which Hope aims are perhaps to be found in "Beware of Ruins." His six-line stanzas proceed according to a rigid ABCABC rhyme scheme, creating and fulfilling the expectation of particular end-word sounds. Of the twelve rhymed pairs in the poem, eleven are true rhymes: in the first stanza, for example, "charm" rhymes perfectly with "arm," "stones" with "bones," and "soared" with "restored." Only one minor violation of our expectations for the rhymes appears in the poem. In the final stanza Hope couples "place" with "alas," creating a slant rhyme. After the regularity of the true rhymes, this slanted pair calls particular attention to these two terms and their relationship to each other. The consequences of visiting the places of our past, Hope has contended throughout the poem, are self-delusion and disappointment. Just as our expectations for a true rhyme are frustrated, so are our expectations for a permanent link to the past. However, the poet does not assign blame to the place, but to us: for it is the expression of "alas" that violates the sound established by "place," not the other way around. That is to say, it is our perception of the past (verbalized by the single word "alas"), not the past itself, which creates discord and grief.

Though Hope's poems are often traditional in form, their effect is not altogether conventional. His voice is often humorous and even sardonic, as in the poems "Australia" and "The Bed," and he frequently addresses themes of sexuality and romantic passion, as in the poems "Imperial Adam" and "Meditation on a Bone." However, humor is absent in "Beware of Ruins," and sexuality exists in this poem in the more muted hues of bygone loves. Though the poem begins with the poet imploring us to beware of our penchant for nostalgia, its final effect is more subtle. The earnestness of the first three stanzas is replaced by a more measured humility in the last stanza. The poet confirms the necessity of allowing ourselves to try to relive the past and to revisit lost loves, even though that endeavor will inevitably cause us some pain: Hope

implicitly admits that to try to prevent us from doing so would be to try to deny what it means to be human.

Source: Jeannine Johnson, in an essay for *Poetry for Students,* Gale Group, 2000.

Sources

Darling, Robert, *A.D. Hope,* New York: Twayne, 1997.

Ellman, Richard, and Robert O'Clair, eds., *The Norton Anthology of Modern Poetry,* second edition, New York: Norton, 1988.

Graves, Robert, *The White Goddess,* New York: Farrar, Straus and Giroux, 1966.

Hart, Kevin *A. D. Hope,* Melbourne: Oxford University Press, 1992.

Hope, A. D., *The Cave and the Spring: Essays on Poetry,* Rigby Limited, 1965.

Hope, A. D., *Selected Poems,* selected and introduced by Ruth Morse, Manchester: Carcanet, 1986.

Ward, Russel, *Concise History of Australia,* Queensland: University of Queensland Press, 1992.

For Further Study

Hope, A. D., *Australian Literature 1950-62,* Melbourne: Melbourne University Press, 1963.
   This is a chapbook that briefly mentions names, publications, dates, and characteristics, the latter in terms of themes and techniques used by authors. It is divided into sections on poetry, novels, short stories, drama, and criticism. There is also an overview of magazines and anthologies.

Hope, A. D., *Collected Poems, 1930-1965,* New York: Viking Press, 1966.
   Hope's poems are printed chronologically but what poems belong to what collections is not indicated. A short preface by the poet introduces the volume.

Hope, A. D., *The New Cratylus: Notes on the Craft of Poetry,* Melbourne: Oxford University Press, 1979.
   Hope gathers together his conclusions on the nature of language and the way it operates in poetry. The work is more of a workshop manual than a treatise because it is primarily aimed at recruiting potential poets.

Pietrangeli, Carlo, *The Sistine Chapel: A Glorious Restoration,* New York: Harry Abrams, 1994.
   Michelangelo's creation of the monumental frescos in the Sistine Chapel marked a revolutionary event in Western art. A nine-year restoration, carried out by experts at the Vatican Museums, is described and illustrated in this work.

The Constellation Orion

Ted Kooser

1975

"The Constellation Orion" was originally published in 1975 in *Three Rivers Poetry Journal,* and then reprinted in Kooser's 1980 collection, *Sure Signs: New and Selected Poems.* The poem typifies Kooser's style: short, descriptive, and literal. Its brevity (only 14 lines) and "artless" manner make it easy to read and accessible to those who are not regular readers of poetry. It also addresses a favorite Kooser subject: the relationship between the natural and the human worlds.

Written in 1970, the poem literally describes an experience Kooser had while driving his son, then about three years old, back to Lincoln, Nebraska from just outside Ames, Iowa. Kooser would make the trek on weekends to pick up his son from his ex-wife, who lived in Marshalltown, Iowa. He would then sometimes visit his parents in Cedar Rapids before returning to Lincoln. The highway, the car, and the night sky made up their world at this time.

The poem relates a brief address by the speaker to the constellation Orion. In the address the speaker imagines his son waking up (he's napping on his father's lap) and mispronouncing the constellation's name, calling him "Old Ryan." We have all been guilty of mispronouncing words; it is frequently part of the process of learning new vocabulary. Therefore, we can smile at the mistake the father imagines his son would make and, indeed, probably has made before. The fact that a child makes the mistake is endearing. Kooser writes only occasionally about other people. Most of his

poems are descriptions of things or animals, or of the rituals of daily life in the Midwest.

Author Biography

Like Wallace Stevens, Ted Kooser made his living as an insurance company executive, retiring from Lincoln Benefit Life only recently. Unlike Stevens, Kooser writes for everyman in an accessible and non-literary manner. Considered one of Nebraska's leading poets, Kooser was born to merchant Ted, Sr. and Vera Moser Kooser in 1939 in Ames, Iowa, and educated in the Ames public school system. At Iowa State University in Ames he took his BS in English Education in 1962. Six years later he received an MA in English from the University of Nebraska at Lincoln. Both Iowa and Nebraska are Great Plains states, and with their flat expanse, and relatively small populations, they provides stargazers with a view of the heavens unobscured by city lights and smog. Light, particularly starlight and moonlight, is a recurring image in many of Kooser's poems.

Kooser married Diana Tressler, a teacher, and had a son, Jeffrey Charles, in 1967, the son in "The Constellation Orion." In 1969 Tressler and Kooser divorced, and Kooser remarried afterward. He writes about both of his marriages in his 1978 collection of poems, *Old Marriage and New*.

Kooser has authored many volumes of poems including *Sure Signs: New and Selected Poems* (1980), *One World at a Time* (1985), and *Weather Central* (1994), all from the University of Pittsburgh Press, and has published pamphlets and books of his own with Windflower Press, a small press started by Kooser which specializes in contemporary Midwestern poetry. The recipient of many national awards including two National Endowment of the Arts fellowships, Kooser's poetry has been featured on National Public Radio and has been reprinted in a number of textbooks and anthologies. Ted Kooser lives in Garland, Nebraska, just outside of Lincoln.

Poem Text

The Constellation Orion

I'm delighted to see you,
old friend,
lying there in your hammock

Ted Kooser

over the next town.
You were the first person   5
my son was to meet in the heavens.
He's sleeping now,
his head like a small sun in my lap.
Our car whizzes along in the night.
If he were awake, he'd say,   10
"Look, Daddy, there's Old Ryan!"
but I won't wake him.
He's mine for the weekend,
Old Ryan, not yours.

Poem Summary

Lines 1-4:

Stargazing is an ancient activity. Greeks practiced it widely, often assigning names to groups of stars and telling stories about those stars. These stories, myths, were an attempt to explain natural phenomena. By the 5th century BC, Eratosthenes compiled the *Catasterismi* which contained a number of these myths, most of which were connected to one another in some way. There are a few myths about the Constellation Orion. One of them names the sea-god Neptune as Orion's father and the great huntress Queen Euryale of the Amazons as his mother. Taking after his mother, Orion became the world's greatest hunter. But in his arrogance he

Media Adaptations

- The Nebraska Center for Writers has an informational website on Ted Kooser and his poetry: http://mockingbird.creighton.edu/NCW/kooser.htm

- For a real-time look at Orion and other constellations on the World Wide Web, visit the following site: http://math1.uibk.ac.at/~werner/light/stars/orion.html

- Visit the following website which satirizes the use of malapropisms: http://www.execpc.com/%7Ejab2/MainPage.htm

- This World Wide Web site provides useful information on the myths behind the names of the constellations:http://www.dibonsmith.com/stars.htm

- An online message board designed to help single fathers with day-to-day issues of child rearing can be accessed at http://www.angelfire.com/ks/singlefather/

- *The Fathering Magazine* contains many useful articles on single fathers and the joys (and pitfalls) of fathering. http://www.fathermag.com/SingleFather.shtml

---

bragged that he could catch any animal in the world. A scorpion eventually stung and killed him in response to his boasting. A second story holds that Orion was motherless, and was given as a gift to a peasant by Jupiter, Neptune, and Mercury, and grew up to be a great hunter. After failing to win the permission of King Oenopion to marry his daughter, Merion, Orion tried to take her by force. Oenopion tricked Orion and blinded him, casting him out on the seashore, where his sight was eventually restored by the sun-god. After many adventures, Orion dwelt with Diana, whom he wanted to marry. However, her brother, Apollo, did not want her to marry Orion and one day tricked her into shooting him with her bow and arrow. When Diana discovered what she had done she wept, then

placed Orion among the stars, where he remains today.

The poem begins with the speaker addressing the constellation Orion, sometimes called Orion the Hunter. Orion is located on the celestial equator and can be seen from every part of the Earth. The Belt of Orion, consisting of a short straight row of three bright stars, is the most noticeable part of the constellation. When you look at them, you're looking in the direction opposite the center of our Milky Way galaxy. These stars are what the speaker refers to when he says "hammock." The speaker obviously takes joy in stargazing as he says that he is "delighted" to see Orion. The neighborliness of the speaker's greeting also underscores that the speaker sees the constellations as a dependable and everyday part of his universe. Many people are so consumed with the daily activities of their lives, particularly indoor activities, that they are not always aware of the world outside, especially the heavenly bodies. This is often true of city dwellers, who have to fight not only the distractions of incessant human activity but light and smog pollution as well to view the stars.

Lines 5-8:

The speaker continues to address Orion, now calling him a "person." His tone is intimate, as if he is addressing a close friend, a godparent, maybe. He tells the constellation that it is the first constellation that his son "was to meet." This makes sense when we understand that Orion is one of the most visible constellations in the sky. This is especially true during January and February for those of us who live in the northern hemisphere. One needs only to look toward the southeast for the three bright stars that make up Orion's belt. Foreshadowing his son's own (unintentional) pun, the speaker refers to his son's head as a "small sun." This simile underscores the boy's importance to his father, and draws attention to the idea that his son himself is a constellation of sorts, a heavenly body on earth. Life on earth depends on the sun for sustenance, just as the father depends on his son for emotional sustenance.

Lines 9-11:

The speaker locates himself and his son in a car, "whizz[ing] along in the night." Such a scene is typical for the Midwest, as long drives are common because towns are often few and far between. Continuing his address to the constellation, the speaker uses the conditional "if" to guess at what his son would say were he awake. By having his son mispronounce Orion's name, the speaker clues us into his son's probable age (3-4). Such a humorous and endearing response from the son only deepens the reader's sense of intimacy between father and son.

Lines 12-14:

The father's refusal to wake his son, stemming from an imaginary conversation with the constellation, also implies that he has competed in the past for his son's affection or attention. That he has his son "for the weekend" also suggests that the speaker is estranged or divorced from the son's mother, and that he has visitation rights for the weekend. This possibility makes the poem all the more endearing, while also bringing it closer to sentimentality.

Themes

Language and its Meaning

The effect of Kooser's poem "The Constellation Orion" rests on two puns. The first one is intentional, the second one accidental. These puns focus our attention on the practice of naming, something that human beings do to make sense of their world, but also something that poets especially have been noted for doing. Foreshadowing his son's mistake, the father says that the boy's head is "like a sun." Such punning underscores the slippery nature of language itself, emphasizing the fact that there is no inherently natural relationship between the idea of the thing named (the signified) and the word (either speech sounds or marks on the page) used to name it (the signifier), but that meaning in language resides in how linguistic elements are different from one another in a given system. Such a view of language, first theorized by linguist Ferdinand de Saussure, suggests that reality, rather than being "out there" waiting to be seen and named, is in large part constructed by the act of naming itself. The son's mispronunciation can also be read as a malapropism, a term derived from the character Mrs. Malaprop in Sheridan's *The Rivals* (1775). A malapropism occurs when a speaker misuses words, most often unintentionally, because they sound alike. Usually the malapropism is close enough to the correct word that the listener knows what the speaker intended. This is certainly the case with the speaker of Kooser's poem, who understands what his son means when he says "Old Ryan." Someone not close to the child and with no

Topics for Further Study

- Research the Greek myths behind at least three other constellations and then construct an outline or a chart detailing the relationships among the characters in those myths. Now write a short essay explaining those relationships.

- Write an essay comparing and contrasting how Kooser represents Orion and how Adrienne Rich represents Orion in her poem, "Orion."

- Probe your earliest memories of how the stars were explained to you, by adults or other children, and write a narrative account of those memories.

relationship to him might not understand the mistake, so in this case, the malapropism and the speaker's recognition of it serve as evidence of the father and son's closeness.

Imagination

"The Constellation Orion" is an act of imagination. It also describes an imaginative act: that is, the speaker having a conversation with the stars, as well as with his sleeping son. Although some critics consider Kooser to be a realist, he is, in fact, a romantic. Before the Romantics, poetry was considered an art designed to mirror human activity. Good poetry also mirrored, or modeled itself after great poetry of the past, specifically poetry of ancient Greece and Rome. William Wordsworth, however, helped initiate a change in how people began to think of poetry. In his *Preface to Lyrical Ballads* he claimed that poetry's primary material was a poet's *feelings,* and that poems arose out of "a spontaneous overflow of powerful feelings." Samuel Taylor Coleridge elaborated on this, claiming that the poems grew organically, much like a plant, rather than being plotted according to rules of past works. The imagination, Coleridge argued, had laws which developed along the lines of its own internal principles. Nature, as well, became a favored subject of poetry, meditation on which often prompted the poet to think about other common human experiences or problems. Kooser's poem, then, can be seen as a quintessentially romantic poem. Like much romantic poetry, it employs the lyric "I," and uses inspiration from nature, in the form of the stars, to meditate on the love of a parent for his child, a universal human experience. The organic nature of Kooser's poem is embodied in its loose conversational style and, as if to underscore the primacy of the imagination itself, the speaker, rather than talking directly to his son who is right next to him, engages in a fantasized dialogue with the youngster.

Style

Though it is told in the present tense, "The Constellation Orion" functions as a humorous anecdote. Anecdotes are short stories, often conversational, told about a particular event. The use of dialogue in this poem also underscores that conversational quality, and its use of non-literary language. This anecdote also includes puns, in the form of the father's calling his son's head "a small sun" and the son's mispronunciation of the "constellation Orion." Puns work when words have identical or similar sounds, but are very different in meaning. The effect of Kooser's puns is to render the child "cute" for readers, and to highlight the intimacy among the father, son, and constellation.

The poem employs figurative language throughout. He uses personification and metaphor to describe the constellation's appearance, saying that he sees Orion "lying there in your hammock." In addressing the constellation directly, Kooser employs apostrophe. Apostrophe is a direct address to an abstract entity or to an absent person. Keats, for example, apostrophizes a Grecian urn in his well-known poem, "Ode on a Grecian Urn."

In comparing his son's head to "a small sun in my lap," Kooser uses a simile. Similes are "like" metaphors in that they compare two distinctly different things, but they are indicated by the word "like" or "as." This comparison also parallels his description of Orion in that both son and Orion are resting: Orion in his hammock, the son in his father's lap.

Historical Context

Kooser was a single parent when he wrote this poem in 1970, and the love that he expresses for his son elicits a warm feeling in readers. The United States in the 1960s and 1970s witnessed a dramatic rise in the divorce rate. In 1970 in the United States there were 709,000 divorces, or 3.5 for every 1,000 marriages, up from 393,000 in 1960, or 2.3 for every 1,000 marriages. Custody of children, though, was most often awarded to mothers, with father's granted visitation rights, often on weekends. As such, the image of the speaker in his car with his son, expressing the joy he feels at having him for the weekend, is a familiar one for Americans. A number of films dealing with the trauma of divorce and custody came out during the 1970's, the most notable one being 1979's *Kramer Vs. Kramer,* starring Dustin Hoffman and Meryl Streep. Kooser's most autobiographical work came out of his own experience with divorce. In 1978 he published *Old Marriage and New* with Cold Mountain Press. This collection of 13 "scenes" recounts the difficulty of that period in his life.

Kooser wrote "The Constellation Orion" in 1970, just three years after M. L. Rosenthal's study, *The New Poets* was published. In that book Rosenthal coins the term "confessional poetry" to designate a kind of poetry which foregrounds open and honest communication between writers and their audience, and frequently eschews what they consider artifice in their craft. Confessionalism had been in vogue for some time before then, as evidenced in Beat writers such as Allen Ginsberg, Jack Kerouac, Anne Sexton, Sylvia Plath, John Berryman, and Robert Lowell, whose *Life Studies* is widely considered to be a hallmark of confessional poetry. Confessionalism was a response to much of the formal poetry being written during the 1940s and 1950s, but it also embodied an air of possibility, and assumed that direct transcription of experience itself was a poetic act. The popularity of psychoanalysis during this period also helped the "cause" of confessional poetry, as poets frequently packed their work with personal details not traditionally included in poems. Kooser, though not a confessional poet in the traditional sense, does share the impulse to literally transcribe personal experience in his poems, though much of that experience rests on literal descriptions of the natural world, and not always or necessarily his emotional responses to that world.

Critical Overview

There has been no criticism written on "The Constellation Orion" and very little written on Kooser

Compare & Contrast

- **1971:** Henry Kissinger secretly visits China to arrange visit for President Nixon, marking the beginning of an era of detente between the two countries. China is admitted into the United Nations.

  Today: Although tensions remain, diplomatic relations between China and the United States have been largely normalized, and it appears likely that China will gain entry into the World Trade Organization.

- **1971:** U.S. Apollo 14 and 15 crews become the third and fourth groups to explore the moon's surface. In the same year three Russian cosmonauts die when their Soyuz 11 capsule develops an air leak when reentering the earth's atmosphere.

  1971: American astronomers discover two "new" galaxies adjacent to the earth's own galaxy, the Milky Way.

1972: The crew of Apollo 17 spends a record 75 hours on the moon's surface.

1998: The Lunar Prospector is launched. This is the first time in 25 years that NASA sent a probe to the Moon.

Today: The Mir Space Station floats above the earth, having completed to date over 77,300 trips around the Earth. In its thirteen years in orbit, cosmonauts and astronauts from dozens of nations have lived on the station and performed experiments of historical significance.

- **1971:** Legalized off track betting is introduced in New York.

  Today: The institution of gambling has become naturalized and legal in most states. Casinos, state sponsored lotteries, video poker, and horse and dog track betting generate large sums of revenue for states.

---

in general apart from reviews for book-length collections of poetry. Critic and poet Dana Gioia has written the most sustained piece of criticism on Kooser's career in his collection of essays, *Can Poetry Matter?*. In "The Anonymity of the Regional Poet," Gioia argues that Kooser is a popular poet because he writes for a nonliterary audience in accessible language, and deals with subjects from everyday life, albeit everyday life in the Midwest. Claiming that Kooser has not received much critical attention because his poetry "poses none of the verbal problems critical methodologies have been so skillfully designed to unravel," Gioia offers a paradox: "the simpler poetry is, the more difficult it becomes for a critic to discuss intelligently." For Kooser, however, it has not been a matter of whether or not critics discuss his poetry intelligently or not, but of whether they discuss it at all. Gioia examines Kooser's limitations *and* virtues as a poet, concluding that "while one would not claim that Kooser is a major poet, one could well make the case that he will be an enduring one."

Sure Signs: New and Selected Poems, the volume in which "The Constellation Orion" appears, received The Society of Midland Authors Prize for the best book of poetry by a Midwestern writer published in 1980 and also carries words from reviewers. Karl Shapiro, himself a Nebraskan poet, compares the collection to other regional poets and poetry, claiming that it is "a lasting work, comparable to the best of the *Spoon River* or Frost in his richest vein." Theodore Weiss seconds that opinion, saying "[Kooser] has, with his wit and his earthiness, his imagination and his lucidity, staked out as his own region—western as it is—somewhere poetically between Frost and Williams." Russell Edson calls the book "a wonderful collection."

Criticism

Pamela Steed Hill

Pamela Steed Hill has had poems published in over 90 journals and magazines and is the author of In Praise of Motels, *her first full-length collection, published in 1999. She is an associate editor for* University Communications *at The Ohio State University. In the following essay, Hill notes how the speaker "talks to" the stars to demonstrate his love and affection for his son, as well as to reveal the reason for the sadness that underlies an otherwise tender moment.*

Born in Ames, Iowa, in 1939, Ted Kooser is one of America's and, in particular, one of the Midwest's most highly regarded poets, especially for the states of Nebraska and Iowa. What has primarily led to his popularity is his consistent ability to turn everyday language and everyday events into poetry. One doesn't need to have lived a fairly quiet, unremarkable life on a small midwestern farm to appreciate or understand Kooser's work. The poet does, however, have a special affinity for the pastoral, for all things natural and simple. And while the poems may reflect that ease and simplicity on the surface, many take the reader on a deeper journey, one in which we can honestly say, "Yes, I know exactly what he means."

"The Constellation Orion" is one of those poems. It is rather brief and seemingly to the point: while a child sleeps, his father drives and takes note of one of the constellations above, fondly recalling the boy's mispronunciation of "Orion" as "Old Ryan." But if we back up and take a slower look at the lines, we find a carefully crafted use of a literary device that is both uncomplicated and powerful at the same time.

Anthropomorphism is an attribution of human characteristics to things not human, such as animals, inanimate objects, or natural phenomena. When we say the couch beckoned us to lie down and take a nap or when we call a tree a weeping willow, we are being anthropomorphic. Ted Kooser gives human characteristics to a collection of stars in the night sky throughout the entire poem, starting with the first two lines: "I'm delighted to see you, / old friend,...." From beginning to end, the speaker addresses the Orion constellation, also known as the "hunter" constellation because the group of stars it contains appears to form the shape of a man holding a bow and arrow, about to shoot. In Greek mythology, Orion was a very handsome, virile giant and an expert at hunting. Tales vary, but most relate that the hunter fell in love with Merope, the "wrong woman," and he was eventually blinded by her outraged father. Orion's sight was later restored but he would ultimately fall victim to yet another disgruntled family member. When Artemis,

goddess of the hunt and not a bad shot herself, showed great affection for him, her jealous brother, Apollo, tricked her into killing Orion when she fired an arrow into his head, thinking that a distant object was a sea creature. Realizing her mistake, she grieved for the giant hunter and placed his image in the sky as a constellation along with his faithful dog, Sirius. One can read, comprehend, and enjoy Ted Kooser's "The Constellation Orion" without knowing any of that. But it is interesting to speculate on what subtle significance this set of stars and its mythological allusions may play in the poem. The speaker seems to have a very pleasant relationship with Orion, noting that it's good to see the old friend "lying there in your hammock / over the next town." Although we typically visualize the constellation's form in an "upright" position, from the perspective of someone gazing through the windshield of a car at the night sky ahead, Orion may appear to be lounging on his back with an arm carelessly slung out to the side. This viewpoint gives the stars a direct connection to the child who is also "sleeping now" and who apparently had his first experience with astronomy when he was shown this very constellation at some point earlier, probably by his father. Orion was "the first person" the son "was to meet in the heavens," and the poet injects an apt simile in saying the boy's head is "like a small sun" in his lap.

We do not actually realize that this poem takes place in a car until the ninth line in which the speaker says, "Our car whizzes along in the night." The word "whizzes" is appropriate here in that it too links the man and his son on earth to events in space occurring all around them. Stars, planets, entire galaxies, and, it is now believed, entire universes also whiz along, and, with speeds incomprehensible to most, the descriptive word is as good as any.

Toward the end of the poem, the father thinks of how his son would react if he were awake and spotted the familiar constellation in the sky. The child would exclaim, "Look, Daddy, there's Old Ryan!" but he is not given the chance to see Orion tonight. For obvious reasons, a father prefers to let his child sleep when he's tired, but there is more going on in this father's mind than simply allowing the boy to rest. The last two lines tell us that the time the man has with his son is very limited and that this is a source of both sadness and possessiveness on the part of the father: "He's mine for the weekend, / Old Ryan, not yours." Now we know that this is not just a casual drive back home after an outing between father and son, but rather a weekend trip to the father's house after he has retrieved his son from wherever the boy now lives, presumably with his mother. There is an understandable sense of proprietorship here as the speaker has lost the pleasure of seeing his child everyday and must resign himself to spending time with the boy only on weekends. In order to make every minute of those weekends count, the father doesn't want to share his son's attention with anyone or anything—not even the stars.

Perhaps Ted Kooser selected Orion as the constellation to appear in this poem because that's really the one he saw while driving home on a starlit night and was inspired to write about it. This is the most likely scenario, given that Kooser is known for capturing the things he actually sees, hears, and experiences and turning them into very lucid verse. We may also, however, consider the possibility that the mythological Orion is a good choice for a poem in which the speaker has apparently lost at love and is feeling exiled from those dear to him, in this case via divorce. The giant hunter of Greek legend may not have gone through any legal proceedings, but he most certainly had his share of problems with women. As well, this poem does not stand in isolation in its theme, for Kooser also wrote "At the End of the Weekend" (from *Sure Signs*), which contains the lines, "It is Sunday afternoon, / and I suddenly miss / my distant son …," and he is the author of "The Witness" (from *One World at a Time*), which states, "The divorce judge has asked for a witness, / and you wait at the back of the courtroom / as still as a flag on its stand." Whether the placement of Orion was by intent or by accident, the image and the allusion serve the poem well, both in literary device and in content.

"The Constellation Orion" first appeared in *Sure Signs,* Kooser's collection of new and selected poems published in 1980. It is one of several in the collection that makes reference to various types of signs—astrological, street, "No Hunting," and signs from nature, such as in the title poem which tells us that "Crickets and cobwebs" are sure signs of "A long hard winter ahead." Whether Orion is intended as a "sign" of something in the poem— bad relationships, heartbreak, loss, etc. is just as nebulous as its selection in the first place. We do know, however, that it has been a much studied and much romanticized constellation with many earth-sky links proposed over the years. Recent speculation even connects this group of stars to the ancient pyramids of Egypt. In *The Orion Mystery,* Robert Bauval suggests that these remarkable structures

> *Perhaps Ted Kooser selected Orion as the constellation to appear in this poem because that's really the one he saw while driving home on a starlit night and was inspired to write about it.… We may also, however, consider the possibility that the mythological Orion is a good choice for a poem in which the speaker has apparently lost at love and is feeling exiled from those dear to him, in this case via divorce."*

are actually mirror images of the "belt stars" of Orion and that the air shafts built into the pyramids point toward the constellation so that the soul's of the dead kings can be projected directly there!

Regardless of how much historical or astrological reference went into the making of "The Constellation Orion," Ted Kooser effected a strong and sensitive poem that makes us feel both warm and sad at once. After reaching the end, we have to question whether the speaker is really as "delighted" to see his "old friend" as he claims to be in the beginning. Second thought seems to be at work here, for "old friend" eventually becomes "Old Ryan," and delight appears to turn to jealousy and possessiveness. Throughout this poem and many others in the collection, a subtle turn of events or a striking juxtaposition of emotions keeps the poetry alive and keeps us considering underlying meanings.

Sure Signs was awarded The Society of Midland Authors Prize for the best book of poetry by a midwestern writer during 1980. While not many

What Do I Read Next?

- Sandhills Press has put out a collection of essays on Nebraskan poets called *On Common Ground: The Poetry of William Kloefkorn, Ted Kooser, Greg Kuzma, and Don Welch*, which offers background and critical insight into a group of neglected writers.

- Dana Gioia's *Can Poetry Matter?* is a collection of essays which offers critiques on the state of contemporary poetry in America as well as reviews of some modern poets such as Weldon Kees, Robinson Jeffers, and Ted Kooser. This is an uneven collection, but the title essay is well worth reading, as it tackles issues immediately relevant to today's poetry, as well as poetry of the past. Gioia's essay on Kooser is the most substantive evaluation of Kooser's work to date.

- *The Poetry of Business Life: An Anthology,* contains poetry from seventy poets who also work in the business world. Poems by writers such as James Autry, Harry Newman, and Dana Gioia, are included, as well as work by Shakespeare, Chaucer, and Kipling.

- Robert Graves's often reprinted *Greek Myths* remains the classic text for those wanting to learn more about the lives of the Olympian Gods. Graves's modern retelling of Greek myths and heroes is both scholarly and accessible.

of the poems have been singled out for lengthy criticism, the book as a whole has met very favorably with critics nationwide. According to a World Wide Web site sponsored by the Nebraska Center for Writers, Dana Gioia, author of the controversial book *Can Poetry Matter?* had this to say about *Sure Signs:* "I found it impossible to put down until I had finished the entire book. It was like sitting next to a box of chocolates before dinner … a collection alternately delightful and mysterious."

We cannot know whether Gioia had "The Constellation Orion" in particular in mind when he wrote this description, but we do know that this poem certainly does contain elements of both delight and mystery. And it is clearly in keeping with Kooser's knack for turning a single, simple moment into a thoughtful and provocative piece of work.

Source: Pamela Steed Hill, in an essay for *Poetry for Students,* Gale Group, 2000.

Cliff Saunders

Cliff Saunders teaches writing and literature in the Myrtle Beach, South Carolina area and has published six chapbooks of verse. In the following essay, Saunders explores the symbolic nature of Orion the Hunter and how the constellation figures into the father-son relationship portrayed in the poem.

Many times over the past 15 years, I have exposed college students in my Composition and Literature classes to Ted Kooser's "The Constellation Orion," and not once has the poem failed to spark a spirited class discussion on the cost and consequences of parental separation and divorce. This is not surprising, considering that many of today's young adults have experienced firsthand the trauma of family dissolution. What is surprising about students' reactions to "The Constellation Orion" (and I've seen it time and time again) is the impassioned depth to which they respond to what is essentially an ordinary poem that captures a meaningful but not-so-rare moment between a father and estranged son he can be with only "for the weekend." The poem is unquestionably tapping into some resonant chord deep within the souls of these students and doing so in a way no essay or article on the subject has been able to touch. How can this be? How can such an unassuming and plainspoken poem have such a powerful, soul-stirring impact on young readers?

One key ingredient in the poem's success is the speaker's upbeat attitude in the face of a situation that can't help but be painful for him. Perhaps the time for recrimination and remorse has passed for this father, and by accepting the situation, he has moved beyond such negative feelings and can treasure what limited time he is allowed to spend with his son. Whatever the reason, the speaker reveals right away that he is overjoyed to be in the presence again of his son, even though his son is fast asleep in the front seat as his father "whizzes along in the night." Unable to convey this joy to his sleeping son, the speaker directs it at a human-shaped constellation in the night sky, that of Orion the Hunter. Notice how Orion, like the speaker's son, is asleep—or at least peacefully at rest—in his "hammock / over the next town." But why *this* constellation? Why Orion?

It may have something to do with the Orion legend. According to Greek myth, Orion was cast into a deep sleep by Dionysus after insulting a maiden, and he was blinded by the maiden's enraged father. Although Orion regained his eyesight by allowing the rays of the rising sun to grace his eyes, he was eventually killed by the goddess Artemis and placed in heaven as a constellation. Could Kooser have seen a little of himself in the Orion myth at the time of the poem's writing? Had he, in a sense, been cast into a "deep sleep" by the divorce from his first wife, been blinded for a time by his own rage, and at some point regained his sight by allowing the rays of the sun (son?) to "grace his eyes"? We can only speculate, but even if the myth of Orion has no direct bearing on the poem, the constellation itself does, and in a highly symbolic way.

From the poem, the reader can infer that the speaker and his son have talked previously about Orion, one of the brightest and most visible constellations in the night sky. One can imagine a happier time when Kooser, who has touched on things celestial elsewhere in his poetry, may have taken his son out to the backyard and pointed him in the direction of some of the night sky's high points, with Orion surely being one of them. That night—or a later one, perhaps—Kooser's son may have first spoken aloud his endearing mispronunciation of the constellation's name ("Old Ryan," which, when you think about it, sounds like just the name a Midwestern family would give their pet hound—"Ol' Ryan! Come here, boy!"), thus creating a private family joke that Kooser puts to memorable effect in his poem. Clearly, therefore, the constellation serves as a touchstone for the two, an icon of a time when Kooser and son enjoyed a special bond that seemed eternal and inviolable. Later, of course, this special bond would be torn asunder by the divorce, but whenever father and son were allowed to see each other, Orion could, on certain nights, remind them of what they once had and what they could still have, if only for a day or two.

The poem sets up a fascinating dichotomy between the eternal (as represented by Orion) and the temporal (as represented by the father and his sleeping son speeding together down a highway in the night). At times of great pain (as would be the case when a beloved son is taken away from a father), a person often looks to the heavens for guidance. Great comfort can be found there when life on earth

> *What is surprising about students' reactions to 'The Constellation Orion' … is the impassioned depth to which they respond to what is essentially an ordinary poem that captures a meaningful but not-so-rare moment between a father and estranged son he can be with only 'for the weekend.'"*

and its personal "injustices" become too unbearable to face. Kooser may have felt this way at the time of the poem's genesis, and so Orion gives him no small measure of solace. Kooser even calls him "old friend," and perhaps that is what Orion truly is to him: a reliable friend with whom he can commiserate at a time of personal turmoil in his life. Orion, moreover, likely represents stability to Kooser; after all, the constellation is a fixture in the night sky—an emblem of permanence, so to speak—and Kooser may have been in great need of this reminder at a time when much else in his life that he had considered "permanent" (i.e., his marriage, his family, a stable domestic life) seemed anything but lasting.

Orion may indeed be an "old friend" of sorts for the poem's speaker, but the constellation, as Kooser points out in the poem's final two lines ("He's mine for the weekend, / Old Ryan, not yours"), constitutes a threat as well. On one level, Kooser may be merely expressing some well-deserved selfishness in those lines, given that he can have his son only "for the weekend" and is on guard against anything that might intrude and divert his son's attention from "Daddy." Of course, in such a situation, every moment spent with an estranged son would seem fleeting and precious. There may be more to the story, however. What if the speaker's ex-wife has remarried or is seeing another man?

What if the speaker is engaged with another man in a battle for the boy's affections? Certainly not an uncommon scenario in this day and age. And though Orion would certainly be innocent of any charge of undue influence, the constellation is nevertheless a representational *male* figure and thus could be construed, in the eyes of a jealous father, as a competitor for the boy's affections and need for a mentor. Logic, of course, would dictate that Orion poses no direct threat to Kooser in this regard, but oftentimes in such situations, men are anything *but* logical. In fact, a loss of control over family can lead men to perform some desperate acts. The poem's speaker does not appear to be such a man, since he acknowledges that he will have to surrender his son at the end of the weekend, but the situation portrayed in the poem serves as a reminder of how fragile the human condition is.

Indeed, it could be argued that this fragility extends even beyond the confines of a tenuous father-son relationship, though this argument would be difficult to prove because of a certain ambiguity within the poem. I call your attention to lines 5 and 6: "You were the first person / my son was to meet in the heavens." These two lines are the only ambiguous ones in the entire poem, and although it is impossible to know for certain what Kooser means by them, they could refer to the possibility that the boy was gravely ill at one time and may have come close to dying. If Kooser had said "You were the first person / my son ever saw in the heavens," I would dismiss this interpretation outright, but by saying "were to meet" rather than "ever saw," he may be implying that there was a time when his son could have met Orion on his way to heaven. Seen in this light, no wonder Kooser seems so protective of his son in the poem, for perhaps the possibility once arose that his son might have been whisked away from him in a more permanent sense. And nothing, of course, makes life seem more fragile than the spectre of death hovering nearby.

Then again, perhaps I am reading too much into this ambiguity, for the poem seems to end on a more joyous note (though the joy looks to be temporary) than a despairing one. Kooser may only be suggesting that in the grand scheme of things (as represented by Orion), all we humans truly have are a few precious moments together as we whiz along in the great darkness that surrounds us. Perhaps Kooser sees Orion not as a threat but as a cosmic mirror image of himself. Perhaps, like the small "sun" Kooser has in his lap, Orion has a much bigger sun in his own lap as he relaxes in his giant hammock in the sky, and if Orion can have his own sun, why can't Kooser have his?

Source: Cliff Saunders, in an essay for *Poetry for Students,* Gale Group, 2000.

Chris Semansky

Chris Semansky's most recent collection of poems, Blindsided, *has been published by 26 Books of Portland, Oregon and nominated for an Oregon book award. In the following essay Semansky examines Ted Kooser's poem "The Constellation Orion" in light of his ideas on truth-telling and poetry.*

"The Constellation Orion" is a typical Ted Kooser poem. Not only because it is short and accessible to the unschooled reader of modern or contemporary poetry, but because it embodies Kooser's idea of truth-telling in poems. Kooser was born in Iowa and has lived in Iowa and Nebraska for his entire life. His poems exhibit what we might expect of a (stereotypical) Midwestern sensibility: they are direct, descriptive, and very often, literal.

In "Lying for the Sake of Making Poems," an essay which appeared in *Prairie Schooner,* Kooser outlines his ideas on truth-telling and poetry. Admitting that he may be"hopelessly old-fashioned," Kooser says that he "grew up believing a lyric poet was a person who wrote down his or her observations." After detailing obvious exceptions to the use of the "I" which might twist the truth in the name of imagination (e.g. persona poems), Kooser bemoans what he considers to be the increasing deception in contemporary poetry by poets who do not tell the literal truth about their lives. Since he never names such poets, readers are left to wonder about whom he is writing. At the root of Kooser's lament is his suspicion that "lying" in contemporary poetry might be tied to the proliferation of academic poets (Kooser himself made his living as an insurance executive) who need to publish in order to advance their careers, and who spice up their lyric poems with racy or provocative events or descriptions which have no basis in reality. Or worse, Kooser writes, this propensity for "lying" in contemporary poetry might be "indicative of some bigger ethical or moral problem."

Kooser's attitude towards what he believes lyric poetry's function should be is rooted in assumptions about language and experience which themselves have changed considerably in the last century. Kooser assumes that language itself is a transparent medium through which experience can be accurately described, whereas much recent critical theory (in which many practicing contemporary poets have been steeped) shuns such an equation. Twentieth-century theories of language and literature from the New Criticism to poststructuralism do not posit a necessary relationship between the "I" of a poem (or a story or an essay or any other collection of words) and its writer's literal experience. The words themselves carry a kind of subjectivity quite apart from the writer. Indeed, the intentionality of the writer is rarely a question for those who read without the expectations Kooser brings to a poem. In "The Anonymity of the Regional Poet" poet and critic Dana Gioia claims that Kooser's poetry has attracted so little critical attention because his work is *so simple.* "Critics," Gioia says, "who have been trained to celebrate complexity, consider him an amiable simpleton." I certainly have not made this judgement, but I admit it is difficult to say much about Kooser's poetry. Even Gioia, whose essay is ostensibly a critical appraisal of Kooser's work, has little of substance to say about it, apart from repeating the obvious. An examination of a typical Kooser poem underscores this point. "The Constellation Orion" appears in *Sure Signs: New and Selected Poems,* published by the University of Pittsburgh Press:

I'm delighted to see you,
old friend,
lying there in your hammock
over the next town.
You were the first person
my son was to meet in the heavens.
He's sleeping now,
his head like a small sun in my lap.
Our car whizzes along in the night.
If he were awake, he'd say,
"Look, Daddy, there's Old Ryan!"
but I won't wake him.
He's mine for the weekend,
Old Ryan, not yours.

What's to know here? This poem, a straightforward and simple anecdote about an experience the speaker had with his son, leaves little to the imagination. Consisting of figurative language which is unsurprising at best, the "point" of the poem turns on the son's mispronunciation, or at least what the father imagines his mispronunciation would be were he awake, and allows the speaker to express his love for his son. The poem is cute, almost goofily sentimental, but what more can be said about it? A phone call to the poet unearthed that his son's name is Jeffrey Charles, his only child, who was about three years old when the poem was written in 1970. The poet, who is one

and the same with the speaker, had just picked him up from his ex-wife (as we might infer from the fact that the father has him for the weekend) and was taking him home for the weekend; the two of them made regular road trips between Nebraska and Iowa. He was not aware that stars and starlight appear regularly in his poems. It was just as I had feared: the poem was a literal transcription of an experience of the poet. Transcribing personal experience is a staple for confessional poets, but often the experience transcribed has some inherent interest—especially with poets such as Anne Sexton or Sylvia Plath—or the language used is interesting or provocative, but with Kooser's poetry it is just the opposite. Many of his poems deal with subject matter so mundane, they almost dare the reader to care, or to continue reading. That they are so brief, rarely more than thirty short lines, makes that task easier. Indeed, Kooser's allusion to the name of a constellation is rare for his poetry, as that might require the reader to refer to a source outside the poem for information.

Gioia describes Kooser as a "popular" poet, meaning that one does not need a graduate degree in modern poetry or linguistics to understand him. His "popular-arity" carries with it a regional quality as well. Gioia points out that although "His language, imagery, ideas, attitudes, even his characteristic range of emotion reflect the landscapes, climate, and culture in which he has spent his entire life …. In hundreds of precise vignettes Kooser has created a poignant mosaic … no less relevant to Abidjan or Osaka than to Omaha or Des Moines." The fact is he has not. The slightness of Kooser's poems, and the fact that his vignettes often amount to little more than coffee house observations demean the very idea of the popular, which rests on more than simply the idea of accessibility. Perhaps Kooser and Gioia misjudge Kooser's readers because it is so hard to know who they are. Contemporary poetry has very few readers outside of the academy itself, and most of the much-celebrated poetry comes from those who publish with university presses, most of whom are academics. Kooser, however, conceives of his audience as those very people he writes about—farmers, barbers, old soldiers, salesmen, businessmen—rather than academics. It would be interesting to know if such an audience actually exists. My instincts tell me no. For such an audience, "unschooled" in reading poetry, a question like "Did this really happen to you?" is important. But for Kooser's actual audience, graduate students, other poets, academics, the people who actually read the literary journals and university presses in which Kooser publishes, this question, for the most part, is moot. When Kooser says "It is despicable to exploit the trust a reader has in the truth of lyric poetry in order to gather undeserved sympathy to one's self," he is addressing the audience he imagines reads his poems, or whom he wants to read his poems, not the actual audience. In lyric poetry especially, contemporary readers look for a truth beyond mere literal description; they look for emotional truths, whose vehicle may or may not be the literal experience of the writer. At root, Ted Kooser's idea about truth telling in lyric poetry says more about his identity as a regional Midwestern poet than anything else. What it says, however, is not good, for it merely reinforces stereotypes about the Midwest and Midwesterners that do not need to be reinforced.

Source: Chris Semansky, in an essay for *Poetry for Students,* Gale Group, 2000.

Sources

Bauval, Robert, *The Orion Mystery: Unlocking the Secrets of the Pyramids,* Great Britain: William Heinemann, 1994.

Gioia, Dana, *Can Poetry Matter?,* St. Paul, MN: Graywolf Press, 1992.

Graves, Robert, *Greek Myths,* New York: Penguin, 1990.

Kooser, Ted, *One World at a Time,* Pittsburgh: University of Pittsburgh Press, 1985.

Kooser, Ted, *Sure Signs: New and Selected Poems,* Pittsburgh: University of Pittsburgh Press, 1980.

Kooser, Ted, *Weather Central,* Pittsburgh: University of Pittsburgh Press, 1994.

Moore, Patrick, *Passion for Astronomy,* New York: W. W. Norton & Company, 1992.

"Nebraska Center for Writers," http://mockingbird.creighton.edu/NCW/kooscrit.htm.

Rosenthal, M.L., *The New Poets,* New York: Oxford University Press, 1967.

Sanders, Mark, *On Common Ground: The Poetry of William Kloefkorn, Ted Kooser, Greg Kuzma, and Don Welch,* Lincoln, NE: Sandhills Press, 1983.

Windle, Ralph, *The Poetry of Business Life: An Anthology,* Berrett-Koehler Publishers, 1994.

For Further Study

Bauval, Robert, *The Orion Mystery: Unlocking the Secrets of the Pyramids,* New York: Crown, 1994.

This archaeological detective story argues that the great pyramids of Egypt's Fourth Dynasty (c. 2600-2400 b.c.) were vast astronomically sophisticated temples. Using astronomical data about stellar movement, the book argues that the Orion stars coincide exactly with the pyramids' positions in approximately 10,400 b.c.—a period the Egyptians called the First Time, when they believed the god Osiris ruled the Earth.

Kooser, Ted, *Sure Signs: New and Selected Poems,* Pittsburgh: University of Pittsburgh Press, 1980.

This collection includes "The Constellation Orion" and poems from a number of other Kooser titles, many of them out of print. Readers will get a full sense of Kooser's range from this collection.

Kooser, Ted, "Lying for the Sake of Making Poems," in *Prairie Schooner,* Vol. 72, No. 1, spring 1998, p. 5.

This is a valuable essay for understanding how Kooser conceptualizes the writing of his poems. He discusses lyric poetry and what his own expectations for it are, as well as what he believes readers expect from it.

A Drink of Water

Seamus Heaney

1979

"A Drink of Water," collected in the 1979 volume *Field Work,* is part of a series of elegies, or poems composed to lament the dead, that comprise much of the first part of the book. In it, the speaker reveals through images and sounds the character of an old woman, presumably a neighbor, who used to come to his well each morning to fill her water bucket. The descriptions in the first eight lines are ones of old age and decrepitude, foreshadowing the woman's death: she is "like an old bat staggering up the field," the pump's sound is a "whooping cough," the woman wears a "gray apron." In the last six lines, she has vanished from the poem physically, but while in life she depended on the favors of the speaker, in death she has become the "Giver," providing the poet with inspiration and perhaps representing to him the maturing process of poetry itself—the aging of his muse. Filled with careful rhythms and intricately patterned sonic elements, the poem is a good example of the sonnet in contemporary poetry—a form Heaney explores extensively in *Field Work.*

Author Biography

Heaney is generally regarded as one of Ireland's preeminent poets of the late twentieth century. His verse frequently centers on the role poets play in society, with poems addressing issues of politics and culture, as well as inner-directed themes of self-discovery and spiritual growth.

Seamus Heaney

sumed a post at a secondary school and later served as a lecturer at Queen's University. As a poet, he published his first collection, *Death of a Natural-ist* in 1966; the volume quickly established him as a writer of significance.

As Heaney's stature increased, he was able to use his literary works to give voice to his social conscience. Of particular concern to him was the 1969 conflict between Catholic and Protestant fac-tions over religion and national autonomy. Living in Belfast, the epicenter of the fighting, Heaney had a front-row seat for much of the ensuing violence, and his poetry of this period reflects his feelings on the causes and effects of the upheaval. Although he moved out of Belfast in 1972, his work contin-ued to address themes directly relevant to the con-flict. After a brief period in the early 1970s during which he wrote full-time, Heaney returned to teach-ing in 1975 as head of the English department at Caryfort College in Dublin. Throughout the 1980s and early 1990s, he divided his time between writ-ing, teaching, and reading tours. His subsequent academic posts have included professor of poetry at Oxford University and Boylston Professor of Rhetoric and Oratory at Harvard University.

These topics are unified by Heaney's Irish sensi-bilities and his interest in preserving his country's history. Using language that ranges from, and of-ten mixes, sexual metaphor and natural imagery, Heaney examines Irish life as it relates to the past and, also, as it ties into the larger context of human existence. He was awarded the Nobel Prize for lit-erature in 1995 for, as the Swedish Academy noted in its press release, "works of lyrical beauty and ethical depth, which exalt everyday miracles and the living past."

Heaney was born in 1939 in Mossbawn, County Derry, Ireland. The eldest of nine children, he was raised as a Roman Catholic and grew up in the rural environment of his father's farm. Upon receipt of a scholarship, he began studies at Saint Columb's College in Northern Ireland and subse-quently attended Queen's University in Belfast. It was at Queen's University that he became familiar with various forms of Irish, English, and American literature, most notably the work of poets such as Ted Hughes, Patrick Kavanagh, and Robert Frost. Like these poets, Heaney would draw upon child-hood memories and past experience in his works. Using the pseudonym Incertus, Heaney began con-tributing poetry to university literary magazines. Upon graduating, he directed his energies toward both his writing and a career in education. He as-

Poem Text

She came every morning to draw water
Like an old bat staggering up the field:
The pump's whooping cough, the bucket's clatter
And slow diminuendo as it filled,
Announced her. I recall   5
Her gray apron, the pocked white enamel
Of the brimming bucket, and the treble
Creak of her voice like the pump's handle.
Nights when a full moon lifted past her gable
It fell back through her window and would lie   10
Into the water set out on the table.
Where I have dipped to drink again, to be
Faithful to the admonishment on her cup,
Remember the Giver fading off the lip.

Poem Summary

Lines 1-4:
While certain specifics of the sonnet's situa-tion are never revealed—the identity of the woman, for instance, and the precise nature of her relation-ship with the speaker—the first lines' implications establish nearly all we need to know in the poem. The verb "came" in line 1 suggests two important possibilities. First, since it is in the past tense, we

infer that the action described no longer takes place—she no longer comes to the well. Combined with the images of old age and decrepitude that follow in the first quatrain —"old bat," "staggering," "whooping cough," "slow diminuendo"—this past-tense description suggests that the old woman has died. Second, the use of "came" instead of "went" implies that the speaker is already at the well when the woman arrives. From this, it is possible that the speaker owns the well and allows the woman to draw from it: that, at the beginning of the poem at least, he is the "Giver."

Lines 5-8:

Throughout the first eight lines, the reader should note the poem's use of the sense of sound to convey the emotional appeal of an elegy. First, consider how the poet plays upon the traditional rhyme scheme of a Shakespearean sonnet. According to that form, the first and third as well as the second and forth lines of each quatrain must be set in end rhyme—that is, the lines' final vowel and consonant sounds must agree exactly. Here, however, Heaney sets his lines in half rhyme, the vowel sounds suggesting one another but not agreeing exactly: "field" (line 2) and "filled" (line 4) as opposed to, for instance, "field" and "wield." This technique allows the poet to achieve the musical sound of a sonnet without sacrificing word-choice or falling into the type of overt lyricism that would be inappropriate to the mood of the poem. The reader should also note the sound elements that work within lines. One of these is assonance , the internal repetition of many vowel sounds in words close to one another: "draw" and "water," "bat," "staggering" and "clattered," "gray" and "apron," and so on. Another sonic device is the consonance, the internal repetition of certain consonant sounds: the p's in "pump" and "whooping;" the l's in "field," "filled," "recall" and other line-ending words; the b's in "brimming bucket" and "treble." These sonic devices reflect the speaker's sound-oriented memory of the woman: she is revealed in the octave through "the pump's whooping cough," the "bucket's clatter," the sound of running water's "slow diminuendo," or decrease in sound, and the "creak" of the pump's handle that sounds like her "treble" voice.

Lines 9-14:

In the sestet, the situation shifts from morning to night and from the well to the woman's house, but the woman herself, who predominates the sonnet 's first eight lines, has vanished physically from

Media Adaptations

- In 1994 Faber and Faber released a cassette of Heaney reading his poems along with several other poets.

- In Harvard College's 1990 recording Heaney reads not only his work but also selections from other poets, including Yeats, Shakespeare, and Wyatt.

- The Lannan Foundation produced a videotape of Heaney reading from his *Selected Poems* and talking about his poems and Irish political history. The conversation took place in 1991, the year the video was also released.

the poem. Further, while the speaker is clearly present at the well in the octave, the relationship between him and the scene in lines 9 through 11 becomes a matter of interpretation. In line 9, the perspective seems to be from outside the woman's house: the full moon lifts "past her gable." Yet in lines 10 and 11, the perspective seems to move inside: the speaker observes (or imagines) the way the moonlight appears to "lie / Into the water set on the table." Whatever the speaker's point of view, the verb "would lie" suggests a continuity in time from the first eight lines to the next three. Yet in line 12, the verb "have dipped" marks a transition to the present perfect tense, suggesting a change in both the time and focus of the poem. With the time-shift and the woman's sudden physical absence, the implication is that she has died.

The reader may consider a number of possibilities when interpreting the last lines. First, the personification of moonlight lying "into the water" might suggest a religious connotation—that of baptism, which marks a person's entry into the Christian faith. This suggestion coincides with the speaker's intent to be "faithful" to the phrase on the woman's cup, itself a religious saying: "Remember the Giver." But while the woman was apparently a believer, it is clear the speaker has doubts about religion. To him, the cup's phrase is an "ad-

Topics for Further Study

- Write a descriptive essay on the old woman in "A Drink of Water." Describe her life, including major events from Irish history.

- Expound on what you think the injunction in the last line, "Remember the Giver," means. Who do you think "the Giver" is?

- What is the role of the moon in this poem? What does it tell you about the woman? What does it tell you about the speaker?

- Examine the references in the poem to different sounds and discuss the effect each sound has on your interpretation of the poem.

monition"—implying that he is guilty of not remembering the "Giver" to which the saying refers—and it is "fading off the lip." That he is "faithful" to something he seems not to believe suggest an irony that might seem flippant. Yet another implication must be considered: while the speaker—the poet—once was the "Giver," allowing the woman to use his well, now her memory has become the source of his poem. She is the "Giver" because the poet remembers her. In this sense the woman takes on a symbolic value that can be traced back through the sonnet. The idea of a female muse—and indeed of a female Ireland, traced back through the ancient goddess-cult—is one Heaney returns to throughout his work. In terms of this symbolic system, the poem may address the maturing process of the poet himself, the "aging" of his muse, his "Giver," who like all things must someday fade and die.

Themes

Memory

Field Work is filled with elegies, some poignant, others gruesome, for victims of "The Troubles," the resurgent violence that swept through Northern Ireland in the 1970s. As many

readers have noted, "A Drink of Water" appears a bit anomalous in this volume. Instead of contemplating the recent violence's terrible effects, the poem returns to a literally and metaphorically more peaceful time. In this childhood remembrance, the poet draws sustenance from the memory of kindness. To put this idea in slightly different terms, memory acts as refreshment in a time of violence.

The poem begins simply, with a conversational tone and a simile that establishes a high degree of familiarity and intimacy: "She came every morning to draw water / Like an old bat staggering up the field." The underlying tenderness cannot be missed; the speaker knows not only the woman's routine but also her particular gate and the various sounds the pump and the bucket make. Even the less-than-flattering comparison of the woman to "an old bat" underscores the shared intimacy. This gentle gibe does not mock her but celebrates the admirably determined way she carries out her morning chores.

The next several lines pursue a similar strategy. The speaker conjures the woman by remembering various details about her: her apron down to its color, the particular "treble / Creak of her voice." These are details stored from years of watching. The poem moves to a moment of illumination within darkness, as when "a full moon" shines upon the water. The speaker peers into the house from outside of it.

Ultimately, the poem argues that to remember is to remain faithful. Honoring the woman's caretaking, the poet fulfills the injunction etched upon her cup, "Remember the Giver." Memory also acts as a kind of sacramental renewal, returning the speaker to his boyhood days. He drinks from the water of memory and, by doing so, lets memory refresh his spirit.

Typically for a Heaney poem, nature furthers this process of renewal. Raised on a family farm, Heaney, like his poetic model William Wordsworth, often depicts nature as a force for regeneration from the miseries of modern life. The woman draws water by hand from deep within the earth; the moon illuminates it so the young boy can catch a glimpse of the pail. The intervening years place a considerable distance between the poet's boyhood state of what one might call "innocence" and his more mature understanding of life's difficulties and frustrations. When the poet casts back to the family farm, though, he dips again into its reservoir of comfort and safety.

Love

"A Drink of Water" is a sonnet, the most distinguished and popular metrical form in English-language verse. A sonnet consists of fourteen-lines; it may, or may not, adhere to traditional rhyme schemes. From the sonnet's origins in Renaissance Italy to its recent revisions by modern poets, one of the major themes that poems in this form express is love.

In "A Drink of Water," the depicted love is familial, not amorous as in many other sonnets. Perhaps the best analogy is one that "A Drink of Water" implicitly draws: the poem as a toast. A toast is an act of love: one only toasts those of whom one feels fondly. Yet, if shared affection inspires a toast, it also requires a certain level of formality. As wedding attendees know only too well, the best man usually begins his required duty with a amiable joke about the groom, moves to a more tender illustration of the bride and groom's compatibility, then concludes with a wish for their continued happiness. In "A Drink of Water," the sonnet form also gives a certain degree of formality to the proceedings; the depicted love follows a well-established tradition of poems in this form about this subject. Just as the memory refreshes the speaker, the sonnet form inspires the poet, guiding his thoughts into a fully formed poem.

Style

"A Drink of Water" is a sonnet, a traditional poetic form characterized by its fourteen-line length and its use of a set rhyme scheme. Although there are many variations on the sonnet form, most are based on the two major types: Petrarchan (Italian) and Shakespearean (English). In different ways, "A Drink of Water" resembles both. While its rhyme scheme is that of the Shakespearean form—three quatrains rhyming or half-rhyming *abab cdcd efef,* followed by a couplet rhyming *gg*—its thematic division most closely follows the Petrarchan model. In this type of sonnet, the first eight lines, or the octave, generally present some kind of question, doubt, desire, or vision of the ideal. The last six lines, or the sestet, generally answer the question, ease the doubt, satisfy the desire, or fulfill the vision. In Heaney's poem, the first eight lines examine the image of the old woman who comes to the speaker's well to collect water. The octave's images are filled with reminders of old age and death. In the sestet, the sonnet shifts to night, focusing on

the image of the woman's moonlit water-bucket and her cup that bears the inscription "Remember the Giver." Now the woman is dead, and while the speaker once was the "giver," allowing the woman to draw from his well, now it is he that remembers and she that gives—in the form of memories and poetic inspiration.

Historical Context

In *The Government of the Tongue: Selected Prose 1978-1987,* Heaney describes the contrary demands that "Song and Suffering" place upon a poet. In a question that has long puzzled poets, he wonders if his primary allegiance as an artist is to beauty or to truth. Especially when read outside its political context, "A Drink of Water" may seem to be a rather nostalgic, overly dreamy poem, too much "Song" and "beauty" and too little "Suffering" and "truth." Yet, it is important to keep in mind the campaigns of violence that form the poem's backdrop in order to see how the poem's peaceful evocations of childhood stand in contrast to contemporary realities.

Among the landmark moments in the violence that has plagued Northern Ireland was "Bloody Sunday," January 30, 1972. In November, the Irish Republican Army (IRA), a Catholic terrorist organization dedicated to independence for Northern Ireland, killed eleven unarmed soldiers. On "Bloody Sunday," British paratroopers killed thirteen unarmed civil rights marchers in Derry. The world viewed these murders with outrage. In addition to Heaney's own poems on the subject, other artistic responses include the Irish band U2's song "Sunday Bloody Sunday."

In his poetry and essays, Heaney is always quick to point out the various absurdities of violence. For example, in "Casualty," a poem that appears with "A Drink of Water" in *Field Work,* Heaney elegizes a fellow Catholic who was murdered by Catholics. On the day of the funeral for those killed on January 30, the Irish Republican Army sets a curfew. However, the victim in Heaney's poem decides to go to the bar only to be killed by another Catholic's bomb.

This violence in Northern Ireland continued throughout the 1970s in spurts and even during more hopeful periods of relative calm. In his book, *Seamus Heaney: The Making of a Poet,* the scholar Michael Parker cites some illustratively grim sta-

Compare & Contrast

- **1972:** Fourteen men die after British troops open fire on a civil rights demonstration in Derry. Later in the year, the IRA sets off a series of bombs in the capital of Belfast that kill 11 people.

- **1979:** The IRA assassinates Earl Mountbatten, a World War II hero and a cousin of England's Queen Elizabeth.

- **1981:** Ten IRA prisoners gain worldwide attention and become martyrs when they die in a hunger strike.

- **1985:** The Anglo-Irish Agreement allows the Republic of Ireland's government a consultant's role in matters concerning Northern Ireland.

- **1993:** The Downing Street Declaration, presented by Irish leader Albert Reynolds and British Prime Minister John Major, stipulates that the people of Northern Ireland will decide their own future. Sinn Fein, the political arm of the IRA, is promised roles in peace talks if they declare a cease-fire.

- **1996:** Former U.S. Senator George Mitchell chairs multiparty peace talks concerning Northern Ireland. Sinn Fein joins the talks in 1997.

- **1998:** Britain announces an independent inquiry into the "Bloody Sunday" killings of 1972. In April, Northern Ireland's political leaders negotiate a deal that includes retaining ties with Great Britain while still having self-rule in Northern Ireland. The plan is presented to voters, who overwhelmingly approve it.

---

tistics. In 1975 and 1976, while Heaney wrote many of the poems that would comprise *Field Work,* sectarian violence in Northern Ireland killed more than 545 people and inflicted major injuries upon more than 5,000 people. Among those killed were cousins of Heaney's.

In 1980, one year after *Field Work* was published, the strife in Northern Ireland again received worldwide attention, as several prisoners in favor of independence from England went on a hunger strike, demanding the status of political prisoners. The American press tended to report the situation as a kind "war of wills" between the hunger strikers and British Prime Minister Margaret Thatcher. Eventually ten hunger strikers died. In Section IX of Heaney's "Station Island," one of the deceased describes the agony of his death: "My brain dried like spread turf, my stomach / Shrank to a cinder and tightened and cracked."

Critical Overview

In his 1988 book *The Poetry of Seamus Heaney,* critic Elmer Andrews explores the development of Heaney's vision in *Field Work.* In poems like "A Drink of Water ," Andrews writes, "Heaney's muse is no longer the mythological goddess of Irish history, the implacable 'black mother.' Instead he develops the image of the domestic muse or sibyl." "A Drink of Water" is a "haunting little poem," Andrews writes, and an example of Heaney's rededication to "the life-giving sources, to his role as diviner through whom the water used to broadcast its secrets." Here, the female figure present throughout Heaney's poetry has grown old, and as a result "the imagery suggests difficulty, noisy effort, disease and decline." But ultimately, Andrews argues, the poem centers on the notion of faith: "Despite the poet's faithlessness, the old woman still provides a drink of water. At the end the poet has 'dipped to drink again to be / Faithful.' " Robert Fitzgerald similarly observes in a 1976 *New Republic* article that the poem demonstrates "Heaney's piety toward the life of his boyhood" and calls "A Drink of Water" an "excellent" poem. The critic adds that "Heaney's best poems in their purity are certainly fresh esthetic objects; at the same time his manner is large and open, his intent a publicly conducted meditation among the living and the dead."

Criticism

Aviya Kushner

Aviya Kushner, the poetry editor for Neworld Renaissance Magazine, *earned an M.A. in creative writing from Boston University. In the following essay, Kushner discusses Heaney's portrayal of the turmoils in Irish history against the beautiful backdrop of Ireland in his writings. She also presents the argument that "A Drink of Water" is actually alluding to the struggles of an Irish poet writing in the poetical form and language of his enemy.*

"The Irish thing," as Nobel Prize-winner Heaney calls it in one of his poems, never seems to go away, both in Heaney's poetry and in his personal life. In stanza after stanza, Heaney addresses the political and religious conflicts of his birthplace—the blood, the gore, and the deep divisions between neighbors.

Heaney's poetry and prose also reveal a strong need to depict a personal heritage. He must write about the land, the heritage of the farm, and his father's spade. He must make poems out of the numerous wells, hills, and schoolrooms of his childhood. As a poet of the land and a poet of the nation, Heaney has a double mission, and this tension of being pulled in different directions may partially explain Heaney's power as a writer.

None of this is lost on Heaney. In his writing and conversation, Heaney frequently describes the pull of Ireland's beauty and the pain of her troubled history as he ponders his role as a poet. In everything from a Nobel acceptance speech to newspaper reviews of others' poetry books, he asks himself: Is the poet obligated to take a stand? What is poetry's "job," anyway? Sometimes, it seems that Heaney is clawing for a poet's right to simply sing, to spend a page praising a tiny white cup. Sometimes, as in the poem "Act of Union," everything from a woman's body to the countryside's rolling hills seems doused in imperialism and political strife.

In "A Drink of Water," written when Heaney was already an established poet and an established destination for journalists looking for views on "the Irish thing," there are several signs of a man caught between two competing forces. The first sign is form. The fourteen lines are in English sonnet form, clearly not an Irish form, though the subject is a seemingly Irish woman. Heaney is using the oppressor's language and the oppressor's form to depict an Irish scene. While this paradox might seem

- Seamus Heaney's *New and Selected Poems 1966-1987* offers a generous selection of his poetry.

- In addition to his skills as a poet, Heaney writes very lucid criticism. In *The Government of the Tongue: Selected Prose 1978-1987,* he discusses the work of Robert Lowell, Sylvia Plath, and several Eastern European poets, among others. The introductory essay, "The Interesting Case of Nero, Chekhov's Cognac, and a Knocker," meditates upon Heaney's responsibilities as a poet and is particularly compelling.

- Two good critical studies of Seamus Heaney's poetry are *Seamus Heaney,* edited and introduced by Harold Bloom, and Helen Vendler's *Seamus Heaney.* Vendler, a former colleague of Heaney's at Harvard, remains one of the most sympathetic and insightful readers of Heaney's work.

- In *The Rattle Bag: An Anthology of Poems,* Seamus Heaney and fellow poet Ted Hughes offer their favorite poems. This lively anthology is a fascinating glimpse into two poets' (sometime idiosyncratic) taste.

subtle at the beginning of the poem, it will get more and more obvious as the poem goes on.

One of Heaney's trademarks is the use of agricultural, natural images that allude to larger issues. Here, he begins a poem that takes place in the outdoors with a simply worded title that doubles as a request—"a drink of water." The opening two lines are similarly low-key, describing a daily scene in a country location:

> She came every morning to draw water
> Like an old bat staggering up the field

The words "every morning" indicate routine, something done over and over—like the sonnet form itself. The title reinforces that sense of routine, since "a drink of water" is something to be had over and over. However, the second line gives

> *Heaney's poetry ...
> reveal[s] a strong need to
> depict a personal heritage.
> As a poet of the land and a
> poet of the nation, Heaney
> has a double mission, and
> this tension of being pulled
> in different directions may
> partially explain Heaney's
> power as a writer.*"

much more information and changes the tone completely. Heaney is expanding the vista, as he often does. "Like an old bat staggering up the field" reveals the woman is probably old and that whatever she is doing is labor for her. It is difficult, and so the poem will to some extent address difficulty.

Heaney tends to use certain words, such as "north," "digging," and "union"; "field" is another word that appears often. Here, "field" provides the first sense of place in the poem, and it establishes a rural feeling—a country ode. "Up the field" means the woman is walking uphill. The first two lines are all visual, but by the third line, sound—what is heard—is introduced.

> The pump's whooping cough, the bucket's clatter
> And slow diminuendo as it filled,
> Announced her.

"Whooping cough" is a fabulous example of the power of personification when it is combined with an element of surprise. "Whooping cough" is a loud, distinctive noise. In addition, "whooping cough" implies severe illness or poverty and fits with "staggering," "old," and the general sense of struggle. The third line makes it clear that for this woman, the seemingly simple task of procuring a drink of water is in fact a difficult task.

What's "coughing" here, though, is not the old woman, but the pump itself, perhaps in sympathy. The speaker must know that particular pump intimately well to use a phrase as specific as "whooping cough." Of course, the downward motion required to pump water matches the swooping undertones of a distinctive word like "whooping."

The focus on sound continues with "the bucket's clatter" and the "slow diminuendo." The struggle is unfolding into a scene of calm, as the bucket fills with water. This mix of brash "whooping" and slow, soothing "diminuendo" is what "announced her." What the woman looks like remains a mystery, but the shorter line indicates that the poem is about to change. The fourth line is also split by a caesura—a pause, in this case a period, that heralds a switch. The phrase "I recall" signals a further change, as the poem moves from describing a routine into a riff on the specifics of the past.

Sight and sound begin to blend in this section. "I recall / Her gray apron, the pocked white enamel / Of the brimming bucket, and the treble / Creak of her voice like the pump's handle." Interestingly, two musical terms have now appeared—"diminuendo" and "treble." Both are Italian words, showing a willingness and perhaps a need to use non-Irish words to describe an Irish scene.

Like many sonnets, "A Drink of Water" turns in the last six lines. Instead of describing a morning, it switches to evening. The profound meaning for the speaker of this individual woman and her daily routine has not been explained yet, and so in this brief poem the pressure is on at the end.

> Nights when a full moon lifted past her gable
> It fell back through her window and would lie
> Into the water set out on the table.

When the full moon is out, the speaker thinks of this particular woman. Something about her haunts him, and something about her makes him remember her:

> Where I have dipped to drink again, to be
> Faithful to the admonishment on her cup,
> Remember the Giver fading off the lip.

In the last three lines, the latent power of water as an image becomes obvious. Water carries religious overtones, with immersion rituals in particular, as the verb "dipped" suggests. Water is frequently associated with purification, and something about this woman's water ritual offers the speaker both "admonishment" and purification. Something about her reminds him of sin and the need to erase it. However, the meaning of the old woman is still ambiguous.

In the last line, the power of this lone old woman getting her water is finally explained. Her cup had a phrase on it—"Remember the Giver." Who the Giver is, of course, is the immediate question. Who gives water, who gives life? These questions might refer to God. However, in Heaney's unique context of an Irish poet writing in English, it is possible that the "Giver" is England, the source of the words he uses as tools to create a self. Like a man dependent on God's water for survival, for the gift of life, this is the tale of a poet dependent on a ruler for the gift of language and the sustenance of words.

Finally, what is most fascinating is that the motto is fading. As Heaney the poet grows in fame and in control over the English language, the fact of ownership—of who actually "gave" him that language—may fade. But wherever he "dips to drink again," whenever he sets pen to paper and starts sipping at the English language, he is nevertheless forced to remember the giver, to think about ownership, nationhood, and what "the Irish thing" means to him as both person and poet.

Source: Aviya Kushner, in an essay for *Poetry for Students,* Gale Group, 2000.

Carolyn Meyer

Carolyn Meyer holds a Ph.D. in modern British and Irish literature and has taught contemporary literature at several Canadian universities, including the University of Toronto. In the following essay, Meyer expounds on the symbolism of the pump and the old woman that draws the water in Heaney's "A Drink of Water" as well as the writer's use of the sonnet form for the poem. She also describes the elegiac nature of the verse.

"A Drink of Water," from Heaney's 1979 collection *Field Work,* is a poem about the strength to be drawn from what lies closest to home. Elsewhere in the volume Heaney mourns the friends and relatives lost to the hatreds and bloodlusts of Northern Ireland's "Troubles" and earnestly reflects on issues of the artist's social responsibility. Here, however, he finds solace and respite from that crisis in the solid traditionalism of the sonnet form and in the recollection of the family pump around which his rural childhood was centered and according to whose rhythms the life of his first community was measured out. In a discussion originally broadcast on the radio by the BBC and later published as "Mossbawn" in *Preoccuptions: Selected Prose 1968-1978,* Heaney refers to the pump as a symbol and touchstone, numbering it among his earliest memories. In its utilitarian simplicity and encapsulation of the local, the ordinary, and the immediate, it stands imperturbable and resolute against the "the great historical action" of World War II, much as the subsequent memory of it has the power to at least temporarily obscure and as-

suage the unconscionable barbarities of sectarian violence:

> I would begin with the Greek word, omphalos, meaning navel, and hence the stone that marked the centre of the world, and repeat it, omphalos, omphalos, omphalos, until its blunt and falling music becomes the music of somebody pumping water at the pump outside our back door. It is Co. Derry in the early 1940s. The American bombers groan towards the aerodrome at Toomebridge, the American troops manoeuvre in the fields along the road, but all of that great historical action does not disturb the rhythms of the yard. There the pump stands, a slender, iron idol, snouted, helmeted, dressed down with a sweeping handle, painted a dark green and set on a concrete plinth, marking the centre of another world. Five households drew water from it. Women came and went, came rattling between empty enamel buckets, went evenly away, weighed down by silent water. The horses came home to it in those first lengthening evenings of spring, and in a single draught emptied one bucket and then another as the man pumped and pumped, and the plunger slugging up and down, omphalos, omphalos, omphalos.

Heaney's poetry, much like this passage of prose, is concerned with roots, origins and wellsprings—enacting quests downwards and backwards to the sources of personal, creative, and national identity. In "A Drink of Water" the poet assumes the role of diviner, as he has often done, revisiting scenes from his childhood in rural County Down, but in this case the past becomes, as critic Carlanda Green noted in *Seamus Heaney,* "the lens through which he looks at the present" to understand the steadying faithfulness and grace that revive and sustain the creative impulse. The source to which he returns, according to Michael Parker in *Seamus Heaney: The Making of the Poet,* is "life-giving" in both the actual and figurative sense, the communal pump offering not only physical refreshment but spiritual replenishment.

While poets of classical Greece and Rome may have looked for inspiration to the daughters of Mnemosyne who tended a sacred spring atop Mount Parnassus, Heaney, according to Elmer Andrews in his *The Poetry of Seamus Heaney,* is heartened by the memory of an aging "domestic muse," an old woman who presides over the farmyard pump and applies herself to her daily ritual of drawing water with clumsy yet unwavering devotion. Heaney's evocative description of her and her legacy brims with a joy in the phenomenal world and in the naming of its objects, lending support to his belief, which he extolled in an interview in *Viewpoints,* that "poems with rural or archaic images" can "engage with the modern world." What the old neighbor teaches him by example and injunction ("Remember the Giver") is exactly what Heaney sets out to achieve in *Field Work* (as quoted in a *Critical Inquiry* interview): "to trust melody, to trust art as reality, to trust artfulness as an affirmation." Like a shade from Dante's *Divine Comedy,* a work Heaney was reading at the time of writing *Field Work,* she is one of his guides, allowing him to negotiate the underworld of modern-day political strife and the minefield of opinion as to what the writer's role in that conflict should be. Her salutary message makes for what critic Blake Morrison, in his book *Seamus Heaney,* called "a moment of grace that blocks out the island's 'comfortless noises.' "

As Heaney pointed out in an interview with James Randall in *Ploughshares, Field Work* marks his return to traditional verse forms and their "rhythmic contracts" after his experiments with the slender, curt and volatile half-lines of his previous collection, *North.* The thirteen sonnets of *Field Work,* "A Drink of Water" among them, accommodate Heaney's natural lyricism—his insistence that "the first person singular" should "mean me and my lifetime"—and serve as formal metaphors for control and order against a backdrop of political aggression and elegiac lament.

Heaney's recourse to the sonnet comes with recognition of the form's flexible rigidity and of the adaptability of its conventions. Given the issues of responsibility and commitment with which Heaney wrestles throughout the collection, the sonnet is in many ways an ideal vehicle for his relentless questioning since its structural division into octave and sestet, comprising statement and counterstatement or problem and solution, satisfies a need for resolution within its tidy span of fourteen lines. The sonnet's reputation as chiefly a love poem "historically filled" with what feminist critic Rachel Blau Du Plessis called, in an article for *(How)ever* magazine, "voiceless, beautiful females in object position" is playfully recast in Heaney's hands, for the feminine principle that assumes many guises in his poems has now grown old and artlessly wise. Closer to the Irish cailleach (hag) than to any object of erotic desire, this unlikely sibyl versed in the traditional ways of living close to the land instead instills a need for mindfulness and circumspection, together with a renewed appreciation for life-giving sources and the restorative gifts of charity, kindness, and reverence.

"A Drink of Water" reinvents the sonnet as a love poem, effectively widening its scope to express a love of this world and its possibilities as sustained by acts of fortitude and faithfulness. Writ-

ing in *The Poetry of Seamus Heaney,* Andrews observed that Heaney's bending of familiar sonnet conventions comes about in part from his effort to find what is poetic in the more unpoetic dimensions of daily and domestic experience. Half-rhymes (field/filled, lie/be, cup/lip), enjambments, and shortened lines (line 5) lend an easy naturalism to the highly wrought artifice of the Shakespearean sonnet form (rhyming ababcdcdefefgg) much as the transition from octave to sestet becomes, in Heaney's hands, as ordinary as the passage from day into night.

The first eight lines concern the water drawer herself, whose identity is inseparable from the task she performs and the place she inhabits. The opening states her business matter-of-factly—"She came every morning to draw water"—but the ensuing description, as richly evocative as it is in its detail, makes her a figure more to be pitied than revered. The imagery Heaney invokes to describe her morning ritual suggests, as Andrews noted, "difficulty, noisy effort, disease and decline," hardly foreshadowing or justifying the abiding influence for which the speaker ultimately credits her. With her drab "gray apron" and "creak" of a voice, she is likened to "an old bat staggering up the field." Her laborious effort engenders "the pump's whooping cough" and "the bucket's clatter / And slow diminuendo." The bucket itself has "pocked" enamel, as though scarred by disease. Even the moon, rising in the night sky and shining into her window, falls back and "lie[s] / Into the water." The inscription on her cup is said to be "fading off the lip," as though the vessel itself is not simply worn but the words themselves, like those spoken by the dying or by the ghosts of Dante's Purgatorio, are being uttered in final, breathless warning or valediction.

What is easily lost in the cacophony of her exertion is the underlying harmoniousness of her undertaking. To suggest this, Heaney modulates his appropriately sturdy, homespun, and at times harshly consonantal language with terms raided from the musical lexicon—the "slow diminuendo" of the filling bucket and the "treble / Creak" of the old woman's voice that is indistinguishable from the music of the pump itself. It is this sound that makes her presence known to the speaker, whose deepening awareness of her and her craft is dramatized by the halting medial caesura of line 5— "Announced her. I recall." This line remains two 2 feet short of its required length, as though the speaker is pausing to collect his thoughts while his distant memory of her comes into sharper focus.

What emerges is a portrait not of the woman herself, for she remains nameless and largely featureless, but of her dedicated triumph over adversity, a legacy that proves inspiringly creative.

The sestet makes it abundantly clear that the old woman, despite all appearances, is not merely an enduring presence but in fact a muse to the poet. The images associated with her—the full moon and its reflected image—are symbols long associated with feminine power and the poetic imagination. Along with similar circle images throughout *Field Work,* including everything from eyes and rings to sunflowers and vaccination marks, they embody what critic Blake Morrison cited as the notion of "artistic perfection", not to mention the finiteness of "artistic self-enclosure." Altogether, the monthly full-mooned nights and the endless chore-filled mornings make for a reassuring sense of continuity that anchors the poem and unifies its constituent parts.

In the sestet, the clatter of the previous eight lines subsides, replaced by a calm interiority and serene domestic orderliness that is presented with the imagistic power of a haiku. The "water set out on the table" as if in offering reflects a moon that seems meant for the old woman's circumscribed world alone, lifting "past her gable" and falling back "through her window." It is, after all, the old woman's labor that makes such poignant beauty possible. The image of the moon lying "into the water" is one akin to baptism, suggesting renewal, rebirth, and purification. For the speaker, the image is a sustaining one, a consolatory moment from which to draw and draw again. Had Heaney placed a comma or omitted the punctuation entirely at the end of line 11, instead of using a period, the syntax of the final lines would invite a far more limited reading. As it stands, the "Where" of "Where I have dipped to drink again" refers not simply to the "water set out on the table" of the previous line but to all that precedes it.

Like any good parable, this brief narrative of the woman's simple life takes on metaphoric relevance and provides the standard against which the speaker measures his fidelity to life's sustaining values. When he drinks, he drinks in and is fortified by the remembrance of her example, in an act that imitates and secularizes the ritual of communion. Heaney seizes upon the problem-solving function of the sonnet's counter-statement, in this case confined to the final three lines, to suggest that the healing affirmations he seeks elsewhere in *Field Work* are to be had by "bowing down to, by offering up"—by rededicating and pledging himself to the life-giving sources according to the cup's ad-

> *Like any good parable, this brief narrative of the woman's simple life takes on metaphoric relevance and provides the standard against which the speaker measures his fidelity to life's sustaining values."*

monishment, "Remember the Giver." This parting motto, haunting in its discernable Dantesque influence, reveals "A Drink of Water" for what it actually is—an elegy—so that the entire poem becomes what Andrews called "a formal enactment" of the old woman's warning. True to his word, Heaney pays tribute to the giver and her gift

Source: Carolyn Meyer, in an essay for *Poetry for Students,* Gale Group, 2000.

Sources

Andrews, Elmer, "Field Work," in his *The Poetry of Seamus Heaney: All the Realms of Whisper,* London: Macmillan Press Ltd., 1988, 219 p.

DuPlessis, Rachel Blau, "Thinking about Annie Finch, On Female Power and the Sonnet," *(How)ever,* Vol. 1, No. 3, Summer 1991, p. 16.

Fitzgerald, Robert, "Seamus Heaney: An Appreciation," in *New Republic,* March 27, 1976, pp. 27-9.

Green, Carlanda, "The Feminine Principle in Seamus Heaney's Poetry," in *Seamus Heaney,* edited by Harold Bloom, New Haven, CT: Chelsea House, 1986, p. 149.

Heaney, Seamus, *Field Work,* London: Faber, 1979, p. 14.

Heaney, Seamus, *The Government of the Tongue: Selected Prose 1978-1987,* New York: Farrar, Straus and Giroux, 1988.

Heaney, Seamus, interview with Frank Kinahan in *Critical Inquiry,* Vol. 8, No. 3, Spring 1982, pp. 405-14.

Heaney, Seamus, interview with James Randall in *Ploughshares,* Vol. 5, No. 3, 1979, pp. 21.

Heaney, Seamus, interview with John Haffenden in *Viewpoints,* London: Faber, 1981, p. 66.

Morrison, Blake, *Seamus Heaney,* London: Methuen, 1982, p. 82.

Parker, Michael, *Seamus Heaney: The Making of the Poet,* London: Macmillian, 1993.

Vendler, Helen, *Seamus Heaney,* Cambridge, MA: Harvard University Press, 1998.

For Further Study

Andrews, Elmer, *The Poetry of Seamus Heaney: All the Realms of Whisper,* London: Macmillan Press, 1988.
Andrews analyzes Heaney's poetry and identifies its primary themes through the 1985 collection *Station Island.*

Buttell, Robert, *Seamus Heaney,* Cranberry, NJ: Associated University Presses, Inc., 1975.
Provides critical analyses of the poems included in Heaney's first three volumes and considers how Heaney's personal experience and literary education have influenced his poetry.

Hildebidle, John, "A Decade of Seamus Heaney's Poetry," *The Massachusetts Review,* Vol. 28, No. 3, autumn 1987, pp. 393-409.
Hildebidle describes Heaney's exploration of both personal experience and Irish history in his poetry.

Parker, Michael, *Seamus Heaney: The Making of the Poet,* Iowa City, IA: University of Iowa Press, 1993.
Provides historical contexts and analyzes the biographical, literary, and political influences within Heaney's poetry.

Drought Year

Judith Wright
1953

If Americans know any of the work of one of Australia's premier poets, Judith Wright, they are likely to know "Drought Year." The main reason is the poem's inclusion in the popular American collection *The Norton Anthology of Modern Poetry* (1988). "Drought Year" is among Wright's most distinctively Australian poems because of its use of plants, animals, and sites specific to Australia. As such, the poem serves as an excellent introduction to not only the work of Wright, but modern poetry from the "land down under."

"Drought Year" is from Wright's third volume of poetry, *The Gateway* (1953). The poem's narrator finds herself witness to a drought in the Australian outback, a witnessing that becomes a warning, one repeatedly punctuated by the cries of dingoes, wild dogs indigenous to Australia. Wright represents the drought as nature, powerful and intimidating, a nature to be avoided. At the same time, the animals and plants subject to the drought represent another side of nature: nature as victim—except, that is, the poem's wagtail, an Australian bird taking advantage of the drought's killing fields by pecking out the eyes in a "seething skull." While Wright's drought is, in no uncertain terms, a hellish matter, the multiple kinds of nature she portrays (frightful drought, tormented animals, opportunistic wagtail) renders nature too complex to easily sum up. This is most likely the reason Wright selected the dingoes' enigmatic cries as the poem's recurrent and eerie motif.

Author Biography

Wright was born May 31, 1915, and raised outside Armidale in Australia's most populous state, New South Wales. She grew up in the rural Australian landscape, the oldest child of three in a well-off and literate family. Wright was fortunate enough to spend her childhood reading a great deal, especially poetry, which her mother had read to her since Wright was very young. Wright's first formal education was through correspondence courses furnished by the New South Wales government to those in rural areas. This afforded the young Wright the advantage of lessened regimentation, a trait often advantageous to a career in poetry. At twelve, the year her mother died, Wright attended the New South Wales Girls' School and there met a teacher who encouraged her to write poetry.

In 1933, Wright, now a teenager, left school. However, she did take one class at the University of Sydney. The light schedule enabled her to read heavily and widely outside class requirements. At twenty-two, Wright traveled through Europe and later, Sri Lanka. The next few years saw her at an array of office jobs, the last as an assistant to a geography professor. With the onset of World War II, she returned home to help out on the family property. In 1943, Wright, now twenty-eight, joined the administrative staff of the University of Queensland. Here, she helped the editor of *Meanjin* produce what would become Australia's most influential literary magazine. In 1946, the editor of *Meanjin* published Wright's first book of poems, *The Moving Image,* a major success in Australian poetry. Two years before, Wright had met her husband, the philosopher J. P. McKinney, who was a large influence on Wright's work. Before McKinney died in 1966, he and Wright became the parents of one daughter.

Wright has published numerous books of poems, including *The Gateway* (1953), which contains her acclaimed "Drought Year." She has also published children's literature and short stories, edited anthologies of poetry, recorded her family's history, and written in the field of conservation. In 1962, she became cofounder and president of the Wild Life Preservation Society of Queensland and served as its president several times thereafter. In this capacity she was instrumental in the effort to save The Great Barrier Reef located off Australia's northeastern coast.

The recipient of numerous important honorary doctorates and awards, Wright eventually garnered Australia's most prestigious literary prize, the Australia-Britannica Award for Literature. In 1970, she was made a fellow in the Australian Academy of the Humanities, the only member elected on the basis of a literary career alone. She also traveled to Canada and India as a representative of the writers of her country, and guest-lectured at numerous universities. In 1992, Wright won the Queen's Prize for Poetry, and in 1995, the Human Rights for Poetry Award, especially for her work for the Aboriginal cause. She sums up her ethos this way: "I have, I suppose, been trying to expiate a deep sense of guilt over what we [white settlers] have done to the country, to its first inhabitants of all kinds, and are still and increasingly doing."

Poem Text

> That time of drought the embered air
> Burned to the roots of timber and grass.
> The crackling lime-scrub would not bear
> and Mooni Creek was sand that year.
> The dingoes' cry was strange to hear.   5
>
> I heard the dingoes cry
> in the whipstick scrub on the Thirty-mile Dry.
> I saw the wagtail take his fill
> perching in the seething skull.
> I saw the eel wither where he curled   10
> in the last blood-drop of a spent world.
>
> I heard the bone whisper in the hide
> of the big red horse that lay where he died.
> Prop that horse up, make him stand,
> hoofs turned down in the bitter sand   15
> make him stand at the gate of the Thirty-mile Dry.
> Turn this way and you will die—
> and strange and loud was the dingoes' cry.

Poem Summary

Lines 1-4:

These lines depict the drought-benighted landscape. "Embered" and "burned" vividly describe the hot, dry air. The word "bear" in line three can be read in at least two ways: 1) the lime-scrub cannot bear the heat or 2) the lime-scrub cannot bear fruit. "Lime" suggests a certain tartness, which contributes well to the dry scene, and the "Mooni" of dried-up Mooni Creek brings to mind a picture of a waterless moon, a desert landscape where every year is a drought year.

Line 5:

The "dingoes' cry" gives the drought conditions a sense of mystery. Since most Americans have probably never heard a dingo's "cry," an American's likely response is, therefore, to think of a coyote, wolf, or dog's cry instead of a dingo's. Similar in character or not, America's canines can be said to have a strange cry, almost like human wailing. Perhaps then, the association of an Australian dog with its American cousins is not wholly mistaken.

Lines 6-11:

Three animals are present in the second stanza: the dingo, wagtail, and eel. The wagtail benefits from the drought by dining on the dying creatures ("seething" with maggots), the eel is one of those dying, and the dingo's condition is uncertain, strange. The Thirty-mile Dry is the name of the dried up creek or river, and the word "scrub" refers to low trees and bushes, also known as "brush," perhaps because the branches of such shrubs have been used as brushes or scrubbers. "Whipstick scrub" enhances the feeling of a dried up landscape sparse with plants having bare, stickish stems: a brushy, scrubby, bristly plantscape. With the occurrence of the word "blood-drop" in line 11, the ground becomes the flesh of the organism Earth whose lifeblood is water. Thus, the last drop of water/blood means a "spent world," both tired and destroyed by drought.

Lines 12-16:

What is the whispering bone of the dead horse saying? Likely it warns of the drought in the area of the Thirty-mile dry. This is borne out by the narrator's bidding to turn the horse into a kind of standing, speaking sign. Placed at the entrance of the area, the narrator knows that the horse's horrific presence would effectively warn travelers to stay away. The image of a standing horse carcass is a disturbing gatekeeper to an eerie landscape strewn with rotting carcasses, reverberating with crying dingoes. This is nature both intimidating and victimized, a nature humans should avoid.

Lines 17-18:

Now the horse's whispering becomes manifest: "Turn this way and you will die." As if there were any mistaking the dead horse's warning, the dingoes' cries once again waft through the parched land. In this poem and in this landscape, both the horse's whispering bone and the dingo's throaty howl suggest nature and death as siblings. The whispering and howling warn us that when we meet nature, we should keep our eyes peeled for death, possibly hidden behind the very dry bushes.

Media Adaptations

- *Judith Wright Reads from Her Own Work* is the title of a recording from the University of Queensland Press, 1973.

Themes

Nature and Its Meanings

Wright is a conservationist as well as a poet. A drought, therefore, might seem a strange subject for an environmentalist intent on giving nature a positive image. Perhaps then, the drought in "Drought Year" is primarily anthropogenic (human-caused), like the Dust Bowl disaster in Thirties America. This would show nature as victimized by human action, something a conservationist might want to stress. There is, however, no evidence for this. Wright's drought seems solely due to lack of rain.

Perhaps Wright meant to reinvigorate nature with awesome power so as to make humans cower, to stop people from swaggering because they dominate the earth. Readers would therefore be meant to identify with the poem's victims: horse, eel, and "seething skull." Still another theory why a conservationist would risk giving nature a negative image is that Wright might have felt she was too romantic about nature. Thus, she decided to depict nature's terrifying aspect, one just as valid as nature with a kindly mien, a nature known as nurturing, beautiful, and victimized. Whatever Wright's motives were, after reading "Drought Year," one is apt to feel glad to be separated from nature, grateful to be sitting under a protective roof, comfortably reading, while piped-in water awaits release behind shiny taps. After reading "Drought Year," one is sure to be happy to be nowhere near the Thirty-mile Dry, relieved he or she is protected from nature by the architecture of culture.

Death

This poem is not so much about drought as about death. However, Wright reminds us that a hot, dry landscape of death, while deadly to some,

Topics for Further Study

- Compare "Drought Year" to "Flood Year," another of Wright's poems from 1953. What is the central image in each? What is similar about both the poems' "characters" and setting?

- Explain the meaning behind the speaker's desire to have the dead horse in the third stanza standing at the entrance of the Thirty-mile Dry.

- What do the cries of the dingoes signify?

- Do some geographical and historical research: attempt to find a particular locale in Australia that matches Wright's description in "Drought Year" and a drought that occurred in Australia in the late 1940s or early 1950s.

means life to others, specifically, the wagtail. In "Drought Year," the wagtail is the lone beneficiary of others' dying. The name, "wagtail," would indeed have a cheery effect if it were not for the bird pecking out the eyes of the "seething skull." The horrific image might cause one to ask why Wright put the wagtail in the poem. Was it to show the double-edged nature of drought and death, that some animals benefit while others die? Whether or not this was the case, Wright's depiction of the wagtail might cause the reader to imagine Death, itself, as a wagtail, with horse, eel, and skull as its victims.

The dingoes can be viewed as victims as well, that is, if their cry is read as agonized. While readers are likely to distance themselves from the wagtail, the other animals' deaths and strugglings could function to bring readers closer to animals in general. For animals, like humans, can fall victim to drought. Perhaps this is what Wright, the conservationist, was working on: connecting humans with nature by showing that animals and people are very similar. The human flesh is subject to the same vicissitudes: will a human not curl in a chair as the eel curls in the mud or sympathize with the fallen horse and the dingoes' agonized cries? On the other hand, others might identify with the wagtail, the survivor turning others' calamities to his own advantage.

Wilderness

While the word *wilderness* in the past commonly signified danger and death, the word has increasingly come to mean a good place, one absent from the harmful influence of humanity. This is a meaning Wright would be likely to support as an environmentalist. However, "Drought Year" was written in 1953, before *wilderness* suggested an undeveloped nature. Wright's wilderness is closer to the older brand: dangerous and deadly, one to avoid, not to seek out, or preserve. However, this depiction does not coincide with Wright's love of nature, thus making it more difficult to understand Wright's portrayal of *wilderness*. Is it deadly and dangerous? Fragile and victimized? Perhaps the answer is: all this and more.

A scientist has been quoted as saying that the reason nature is so variously interpreted is because it can amply accommodate almost any meaning one gives to it. So full of variety is nature that it can be represented by the parks of paradise or the wastelands of hell. The same is almost as true for wilderness, equally represented by droughty desert or life-sustaining rain forest, which suggests that wilderness and nature are probably best summed up by images difficult to decipher. American poet Emily Dickinson (1830-1886) had already spoken to this issue: "Nature," she said, "is a haunted house. Art, a house that wants to be haunted."

Style

"Drought Year" contains three stanzas that successively increase by one line: the first stanza has five lines; the second, six; the third, seven. The overwhelming majority of the poem's lines are in iambic tetrameter and the rhyme scheme, though necessarily different because of variances in each stanza, consists of three sets of end-rhymes: *abacc* in the first stanza, *aabbcc* in the second, and *aabbccc* in the third. All the poem's rhymes are of one syllable and thus "masculine." In the second stanza, *b* lines end with a slant rhyme. The poem has no enjambment (usually making a poem more like prose and conversation), and this gives "Drought Year" more the character of a lyric, or song-like poem, enhanced by the poem's regular meter and rhyme pattern. The dingoes' cries within the poem also help create a kind of song, like the howls of wolves and coyotes, or the wails of whales and humans—a somewhat strange, tortured, and more importantly, *dry* song, wailing not sobbing.

Compare
& Contrast

- **1953:** Secret British nuclear weapons tests begin at the Maralinga test range in southern Australia. Aboriginals are moved from the immediate area during the test years, but nearby, others are exposed to radiation, as are the evacuees after they begin returning in the mid-1980s. British nuclear tests are also conducted at the Emu test range and on the Monte Bello Islands, and at Christmas Island in the South Pacific.

  1999: About 90 invited visitors tour the outside of Tsuruga nuclear power plant in Fukui Prefecture, Japan, just four hours after a leak occurred at its No. 2 reactor. Though the Japan Atomic Power Co. (Genden) stated there would

be no danger to visitors—and its officials explained there would be no exposure to radiation—its decision to conduct a tour in the aftermath of an accident is thought controversial.

- **1953:** A drought in far western Australia ends a plan by the Air Beef enterprise to establish itself in the Kimberley Downs.

  1999: The National Farmers Federation of Australia believes that the current five-year Australian drought will cost the economy 2 billion in Australian dollars. The drought is spreading south, and without good rain before December, summer crops will be threatened and the economic situation will worsen.

Historical Context

During World War I, Australian forces fought along with the British in Europe. Years later, in the Second World War, between 1940 and 1942, Australian forces again supported the United Kingdom, this time in the Middle East; after the Japanese attack on Pearl Harbor, Australia played a major role in the Pacific theater. Following World War II, the Australian government embarked on a massive immigration program to fill the jobs created by a booming war economy. The success of this program radically altered Australia's demographic composition. Before the war, almost all Australians traced their ancestry to the British Isles, but between 1947 and 1961, nearly half the new immigrants came from southern and eastern Europe, increasing the population of Australia from 7.5 million in 1947, to 11 million in 1966. The increase was due either to immigration or to the children born of immigrants. As expected, with an exploding economy and population, the development of Australia followed apace.

Australia's Labour government was voted out of office in 1949, and beginning in 1950, Australia was ruled for 23 years by the Liberal Country Party (later National Country Party and now National

Party) coalition headed by Robert Gordon Menzies (1894-1978). During that period, Australian foreign policy stressed collective security and support for the U.S. presence in Asia. Australia even signed the ANZUS Treaty of mutual military cooperation in 1951 between itself (A), New Zealand (NZ), and the United States (US).

The Menzies years were times of economic expansion, continued population increase, and development. Menzies's government pushed forward the previous administration's initiation of the huge Snowy Mountain hydroelectric project, one of the world's largest civil engineering ventures. When completed, millions of tons of snowmelt annually running down the Australian Alps, through the Snowy River, and into the Pacific Ocean were used to supply much of Australia's electric power. An additional part of the project involved the diversion of water into tunnels to irrigate the dry western plains of New South Wales. A number of roads and freeways were constructed and mineral development—especially uranium production—proceeded as well. Menzies even allowed Britain, from 1952 to 1957, to use Australian land for secretly testing Britain's nuclear capability. Aboriginals were the most affected; they were made to relocate without compensation and many suffered the effects of radiation.

Partly because of subsidies that the Menzies's government offered for oil exploration, a major oil industry arose, particularly after oil was discovered in the new "Royal Range" area. Wool growers also prospered. Between 1945 and 1950, Australia joined Britain, New Zealand, and South Africa in cooperative wool marketing to keep up the price of wool, which rose 30 percent from 1949 to 1950. Pastoralists and graziers especially benefited when scientists introduced myxomatosis into the rabbit population, a disease that decimated wild rabbits to make way for domesticated sheep.

Land devoted to dairy and beef cattle also increased. Primary producers of dairy and meat products snapped up cheap transport, such as trucks and planes, from a downsizing military. Not only did the Royal Flying Doctor Service expand, but between 1949 and 1953, the Air Beef enterprise attempted to establish itself in the Kimberley Downs to eliminate the waste of droving cattle. The Air Beef enterprise slaughtered the animals at an inland center and then flew the carcasses to market. Though drought ended the scheme, the plan was a harbinger of the new technologies of transportation and communication that would begin changing the face of Australia.

Critical Overview

Few critics appear to have written about "Drought Year," the exception being Richard Ellmann and Robert O'Clair who selected the poem for *The Norton Anthology of Modern Poetry* (1988). Ellmann and O'Clair wrote, "The dingoes' cry in 'Drought Year' reminds us of the unseen world that remains a part of us." Is what Ellmann and O'Clair mean by "unseen world," natural impulse? It is difficult to know since "unseen world" is about as cryptic as the "dingoes' cry."

With so little criticism written on "Drought Year," it helps to examine the critical discussions about the book— *The Gateway* (1953)—in which the poem appears. Vincent Buckley, in 1957, compared *The Gateway* with Wright's first two books of poems. He provided an analysis of *The Gateway* also applicable to "Drought Year": "*The Gateway,* however, reveals an inversion of the earlier values—an inversion which is not so complete as it may at first sight appear. In the latest poems [i.e., those in *The Gateway*], nature is seen as possessing a different kind of power, the power not of an-

imistic force but of archetypal symbols. Nature in the first case is a threat; in the second it is a sort of Gnostic script. But in both cases it is equally hypnotic, equally transcendent, and even contemptuous, of ordinary human life." Buckley concluded his commentary with the following assessment: "By the time we get to *The Gateway,* we find a more seriously disabling kind of lapse—a lapse caused by the fact that she [Wright] is using her key ideas and images as talismans. The idea is this: 'When you hear the theme music strike up, you know that an important spectacle is going to be presented for your edification and uplift.'" In other words, Buckley suggests Wright is too didactic in *The Gateway,* which is most likely signified in "Drought Year" by its message that nature can be cruel and indifferent.

A. D. Hope, Australia's foremost poet, writing about his friend and colleague in his long essay, *Judith Wright* (1975), mostly concurs with Buckley's evaluation of *The Gateway:* "Judith Wright sometimes forgets another saying of William Blake's: 'The tygers of wrath are wiser than the horses of instruction.' In fact, from this point on in her poetry and in one way or another, there are moments when the poet seems to lose her certainty, her sureness of touch, her instinct for the right phrase." Hope then breaks off into the way poets are judged, not by low points, but by high ones: "It is the peaks that matter, not the hollows of the plain. Think what a mass of rubbish Wordsworth wrote and took the trouble to publish; and then think again that Wordsworth is one of the great poets of all time. I do not wish to be censorious with Judith Wright because she sometimes writes dull or bad poems and because she sometimes cannot tell the good poems from the bad. But I do wish to say that she seems to me to have been damaged at times by two sterile and destructive poets for whom she has avowed a deep interest: T. S. Eliot and Ezra Pound."

Criticism

Jhan Hochman

Jhan Hochman, who holds a Ph.D. in English and an M.A. in cinema studies, is the author of Green Cultural Studies: Nature in Film, Novel, and Theory *(1998). In the following essay, Hochman finds that Wright's portrayal of nature is one not easily summed up, and for that very reason, it is a depiction that could serve environmental concerns.*

"Drought Year" describes a nature that is not one. Multiple players—animals, plants, and elements—might appear to yield a unified image of harsh nature, but subtler and more varied forces are at work. This analysis will begin with the poem's four elements (earth, air, fire, and water), then proceed to the poem's four flora, and finish up with its four fauna. This essay will show that the relationships between the three sets of four characters—four as a traditional symbol of multiplicity within a wholeness represented by twelve—work against understanding nature as an indivisible oneness, a nature identifiable as Mother Nature, or Nature with a capital "N".

All four elements—earth, air, fire, water—discussed by the pre-Socratic, Greek thinker Empedocles, are represented in Wright's "Drought Year." The poet begins with "embered air," an image combining the extreme heat of embers (as in fire) with air. Sand, called "bitter," can be said to represent earth. The attribution of *bitter* to sand can be read in at least three ways: 1) bitterness of taste, as if one were so thirsty as to eat sand in hopes of water; 2) bitterness of emotion, as when water, not sand or dirt, is expected; or most interestingly 3) bitterness of earth against fire and air, the latter two which show no mercy when they dry up earth's supply of water. These then, are the four elemental characters in Wright's drama.

If Wright's "bitter sand" (earth) is read as bitterness toward Air and Fire for drying up Water, then elemental nature is not a unified entity as is commonly conceived. Instead, nature is multiple, like the gods of Greek myth. In fact, nature, as represented by the four elements, becomes plural enough to be in conflict, or as the expression goes, "at sixes and sevens." Indeed, Wright shows that the expression, "at fours," might work just as well. Empedocles had already configured nature as not one, but four elements, now in conflict (strife), now in cooperation (love). Humans were not important actors in this humanlike soap opera of elemental characters, relationships, and stormy emotions.

In the nature of "Drought Year," as in the philosophy of Empedocles, the elements are also not unified. For this reason: earth is a victim of air and fire; or a victim of air, fire, and water; or, earth and water are victims of air and fire. With this kind of fourfold configuration of elemental nature, blaming an indivisible Nature for drought becomes difficult. Equally difficult is perceiving the universe as a battlefield wherein Nature is pitted against Man. With Wright, nature is a multiple in conflict, a struggle in which humanity does not figure as na-

> *With Wright, nature is a multiple in conflict, a struggle in which humanity does not figure as nature's pawn, victim, or enemy."*

ture's pawn, victim, or enemy. Wright's multiple nature is in line with an environmental agenda (not surprising since Wright has been an influential environmentalist) because nature, as multiple and in conflict, can no longer be construed as something humanity must constantly defend itself against or subdue in order to flourish. Wright's (and Empedocles') nature is simply too busy with its own selves to be concerned with, or even cognizant of people. Such an elemental nature is not an enemy but, instead, something to pay attention to (as in spectacle) or something to understand and respect (as with knowledge and people).

And now, the flora of "Drought Year": the "roots of timber and grass" are, Wright says, "burned." So dry is the "lime-scrub," it is "crackling." Even without the word, "crackling," *scrub* already connotes a dry, stunted plant. Couple "scrub" with "lime"-sour bushes, and you not only have a plant unfit to eat but a complement to the "bitter sand" discussed above. Finally, dryness is furthered by "whipstick scrub," a plant imagined as more sticks than leaves. Sticks for whipping yields an image of drought as torture. The association is potent since whipstick scrub can be figured as the victim of drought's elemental torture, or, itself, the torturer of animals trying to eat it. Timber, grass, lime-scrub, whipstick scrub—these are Wright's four plant characters.

These floral actors are not in conflict with each other as were the four elemental characters. Instead, the plants are in conflict with either elements or animals. All the plants are indeed victimized by drought (some or all the elements), but two of the plants can be seen to be also somewhat complicit with the drought. In the line, "the crackling lime-scrub would not bear," the lime-scrub can be read as sour and stingy. Likewise, the whipstick scrub might be viewed as cruel and miserly. Both plants are so devoid of moisture or nutrients that it is understandable that during a drought they might be

What Do I Read Next?

- R. McNeill Alexander's *Bones: The Unity of Form and Function* (1994) contains magnificent photos of teeth, horns, bones, and skeletons, mostly of animals. The important thing about this volume is the way it dissociates the skeleton from death and associates it with form, function, and life.

- *The Machine in the Garden* (1964) by Leo Marx is an important milestone in the study of nature in American literature. Marx's focus is how the invasion of technology into nature was perceived in literature at the time the events were unfolding.

- *The Idea of Wilderness* (1991) by Max Oelschlaeger is a study of humankind's relationship with nature from early totemism, through Egyptian, Greco-Roman, and Judeo-Christian supernaturalism, and finally to the rise of materialism and modernism.

- *The Dirty Thirties: Tales of the Nineteen Thirties during Which Occurred a Great Drought and a Lengthy Depression* (1991) by William H. Hull is a book about the Dust Bowl, the aftermath of which became famous in John Steinbeck's novel *The Grapes of Wrath.*

---

hated. Again, because Wright's nature is not one (all plants are victims but some, lime-scrub and whipstick scrub, are also villains), nature becomes too divided and conflicted to muster a unified force against humanity, or animals. While individual elements and plants can still be construed as friend or enemy, nature, as a whole, cannot be. Such a conception of nature resembles our impression of our own species (probably an improvement over the way humans think about nature). And though it is true that people still have a long way to go in their treatment of each other, Wright's multiple approach to nature is likely a step in the right direction.

Finally, there are the four fauna: horse, dingoes, wagtail, and eel. The wagtail is a bird with a happy name. It might even be wagging its tail as it eats the eyes or maggots out of that "seething skull." While everything else dies, the wagtail is able to "take his fill." The image is likely to be horrific. But the wagtail is the one animal flourishing during the drought, a situation going against the grain of suffering prevalent throughout the poem. Here, the wagtail, a "good" animal (most birds having good reputations) lives well off the fallen-unfortunate, perhaps humans among them. Even if this is a good animal, it will be hard to like it. On the other hand, there is the eel, an animal most people think is "bad," but whose suffering and dying in "the last blood-drop of a spent world" makes it worthy of sympathy. Where Wright depicts a "good" bird luxuriating on a rotting skull, she also shows a "bad" eel struggling to live. If readers are confused by their dislike of a cheery bird, they are also likely to be about their sympathy for an icky eel. Wright does a marvelous job of mixing up preconceptions of nature. The result is a difficulty in calling nature either good or bad.

Now the last two animals. First, the horse. The dead horse is a rather uncomplicated image in "Drought Year." It is an animal with whom to sympathize, since the horse is considered a "good" animal, and because it has died. What better sign than a propped-up horse carcass to give people the willies, keep them outside the gate of the Thirty-mile Dry? Perhaps only a propped-up human corpse. But if the horse is simple to understand, the dingo is just the opposite. Richard Ellmann and Robert O'Clair, in their introduction to Judith Wright in *The Norton Anthology of Modern Poetry* (1988), wrote that "The dingoes' cry in 'Drought Year' reminds us of the unseen world that remains a part of us." What this has to do with drought is anyone's guess. A different interpretation from Ellmann and O'Clair might posit the dingoes' cries as vaguely deathlike because the cries (if, that is, they sound like wolves and coyotes) sound like human wails or ululations. Such an attribution is, by the way, in stark contrast to most American horror films, in which howling coyotes and wolves are deathlike because they threaten humanity with death. Wright's dingoes, unlike coyotes and wolves in horror films, do not seem threatening themselves, but instead, seem to warn of threat, specifically of drought conditions. If this is accurate, then the dingo, a *wild* dog, is a version of the domestic dog, "man's best friend," warning and advising us to beware. Whether Ellmann and O'Clair's interpretation of the dingo's cry as "a part of us" is favored, or the dingo's cry as a warning call is preferred, the dingo is an animal readers will likely favor instead of fear. Perhaps the reason is little more than Wright's use of the word "cry" for the dingo's call, a word applicable to mourning the dead or the lack of water.

Still, Wright does make it difficult to attribute to the dingo any particular character, either for or against humans, or for that matter, for or against any of the animals, plants, and elements. This makes the dingo difficult to hate or love, or about which to have any particular feeling. The dingo is nature as strange and difficult to sum up as friend or enemy. Perhaps this was Wright's point all along: that drought, like the dingoes' cries, is so complex as to be strange, so multiple as to make impossible painting the drought landscape with a single brush. And so, nature as well. In the final tally, the single *four*-legged dingo is, itself, a mysterious multiplicity, and, therefore, the best single candidate for a nature whole but not wholly one.

If "Drought Year" is first read as a poem warning of a harsh and punishing Nature, a later reading may show the poem as a complex depiction of a complex landscape of victims and victors, sometimes different, sometimes one and the same—a nature never one, but many. To be sure, after reading "Drought Year," humans will still avoid drought conditions with due caution. But a drought may not be interpreted as just another example of a hostile or indifferent nature, one that must be subdued to stay alive. It may prove difficult to speak the word "nature" at all without realizing this one word or concept represents an immensely complex situation. If this ever becomes the case, then Wright and the dingoes' cry may be remembered and the dingoes' complex and mysterious utterance may be recalled as a more suitable description for what is called "nature."

Source: Jhan Hochman, in an essay for *Poetry for Students*, Gale Group, 2000.

Sources

Bolton, Geoffrey, *The Oxford History of Australia,* Melbourne: Oxford University Press, 1990.

Brooks, David, and Brenda Walker, *Poetry and Gender: Statements and Essays in Australian Women's Poetry and Poetics,* St. Lucia: University of Queensland Press, 1989.

Buckley, Vincent, *Essays in Poetry, Mainly Australian,* Melbourne: Melbourne University Press, 1957.

Ellman, Richard, and Robert O'Clair, eds., *The Norton Anthology of Modern Poetry,* New York: W. W. Norton, 1988.

Hope, A. D., *Judith Wright,* Melbourne: Oxford University Press, 1975.

Strauss, Jennifer, *Judith Wright,* Melbourne: Oxford University Press, 1995.

Walker, Shirley, *Flame and Shadow: A Study of Judith Wright's Poetry,* St. Lucia: University of Queensland Press, 1991.

Ward, Russell, *Concise History of Australia,* St. Lucia: University of Queensland Press, 1992.

For Further Study

Beach, Joseph Warren, *The Concept of Nature in Nineteenth-Century English Poetry,* New York: Macmillan, 1936.
> One of the few extended studies of the meanings of nature in poetry. The volume covers Wordsworth, Coleridge, Shelley, Goethe, Carlyle, Emerson, Whitman, Arnold, Tennyson, Browning, Swinburne, Meredith, Hardy, Jeffers, and Eliot. The book is an invaluable source for reading about representations of nature in the nineteenth and twentieth centuries.

Darwin, Charles, *The Origin of Species by Means of Natural Selection or The Preservation of Favored Races in the Struggle for Life,* New York: Modern Library, 1974.
> A crucial text, containing one of the modern world's most indispensable concepts: natural selection. Darwin here helps readers to understand the workings of the natural world.

Ellmann, Richard and Robert O'Clair, *The Norton Anthology of Modern Poetry,* New York: W. W. Norton, 1988.
> From the verse of Walt Whitman to Cathy Song, this anthology features the best of modern poetry in English. Includes poetry by Australian poets like A. D. Hope and Wright.

Wright, Judith, editor, *A Book of Australian Verse,* London: Oxford University Press, 1956.
> The work includes an introduction written by Wright and spans a period of time from Charles Harpur (1813-1868) to Ray Mathew (1929-), and includes 72 poems. Wright includes seven of her own poems, but "Drought Year" is not one of them.

Ethics

Linda Pastan
1981

"Ethics" appears in Linda Pastan's sixth volume of poetry, *Waiting for My Life* (1981), a title that hints at the tensions for which the New York-born poet is best known: the challenges of living in that "waiting" place between the magic and the tedium of the ordinary; between the artistic and the domestic life; between the rewards and the losses of aging and death. A kind of "aesthetic ethic" itself emerges from the body of her poems, one proclaiming that simple language and images of the ordinary are especially capable of bearing mystery and of resisting easy answers.

"Ethics" itself embodies this resistance. The poem takes shape first in a memory from school days and is then bridged, through images of frames and fire, to an understanding acquired in the poet's older years. The question the ethics teacher poses "so many years ago" is unanswerable partly because it is not "real"; the students answer it "half-heartedly," at best. Having posed a hypothetical fire in a museum, the teacher wants the students to make a clear choice, between saving "a Rembrandt painting / or an old woman who hadn't many / years left anyhow." The surprising answer for the poet arrives years later, in a "real museum," as the poet stands "before a real Rembrandt."

Several readers have noted Pastan's similarity to the nineteenth-century poet Emily Dickinson. Both share an ability to express complexity and mystery in the language of domestic life. However, unlike Dickinson, Pastan has struggled with the issues of raising children and being married. Pastan

is a poet of the home even while she is clearly in the world. "Meditation by the Stove" shows she has trained her eye on the realities of her own life:

> ... I have banked the fires of my body
> into a small domestic flame for others
> to warm their hands on for a while.

However, she has also looked up and out of her home into the "darkness of newsprint." In "Libation, 1966," the sacrifice of young men to the Vietnam War reminds her of cruel, ancient rituals:

> They dance as delicately
> as any bull boy
> with bayonet,
> in a green maze,
> under a sky as hot as Crete.

The ethics of being an artist in the world is of concern to Pastan, a world where what one "saves" is crucial, but not simple.

Author Biography

Pastan was born in New York, New York, on May 27, 1932, the only child of Jacob and Bess Schwartz Olenik. A melancholy poem about her parents, "Something about the Trees," records Pastan's childlike faith that her father would "always be the surgeon," her mother, "the perfect surgeon's wife," and that "they both would live forever." She began writing, she says, around age ten or eleven: "As a very lonely only child, reading and writing was my way of being part of the world." The world of her poems is a peopled world, inhabited by parents, grandparents, husband, children, and lovers. It is also inhabited by mythic figures—Eve, Adam, and Noah, Odysseus, Penelope, Circe, and Achilles. These people, mythic and real, are often connected by Pastan's ability to tell stories of loss and change. They are also connected through metaphors from ordinary times and common places, images of "ordinary weather / blurring the landscape / between that time and this." Pastan writes many of the poems in *Waiting for My Life,* including "Ethics," from this landscape of "between"—between past and present, youth and age, home and world. Metaphors from kitchens, closets, gardens, and porches inform the sense that Pastan's life is rooted in the home, but that home is not necessarily a safe haven:

> I tell you household gods
> are jealous gods.
> They will cover your windowsills
> with the dust of sunsets;

Linda Pastan

> they will poison your secret wells
> with longing. ("Who Is It Accuses Us?")

The "between" places are at once familiar and strange, irreducible, and resistant to cliche.

The longing for a life of creative passion and fulfillment in the midst of domestic demands is palpable in *Waiting for My Life.* "There are poems / that are never written," laments one poem in the book, but the ones that fill this volume and eleven other books counter the claim that her art has truly had to wait. In fact, Pastan has been the recipient of numerous awards for her poetry, beginning with the *Mademoiselle* poetry contest, which she won during her senior year at Radcliffe. Honors have followed nearly all of her major publications, including the De Castagnola Award in 1978 for *The Five Stages of Grief,* an American Book Award poetry nomination in 1983 for *PM/AM, Poetry* magazine's Bess Hokin Prize in 1985, *Prairie Schooner's* Virginia Faulkner award, a Pushcart prize, and appointment as the poet laureate (1991-1995) of Maryland, the state where she currently lives.

Pastan's gift was recognized early. When she was a senior in high school, one of her poems was chosen to be printed on the back of the graduation program. She recalls that her English teacher tried to make editorial suggestions and persuade her that a tree couldn't have both "antlered branches" and "summer-scented fingers." But the young poet re-fused to change a word. "My infatuation with metaphor has remained with me, though of course, my teacher was absolutely right," admits Pastan to-day. Her childhood love of reading and writing was nurtured at Radcliffe where she was an English ma-jor, and "constantly amazed to be given college credits for what I would have chosen to read any-way." She claims no particular influence on her writing, rather that her wide reading from child-hood on has given her "the models of great poetry to love and to strive towards."

Linda Olenik married Ira Pastan, a molecular biologist, in 1953, a year before she finished her degree at Radcliffe. She temporarily "relinquished" her writing, Pastan tells Michael Kernan of the *Washington Post,* for the "whole '50s thing, kids and the clean floor bit." Yet, she confesses, "I was unhappy because I knew what I should be doing." Once her children reached school age, Pastan be-gan to devote her "free" hours and energy again to poetry. Soon she found that family, marriage, and home had put their indelible mark on her material, and that they had the power to shape her work "by allowing themselves, albeit reluctantly, to be sub-jects of my poems." The Pastan children, Stephen, Peter, and Rachel, often show up in poems that ex-press with both tenderness and anguish the strug-gle between raising children and tending to one's art. Pastan established the habit in those years of rising earlier than the rest of the household to write, and often stayed up late to draft or revise, hence the title of one book, *PM/AM.* For twenty years, she was a teacher at the renowned Bread Loaf Writer's Conference in Vermont. Being on staff at Bread Loaf "gave me a feeling of belonging to the com-munity of writers," says Pastan. "And I loved teach-ing for just twelve days a year. I could enter the class with enthusiasm and leave it before I became weary." Pastan continues to write from her home in Potomac, Maryland. Her latest volume is *Carni-val Evening: New and Selected Poems, 1968-1998.*

Poem Text

In ethics class so many years ago
our teacher asked this question every fall:
If there were a fire in a museum
which would you save, a Rembrandt painting
or an old woman who hadn't many   5
years left anyhow? Restless on hard chairs
caring little for pictures or old age
we'd opt one year for life, the next for art

and always half-heartedly. Sometimes
the woman borrowed my grandmother's face   10
leaving her usual kitchen to wander
some drafty, half imagined museum.
One year, feeling clever, I replied
why not let the woman decide herself?
Linda, the teacher would report, eschews   15
the burdens of responsibility.
This fall in a real museum I stand
before a real Rembrandt, old woman,
or nearly so, myself. The colors
within this frame are darker than autumn,   20
darker even than winter—the browns of earth,
though earth's most radiant elements burn
through the canvas. I know now that woman
and painting and season are almost one
and all beyond saving by children.   25

Poem Summary

Lines: 1-2

"Ethics" begins with the memory of an ethics class that Pastan herself attended. The focus of this memory is a question the teacher posed, and the rest of the poem is given to unfolding its answer. The poem's language is specific. The question was asked, not simply every "year," but "every fall," and the image of autumn also unfolds in important ways as the poem proceeds.

Lines: 3-6

In these lines, the question is put forth as the poet recalls it, in concrete, straightforward lan-guage that gives the past a sense of immediacy. It is a typical "values clarification" question, de-signed to stir a conversation about the relative value of life and art: which is of greater worth in "sav-ing," a famous painting or an old woman? The choice is obviously difficult and contains the seeds of several large ethical issues. However, the stu-dents are not engaged. So, instead of providing their response, the poem instead suggests their restless unreadiness to answer with any sort of conviction.

Lines: 7-9

A clear sense of the students' apathy is ex-tended in these lines. As the poet remembers it, nei-ther art nor old age seemed particularly worth their passion or time. Choosing life one year and art the next has little to do with authentic engagement in the question.

Lines: 10-12

A sudden shift from the external classroom scene to the poet's private thoughts occurs in lines

9 and 10. The poet lets the reader into her imagination of that hypothetical old woman, who is no longer anonymous; she has "borrowed my grandmother's face." The kitchen is the site of many images, if not whole poems, in Pastan's corpus. Here, the grandmother leaves "her usual kitchen" in the poet's internal reverie, and is relocated in a vague, rather unappealing museum. Leaving the "usual" is clearly uncomfortable for the old woman; she can only "wander" around the museum. This interior picture shows how unacquainted the young "Linda" really is with both art and old age. In her mind, the two prongs of the question are still determined by stereotypes, by the "usual."

Lines: 13-16

At the middle of the poem another shift occurs, from inside back to outside, as the poet herself actually replies to the teacher's question. The "usual" gap between professor and student is dramatically rendered in these spare lines. The poet-student makes a sophomoric suggestion that the old woman should "decide herself." In rather pedantic language, the teacher replies to the class that this response is an evasion of moral responsibility, that "Linda … eschews" its burdens. Line 15 leaves little doubt that the poem's point of view and experience are Pastan's own.

Lines: 17-19

With line 17, the poem is lodged no longer in the past, but in the here and now. The verb tense is simple present, and the "every fall" of past years has become "this fall." The hypothetical museum and painting have vanished, and in its place is a "real Rembrandt" in a "real museum." However, this view is now framed through the eyes of someone "nearly" an old woman herself, and autumn obviously means more than calendar time. It is the season of her life.

Lines: 20-23

However, lest the correspondence between autumn and aging devolve into a cliche? the poet observes that the colors she sees in the painting are actually "darker than autumn." In fact, they are "darker even than winter," the darkest of seasons. The poet is seeing both painting and experience with the inner eye, led by the painting's radiant darkness to a kind of mystical vision. In the process, the "browns of earth" become much more than paint and color. In an image echoing the fire that frames the teacher's question, those elements "burn" beyond the frame of the Rembrandt to impart a knowledge unattainable during the poet's restless youth.

Media Adaptations

- *The Cortland Review, an Online Literary Magazine* includes a new poem by Pastan, "The New Dog," in its May 1999 issue. *The Cortland Review* features poetry, fiction, and essays, and is issued monthly in both text and audio format at www.cortlandreview.com.

- Pastan's poetry also appears online at several other sites, including *Poetry Daily,* www.poems.com, and *Atlantic Unbound, Atlantic Monthly*'s online site, featuring Pastan and many other poets reading their own work in RealAudio. See www.theatlantic.com/poetry.

- Reader reviews of *Carnival Evening* can be found through the large online bookseller, Amazon.com. Unlike book reviews published in literary journals and magazines, Amazon's short "reviews" are unsolicited and quite varied.

- Watershed Tapes recorded Pastan in 1986 reading poems about family life from several volumes of her work. The audiocassette tape, *Mosaic,* is available from The Writer's Center. For listings and ordering information on the Web, go to www.writer.org/poettapes/pac15.htm.

Lines: 24-25

The last two lines tell us what the poet has learned, and it appears to be larger than "ethics," larger, at least, than the academic question posed by the teacher. It is not unusual for a mystical experience to impart a sense of unity where once there was division. Thus, what the poet knows, with a knowledge greater than either her senses or reason can provide, is that there is "almost" oneness among "woman / and painting and season." This mysterious unity makes rescue or salvation almost irrelevant. Even so, that subtle word "almost" keeps such knowledge away from any easy absolute, even that of "oneness." Neither woman nor painting nor season loses the force of their particular existence, to which the poet, through language, must be responsible. Therein lies the "ethics" of the poem.

Themes

Ethics

Besides being a memoir and a reflection on art, this poem is the story of its title, "Ethics," in the life of one woman. It not only tells a story about the passage from youth to old age, but also about a maturing morality that perceives the unity among all things and takes responsibility for the "real." To put it in the language of the poem, it is about making the passage from "half-hearted" and "half imagined" to an ethical landscape that has features that are "almost one."

At the beginning of the poem, the poet-speaker and her classmates are equipped with partial knowledge, producing their "half-hearted" response. The typical strategy of a philosophy teacher is to introduce students to a variety of moral theories and posit situations that test their implications. An ethics class might examine the conduct of an individual or group in light of Jean-Jacques Rousseau's philosophy of innate goodness, for example, or its opposite, in the writing of Thomas Hobbes, who declared the human life is "short, brutish, and nasty." They might explore the "instrumentalism" of John Dewey, who held that truth is a tool for solving problems, and therefore "truth" changes as the problems change. Such moral relativism could be contrasted easily with Plato's idealism, an understanding of virtue as inseparable from knowledge and happiness, and rooted ultimately in an absolute good. "Every year" this ethics teacher offers the same moral dilemma, and presumably looks for an increasing sophistication in the students' response.

However, as the poem proceeds, we learn that such an outcome is not feasible due to the apparent apathy of the young people, not only toward "pictures" and "old age," but more fundamentally, for the question itself. For reasons the poem refuses to judge, the heart and the imagination come to class incomplete. It takes the very "real," personal experience of aging, and the contemplation of a "real" Rembrandt to bring the poem's speaker, Pastan herself, to a knowledge of wholeness, which both includes and surpasses moral theories and systems. The repeated use of the word "real" is no accident in the latter part of the poem, as "real" becomes a temporary antonym, or opposite, for "half." The "real" is whole and complete. It embodies an inseparable totality of thought and experience, mind and body. The implications of the last line are not that the "real" lies beyond human responsibility, only that its "salvation" is beyond those still "restless on hard chairs."

Art and Experience

Pastan's interest in art shines through her work. In fact, the question that is central to "Ethics" concerns the value of a piece of art in relation to human life. Pastan's passion for the arts influenced her writing throughout her career. Ten years after the publication of "Ethics," Pastan began an essay with a group of painters who were engaged in self-portraiture—Rembrandt, Vincent van Gogh, Pablo Picasso, Diego Velasquez, and Jan Vermeer. At that time, she was quoted as saying, "This has been a year of looking at pictures for me," confessing that her "obsession" with artists' self-portraits is akin to her interest in "writers writing about writing."

Whether it is poetry, painting, music, sculpture, or dance, there is hardly an art form of any place or time that has not drawn attention to its own materials, making, and reception. As a particularly good example of this aesthetic "self-reference," Pastan points to Picasso's *The Painter and His Model,* wherein Picasso "almost as nude as the model herself, is at his easel hard at work." Her own poem "Ars Poetica" draws attention to the process of writing a poem through a series of surprising metaphors. In Pastan's experience, the Muse is not the elusive goddess of many cliches, but more often "just / a moth"; writing is a battle whose warhorse "would rather be / head down, grazing"; and a poem should be offered, finally, as "a chair / on which you've draped a coat / that will fit anyone."

Within the body of modern poetry, examples abound of poets, like Pastan, who have looked to painters, sculptors, and musicians for guiding both the depths and surfaces of their own aesthetic. The work of poets Denise Levertov and William Carlos Williams pays homage to the painter Paul Cezanne, that of Langston Hughes to jazz-man Charlie Parker, and Rainer Maria Rilke to the sculptor Rodin. Likewise, Pastan's garden and kitchen are not the only sites of inspiration; there are also the landscapes of feeling she enters standing before Rembrandts, Rousseaus, and Magrittes. Her focus on "woman / and painting and season" is not unique to "Ethics."

As early as 1975, there is poetic evidence that Pastan had been looking at pictures in "real" museums, for her work is filled with references to paintings. Masaccio's fresco *Expulsion from the Garden of Eden* provides the loci for reflection and memory that becomes the poem "Fresco." Much like "Ethics," "Fresco" is about the contrast between knowledge learned at school and knowledge gained from life experience. In both cases, a "real" work of art provides the pivot point. In "Fresco," Eve loses her innocence and awakens to the painful recognition that both good and evil, Abel and Cain, will be nourished at her breasts.

In Pastan's most recent writing, there are numerous art-inspired poems which, like "Fresco," mark a subtle, but certain shift from the "usual" kitchen of earlier work. Gustave Courbet's *Still Life with Apples and Pomegranate* makes the poet grieve for her father. "Le Sens de la Nuit," named after a Magritte oil painting, explores the meaning of night. "Still Life" and "Nature Morte," titles that come from a particular genre of painting, lament that both Eden and the "actual" have been lost somehow, "cut off / at the stem or wrenched / from the earth." Her most recent collection, *Carnival Evening,* takes its title from an oil painting by Henri Rousseau.

Like Picasso, Pastan engages in artistic self-portraiture in "Woman Holding a Balance." In the process of describing a Vermeer painting, the poem draws attention to the essential character of Pastan's own work:

> It is really the mystery
> of the ordinary
> we're looking at—the way
> Vermeer has sanctified
> the same light that enters
> our own grimed windows
> each morning, touching
> a cheek, the fold
> of a dress, a jewelry box
> with perfect justice.

In another recent poem, "Lost Luggage," the theme of "waiting for my life" is once again taken up, this time inside a museum where the aging poet is "in transit" from one landscape to another. The poem eventually confesses that the "real" woman behind the "tourist" disguise is "merely myself" and the art she would lose herself in becomes, instead, the mysterious agent of redemption:

> … ghosts clothed in tempera
> follow me everywhere,
> as if art itself were a purpling shadow
> whose territory I must step back into,
> a place where I can hide myself
> over and over again, where what is lost
> may be found, though always
> in another language and untranslatable.

Topics for Further Study

- Choose a painting by Rembrandt or another well-known artist and trace the path of its acquisitions, from studio to museum, private collector, or gallery, in as much detail as possible. What is its estimated worth today?

- As a student "feeling clever," Pastan posed the question, "why not let the woman decide herself?" in response to the question of whether an elderly woman or a Rembrandt painting should be saved in a museum fire. Render the old woman's decision-making in the form of a dramatic monologue, poem, short story, or song.

- Hold a debate using the question posed by the teacher in "Ethics" ("If there were a fire in a museum / which would you save, a Rembrandt painting / or an old woman who hadn't many / years left anyhow?"). Prepare by becoming acquainted with several moral philosophies of famous philosophers, such as Plato, John Locke, Jean-Jacques Rousseau, Thomas Hobbes, and John Dewey.

- Write a story based on your own encounter with an ethical dilemma. Let the story reveal the processes involved in seeking a resolution, whether it is found or not.

The conviction behind Pastan's art is that the ordinary is almost always extraordinary, that behind the familiar lies an unnamable terrain, and there "earth's most radiant elements burn / through the canvas."

Style

"Ethics" is written in the form called "free verse," which depends on images and the natural rhythms of speech for its expression, not on meter or rhyme. Many modern and contemporary American poets in the last two centuries have written in free verse, revealing the range of its powers in the relative absence of "formal" patterns. Walt Whitman, for example, drew upon the "music" inherent in free verse, Robert Frost explored its capacity for drama, and William Carlos Williams explored the power of the image to provide meaning and design.

Pastan's free verse poem tells a story about knowledge, beginning in a classroom in one kind of institution, and ending in another, a museum. However, the experience is not expressed academically or in institutional jargon. Most of the poem-story is told in the simple language, rhythm, and tone of a conversation. Pastan's diction, or word choice, comes from accessible, everyday language. The first person pronouns *I, we, my,* and *our* increase the sense of intimacy by drawing the reader-listener into the poet's experience. There are no stanza breaks, and the line breaks follow a natural breathing or pausing pattern. Punctuation is sparse, increasing the sense that this memoir is being spoken *sotto voce* to a listener close-by. Only the essential commas are retained, and there are no quotation marks to set off the spoken lines. Punctuation in a poem is analogous to the rhythmic markings and rests in music. Thus, if this poem were to be sung, it would probably be marked *rubato* or "freely."

Writers of free verse often create design in their poems through patterns of images. The images of fire and autumn in "Ethics" frame the speaker's growth of conscience and wisdom—from a hypothesized fire to a real Rembrandt aflame with the elemental power of art, from a routine September question to the darkening autumn of age. Pastan's poem derives much of its vitality from the inflections of these images.

Historical Context

"Ethics" was published in the early 1980s, when the U.S. economy experienced a decided upturn after two decades of civil unrest and an uncertain position in the global market. Perhaps it is no accident that an economics of worth is what drives the poem's ethical question, "which would you save, a Rembrandt painting / or an old woman who hadn't many years left anyhow?" When Republican Ronald Reagan became President in 1980, the country was ripe for economic reform. The former actor's plan, later dubbed "Reaganomics," involved drastic cuts in taxes and social spending, and resulted for a while in steep declines in interest and inflation rates, and the appearance of millions of new jobs.

In retrospect, however, that economic prosperity benefited only a few. The wealthiest five percent of Americans celebrated twenty percent gains, while three-fifths of the population, at the lower end of the economic scale, watched their income fall by nearly eight percent. Child poverty and homelessness increased exponentially. Not until October 19, 1987, the date of the biggest stock market crash on record, did Wall Street end its eight-year-long "party." The nation's apparent prosperity had thinly veiled its enormous trade and federal budget deficits, and there were signs that inflation and high interest rates were making a comeback. These trends were blamed for "Black Monday," as it was called, when total share values plunged half a trillion dollars. Some 37,000 Wall Street employees were laid off in its wake, and it wasn't until the end of the decade that the state of the U.S. economy improved.

Meanwhile, those who rose high on the wheel of fortune in those years composed lives and "lifestyles" that have given history permission to call the 1980s the "the decade of greed," inhabited by the "me generation." Where "hippies" had been a prevailing stereotype of the radicalized sixties and early seventies, the "yuppies," or "young urban professionals," of the eighties were characterized by their liberal spending on clothes, entertainment, travel, transportation, fitness, and housing. While poverty among the nation's children rose alarmingly, one in every five, and increasing numbers of homeless men, women, and children found shelter under bridges in cardboard lean-tos, many of the nation's upper-middle class, according to the stereotype, sat in chic cafes debating where to spend their "discretionary income."

The world of entertainment and sports were clearly among the benefactors of such prosperity. Steven Spielberg's *E. T.: The Extra-Terrestrial* made movie history in 1982 when it grossed more than a billion dollars. By 1987, the sports industry had garnered an unprecedented 1.1 percent of the nation's gross national product (GNP). The fine arts also felt the results of new spending trends. Not to be outdone by the sorts of world records being achieved in other cultural arenas, brokers and collectors of fine art set the bars for purchases ever higher: a Picasso that sold in 1981 for $5.8 million was sold nine years later for nine times that amount. Van Gogh's *Irises* achieved fame overnight in 1987 when it sold for the highest price ever paid for a work of art, $53.9 million.

It is in the context of this "prosperity phenomenon" that "Ethics" resonates beyond Pastan's story

Compare & Contrast

- **1979:** The Metropolitan Museum of Art in New York City experiences its first theft in the museum's 110-year-old history on February 9 when an ancient Greek marble head valued at a quarter of a million dollars is stolen.

  1988: Exactly nine years later, on February 9, two valuable Fra Angelico paintings are among the works stolen from a gallery in New York's wealthy Upper East Side, in the city's largest single art theft to date. Eighteen paintings and ten drawings valued at a total of $6 million are taken from the Colnaghi Ltd. gallery.

  1990: The night of March 18, thieves enter Boston's Isabella Stewart Gardner Museum and make off with $300 million worth of art, including three paintings by Rembrandt, five by Edgar Degas, Edouard Manet, and the most valuable, *The Concert,* by Jan Vermeer. None of the paintings has been returned.

  1997: In December, the Department of Justice and the FBI issue a statement regarding reports that certain individuals could broker the return of art stolen in March of 1990 from the Gardner Museum. The Department denies that any such reports are legitimate, and that photographs and paint chips purported to be that of the stolen paintings are carefully analyzed by museum officials and deemed fraudulent.

  1999: On July 13, the night before Bastille Day, thieves steal Rembrandt's *Child with Soap Bubble,* worth unspecified millions, from a municipal museum in the Toulon region of France.

  Today: A $5 million reward is still being offered for the safe return of the art stolen from the Isabella Stewart Gardner Museum in 1990.

- **1791:** The nation's first internal revenue law requires a tax on distilled spirits, at 20 to 30 cents per gallon. The legislatures of North Carolina, Virginia, and Maryland pass official resolutions of disapproval.

  1861: Four months after the Civil War begins, Congress adopts an income tax law to help finance the war. Incomes from $600 to $10,000 are taxed at 3 percent, and those $10,000 and above, at 5 percent.

  1916: The federal income tax is ruled constitutional by the U.S. Supreme Court.

  1960: US taxpayers pay federal, state, and local taxes worth 25 percent of their earnings.

  1969: On December 22, Congress passes a far-reaching tax reform bill that removes 9 million of the nation's poor from its income tax rolls. The bill draws criticism that it ultimately aids the rich, not the poor.

  1981: Shortly after his election, President Ronald Reagan proposes a 10 percent income tax cut in each of the next three years. The plan is modified by Congress to begin with a 5 percent cut the first year.

  1995: An average lawyer's income is $1,116 per week. A child care worker makes an average of $158 per week.

---

and its personal conclusions. The poem is not only about growing older and wiser about some things; it is also about the necessity of becoming *dis-illusioned.* The 1980s in the United States left in its wake an increasingly polarized economy, proving it an illusion that any one strategy, economic or otherwise, can unlock the American dream for all. To put it in the intellectual language of the decade, the American dream itself is being "deconstructed" along with its illusions of privilege and power. In the terms of "Ethics," it is an illusion that the worth of a life can be pitted, with any validity, against the worth of a famous painting. Pastan's poem suggests that a "real" ethics can never be rooted in anything but a "real" life in the world, that part of the task of being human is to become disillusioned without growing cynical, awakened to what is both worth saving and "all beyond saving."

Critical Overview

Beyond reviews of her books, there is relatively little criticism of Pastan's poetry, despite the fact that she has been widely and steadily published for thirty years, and has received numerous awards. In his review of *PM/AM: New and Selected Poems* (1983), critic Peter Stitt of *The Georgia Review* may have suggested the simplest reason for this phenomenon: "Pastan does not write about ideas nor about things."

Pastan writes about people—their bodies and their minds—and because of the nature of her centeredness, she offers less for critics to talk about; these poems are more readily accessible to the reader. Pastan is "accessible" because she writes about people going about their "dailiness," a subject that is presumably uninteresting to the average critic. Stitt's comment (and his review in general) may ultimately have more to say about the perceived difference between "reader" and "critic" than it does about the substance of Pastan's poetry.

The content of Pastan's poetry is frequently concerned with the life of a woman trying to be an artist amid the demands of home and family. Feminist critic Sandra Gilbert is generally unsympathetic and, in an article for *Parnassus: Poetry in Review,* finds the author of *Waiting for My Life* to be a poet not only of the "melody of the quotidian" but of its "malady." Writing in *Washington Post Book World,* Mary Jo Salter finds Pastan's poems "sometimes simple to a fault." Amidst these criticisms, Gilbert discovers Pastan's strength in those moments when, like Emily Dickinson, "this artist of dailiness stresses the mystery of the ordinary." Fellow poet Dave Smith, writing in *American Poetry Review,* goes as far as to suggest that "Dickinson is Pastan's ghost," and celebrates her ability to depict "those moments spent at windows in kitchens or gardens where we are astonished at the speed and movement that is all the not-us."

Smith and others—L. M. Rosenberg, Edward Morin, Hugh Seidman—stress that as Pastan's work has matured, the "low heat" she has banked "into a small domestic flame for others" has become, in Smith's words, "a radiant heat nonetheless." Donna Seaman, a reviewer for the American Library Association, finds Eve, not Emily Dickinson, Pastan's alter ego in her most recent collection *Carnival Evening: New and Selected Poems, 1968-1998.* New poems and old from nine previous volumes, culminate, says Seaman, in a portrait of domesticity that is "both a temple and a prison," an Eden which Eve herself likely found "too confining, too orderly." Pastan's more mature art and its resistance to cliche has made earlier charges of her poetry being too "simple" more difficult to sustain.

Criticism

Alice Van Wart

Alice Van Wart teaches literature and writing in the Department of Continuing Education at the University of Toronto. She has published two books of poetry and has written articles on modern and contemporary literature. In the following essay, Van Wart discusses the mode in which Pastan writes, examines the oppositional nature of the poem, and discusses the moral issues presented in "Ethics."

Pastan received her first honor for a poem while she was a student at Radcliffe College in 1954 by winning the *Mademoiselle* poetry contest. Sylvia Path was the runner up. Though Pastan went on in school and received an M.A. from Brandeis University in 1957, she married young and had three children. Like many other women of her generation, who put aside their aspirations for domestic life, Pastan set aside her writing to concentrate on her children and home. Yet the desire to write remained, and eventually she returned to it, publishing in 1971 *A Perfect Circle of Sun,* the first of her many collections of poetry.

Pastan writes in what is referred to as the confessional mode, but unlike the more well-known confessional poets, her contemporaries Sylvia Plath and Anne Sexton, Pastan uses the personal not only to understand the self, but also as a means to understanding the nature of the world around her. Pastan's poetry is rooted in the common; it is filled with humor, passion, delight, despair, rebellion, and hope. As a woman who has lived the multiple roles placed on women, she grapples with the issues facing contemporary women, specifically the problems associated with love and domestic life. The war between desire and dealing with daily issues permeates her work as a common theme. It is, however, in the world of the everyday where she finds the small miracles in life and learns the nature of humanity.

Published in her fourth collection *Waiting for My Life* (1981), "Ethics" is a poem that is generally representative of much contemporary free verse. Told from a first person point of view in a

What Do I Read Next?

- The opening poem of Barbara Ras's *Bite Every Sorrow* argues that "you can't have it all," contrary to the myth, spawned by the American dream, that you can. However, says the poem, which is titled "You Can't Have It All," you *can* have "the fig tree and its fat leaves like clown hands / gloved with green," as well as a host of other gifts the world freely gives: "You can't count on grace to pick you out of a crowd, / but here is your friend to teach you how to high jump, how to throw yourself over the bar, backwards, / until you learn about love, about sweet surrender." Though not yet as well known as Pastan, Barbara Ras has been spoken of as a poet who "accurately captures the tug of war between the quotidian and the miraculous." *Bite Every Sorrow* won the prestigious Walt Whitman Award in 1997 for a first book of poems.

- Pastan's most recent collection, *Carnival Evening,* spans thirty years of the poet's career, and contains both new poems and a selection from nine previous volumes. If one reads through *Carnival Evening* chronologically, Pastan's evolving skill with metaphor and her changing preoccupations with art, marriage, family, and aging become apparent.

- One could argue that Pastan's poetry is "confessional" in its treatment of personal, often private, emotions and situations. "Confessional poetry" emerged as a genre of American contemporary poetry in the mid-1950s through the work of Robert Lowell, Anne Sexton, and Sylvia Plath, and is embodied today in the poems of Sharon Olds and others. The poems in Robert Lowell's *Lord Weary's Castle* (1946) and *Life Studies* (1959) are peopled with family members and poets, both living and dead, whose lives and words provide a terrain for the self to be revealed, often painfully.

- In some ways, Pastan has answered the imperative in *A Room of One's Own* (1929) that a woman of "genius" must have the means to exercise her gift. Virginia Woolf's landmark "feminist" essay urges that a woman must have "a room of her own," the necessary time, privacy, and freedom from financial concerns to satisfy the call of her art. Woolf believed that men and women experience life quite differently, and that the form of their artistic expression, therefore, must also differ. To put it in Woolf's writerly terms, a woman's "sentences" will reflect the unique shape of her experience. Many of Pastan's poems reveal the tensions in finding such a "room," even while they provide examples of "sentences" distinctly feminine in both form and content.

- In *Storyteller,* Leslie Marmon Silko has assembled a collage of stories, poems, and photographs that provide a portrait of Laguna Indian life, and specifically, that of several generations of her own family. Native American legend and voices from the land are woven seamlessly into this "family album." Silko's book, published the same year as Pastan's *Waiting for My Life* (1981), provides a glimpse into the "extraordinary ordinary" life of the Laguna people in this century.

---

colloquial idiom and conversational tone, the poet relates a personal experience from the past that takes on new significance in the present. It is also typical of Pastan's poetry in that the poem works around opposed elements. Written in a simple language, devoid of figurative language, the poem tells a story in two parts, the second part drawing meaning from the first. Though there are no stanza breaks, the poem works through the opposition of its two parts, defined as clear rhetorical units, parallelism, repetition, and irony to suggest that it is beyond the ability of children to determine complex moral issues.

The poem's title points to its central concern—ethics. What is meant by ethics is a general system of moral principles, the study of which is the branch of philosophy concerned with right and wrong of

> "*The final lines of the poem evoke a mature awareness on the part of the poet. They suggest a wisdom and a comprehension that only comes with age.*"

certain actions and behavior. A system of ethical or moral behavior is essential to a civilized society, and we learn early through instruction many of its moral precepts. However, in the course of life people find themselves in situations in which they must decide for themselves what is the right way to act or the right choice to make. It is an individual's responsibility to make the right choice and to be accountable for that choice. A part of growing up is learning how to make the right choices.

In Pastan's poem "Ethics" the poet, while visiting a museum and looking at a Rembrandt painting, remembers an ethics class she had taken "many years ago." Each fall the teacher posed the same question to the students: Which would they choose if they were forced by a fire in a museum to save either "an old woman who hadn't many / years left anyhow" or "a Rembrandt painting." The question had little meaning for the students, who were "restless on hard chairs" and who "car[ed] little for pictures or old age," but each year they would "half-heartedly" alternate their answers, "one year for life, the next for art." To try and make the question more relevant to her life, the poet admits she would try to picture the old woman as her grandmother, or as Pastan puts it, "the woman borrowed my grandmother's face / leaving her usual kitchen to wander / some drafty, half imagined museum."

The poet's use of the phrase "half imagined" shows her awareness of her inability as a young student to conjure up the image of a museum, let alone to understand the complex implications of the question. Much more real were hard chairs and restlessness as she struggled with the problem. One year "feeling clever" the poet responded to the question by asking the teacher, "why not let the woman decide herself?" Later, the teacher "would report" that she (the poet) "eschews / the burdens of responsibility." The teacher meant that the poet was avoiding the process of learning to make responsible choices by suggesting they let the woman decide for herself; she was placing the burden of the "responsibility" of choosing on someone else.

The poem turns on the word "responsibility" and moves to the second part. In the syntactical integrity of the poetic line, the poet puts the word at the end of the line placing emphasis on it. Though the progression in the poem moves in time from past to present, from when the poet is a child to when she is a mature woman, the action in the poem is implicit in the juxtapositioning of or opposition between the two parts of the poem.

The second part of the poem begins "this fall," which brings the time back to present. This fall the poet finds herself in "a real museum" as opposed to some "half imagined museum," standing before "a real Rembrandt," as opposed to just a picture. The repetition of the word "real" shows the contrast between the theoretical and the concrete and the poet's awareness of the irony of her situation as she recalls the question posed to her as a student. She is now an old woman herself, or "nearly so," in a museum, before a Rembrandt. She no longer needs to find a face for the old woman to help make the theoretical personal; she is the woman, the painting is a real Rembrandt, an invaluable work of art painted by one of the great masters centuries ago.

As she studies the painting she notices "the colors / … are darker than autumn, / darker even than winter." The painter's colors on the canvas are those deep colors seen at the end of a season, "the browns of earth." The poet is also probably aware that the pigment in the colors has darkened over time (a particular problem in the preservation of the work of the old masters). In the next line, however, she sees that through these dark colors "earth's most radiant elements burn." The verb placed at the end of the line accumulates with weight, placing the importance of the line on the active verb "burn," and evoking an image of a smoldering fire with deepened burnished light and heat. The syntax of line nineteen, which reads from the previous line as "old woman, / or nearly so, myself. The colors," points to the poet's awareness of the parallel she sees in the painting's frame and in her own life. In a sense the painting acts for the poet as an objective correlative mirroring the inner state of her being, suggesting that though she has reached the later part of her life she still "burns" with life.

The final lines of the poem evoke a mature awareness on the part of the poet. They suggest a wisdom and a comprehension that only comes with age. To begin with she understands the value of the painting as she could not as a young girl. She remembers how little meaning either "pictures or old age" then had for her. The question posed by her ethics teacher was merely theoretical, an abstract exercise that had nothing to do with real life, which is full of paradox, irony, and contradiction. The restless student, now a mature woman, says in the concluding lines, "I know now that woman / and painting and season are almost one / and all beyond saving by children." In the last two lines the poet's use of the coordinating conjunction "and" to link "woman / and painting and season" places equal value through parallel structure on life, art, and nature.

The final lines also attest to the poet's awareness of the complexity of the moral issue posed to her as a young and callow girl in the form of a choice between life and art. Furthermore, she understands the ironic nature of value itself. The season is at its richest in fall just before its end, and a painting acquires value with age. But what is the value of an old woman in a society that has little respect for old people, in general, and women, in particular? (In the first part of the poem the theoretical old woman "hadn't many years left anyhow.") The poet implies it is not society that makes "woman / and painting and season" "almost one," but a much stronger force hinted at throughout the poem. The season is fall; the poet is almost old; and the painting, which is "darker even than winter," is fading into blackness, and as such they are "all beyond saving by children." The inexorable, equalizing force of time is with them all. By using the coordinating conjunction to link "woman / and painting and season" the poet places equal value through parallel structure on life, art, and nature and, in effect, still refuses to play the game in choosing one over the other.

Source: Alice Van Wart, in an essay for *Poetry for Students,* Gale Group, 2000.

Sources

Gilbert, Sandra, "The Melody of the Quotidian," *Parnassus: Poetry in Review,* Vol 11, No. 1, spring/summer 1983, pp. 147-56.

"Linda Pastan," *Contemporary Authors: New Revision Series,* Vol. 61, Detroit: Gale, 1998, pp. 364-67.

"Linda Pastan," *Dictionary of Literary Biography,* Vol. 5, Part 2: *American Poets Since WWII,* Detroit: Gale, 1980, pp. 158-63.

Our American Century: Pride and Prosperity, the 80s, Alexandria, VA: Time-Life Books, 1999.

Pastan, Linda, *Carnival Evening, New and Selected Poems, 1968-1998,* New York: W. W. Norton & Co., 1998.

Pastan, Linda, letter to the contributor, September 22, 1999.

Pastan, Linda, *Waiting for My Life,* New York: W. W. Norton, 1981.

Salter, Mary Jo, review of *Waiting for My Life,* in *Washington Post Book World,* July 5, 1981.

Smith, Dave, article, in *American Poetry Review,* January 1982.

Still, Peter, "Stages of Reality: The Mind/Body Problem in Contemporary Poetry," *The Georgia Review,* Vol. 37, No. 1, spring 1983, pp. 201-10.

Student Handbook: What Happened When, Nashville: The Southwestern Co., 1996.

For Further Study

Pastan, Linda, "Response," *The Georgia Review,* Vol. 35, No. 4, winter 1981, p. 734.

> Pastan was chosen along with several other poets to respond, in colloquium style, to a statement made about the changing audience for poetry. Though quite brief, her comments reveal much about her detachment from literary criticism and her stance on the political power of poetry.

———, "Writing about Writing," *Writers on Writing, A Bread Loaf Anthology,* edited by Robert Pack and Jay Parini, Hanover, NH: Middlebury College Press, 1991, pp. 207-20.

> Pastan's love of painting and interest in self-portraits provide the entree into this essay, which has a simple thesis: Pastan likes to write about writing, and so do many other poets. She creates some useful categories for poems about poems, such as "How to Do It" poems, "writer's block" poems, "invocations to the muse," and poems that define either poetry or the poet's task. The anthology itself is full of lively essays by a variety of fiction writers and poets on the subject of writing, from many different viewpoints.

———, "Ask Me," *On William Stafford: The Worth of Local Things,* edited by Tom Andrews, Ann Arbor: The University of Michigan Press, 1993, pp. 253-54.

> This is Pastan's tribute to the late poet William Stafford. It is short, intimate, and honest in her open affection for the late poet, and her discomfort in "writing about poems." Pastan focuses on Stafford's poem "Ask Me," "because it seems to give me permission to be almost silent, to stand with him a moment quietly at the edge of the frozen river and to just wait."

"Women & the Arts", *The Georgia Review* (special issue), Vol. 44, Nos. 1 & 2, spring/summer 1990.

Occupying the center pages of this issue of *The Georgia Review* is a series of paintings, "Homescapes," by Georgia artist Mary Porter. Porter's work, like Pastan's, finds domestic themes, places, and objects to be worthy of art. In Porter's lively watercolors and acrylics, the common porch, kitchen, stovetop, sink, laundry basket, and coffeepot are transformed "into enigmatic metaphors." Several of the fiction writers, essayists, poets, and graphic artists in this issue are well known—Eudora Welty, Naomi Shihab Nye, Joyce Carol Oates, Maxine Kumin, Rita Dove, Eavan Boland, and Pastan, to name a few. The editors of this special issue hope that the contributors' engaging, "varied energies," will invite a "fresh reassessment" of women artists in our society.

The Force That through the Green Fuse Drives the Flower

Dylan Thomas

1934

Dylan Thomas made a dramatic impact on the literary world when his first collection of poetry, with the unassuming title *18 Poems*, appeared in December of 1934, when he was only twenty years old. Although he had published a few poems in literary magazines during the previous year, Thomas was basically an unknown figure. From the beginning, he was a controversial poet. Not part of the conventional literary establishment, unconnected with any particular poetic movement, his work was difficult to categorize. Although Thomas's poems received critical acclaim for the force and vitality of their language and imagery, he was also criticized for obscurity. Because of this, he was often identified with the Surrealist movement, where images and language violated the rules of logic, frequently imitating the landscape of dreams, or even nightmares. On the surface, Thomas seems to have much in common with Surrealism; however, he vehemently denied the relationship, insisting that his poetry was carefully planned and controlled. Thomas fully intended his images to be understood. Unfortunately for the reader, the intensely personal nature of many of his metaphors makes this difficult.

"The Force That through the Green Fuse Drives the Flower," one of the most popular and least obscure of the poems in the collection, illustrates both the vivid language and the complex, powerful, but often confusing imagery. While it is easy to get caught up in the rhythm and drama of the language, it is far more difficult to unravel meaning. On its most basic level, however, the poem describes the cycle of life and death, noting that creation and destruction are part of the same process, both for man and for nature. Each stanza presents the flow of time moving to its inexorable conclusion.

Author Biography

Thomas was born at home in the Uplands district of Swansea, Wales, on October 27, 1914, the second child and only son of middle-class parents. His sister Nancy was nearly nine years older than he. His father was a schoolmaster in English at the local grammar school. Though considered a cold and bitter man who resented his position as a teacher, the elder Thomas's love for literature encouraged a similar devotion in his son. Thomas feared, respected, and deeply loved his father, and in some sense his life appeared to be an attempt to realize his father's frustrated dream of being a great poet. In contrast to his father, Thomas's mother was loving, overly protective, and inclined to over-indulge her son. Even at the end of his life, she found no fault in his public behavior and the drinking habits which ultimately led to his death.

Thomas enjoyed his childhood in Wales, and his work in later years would reflect a desire to recapture the relatively carefree years of his youth. A generally undistinguished student, Thomas entered the Swansea Grammar School in 1925. In 1931 he left school to work for the *South Wales Daily Post* in Swansea. He would later say that his real education came from the freedom he was given to read anything in his father's surprisingly well-stocked library of modern and nineteenth-century poetry and other works. Following his resignation from the paper early in 1933, poetry became Thomas's primary occupation. By all accounts, he was not a successful news reporter: he got facts wrong, and he failed to show up to cover events, preferring instead to loiter at the pool hall or the Kardomah Cafe. During the early 1930s Thomas began to develop the serious drinking problem that plagued him throughout the remainder of his life. He also began to develop a public persona as a jokester and storyteller. However, his notebooks reveal that many of his most highly regarded poems were either written or drafted during this period and that he had also begun to experiment with short prose pieces. In May of 1933 his poem "And Death Shall Have No Dominion" was published in the *New English Weekly,* marking the first appearance of his work in a London journal, and in December of the following year his first poetry collection, *18 Poems,*

Dylan Thomas

was issued. During this period he established a life-long pattern of travel between London and some rural retreat, usually in Wales. As the decade progressed he gained increasing recognition for both his poetry and his prose.

In the summer of 1937 Thomas married Caitlin Macnamara, a young dancer of Irish descent whose Bohemian lifestyle and behavior rivaled Thomas's own. For the next twelve years the couple led a nomadic and financially difficult existence, staying with friends, relatives, and a series of benefactors. The stories later collected in *Portrait of the Artist as a Young Dog* (1940) were written primarily during the couple's stay in the Welsh coastal village of Laugharne in late 1938 and early 1939. Too frail for active military service and needing to support himself and his wife, Thomas took work writing scripts for propaganda films during World War II, at which time he also began to participate in radio dramas and readings for the BBC. His financial burdens increased during this time. In January 1939 Thomas's first child, a son named Llewelyn, was born. Daughter Aeron followed in March 1943. Thomas emerged from the war years a respected literary figure and popular performer; however, his gregarious social life and the excessive drinking it encouraged seriously interfered with his writing. Seeking an environment more conducive to poetic production, Thomas and his family returned to Laugharne in 1949.

During the early 1950s Thomas wrote several of his most poignant poems, including "Do Not Go Gentle into That Good Night" and " Lament." Nevertheless, fearing that his creative powers were rapidly waning and seeking to avoid the pressures of writing, he embarked on a speaking tour of the United States in the spring of 1950. During the final years of his life he traveled to the United States four times, each time engaging in parties and readings in and around New York City, followed by readings and more celebrations at numerous universities throughout the country. Thomas's personal charisma and self-described public reputation as a drunkard, a Welshman, and a lover of women seemed to serve only to enhance his standing in literary circles. His fourth and final American tour began on October 19, 1953, and ended with his death from a massive overdose of alcohol on November 9.

Poem Text

The force that through the green fuse drives the
    flower
Drives my green age; that blasts the roots of trees
Is my destroyer.
And I am dumb to tell the crooked rose
My youth is bent by the same wintry fever.   5

The force that drives the water through the rocks
Drives my red blood; that dries the mouthing
    streams
Turns mine to wax.
And I am dumb to mouth unto my veins
How at the mountain spring the same mouth sucks. 10

The hand that whirls the water in the pool
Stirs the quicksand; that ropes the blowing wind
Hauls my shroud sail.
And I am dumb to tell the hanging man
How of my clay is made the hangman's lime.   15

The lips of time leech to the fountain head;
Love drips and gathers, but the fallen blood
Shall calm her sores.
And I am dumb to tell a weather's wind
How time has ticked a heaven round the stars.   20

And I am dumb to tell the lover's tomb
How at my sheet goes the same crooked worm.

Poem Summary

Line 1:

"The Force That through the Green Fuse Drives the Flower" is a complicated poem. On the

first reading, it may seem almost too difficult for a beginning reader to understand. However, careful analysis will make much of the imagery clearer. As a survey of critics reveals, there is no one right explanation for the more complicated ideas in the poem. Even critics interpret lines in different and often contradictory ways. Since the poem is about contrast, change, and paradox, this may prove part of the poem's meaning.

The first stanza in the poem is the easiest to understand. It is important to be aware of the pattern that Thomas develops in this stanza, in order to look for variations that appear later. The first three lines contrast the creative and destructive forces that surround man. Thomas's imagery emphasizes the explosive nature of this power. The green fuse is obviously the flower's stem, yet the word "fuse" gives the connotation of explosive growth, rather than gentle development. In this line, Thomas introduces the creative force in nature.

The rhyme scheme in this stanza is *ababa*.

Line 2:

In the first four words of this line, the power that causes growth in nature is revealed as the same force that causes the speaker to grow. Like the flower, the speaker is still in the process of growing. Green age implies youth, since the word *green* has connotations of spring and renewal. Although green is often used in poetry to convey youth, this phrase also contains a sense of opposites; *green* conveys youth, while *age* often speaks of being old. Throughout the poem, Thomas will combine many seemingly opposite words.

After the caesura—the pause or break in the rhythm at the semicolon—the destructive power is unleashed. Grammatically, the phrase refers back to the force in the first line. However, now it is a destructive power, obliterating trees by their very roots. Thomas makes it clear that the fuse which blasted the flower into existence is also the blast which destroys it.

Line 3:

Like nature, the speaker is also subject to the same fate. The change in length helps to emphasize the line's power. With three words, the speaker describes his ultimate fate.

Line 4:

The fourth line in each stanza begins with the same four words indicating that the speaker is unable to convey his insight. *Dumb* has several mean-

Media Adaptations

- *The Caedmon Collection of English Poetry,* released in 1996, includes several poems by Dylan Thomas.

- In 1995, Harper Collins Audio released a cassette version of *Under Milk Wood* with Dylan Thomas reading one of the roles.

- In 1988, Vestron Video released a dramatization of Thomas's childhood memoir, *A Child's Christmas in Wales.*

- An audiocassette, *Dylan Thomas Reads "A Child's Christmas in Wales" and "Fern Hill,"* which also contains other poems, was released by Caedmon in 1992.

- CBS/Fox released a 1971 film version of *Under Milk Wood,* which is based on a Dylan Thomas radio play about a Welsh fishing village.

ings which could be applicable. While the speaker may be unable to "tell" for physical reasons, it is more likely for emotional ones, a sense of inadequacy to express the idea.

Once again, Thomas combines words with opposite connotations. The rose is a symbol of beauty, of the growth described in the first line; using the adjective *crooked* to describe it changes our impression of the flower. Like much of Thomas's imagery, this phrase is not precise. It relies on the reader's feeling or impressions. The entire stanza leaves the reader with the impression that the crooked rose is blighted.

Line 5:

The speaker shares the same fate as the flower. The verb *bent* furthers the connection between the speaker and the rose, as the reader understands that the vigorous youth will become stooped and crooked with age, like the rose. In *wintry fever* Thomas includes still another paradox as the cold of winter is blended with a fever's heat.

Line 6:

The pattern in this stanza is the same as the first, both grammatically and in the organization of ideas. However, the focus now changes from relationship between man and the biological world to man and the geological world. The force that was introduced in the first stanza pushes the water from under the earth's surface through the rocks to give birth to the mountain stream.

Line 7:

Once again, Thomas compares the speaker to nature in the first four words; the line opens with "drives" just as line 2 did, emphasizing the similarity. Blood is pushed through man's veins just as the water coursed through the rocks. Thomas frequently uses color in his poems; the red blood in this line is a counterpart to green age in the previous stanza. The contrasting element following the caesura describes these same streams dying. The alliterative half-rhyme of *drives* and *dries* reinforces this contrast.

Thomas is noted for his ability to combine words to create arresting images, such as *mouthing streams,* which are open to a variety of interpretations. A stream's mouth is the place where it enters another body of water. Rather than being destroyed at the source like the trees in line 2, the stream dries before it reaches its destination; it is thwarted from completing its route. The word *mouth* will appear in two different contexts later in the stanza.

Line 8:

Mine in this line refers to the speaker's blood. It is turned to wax by the embalmer; it will flow no longer to sustain life but will become as solid as wax.

Line 9:

In the previous stanza, the speaker was unable to communicate with the rose. In this line, his inability to express his feelings is even more poignant, since he cannot communicate with his own body. The word *mouth* again is used, and while to "mouth" in this line literally means to speak, the phrase takes on extra significance because of the repetition and variation in the use of this word.

Line 10:

Again the speaker shares nature's fate. *Mouth* in this line takes on an almost vampirish quality, as it sucks away life, the water from the stream, the blood from the speaker's veins.

Line 11:

The first two stanzas were extremely similar. The rhyme pattern was the same. Each image in the first found a parallel in the second. The third stanza, however, varies the pattern in several ways. The rhyme scheme will shift to *ababc,* leaving the last line unconnected to this stanza and to the previous ones.

Force is replaced by *hand. Force,* as an abstract and general term, is easier to understand as a controller of human destiny than the very specific word *hand.* In the previous stanzas, the contrasts were clear. The first line in both previous stanzas described growth and creation; the images Thomas uses here are not as clear. Water may be life-giving, but as the hand whirls it in the pool, the words join to convey a sense of danger, of the whirlpool.

Line 12:

The first four words of the second line in previous stanzas connected the speaker's growth with nature's. In this line, the pronoun is left out. Instead, the hand stirs quicksand. Like the whirlpool, it is a destructive force. Both however, are limited in their ability to damage. All flowers will die; few individuals are caught in quicksand or a whirlpool. As the first half of the comparison is longer clear in its constructive nature, the destructive element is also less obvious. To rope the wind only implies control over nature.

Line 13:

Thomas includes the personal pronoun again, in the second half of the comparison. The destructive nature of the phrase is clear; the shroud means death. Indeed, the phrase conjures up visions of a type of Viking funeral as the corpse is sent to sea. Interestingly, a secondary meaning of *shroud* is a rope used to take pressure off a mast; this use ties the line to the ones before and after it.

Lines 14-15:

In each previous refrain, the speaker failed to communicate: to the rose, to his veins. Neither of those were new images; they followed from the first part of the stanza. The hanging man is introduced for the first time in this refrain. His connection with the details in the previous lines is vague, unless the image of a rope can be counted. Even the words *hanging man* are imprecise. The obvious conclusion is that he is the man who has been hung, but that is not specifically stated. He could be the hangman himself. Perhaps it even refers to both. In the previous stanzas, the speaker looked ahead to his ultimate fate. Line 15 looks back from a future when the speaker is already clay, part of the lime-filled pit where the hangman disposes of his victims. The unattached rhyme in this line looks ahead to *time* in line 16.

Line 16:

This is the most difficult of the stanzas. The punctuation is different; the semicolon isolates this line so that the first four syllables of the next line are no longer directly connected. Time is the creative and destructive force that has been operating in the previous stanzas, and now time itself becomes the focus of the poem, as time joins with the fountainhead or source. There are obvious sexual connotations in this line; the lips represent the vagina, while the fountainhead is a phallic image. The use of *leech* as a verb here connects this line to the *sucking mouth* of stanza two.

The rhyme scheme joins the first two lines, *head* and *blood*; the third and fifth lines are also connected. The fourth line refers back to line 12 in the previous stanza.

Lines 17-18:

Thomas again combines positive and negative images in these lines, which are open to varied interpretations. The fallen blood may have sexual or birth connotations; it can be connected with Christ's blood and salvation, as well, in its calming power. These lines also foreshadow the final couplet, connecting love and death.

Lines 19-20:

Thomas has moved from a single flower to the cosmos. The speaker cannot tell the wind about the nature of time or of the heavens. The image of speaking to the wind is a powerful one. Much of this stanza is more easily felt than defined.

Lines 21-22:

The final couplet restates Thomas's theme of creativity aligned with destruction. *Lover's tomb* is an almost perfect symbol for love and death. The speaker, too, shares the same fate as the lovers. The last line may be interpreted in two different ways. The sheet may be viewed as a shroud, and the worm that which feeds on the corpse. The worm may also be seen as a phallic symbol and the sheet a bed sheet. Both images are integral parts of Thomas's theme. The crooked worm also returns the poem to the first stanza and the crooked rose. The poem, itself, becomes a cycle, combining conception, birth, growth, and death, all part of the same process.

Topics for Further Study

- The Eisteddfod, a competition among poets, has been a Welsh tradition for over eight hundred years. Find out how it is celebrated in Wales today. Note: the most effective way to research this is by using the Internet.

- Sometimes it is "dumb" to tell. In either a story or an essay, describe an incident where someone spoke hastily and wished they had remained silent. You may choose to describe the reverse, a situation where someone remained quiet and later regretted it.

- The poem mentions a lover's tomb. Both literature and history are filled with famous lovers who died tragically: Romeo and Juliet, Antony and Cleopatra, Bonnie and Clyde. Select a pair of fictional, historical, or modern-day lovers and retell their story in a poem, song, or narrative.

Themes

Cycle of Life

"The Force That through the Green Fuse Drives the Flower" describes the cycle of birth and death. It is one of several poems by Thomas which explores this pattern; in fact, the pattern provides such a consistent theme throughout his work that some critics have categorized this group as process poems. As the poem opens, the speaker presents the creative and destructive forces in life and nature. In the first two stanzas, Thomas clearly indicates that birth and blight are simply aspects of one continuum. The opening lines of these stanzas make this evident to the reader. The same force creates the flower, the child, the mountain spring, the circulatory system. However, the force which brings life also brings death. The force which "drives the flower" is also the force which "blasts the roots," killing the tree.

This process, although in more complex form, occurs in the third stanza as well. However, the contrast between life and death imagery is less clear. The destructive elements seem more dominant. In place of the unmistakable positive images in the first stanzas, the whirling water hints at a whirlpool; it is followed by quicksand, another destructive element. Yet the poem continues to indicate that out of death comes conception. Consider the stanza's final line, "How of my clay is made the hangman's lime." Although the initial impact of the phrase may be negative, upon reflection, it demonstrates the cycle in practice. Man is born, dies, is buried and then joined with nature as dust or clay. This clay is used to create the pit where the hangman buries his corpses. The lime, a cleansing agent, soon reduces the corpse to bone, then dust or earth or clay. Eventually from that earth, "the force … drives the flower." The poem indicates that the process does not end with death. Both the creative and destructive aspects of life are steps in a process, part of a continuous cycle. Thus, in every birth there is an element of death; every death somehow holds the intimation of rebirth.

Balance

The process described in the poem is expressed by using positive and negative imagery as counterparts. This contrast or balance becomes a secondary theme; in fact, Thomas uses this principle to structure his poem. This balance serves as an underpinning, reinforcing his main theme, the cycle of life and death. The first two stanzas begin with lines describing the polar opposites in the process. Even the lines themselves are balanced, as a semicolon provides a physical demarcation between the two aspects of the force. This balance is extended to the imagery as well. The crooked rose of the first stanza may be paired with the crooked worm in the last, neatly joining the poem's opening and closing stanzas. The fourth stanza, while complex, also contains balance in its imagery. "Love drips and gathers, but the fallen blood / Shall calm her sores" is a passage that is open to several interpretations. Critics have seen both religious and sexual overtones in the language. In either case, however, the line contains the pairing of both positive and negative forces. The use of the conjunction *but* provides a clear indication of this. Even if love should falter, it shall be redeemed. Whether the calming blood is that of the crucifixion or of menstrual blood, both suggest the image of birth or rebirth. Thomas continues this balance even in simple phrases, such as "wintry fever," "green age," and "lover's tomb." The pairing of these last two words, in many ways, effectively sums up the poem's theme of life and death.

Microcosm/Macrocosm

An additional theme in the poem involves the relationship, the interconnectedness, among all living things as the poem introduces the reader to the role of the microcosm and the macrocosm. The speaker makes clear that all living matter follows the same pattern. What is true for the flower is also true for man. The poem extends the premise of interconnectedness beyond organic matter, which is of course subject to life and death, in the second stanza. The geological world, rocks and water, is also subject to the universal pattern. Later, the poem includes the "weather's wind" and the stars. The pattern of creation which applies to the smallest cell foreshadows the fate of the universe.

These three themes work together to create a picture of a universe where all matter is linked together, intricately united and balanced. Interestingly, critics are divided on whether the poem's ultimate message is one of hope or despair. For some, the final two stanzas reveal an impenetrable barrier between the universe and its governing force. Others find that the poem itself, a balanced cycle, presents a message of hope, illustrating that life will survive.

Human Isolation

A final theme deals with one's inability to express one's feelings and thoughts. Throughout the poem, the final couplet of each stanza begins "And I am dumb." The speaker indicates that although he is aware of the process, he is unable to share that knowledge with the rest of nature. He may be part of the same cycle as the rose and stream, but he cannot speak to them. He cannot even tell his own veins, his own body, about this knowledge. Although the entire universe is part of one continuum, each individual, in many ways, remains ultimately alone.

Style

"The Force That through the Green Fuse Drives the Flower" is made up of four stanzas, each with five lines, followed by an ending couplet. Its meter is often described as iambic pentameter, a line of verse featuring five segments of two syllables ("feet") where the first syllable is unstressed and the second is stressed, as in the word "above." But Thomas's poetry seldom fits neatly into conventional metric analysis. While most poems contain some irregularity in meter, Thomas's poetry uses more variation than most. Thus many critics choose

to view his poetry in terms of the number of syllables in each line, rather than by metric feet. Thus "The Force That through the Green Fuse Drives the Flower" may also be described as decasyllabic, having ten syllables in a line. Thomas's predominant use of one-syllable words frequently means that the stress or emphasis in a line depends on the reader's decision about which syllables should be emphasized. Notice, for example, the first four words in the second line of the poem, "Drives my green age." Read them aloud to see which ones you emphasize. The result will vary from person to person. In fact, William Lord Tindall remembers that when Thomas himself read another phrase from the poem, "And I am dumb," he stressed the words equally, giving separate emphasis to each one.

More important than meter for Thomas is the poem's pattern. "The Force That through the Green Fuse Drives the Flower" is a very complicated poem, but each stanza is organized in a similar manner. When there are alterations in the pattern, it provides a guideline for the reader to look for changes in the poem's imagery and meaning as well. The first two stanzas set the basic pattern; the first three lines in each provide a contrast between a creative and a destructive force. This contrast is marked grammatically with a semicolon after the fourth syllable in the second line. The final two lines are a refrain describing the poet's inability to articulate the extent of the contrast he has just described. Similarities in the opening words of the lines in the stanzas also help to reinforce the pattern of the poem. When the structure shifts, slightly in the third stanza and more noticeably in the fourth, this indicates a shift in Thomas's thematic development.

The use of rhyme is also an important element in Thomas's poetry. In this poem, he uses end rhyme in each stanza. The first two stanzas, using half-rhyme or slant rhyme, follow an *ababa* pattern, where the first, third, and fifth lines are based on one rhyme and the second and fourth lines on another. Alliteration and assonance are also very important in the poem's rhyme. The first two lines provide numerous examples. With their initial letter *f*, *force, fuse,* and *flower* are all alliterative, while *drives, blast,* and *trees* show assonance, or similarly located vowel patterns.

Historical Context

Just as the poetry of Dylan Thomas is difficult to characterize as springing from any particular po-

Compare & Contrast

- **1934:** The Dionne quintuplets were born.

  1997: The McCaughey septuplets were born.

  1998: Nkem Chukwu gave birth to octuplets; the smallest one, weighing only 10.3 ounces, died of heart failure one week after birth. This renewed the debate about the medical ethics of the prescribing of fertility drugs.

- **1934:** The Hayes Office was established by the Motion Picture Producers and Distributors to create a code for behavior in the movies. Female breasts and "unconventional" kissing were banned from the screen.

  1969: Jack Valenti developed the current rating system for movies.

  1999: The movie rating system came under attack for allowing too much violence in movies after the shooting at Columbine High School. President Clinton challenged the industry to improve and enforce their system.

---

etic movement, it is also problematic to pin down his poetic roots, his literary heritage. Although he is Welsh, his poetry seldom reflects this, since his themes are intensely personal, having little relation to either his Welsh background or his historic period. Even in poems such as "Fern Hill," which is based on a childhood location and memory, the setting is more deeply rooted in the world of the imagination than in the countryside of Wales.

Because of this, critics are often bitterly divided about the description of Thomas as a Welsh writer. Many feel that he should not be characterized as such since he was unable to speak Welsh and stated that he had no interest at all in the language. He rejected the cause of Welsh nationalism and was reported as saying, "Land of my fathers, and my fathers can keep it." Other critics, however, believe that Thomas is the product of a long tradition of Welsh poetry. They find traces of this rich Welsh heritage in Thomas's passion, celebration of wild nature, elaborate play with meter, and highly structured poetic forms. A review of the role which language and literature have played and continue to play in Welsh history may help illuminate both sides of this argument.

Wales, like most of western Europe, was overrun by successive waves of invaders who eventually settled the land. Gradually, however, the people of Wales began to forge a national identity. By the sixth century, the Welsh language had evolved. A century later, the people of the land—who were called "Welsh" or "foreigners" by the inhabitants of Britain—described themselves as Cymry, or compatriots. During the seventh and eighth centuries, four main kingdoms were established: Gwynedd, Powys, Deheubarth, and Morgannwg. By the ninth century the country had a national name and identity, Cymru.

During the period while these kingdoms were being forged, poetry played an important role in the forming of a national consciousness. Two famous sixth-century poets celebrated the valiant struggles of Welsh heroes. Taliesin created odes praising the passion of the leader Urien. Anerin also wrote of the valorous exploits of Welsh warriors. They are often considered the fathers of the intricate rhyme and rhythm schemes which characterize modern Welsh poetry. The Welsh literary heritage is one of the oldest and most consistent in the world.

During the next few centuries, the bardic tradition played an increasingly important role in the development of the society. Bards were poets trained in metrics and the conventions of poetry, such as alliteration and complex internal rhyme; frequently the role of bard was a family tradition, passed down through successive generations. The role of these poets was highly honored, since bards served to heighten national pride and unity. In addition, many households kept their own bard to record the family's private triumphs and celebrations.

The period of the Norman invasion of Wales during the eleventh and twelfth centuries became the heroic age of Welsh poetry. Court poets played an official role in government, and verse assumed an integral role in the royal court. It celebrated the feats of national heroes such as Owain Gwynedd, who resisted the Normans in North Wales. His son, Hywel ab Owain, further strengthened the importance of the role of the bard, since he was respected not only as a prince and warrior but also as a poet.

This esteem for poetry was strong throughout Wales. In the southern section of the country, Lord Rhys, who was the last of the kings of Deheubarth, exchanged his royal title to take over for the English monarch, becoming Henry II's Justice of South Wales. Like other Welsh people, he placed a great value on poetry. Therefore, in 1176, he declared the first eisteddfod, a contest to acknowledge the nation's best poet and best musician. This accolade became one of the country's highest honors.

The next few centuries saw the decline of the power of the bardic tradition. The gentry no longer supported poets, and the role of the bard diminished in importance. Nominal English control during the fourteenth and fifteenth centuries allowed Welsh to remain the dominant language and culture. However, when Henry VIII passed the Act of Union in 1536 declaring Wales "for ever ... annexed" to Britain, Welsh ceased to be the official language of the country. Although Elizabeth I declared an eisteddfod to be held at Caerwys to bolster the strong Welsh poetic tradition, this had little effect on the gradual encroachment of the English language and culture in Welsh society.

By the eighteenth century, the industrialization which flourished in many portions of South Wales helped to create a kind of cultural divide, since the language of business was English. This was countered by a movement to honor the language, art, and culture of Wales. The Honourable Society of Cymmrodorion, founded in 1751, dedicated itself to this purpose. Unfortunately, the Welsh language found itself increasingly under attack. Another blow came in the latter part of the nineteenth century, when English was ordained as the official language taught in schools.

At the beginning of the twentieth century, many Welsh parents were convinced that English was the language of success and prevented their children from speaking Welsh. This was true for Thomas. Although both of his parents spoke Welsh, his father discouraged him from learning the language. At the same time, however, a strong nationalist movement began to form. By 1934, when Thomas wrote this poem, there was a renewed interest in reaffirming the strong traditions of the Welsh language and poetry.

Critical Overview

Critics interpret "The Force That through the Green Fuse Drives the Flower" in a number of different ways. For M. L. Rosenthal, it is basically a tragic poem. In *The Modern Poets: A Critical Introduction,* he analyzes Thomas's style, asserting that the power of his poetry, particularly in his early work such as this poem, lies not in his themes but in the grandeur and power of his language. Like many critics, he finds the poem's ideas about the cycle of birth, growth, and death in man and nature the least compelling aspect of the poem. Rosenthal traces the comparison between man and nature and man and sub-organic nature through the first three stanzas. The fourth stanza reveals the tragic premise he finds in the poem. Although it reveals a passionate desire for a union, or communion, between all living things and the force which governs them, this is not possible. "The poem ends in despair, with a bizarre and deliberately ugly phallic image that, in degrading the symbolism of the fourth stanza, doubly underlines the anguish out of which it has arisen."

In *Entrances to Dylan Thomas's Poetry,* Ralph Maud sees "The Force That through the Green Fuse Drives the Flower" as an expression of the unity of life. He classifies it as one of Thomas's process poems, using the balance of symbols such as the crooked rose and the crooked worm to support the poem's antithetical organization. The shift in positive and destructive imagery in stanza three, instead of being "subversive," develops the point that the life and death forces are the same. For Maud, the poem shows that positives flow from negatives. The lime pit where the dead are placed has a cleansing function. *Leech* is an archaic term for a doctor, and a loss of blood may be beneficial. For him, the central focus is "the idea of the unity of contrary forces."

Criticism

Aviya Kushner

Kushner, the poetry editor for Neworld Renaissance Magazine, *earned an M.A. in creative writing from Boston University. In the following es-*

What Do I Read Next?

- *A Reference Companion to Dylan Thomas,* by James A. Davies, is an extremely helpful resource which includes a biography, discussion of each book, analysis of Thomas's techniques, and discussion of the critical reaction to his work. It was published by Greenwood Press in 1998.

- Thomas is frequently mentioned in *Anglo-Welsh Literature: An Illustrated History,* by Roland Mathias, a 1986 publication of Poetry Wales Press that presents an overview of Welsh writers who wrote in English.

- Although David Holbrook, the author of *Llareggub Revisited,* a 1962 publication by Cedric Chivies Press, noted in later editions of this work that his criticism of Thomas was too hostile, his negative comments on "The Force" remain interesting.

- In 1962, Noonday Press published William York Tindall's *Reader's Guide to Dylan Thomas,* which provides one of the best overall introductions to Thomas's work. It is an invaluable resource for readers seeking insight into Thomas and his poetry.

- Constantine FitzGibbon's 1965 biography, *The Life of Dylan Thomas,* provides a compassionate portrait of Thomas's life and reveals much about the sources and complexity of his poetry.

- *The Land Remembers: A View of Wales,* by Gywn Williams, provides a clear history of the complex background of Welsh culture and society. This is a 1977 book from Faber & Faber.

- In his 1960 work, *A Casebook on Dylan Thomas,* John Malcolm Brinnan has collected essays in which some of the most prominent writers and critics of the twentieth century discuss Thomas's poetry.

---

say, Kushner describes how "The Force That through the Green Fuse Drives the Flower" "can be read as an ode to life or a meditation on death."

A legend. That's what Dylan Thomas remains for the thousands of people who heard him read during several U.S. lecture tours in the 1950s. Thomas's trance-inducing, powerful voice, which rolled *r*s and trilled *l*s, has been described by dozens of enthralled American writers and also chronicled by all kinds of ordinary folks who felt personally touched by a genius. In those electrifying readings, Thomas reportedly began by reading poems by greats like William Butler Yeats and T.S. Eliot and then moved on to his own work.

But the hypnotizing "genius effect" of Thomas the man had an equally well-chronicled downside. His trouble with alcohol and his often embarrassing tendency to pursue very young women has also been detailed by a variety of literary types. All this background information, however, pales next to the poems themselves. What matters is the words in front of us, the work the man left before he died at age thirty-nine in an emergency room in New York City, a casualty of alcoholism.

"The Force That through the Green Fuse Drives The Flower" is one of Thomas's most famous poems, and it is propelled by his trademark lush, gorgeous sound. The ear is king for Thomas, and the immediate first impression this poem gives is a rush of consonants, kneaded into a relatively strict yet graceful form that Thomas created for the occasion.

Thomas's early critics often berated his work as difficult and obscure. Here, it's possible to read the entire poem several times through, utterly in love with the sound of it, without understanding a word. This confusion requires a global look at the poem's structure, followed by slow first impressions and a grasp toward meaning. While Thomas may not be easy, he is certainly comprehensible.

First, a look at overall form. Thomas veered between strict and lovely villanelles like "Do Not Go Gentle into That Good Night" and rifts into free verse. Here, he falls somewhere in between with a

---

form that has a little flexibility. The first four stanzas each have five lines. Each of the first four stanzas has a second line which is split by a semicolon or comma, followed by a much shorter third line. The last stanza is a couplet, for a total of twenty-two lines.

Right from the title, which doubles as the first line, there is a palpable power here, an obvious comfort with the big subjects—another Thomas hallmark. Birth, death, and sex are his themes, and he frequently refers to all three in a single poem. Above all, poetry itself is his terrain, and the beauty of letters, consonants, vowels, and the life they depict is his great obsession.

Thus the title and the first line are about power—both poetic power and the power of the world's beauty. *Force, fuse, drives,* and *blasts* are all cyclical, whooshing words. *Age,* also appearing in the first stanza, establishes that this is a big poem, one that aims for the fences. Against this huge, complex backdrop of a sweeping look at the entire world is the rather small "I," who is "dumb to mouth"—a speechless speaker.

But also from the start there is a definite density to the poem, along with that sense of known destiny. The words are piled on thickly, as are their connotations. Thomas is a poet of double meanings, and this poem is a classic example:

> The force that through the green fuse drives the
>   flower
> Drives my green age; That blasts the roots of trees
> Is my destroyer.

The force that brings life to the flower and to the trees is the same force that "destroys"—or brings death. This idea repeats throughout the poem, as each stanza presents a variation on the theme of a huge force that both gives life and removes it. Despite all of the power of the poet to notice something as magnificent as "the force that through the green fuse drives the flower," or "the force that drives the water through the rocks," or "the hand that whirls the water," he still feels inadequate. He still feels "dumb to mouth" or "dumb to tell."

While this feeling of inadequacy is clearly expressed, readers cannot help but notice the tour-de-force of sound, which indicates that the poet was anything but inadequate at his work. Thomas, however, operated by different standards. In an interesting piece written decades after Thomas's death, well-known poet Donald Hall told of talking to Thomas and praising his work. Thomas was not pleased with Hall's praise and answered that only

> *The ear is king for Thomas, and the immediate first impression this poem gives is a rush of consonants, kneaded into a relatively strict yet graceful form that Thomas created for the occasion."*

three of his poems were good. As Hall explained, Thomas compared himself to greats such as Yeats and Hardy, so in his mind, he was always coming up short. And so the only two-line stanza here again emphasizes that "I am dumb"—that huge helplessness and inadequacy of the poet against the great world.

As is typical in a Thomas poem, a few words repeat throughout, giving the poem both structure and rhythm—and making it easy to memorize. *Force, drives,* and *dumb* show up again and again, as do related words that share a consonant with them, such as *dries* next to *drives.*

Many words are related to death, though death itself is never named. *My green age, destroyer,* and *youth* are mentioned right in the first stanza. In the third stanza, *shroud, hangman,* and *quicksand* are introduced. By the fourth stanza, *time* and *heaven* come in, and in the penultimate two-line stanza, *tomb, sheet,* and the *same crooked worm* have made their way in.

It is possible to read the poem as a meditation on death, but it is also possible to read the same poem as an ode to the glory of life. British literary editor Anthony Thwaite wrote that Thomas believed that beings begin to die the moment they are born and that all of his poems express this idea. Thus Thomas's interest in death is the same as his interest in birth—all life leads toward that final ending.

Thomas, however, is not just a poet of thick sounds, with like letters piled one on top of the other. He is also a poet of layers, of thick meanings. Half an hour spent with a dictionary reveals an interesting undercurrent to the poem. Many of the words here have secondary nautical meanings.

Fuse, shroud, and *lime* are all words related to the sea.

In fact, water itself is a major force in the poem, beginning in the second stanza.

> The force that drives the water through the rocks
> Drives my red blood; that dries the mouthing
>   streams
> Turns mine to wax.
> And I am dumb to mouth unto my veins
> How at the mountain spring the same mouth sucks.

By stanza three the water imagery has reached full force:

> The hand that whirls the water in the pool
> Stirs the quicksand; that ropes the blowing wind
> Hauls my shroud sail.

By the fourth stanza, "love drips and gathers." This view of water as life-giver and life-taker is related to the cyclical view of both life and water expressed in Ecclesiastes and quoted in the epigraph to Ernest Hemingway's 1926 novel *The Sun Also Rises,* published a few years before "The Force That through the Green Fuse Drives the Flower":

> All the rivers run into the sea; yet the sea is not full;
> unto the place whence the rivers came, thither they
> return again.

Much of Thomas's poetry sounds prophetic, with a span and largeness that, to a certain extent, draws on the Bible—the original bastion of double meanings that have occupied scholars for centuries. Practically every word here can be read in at least two ways. In this poem which can be read as an ode to life or a meditation on death, a key example of how one word packs two divergent possibilities is *leech.* A leech, according to the *Shorter Oxford Dictionary,* can be either a rapacious, exploitative, blood-sucking person or animal—or it can be a physician or a healer. Like water, or the mysterious "force" blasting through the poem, nearly every word carries the possibility of connoting either death or life. And in another twist, *leech* also has a nautical meaning—the vertical edge of a square sail.

All of these meanings seem to prove the early critics wrong. If Thomas's poetry seems difficult, it is not because of a lack of meaning but rather because of an abundance of meaning. In creating layers of possibility within a brief twenty-two-line poem, Thomas has—despite all the self-deprecating remarks about being "dumb to tell" and even "dumb to mouth"—succeeded in his mission of capturing life in words. The memorable, water-like rush of sound creates a "force" that beautifully mimics the brute power and frequently baffling ten-

dencies of the natural phenomena the poem describes. In its thick twists and turns that somehow plough forward, Thomas's artful explosion of sound mirrors life itself.

Source: Aviya Kushner, in an essay for *Poetry for Students,* Gale Group, 2000.

Bruce Meyer

Bruce Meyer is the director of the creative writing program at the University of Toronto. He has taught at several Canadian universities and is the author of three collections of poetry. In the following essay, Meyer explains how Thomas "attempts to capture a portrait, in miniature, of the scope of life itself."

There is an overwhelming sense of the emphatic that pervades Dylan Thomas's poetry. There is a feeling of passionate insistence that results from his use of an elliptical syntax, where nouns and their accompanying adjectives work against the preconceived notions of phraseology not only to express but to plead for their subject matter. He rarely addresses his subject matter frontally; instead he talks around his issues and concerns by inverting the expected relationships between nouns and adjectives and by describing the energy and the processes behind an idea rather than just the elements that comprise the action. This approach to poetry refocuses the reader's attention away from the "things" of a poem's content and onto the actions, processes and verbs to the point where it can be said that Dylan Thomas is a poet who is fascinated by the inner workings, the deep energies and the intense modus operandi that lie behind both human and natural events.

"The Force That through the Green Fuse Drives the Flower" is a good example of Thomas's poetry of process. What emerges from the poem is not simply an examination of the botanical life force that makes a flower bloom, but the connectedness of that same life-energy between all living things. The poem starts with an inquiry into what "drives the flower"—life itself—and ends with an understanding that the same active presence in the world inhabits "the same crooked worm" that eats his shroud in death. What is evident throughout the rhetorical movement of the poem is not just the connectedness of things but the strange, paradoxical mystery behind the blurred relationship between life and death. Between the alpha and omega of this poem, Thomas attempts to capture a portrait, in miniature, of the scope of life itself. This is a tall order for such a short poem. Indeed, it is a tour de force of sorts, where the reader is asked to make large leaps of logic between a very disparate set of images within the poem's system; yet what must be recognized is that Thomas's poem is not operating by linear logic per se but by a system of imaginative "leaps" and gaps (created through his metaphors and his unique syntax).

To understand how the poem works rhetorically and how it operates as a piece that plays upon the paradox between what we know and what we do not understand, we have to go all the way back to the way texts were read in the Middle Ages. In medieval times, especially in the context of Romance literature, the reader was expected to approach the text on four levels. The first level, the literal reading, simply asked the question "what is happening?" The literal reading was meant to establish narrative, events, and settings. The second level, the symbolic reading, asked the reader to examine the images and perceive the range of possibilities and specific associations that certain objects or situations represented. The third level, the allegorical reading, demanded that the reader examine the dynamics of a situation and find parallels in other stories where the moral attributes from, say, a biblical story could be applied to the specific situation in the text. The first three levels of reading were intended to help the reader understand the logical and moral meaning of the text. But a final demand was usually placed upon the reader, a demand that required the reader's mind to leap beyond logic and make emotional, spiritual and even mystical connections to sizable abstract concepts such as truth, God, faith, and love. This fourth level was called the anagogic reading. It was meant to take the reader beyond the text and into a deep sense of comprehension, where the reading took on profound resonances. Dante constructed his *Divine Comedy* to be read in this fashion, as did the authors of such medieval Romances as *The Quest of the Holy Grail.* It was the approach that was used to interpret passages from the Bible and formed the basis of Scholastic theological arguments and critiques.

Thomas's poem asks the reader to make a whole series of anagogic leaps. In the first stanza, the persona says that "the force that through the green fuse drives the flower / Drives my green age; that blasts the roots of trees / Is my destroyer." In other words, he is paraphrasing T. S. Eliot's epigram to "East Coker" (a quote Eliot stole from Mary Queen of Scots' last words), "In my beginning is my end; in my end is my beginning." Thomas, in a very poetic if not roundabout man-

> *'The Force That through the Green Fuse Drives the Flower' is a good example of Thomas's poetry of process. What emerges from the poem is not simply an examination of the botanical life force that makes a flower bloom, but the connectedness of that same life-energy between all living things."*

ner, is attempting to show that the energy that animates nature is both the cause and the effect of things, that it propels both the beginning of life and the end of life. He asks the reader to make this connection, to see the beginning as the end and the end as the beginning, but as is often the impact of the anagogic moment, he confesses that "I am dumb to tell the crooked rose / My youth is bent by the same wintry fever." In other words, he can no more explain his perception of the way the universe operates to that most "eternal" of images, the rose, than he can explain that same understanding to himself. And in his universe, where explanations fail and so much has to go unsaid, the rose is not the "sacred, most inviolate rose" of Yeats's poetry, or even the beautiful love-object rose of Romance (as is the case in Guillaume de Lorris and Jean de Meun's *Romance of the Rose*) but a "crooked rose" that is bent and shaped by the same forces that act upon the persona.

He searches for an exemplum of the way the world operates and finds yet another useful parallel, an allegory, in "The force that drives the water through the rocks / Drives my red blood." His circulatory system is based upon the same tidal forces that make the oceans rise and fall with an almost uncanny predictability. What Thomas is again emphasizing is the cyclical manner in which a human being is caught up in the processes of nature—an idea not unlike another rendering of the same notion in his poem "Fern Hill."

In each of the stanzas he repeats the phrase "I am dumb." The process of explaining the relationship between mankind and nature is not something that can be explained. It is not a matter of science and rational discussion, and it is a question that exceeds the capabilities of poetic utterance. The mystery stems from the insistence that life leads to death and that everything, all human experience and all of nature, from the small life of a plant to the movement of the constellations in "heaven," is caught up in this unspeakable mystery. Yet the reader is left with the impression that, having witnessed this encapsulation of the machinations of totality, there is some sort of wisdom that can be drawn from it all. What Thomas is attempting to describe, on a very simple level, is life, the time-limited animating principle that governs all things. On a symbolic level, nature itself, in all its splendor and symbolic possibilities is really a series of perceptual reverberations—just as the stanzas of the poem are a series of reverberations—what the complex system of the cosmos is being driven by—a kind of mystical and elusive energy. On an allegorical level, the reader is meant to come away from the poem with the same sense of acceptance of the way things are that is offered by Ecclesiastes—a simple acceptance that to buy into life is also to buy out of it when things have run their course and that everything is all part of some wonderful divine operating system. But on the anagogic level, when the persona is struck "dumb" by it all, there is still an incredibly moving sense of wonder at the complexity of the universe and the subtle sense of empathy not only between the persona and his cosmos but between the reader and all of nature.

Thomas's sense of the emphatic is achieved not only through these repetitions of stanzas or through his rather unique phraseology or even through his rather cheeky attempts to encapsulate the meaning of life in a single poem, but through his linguistic desire to echo the "forces" of nature through the forcefulness of his argumentation and through the concreteness of his language and images. If he loses the reader in the final stanza, where he declares, "The lips of time leech to the fountain head; / Love drips and gathers, but the fallen blood / Shall claim her sores," he can be forgiven. He has already warned the reader that he is struck dumb by his comprehension of things, and by this point in the poem we are far beyond the point where the statements can be read logically. Like the persona, we are moved with a wonder we cannot fully explain.

Source: Bruce Meyer, in an essay for *Poetry for Students*, Gale Group, 2000.

Alice Van Wart

Alice Van Wart teaches literature and writing in the Department of Continuing Education at the University of Toronto. She has published two books of poetry and has written articles on modern and contemporary literature. In the following essay, Van Wart offers a biographical perspective on "The Force That through the Green Fuse Drives the Flower."

Poet Dylan Thomas was a legend in his lifetime, a legend that grew from both his success as a writer and from a certain notoriety. Though thought by some to be a genius and by others a charlatan, he was neither. Despite criticisms of obscurity and ambiguity, Thomas's literary abilities have never been in doubt. As a writer of poetry, drama, stories, and reminiscences, Thomas was one of the most popular poets of his day. Known for his extravagant rhetorical style, he was a lyrical writer who thought in unusual images. His work offered to many readers a welcome contrast to what was perceived as the stark desolation of much early modern poetry, such as T. S. Eliot's *Wasteland* and the early cantos of Ezra Pound, for example. In the early 1930s Thomas moved to London, where he lived a flamboyant life and where his work, helped along by his work in the mass medium of radio, gained wide public recognition. Despite the success of his work and a loving relationship with his wife, Caitlin, Thomas lived a turbulent life. He died an ignominious death from alcoholism, under sordid circumstances, at the young age of thirty-nine while working in New York.

Thomas was born in Swansea, Wales, to country people in 1914, the first year of the Great War. He grew up in an atmosphere of war, mass unemployment, amid industrial ugliness and social protest and lived through two world wars. It was an age when much of the poetry being written was poetry of social protest. There are few social references in Thomas's work, however, but this does not mean he had no social awareness; in fact, he was very much aware of the social realities of his time, but he was not politically minded, like his contemporaries W. H. Auden, C. Day Lewis, and Stephen Spender. Thomas celebrated life in his writing, inspired not by the world of politics or social unrest, but by the natural world itself. Though he was not a nature poet per se, his imagination was rooted in the countryside of Wales. In much the same way that James Joyce's writing is rooted in Dublin and William Faulkner's in Mississippi, Thomas's work was rooted in his recollections of the people, the places, and the language of south Wales and particularly of his happy early childhood there.

As Thomas matured, so did his awareness of his own human nature and his ability to present the human nature of other people in his work. At the core of his writing is his attempt to evoke the physicality of life. As a poet, Thomas had considerable technical skill and command of structure, but what finally makes his work powerful is the kinetic power of his language, his use of imagery, and his ability to evoke the sensations of experience—its very smells, sights, and sounds.

Thomas's themes were the universal ones of love, birth, death, and the mutability of physical existence. In a well-known early poem, "If I Were Tickled by the Rub of Love," the poet asks in the last stanza, "And what's the rub?" After supplying three possible answers he concludes: "I would be tickled by the rub that is: / Man be my metaphor." In the Note prefixed to his Collected Poems (1952), Thomas also writes, "These poems with all their crudities, doubts and confusion, are written for the love of Man and in praise of God, and I'd be a damn' fool if they weren't." Both remarks are telling; man as representative of the human condition is the final subject of all his writing.

For Thomas the human condition was a struggle from darkness to some form of light. The spiritual was not separate from the physical but contained in it. Though his poetry is not overtly spiritual, there is a pantheistic sense of the divine in the natural world. This sense is evident in "The Force That through the Green Fuse Drives the Flower," collected in his second volume of poetry, *Twenty-five Poems* (1936).

Thomas shows considerable technical skill in this poem to show the integral connection between the creative and the destructive forces in life. The poem turns on a single idea established in the first stanza and reiterated through each succeeding stanza. Composed of four five-line stanzas and two concluding lines, the poem conforms to a regular metrical and syntactical pattern, appropriate to conveying the single idea contained within the poem.

"The force" in the first line is "the green fuse" that "drives the flower." The action of the verb *drive* evokes the power behind "the green fuse." The image of "the green fuse" suggests an electrical current; it is what produces the green chloro-phyll of the plant, which will result in a flower. In this case the force is the energy from the sun, a power of irradiating energy that animates and brings the flower to life.

The enjambment between the first and second line connects the force that drives the flower to the force that "drives my green age." The repetition of the color green in "green fuse" and "green age" provides a correspondence between the two images. The energy of the green fuse is also the one behind the "green age." Green in this context, however, means unseasoned or unripe and points to the unformed youth of the poet. A semicolon completes the first syntactical unit connecting the two parts of the second line so that the force that "drives my green age" also "blasts the roots of trees" and "is my destroyer." The semicolon provides a stronger break than a comma, but it also connects the two images to the third line. The force associated with the green fuse and green age is the same one that "blasts the roots of trees."

The verb *blasts*, however, not only suggests the constructive force that drives the flower and the tree, but also a violent force with the potential to destroy. Another enjambment between the second and third lines connects "the force that blasts the roots of trees" to the short next line, "Is my destroyer." The dramatic shift from constructive to destructive force is emphasized by the metrical shift from the iambic pentameter of the first two lines to the iambic dimeter of the third. The effect creates a structural tension in the stanza that corresponds to and emphasizes the thematic tension.

The fourth line begins with the coordinating conjunction *and*, which connects the line syntactically to the preceding ones and to the final two lines of the stanza: "And I am dumb to tell the crooked rose / My youth is bent by the same wintry fever." The lines turn on the word *dumb*, suggesting the poet's inability to express what seems a paradox, to comprehend what is a fundamental fact of life—the force that gives also takes away. More fittingly, the flower is truly dumb in its cycle of flowering and death. The poet is aware that the force that makes the rose grow crooked will also end it in a "wintry fever." The oxymoron compresses the symbolic meaning of winter as death and the fever of the cycle that pushes the flower to its inevitable conclusion. The poet intuits that his "green age" is subject to the same "wintry fever," that it will bend his body too as he grows old.

The following three stanzas employ the same structural and metrical form to reiterate this dichotomy. In the second stanza, the force "that drives the water through the rocks" also "drives my red blood." The strength of the force, expressed through the repetition of the verb *drives*, is suggested in the image of water breaking through the rocks. Again, however, the same force that drives the water through the rocks also "dries the mouthing streams" and turns the healthy red blood of the poet "to wax." As in the first stanza, the third line creates contrast and tension between the healthy red blood of a living being and wax, a lifeless, insoluble substance suggestive of death.

The beginning of the fourth line repeats the phrase "And I am dumb," changing "to tell" in the first stanza to "to mouth unto my veins / How at the mountain spring the same mouth sucks." In the third line the image of "the mouthing streams" suggests a gushing spring in a mountain. Water is traditionally a symbol of the life-force. In the final line "the same mouth sucks" refers back to "the mouthing streams," but is also the force that sucks it dry. "I am dumb to mouth," on the other hand, simply means as it did in the first stanza the inability to speak, but again the poet comprehends "how at the mountain spring the same mouth sucks." The red blood that flows through the poet's veins giving him life will, like the water from the mountain spring, eventually dry up.

In the third stanza "the force" becomes "the hand that whirls the water in the pool." The force that makes the water whirl is not a hand but some physical power, the same one that "stirs the quicksand" or gives it its dangerous sucking property, the same force "that ropes the blowing wind." The image of quicksand again suggests a destructive force, one that "hauls my shroud sail." The isolated image of the shroud—a cloth wrapped around a body before it is buried—being blown by the wind is parallel to the destructive powers in the third lines of the previous two stanzas and is equated with death.

The final two lines—"And I am dumb to tell the hanging man / How of my clay is made the hangman's lime"—also work in a manner similar to those of the preceding stanzas. Yet there is a more concrete acknowledgment of the connection between the constructive and destructive natures of the force. The hanging man—literally, the man who hangs others—is a symbol of death. The body of the person hanged is placed in the "clay," which is associated with earth covering the dead. The breakdown of the body in the earth, however, enriches the soil and helps plants grow.

In the third stanza the cycle from birth to death has come full circle from the "green age" through the "wintry fever" and the "shroud" to "lime." The force here is regenerative, and the polarities of life and death are integrally connected: in life there is death, and death brings new life. In the final stanza the poet makes this paradox even more explicit. The force is referred to as "the lips of time." The image recalls the imagery of the second stanza. Like the mouth that sucks the mountain stream dry, the lips of time "leech to the fountain head." The fountain head, often equated with the source of inner life and spiritual energy, is where "love drips and gathers."

The image of the fountain head is also sexual, the source from which life pours forth. In this respect it echoes the image of "the mouthing streams," now associated with fertility and fecundity. The sensuous image of love dripping and gathering suggests the act of coitus and the spilling of semen, while "the fallen blood" suggests both the hymen breaking and the menstrual cycle, and "the fallen blood / Shall calm her sores" implies the bringing forth of new life through the sexual act. The final two lines of the stanza suggest a connection between the sexual and the cosmic, if not the spiritual. The lips of time that suck like a leech at the substance of life are ceaseless like the "weather's wind." The expansive image of time ticking "a heaven around the stars" suggests a never-ending process, since heaven and its stars are thought to be infinite.

The concluding lines of the poem connect the image of ceaseless time ticking a heaven around the stars back to the sexual act of love and to the regenerative process suggested in the third stanza. The lines begin by repeating the first six words of the last two lines of the fourth stanza: "And I am dumb to tell the lover's tomb / How at my sheet goes the same crooked worm." "The lover's tomb" is where the lovers will finally lie together after the "wintry fever." In this context, "fever" suggests the end of physical passion. The "crooked worm" echoes the image of "the crooked rose" and recalls the leech of time at the fountain head. The "crooked worm" now goes "at my sheet," with the implication being that, even though the sexual act may bring forth new life, the end of life is contained in conception, just as the death of a plant is contained within its seed. The "crooked worm" is both the phallus that contains the seed of life and the worm that eats away at it. As such it is the double image of regeneration and degeneration.

In his poem Thomas not only uses structural and metrical parallelism to convey his idea, but he also exploits the resources of figurative language to create a powerful incantatory effect. He uses repetition and alternates alliteration ("the force that drive my green fuse drives") with assonance ("And I am dumb") to heighten his diction; he uses strong active verbs such as *drives*, *blasts*, *whirls*, and *leech* to create a powerful dramatic effect; and he uses startling images such as *green fuse*, *green age*, *mouthing streams*, *shroud sail*, *weather's wind*, and *lover's tomb* and the oxymorons of *wintry fever* and *lover's tomb* as well as a pun in *the hangman's lime* to enhance and reinforce the contradictory nature behind "the force" that is, in fact, one and the same thing.

Source: Alice Van Wart, in an essay for *Poetry for Students*, Gale Group, 2000.

Sources

Jones, T. H., *Dylan Thomas,* London: Oliver and Boyd, 1966.

Maud, Ralph, in his *Entrances to Dylan Thomas's Poetry,* Pittsburgh: University of Pittsburgh Press, 1963, 175 p.

Rosenthal, M. L., "Exquisite Chaos: Thomas and the Others," in his *The Modern Poets: A Critical Introduction,* Oxford University Press, 1960, pp. 203-72.

Thomas, Dylan, *Collected Poems,* London: Dent, 1952, p. 163.

For Further Study

Ackerman, John, *Dylan Thomas: His Life and Work,* New York: Oxford University Press, 1964.
> The book discusses Welsh and Anglo-Welsh literature along with Thomas's role in both traditions.

Davies, Aneirin Talfan, *Dylan: Druid of the Broken Body,* Swansea: Christopher Davies, 1977.
> Davies analyzes Thomas's poetic craftsmanship as well as discussing major influences on his poetry.

Dodd, A. H., *A Short History of Wales,* London: B. T. Batsford Ltd., 1981.
> This concise history explains the development of Welsh culture and national pride throughout the centuries.

Kershner, R. B., *Dylan Thomas: The Poet and His Critics.* Chicago: American Library Association, 1976.
> Kershner focuses on the critical response to the major issues dealing with Thomas's life and poetry. The extensive list of references following each chapter provides a helpful resource for students.

Maud, Ralph, *Entrances to Dylan Thomas' Poetry.* Pittsburgh: University of Pittsburgh Press, 1963.
> In this excellent introductory source which analyzes each poem, Maud evaluates the poem's themes, structure, and unity.

Peach, Linden, *Ancestral Lines: Culture and Identity in the Work of Six Contemporary Poets,* Bridgend, Mid Glamorgan, Wales, Seren Books, 1993.
> Peach provides an interesting analysis of the influence of politics, history, myth, and culture on several poets, including Dylan Thomas.

Tedlock, E. W., *Dylan Thomas: The Legend and the Poet,* Westport, CT: Greenwood Press, 1960.
> This collection of biographical and critical essays attempts to summarize the most important aspects of Thomas's life and poetry.

Music Lessons

Mary Oliver

1979

Mary Oliver is usually and conveniently referred to as a New England nature or pastoral poet and thought to descend from a line of other New England pastoralist writers, from Thoreau to Robert Frost. "Music Lessons," from Oliver's third volume of poetry, *Twelve Moons* (1979), however, is somewhat uncharacteristic since its inspiration and situation begin in a house at a private music lesson where a teacher takes a break from teaching and plays for her probably younger student and for herself. Perhaps the poem documents a memory from Oliver's childhood.

In "Music Lessons" a teacher, perhaps growing tired with the student's fumblings or imperfections, decides to take over the keyboard. The music acts upon the student as challenge and adventure and upon the pianist as escape from domesticity and mortality. Quietly feminist and more loudly a paean to music, the title, "Music Lessons," is apropos in that the paean was, in its earliest known instance in *The Iliad* of Homer, a song praising and calling for Apollo, the *Paian,* or "healer." Apollo is the ancient Greek god of arts and civilization, and specifically, patron of music (whose instrument is the lyre which is also the name of the frame holding the strings of the piano). Music, Apollonian or otherwise, may not serve as healer of life's ills, but it does depict an act that seems to defy the duties of life and the inevitability of death—at least temporarily.

Author Biography

Mary Oliver was born September 10, 1935, in Maple Heights, Ohio, to Helen and Edward Oliver (a teacher). Oliver has described herself as a serious thirteen-year-old who wanted to write. At the age of fifteen, she wrote a letter to Norma Millay Ellis, the sister of the then recently-deceased Edna St. Vincent Millay to ask permission to visit Millay's home in upstate New York. This visit was followed by more and eventually a longer stay at which time Oliver assisted in organizing Millay's papers. The influence of Millay upon Oliver is apparent, and similarities can be seen in the lives of Millay and Oliver: both were familiar with country life, studied at Vassar, and moved in the bohemian circles of Provincetown, Massachusetts. Oliver studied at Ohio State University from 1955-56, and then at Vassar from 1956-57. Since then, she has had a series of scholarly engagements at various academic institutions including Case Western Reserve University, Sweet Briar College, and Duke University. Her last appointment, in 1996, was to the Catharine Osgood Foster Chair for Distinguished Teaching at Bennington College. In 1998, Oliver completed a second poetry handbook, *Rules for the Dance,* on metrical poetry to compliment *A Poetry Handbook* (1994), which discussed free, as well as metered, verse. Oliver is writing another volume of essays titled *Winter Hours,* which she expects to publish in 1999. Among Oliver's many honors are a National Endowment for the Arts Fellowship (1972), a Guggenheim Foundation Fellowship (1980), and an American Academy and Institute of Arts and Letters Achievement Award (1983). In 1984 Oliver was the recipient of the Pulitzer Prize for her volume of poetry, *American Primitive* (1983). Another book of poems, *House of Light* (1990) won both the Christopher Award and the L. L. Winship Award in 1991, and *New and Selected Poems* (1992) won the National Book Award that same year.

Mary Oliver

vanished as new shapes formed. Sound
became music, and music a white
scarp for the listener to climb

alone. I leaped rock over rock to the top
and found myself waiting, transformed,   10
and still she played, her eyes luminous and willful,
her pinned hair failing down—

forgetting me, the house, the neat green yard,
she fled in that lick of flame all tedious bonds;
supper, the duties of flesh and home,   15
the knife at the throat, the death in the metronome.

Poem Text

Sometimes, in the middle of the lesson,
we exchanged places. She would gaze a moment at
   her hands
spread over the keys; then the small house with its
   knickknacks,
its shut windows,

its photographs of her sons and the serious   5
   husband,

Poem Summary

Lines 1-3:

From the title we know this is a music "lesson" (line 1). The first line immediately alerts the reader to a shift in the action when the narrator says "Sometimes, in the middle ..." (line 1) "we exchanged places" (line 2). The reader can guess that the student and the teacher are the "we." And perhaps this is a private lesson. Oliver further evokes a shift in the reader's experience by starting the poem as if it were the middle of a larger piece. At this point, the teacher takes her place at the keyboard, and the reader can safely conclude that the poem's narrator is the student when the teacher prepares herself before playing as "She would gaze a moment at her hands / spread over the keys" (line 2).

Lines 3-6:

In concentration and in playing, the piano teacher's house vanishes from her mind, or from another perspective, she escapes her home as it vanishes from her mind. The parts of the house the narrator mentions suggest the teacher's rather insular life focused on family and home.

Lines 6-9:

What takes the place of house and home is sound and then music as the sound begins to become shapely, become an object, an object the student-narrator describes as a "scarp," also known as an "escarpment," a wall of high rocks, a cliff. The musical piece, as scarp, is white to give it the insubstantiality of an imagined thing and give it a positive sense as well. The narrator also points out that this scarp can only be climbed "alone" (line 9), as if listening to a piece of music were like scaling a cliff. The word *scale,* in fact, could have been what connected a musical piece on one hand with the cliff on the other.

Lines 9-10:

The metaphor might now become difficult to follow, for instead of climbing a wall of music to the top, the narrator is leaping over rocks to the top. Perhaps after climbing awhile, the way to the very top became a gentle incline that could have been run or walked? Whatever the case, the narrator arrives at the top transformed, and waits as if she had reached the destination before her teacher, and as if she must now wait for her teacher to catch up. It is possible that the student has realized, before the musical piece ends, where it is going and how it will get there. The student has learned something about music by listening as well as by playing.

Lines 11-12:

The teacher, in these lines, is losing herself to the music, becoming, as they say, wild and abandoned, quite a different thing than what most people think of when they think "piano teacher," an image that may conjure up something like "librarian." The loosening of the hair is the loosening of bonds in general.

Lines 13-16:

But if the student is waiting for the piano teacher to meet her, the teacher seems to have for-

gotten her student, perhaps has even forgotten herself in her playing. Both teacher and student appear to have transcended their circumstances in different ways (playing and listening) but by experiencing the same piece of music. A difference between them, however, remains: while the teacher has figuratively transcended "the duties of flesh and home" and even danger and death, the student apparently has not, for she notices—in the metronome—time moving relentlessly toward death. The music that had become the pinnacle of living (adventure and challenge) now becomes a reminder of death, which the student connects with the metronome that describes an arc like the scythe of Time, or a pendulum connected to a morbid clock just beneath the music.

Themes

Creativity and Imagination

Several layers of creativity and imagination are at work in "Music Lessons": the composer having created a musical composition out of his/her imagination; the pianist recreating the score in her imagination and on the keyboard; and the listener processing the music in her imagination to create a poem that readers imagine, and may one day play a part in reimagining and creating a further object of attention. The playing of a piece of music inspires in the student an image of rockclimbing, and the metronome provokes her to imagine death. Other things inspire their opposite in a kind of counterpoint: inside inspires imaginings of outside, relative inactivity of the lower torso inspires imaginings of intense physical activity of the same area, culture (music) inspires an image in nature, constant motion of the metronome inspires the stillness of death. And this is just the point of the poem: that the playing of music allows one to transcend one's circumstances, to flee to, in many cases, to what seems farthest, most opposite. The imagination is under no commandment to compromise its desire, can travel as far as it wants to get what it needs to soothe lived experience. The teacher uses the piano, a time machine, to do her travelling, to leave her domestic circumstances and duties, even leave the confines of her own body so she can escape death. But while the teacher is able to escape her circumstances, empty out her existence in a kind of heavenly death that is the furthest state away from morbidity, the student cannot forget (that incessant metronome!) what music is: a stalling, a delay, a detour along the way to a death whose time it tries to delay with imagination and creativity.

Time

A metronome is a time machine, a serious time machine unlike the more playful time machine, the piano. A metronome can be adjusted to go faster or slower; it cannot be played; it either works or it does not. While the piano transports teacher and student to another place and another time—a time devoid of responsibility and duty, a time devoid of time—the metronome brings the student back to the teacher's insular home, to a reminder of time passing (already indicated with family photos and knickknacks), of time, like a shadow at the end of day, lengthening behind and shortening ahead. The metronome is a pendulum without a clock. A clock can be a kind of taskmaster keeping one from thinking of death because of its marking of appointments and opportunities. The metronome, however, is a more severe taskmaster than the clock, for no matter how one tries to play with or around the time of the metronome one inevitably returns to it, the mind numbing, tick-tocking of time passing. In a musical piece played on the piano one knows or can find out where one is either in the piece or on the piano. But with the metronome one might as well be here as there. Finally, while piano and composition allow one to know where one is, the effect can be a feeling of timelessness in the best sense of the word: time without concern. But the metronome produces no sense of timelessness, only incessant and eternal monotony, marking time without reason, here (tick) and there (tock) as different places without difference.

Death

Both piano and metronome mark time but only the piano yields timelessness: the piano produces the timelessness of a pleasurable, transcendent state of death while the metronome produces never-ending time in a miserable and mired state of hellish death. This may be the reason for Oliver's, or if you must, the student's association of the metronome with death, and the piano with vigorous activity allowing one to forget time. The metronome is a kind of upside down or standing pendulum, a pendulum that might remind one of Poe's story "The Pit and the Pendulum" (1842), where the pendulum is fitted with a blade like Oliver's "knife at the throat." Or the metronome might remind one of a pendulum inverted so as to give primacy to the constant beating of time. The metronome, then, is both a symbol of terror and

Topics for Further Study

- Imagine the metronome as a symbol of life and the piano as an object of death. Write a small essay on how these objects might be so configured. For help, see the Themes section where the opposite is argued.

- Do research on the word *scale,* on its derivations and meanings and how those meanings might be related and how understanding the word might help in a discussion of this poem.

- Attempt to tie "Music Lessons" to the history of the 1970s supplied above, or to your own research or knowledge of the seventies. While this might seem futile in illuminating Oliver's (timeless and timefilled) poem, it can be done and might be further effectual for tying other objects and events to their times.

eternal boredom. But one might conclude—as does Oliver—that the metronome is as necessary an evil for the joys of music-making as death is necessary to produce and maintain life. Music reminds us of time, time reminds us of life and death, and life and death provoke many of us to seek transcendence from time through a medium such as music— founded, paradoxically, on time. If the paradox works, it is because people usually find in music a greater amount of life than death.

Style

"Music Lessons" is a free verse poem, that is a poem without rhyme (except the last two lines whose rhyming promotes finality) and without regular meter. But the poem does have a kind of 4/4 time—a common time signature in music—since it has four stanzas of four lines (quatrains). The poem makes occasional use of enjambment as in lines 6-7 and 7-8, but why? As Mary Oliver writes in *A Poetry Handbook:* (1994) "We leap with more energy over a ditch than over no ditch." But an additional reason is that Oliver's enjambed lines make "Music Lessons" consistent, since no line, except the last, ends in the full stop of a period. Such a technique keeps the reader moving, even over gaps (the ends of lines), somewhat like music, an art-form that does not allow the listener to speed or slow the pace. Or for that matter, like film or dance which move at their own speed over gaps or pauses and must be followed or lost. Unlike the usual experience of reading (or of viewing fine art) where one has some choice in pacing, "Music Lessons" might be attempting the character of the more "coercive" arts (film, music, dance) by making us leap whether we are ready or not. In this way, "Music Lessons" is more like a poem being read to us, turning it into a "coercive" experience like heard music and watched film, rather than the less coercive experience of reading it ourselves.

"Music Lessons" is heavy with sibilants, the sound perhaps evolving out of the writing of the poem and then developed further to help keep the poem a unified whole. If there is another reason why whispering, buzzing, and hissing sibilants, say, instead of liquids, were employed it might be their connection to vibration, especially the vibration of the strings in the piano. Once in a while, the poem also employs assonance, as in "rock over rock to the top" or "neat green," which seem little more than pleasurable sound symmetries to keep one interested in reading.

To illuminate the free verse aspects of "Music Lessons," it seems best to quote Oliver on free verse. The following passages are taken from her work of criticism, *A Poetry Handbook:* "The free-verse poem sets up, in terms of sound and line, a premise or an expectation, and then, before the poem finishes, it makes a good response to this premise. This is the poem's design. What it sets up in the beginning it sings back to, all the way, attaining a *felt* integrity." This, by the way, is often a characteristic of metrical verse, as well. But what is far less characteristic of metered verse is Oliver's statement about the tone of a free-verse poem. This has to do with poetry changing, in modern times, from metered to free verse because of the onset of printing which produced a trend away from hearing a poem read in performance to reading a poem oneself, alone. In reading poetry alone, Oliver says, "What was needed was a line which, when read, would feel as spontaneous, as true to the moment, as talk in the street, or talk between friends in one's own house…. Speech entered the poem. The poem was no longer a lecture, it was time spent with a friend. Its music was the music of conversation."

Free verse's more conversational feel then, might be said to fill the gap left by the increasing individuation, privacy, and loneliness of lived life, including the loneliness always threatening reading (and writing).

Historical Context

From the Kent State shootings (1970), to the Watergate scandal (1972-74), to the end of the Vietnam War (1965-73), to the Three Mile Island disaster (1979) and the Iran hostage crisis (1979), the dominant key of seventies America can be characterized as skepticism—about the rightness of U.S. expansionism on the one hand, and about possibilities for substantive change in U.S. domestic affairs on the other. Both instances of scepticism point to the decade's overall disenchantment with big government, a feeling which, by the nineties, would split into a left-winged critique of big corporations thought to control big government with big money, and a right-winged reaction against big government (controlled by international elements?) thought to infringe on the rights of individual American citizens. The American seventies, from other perspectives, however, wore an expression hard to read because it was in transition; from this perspective, the seventies was less a decade with its own cultural countenance than one with a slowly changing expression: from an extrovert sixties—angry and anguished—to an introvert eighties—withdrawn and self-centered. Some historians, unwilling to give the 1970s its due, demarcate 1965-75 as "the sixties," even call the seventies the "five-year decade."

The most obvious blow to common political assumptions in the seventies was the defeat (in terms of traditional twentieth-century warfare) of the United States in the Vietnam War, a defeat covered up by the Nixon administration with a 1973 "peace treaty." The war forced Americans to begin to question two basic assumptions about their place vis a vis the world. The first—in place since at least the 1840s—assumed that the United States possessed the world's best form of government. The second held that American corporate capitalism was the best method of economic organization and should control a world still full of inefficiency. By the seventies, Nixon knew that the strategy of communist containment, the Cold War, and the Vietnam War was overextending U.S. resources, crippling U.S. competitiveness with nonmilitary

Compare & Contrast

- **1979:** A new study linked lead in children's blood, even at low levels, with lower intelligence scores. A ban on lead-containing paint in 1980, and successively lower maximum acceptable lead blood levels followed. Lead had been banned in Europe in the 1950s.

  June, 1999: Several cities across the U.S. sue companies for using lead in house paint. Hiring lawyers fresh from state victories over big tobacco companies, cities claim that the paint companies were well aware of lead's dangers.

- **1979:** Shah Mohammed Reza Pahlevi fled Iran on January 16, appointing Shahpur Bakhtiar prime minister of a new democratic government. But Ayatollah Rhuollah Khomeini returned to Iran on February 1 and quickly took power. Iran took 66 American hostages at the Tehran embassy on November 7 and held 52 of them for 444 days, winning several concessions from the U.S. and greatly harming American prestige and the Carter presidency.

  June, 1999: Tens of thousands of Iranians crowd the mausoleum of the former Ayatollah to commemorate the tenth anniversary of his death.

- **1979:** At the Three Mile Island nuclear plant near Middletown, Pennsylvania, a partial core meltdown occurs on March 28 after equipment failures and human errors caused overheating of the reactor. A major containment-breaching explosion like what happened at Chernobyl in 1986 was averted. The state ordered the evacuation of pregnant women and children nearby. After this event no new U.S. orders for nuclear plants were placed, and those ordered after 1973 were canceled.

  1999: A leading U.S. scientific organization produces new findings supporting the suitability of Nevada's Yucca Mountain nuclear site for the long-term storage of spent nuclear fuel. The reason for the news is that water is not expected—based on research into the geologic past of the site—to seep into the area.

- **1979:** Charles Mingus (b. 1922), a leading jazz composer, bandleader, and bassist, is found dead.

  1999: New Jersey mother, wife, and composer Melinda Wagner receives the Pulitzer Prize for music.

---

nations like Japan and Germany, and turning the domestic sphere into a war zone with police and national guard on one side, anti-war protesters on the other. The war forced the American coalition of big business and big government to abandon grand designs for a world economy and re-concentrate itself on maintaining competitiveness in an increasingly competitive world—that is, if it wanted to remain stable and prosperous at home.

The seventies was a decade of self-centeredness (the "me decade" was a term coined by author Tom Wolfe in 1976). The characterization was a response to magazines, paperbacks, pop music, television, and movies filled with discussions of human sensitivity and feelings. Looking good, feeling right, and eating healthy became ritualistic preoccupations of increasing numbers of people.

Folksingers moved from protest songs to confessional ballads. The psychologist Heinz Kohut made the narcissistic personality the focus of his clinical study; John Ashbery published his Pulitzer Prize-winning poetry collection *Self-Portrait in a Convex Mirror;* cultural critics such as Christopher Lasch and Daniel Bell weighed in against narcissism in culture; even artists such as Vito Acconci's manipulation of his skin, and Lucas Samaras's resourceful Polaroid self-portraiture gave expression to the period's self-obsession. But running counter to the skepticism and self-centeredness of the seventies was an inconsistency: the environmental movement was picking up strength (even to the point that some think that twentieth-century environmentalism began with the first Earth Day in 1970, rather than 1962, the year Rachel Carson's

Silent Spring was published). While it can be convincingly argued that Americans never escaped the me decade with regard to the environment-damaged nature still being understood primarily as an entity *for us,* as either a spectacle for human entertainment, or threat to human health, Americans did become apprised of at least some of the damage being done to plants, animals, land, and of course, themselves, from Love Canal to Three Mile Island to numerous publicized oil spills, including the largest ever near Trinidad and Tobago (97 million gallons). The American public's political and social response was tremendous: Earthfirst!, Greenpeace, Worldwatch, The Cousteau Society, League of Conservation Voters, National Resources Defense Council, and Ralph Nader's PIRGs (Public Interest Research Groups) were established. Even the federal government wanted to show its concern by establishing the Environmental Protection Agency (1970), passing the Endangered Species Act (1973), and passing emendations to strengthen the Clean Air and Clean Water Acts (1977). But though the song of the environmental seventies was played with passion and conviction, Americans continued to adhere to life-as-usual, never escaping me-ness, arguably the most lasting legacy of the seventies and before.

Critical Overview

Robert DeMott writes that Oliver, along with Theodore Roethke and Galway Kinnell, is "sensitive to visitations by the 'dark things' of the wood." Two characteristics emerge here: that Oliver is a poet of death and of nature. But Diane Wakoski notices that "If Oliver writes of 'dark things,' they are friendly, benevolent dark things. Even her vision of death is gentle, pastoral and haunting, rather than fearful or violent." Perhaps Wakoski forgot the "knife at the throat" in "Music Lessons."

As to nature, the ambitious collection of fifty-one poems entitled *Twelve Moons* (1979), from which "Music Lessons" comes, primarily concentrates on the imagery and cycles of nature, including twelve poems dedicated to different lunar phases. Oliver celebrates the natural cycles of birth, decay, and death as flourishing in all life. In the poetic landscape of Oliver's mythic worlds, starry realms are connected to the realms of flora and fauna, including humans. The poet invites the reader to become engulfed in the natural world, become connected to all things, all creatures. "Music

Lessons" generally fits this description since the teacher escapes the world of domestic culture and the student immerses herself in climbing the scarp. But it is through music that such an immersion is made. "Music Lessons" is therefore less a nature poem of connection than a culture poem of connection. In "Music Lessons" music links player and listener to human movement, the outside, to life, to death. Jean B. Alford writes that "To Oliver, man's inward struggles to be immortal through art, work, or love do not cancel mortal existence but rather create a fleeting sense of stay. In 'Music Lessons,' when the teacher takes over the piano, 'sound becomes music' that flees 'all tedious bonds: / supper, the duties of flesh and home, / the knife at the throat, the death in the metronome.' The grand finale, though, is only a momentary transformation." In Alford's eyes, though the music in "Music Lessons" fills the pupil with images of life lived at the frontiers, in the end, she is brought back to its connection with the ultimate unknown and unexplored frontier: death. Here, it might only be added that while the piano catapults the student into life, when it stops, the ticktock of death in the metronome is all that is audible. In a way, "Music Lessons" is the ultimate unsentimental culture poem, for while it romanticizes music, and in so doing culture, the poem also exposes culture's underbelly—the pulse—which in one direction indicates life, while in the other it points to death. This is only to say that culture emerged but never escaped from nature.

Criticism

Alice Van Wart

Alice Van Wart teaches literature and writing in the Department of Continuing Education at the University of Toronto. She has published two books of poetry and has written articles on modern and contemporary literature. In the following essay, Van Wart analyzes the relationship between the teacher and student in "Music Lessons" while elaborating on Oliver's exploration into human nature (and nature) and the fleeting transcendence of life's tedious experiences inspired by the medium of music (or culture) and its playing.

Mary Oliver caught the attention of the public with her third collection of poetry, *American Primitive,* for which she won the Pulitzer Prize in 1984. The poems in this collection pulse with the drama of human life and nature, and with wit, love, yearning and grief, qualities that define Oliver's poetry. Writing on a wide range of subjects in both free verse and in the traditional discipline of rhyme and meter, her poems are immediately accessible and flawless in their craft.

Oliver's poetry provides an intimate exploration of nature and human relationships. She sees in life an ancient need for union both with the natural world and other people. Profoundly aware of nature's unaffected beauty, she never sentimentalizes it and though well aware of the dark side of life she never loses sight of the rich physical landscape we inhabit—its beauty, its terror, and its persistent promise of renewal. Oliver's poems illuminate by revealing to us anew the world we live in, but often do not see or feel.

There is a persistent spiritual quality in her work that is neither pantheist nor transcendental in nature, but a result of the poet's sense of the vital force that animates life. "Music Lessons," published in *Contemporary American Poetry* (edited by A. Polin Jr., Houghton Mifflin, 1985) and never collected into a book reveals the poet's awareness of her need to be close to the intense vital forces of life. In this economical poem of four quatrains using image, enjambment, contrast, and opposition, Oliver interweaves subject and technique to reveal the poet's unconscious fear of losing her own intense, passionate engagement with life.

At the center of the poem is the relationship between the student and the teacher. The portrait the poet creates of her music teacher is based on what she thought were the opposing, antithetical qualities she saw in her teacher when she was a music student. In the first part of the poem the poet presents her teacher as someone who lives in a "small house" full of "knickknacks" with her sons and "serious husband," giving an impression of a prim and serious woman. The images convey a sense of stiffness and stuffiness. On the few occasions when the student and teacher "sometimes" exchanged places "in the middle of a lesson," and the teacher played for the student, the poet became aware of another side of her teacher.

The second part of the poem shows the poet's picture of the teacher as she played on, forgetting her student, and her stiff role as a teacher fell away, as does her "pinned hair." She forgets "the house, the neat green yard;" her eyes became "luminous and willful." The student sees her teacher transformed by the passion she feels in her playing for the music, what the poet calls "that lick of flame."

What Do I Read Next?

- *Aesthetic Theory* (1970), by Theodor Adorno is a philosophical treatise by the most important thinker of the Frankfurt School. Adorno was a musician and composer as well as one the twentieth century's greatest theoreticians. A great deal in this volume addresses the meanings of music.

- *Critical Theory and Performance,* edited by Janelle G. Reinelt and Joseph R. Roach is an anthology of essays about performance under the rubrics of cultural studies, semiotics and deconstruction, post-Marxism, feminism, theater history, psychoanalysis, and philosophy.

- *An Equal Music* by Vikram Seth is a wonderful novel about a string quartet and the experience of music. Seth is also a poet.

- *Godel Escher Bach: An Eternal Golden Braid* by Douglas R. Hofstadter (1979) is a consistently engaging and challenging meditation on puzzles and paradoxes of logic, mathematics, physics, music, art, and philosophy, presented in a series of essays and dialogues. The book won the 1979 Pulitzer Prize.

As a student the poet saw her as escaping "the knife at the throat, the death in the metronome." Contained in the structure of the poem, however, is not just the sense of the teacher being surveyed by the student, but also the poet's unconscious response to her teacher and her music lessons.

This is not a usual music lesson as the poet makes clear by their exchanged position. Usually it was the poet, who as a student "would gaze a moment at her hands / spread over the keys" and look about the room before beginning to play. Now it is the teacher who looks about "the small house with its knickknacks" and "its shut windows." The shortened final line of the first stanza draws attention to the "shut windows," suggesting a tight, closed atmosphere that is airless and stuffy. The enjambment between the first and second stanza shows the poet's recollection of her response to the room, as well as her perceptions of her teacher's life. It is clear, however, that the responses are not those of the teacher but of the student. Before beginning her lesson, it is the student who noticed the "photographs of her sons and the serious husband."

The continuation of the first line of the second quatrain into the second line shows the poet's response to her teacher when the teacher begins to play. The knickknacks, the shut windows, and the photographs suddenly "vanished," and in their place "new shapes formed." By placing the active verb "vanished" at the beginning of the second line, the poet reinforces the sudden shift in focus from the teacher to the poet as the student.

When the teacher begins her playing the trivial, domestic details of the teacher's life that have been bothering the student disappear. Her focus changes from the details of her teacher's life to the sound of the music. Her previous thoughts vanish as "new shapes formed. / Sound" and as "Sound / became music." Clearly it is the student, not the teacher, who saw "new shapes formed." By ending the second line with "sound" and using an enjambment between the second and third line, the focus turns into the interior consciousness of the student.

As she listens to her teacher's playing, the student's mind takes off in a flight of fancy. The music becomes "a white / Scarp for the listener to climb." Initially the image of the "white scarp" seems an unlikely one to describe the student's response, but in the context of the second stanza, with its suggestion of rugged, fractured cliffs, the image is apt. It perfectly reveals the student's inner consciousness as she imagined herself leaping, "Alone ... rock over rock to the top."

The enjambment connecting the last line of the second stanza with the first line of the third creates a complex interplay of meanings. The shift in the poem is into the subjective consciousness of the

student as she imagines herself leaping rock over rock. Both the student and teacher seem momentarily alone, isolated by the music from the world around them. The image the student has of herself leaping freely over the rocks stands in direct contrast to what she feels about the small airless room full of knickknacks and photographs, where she feels stifled.

As the energy of the music pushes her in her thoughts and she reaches the rock's pinnacle, she realized her teacher is still playing on, so she waits "transformed." The syntax of the lines in the third stanza not only connects the exterior and interior focus, but also shows an identification on the part of the student with the teacher; they are, in fact, both "transformed." The music has carried the student out of the small, airless room into a place in her imagination where she feels free of the constraints put on her by her music lesson. The teacher is lost in her playing.

In the third line of the stanza the focus returns to the student's perceptions of the teacher as the student waits for her to finish playing. She noticed her eyes are "luminous and willful / her pinned hair falling down—." The poet's description of the teacher's eyes as "luminous and willful" reinforces the poem's interplay between external and internal focus and suggests further it is the poet's own sense of herself she saw. At the sight of her teacher's "pinned hair falling down," completely engaged in her playing, the student imagines her teacher "forgetting me, the house, [and] the neat green yard."

The student's perceptions are again purely subjective, based on what she feels. She sees in her teacher's passionate playing an escape from "all tedious bonds; / supper, the duties of flesh and home." The use of the verb "fled" and the syntax of the second line, however, show it is the student who imagines fleeing the stifling room and "all tedious bonds" in "that lick of flame." The student has projected onto her teacher her own fears of the "tedious bonds" and the "duties of flesh and home."

In her choice of diction the poet reveals the unconscious fear she had as a student. She feared becoming like her teacher, living in a small house full of knickknacks, and teaching music in a room with shut windows. The enjambment in the poem between the last two lines of the final quatrain with its rhyming couplet underlines the student's unconscious fear, as "the tedious bonds" and "the duties of flesh and home" become "the knife at the throat, the death in the metronome."

The image of the "knife at the throat" is particularly poignant, suggesting the poet's unconscious awareness at the time that she would have to make a choice in her own life, perhaps between the artistic and the domestic life. The metaphoric linking of the metronome, and its use for beating out time, with death suggests the poet's awareness even as a young student of the eternal ticking of time. For the poet it was symbolic of the incessant repetition of the music lessons as she sat in the airless room. For the poet the music lessons and her teacher's life represented a form of death.

Though the focus on the poem appears to be on the music teacher and the different sides of her nature. In fact, the teacher represents what the student believes she does not want to become. The brief identification between the student and her teacher points to what the student believed the teacher had lost to domestic life. In the poet's recollection of her teacher and her music lessons she reveals more about her own feelings at the time than about her music lessons.

Source: Alice Van Wart, in an essay for *Poetry for Students,* Gale Group, 2000.

Sources

Alford, Jean B., "The Poetry of Mary Oliver: Modern Renewal Through Mortal Acceptance," *Pembroke Magazine,* Vol. 20, 1988, pp. 283-88.

De Mott, Robert, "Recent Poetry: 'The Night Traveler'," in *Western Humanities Review,* Vol. XXXIII, No. 2, Spring, 1979, pp. 185-186.

Graham, Vicki, "Into the Body of Another: Mary Oliver and the Poetics of Becoming Other," *Papers on Language and Literature,* Vol. 30, No. 4, Fall, 1994, pp. 352-72.

Oliver, Mary, *New and Selected Poems,* Boston: Beacon, 1992.

Oliver, Mary, *A Poetry Handbook,* San Diego: Harcourt, Brace, 1994.

Scully, James, ed., *Modern Poetics* New York: McGraw-Hill, 1965.

Wakoski, Diane, "Oliver, Mary," in *Contemporary Women Poets,* edited by Pamela L. Shelton, Detroit: St. James, 1998, pp.270-271.

For Further Study

Runciman, Lex, "Knocking on Nature's Door: Religious Meaning in Twentieth Century U.S. Poetry," *Literature of Nature,* Patrick Murphy, editor, Chicago: Fitzroy Dearborn, 1998.
 This essay has a section devoted to Oliver discussing her notion of nature as "an ever-renewing and endlessly elemental present."

Oliver, Mary *American Primitive,*Boston: Little Brown, 1983.
 This collection of Oliver's poems won the Pulitzer Prize and is primarily concerned with pastoral subject matter.

Oliver, Mary, *House of Light,* Boston: Beacon, 1990.
 This volume contains poems of air and seaside and is dominated by poems about birds.

Oliver, Mary, *Rules for the Dance: A Handbook for Writing and Reading Metrical Verse,* Boston: Houghton Mifflin, 1998.
 While the title of this book is self explanatory, the book also includes a hundred pages of poems that serve as examples. The book is written clearly and simply for those without a background in technical language about metrical verse.

My Life Closed Twice Before Its Close

Emily Dickinson
1896

"My Life Closed Twice Before Its Close" was first published in Dickinson's posthumous third collection, *Poems by Emily Dickinson, third series,* in 1896. Scholars do not know when it was written. The poem has also been published in some other anthologies under the name "Parting." Like much of Dickinson's best work, this poem is simultaneously personal and universal. On a personal level, the poem's speaker is telling of the losses he or she has suffered, so painful that they were like death itself. Though the speaker has not yet experienced real, physical death, he or she cannot bear to imagine anything that could be more terrible than the two deprivations already experienced. The speaker does not tell us what these losses were, but one might imagine some bereavement—the death of a loved one, the end of a passionate affair.

On a universal level, the poem poignantly describes the great tragedy of human life, for to be human is to suffer loss. In the final two lines of the poem, Dickinson creates a brilliant paradox, a statement that seems contradictory but might really be expressing a truth. Here heaven and hell, great symbolic opposites according to conventional wisdom, come together in their relationships to the word "parting." If there is a heaven, all we know of it is that we must leave behind our loves and lives on this earth in order to enter there. At the same time, all human beings, to some degree, have known the misery of the private hell of separation and loss because that is an unavoidable part of human experience.

Author Biography

Emily Elizabeth Dickinson was born on December 10, 1830, in Amherst, Massachusetts, the second of three children to respectable, upper-middle-class Puritan parents. She would later describe her father as domineering and her mother as emotionally distant. Early on, she was a great admirer of and a great rival to her brother, Austin, born nearly two years previously. She was active, precocious, and strong-willed as a child. But in time, she would become increasingly sensitive, shy, and retiring.

After two years at Amherst Academy, Dickinson entered the Mount Holyoke Female Seminary (now Mount Holyoke College), where she studied for one year until homesickness drove her home. Although only seventeen at the time, Dickinson quietly defied both official and peer pressure to experience a conversion to Christianity. Dickinson later admitted in a letter that she secretly worried that somehow she had willfully put herself beyond God's grace by her rebellion.

Despite the brevity of her formal education, Dickinson voraciously read all of her father's books and subscribed to the great literary journals of her time. In fact, her struggle with social Christendom may have actually propelled her into a quest for the sublime in literature. (This Romantic transference from orthodox Christianity to a worship of nature and the powers of the imagination has been described by M. H. Abrams in *The Mirror and the Lamp*.) By the late 1850s, Dickinson had begun to take herself seriously as a poet, inspired by the successes of George Eliot, George Sand, and Elizabeth Barrett Browning, the great women writers of her time.

Many speculate that a tragic end to a love affair caused Dickinson's prodigious poetic output in the early 1860s. The story goes that Dickinson's heart was broken when clergyman Charles Wadsworth told her, in 1860, that he was journeying to California. There are, in fact, many poems from this period that accurately describe the processes of a severe mental breakdown. Nevertheless, all such speculations are just that—speculations. What is more interesting is that Dickinson so successfully portrayed various life experiences and mental states considering that, by the early 1860s, she had chosen to live in almost total physical isolation from the outside world.

In 1862, Dickinson sent Thomas Higginson, editor of *The Atlantic Monthly,* a letter and included some of her poems. She internalized his observa-

Emily Dickinson

tion that she was not ready for publication in a way he never would have suspected. She resolved to continue writing in her own unique style and await future readers that would appreciate her voice, while still sending Higginson poetry for advice she never followed. She lived out the remainder of her life in relative obscurity, caring for her invalid mother until her death in 1882. Emily Dickinson's own death—from a kidney ailment called Bright's Disease—followed nearly four years later, in 1886.

Poem Text

My life closed twice before its close—
It yet remains to see
If Immortality unveil
A third event to me

So huge, so hopeless to conceive   5
As these that twice befell.
Parting is all we know of heaven.
And all we need of hell.

Poem Summary

Line 1:

The poem begins with a powerful statement: The speaker's life has already "closed" two times. Here, the use of the verb "closed" might be inter-

Media Adaptations

- In 1993, Atschul Group Corp. released a video cassette entitled *Emily Dickinson.*

- In 1994, Kino International released a video cassette entitled *The Belle of Amherst.*

- In 1977, Aids of Cape Cod released a film strip entitled *Emily Dickinson: I'm Nobody! Who Are You?,* for the "Americans Who Changed Things" series.

- In 1996, Mystic Fire Audio released an audio cassette entitled *Emily Dickinson,* for the "Voices and Visions" series, volume two.

- In 1999, Dove Audio released an audio compact disk entitled *Poems of Emily Dickinson.*

- In 1996, EMILY released an audio cassette entitled *Emily Dickinson: Selected Poems.*

- In 1960, Caedmon released an audio record album entitled *Poems and Letters of Emily Dickinson.*

- In 1993, Marion Woodman recorded an audio casssette entitled *Emily Dickinson and the Demon Lover.* The cassette was released by Sounds True Recording.

- In 1998, Monterey Home Video released a video cassette entitled *The World of Emily Dickinson.* The video cassette belongs to The Master Poets Collection, volume 1.

preted in two ways. One meaning might be "finished or concluded," but another could be "closed on all sides; shut in." Either or both meanings seem appropriate, inasmuch as Dickinson 's poetry is often concerned with both the theme of death and the theme of isolation. "Before its close" most likely means "before its conclusion," or before that final closing act of every life—the concrete, physical death of the body.

Lines 2-4:

In these lines, the speaker expresses concern about what the future might hold. The poem's speaker, having already suffered two life "closes," is left to deal with whatever will happen next. "Immortality" is the only capitalized word in the poem which does not fall at the beginning of a line. One might have expected her to use the word "Mortality," as that is the way that most people talk about the end of life, but the use of "Immortality" shows the spiritual depth of the poem's speaker. "Immortality," or endless life, is a sacred mystery that may or may not "unveil," or reveal, a third and final "close" to the speaker. There is a certain tone of courage in these lines, perhaps the courage that enables people to go on living in spite of overwhelming losses.

Lines 5-6:

In these lines, the speaker wonders if the next "event," if it ever occurs, could possibly be as "huge" and as "hopeless to conceive" as the two "events" or "closes," that have already happened. Here, "huge" is probably used in the sense of one of its synonyms, "tremendous," meaning capable of making one tremble. "Hopeless to conceive" indicates impossible to imagine. In other words, the speaker knows that there is no way to prepare for the next, perhaps inevitable, "close." In addition, the speaker cannot imagine that anything, even death, could be more unbearable than what has already happened. Though most people know that grief and loss are an unavoidable part of the human experience, there is no way to really prepare for it before it happens.

Lines 7-8:

The word "parting" is a clue to the meaning of "closed" and "close" in the first quatrain of the poem. Like most of the words Dickinson uses, "parting" is rich with meanings. On one level, it means departure or leave-taking. In this sense, when the speaker's life "closed," it might have been because of some terrible separation from a loved one—relative, lover, or friend. On another level, "parting" is used as a euphemism for the act or time of dying. In this sense, the mysterious, unavoidable "close" which the speaker awaits is the permanent separation that occurs at the end of life. "Heaven" and "hell," traditionally characterized as extreme opposites, meet each other on earth in the context. When a loved one is lost to death, people comfort themselves with a faith that the deceased is "in heaven;" however, no one *knows* this to be true. All that is concrete and tangible about the afterlife is the separation of the living and the dead. On the other hand, though there are many interpretations of what "hell" is in various religions, it is universally understood that hell is somehow the absence, or separation from, God and love. On earth, the word "hell" is used to describe anything that causes great torment and anguish, such as the loss of love.

Themes

Permanence

With its use of the word "Immortality," this poem presents a contrast that seems simple at first but more complex as it is examined more closely. The poem deals with the fact that life ends—one of the few things that is certain about life. The speaker of the poem says that her life has been cut short twice, and that she expects it to happen at least once more at life's end. The ironic thing is that life will eventually be limited by the soul's limitlessness—its immortality. The word "Immortality" is used in the poem, for the most part, in the same way that it is used in common discourse. There is a key difference, however. Dickinson capitalizes it, and relates it to God and heaven. In Christian doctrine, heaven is where those who have died in this world will go to join God and to live eternally. To reach this state of permanence in heaven requires going through the troubles associated with life's uncertainty. However, as the poem points out, life is so unstable that it can close more than once—three or more times—without reaching any state of stability. It is life's frustrating tendency to go on and on after reaching its end that makes the permanence of the afterlife "hopeless to conceive" for the speaker of this poem.

Alienation and Loneliness

Whether one interprets the phrase "my life closed twice" as death, as traumatic events, or as revelations, it seems to indicate that the speaker of the poem feels separated from all that came before. The word "closed" appears final, absolute, leaving no possibility of going back. The implication is that everything the speaker knew prior to each "closure" is left irreversibly behind, inaccessible to the person she grew to be each time. Old ideas, former relationships, and familiar ways of doing things are all sealed off in the past, as if locked behind a closed door. Each time that the speaker's life closed, she had been left alienated from what had gone before. Furthermore, the speaker of the poem is tortured by the loneliness she has suffered each time her life closed. The line "Parting is.... all we

Topics for Further Study

- Write a letter from the point of view of one of the people involved in the two awful partings mentioned here. Imagine that in the circumstances you felt it was right to part, but that you also want to comfort the speaker of "My Life Closed Twice before Its Close."

- Some people say that bad news comes in groups of three, like the three events that this poem talks about. Do you agree? Why or why not? Use examples to support whichever side of the argument you are defending.

- What exactly does the speaker mean by "Immortality"? Why do you think this word is used, rather than "God"?

- Examine an example of an artistic piece that seemed to close, to reach its end, but then continued on—a movie or a song, perhaps. Analyze what you think the artist was trying to say by this, and how you think it relates to Dickinson's point in this poem.

need of hell" expresses the pain of hell in present life caused by parting and closing.

Death

Although death is often presented as an end and what comes after death is seen as mysterious, Dickinson presents the end of life as the beginning of Immortality. In comparison with the eternal afterlife suggested in the poem, life itself seems puny. The poem does not celebrate life, but does not accept death with open arms either. Rather, death is presented as having terrible consequences. It separates one from the things one loves in this world. Although "Parting" (the word used to indicate death) suggests a non-violent end to life, it is an ending that creates the agonies of hell.

Style

" My Life Closed Twice Before Its Close" is written in two quatrains, or stanzas of four lines each, arranged in iambs. The iamb is a metric foot of two syllables in which the first syllable is unstressed and the second stressed. It is the basis for the most common line pattern in English verse.

The first and third lines of each quatrain are in iambic tetrameter , which means that there are four iambs in each line ("tetra" meaning four). In the alternate, and rhyming, lines, Dickinson changes to a three-foot meter called iambic trimeter ("tri" meaning three). For a lesser poet, such a fixed metrical pattern might have been a creative limitation. However, Dickinson, whose genius was her ability to choose the perfect word above all others, used the simplicity of the this familiar stanza pattern to showcase the power of language without distraction.

One interesting aspect of this poem is Dickinson's use of traditional punctuation. In many of her poems, Dickinson substitutes dashes for periods, commas and other punctuation marks. However, this poem consists of two complete sentences, one long and the other short, punctuated with a semicolon, two commas and two periods.

Historical Context

Critics and historians frequently draw a connection between Emily Dickinson's poetry and the New England Transcendentalist movement. Dickinson was growing up and formulating her own ideas when the Transcendentalist movement was reaching its peak between the 1830s and the 1860s. Dickinson lived in Amherst, only seventy-five miles away from the center of Transcendentalism in Boston. Furthermore, Dickinson openly discussed the influence of Transcendentalism, especially the influence of the ideas in the essay called "The Poet" by Ralph Waldo Emerson, a key figure in the movement. However, literary critics point out that, although Dickinson's poetry reflects aspects of Transcendentalism it also reflects many of the Puritan religious beliefs that Transcendentalism supposedly contradicted and replaced. Some interpret this duality as a sign that Dickinson, in her devotion to her family's religious heritage, allowed herself to be trapped in the contradiction of embracing both modern thinking and a putatively antiquated way of thinking.

The Puritans were a religious sect emerging as a splinter faction of English Protestantism during the sixteenth and seventeenth centuries. Protestantism itself began as a protest against the Catholic Church because of its emphasis on ceremony and on the powers of the church hierarchy, with too little attention being given to God. Puritans felt that mainstream Protestants were themselves distracted by the things of the world. Turning their backs on political activity and social interaction, Puritans focused on theories of heaven and hell and who would end up spending eternity in each when their lives were over. Hard work was valued by Puritans as a way of striving toward one's salvation, and worshipping God was a constant element of everything they did. The Puritans came to power in England under Oliver Cromwell, but eventually lost power in a resurgence of royalist forces. As a result the Church of England regained control. At that time, North America was being colonized, and hundreds of Puritans made the decision to move to the New World, where they could practice their religious beliefs freely. The Puritans founded Jamestown, the first permanent settlement in North America, and the majority of those who came to America on the Mayflower were Puritans. In 1620, off the shores of Provincetown Harbor in what came to be Massachusetts, the Mayflower Compact was signed, representing the first form of European-style government in America and influencing the country's political development. Because Puritans valued hard work and disdained comfort or pleasure, they were able to survive the wilderness conditions that other Europeans could not tolerate. American capitalism has been influence by Puritan ethics, particularly in the economic principle that wealth is the reward of hard work and that poverty and suffering are the deserved rewards for failing to work hard. In Massachusetts, among the descendants of the original Puritans, the Puritan influence would have been especially keenly felt.

In some ways, Transcendentalism was a response to Puritan beliefs, although it was also influenced by the literary trend of Romanticism that was sweeping European literature at the same time. Romanticism had grown throughout the late 1700's, as seen most clearly in the works of the French philosopher Jean-Jacques Rousseau and the German poet Johann Wolfgang von Goethe. The ideas of Romanticism were crystallized into a distinct statement of beliefs in the introduction to William Wordsworth's and Samuel Taylor Coleridge's *Lyrical Ballads* in 1798. Romanticism emphasized freedom and nature, presenting human beings as innate geniuses in their capacity to understand the natural world and dismissing society as a form of corruption. In America, the Romantic ideal made its strongest impact in the way it influenced the New England Transcendentalists. This

Compare & Contrast

- **1896:** Entrepreneur Henry Morrison Flagler, one of the founders of Standard Oil, dredged the south Florida swamp to extended his railway, reaching the newly-incorporated town of Miami. The year before the unincorporated territory consisted of only three houses. Flagler owned a cluster of Florida resorts, with major hotels in Daytona and Palm Beach.

  1990s: Miami is the largest metropolitan area in Florida. Over 40 million tourists visit the state each year, mostly to visit the cluster of theme parks around Orlando.

- **1896:** The first public showing of a motion picture occurred in New York, at Koster and Bial's Music Hall.

  1956: The first successful videotape recorder was demonstrated at Ampex Corp. in Redwood City, California.

  1990s: Advanced home theater technology threatens to make public move viewing obsolete.

- **1896:** The discovery of gold in the Klondike Territory, near the Alaskan border, led to a gold rush that brought miners from around the world. By the end of the next year, over $22 million had been mined, and many of Alaska's major cities had been settled.

  1973: When the OPEC oil embargo cut off the United States' main source of inexpensive oil, Congress authorized the nine billion dollar Alaska Pipeline to pump crude oil from Alaska's Arctic coastal plain to the accessible port of Valdez.

  1990s: Oil is the main economic force in Alaska.

- **1896:** The first continuing comic strip, "The Yellow Kid," began as a one-panel feature in Joseph Pulitzer's newspaper *New York World.*

  1990s: Readers expect at least a page of comics in any reputable metropolitan newspaper.

- **1896:** In the case of *Plessy v. Ferguson* the U.S. Supreme Court upheld segregation of blacks and whites. The ruling called for "separate but equal" access to accommodations such as transportation and education, but common practice quickly established the practice of offering blacks inferior services.

  1954: In the case of *Brown v. the Board of Education of Topeka, Kansas,* the Supreme Court ruled that separate accommodations would never be equal, and overturned the decision of *Plessy.* The Chief Justice of the Court, Warren Berger, ordered that schools across the country be integrated "with all deliberate speed."

  1990s: Debates continue about what school systems should do to narrow the discernable gap in test scores between blacks and whites.

---

was a movement begun in 1836 with the Transcendental Club in Boston. Members included such noteworthy intellectuals as Bronson Alcott, William Ellery Channing, Margaret Fuller and Henry David Thoreau. Thoreau's book *Walden,* about the years he spent living in a shack in the woods relying on nature and limiting his involvement with people, is still read in schools today. The most direct and influential spokesperson for Transcendentalist beliefs was Ralph Waldo Emerson, a poet and the author of such essays as "Self-Reliance" and "Nature." The Transcendentalists were like the Puritans in the way that they emphasized the individual's relationship to God without the need for a priest or other religious figure to be involved in the middle. However, they did not picture God as a stern, vengeful father figure. Instead of using the word "God," Emerson coined the word "Over-Soul," implying that this was an entity present in all of nature and that all people and all components of nature were part of this cosmic force equally.

With its emphasis on Nature as something to be approached and experienced, the Transcendentalist movement faced considerable difficulties in nineteenth century America. As the Industrial Revolution developed, Americans became too busy and too excited with production and economic growth to give much attention to the Transcendentalist worship of nature. As the Civil War approached, citizens chose up political sides, and the Transcendental goal of individuality and self-reliance was seen as naive and self-indulgent. By the time that Emily Dickinson wrote most of her poems and the Civil War was approaching, the influence of the Transcendentalist movement was declining. Both Puritanism and Transcendentalism can be seen as influences on Dickinson's thought, and her poems show a unique mind that was able to use and blend important ideas from several sources.

Critical Overview

"My Life Closed Twice Before Its Close" has been viewed by many critics as a poem about the act, by God or man, of revealing something surprising and not known before. The critic Martha Hale Shackford, writing in the *Atlantic Monthly,* sees the poem's speaker as a "voice of tragic revelation." Shackford explains that Dickinson was not so much a philosopher as she was an observer of life, gifted with the ability to express profound emotions.

Another critic, Conrad Aiken, offers an interesting interpretation of the poem in his book *Collected Criticism.* He points out Dickinson's obsession with death, noting it as a persistent theme in her poetry. He writes, "she seems to have thought of it constantly—she died all her life, she probed death daily." Aiken goes on to explain how the theme of death is present in some of her "sharpest" work, noting that her poems tend to be more lyrical, or musical, when they deal with the subject of death and the question of immortality.

A third critic, Kenneth Stocks, writing in *Dickinson and the Modern Consciousness,* views the poem from a very intriguing angle, calling it "one of the greatest love-poems ever written." According to Stocks, "love, death, heaven and hell" come together in the poem, and the result is a deep and powerful insight into a universal human experience.

Criticism

Jeannine Johnson

Jeannine Johnson currently teaches writing and literature at Harvard University. She has also taught at Yale, from which she received her Ph.D., and at Wake Forest University. Her most recent essay is on Adrienne Rich's "To a Poet," published in the Explicator. *In the following essay, Johnson discusses Dickinson's vision of isolation in "My Life Closed Twice before Its Close."*

"A letter always feels to me like Immortality because it is the mind alone without corporeal friend" (*The Letters of Emily Dickinson*). When Emily Dickinson wrote these lines to the author and editor Thomas Wentworth Higginson, she might as well have been describing the nature of her poetry. Dickinson reveals that a letter provides her a link with "immortality," which in this context does not mean life after death but a sense of infinitude in this life. The "friend" to whom she writes is not physically present and thus, though she imagines another person who will eventually read her thoughts, her own experience in writing is one of solitude. Dickinson describes poetry writing in much the same terms. In "My Life Closed Twice before Its Close—" (Poem 1732), the poet also refers to "Immortality" and the way that her encounter with it may expand her mind. In the letter quoted above and in other poems, such as "The Brain—is wider than the Sky—" (Poem 632), Dickinson extols the virtues of pursuing her intellectual goals in isolation and of driving her mind beyond the rational. However, in "My life closed twice," the poet does not celebrate this confrontation with the incomprehensible, and her solitude here is accompanied by a marked sadness.

The poet's mind is alone and she is mourning the fact that her life has already "closed twice," or in other words that the poet herself has symbolically died two times before her bodily death. This poem recalls an earlier work, "I never lost as much but twice" (Poem 49), likely written in 1858. The loss in "I never lost as much" is the literal death of two persons close to the poet, as these privations are likened to bodies that lie buried "in the sod." However, in "My life closed twice," the cause of the poet's anguish is not so clear: while it is certain that these two "closings" were very painful, the poet declines to identify them explicitly. The poet anticipates but does not quite experience a third and final wound: "It yet remains to see / If Immortality unveil / A third event to me." The incidents to which she refers are "So huge, so hopeless," that the poet's imagination fails her when she tries to utter how much worse a third similar "event" might be.

Based on the subjects of other Dickinson poems, we could imagine that the afflictions in "My

What Do I Read Next?

- For thirty years Emily Dickinson corresponded with her sister-in-law and next-door-neighbor Susan Huntington Dickinson. The resulting mix of letters, notes, and poems was finally published in 1998 as *Open Me Carefully,* edited by Ellen Louise Hart and Martha Nell Smith, who wrote the introduction.

- John Donne was a metaphysical poet who died nearly two hundred years before Dickinson was born. His themes and reflections on the nature of God resemble Dickinson's, as well as his irregular poetry patterns. One of several good collections of his works is the Modern Library 1994 publication of *The Complete Poetry and Selected Prose of John Donne.*

- Because the author herself never arranged for the publication of her works, the process of gathering her poems for publication has been slow. The current definitive text is *The Complete Poems of Emily Dickinson,* published by Little, Brown and Company, edited by Thomas H. Johnson. The paperback edition was published in 1976.

- Students interested in New England Transcendentalism, which is the intellectual background that Dickinson came from, will be interested in the writings of Ralph Waldo Emerson, who is considered to be the main figure of this philosophical movement. His writings have been collected in one definitive volume, *Ralph Waldo Emerson: Essays and Lectures,* published by the Library of America in 1983.

- Because Dickinson was a recluse in her lifetime, the question often arises regarding who she thought would read her poems. The University of Michigan Press has collected essays on this subject from a wide variety of critics and historians in *Dickinson and Audience,* edited by Martin Orzek and Robert Weisbuch, first published in 1996.

---

life closed twice" were emotional losses, spiritual injuries, or even artistic disappointments. But, since the poet mentions "parting" in the final stanza, she hints that the two events were instances in which she was separated—by death or by the dissolution of a relationship—from another person. Critics have routinely claimed that the two closings in this poem likely refer to the real death of Dickinson's father in 1874 and to the figurative death, around 1861, of her romantic interest in Charles Wadsworth, a Philadelphia clergyman. However, there are too many risks and not enough rewards in making such speculations. There is no firm evidence as to the date of the poem, so we cannot limit with any certainty the time period during which the events referred to in the poem might have occurred. Furthermore, Dickinson suffered more than two major "closings" in her life: we could just as easily—and as plausibly—claim that the painful incidents to which the poet alludes are those of the death of her mother (in 1882) and of Susan Hunt-

ington Gilbert's marriage to Emily's Dickinson's brother, Austin (in 1856).

Emily and Susan shared a lifelong romantic passion for one another, as letters and other evidence reveal, and Emily was devastated by Susan's marriage. Though afterward they renewed their emotional bonds and, for most of thirty years, lived next door to each other, Emily was forever changed by her friend's marriage. In a letter from the mid-1850s, Emily wrote to Susan, "You need not fear to leave me lest I should be alone, for I often part with things I fancy I have loved,— sometimes to the grave, and sometimes to an oblivion rather bitterer than death—thus my heart bleeds so frequently that I shant mind the hemorrhage, and I only add an agony to several previous ones ..." (*Open Me Carefully*). Here Dickinson makes it clear that her personal sufferings have been many and that they are not confined to the two most often cited by critics. In addition, in this letter Dickinson confirms that the loss of a re-

---

> *Dickinson's ironic revision of Shakespeare suggests that the verbal devices we employ as consolation are inadequate to their task, and it further indicates that there is little redemptive value in undergoing enormous emotional distress.*"

lationship can cause as much anguish as the death of a loved one.

In the end, it makes little difference whether we can accurately identify the two milestones mentioned in the poem, for to claim a strict parallel between Dickinson's life and her work reduces the value of her poems to biographical history. In fact, Dickinson herself discouraged such biographical readings of her poems when she offered this warning to Thomas Higginson: "When I state myself, as the Representative of the Verse—it does not mean—me—but a supposed person" (*The Letters of Emily Dickinson*). From very early in her career, Dickinson was conscious of creating a poetic persona in her writing, and though the experiences in her poems are genuinely human, the speaker who relates these experiences is a fictional character.

Although there seems to be a personal motive behind "My life closed twice," its primary goal is to reveal larger truths about the human condition. The final lines contain an aphorism, or succinct statement of a general principle: "Parting is all we know of heaven / And all we need of hell." This aphoristic quality is characteristic of Dickinson's poetry, but the simplicity of her language can be misleading, and the meaning behind this couplet is complex. In two lines, the poet encapsulates the pain of being kept apart from someone she loves. The lines echo Juliet's observation, in Shakespeare's *Romeo and Juliet,* that "Parting is such sweet sorrow." This allusion to a play about a romantic relationship reinforces Dickinson's idea that the separation caused by physical death is no worse than the separation of lovers.

Yet Dickinson's statement does not contain the hopefulness of Juliet's protest. Parting is sorrowful for Juliet, but it is also sweet because she looks forward to a future reunion with Romeo. In Dickinson's formula, "sorrow" is represented by "hell," but, unlike Shakespeare's heroine, Dickinson finds little relief in the sweetness that should be delivered by "heaven." The only benefit in experiencing the parting that Dickinson depicts is that our knowledge of heaven may be slightly increased. That is to say, when someone dies we might console ourselves with the idea that that person has gone to a better world, and in that moment we might contemplate what heaven is like and imagine that we have come to better understand it. However, the poet did not subscribe to conventional religious beliefs of her day, and she would not have placed much value on learning about the hereafter, especially at the high cost of a loved one's death.

Juliet's observation ends on a positive note, and, though she is ignorant of the tragedy that is to befall her, she looks forward to the future, as the second part of the couplet reveals: "Parting is such sweet sorrow, / That I shall say good night till it be morrow." However, Dickinson's poem ends with the word "hell," and its woe resounds without interruption or expectation. Dickinson's ironic revision of Shakespeare suggests that the verbal devices we employ as consolation are inadequate to their task, and it further indicates that there is little redemptive value in undergoing enormous emotional distress.

The poet in "My life closed twice" seems to be left alone with her incomprehensible sadness, but the structure of the poem tries to counteract her solitude. The piece is composed of two four-line stanzas, or quatrains, that follow an ABCB rhyme scheme. (These are the ballad stanzas typical of Dickinson's poetry.) But even though the poem is split into two groups of four lines, the meaning of the poem is divided between the first six lines and the last two lines: the first six constitute one full sentence and the last two constitute another. The final couplet is distinguished from the rest of the poem, yet these two parts are still linked by the stanzaic structure. In the couplet, the poet changes the first person singular ("I") to the first person plural ("we"), a gesture that marks her as a member of a community rather than an isolated individual. Though a period separates the poet from her identification with others, this is not as absolute a division as a stanza break would be. Nevertheless, the community toward which she signals is absent, just like the "corporeal friend" to whom one writes a letter. Dickinson's rather solemn work suggests that though a poem, like a letter, confirms both the existence of its addressee and the poet's separation from that person, there is some solace in reaching out to others by writing to them, if only to temporarily stanch the "hemorrhage" of a lifetime of partings.

Source: Jeannine Johnson, in an essay for *Poetry for Students,* Gale Group, 2000.

David Kelly

David Kelly teaches literature and creative writing at several community colleges in Illinois. In the following essay, Kelly argues that it is usually unfair to invade an author's privacy by using her life to interpret her poetry, but that it might be acceptable or even necessary in the case of Emily Dickinson.

In the poem "My Life Closed Twice before Its Close," Emily Dickinson raises the particularly daring question of whether anything that happens after death will, or could, outdo the startling events of her life, in terms of hugeness and inconceivability. In a way, she is playing the role of the humble, timid questioner, adopting the passive pose of one who is just wondering about things, not speculating about what *will* happen but curious about what might. However, as in all of Dickinson's poetry, this demure casing serves to cushion a steely temperament. The allure of her poetry has always been that she reaches the same conclusions as organized religions but that she skips past the easy answers and addresses the more troubling uncertainties. It is in part the nature of organized religion that some people might possibly fool themselves and others by mouthing the right words without understanding the deeper implications. In the case of this poem, Dickinson skips past the intellectual ease of praising heaven and rejecting hell: anyone knows well enough to do that. She even goes past the uncomfortable question of whether the afterlife will be a good experience or not. Even worse than Eternity being bad would be if it were irrelevant: the very unsettling question this poem asks is whether heaven or hell will be as potent or as startling as our experiences here on Earth. The Afterlife less interesting than life? You might know someone who has made such a bold claim so eloquently, but probably not.

Each year, millions of words are published about Emily Dickinson and her poetry, and easily ten times more appears as unpublished works, such as school assignments and chat-room banter. Most

> *Reading poetry would not, after all, be much of an experience if we had to count on a one-to-one correlation between the events depicted in the poem and some definite external reality. If too much of the poem's impact depended on its relationship to reality, then it would mean a lot more to the author who lived it, but the reader's experience would be much less potent."*

of what people write concerns her life. She did indeed have a fascinating life. She was an archetype: there is something of the recluse in every poet, and something of the poet in every recluse. People hearing for the first time about the woman who shuttered herself away from the world and scribbled off hundred of poems, with no concern for publication, have the sense that they have heard this story before. The themes in her poems interconnect and contradict in a bewildering pattern. Readers feel that they need to look beyond the poetry for clues, and that the poet therefore deserves to have her mysterious life picked apart, in payment for the trouble that she has caused everyone by leaving her ideas poorly explained. If Dickinson had published during her lifetime, her fans could have written to her and gotten her own responses to the questions that plague us all today; if she had socialized more, maybe someone would have kept a record of what their friend Emily thought, the way Boswell did for Johnson; if she had earned a living, it would probably have been as a scholar, and we would have the benefit of her analyses of other works to help us analyze her own. As it is, we make do with what we have, plugging the gaps in the ideas the poetry insinuates with details plucked from her life.

In general, it should be considered unfair to reach into an author's private life in order to get a better view of their works. There is, after all, a reason that writers use poems and autobiographies to set down their ideas. I think it is safe to assume that a similar lack of exhibitionism compels an author like Dickinson to lock herself away in her house. Neither writing nor solitude can be construed to mean the author welcomes the scrutiny of the world. Shouldn't we respect the desires of authors that we like? Too often, though, we don't. Maybe, as already noted, we feel that any debt to the writer's wish is overruled if he or she makes the poetry too challenging, or maybe we feel that there are writers who are just so completely fascinating that we become irrationally ravenous for any minute detail about them, whether it concerns their life, work, discarded drafts, distant relatives or whatnot. Still, it seems only respectful to leave the life of the author, especially one who valued her privacy, like Dickinson, out of the conversation when we can.

When we can. But what can we do about a case like "My Life Closed Twice before Its Close"? Emily Dickinson does, after all, tease readers' curiosity by referring to a mystery in her past—two of them, actually. In daily life, if someone tells me something enigmatic, such as the fact that her life closed twice, I consider it an opening to conversation. Even if I were not interested in what she is hinting at, politeness requires me to show some interest in the open-ended tow line that has been thrown out. Maybe the issue shifts away from respect for privacy once the author has invited us in. Assuming this freedom has led scholars to amass mountains of information about Dickinson's relatives and acquaintances, hot on the trail of what it is that she *means*. I myself am not entirely comfortable with this assumption, but I can see why others believe in it. I would rather try understanding the poem on its own merits, without having to consider the author along with it. I think we can glance toward Dickinson's personal story, nod, and then understand her poem without any biography.

It is not at all far-fetched to say that it was the poet herself, a coy recluse, who began this line of inquiry. Emily Dickinson was a very smart person. I would venture to guess that, intensely aware as she was about all other things in her life, she knew how the obscurity of her words would raise interest in her beyond the page. The same faith in her genius makes me just as sure that she was not limited to herself when she wrote "me" and "my": a forceful imagination like hers could not be corralled

into just one person's lifetime. The situation in "My Life Closed Twice before Its Close" probably is not imaginary—there are enough traumatic events in Dickinson's life for us to accept that at least two qualify as "closings." Isn't it is enough for readers, though, to realize that she *could have* imagined them? The impact of this poem would be the same no matter what her sources of inspiration were. We do not need to know whether it refers to a broken love affair, a friend's death, a nervous breakdown or a relative's disability, or if she felt her life closed because of some smaller, unrecorded personal loss, something that went deeper into her soul than we could ever understand. Maybe one particular look in the mirror one particular day did it. Maybe someone left her cake out in the rain. I doubt the significance of the answer almost as much as I doubt the possibility of finding what it is.

Reading poetry would not, after all, be much of an experience if we had to count on a one-to-one correlation between the events depicted in the poem and some definite external reality. If too much of the poem's impact depended on its relationship to reality, then it would mean a lot more to the author who lived it, but the reader's experience would be much less potent. This idea becomes clearest in a case like "My Life Closed Twice before Its Close": if we could not all place our life's closings into the first few lines—if we believed that it was about only *her* life and the events surrounding it—then there wouldn't really be any reason why anyone but Dickinson herself should care. But we *do* care, because, as with all great works of art, the situation stirs our sense of empathy. We all feel we have been in the situation she is writing from. There is a good reason why Dickinson was so mysterious about the personal, biographical source of the poem: it piques readers' curiosity, drawing us in. There is also a good reason to not think too hard about the author's real life beyond what is presented on the page, for that tends to distance the reader, freezing the poem as an inanimate object. It becomes Emily Dickinson's problem, not one's own.

Emily Dickinson lived in a world created by her own mind, in a universe that followed the exact same rules of physics and emotions as ours. We have learned a lot from her world, but for some reason we keep trying to drag her into this one. We find lovers for her, we try to recreate incidents that may have been the "reality" behind the incidents she talks about in her poetry. I doubt that this is what she would have wanted, and I don't think that she owes it to us. In a way, playing with her life after she is gone is a little like picking up her hollowed-out skull and using it as a puppet to tell jokes. It is awfully disrespectful, and it is unnecessary. Her poems stand well enough on their own: in fact, they have even more to offer if they are appreciated for their own wisdom and are not taken as signposts to points in her biography. It can hardly matter what closed her heart twice in life. If readers cannot figure those enigmatic words out by looking within themselves, there is nothing in Dickinson's life that will help.

Source: David Kelly, in an essay for *Poetry for Students*, Gale Group, 2000.

Aviya Kushner

Aviya Kushner, the poetry editor for Neworld Renaissance Magazine, *earned an M.A. in creative writing from Boston University. In the following essay, Kushner elborates on the quality of mystery found in the poem.*

Many details of Emily Dickinson's life remain a mystery, from what she looked like as an adult to the nature of her love life. Similarly, mystery is a major part of her immensely accomplished, spare, and often easy-to-memorize poetry. Riddles, secrets, and lines which can be read in at least three ways abound. What's more, Dickinson's distinctive poetry is filled with dashes which hang, leaving the breathless and sometimes baffled reader to fill in the mysterious black blanks.

"My Life Closed Twice Before Its Close" is a typical Dickinson mystery—a tight package waiting to be unraveled. Clearly, as every child learns, a person dies only once. But as a quick thumbing through her copious collected works reveals, Dickinson was fascinated by death and subjects related to it. She was especially gripped by the idea of the soul and the afterlife. Interestingly, this preoccupation with immortality and the next world leaked into her view of words and language. In fact, Dickinson seemed to believe in the power of words to expand on life, to make life more colorful and larger than it really was. One of her shortest poems articulates this belief in the strength and inherent life force of the spoken and written word:

> A word is dead
> When it is said,
> Some say.
> I say it just
> Begins to live
> That day.

Life, for Dickinson, begins on the page. Her standard biography of a shut-in who never had a

> *... Dickinson may not only be defining her view of death, but also explaining her feelings about mystery. Mystery is part pleasure and part pain—one-half delight and one-half deprivation. The delight of the unknown is quite possibly all we know of heaven, while the pang of secrecy is sheer hell—or at least 'what we know of it.'*

romantic relationship may strengthen this view, but what's most amazing is the way Dickinson straddles between an absolutely strong written voice and a plot with huge holes in it. That short poem is also noteworthy because it is composed entirely of one-syllable words, except for "begins." Because "begins" is the longest word in the poem, it carries extra emphasis—which is appropriate for the plot of the poem. Dickinson manages to leave what happens to the word an utter mystery, but she lets us know that that word will have an exciting life as it "begins to live."

Here, the first line of the masterful "My Life ..." states a mystery, but states it with absolute clarity: "My life closed twice before its close." Again, with just one word carrying two syllables—"before"—that word carries extra strength. And again, quite typically, Dickinson doesn't reveal what those two times were. Instead, she states that there is a possibility of even more mystery:

> It yet remains to see
> If Immortality unveil
> A Third event to me

With Dickinson, it always "remains to see." That first line is composed of delicate, masterful sound without a syllable wasted. "Life" and "twice" form a sweet, internal rhyme, and of course, "closed" and "close" lay out a rhythm which immediately sticks in the mind. The next three lines are shorter and sweeter. "See" and "me" are rhymed, but the poem moves swiftly to the second stanza—the seat of the largest mystery here.

> So huge, so hopeless to conceive.

This mystery will be as heavy as immortality, and the alliteration of huge and hopeless hints at the heft of this unknown quantity. Of course, it is impossible for the reader to conceive the "hugeness" of the third mystery with no concept of the first two.

This type of gap is certainly frustrating. But Dickinson liked her poetry—and perhaps her life—that way. At one point, she wrote to a friend: "The Riddle marks we can guess / We speedily despise," which often seems like her motto.

There are numerous possibilities for what the two "closes" mentioned here really are in Dickinson's biography, which is full of question marks. Dickinson never married, and it is possible that the two "closes" refer to failed love affairs. They may refer to unreturned love. Some biographers claim that Dickinson was in love with her best friend, Susan Gilbert, who eventually became Dickinson's brother's wife.

Reading Emily Dickinson's letters, it's easy to imagine that she would have enjoyed all of this speculation. In one letter, for example, Dickinson expressed her love of mystery and riddle to Susan Gilbert: "In a life that stopped guessing, you and I should not feel at home." Death, of course, was the ultimate mystery for Dickinson, and she refers to death and related terms like immortality repeatedly in her poem.

But another key element of Dickinson the person and the poet becomes crucial in the second stanza. Dickinson loved dictionaries and once revealed that for years, a dictionary was her only companion. Many of her poems, then, aim for definitions. (In a biographical aside, Amherst College was founded by Dickinson's grandfather and Noah Webster, of Webster's Dictionary.) She tries to explain terms, and here, she grasps at death and immortality through the means of definition:

> Parting is all we know of heaven
> and all we need of hell.

This defines "parting," and does so in the most mysterious way. Interestingly, there are two main dictionary meanings for "parting." The first is a "leave-taking." But the second—"a place where things part or are parted"—makes sense for this line. Parting is a place, just as heaven is. Heaven is the destination of the dead—those separated, or parted from, the living. In that sense, a parting as a place where one parts from another is exactly the element of heaven which we can "know."

In their essence, of course, "heaven" and "hell," like immortality, are unknown quantities. A trip to a basic dictionary—the New Shorter Oxford—reveals six definitions for "heaven" and eight for "hell," along with dozens of individual examples. With that definition-like line, it seems that Dickinson may not only be defining her view of death, but also explaining her feelings about mystery. Mystery is part pleasure and part pain—one-half delight and one-half deprivation. The delight of the unknown is quite possibly all we know of heaven, while the pang of secrecy is sheer hell—or at least "what we know of it."

Thinking of the poem as a comment on mystery allows one to return to the first line and see that it is not as morose as it sounds: "My life closed twice before its close" might not mean a triple death. It's quite possible that the "close" was a delightful or heavenly moment. But one thing is nearly certain—Dickinson enjoyed planting the mystery in that first line, just as she enjoyed arranging the sounds of "closed" and "close" and the double "all"s preceding heaven and hell. What makes Dickinson memorable is not only her masterful command of sound and line, but her ability to present and sustain a mystery.

Source: Aviya Kushner, in an essay for *Poetry for Students,* Gale Group, 2000.

Sources

Aiken, Conrad, "Emily Dickinson," in his *Collected Criticism,* Oxford University Press, 1968, pp. 156-63.

Hart, Ellen Louise and Martha Nell Smith, eds., *Open Me Carefully: Emily Dickinson's Intimate Letters to Susan Huntington Dickinson,* Paris Press, 1998.

Johnson, Thomas H. and Theodora Ward., eds., *The Letters of Emily Dickinson,* Belknap Press of Harvard University Press, 1958.

Lucas, Dolores Dyer, *Emily Dickinson and Riddle,* DeKalb, IL: Northern Illinois University Press, 1969.

Shackford, Martha Hale, "The Poetry of Emily Dickinson," in the *Atlantic Monthly,* Vol. III, No. 1, January, 1913, pp. 93-97.

Stocks, Kenneth, "The Realism of Love and Death," in his *Emily Dickinson and the Modern Consciousness,* St. Martin's Press, 1988, pp. 102-12.

Suchard, Alan, *American Poetry: The Puritans Through Walt Whitman,* Boston: Twayne Publishers, 1988.

Tate, Allen, "New England Culture and Emily Dickinson," in *Critical Essays on Emily Dickinson,* edited by Paul J. Ferlazzo, Boston: G.K. Hall & Co., 1984, pp. 81-93.

For Further Study

Capps, Jack L., *Emily Dickinson's Reading: 1836-1886,* Cambridge, MA: Harvard University Press, 1966.
    This meticulously researched book examines Dickinson's career from the point of view of what she read and what the author concludes she would have read, ranging from the King James Version of the Bible to the important topics in contemporary newspapers.

Diehl, Joanne Feit, *Dickinson and the Romantic Imagination,* Princeton, NJ: Princeton University Press, 1981.
    A solid interpretation of Dickinson's thought in terms of Romanticism.

Ford, Thomas W., *Heaven Beguiles the Tired: Death in the Poetry of Emily Dickinson,* University, AL: University of Alabama Press, 1966.
    Surprisingly, this poem is not included in Ford's study about the ways in which Dickinson's poems display her feelings about death; it nonetheless provides a good background understanding of how she approached the subject in general.

Johnson, Greg, *Emily Dickinson: Perception and the Poet's Quest,* University, AL: University of Alabama Press, 1985.
    This is a scholarly work that examines the concept of perception, of the line between the knowable and the unknowable, as the key to understanding this poet's work.

Gilbert, Sandra M., "The Wayward Nun Beneath the Hill: Emily Dickinson and the Mysteries of Womanhood," in *Feminist Critics Read Emily Dickinson,* edited by Suzanne Juhasz, Bloomington, IN: Indiana University Press, 1983.
    Dickinson has been a favorite for feminist writers, and this essay, along with the other essays in this text, makes it easier to understand the myth around her and the ways that the myth obscures our understanding her as a living breathing woman.

Juhasz, Suzanne, *The Undiscovered Continent: Emily Dickinson and the Space of the Mind,* Bloomington, IN: Indiana University Press, 1983.
    Juhasz offers a feminist interpretation of Dickinson, proposing that the poet's way of dealing with the problem of being an artistic woman in the nineteenth century was to create a new terrain, a free space, in her mind.

Lundin, Roger, *Emily Dickinson and the Art of Belief,* Grand Rapids, MI: William B. Eerdmans Publishing Co., 1998.
    Most biographical works about Dickinson mention her religious beliefs, but Lundin's is one of the few book-length works to concentrate on that aspect of her life exclusively.

Small, Judy Jo, *Positive as Sound: Emily Dickinson's Rhyme,* Athens, GA: The University of Georgia Press, 1990.
    A book-length analysis of the poet's rhyme patterns might seem to some to be too narrowly focused, but Small manages to weave her material into a fascinating story that helps make sense of Dickinson's life and ideas.

Wolosky, Shira, "A Syntax of Contention," in *Emily Dickinson,* edited by Harold Bloom. New York: Chelsa House, 1985, pp. 161-85.
    This essay does not specifically examine the poem called "My Life Closed Twice," but it does provide a good clear analysis of the poet's use of language and the way she gave life to abstract ideas.

Names of Horses

Donald Hall

1977

Donald Hall began writing "Names of Horses" in 1975, and it was first published in the *New Yorker* in 1977. In this poem, Hall revisits his past and pays tribute to the horses that worked his grandparents' farm in New Hampshire. While poets often change the facts of memories from real life to fit their creative purposes, Hall is faithful to his memories. With the exception of the last, the names of the horses in the poem refer to actual horses Hall knew of as a child at Eagle Pond Farm. Thus the poem has a highly autobiographical dimension.

The first half of the poem reads like a list, a summary of the life of a work horse. Day after day, season after season, the same set of chores needed to be performed if the farm was to thrive. Summer meant haying, Sundays meant driving the family to church, and the horses were always present to lend their power in the service of man. In its direct address, the poem narrates the life of these horses, indirectly giving voice to otherwise mute creatures. At the same time, it educates the reader as to the details and harsh realities of life on a New England farm.

But the poem offers much more than a cataloging of farm chores. When the horse's period of service is over, when its body can no longer bear the workload, it is taken to a field, shot, and buried. Farm work was often very hard, and trying to squeeze a living out of the rocky and sandy soil of Eagle Pond Farm left little room for sentimental attachments, little room to regard the older animals as pets. The unwritten law of the farm demanded that the horses no longer holding their own, those no longer contributing to the success of the farm, must be euthanized. Part story, part meditation on memory and time, in "Names of Horses" the life of a typical horse becomes Hall's means of expressing his complex vision of mortality and the inherent worth of these unsung creatures.

Author Biography

Donald Hall was born on September 20, 1928, in New Haven, Connecticut. Although he grew up in the depths of the Depression, the elder Halls never felt its full effect, and they never shirked on their son's education. Boyhood summers were spent on the farm in New Hampshire where his mother was raised, Eagle Pond Farm, where Hall heard his grandfather reciting poetry as they worked in the fields. At twelve, Hall made his first attempt at writing, and his first poem was published when he was sixteen. Hall enrolled in Harvard at a time when the university was a Who's Who of present and future American poets. Robert Bly, Adrienne Rich, John Ashbery, and Frank O'Hara were among Hall's classmates, young writers honing their craft and establishing the styles by which they would become well known. In addition, two giants, Robert Frost and Archibald MacLeish, were on the Harvard teaching staff. Hall's poetry received several prizes during these years, and his winning streak continued at Oxford, where he was awarded the prestigious Newdigate Prize. This award gave Hall a welcome endorsement and led to more publications back in the United States, a residency at Stanford, and a three-year stint at Harvard's Society of Fellows. In 1957, Hall accepted a position at the University of Michigan, where he was employed for seventeen years, and continued to produce his distinctive collections of poetry, moving slowly away from writing exclusively metrical, formal verse to adopting free verse and a diversity of styles. In addition, Hall branched out into a variety of genres, producing prose memoirs, art criticism, drama, and children's books. In 1975, Hall resigned his professorship and purchased Eagle Pond Farm, the setting for "Names of Horses." There he lived with his second wife, the poet and translator Jane Kenyon. The rural setting afforded them the time and seclusion to dedicate themselves to their writing full time. Hall's 1988 collection, *The One Day,* won the National Book Critics Circle Award, the *Los Angeles Times* Book Prize, and was a finalist for the Pulitzer Prize. Donald Hall still resides at Eagle Pond Farm, where he is as prolific as ever.

Donald Hall

Poem Text

All winter your brute shoulders strained against
    collars, padding
and steerhide over the ash hames, to haul
sledges of cordwood for drying through spring and
    summer,
for the Glenwood stove next winter, and for the
    simmering range.

In April you pulled cartloads of manure to spread   5
    on the fields,
dark manure of Holsteins, and knobs of your own
    clustered with oats.
All summer you mowed the grass in meadow and
    hayfield, the mowing machine
clacketing beside you, while the sun walked high
    in the morning;
and after noon's heat, you pulled a clawed rake
    through the same acres,
                                      10
gathering stacks, and dragged the wagon from
    stack to stack,
and the built hayrack back, uphill to the chaffy
    barn,
three loads of hay a day from standing grass in the
    morning.

Sundays you trotted the two miles to church with
    the light load
of a leather quartertop buggy, and grazed in the
    sound of hymns.
Generation on generation, your neck rubbed the   15
    windowsill

of the stall, smoothing the wood as the seas
    smooths glass.

When you were old and lame, when your shoulders
    hurt bending to graze,
one October the man, who fed you and kept you,
    and harnessed you every morning,
led you through corn stubble to sandy ground
    above Eagle Pond,
and dug a hole beside you where you stood   20
    shuddering in your skin,

and lay the shotgun's muzzle in the boneless
    hollow behind your ear,
and fired the slug into your brain, and felled you
    into your grave,
shoveling sand to cover you, setting goldenrod
    upright above you,
where by the next summer a dent in the ground
    made your monument.

For a hundred and fifty years, in the pasture of   25
    dead horses,
roots of pine trees pushed through the pale curves
    of your ribs,
yellow blossoms flourished above you in autumn,
    and in winter
frost heaved your bones in the ground—old toilers,
    soil makers:

O Roger, Mackerel, Riley, Ned, Nellie, Chester,
    Lady Ghost.

Poem Summary

Lines 1-4:

The first stanza begins with a list of grueling labors. The reader determines quickly that the identity of the being addressed as "you" (or "your") is not a person, but a horse. The animal is a beast of burden, a "brute" performing the farm chores that are too difficult for humans alone. The chores are not easy for the horse either, who must "strain" against its burden.

The inclusion of the horse's devices, its network of harnesses, collars, and padding, are important details. They lend the speaker of the poem an air of authority, giving the reader access to the life and procedures of a working farm, a world foreign to most. But most importantly, the contraptions the horse is wearing show the animal is physically linked to its owner, is under the master's complete control. The "ash hames" are the curved supports (here, made of the wood of the ash tree) that are attached to the collar. These are in turn fastened to the traces, which connect the horse to the sledge, or sled, and allow the animal to pull it along.

In other words, the horse is tied directly to the heavy load it is hauling.

A strong sense of time and process also informs this stanza. The hauling here is just one link in a chain of necessary chores. The wood is being collected and stockpiled for drying, in preparation for the next winter.

Lines 5-8:

Notice how the first two words mirror the opening of the first stanza, except this time "All winter" has become "In April." Time is moving on, and with the passing of the seasons there are new and different duties to be tackled on the farm. Fertilizer needs to be spread on the fields. With "all summer" the poet matches even more closely the poem's opening words. Without a moment of rest, it is summer and time to cut and gather the hay. In capturing the rigors of the hayfield, Hall employs two distinct poetic devices. The first is the use of onomatopoeia, or a word that attempts to imitate the sound it describes. (Hiss, hum, and click are also examples of words that capture sounds.) Here, Hall has invented a word, "clacketing," in an attempt to replicate the noise and rumble of the mowing machine. The word is similar to another actual word, clack, meaning to make a clatter. But Hall extends his word into clacket, which rhymes with racket, also meaning a loud outburst. The invented word has more dimensions and a stronger impact in conveying the sense of a constant, jarring sound.

Hall ends the stanza with a second imaginative use of language: personification. This is when a writer attributes human qualities to an otherwise lifeless object. Here, the sun is said to have "walked high" in the summer sky. While this is a unique and original description of the sun rising across the sky, it also accentuates the role of time, which is so important to the poem, and the slow progress of the horse's endless labor. As the horse performs the same monotonous actions, the sun slowly creeps higher in the sky, sending more and more heat down upon the laborers, making their jobs even more difficult.

Lines 9-12:

This stanza continues the account of the hay season. While there are hints of repetition in the second stanza ("manure" and "mowed/mowing" appear twice), the use of rhyme and sound come to the forefront here. The repetition takes on two forms: full rhyme ("stack," "hayrack," and "back"; and "hay" and "day") and internal rhyme, or sounds that rhyme within a word. This is evident in "rake" and "acres" and in "dragged" and "wagon." As the sounds cascade through the poem, creating linkages in the rhyme and repetition, Hall's rhymed word-play adds rhythm and unity to the work and aids the reader's movement through the poem. Not only are the sounds pleasing to the ear, they form the bond that holds the poem together, with each line or stanza flowing effortlessly into the next. The repetition of words and sounds allows the poet to make an important, yet unspoken, point: The work never ends, and each task is comprised of the same movements repeated endlessly. Here, the repeated sounds reflect or enact the repeated chores of the horse.

Lines 13-16:

Hall chose not to focus on the people who work the farm, who must brave the elements as well as the horses to keep the farm running. But if the reader extends any sympathy to them as well, the poet attempts to downplay their significance in this stanza. While the people, the horse's masters observe the Sabbath, the day of rest, there is no such rest for the animal. Although their Sunday task is hardly as grueling as the farm-work, the horse "trotted" carrying its "light load." Whether it is for work or recreation, the horse is a human tool.

Again, the vast sense of time is evoked here as the poet notes that "generation on generation" the horses have brought their masters to church. Now the reader is fully aware that Hall isn't addressing a single horse, but all the animals that have worked and died on his grandparents' farm. The stanza closes with a simile, a comparison using the word "like" or "as," to further this sense of constant work performed over long stretches of time. He claims that as long as it takes for the sea to smooth the edges of glass through a long process of erosion and the wash of waves, generations of horses have rubbed smooth the sill of the stall.

Lines 17-20:

Now many seasons have passed, and the horse has outlived its usefulness to the owner. There is no sentimentality on the part of the farmer. The horse was never a pet but a "machine," no different from the hay rake. Having become more a liability than an asset to the farmer, the horse is led out for the last time through the fields it helped to till. Hall's tone is straightforward and matter-of-fact. The reader is unsure of the attitude of "the man who fed you and kept you, and harnessed you every morning." These are the actions the farmer could have done fondly, out of love of the animal,

Media Adaptations

- An audio recording of Donald Hall reading "Names of Horses" was released by Watershed Tapes in 1985.

- *Donald Hall: Poetry and Prose* is a two-cassette selection of the author's work, available from Audiobooks.

- There are also several recordings of Hall reading the work of other poets.

or just to protect his investment and to ensure he got as much work out of the horse as possible. As the farmer prepares the horse's grave, the animal stands "shuddering," a well-chosen word that contributes an ambiguous note to the stanza. Is the word meant sentimentally, as if to suggest that the horse perceives its life is nearly over and waits in fear for its final moment? Or is the shuddering meant to highlight the horse's uselessness and justify the killing, as the once powerful muscles have succumbed to old age and now been reduced to uncontrollable twitches? It is this lack of perfect clarity that helps drive the poem, piquing the reader's curiosity to read on in search of answers.

Lines 21-24:

The poem is very direct and explicit in its portrayal of the horse's death. One gunshot and the animal is rolled into its grave and buried. Hall continues to employ the repetition of sounds and phrases to great effect. However, the recurrence of similar structures ("into your brain" and "into your grave") and the use of internal rhyme ("shoveling," "cover," and "above") serve a new function in the poem, one of larger significance. Now it is not the monotony of performing the same tasks Hall is attempting to convey, but a larger cycle: the life-cycle of the horse from its seasons of labor to the moment, now, when its body has given out. So the poem does not end with the horse's death. It is just part of a larger chain of events that encompass, or surround, the animal's life. Hall does not pause to sentimentally eulogize the animal's years of service to the farm. By the end of the stanza, half a year has passed, and the only trace of the horse's existence is a "dent in the ground."

Lines 25-29:

The scope of the poem broadens with this stanza. The story of the horse's life is also a comment on time, the seasons and years that have marked each horse's regimen on the farm. But now, time has accelerated even further. It is 150 years later, and the pasture has become a veritable horse cemetery. The stanza ends with a subtle, yet ironic, comment on the horses' lives of servitude. Even in death, they are still working; they are "soil makers," their bones churning and tilling the earth from within as the soil expands and contracts with each change of seasonal temperature.

Line 29:

Hall ends the poem with its only single-line stanza, interrupting the expected pattern of quatrains, or four-line stanzas, to present a roll-call of horses that have worked the farm. With this list of names comes the full explanation of the title. The reader more fully understands the scope of the "you": that Hall is not addressing a single horse, but many. In telling the story of one, he is telling the story of all.

Themes

Mortality

"Names of Horses" has been called an animal elegy. The elegy typically centers upon the death of a person. But Hall's poem participates nonetheless in the long-standing tradition of this poetic mode, in praising the lives of the dead horses. The pasture where the generations of animals are buried becomes a sort of potter's field, or Flanders Field, a place where unknown soldiers are laid to rest. But whereas some soldiers who have fallen in the line of duty remain forever anonymous, Hall's poem attempts to rescue from the past the names that would otherwise be forgotten. In writing the poem, Hall honors the dead, recognizing their accomplishments and contributions as we would any virtuous person now deceased. The fact that the poem is addressing horses instead of a departed loved one or famous citizen makes the work all the more original and compelling.

The recitation of the names at the end is like the listing of names on a memorial; though, instead

Topics for Further Study

- Donald Hall has cited Edwin Muir's "The Horses" (1956) as an influence upon "Names of Horses." Read Muir's poem and then compare and contrast this portrayal of the horses to Hall's. Find correlations in the Hall poem for the following lines from Muir: "We had sold our horses in our fathers' time/To buy new tractors" and "Since then they have pulled our ploughs and borne our loads./But that free servitude still can pierce our hearts." How do the themes and tone of "The Horses" differ from that of "Names of Horses"?

- Look at the paintings and prints of Currier and Ives or Grandma Moses, artists who took their inspiration from scenes of New England and rural life. Analyze a piece of your choosing, considering the subject the artists have chosen to portray. How realistically is the subject represented? How does an artist create a sense of tone? Write a poem or prose poem about the scene you've just analyzed, giving voice to an otherwise overlooked element or portion of the composition.

- Nostalgia heavily informs "Names of Horses." Choose a particularly memorable moment from your own past and write a paragraph capturing the event. Then rewrite the scene in the third person. How do the two versions differ?

- Write a poem or prose poem on the life and death of a pet or animal. Address the animal in the second person. How does the "you" affect how the story is told?

of headstones, there are only shallow depressions in the ground, marking the location of each horse's grave. In summer, the goldenrod sprouts "upright above" them. Reciting the names is the best substitute for a memorial the poet can offer. Ironically, it also brings the horses more vividly to life for the reader. The last line gestures to the fact that the horses seemed to occupy an ambiguous role on the farm. Meant only for work, they were still given names as any household pet would. Naming is an attempt to attribute identity, to recognize the value of an entity's life. But this avowal of the horses' inherent worth seems at odds with the brutal treatment they face when their bodies are no longer strong enough for the labors they must perform. In reality, the horses are killed, buried, and forgotten. The poet cannot change the past or the fate each horse faced. But in the world of the poem, it is the poet who has the last word. He can honor the memory of the horses that are so enmeshed in his own reminiscences of his childhood.

Time

No poem could be a meditation of mortality without grappling with the passage of time: the cycle of seasons and the laws of nature, which govern the lives of all living things. The "toilers" on the farm, human and animal alike, are subject to time, powerless to stop its swift progress. With the regimen of chores, there is the sense that the workers are always racing against time, needing to get in enough cordwood to last through the winter, enough hay to feed the animals to fatten them up for sale or to keep them working. And chores, as is typical, are not performed only once; for, like the seasons, chores are a never-ending process, an attempt to stay just one step ahead. Hall loads each stanza with references to units of time. They act as constant reminders of time's passage, like the chiming of a clock: "winter," "spring," "April," "summer," "morning," "noon," "day," "Sundays," "generation," "October." There is so much work to be done on a day-to-day basis for each generation of farmer who works the land; yet, before long "a hundred and fifty years" have gone by. Time is inescapable, larger than any one thing, and life, symbolized in the "roots of pine trees" and "yellow blossoms," moves on in spite of those who have gone before.

Labor

Before there were combines, harvesters, and tractors, farm work was performed by hand. For hundreds of years, worldwide, little changed. The farmer's lot improved somewhat over time, but compared to the revolutionary advances of the twentieth century, technology crept along at a snail's pace. Thus, it is understandable why the farmer relied so heavily on the horse and other beasts of burden. This is one of the ironies that informs the poem. Whether the goal was a successful harvest, the hauling of wood, or getting to town or church quickly, it was the horse that made all of it possible. For a system whose success relied so

heavily on the horse, there is a seeming callousness in ending their lives "when [they] were old and lame."

It is unclear exactly when the opening of the poem is set, but its origins may reach as far back as the early nineteenth century, a time when many upheld the value of hard work as among the highest of ideals. For some, this doctrine had a religious component, as a busy life kept one away from the temptations of sin. For others, it was purely economic: If you didn't work and work hard, you simply couldn't survive. In choosing the workings of a New England farm as his subject, Hall is taking part in the pastoral tradition, in which rural life is idealized for its simplicity and pure connection to the earth. Thus, perhaps for Hall, the listing of the labors of both farmer and horse is its own form of nostalgia. But the lesson learned from these past lives can be bittersweet. Some people face an existence no different from that of the horses: a life of constant labor with no recognition or rewards.

Style

"Names of Horses" is marked by simple, declarative diction. Diction is the specific word choices a poet makes and how the words are used to create a desired tone or effect. The poem's almost plain, matter-of-fact narration fits the subject matter, for the poet would threaten his authority or believability if he presented the horses' life and death in a sentimental way, or tipped-off the reader as to where his true sympathies lie. Instead, Hall just presents the facts of the case, reserving any sort of moral judgment. While there is often a celebratory note to the tone in Hall's praising the horses' feats and endurance, there is no condemnation of the horses' treatment or how their lives are viewed as disposable. That judgment is reserved for the reader.

The unusually long lines form a particularly noteworthy feature of the poem. Some lines are too long to fit the width of a standard page. Each line is intended to be read continuously, as one line of type, but methods of reproduction make it impossible. So, the long phrase is completed by carrying it to the next line and indenting. The visual aspects of the poem, how it looks on the page, are affected. Nonetheless, the intended effects of the long lines are not compromised. The long lines are well suited to the unfolding of a long tale; for although it is evident that "Names of Horses" is organized as a

Compare & Contrast

- **2,500,000 years ago:** Equus, the modern horse, evolves. It spreads across North America.

  10,000 years ago: The horse mysteriously dies out, disappearing from North America altogether.

  1510s-1520s: Horses return to their native land on the ships of Spanish conquistadors. Hernan Cortés is probably the first person to reintroduce the animal, bringing sixteen horses to the New World in his invasion of present-day Mexico.

  1865: Donald Hall's great-grandfather buys Eagle Pond Farm, the setting for "Names of Horses."

  1878: Hall's grandmother Kate is born at Eagle Pond Farm.

  1903: Hall's mother, Lucy, is born there.

  1975: Donald Hall purchases the farm and moves to New Hampshire.

- **1830s:** Horses and horse-drawn vehicles are the most common forms of transportation.

1910s: Use of the horse as a work animal reaches its peak in America.

1917: Henry Ford introduces the Fordson Tractor, the first commercial tractor.

1929-1941: The Great Depression cripples the nation economically. Unemployment and poverty become a national epidemic. Millions of horses and the farmers who own them are "tractored out," slowly replaced by the more efficient machines. By the time the nation recovers, at the end of World War II in 1945, more than one million tractors are in use on American farms, and the golden age of the horse has come to an end.

1919: There are 23 million horses in America.

1939: The horse population drops to 10 million.

Today: There are just over 5 million horses in the United States.

---

poem, it is really telling a story of the otherwise anonymous horses whose labor ensured the livelihood of their owners. Thus, If it weren't for the spaces between stanzas, the poem would look like a piece of prose, perhaps taken from a novel or story. Although the poem accomplishes much more than simply narrating a series of events, the long lines resemble sentences and help to visually cue readers that they are experiencing a version of the horses' history. After all, poems can be an alternative form of storytelling.

Despite the visual effects of the long lines, Hall still chooses to organize his poem into quatrains. This is an example of how form mirrors content. In other words, the regular, expected, and ordered patterns the quatrains establish reflect the essence of what Hall is attempting to relate. The structure of four-line stanzas-regular, repetitive, predictable-adds to the effect of a poem about the recurring cycles of time and the monotonous routine of the farm's chores.

However, at the end the poem abandons its strategy of order and balance with the inclusion of the sole one-line stanza. Again, this single line is another example of form matching content. The poem attempts to upset the order of its romantic, bucolic New England setting by drawing attention to an undervalued and overlooked element: the horses.

Historical Context

In an interview with Donald Hall, critic Alberta Turner asked him how the reception of "Names of Horses" would be affected since the subject had little familiarity for the modern reader. How would a reader approach such a poem "when the experience has become a historical curiosity associated with calendar towels and department store windows at Christmas"? Turner is referring to the nostalgic images of horse-drawn sleighs and teams pulling a wagon full of hay; in other words a romanticized vision of the old-fashioned "simpler" times. Clearly, Hall is writing about an era that has fallen away, a way of life and a style of working that were quickly disappearing from the American landscape in the twentieth century.

But in "Names of Horses," the local mirrors the universal. Telling the story of one farm is a way of capturing and honoring the life of all farms where soil is tilled, and the fields hayed, and where horses once bore the brunt of the labor. Throughout the nineteenth century, America was a largely agricultural nation that relied almost exclusively on the horse. While New England had already been settled and large farms established, vast tracts of virgin soil in the Midwest and Far West were being turned into fields of wheat, corn, and sugar beets. These massive swaths were known as agricultural belts, and they ranged from five hundred to two thousand miles in width. Farmers required huge teams of horses to plant and harvest their crops.

In Hall's part of New Hampshire, local agriculture had been practiced for centuries. But by the 1840s the railroad had come through, making it possible for farmers to ship their milk, corn, and hay to Manchester, Boston, and beyond. Slowly the nation was becoming commercially connected, and the horse was in its heyday.

The poem is intended as an elegy for horses, not as an account of the demise of widespread agriculture in the twentieth century. But with the death of the horses comes the death of an entire way of life: not the passing of the individual animals, but the system of horse-reliant labor as a whole. By the 1920s, farming had become more mechanized, and by the end of the century an increasing number of farmers were forced into bankruptcy, in part because of the cost of owning and operating tractors, combines, and other heavy equipment. So Hall's poem, in focusing on the life of the farm, cannot avoid including by association the people who labored there as well, and the proud tradition of which they were part. In answering Alberta Turner's question, Hall stated that his poem is "an elegy not merely for horses but for people who hayed and cut ice and went to church and spread manure and shot horses, by extension for the whole country of the dead." The horses do not work the farm alone. They are inextricably linked with their owners, with each dependent on the other for survival. When the horse ages, is injured, or is replaced by more efficient machines, the farmer's life is greatly impacted as well.

Critical Overview

"Names of Horses" can be counted among Donald Hall's best-known and most accomplished poems. Critics are drawn to the complexity of its vision as it addresses the large questions of time and mortality while exploring the events in the life span of a horse. As evidence of its complexity, critics have identified two seemingly opposite currents that course through the poem: the harsh reality of death (through the killing of the old and weak) and the comfort the poet draws from reviving memories of the past, no matter how painful. Writing in the *Harvard Advocate,* Richard Nalley notes how the poem engages overtly with death, and yet "there is a certain sentimentality and longing for the past" evident as well. The blending of these concerns creates a sense of bittersweet nostalgia. In the poem, Nalley states, "Hall wishes to make one feel an inclusive warmth and a fine sadness."

In a notice published in *National Review,* Guy Davenport looks at a very specific mode of death present in the poem: death by violence. The heartless killing of the horse serves as a reminder of how brutal reality can often be. "The taste" the poem leaves "in the mind is the bitterness of life's brevity." The comfort and luxury of remembering the past often comes at the expense of others. "Against the goodness of being alive," Davenport writes, "runs the harshness of the bargains by which we live: the toil and death of other creatures."

In *Poet and Critic,* Brent Spenser takes a much lighter spin on the poem, noting that the recuperative power of memory is the main theme of the collection, *Kicking the Leaves: Poems,* of which "Names of Horses" is a part. The lessons learned from the past eventually erase the sadness of death or the sting of mourning for those lost. "The effort in these poems is to look for that part of the past that lives on into the present. They are, for the most part, poems about the gifts the past brings us, the gifts of the dead."

Criticism

Chris Semansky

Chris Semansky's most recent collection of poems, Blindsided, *published by 26 Books of Portland, Oregon, has been nominated for an Oregon Book Award. In the following essay Semansky examines ways in which Hall represents the idea of work in "Names of Horses."*

What Do I Read Next?

- Another famous literary horse is Gabilan from John Steinbeck's *The Red Pony.* This collection of four related stories center around young Jody Tiflin. In "The Gift," the best-known of the stories, Jody is presented a red pony by his rancher father. With the help of ranch hand Billy Buck, Jody learns the responsibility of raising and training the sorrel colt. The story traces the maturation of both the boy and his pony. The impact of Gabilan's death upon Jody informs the collection's subsequent tales.

- Those who would like to learn more of Donald Hall's New Hampshire roots or sample some of his nonfiction should read his memoir *String Too Short to Be Saved: Recollections of Summers on a New England Farm.* In brisk prose, Hall offers a portrait of a world that strongly influenced both his love of nature and his love of poetry. Another good source is Hall's 1987 work *Seasons at Eagle Pond,* a tribute to the place where Hall spent many years which depicts the quaintness and nostalgia of New England life.

- Robert Frost is widely considered the bard of New England, and like Hall he spent a large portion of his life in New Hampshire. Start with his work entitled *New Hampshire* (1923) or his second collection *North of Boston* (1914). Such classic poems as "Mending Wall," "Stopping by Woods on a Snowy Evening," and "Death of the Hired Man" capture not only his rural sensibil- ities but the profound simplicity that was Frost's signature.

- Frost cast a long shadow over the New England writers that established themselves in the latter part of the twentieth century, as is evident in *After Frost: An Anthology of Poetry from New England* (1996), which includes poems by Wallace Stevens, Donald Hall, and many of Hall's contemporaries.

- Some critics have described certain trends in Donald Hall's work as "New Hampshire pastoral," referring to the long-standing tradition of literature that praises the simplicity and innocence of country and agrarian life. Traditional pastoral poetry took shepherds and shepherdesses as its subjects. Among the writers best known for their use of the convention are the classical poets Theocritus (*Bucolics*) and Virgil (*Eclogues*), as well as the English poets Edmund Spenser (*Shepeardes Calendar*), Robert Herrick, John Milton, and Percy Bysshe Shelley. The pastoral has survived into the modern era in a variety of forms, from the ironic eclogues (a poetic conversation between shepherds) of Louis MacNeice to W. H. Auden's *The Age of Anxiety,* which the poet described as "a baroque eclogue." The works of these poets can be found in your library, or for an anthology devoted to the pastoral, read *Field Days: An Anthology of Poetry*(1999).

A seemingly unblinking and unsentimental paean to the generations of horses which have labored on the Hall farm, Donald Hall's poem, "Names of Horses," praises the idea of work, particularly physical work, as much as it praises the horses themselves. By describing the typical life of one family horse, Hall characterizes all of them and their importance to his family.

For Hall, work is what we do during life, both animals and humans. When we can no longer work, we lose much of our usefulness, our reason for being in the world.

Hall begins the poem with a description of the strenuous nature of the horse's work, detailing how the animal "strained against collars, padding / and steerhide" to carry wood that would ensure its owner's warmth for the next winter. By addressing the horse directly, and by cataloguing the various kinds of work the horse did for its owner, the speaker creates a sense of intimacy between himself and the animal. Readers are witnesses to this intimacy, in a position not unlike that of audience members listening to a eulogy. This poem, however, is as much elegy as it is eulogy, celebrating as it (implicitly) laments. By focusing on the physical details of the horse's work, the speaker underscores the effort that goes into the labor. It is this effort which marks the value of the work, and of the horse, for the speaker. Implicit in this poem is the awe that the speaker feels towards the horse, and his gratitude for the work the horse had done to keep his ancestors alive.

In addition to describing the horse's work, the speaker also describes the work of the seasons. In the opening stanza he details the work the horses do in winter, and in the next stanza moves to spring and summer. In the second and third stanzas he names the time of day and the kind of work the horse does during the day. Accretion of this kind of detail underscores the ritualistic nature of the work, both the animal's and the seasons', and it draws attention to the relationship between creature (i.e., human and animal) work and non-creature (i.e., natural processes) work and the relentlessness of time itself. Work, this poems implies, is the defining element of *all* life.

The fourth stanza again highlights the horse's value to its owners, describing its activity in human terms, when the speaker writes how on Sundays the horse "grazed in the sound of hymns" as it waited for its owners to finish the worship service. This metaphor, striking in its use of synesthesia (uncharacteristic for this poem), contributes to the eulogistic tone of the poem. This stanza introduces the idea—only implicit in the poem until now—that it is not one horse we are reading about but rather one horse representing generations of horses. Hall writes: "Generation on generation, your neck rubbed the window sill / of the stall, smoothing the wood as the sea smooths glass." This simile is fitting, for it suggests the ways in which individual identity folds into a kind of generic use-value when considered over time. Put another way, it is not an individual horse that the speaker describes and praises, but rather all horses which work. Just as the ocean's waves wear away the identifying markers of glass (e.g., the ridges, the ink, the shape itself), so too is the horse wearing away the identifying markers of the wooden window sill. Both the original wood and glass can be seen as signifying individual identity which, over time, is leveled into a type.

The fifth stanza develops the speaker's utilitarian attitude towards the horse and towards work. When in the eyes of its owner the horse has outlived its usefulness to its owner, it is time to kill the horse.

> *The work survives the worker."*
> *—Donald Hall*

When you were old and lame, when your shoulders
    hurt bending to graze,
one October the man who fed you and kept you,
    and harnessed you every morning,
led you through corn stubble to sandy ground
    above Eagle Pond,
and dug a hole beside you where you stood
    shuddering in your skin,
and lay the shotgun's muzzle in the boneless
    hollow behind your ear,
and fired the slug into your brain, and felled you
    into your grave,
shoveling sand to cover you, setting goldenrod
    upright above you,
where by next summer a dent in the ground made
    your monument.

Interestingly, the speaker describes the horse's death in such a way that the reader has two conflicting responses. The first one is empathy for both owner and horse because the horse is hurting and because the owner *has* to kill him, there being no alternative. The second one, revulsion at the owner's act of killing, stems from the detailed description of the act and of the owner's calculated approach towards the killing. Hall's use of assonance (lame/graze; shoulders/hurt; brain/grave), consonance (stubble/sandy/pond; summer/dent/ ground/monument), and alliteration (stood/shuddering/skin; fired/fell) underline the visceral and graphic nature of the image and contribute to readers' feeling of shock. That the horse's killer/owner had already prepared the grave for the horse to fall into once shot highlights the owner's—over generations, each a Hall ancestor—own practical attitude towards work, even the work of killing. The matter-of-fact description of the killing, the efficient way in which it was carried out, and the poem's final image before the roll call of names, describing the horses as "old toilers, soil makers," all underscore the primary value of the horses to the Hall family as workers. The horse's work continues even in death. If in life the horse worked on nature, in death nature works on the horse. His bones nourished the "roots of pine trees" and "yellow blossoms flourished above ... [him] in autumn." The last stanza demonstrates that even the speaker's impulse towards eulogizing the horses, towards remembering them as family members, is tempered by his description of what they have done for the family. The final line, a lament cataloguing the names of the Hall family's horses over the last century and a half, is also praise for work well done. Calling out the horses' names can be read as a way of evoking their presence, making their image palpable both to himself and to readers of the poem. Giving the horses names also marks a way of "personalizing" our image of the horses.

Hall himself is consumed with the idea of work, thinking and writing about it often. In his book, *Life Work* (which he thought about naming "Work and Death"), he draws a distinction between himself and manual laborers, claiming that he had never "worked" a day in his life. Hall writes: "I've never worked with my hands or shoulders or legs. I never stood on the line in Flint among the clangor and stench of embryonic Buicks for ten hours of small operations repeated on a large machine." This kind of activity, the "dirty work" of the body, is what the horses do, spreading manure, mowing grass, transporting wood. Hall praises it because it is precisely what he does *not* do. Coming from a farming family who made their living working with their hands, Hall respects manual labor to the point of romanticizing it. For Hall, work is what we do during life, both animals and humans. When we can no longer work, we lose much of our usefulness, our reason for being in the world. And just as work unites humans and animals, so too does death, the great leveler. In "The Black Faced Sheep," a poem appearing in the same volume as "Names of Horses," Hall writes

> that the rich farmer, though he names the farm for
>   himself,
> takes nothing into his grave;
> that even if people praise us, because we are
>   successful,
> we will go under the ground
> to meet our ancestors collected there in the
>   darkness;
> that we are all of us sheep, and death is our
>   shepherd,
> and we die as the animals die.

Hall wrote this poem and "Names of Horses" after quitting academia in 1975 and returning to the place of his birth, Eagle Pond Farm in Wilmot, New Hampshire in 1975. Much of his poetry after this date is rooted in place and family and more concrete, more personal than his previous writing. His poems frequently detail the work of the body, the earth, rather than the mind, and remind us of the material world in which we live and the bodies we inhabit.

Source: Chris Semansky, in an essay for *Poetry for Students,* Gale Group, 2000.

Sources

Braider, Donald, *The Life, History, and Magic of the Horse,* New York: Grosset, 1973.

Davenport, Guy, "New Hampshire Elegies" in *National Review,* March 30, 1979, p. 430.

Hall, Donald, *Kicking the Leaves: Poems,* New York: Harper, 1978.

——, *Poetry and Ambition: Essays 1982 1988,* Ann Arbor: University of Michigan Press, 1988.

——, *Seasons at Eagle Pond,* New York: Ticknor & Fields, 1987.

——, *String Too Short to Be Saved: Recollections of Summers on a New England Farm,* Boston: Godine, 1979.

Nalley, Richard, "Kicking the Leaves" in *The Harvard Advocate,* vol. 112, no. 1, December 1978, pp. 26-7.

Osborne, Walter D., and Patricia H. Johnson, *The Treasury of Horses,* New York: Ridge, 1966.

Poulin, A., Jr., ed, *Contemporary American Poetry* Boston: Houghton Mifflin, 1985.

Spenser, Brent, "Kicking the Leaves" in *Poet and Critic,* vol. 12, no. 30, 1980, p. 77.

Turner, Alberta, *Forty-five Contemporary Poems,* New York: Longman, 1985.

For Further Study

Corbett, William, *Literary New England: A History and Guide,* London: Faber & Faber, 1993.
   This brief overview traces the roots of the New England literary tradition and the literary ancestors who influenced Donald Hall and his generation.

Howard, Robert West, *The Horse in America,* Chicago: Follett, 1965.
   One of strongest works on this topic, it provides a unique interpretation of history through the eyes of the horse. West traces the gradual replacement of human labor by horse power, including the eventual demise of the animal's role as a beast of burden. Also strong is his account of the horse's arrival in the Americas during the seventeenth century and its subsequent transformation of Native American life. Howard's is an indispensable resource for all things horsey.

Rector, Liam, ed., *The Day I Was Older: On the Poetry of Donald Hall,* Santa Cruz, CA: Story Line Press, 1989.
   Rector has collected a series of critical essays which provide the first full treatment of Hall's development as a writer and his overall contribution to American letters.

A Red, Red Rose

Robert Burns
1794

After the 1786 publication of *Poems, Chiefly in the Scottish Dialect*, Robert Burns spent the last ten years of his life collecting and editing songs for *The Scots Musical Museum*, an anthology intended to preserve traditional Scottish lyrical forms. During this time, Burns also composed more than three hundred original works for the volume, songs that relied heavily on forms and sentiments popular in the folk culture of the Scottish peasantry. " A Red, Red Rose," first published in 1794 in *A Selection of Scots Songs*, edited by Peter Urbani, is one such song. Written in ballad stanzas, the verse—read today as a poem—pieces together conventional ideas and images of love in a way that transcends the "low" or non-literary sources from which the poem is drawn. In it, the speaker compares his love first with a blooming rose in spring and then with a melody "sweetly play'd in tune." If these similes seem the typical fodder for love-song lyricists, the second and third stanzas introduce the subtler and more complex implications of time. In trying to quantify his feelings—and in searching for the perfect metaphor to describe the "eternal" nature of his love—the speaker inevitably comes up against love's greatest limitation, "the sands o' life." This image of the hour-glass forces the reader to reassess of the poem's first and loveliest image: A "red, red rose" is itself an object of an hour, "newly sprung" only "in June" and afterward subject to the decay of time. This treatment of time and beauty predicts the work of the later Romantic poets, who took Burns's work as an important influence.

Robert Burns

Author Biography

Burns was born in Alloway, Scotland, in 1759. His father, a poor tenant farmer, tutored his sons at home and sought to provide them with as much additional education as his resouces allowed. An avid reader, Burns acquired a grounding in English before studying the poetry of his Scottish heritage. During his youth Burns endured the hard work and progressively worsening financial difficulties which beset his family as they moved from one rented farm to another. As a young man Burns developed a reputation for charm and wit, engaging in several love affairs that brought him into conflict with the Presbyterian Church. He also angered the church by criticizing such accepted beliefs as predestination and mankind's inherent sinfulness, which he considered incompatible with human nature. In 1786 Burns proposed marriage to Jean Armour, who was pregnant with his twin sons. Her parents rejected his offer and demanded financial restitution. As a result, Burns determined to sail to the West Indies and start a new life. However, with the successful publication that year of his *Poems, Chiefly in the Scottish Dialect,* Burns abandoned his plans and traveled to Edinburgh, where he was much admired in literary circles. While in Edinburgh Burns met James Johnson, a printer involved

in a project to publish all the folk songs of Scotland. Burns subsequently traveled throughout the country, collecting over 300 songs, which were printed in Johnson's six-volume *Scots Musical Museum* (1787-1803) and George Thomson's five-volume *Select Collection of Original Airs for the Voice* (1793-1818). Many of the songs he collected were revised or edited by Burns—as with "John Anderson My Jo"—or, in some cases, newly written by him—as with "A Red, Red Rose." One consequence of his journeys around Scotland was his rise to national prominence and popularity. Burns finally married Armour in 1788 and divided his time between writing poetry and farming until he obtained a government position three years later. He died from rheumatic heart disease in 1796.

Poem Text

O my Luve's like a red, red rose,
    That's newly sprung in June:
O my Luve's like the melodie
    That's sweetly play'd in tune.

As fair art thou, my bonnie lass,   5
    So deep in luve am I;
And I will luve thee still, my Dear,
    Till a' the seas gang dry.

Till a' the seas gang dry, my Dear,
    And the rocks melt wi' the sun: 10
And I will luve thee still, my Dear,
    While the sands o' life shall run.

And fare thee weel, my only Luve!
    And fare thee weel, awhile!
And I will come again, my Luve,   15
    Tho' it were ten thousand mile!

Poem Summary

Lines 1-2:

The reader may be already familiar with the poem's much-quoted first line. Its appeal over time probably stems from the boldness of its assertion—the speaker's love conveyed through the conventional image of the rose and through the line's four strong beats. The poet's choice of a rose may at first seem trite, and the color "red" may seem too obvious a symbol of love and passion. Yet if the comparison between the beloved and the rose verges on cliché, a careful reading reveals the subtler ways in which the speaker expresses his conviction. Why, for instance, is the word "red" repeated? The answer might be found in the second line. While red is the expected hue of the flower, the repetition of the adjective represents the fullest and most lovely manifestation of the rose: its ideal state. Such also is the nature of the speaker's love. "Newly sprung," it exists in its purest and most perfect state—none of its vitality has faded; time has not scarred it with age or decay. Yet this embodiment of love is a temporary one. Like the rose, which can exist in this lush form only "in June," the speaker's feelings and his beloved's beauty cannot remain frozen in time: they, like all other forms of beauty, are passing.

Lines 3-4:

Perhaps it is the speaker's recognition of the rose's brief beauty that compels him to pursue another metaphor for his love. This time he chooses to compare her to a lovely melody from a song, but this is also a temporary form of beauty. While a song may be "sweetly play'd in tune," it too is a product of time, of beats and measures. When the song has ended, its beauty lives on only in abstraction—as the *idea* of the beautiful song.

Lines 5-8:

The second stanza plays on the word "luve," revealing the elusive nature of the concept. When the speaker says "I will luve thee still," he plays on the concept of time. The line seems to indicate that the speaker will love continuously or forever, but the following line does put a limit on the amount of time he will love. His passion will continue "Till" a certain time—when "the seas gang dry." Though the prospect of the seas drying up seems remote, it exists nonetheless. Thus, while the sentiment seems wholly romantic, there remains in it a hint of melancholy: The speaker is saying his love will last a long time—but that it is not eternal in the purest sense.

Lines 9-11:

The repetition here of "Till a' the seas gang dry" is in keeping with the song's musicality. But in it there is also a hint of reconsideration, as if the speaker has just understood the implications of what he has said. From this, he moves to another attempt to express eternity, yet this too depends on the word "Till": he will love until the rocks "melt wi' the sun." But the rocks may indeed melt one day, or erode, in any case, under the effects of the sun, wind, and weather. At that point his love will cease, so again, his sentiments are not wholly timeless.

Line 12:

Line 12 also casts some doubt on the speaker's intentions, since it can be interpreted two ways. In

Media Adaptations

one sense, he could mean that their love is separate—above or beyond—the sands of time. This indicates that it will last forever and won't change or end because of time. On the other hand, he almost seems to emphasize the fact that the sands are running, which is to say time is running out, as sand runs out of the hourglass. This direct reference to time also reminds us of the first two lines in the poem: the momentary, time-bound state of a "red, red rose that's newly sprung in June." Read in this way, the poem becomes more than the simple love ballad that it seemed initially; instead, it can also be a seen as a meditation on the speaker's consciousness of time and on limits that time can place upon human emotions.

Lines 13-16:

The last stanza seems to shift away from the predominant concerns of the first three: the speaker turns from the concept of time to that of parting. He is journeying away from his love, assuring her that he will be true and will return. Yet the concept of time enters here as well: the speaker will transcend not only vast distance ("ten thousand miles") to be with his love, but also time itself, with words like "awhile" and "again" drawing the poem back to the main concerns of the first three stanzas.

Topics for Further Study

- What do you think are the circumstances of the speaker of this poem that cause him/her to leave his/her love? Write a short story or dialogue that explains why the speaker is leaving, and how this poem affects the situation.

- Look through magazines and find at least five examples of red things. Which do you think could be described as "red red"? Why?

- Which of the symbols used to express love in this poem works the best? Why?

- Adapt this ballad to the music of a contemporary song, and explain what elements of the music you think are appropriate to what the poem is saying.

Themes

Love and Passion

Because modern readers are well familiar with the poetic imagery that Burns uses in this poem, and also because "A Red, Red Rose" was originally written to be sung as popular music, some of the poem's impact may be lost to the contemporary audience. The poem expresses love, but it does not try to stir up deep feelings of passion—instead, it reminds readers of love, making the speaker's feelings sound more theoretical than real. In the first stanza, the word "Luve" is used twice as a pronoun, describing a particular person that the speaker has in mind. By talking about this person, the poet draws attention to the other person and to how he relates to that person, rather than examining his own emotions. This raises the impression that the love affair might be more for show, for the approval of other people, than for the experience of it. In the first half of stanza 2, the poem actually says that the amount that the speaker is in love can be measured by how fair the woman is. There is a simpler reading, that because his love is great her fairness (or beauty) must be great too, but it is clearly implied that if she were now or were to become less beautiful then his love would diminish.

Lines 7 and 11 both contain promises that this poem's speaker makes to his lover. The problem, however, is that his promises are exaggerated, made in over-inflated terms that are common among passionate young lovers but are difficult to take seriously. His claim that he will still love her when the seas dry up and the sun melts rocks, or until the sands stop flowing, may or may not be true: no one will be around to see these events, so who would ever know? The final stanza mirrors the first in its use of "my Luve," but this time the phrase is directed directly to the lover. It is here that the speaker makes a specific claim: that he is leaving now, but that he will come back. Given the over-exaggeration that precedes it, readers are invited to question his commitment to love and to question whether, once he is out of sight of her beauty, he will be as committed to her as he says he will.

Time

"A Red, Red Rose" seeks to strike a balance between the temporary and the eternal. It starts with images of things that last for only a short time and then are gone. Any flower can be used by poets to remind readers of the fact that beauty is fleeting, because the life of a flower is so short when compared to human life. Flowers are often used to remind us of the interconnection of life and death because of their quick succession of budding, blossoming, and wilting. In this poem, the flower that Burns uses is especially short-lived: it is not just red but a *red, red* rose. A flower can only stay at its peak brightness for a short time. It is *newly* sprung; it is presented in June, hinting at the fate that awaits it in the autumn. Similarly, the "melodie" used to describe the lover is another image of fleeting time. This sense would have been clearer to readers in the 1700's, a time before recording equipment, when any rendition of a song could only occur once, to be imitated later perhaps but never reproduced exactly. Melodies, like moments, evaporate into the air and become history.

These initial examples of the ways time constantly passes are in conflict with the poem's main claim. By the time they have finished with "A Red, Red Rose," readers are left with the impression that Burns is talking about love as being eternal, not fleeting. In the third stanza he claims that his love will outlast events that will take more time than humans could even imagine: seas going dry, rocks melting in the sun, etc. In the end he claims he will love her after traveling ten thousand miles, which, we assume would have to take place by horseback or sailing ship at a laborious pace. The conflicting images of love as fleeting and also measured by centuries is used to highlight the different uses of the words "my Luve": when the Luve is a person, its life is brief like a melody or a rose, but when the word is used to discuss emotions the poem uses images that time cannot affect.

Duty and Responsibility

The first three stanzas of this poem present the speaker's claims about love, while the last stanza creates an actual social situation in which he is able to act upon this great love. Readers find out at the end that there is a reason why this speaker is telling the object of his affection, his "bonnie lass," how much he cares for her. He is going away, and for some reason he expects her to doubt that his love for her will last while they are apart. Most of the poem is taken up with open-ended, unsupported claims that he loves and reveres her, but it is only at the end that he mentions something that he can take action on. In promising to come back to her, the speaker takes on a responsibility for his future action. The words "I will come again" create a moral commitment. It is not complicated with any qualifiers (such as "I will come again *unless* ..."); in fact, the last line assures that he will allow no unforeseen difficulty to keep him from her.

Readers' faith in his returning, in how serious this speaker is about his responsibility, depends on how much sincerity they see in the words he uses. If the love he describes is sincere, then there is probably no force strong enough to keep him from returning to her. If, on the other hand, the grandeur of his statements is read as a tendency toward exaggeration, then he might just be promising to return because he feels that he ought to promise, just as he is overstating his love because he feels it is what she wants to hear. Love is such a powerful emotion that it would be easy to understand someone being carried away, expressing himself with hyperbolic, flamboyant terms, but in making a promise this speaker has brought upon himself the responsibility to fulfill it.

Style

"A Red, Red Rose" is written in four four-line stanzas, or quatrains, consisting of alternating tetrameter and trimeter lines. This means that the first and third lines of each stanza have four stressed syllables, or beats, while the second and fourth lines have three stressed syllables. Quatrains written in this manner are called ballad stanzas. The ballad is a old form of verse adapted for singing or recitation, originating in the days when most poetry existed in spoken rather than written form. The typical subject matter of most ballads reflects folk themes important to common people: love, courage, the mysterious, and the supernatural. Though the ballad is generally rich in musical qualities such as rhythm and repetition, it often portrays both ideas and feelings in overwrought but simplistic terms.

The dominant meter of the ballad stanza is iambic, which means the poem's lines are constructed in two-syllable segments, called iambs, in which the first syllable is unstressed and the second is stressed. As an example of iambic meter, consider the following line from the poem with the stresses indicated:

That's *sweet* / ly *play'd* / in *tune*.

This pattern exists most regularly in the trimeter lines of the poem, lines which most often finish the thoughts begun in the previous line. The rhythm's regularity gives the poem a balanced feel that enhances its musical sound.

Historical Context

Robert Burns is often considered a writer ahead of his time, who often embraced the idea of using common language to reach the common person just slightly before this idea became popularized as the Age of Romanticism swept across the globe. When Burns published "A Red, Red Rose" in 1794, the Age of Enlightenment was dwindling to an end. As with all historical ages, there is no definitive way of measuring the beginning or the end of the Enlightenment—historians can't point to an exact moment when people across the earth agreed to adopt a set of beliefs, or when they stopped believing—but the term is useful in measuring the prevailing mood of the time. As far back as the 1500s, scientists and philosophers began to believe that it was possible to understand how the universe works by establishing laws and principles: they turned from the religious explanations that were provided by the church to scientific explanations that were supported by reason. Today, people take for granted the idea that scientific inquiry should be conducted according to reason, but in the sixteenth century, nearly two hundred years before Burns's time, the idea was new and bold and slightly dangerous. The

Compare & Contrast

- **1786:** Farmers in Massachusetts, burdened by the debt of the Revolutionary War, participated in Shays' Rebellion in order to protest against having to pay the colonial government with cash. The rebellion was fairly small-scale—rebels broke up a session of the state Supreme Court and tried unsuccessfully to take the state arsenal—but symbolically it was reminiscent of the uprising against oppression that led to the foundation of the country. The rebellion was one of the most glaring proofs that the Articles of Confederation that then governed the United States were inadequate: the following year the Constitution was drafted.

  1990s: Twenty-seven amendments have been added to the Constitution, representing very little change needed in a document written over two hundred years ago.

- **1786:** Inventor Ezekiel Reed developed a machine that could produce nails. Previously, all buildings were held together with wooden pegs or handmade nails.

  1990s: The world's tallest buildings, the Petronas Towers in Kuala Lumpur, stand at 1,483 feet each.

- **1786:** The first public golf club in the United States was opened in Charleston, South Carolina. The game had been popular in Scotland since the 15th Century.

  1990s: There are private golf courses with high membership fees, but the game of golf has been embraced by the general public in the United States, and public courses abound.

- **1786:** The population of the United States was around 3.7 million people. The largest city, New York, had 32,000, with roughly 17,000 more on the surrounding farms that would later be incorporated into the city.

  1990s: The population of the United States is estimated to be around 260 million. New York is still the most populous area, with 7.5 million inhabitants.

- **1786:** Coal miners in Scotland worked under conditions that resembled slavery, under an edict from George III: they were subject to long hours in deplorable conditions and were treated as criminals if they tried to leave. An edict allowing them freedom was signed in 1788 and enacted in 1789.

  1990s: Scotland is still a part of the United Kingdom of Great Britain, having members elected to the House of Commons and the House of Lords.

theory that Earth orbits the sun, which was first put forth by Polish astronomer Nicolaus Copernicus in 1543 and later supported by Galileo, was opposed by the powerful Catholic church, which sentenced Galileo to life imprisonment for suggesting that God did not place humans at the center of the universe. A key discovery that prodded Enlightenment thinking along was Isaac Newton's 1684 Laws of Motion, which included the theory of Universal Gravity that could explain events and physical actions just as clearly as referring to God's divine will could. By the 1700s, writers and philosophers were expanding out from the idea that reason could explain the way the physical universe works. Since rational theory worked so well when applied to the physical universe, they decided that there was no reason that political and social interactions could not be explained with scientific equations in the same way. During the early part of the Enlightenment, writers, based mainly in France, faced social persecution for publishing ideas that challenged the reigning authorities. One of the key figures of the time was Voltaire, who was one of the most versatile writers of his time: his essays, plays, novels and poems supported the belief that neither the church nor the monarchy had any special knowledge of the world that people of ordinary intelligence could not attain. Another key figure was

Jean-Jacques Rousseau, who published his philosophical work *The Social Contract* in 1762: it supported the will of the people over the previously-accepted "divine rights" of the monarchy. Voltaire spent eleven months in the Bastille for his writings, and Rousseau was exiled from France. However, later thinkers, who were strongly influenced by the French thinkers, ended up having enormous impact on how society imagined itself. One example was the German philosopher Immanuel Kant's 1781 book *Critique of Pure Reason,* which argued that moral choices must apply to all people at all times, thereby bringing the Enlightenment worship of logic to every decision a person makes. One of the results of the Age of Enlightenment was the American Revolution: the thinkers who wrote the Declaration of Independence in 1776 did so believing the untested idea that people could rule themselves at least as well as monarchs could. The United States was structured on rationalist principles that derived from the Enlightenment. Following the War of Independence came the French Revolution, from 1789 to 1799: while the American Revolution established a new state according to democratic principles, the revolution in France reorganized an old, established state, taking power out of the hands of the aristocracy and trusting the common people's ability to follow reason.

Overlapping with the Age of Enlightenment is another era which stressed the common people over the rules of the elite: literary historians call this period the Age of Romanticism. Like the Enlightenment, the thinkers of the Romantic Age did not think that one had to come from a certain privileged class to experience the world fully or to understand it. The key difference, though, was that Romantic writers stressed emotion, not reason. Romantic writers were not interested in finding new equations to let them measure and control the world, as Enlightenment thinkers had been. Romanticism was more concerned with experiencing nature, not understanding it. As such, Romanticism allowed for the possibility of an inexplicable, supernatural world. Writers in this movement were drawn to the mysteries of the exotic, the lure of romance. Because of this emphasis on experience, the Romantic poets moved even further than the Enlightenment away from the idea of elitism: they not only rejected the idea that anyone from higher social classes was particularly knowledgeable, they also refused to believe that educated people understood the world better than uneducated people, who felt experiences more deeply. Society was corruption of humanity's natural goodness, so social

success indicated a further distance from nature. Historians generally measure the Romantic period in literature as beginning with the publication of *Lyrical Ballads* by William Wordsworth and Samuel Taylor Coleridge in 1798, although, as "A Red, Red Rose" demonstrates, the Romantics' faith in simple, common, accessible language is one of the ideas that was around before the movement in general took root.

Critical Overview

Critics discuss "A Red, Red Rose" in terms of the delicacy of its craft and the power of its expression. Franklyn Bliss Snyder sees "A Red, Red Rose" as an example of Burns's proficiency at English verse. Calling it "one of the perfectly cut and polished gems in Burns's song collection," the critic points out that "four touches of the vernacular—bonie, gang, a', and weel—are all that save the song from being pure English." Iain Crichton Smith calls "A Red, Red Rose" an example of the sentiments of a by-gone era, suggesting that we cannot enjoy such a direct anticipation of an enduring relationship in modern times. "A poem like 'A Red Red Rose' begs too many questions, is too set in one inflated mood for us to write like it, because we would be far more concerned with the shadows. How could we possibly, in our world, speak of such permanency," he writes, possibly yearning for those by-gone times. In contrast, David Daiches writes fondly of the poem's depiction of the tenderness and swagger of the young man in love.

Criticism

David Kelly

David Kelly teaches courses in Creative Writing, Poetry and Drama at College of Lake County and Oakton Community College, in Illinois. The following essay examines the idea of "simplicity" in "A Red, Red Rose," questioning whether it is really as easy to understand as most readers would like to believe.

I have seen readers bulldoze through Robert Burns's "A Red, Red Rose" in thirty seconds, or however long it takes to sift all of the letters through their visual screen, and then sit back and say they

What Do I Read Next?

- The definitive collection of Scottish ballads, of which Burns is considered the master, is Francis James Childs's collection *the English and Scottish Popular Ballads.* It was originally published by Houghton Mifflin in ten volumes between 1882 and 1898. In 1965 Dover Publications issued a condensed five-volume reprint.

- In 1971 Greenwood Press reprinted the famous multi-volume *Scottish Poetry of the Eighteenth Century,* first published in 1896. The editor, George Eyre-Todd, has assembled the best writings of Burns and his contemporaries, many of whom are not familiar to modern audiences.

- Thomas Carlyle was a famous Scottish historian from the generation after Burns (he was born in 1795: Burns died in 1796). Carlyle's book-length essay on Burns might seem a bit too complex for some modern readers, but, remembering the time it came from, it is a helpful piece for putting the poet in historical perspective. The essay was printed as *An Essay on Burns* in 1910 by Charles E. Merrill Co., and has appeared in several different formats since.

- A handy reference, written for contemporary students, that puts Burns's ballads in historical perspective is *The Penguin Book of Ballads,* edited by Geoffrey Grigson and published in 1975.

- The University of Iowa Press published a collection of essays in 1997 called *Robert Burns and Cultural Authority,* consisting of eleven essays by literary critics about the poet and his relation to social issues, such as "Burns and God" and "Burns and Sex."

- In the 1760's Scottish poet James MacPherson published several volumes that claimed to be translations of ancient stories about a legendary Scottish folk hero, Ossian. Scholars suspect that MacPherson made the stories up himself. Those interested on Scottish literature at the time Burns was writing can read *The Poems of Ossian and Related Works (The Ossianic Works of James MacPherson).* Edited by Howard Gaskill, published by Edinburgh University Press, 1996.

- Alan Bold made life immeasurably easier for students of Robert Burns by publishing *A Burns Companion* in 1991 (St. Martin's Press). This comprehensive volume contains biographical info and literary criticism that covers the poet's career.

- The book *Auld Lang Syne* by Joanne Findon and Ted Nasmith, was written for children, but it serves all ages as an intelligent (if simplified) introduction to Burns and Scotland of his time. This book imagines life in Eighteenth-Century Scotland from the poet's first-person point-of-view. Published in 1998 by Stoddard Kids Publishing.

---

know it. A bad sign is when, asked to explain it, they start with, "It's just …" or "All he's saying is …," to prepare the listener for the fact that there isn't much to be said. I don't know why anyone thinks poetry is something to be understood as quickly as it is read. I do know that sometimes students are forced to read something they do not like, and so want to get the whole experience over as quickly as possible, but if I were them I would be very, very surprised to find a poem that had no secrets, that presented all that it was about to the naked eye. I must admit, though, that Robert Burns, of all poets, tends to make us feel that there is no mystery beneath the surface of his work, and of all his poems "A Red, Red Rose" does the most to make readers feel that they are going over material they already know.

If you are old enough to read, and you grew up in the Anglicized world or have lived long enough in it, then you have either come in contact with Robert Burns's work or have at least encountered some source influenced by it. Poems that might ring a bell include: John Barleycorn: A Ballad," "John Anderson, My Jo," "Coming Thro' the

Rye" (from which J. D. Salinger took the title of his novel *The Catcher In The Rye*), "Tam o Shanter," and "To A Mouse" (from which John Steinbeck took the title of his novel *Of Mice and Men*). On New Year's Eve, as the clock reached the stroke of midnight, you might have sung some form of the traditional folk song "Auld Lang Syne"—perhaps even the rendition that Robert Burns set down in print as a poem. These examples, a mere speck in Burns's canon of hundreds of poems and songs, point to several of the major reasons why Burns is so familiar today. First, other writers quote him often. He was a fun writer who enjoyed using words cleverly, and he was a man of the people and not of the intellectual establishment, and these are both traits that writers often admire and emulate. Second, and perhaps most importantly, is the fact that so much of Burns's writing was taken, either in whole or in part, from songs that had already been around Scotland for years. In those days before copyright law had reached to such diverse forms of intellectual property as songs, popular music was spread by being heard and repeated, for hundreds of years sometimes. If Burns heard a set of lyrics he liked he would write them down, modifying them as he saw fit. In this way he became, not just an important writer in Scottish history, but an integral thread in the weave of Scottish culture. Unlike most authors whose works spawn forward from their time, Burns's poems stretch in both directions, future and past, from the poet himself. The third element to Burns's popularity was his use of the Scottish dialect. This stylistic tendency is often a source of trouble and vexation for non-Scottish readers, who have to slow down their reading with frequent trips to the glossary or dictionary, but it has cemented his eternal popularity among Scots. The love of his fellow citizens is so powerful that it is felt beyond the nation's borders and throughout the world.

"A Red, Red Rose," one of Burns's most popular and most anthologized works, actually has the opposite effect on students than his reputation does. Readers may find themselves to be more familiar with the poet's works in general than they had realized, but they also find that the ideas in this poem are not as familiar as they first seem. The poem is a declaration of love, particularly a vow, upon the occasion of leaving, to keep love alive. It is a situation that does not change throughout the ages, and so impatient readers tend to read this poem once and think that they understand all that it has to say. Too often, readers proceed with a set of assumptions that does not serve them well.

> *There are other indicators that this speaker's concept of love is less heartfelt than presented, but that is not the issue here: the point is to raise the question of whether Burns could have designed this poem to be more than a sincere declaration of love."*

One major mistaken assumption is that life was simpler in the past. The world is always becoming more and more complex, with scientists uncovering more facts, computers enabling us to send the facts around and the arts developing newer ways to turn facts into ideas. People constantly talk about how complicated life is, how simple the good ol' days were. I myself have heard students try to explain how complex modern family life is now, at the turn of the century, contrasting it to the 1970's when the standard was the intact nuclear family of Mom, Dad and two-point-five children: the explanation reminded me of how, in the 1970s, I used that same "Mom, Dad and 2.5 kids" formula to explain how much simpler life had been in the 1950s. We were all drawing on the oversimplification of television. So long as we can understand events in historical perspective better than we understand them as they are happening—that is, forever—we will always look on the past as a simpler time.

And so, many modern readers assume that "A Red, Red Rose" is straightforward, with no particular guile. They write this assumption off to their concept that people in the past did not know how to present a complex relationship, even if they knew how to have one. Such readers give up analyzing after they realize that the red rose symbolizes love in this poem, a realization that any Valentine card could explain. They think that it was all Burns could do, in his backward time, to set his ideas down on paper. Without a historical perspective (and who in American schools has much of a sense of history anymore?), Burns's poem from the late 1700s is as crude and basic as some cartoon caveman in an off-the-shoulder pelt grunting, "Me like."

If the speaker of this poem seems to lack guile, couldn't it be that he wants to seem naive? It is, after all, a love poem, and unfortunately there is as much trickery in love, as much subtext, as in poetry or in the arts in general. There is, for instance, one open and ambiguous line that could be read as an indication of the speaker's deep sincerity, but could also, with a different set of assumptions, be taken to mean that the speaker is shallow and superficial. In the second stanza, the first two lines say, in effect, "As beautiful as you are, that is how much in love with you I am." Readers who accept this poem at face value, thinking that the person's love must be great because he says it is, read these lines to mean that his love and her beauty are of such magnitude that they can only be compared to each other. But the poem does not say that they are huge, just equal: if her level of fairness is mediocre, his love is lukewarm. Equating love and beauty is not necessarily an indicator of great love, and Burns, if his ambiguous phrasing is any clue, knew that his line would be open to many interpretations. There are other indicators that this speaker's concept of love is less heartfelt than presented, but that is not the issue here: the point is to raise the question of whether Burns could have designed this poem to be more than a sincere declaration of love.

Another reason readers assume that the speaker is being sincere is that the average person gets their greatest exposure to poetry in schools, where positive, affirmative values, including honesty, are emphasized. We are taught that, all other things being equal, poets' intentions are most likely noble, and this assumption is fed by the examples of morally uplifting poetry that are, quite properly, used in classrooms. Readers tend to go straight for a poem's uplifting message because experience tells them that poems often affirm goodness. What this assumption ignores, however, is the power of irony. It is quite possible for Burns to make the world a better place by presenting a lover who is fickle, insincere or even downright conniving. We do not have to agree with the speaker of the poem, we only have to understand him the way he understands himself, so that we know how to deal with attitudes like his when we encounter them in our lives. If we fail to wonder whether there are motives beneath the surface, we run the risk of becoming gullible. The same people who would laugh at someone for believing that an advertisement for

"the great American carpet deodorizer" is *really* about patriotism, as it presents itself to be, are for some reason willing to accept this speaker's claim of his great love.

He certainly does talk like someone in love. His language is hyperbolic: he appears to think in extremes, the way lovers do. Someone who is head-over-heels in mere fondness might claim to love his bonnie lass until the creek goes dry, or until the rocks erode, but a lover in the heat of passion uses excessive language, as Burns does here. The fact that the poem is written using the plain vernacular, the common language of the average Scotsman and not the elevated English of the educated, makes the speaker that much more credible. But even while this speaker's excitement about this girl makes us trust that he believes what he is saying, at the same time it raises the suspicion that he does not know himself very well. He might be too infatuated with her to understand whether he is in love or not, or he might be working just a little too hard to convince her of his love. There are a number of things that the poet might be indicating with the simple strong language of love, other than love itself.

Readers who feel that an "old" poem like Burns's "A Red, Red Rose" is a simple piece to understand need to put more effort into their reading. Poets do sometimes state simple truths simply, but there is not much fun in that: we understand the implications of the world we live in by understanding the implications of works of art. If a poem like "A Red, Red Rose" has more to tell us than what we all want to hear—that love is wonderful—we may never know it if we don't look past its surface.

Source: David Kelly, in an essay for *Poetry for Students,* Gale Group, 2000.

Bruce Meyer

Bruce Meyer is the director of the creative writing program at the University of Toronto. He has taught at several Canadian universities and is the author of three collections of poetry. In the following essay, Meyer suggests that the poet desires to multiply the images of his beloved, to elevate her above mortal beings, and to provide a test to prove his love.

It seems extremely clinical, if not criminal to examine something as tender and beautiful as Robert Burns's "A Red, Red Rose" under the scrutiny of critical consideration. So delicately, so intricately is it wrought that the poem is, in itself, a frail rose. Yet the poem's delicacy, its fragility, is achieved through a wonderful series of similes that flow from one image into the next and build an argument picture by picture to form, not only a masterpiece in itself, but a wonderful addition to the ongoing tradition of love poetry.

Love poetry is more than mere flattery. It is a high form of rhetorical persuasion. The Song of Solomon, perhaps the model from which Western love poetry has evolved, is a rare piece of epideictic rhetoric where the beloved is praised. In the dialogue of the Song of Solomon, two characters frantically seek each other out throughout the city. Night is falling, and the urgency and necessity of the search is highlighted by the ways in which each voice describes the other it is seeking through a series of similes. The beloved is not seen in his or her own terms but in comparison to other things— the most beautiful things—and the process of finding the likeness of the beloved in other images only adds to the overwhelming sense of desire that the voices convey. Not only does the reader seek the "beloved" in himself in the Song of Solomon; he is driven to seek him, at least partially in other images. And that is part of the appeal of interwoven similes: the love object to which they are applied draws so much into his or her appearance and reflects that appearance back onto so many other objects to the point that the beloved seems to rise out of himself or herself and become not one thing but many. The comparison, in this process, becomes a much broader process than a mere metaphor might accommodate, and the single image proliferates into many images.

This is the process Burns is attempting to highlight in his poem "A Red, Red Rose." Like John Ruskin, who saw twenty-eight different colors of red in a single rose, Burns is attempting to see a kind of multifoliate array of ideas attached to his beloved. This process of extension, of adding one simile to another can be seen in the way Burns connects one verse to another by repeating the final image from the previous stanza as the first line of the next, either verbally or conceptually. But there is more to Burns's process of epideictic than mere imagistic or conceptual connectivity. The entire poem turns upon a rather commonplace conceit in the vocabulary of love poetry: the comparison of a woman with a flower.

The first stanza opens with the lines "O, my luve is like a red, red rose / That's newly sprung in June, / O, my luve's like the melodie, / That's sweetly play'd in tune." These two comparisons, the love with the rose and the love with the melody, establish not only two consecutive similes, but a juxtaposing of two very essential concepts: beauty

The series of comparisons are intriguing in their own right, but it is the pledging that drives the poem home as a personal note of dedication and an expression of timeless love."

of appearance and beauty of sound. The poem's imagery looks after the matter of the beauty of appearances. But what catches the reader by surprise is that the beloved, in being compared to a "melodie / That's sweetly play'd in tune," is established not only as the subject of the lyric but as the lyric itself. To say that his "luve is like a melodie" is to association the beloved with the poem itself and its very lyricism.

Burns's use of the quatrains gives the poem a wonderful sense of sonic flow and an overwhelming sense of song. The song is something that the persona carries with him through time ("While sands of life shall run") and space ("Tho it were ten thousand mile!") and it is the lyric utterance that connects him to his beloved. But this is no mere song: in the opening stanza Burns repeats the invocative "O" which is another way of calling upon divine assistance for the singing process. The invocative "O", a means of calling upon either the assistance of the Muses or the help of heavenly song as in the opening lines of Shakespeare's *Henry V,* connects the idea of song to the concept of vatic "seeing," the process where the voice of the poet becomes the medium for some sort of higher utterance and observation than mere reality can provide. The invocative "O" also serves to elevate the entire series of connections and comparisons that Burns undertakes in the poem. The song to which the beloved is compared in line two, therefore, is divine song and Burns has very subtly lifted his subject matter above the mortal concerns of time and space. His love for her will last beyond the timespan of the seas and is stronger than any geographical distance that might come between them. It is divine love by process of allusion.

In the scope of love poetry, what the masters of the sub-genre attempt to do is to elevate their subjects not only through praise but through connection. This was undoubtedly the process behind the Provencal poets of the eleventh century when they co-opted the structures of liturgical hymns to the Virgin Mary and applied them to the praise of mortal women. It was the same impetus of comparison that triggered the sonnet tradition—albeit that tradition is more rhetorical and discursive than lyrical—and it is the reason why even the simplest and corniest love poems, such as "Roses are Red, Violets are Blue" refract the beloved through some sort of comparative mechanism.

But beyond the standard conventions of love poetry, what makes this poem so touching is that it is a poem of departure. In the final stanza, he bids "fare thee weel" "a while" to his beloved and promises to "come again" no matter how far he may roam. Parting love poems are always difficult to evaluate because part of their ancestry lies in works such as Ovid's *Remedium* which advises the reader in the ways and means of breaking off a love affair in the classiest way possible. But regardless of the poem's ancestry and possible underhanded intent, what the reader is confronted with in Burns's lyric is a situation that strikes a note of pathos. There is a pledging of love which seems sincere because its value and strengths are compared to the question of tests—"I will love thee still my dear / Till a' the seas gang dry" or "While sands of time shall run." In a very subtle allusion to the language and structure of Medieval love romances such as Guillaume de Lorris and Jean de Meun's *La Romain de la Rose* (yet another nod of acknowledgment to that horticultural wonder and symbol of both martyrdom and divine, blood-pledged love), the lover of "A Red, Red Rose" is pledging himself to a test in order to prove his love, not just proffer it. The tests of time and space, the true tests of love, are laid out with great sincerity because they address considerable magnitudes of temporality and spatiality. Such are the linguistic and imagistic conventions of love poetry.

"A Red, Red Rose," however, is more than a mere exercise in convention. The balance and delicacy of the lyricism, the simplicity of the language in its earthy Scots dialect, and the directness and accessibility of the comparisons make for a very sincere and heartfelt utterance. "So deep in luve am I," notes the persona in the second stanza, that one does not question the profundity or the verity of the emotion. The series of comparisons are intriguing in their own right, but it is the pledging that drives the poem home as a personal note of dedication and an expression of timeless love.

Source: Bruce Meyer, in an essay for *Poetry for Students,* Gale Group, 2000.

Sources

Crawford, Thomas, *Burns: A Study of the Poems and Songs,* Stanford, CA: Stanford University Press, 1960.

Daiches, David, "The Identity of Burns," in *Restoration and Eighteenth Century Literature: Essays in Honor of Alan Dugald McKillop,* edited by Carroll Camden, The University of Chicago Press, 1963, pp. 323-40.

Fitzhugh, Robert, *Robert Burns, The Man and the Poet: A Round, Unvarnished Account,* Boston: Houghton Mifflin Company, 1970.

Smith, Iain Crichton, "The Lyrics of Robert Burns," in *The Art of Robert Burns,* edited by R. S. Jack and Andrew Noble, Vision Press, 1982, pp. 22-35.

Snyder, Franklyn Bliss, *Robert Burns: His Personality, His Reputation and His Art,* 1936, reprinted by Kennikat Press, 1970.

For Further Study

Hill, John C., *The Love Songs and Heroines of Robert Burns,* London: J.M. Dent and Sons, Ltd., 1961.
   Hill's book gives a good sense of Burns the man and of his view of romance by exploring the poems that he wrote for particular women, with biographical background material.

Kinsley, James, ed., *The Poems and Songs of Robert Burns, volumes I—III,* Oxford, England: Clarendon Press, 1960.
   This is the most comprehensive collection of all that Burns wrote: three volumes, each more than 1500 pages, with extensive explanations and references given for each of the works.

Rogers, Charles, *Book of Robert Burns: Genealogical and Historical Memoirs of the Poet, His Associates and Those Celebrated in His Writing,* AMS Press, 1988.
   This scholarly work gives a detailed explanation of the poet's life and his influences.

Smith, Ian Crichton, "The Lyrics of Robert Burns," in *The Art of Robert Burns,* edited by R. D. S. Jack and Andrew Noble, Totowa, NJ: Barnes and Noble Press, 1982.
   This poem was originally a song, and Smith examines it, along with many of Burns's other famous songs.

Sprott, Gavin, *Robert Burns: Pride and Passion: the Life, Times and Legacy,* New York: Seven Hills Book Distributors, 1996.
   This huge overview of Burns's career gives readers and students a useful look at who Burns is and why we still study him today.

The River-Merchant's Wife: A Letter

Ezra Pound

1915

" The River-Merchant's Wife: A Letter" was published in 1915 in Ezra Pound's third collection of poetry, *Cathay: Translations,* which contains versions of Chinese poems composed from the sixteen notebooks of Ernest Fenollosa, a scholar of Chinese literature. Pound called the poems in English which resulted from the Fenollosa manuscripts "translations," but as such they are held in contempt by most scholars of Chinese language and literature. However, they have been acclaimed as "poetry" for their clarity and elegance. They are variously referred to as "translations," "interpretations," "paraphrases," and "adaptations."

Pound's study of the Fenollosa manuscripts led to his preoccupation with the Chinese ideogram (a written symbol for an idea or object) as a medium for poetry. In fact, he realized that Chinese poets had long been aware of the image as the fundamental principle for poetic composition that he himself was beginning to formulate. Pound further maintained that the poetic image did not lose anything in translation between languages nor was it bound by time, but effectively communicated through time and across cultures, accruing meaning in the process. " The River-Merchant's Wife: A Letter," for example, communicates with depth and poignance the human experience of sorrow at separation, the human experience of love.

Working with the literary traditions of other cultures was typical not only of Pound, but of most of his contemporaries, who were not convinced that the only culture of value was European. However,

Ezra Pound

Pound's work has significance not only for its cross-cultural innovations, but for the "cross-chronological" breakthrough notion that the human response to the world links us all, so that an American in the twentieth century can share and learn from the human experience of an eighth century Chinese river-merchant's wife.

Author Biography

Pound was born in Hailey, Idaho, in 1885, and raised in Philadelphia, the son of Homer Loomis Pound and Isabel Weston Pound. He made his first visits to Europe with his family in 1898 and 1902. He attended the Cheltenham Military Academy when he was twelve and soon after attended the Cheltenham Township High School. Just before his sixteenth birthday Pound entered the University of Pennsylvania, and in 1903 he transferred to Hamilton College, receiving his bachelor's degree in 1905. He taught Romance languages at Wabash College in Indiana for a short time in 1907, but was dismissed after a scandal involving a stranded actress that he allowed to stay overnight with him in his room. After this and a failed courtship with Mary S. Moore, Pound decided to leave for Europe, where he privately published his first volume of poetry, *A lume spento*, in Venice in 1908. He then moved to London and by 1911 was immersed in the literary and intellectual milieu and was a respected critic and poet. Around this time Pound founded a poetic movement called Imagism , which linked techniques derived from the Symbolist movement and Oriental poetry, such as haiku.

Pound spent much of his time concerned with promoting the careers of many of the great writers of the time and was a key figure in the publication of many influential works, including Ernest Hemingway's *In Our Time*, and T. S. Eliot's *The Waste Land*. In 1921 Pound moved to Paris and from there to Rapallo, Italy, in 1924. In Italy Pound endorsed the Fascist government of Benito Mussolini and declared his political and anti-semitic beliefs in a series of radio broadcasts during World War II. After the war Pound was arrested by American allies and charged with treason. He was found mentally incapable to stand trial and was committed to St. Elizabeth's Hospital in Washington D.C. in 1946. Upon his release in 1958 he returned to Italy. He died in Venice in 1972 and is buried in San Michele Cemetery on the island of San Giorgio Maggiore.

Poem Text

While my hair was still cut straight across my
forehead
I played about the front gate, pulling flowers.
You came by on bamboo stilts, playing horse,
You walked about my seat, playing with blue
plums.
And we went on living in the village of Chokan: 5
Two small people, without dislike or suspicion.

At fourteen I married My Lord you.
I never laughed, being bashful.
Lowering my head, I looked at the wall.
Called to, a thousand times, I never looked back.   10

At fifteen I stopped scowling,
I desired my dust to be mingled with yours
Forever and forever and forever.
Why should I climb the look out?

At sixteen you departed,   15
You went into far Ku-to-yen, by the river of
swirling eddies,
And you have been gone five months.
The monkeys make sorrowful noise overhead.

You dragged your feet when you went out.
By the gate now, the moss is grown, the different   20
mosses,
Too deep to clear them away!

The leaves fall early this autumn, in wind.
The paired butterflies are already yellow with
    August
Over the grass in the West garden;
They hurt me. I grow older.   25

If you are coming down through the narrows of the 26
    river Kiang,
Please let me know beforehand,
And I will come out to meet you
    As far as Cho-fu-Sa.

Poem Summary

Lines 1-6:

This opening stanza of 6 lines is organized around a central image of the river-merchant and his wife as a child, confirmed by the first component of the central image: the picture of a little girl with her hair cut in bangs. (The mark of an adult woman in the ancient Chinese culture was elaborate arrangements of uncut long hair.)

Each line contributes to a clearer understanding of the central image of the children. The repetition in three separate lines of the verb "playing" to describe the little girl's activity at the front gate, as well as the little boy's presence on stilts and his circling around where she sits, emphasizes the natural, contented activity of children—almost as a part of the natural world referred to here by "flowers" and "blue plums."

This stanza establishes the presence of the "I" and the "you" in the world of the poem.

Lines 7-10:

The second stanza places the girl and the boy, the "I" and the "you," as a woman and man in the adult world. In ancient cultures, and in some cultures today, early marriages are customary, and it is often also the custom for the wife to refer to her husband by a respectful title. In the case of this poem the formality of the title is softened by the direct address of "you" added right after it.

Lines 8–9 establish the child-wife's shyness in this formal adult situation by offering a picture of her bent head and averted eyes, a shyness so extreme that she could not respond to her husband, no matter how many efforts he made.

Lines 11-14:

The central image of this stanza is the growth of love between the young husband and wife. Her face, which in the first stanza has the bangs of childhood across her forehead, in the second stanza is averted and unsmiling, "stops scowling" in the third stanza.

The vows of the marriage ceremony, "till death us do part," are evoked in lines 12 and 13 and poignantly reinforced by the triple repetition in line 13 of "forever."

It is unclear whether "climb the lookout" in line 14 is a reference to a ritual performed in this culture by a wife after death, perhaps to look for other offers to marry that might come her way. If it is, it means that the wife as a widow does not want to do this. In any case, it is clear that there is nothing she wishes for after the death of her husband, so deep is her love for him now.

Lines 15-18:

An image of separation is developed in these lines as the husband takes on his role as a river-merchant and travels the waters, conducting his work in the world on a distant island.

The wife's statement of the length of his absence is expressed in one line, giving it full and emphatic force. And in line 18 the effect of this long absence is brought to full comprehension by the use of the natural image of the sounds of the monkeys that reflect back to her the sound of her own sorrow. The sounds that monkeys make are generally interpreted as chirping, happy sounds, but the weight of the wife's sorrow is so great that she can only hear the monkeys' noise as "sorrowful."

Lines 19-21:

The first three lines of this final 11-line stanza are centered on the image of the river-merchant's absence. Line 19 indicates that he was as averse to this separation as she was. In line 20 the phrase "by the gate" (perhaps the same gate they played about as children), indicates that she has returned to this gate and in her memory sees him reluctantly leaving again. For her it is the scene of the beginning of his absence. And evidently she knows this scene well: not only is there moss growing there, but she is aware that there are different kinds of mosses, which she has not cleared away since his departure. They are now too deep to clear away.

Lines 22-25:

In line 22 the sadness of the river-merchant's wife is again reflected back to her by the natural world, by the falling leaves and wind of autumn. This image becomes more defined with her observation of the butterflies in the garden, for they are

Media Adaptations

- Unapix released a 1995 biography titled *Ezra Pound*.

- *Ezra Pound: Visions and Voices,* a 1988 Mystic Fire Video, presents Pound's life and poetry.

"paired" as she is not, and they are becoming "yellow" changing with the season, growing older together.

The butterflies "hurt" her because they emphasize the pain of her realization that she is growing older, but alone, not with her husband.

Lines 26-29:

In these closing lines of the poem and the "letter" the river-merchant's wife reaches out from her lonely world of sorrow to her husband in a direct request: Please let me know when and by what route you are returning, so that I may come to meet you. This, however, conveys more than it would at first appear. Her village is a suburb of Nanking and she is willing to walk to a beach several hundred miles upstream from there to meet her husband, so deeply does she yearn to close the distance between them.

Themes

Love and Passion

Ezra Pound's "The River-Merchant's Wife: A Letter," a dramatic monologue written in the form of a letter, is a poignant plea from a wife to her husband, a merchant whose journey has lasted far too long for the wife's ease of mind. The poem honors constancy and faithfulness as the wife reflects on the development of their life together and expresses her growing sorrow as she anxiously awaits his return.

One important theme in the poem reveals the process through which the love between the man and woman develops. In the opening lines of the poem, the wife recalls her childhood when her husband was simply a playmate, a companion. The first line gives a vivid picture of the wife as a child. The use of the passive tense, making bangs the subject, helps create the world from a child's perspective, not actively involved in decisions about what to wear or how to look. This creates both a clear physical portrait, as well as indicating the passivity of childhood with its lack of involvement in things other than play. Notice that the second line begins "I played." This also foreshadows the lack of input she will have in her marriage. The poem then moves on to describe the carefree merriment of the speaker and her future husband. The wife reinforces this picture of innocent pleasure with her comment, "Two small people, without dislike or suspicion."

In the second stanza, the reader learns of her marriage, at the age of fourteen. The wife's description clearly suggests that it has been forced upon her, and she is both shy and uncomfortable with her husband. The formality of the phrase, "I married My Lord you," not only indicates the proprieties that would be common in China during that period, but, for the modern reader, emphasizes the emotional distance in the marriage. Her statement that she never laughed contrasts jarringly with her earlier picture of the two companions at ease in their world. In the fourth line of the second stanza, the husband hopes to win her as he calls to her "a thousand times." However, she only looks at the wall, lowering her heard, refusing to look back and answer his summons.

With the final four lines of the stanza, she suddenly indicates that their relationship has changed as "at fifteen [she] stopped scowling." Her next words show how dramatically her love has grown. She now "desired [her] dust to be mingled with [his] / Forever." Their union is not only welcome, but for her the end of their relationship is unthinkable. She wishes it to continue throughout eternity. Ironically, now that this love has developed, the husband's trip separates them, creating the poem's real poignancy. The reader has followed this relationship from childhood joy, through the reluctant wife's initial unhappiness, until their love matures. The two are now torn apart, and the wife is left alone to mourn his absence. The growth and development of this relationship allows the reader a greater understanding of her loss and pain.

Constancy

The portrait of the growth of their love provides a rich context to allow the reader to fully appreciate another of the poem's themes, faithfulness or constancy. When the speaker's husband left, she had just learned to love him. The reader understands her regret that her newfound passion was too brief. She also hints about her fears for his safe return: he has traveled "into far Ku-to-yen, by the river of swirling eddies." It is clear that he has been gone much longer than she had expected. Although she never mentions the possible dangers of traveling such a river, the reader realizes that rapids or whirlpools could explain why he has been gone so long. This would be even clearer to a Chinese reader since an ancient boatman's song tells of the perils of traveling on this particular stretch of river.

The letter makes clear how painful the wait has become for her. The two short sentences in line 25 make a strong impression. Mentioning "the paired butterflies," she simply states, "They hurt me," leaving the reader to fathom her world of pain. She continues by noting that she has grown so much older, an aging that is emotional rather than physical. However, she remains brave in her wait, ending the letter with the message that she will come to meet him, if he will only send word. She holds fast to the thought of his return, despite the hints of trouble that nature has provided: the overgrown moss, the early autumn.

Hugh Kenner, who has written several books about Pound, believes that "The River-Merchant's Wife: A Letter" along with the poet's other verse published in 1915 provide some of the most effective emotional responses to the circumstances of World War I. Indeed, the parallel between the situation of the wife in the poem and women throughout Europe writing letters of love and longing to soldiers called away to war is striking. While this poem has no military theme, it involves the same sense of loss, of fear, of waiting: the insecurity about whether the loved one will, in fact, return. Interestingly enough, this parallel reinforces the universality of the theme in the poem. That a poem composed in the voice of a Chinese woman in the eighth century provides such an accurate emotional description of a wife or lover waiting for news from the World War I front adds to its enormous poignancy.

Nature

In a 1918 essay titled "Chinese Poetry," Pound described the central qualities of the Chinese verse-form. One was the use of nature imagery to explain or indicate human emotion or set mood. He referred to this as "metaphor by sympathy." This use of nature is a major factor in setting the tone of the final stanzas of "The River-Merchant's Wife: A Let-

Topics for Further Study

- In 1948, Ezra Pound won the Bollingen Prize for the best volume of poetry published that year. Many people were highly critical of this award since he had been accused of treason during World War II by the U.S. government. Evaluate both sides of the controversy and explain which position you find most convincing.

- The letter is a common device used in both literature and song. Find some other examples of letters, and discuss whether the author has used the letter form effectively.

- Both Pound and Li-Po found themselves in conflict with governmental authorities. Compare/contrast their difficulties.

ter." While the five months the husband has been gone may not seem a terrible burden to the reader initially, Pound uses nature to cue the reader to mood. The "sorrowful" monkeys mirror the wife's feelings. The fact that the merchant "dragged [his] feet," cutting a path through the moss, shows his reluctance to leave; the fact that the moss has eradicated those marks of his presence, casts a worrying shadow. Much of nature, the wind, the seasons, the leaves, seems out of order reinforcing the wife's foreboding. "The paired butterflies" provide a final, almost unbearable, touch. While these delicate creatures remain together, they torment her with the reminder that her own love is gone.

Style

This translation, "The River-Merchant's Wife: A Letter," is structured into 5 stanzas: the first of 6 lines, and the second, third, and fourth of 4 lines each. Each of the first four stanzas is image-centered, focusing an emotional point in the history of the relationship between the river-merchant's wife and her husband. The final stanza of 10 lines and a dropped half-line begins with the presentation of a similar central image that collects an enhancing detail in each line until line 25 shifts into direct emotional statement. The last four lines mix this direct letter-writing style with the final image closing the physical and emotional distance between the river-merchant and his wife.

It was Pound's belief that the pictorial quality of the Chinese ideogram, in its "closeness to the thing itself," had the capacity for raising the mundane to the poetic. Likewise, Pound's ear for the music of conversational speech raised natural speech rhythms to the level of poetry. In this poem he expertly combines these to create a sense of the conversational naturalness of letter-writing with the focused, direct, and simple presentation of image inspired by the Chinese ideograms in which the poem was originally written.

Pound's insistence on the centrality of image to poetry is in great part responsible for the varied line lengths of this poem written in unrhymed free verse. While each of the first four stanzas concentrates on one image, the individual lines themselves are as long as Pound needs them to be to focus each component of the central image of the stanza in the mind of the reader. This technique is termed end-stopped lines, meaning that a complete idea is expressed in a line, with no spillover into the next line. However, the use of capital letters at the beginnings of each line is a signal that it is the lines of poetry, rather than the sentence constructions, that are the basic units of meaning.

The poet employs direct address throughout the poem, taking on the persona of the wife as the "I" who is writing the letter and thus entering her experience. This use of the first-person "I" also makes it possible for the reader of the poem to enter her experience. In addition, the direct address to the second-person "you" allows the poem also to be experienced as if it is a letter to the reader.

Historical Context

Chinese history presents a rich and complex tapestry. Archaeologists believe that the first organized society, the Shang dynasty, existed from approximately 1500 to 1100 B.C. Excavations reveal an agrarian yet artistic culture. From these beginnings, Chinese civilization developed a sophisticated governmental system, as well as a rich philosophical and artistic tradition. Although similar developments were occurring in the lands sur-

rounding the Mediterranean Sea, there was only sporadic contact between the two cultures, a communication based on trade. While the Silk Road carried caravans between China and the Roman Empire, almost all interactions were limited to commercial exchanges, controlled by the traders who dominated the route.

Because of the economic importance of this trade, the Han dynasty, which ruled China from approximately 200 B.C. to 200 A.D., expanded the boundaries of China, in a successful effort to gain control of the Silk Road. However, they were not interested in cultural exchanges with outsiders. The Han ruled using a tribute system. Since they believed non-Chinese were barbarians, diplomatic relations and trading rights were extended only to those peoples who would recognize the superiority of the Chinese and prove it with the payment of a tribute. This attitude toward the rest of the world continued throughout most of Chinese history. Although visitors came to China to learn from the accomplishments of the various dynasties, they remained outsiders, not assimilated into the society.

This was true during the Tang dynasty, which assumed control in the seventh century. Many historians call this era the golden age of China, which was, at the time, the wealthiest and the most extensive empire in the world. Literature, painting, sculpture, as well as other arts flourished. Scholarship was encouraged and two encyclopedias were produced during that period. The Chinese also made several technological advances, and government was directed by a code of laws based on Confucian principles.

This Chinese culture provides a sharp contrast to the western world at this time. In the eighth century, when Chinese poet Li Po wrote, Europe was struggling to emerge from the chaos caused by the fall of the Roman Empire. Muslim Arabs had invaded Spain; Slavic invaders attacked from the East. Although Charlemagne attempted to recreate a new Holy Roman Empire, the strong nation states of Europe would not emerge for a few more centuries. Ironically, the old trade routes between East and West continued unabated, since the turmoil never diminished the demand for spices from the Orient.

By the twelfth century, however, the power balance was reversed. Warring factions weakened China, and this left the nation vulnerable to the onslaught of the Mongol forces led by the great warrior, Genghis Khan, who extended his empire across Asia. After his death, power was distributed

Compare & Contrast

- **1916:** Einstein announces his general theory of relativity.

  1997: Einstein again makes scientific headlines when astronomers announce signs that could prove the accuracy of the theory of relativity. Spinning bodies twist space and time along with them, which is an inevitable result of Einstein's theory.

- **1915:** The Germans use chlorine gas at the Second Battle of Ypres—the first time poison gas is employed in conflict.

1961: The United States begins "operational field tests," spraying the defoliant Agent Orange over Vietnam. The program continues until 1971.

1995: Twelve people are killed in a terrorist attack using Sarin gas on a Japanese subway.

1999: The Defense Department begins a controversial program to vaccinate all military personnel against anthrax. Several soldiers who have refused on the grounds that not enough is known about the vaccine's safety have been court-martialed.

---

among his sons and China was left to the care of his son, Kublai Khan, who recognized the achievements and scholarship of the Chinese.

Kublai Khan is familiar to westerners because of the writings of Marco Polo who visited the imperial court in 1275. When his accounts of the grandeur, even superiority, of the Asian world first reached Europe, these tales were considered to be more fantasy than reality. However, since there had been commercial contact between East and West for centuries, eventually similar reports reinforced the claims of Marco Polo. The riches of the Orient soon became an irresistible lure to western explorers and adventurers.

Both China and the nations that emerged in Europe during the late medieval and Renaissance periods were proud, even arrogant. The Chinese dynasties, on their part, felt no need to pursue anything beyond their own boundaries. They were self-sufficient, possessors of a rich and elaborate culture. Foreigners were still viewed as barbarians. In the western world, on the other hand, the development of strong nation states fueled the desire for exploration and conquest. Explorers believed that the new worlds that were now discovered were rightly theirs, to claim and plunder. Seagoing journeys revived interest in the East. In fact, Columbus's voyage was supported by Ferdinand and Isabella, the rulers of Spain, because they had visions of great profits to be taken from the Orient.

The Portuguese, who were the first to reach China, in 1514, planned to gain fortunes by seizing control of the rich spice trade, which was dominated by Arab traders. The Chinese authorities were dismayed by the arrival of these "barbarians." Rumors abounded along the areas where the Portuguese sailed that they were cannibals who wanted to buy or steal children to eat them. The Chinese government attempted to limit all foreign influence as much as possible, refusing to permit colonies on the mainland. Only mercantile, not diplomatic, relations existed between China and Europe.

Eventually, as the West sought to force China to allow more trade, conflict became inevitable. Each side felt themselves unfairly treated; each felt themselves a superior culture. England resented the failure of China to respond to its diplomatic overtures. China was insulted by the insensitive behavior of English diplomats. England wanted Chinese tea, but unfortunately produced no comparable item that the Chinese desired. Therefore, they tried to force China to make opium legal so that the English could bring it to China from India in exchange for the tea. The eventual result was the Opium Wars. England eventually won both wars, forcing China to open more ports and allow the importation of opium.

Although China still struggled to resist western aggression, the nation was forced to endure continual attacks on its sovereignty. Eventually resentment caused the formation of secret societies who, in 1899, launched several attacks against westerners in China. Although this movement, the Boxer Rebellion, was quashed within a year, it helped bring about a new government for China. In 1912, just three years before *Cathay* was published, the Republic of China was formed with Sun Yat-sen as its president.

Critical Overview

American critic and poet T. S. Eliot has called Pound "the inventor of Chinese poetry" for the twentieth century. Nevertheless, he sees *Cathay: Translations,* containing the much anthologized poem " The River-Merchant's Wife: A Letter," as more than intelligent literary archaeology of poems from eighth century China. It establishes Pound's particular literary genius "for expressing himself through historical masks" that would become the hallmark of his later major work, the *Cantos.* It is Eliot's critical assessment, furthermore, that the value of Pound's work in this collection is the clarity with which he presents his perception that "the present is no more than the present significance of the past." In fact, Eliot maintains that Pound's translations of ancient Chinese poetry are decidedly Modernist because they affirm the universality of human experience through time and across cultures.

Eliot grants that while Pound's style in these translations might not reflect that of the Chinese originals, his poetic concern for image provides an effective means for "transporting the content" of the original picture-making Chinese ideograms. Thus the value of these poems is not as Chinese translations, but as a stage in the development of Pound's poetic concerns from his original concepts of "luminous detail" and "Imagism," through "vortex" and "haiku" and "metaphor," and ultimately to the "ideogrammatic composition" of his *Cantos.*

Pound is not generally viewed as especially gifted in composing his own original poems, but the accusation of Chinese language scholars that he mistranslates the poems of this volume is brushed aside by such critics of poetry as Hugh Kenner, who is perfectly willing to read them as "Pound's interpretative paraphrases that are informed by his own concerns and background." It is Michael Alexander's estimation that these poems have been "underrated" as mere translations, rather than appreciated for their highly disciplined free verse. In-

deed, as William Pratt has noted, "the relatively pure images of *Cathay* ... seem less and less like translations and more and more like original poems."

William Van O'Connor suggests that Pound's "translations" have a song-like quality, which he notes especially in " The River-Merchant's Wife: A Letter." In this poem Pound's belief that poetry always had and always should reflect the conversational speech of its day combines with his intensive study of musical forms to achieve the composition of lyrical natural lines toward the development of the convincing voice of the poem's persona.

M. L. Rosenthal and Sally M. Gall acknowledge the "rhythmic successes" of such poems as "The River-Merchant's Wife: A Letter" as responsible for a move away from dramatic presentation of character and monologue toward "what the poem before us is creating." It is their contention that these poems go beyond "Imagism" and "phanopoeia" ("the casting of images upon the visual imagination"), engendering a progression of centered images in a sequence, or pattern, of human thought and emotion.

Accordingly, David E. Ward postulates that the guiding principle of Pound's theory is a belief in a shared poetic tradition that allows full expression of the emotional patterns of human experience and response. "The River-Merchant's Wife: A Letter" is an eloquent manifestation of this principle.

Criticism

Jonathan N. Barron

Jonathan N. Barron is associate professor of English at the University of Southern Mississippi. He has written numerous articles and edited a number of books of essays on poetry, and is editor of The Robert Frost Review. *In the following essay, Barron shows why Pound's poem, using free-verse poetic technique, succeeds as a masterpiece of translation.*

It is said that Pound created the Chinese poem in English. The attributes of Asian poetry, particularly of Chinese poetry, that are now familiar to students of poetry—clean, spare, description; quiet tones; precise use of proper nouns and simple active verbs—are familiar in large part because of Pound. Despite this achievement, Pound's contem-

What Do I Read Next?

- Several poems by Li Po are included in the 1975 Anchor Press anthology *Sunflower Splendor: 3000 Years of Chinese Poetry,* which provides an excellent introduction to Chinese poetry supplemented by helpful explanatory materials.

- Ezra Pound noted that "The River-Merchant's Wife" had a style and tone that would make it seem at home in Robert Browning's early collection of poetry titled *Men and Women,* available from Oxford University Press, 1972.

- In *Digging for the Treasure: Translation after Pound,* published by Peter Lang in 1984, Ronnie Apter discusses Pound's ability to remain faithful to the original poem while translating for a twentieth-century reader.

- *Cathay* is included in Pound's *Collected Shorter Poems* (Faber & Faber, 1968), a volume that includes many of Pound more accessible works.

- Simon Elegant's *A Floating Life: the Adventures of Li Po: an Historical Novel* is a beautifully written tale that recreates the adventurous, flamboyant life of Li Po, describing his role in the golden age of Chinese culture.

- *The Case of Ezra Pound* presents documentary evidence, testimony, and the response of many contemporary poets to the trial of Ezra Pound. This fascinating study was edited by Charles Norman and was published by Funk & Wagnells in 1968.

- James Laughlin's 1985 work *Pound as Wuz: Essays and Lectures on Ezra Pound* is a collection of insightful, frequently touching memories based on Laughlin's relationship with Pound in the years before World War II.

- Van Wyck Brooks discusses the influence of Oriental art and philosophy on Western artists in *Fenollosa and his Circle,* a biography of the man upon whose preliminary work *Cathay* is based.

- Published by Oxford University Press in 1999, *Ezra and Dorothy Pound: Letters in Captivity, 1945-46* presents an fascinating picture of their relationship, along with a chilling picture of his captivity.

---

porary, the great American poet Robert Frost, dismissed the very idea of poetic translation as impossible: "Poetry," he said, "is what gets lost in translation." According to Frost, poetry is so specific to its host language that if one translates a poem one loses all that made it poetic in the first place. Poetry, according to Frost, is so dependent on the music of the spoken sound of the actual language, that no foreign language poem could ever be appreciated for its poetry if rendered into English. It would, in effect, be like reading an opera without ever hearing a note of it performed.

"The River Merchant's Wife: A Letter" may well be the best challenge to Frost's theory available in English. In this poem, Pound translates from the Chinese to the English and, as the great critic of Modern poetry Hugh Kenner wrote in *The Pound Era,* he "invents Chinese poetry for our time." The poem is a funny kind of translation because it comes from the notebooks of Ernest Fenellosa, a notable scholar of Japanese and Chinese literature. Because Fenellosa was mostly familiar with Japanese, he, himself, translated the poems' Chinese proper names into Japanese. As a result, all of the proper names, even the name of the poet who originally wrote "The River-Merchant's Wife: A Letter," are given their name in Japanese translation. The note to the poem says the poet was Rihaku but that is just the Japanese name for Li Po. When Pound made this translation, he was living in London, in Kensington. This American living in London, therefore, came across the world of Chinese poetry by reading the work of another American scholar. As Kenner put it: "A Li Po ... reach[ed] Kensington by way of Tokyo, through the intercession of [Fenollosa] a Harvard-educated enthusiast of Spanish descent." Pound knew Fenollosa's work because the scholar's wife had given him his

> *The attributes of Asian poetry, particularly of Chinese poetry, that are now familiar to students of poetry—clean, spare, description; quiet tones; precise use of proper nouns and simple active verbs—are familiar in large part because of Pound."*

notebooks. The notebooks contained translations, or notes on 150 poems. Of them, Pound translated 14 into English, and of them, "The River Merchant's Wife: A Letter" has achieved the status of masterpiece.

This poem is so well regarded because, ultimately, it translates on three distinct levels. First, Pound transcribes the words and their meaning from the Chinese language to the English. Second, he translates one cultural tradition, China and the Far East, into the idiom of another cultural tradition: Anglo-American culture. Third, he translates the ancient past—the events of the original Chinese poem which take place in the eighth century—into the present of the twentieth century. In so doing, Pound manages to convey a culturally specific remote world—eighth-century China—into the modern twentieth century.

How did Pound do it? As Kenner notes about the little volume of translations, *Cathay* (1915), that Pound published and that contains "The River Merchant's Wife: A Letter," its "real achievement" lay in its ability to "rethink the nature of an English poem." In this poem, Pound raised some fundamental questions: must poetry have meter and rhyme, or if not rhyme, meter? Might "free verse" be a source not just for translation but for genuine poetry? Pound's answer was "yes."

"The River Merchant's Wife: A Letter," for example, makes use of "free-verse" technique. That is to say, from one line to the next, the poem follows no consistent metrical or rhyming pattern. Pound is able to maintain a Chinese-language feel-

ing in the poem because of the freedom such verse permits. Again, Kenner tells us that Pound's translations from the Chinese were the very first in English ever to be derived from the transcription of the actual Chinese words, Fenollosa's "detailed notes on Chinese texts." Pound, in other words, did not use some other English translation. More importantly, they were, says Kenner, the first English translations to "abandon rhyme and fixed stress count." What this means is that Pound refuses to mimic a Chinese metrical pattern that would only make sense to Chinese speakers. Had Pound tried to make the poem sound Chinese or conform to Chinese rules of poetry he would, indeed, have lost the poetry in the translation: the poem would sound silly, artificial, even weird to English speakers unfamiliar with Chinese sound patterns. Similarly, Pound also refuses to make the poem fit into one of the many English metrical forms available. Had he done that there would be no Chinese sound to the poem at all. Instead, he resorts to free verse, to no one particular sound or rhyme pattern at all. In so doing, he is able to invent his own formal rules and thus create a Chinese-sounding rhythm, music, and beauty. In short, he makes poetry happen by making up his own set of rules.

How is it possible for Pound to render the Chinese into English? How did he do it? What are the rules he adopted for his poem that enabled him to convey the distinctive quality of Chinese poetry in an English-language poem? The answer is simple: by describing things in exact detail and by focusing on culturally specific images and things in his poem that can only make sense if they are understood in the terms provided by eighth-century China. In this poem, Pound refuses to generalize. His rule is simple. Every poetic line will contain a specific image: new image, new line. Also, every stanza will develop a new chapter in the speaker's life—new period in her life, new stanza. In what follows, then, I offer a guide through the poem by looking carefully at these rules, at the line breaks, and the stanza divisions in order to show how the poem is built entirely out of specifically Chinese references, scenes, cultural assumptions, and imagery.

In the five stanzas that constitute this poem, Pound is able to convey the autobiography of a sixteen-year-old Chinese girl from nearly a thousand years ago (eighth century C.E.) In so doing, he makes her and her story new. In the first stanza, for example, Pound develops the title of the poem: this is, in fact, to be understood as a letter written by a wife to her husband:

While my hair was still cut straight across my
forehead
I played about the front gate, pulling flowers.
You came by on bamboo stilts, playing horse,
You walked about my seat, playing with blue
plums.
And we went on living in the village of Chokan:
Two small people, without dislike or suspicion.

Notable here is the focus on what we can see.
Not only does the surface, obvious imagery reveal
the location: this is China, and this is a Chinese
woman talking, but it also reveals a deeper more interesting psychological story as well. Notice how
this stanza depends on particulars, on visible things,
not on generalizations. Notice that the woman does
not say, "I've know you a very long time husband,
ever since we were kids." Instead, every single line
gives a new image, a new thing to understand. Remember the rule: new image, new line. For example, in the first line she talks about "her hair cut
straight." This implies, and we can only know this
from the context provided both by the poem's note
and by the title, that she is telling us about her life
as a girl. Evidently, this is a hairstyle common to
unmarried Chinese girls. In the second line, she
gives us a new image and in this image the story
moves a little further along. Her childhood was
happy, serene, and pleasant. The simple image of
the flowers conveys this meaning. In the third line
a new image and a new character are introduced.
Now we meet her future husband, a fun-loving kid.
Note that we know this only from the specific objects of his play, "bamboo stilts," "horse": these objects reveal the scene to be in Asia, not in America.
In short, the Chinese aspect of the poem is made
visible to us through the writer's focus on the things
of Chinese life: the customs of the people, the games
of the children. Notice, too, that the tone of this
stanza is quiet. The many commas and pauses force
us to speak the lines quietly, deliberately.

Just as every line conveys one single new image, one new element, so, too, every stanza contains a new chapter in the life of this woman. If the
first chapter, or stanza, depicts her childhood, then,
the second stanza depicts her life as a wife:

At fourteen I married My Lord you.
I never laughed, being bashful.
Lowering my head, I looked at the wall.
Called to a thousand times, I never looked back.

By the second stanza, the poem "feels" Chinese. Why? Because of the quiet tone, certainly,
but more than that because of the specific imagery.
The details, here, depict a traditional, and traditionally submissive wife in eighth-century China,
a girl who becomes a "woman" at the age of four-

teen. By raising these new and culturally specific
points, this stanza also introduces a new set of issues. For why on earth should this wife have to remind her husband that he is her husband and that
they did know each other? If this poem really is a
letter she surely should not have to tell her husband
what he must very well know.

What is happening is that these first two stanzas establish a justification for the rest of the
poem—three stanzas of complaint, of quiet anger.
In the end, what the poem depicts is a portrait of
the inner life of a woman. Ultimately, the poem/let-
ter is meant to remind her husband of her role as
his wife, of her existence, of their relationship. It
is meant to be a gentle way of telling him not to
forget, or betray her. Remember, she is a river-merchant's wife in eighth-century China. This is like
being a traveling salesman's wife today. In those
days, the river was the only major source of travel
and commerce. Her husband, as a merchant, was
more often not at home than at home. Evidently,
his wife is tired of this situation. Therefore, she
writes him a letter. The first two stanzas of this let-
ter/poem establish her role as a good, submissive,
Chinese wife of the eighth century. In effect, she
is reminding him of their relationship so that he
will know that if she complains she does so only
as a good eighth-century partner in marriage. The
first two stanzas, therefore, give her the right to
complain because they say, in effect, "I have been
a good wife and as such a wife I now feel the need
to speak."

The poetry, then, is as much in the story of this
wife's quiet anger directed at her husband as it is
in the way that the story is told. The poem feels as
if it were in another language in part due to the
rhythm, in part due to the tone, but, as I have been
arguing, mostly because of the particular details
and images. These details tell a decidedly old-fashioned culturally specific story of a lonely wife of
a river merchant in a particular time and place. In
stanza three:

At fifteen I stopped scowling,
I desired my dust to be mingled with yours
Forever and forever and forever.
Why should I climb the look out?

This is a crucial stanza to the story of the poem
because here the wife confesses the depths of her
love for her husband. Notice, again, that Pound still
adheres to his own rule: one image per line. Notice, too, that a new chapter has begun and so a new
stanza begins. In this case, the chapter is her life
after a year of marriage: her life at the age of fifteen. But her point here is to confess the depth of

her love. If she "scowled" at first, now she would like to have their "dust" mingled. In these simple images the generalizing cliche, "I love you always and forever," is communicated through the use of specific images. How, then, are we to interpret this stanza's last line?

Three ways. First, the look out is the only means she has of seeing the return of her husband. Therefore, this is a rhetorical, sarcastic, ironic question. She is, in effect, saying: "how could you possibly think I don't miss you. Why should I climb the look out! Are you crazy? How could I not want to climb it?" Second: "I love you so much, our love is so eternal, my trust in you is so absolute that I have no need to climb the look out. Of course you will come back. Why should I climb a lookout to see if you are coming?" That would imply that she thinks he might not be coming back. She says, in effect, "since I know you will return I have no need to climb the look out. Why should I climb it?" This is my own personal reading of that line but a third reading is possible: "I don't know if you will come back. Will you? Give me a reason. Why should I climb the look out?" Whatever reading one assigns to that line, its position as the last line of the stanza is a kind of gauntlet thrown down to her husband. All three readings, after all, say, in effect, that she loves him dearly and hopes he loves her enough to return.

In the fourth stanza, therefore, the story moves to the result of such love. If the third stanza is an awakening to consciousness of the wife's love for her husband then the fourth stanza communicates her sadness. Both stanzas are remarkable because a wife in the eighth century had no right to confess her feelings about anything. If her husband abandons her to go on business, her job as a "good wife" was to suffer in silence and wait. Yet, she decides, despite the cultural tradition against such talk, to express her feelings. And, not only does she express the depths of her love, but she dares even to complain. For her to say that she is lonely, that, in fact, she is also a little angry as well, is, in the terms of the time period, all but heresy:

> At sixteen you departed,
> and you went into far Ku-to-yen, by the river of
>   swirling eddies,
> And you have been gone five months.
> The monkeys make sorrowful noise overhead.

In this stanza, we are brought into the present moment. This chapter of her life is now, the present telling of the tale. Here she says that she is now 16 years old. What she implies, then, is that just as she grew accustomed to their life as a mar-

ried couple (the past year), he left. The third line of this stanza is quiet and seems to be nothing more than description. But the tone here must be read in terms of the larger context. For her to say, "you have been gone five months" is another way of saying, "I am so lonely!" It is even a complaint: "how could you abandon me, your own wife, for so long!" We are trained to see this because of the final image concluding the stanza. The monkeys, in a way, become a metaphor for the emotional state of the wife. Their "sorrowful noise" merely speaks aloud what she feels.

The most interesting and poignant section of the poem is the concluding fifth stanza. For here, the new chapter is not a new period in her life but a new awareness, a realization, a new sense of what it means to be a wife, and especially this Chinese wife. This stanza is a particular triumph of the one new image, one new line rule. And of the all the images in this stanza the following should be singled out:

> The paired butterflies are already yellow with
>   August
> Over the grass in the West garden;
> They hurt me. I grow older.

This girl's contemplation of the butterflies, of the natural order of things, of continuity in nature, of growth and renewal, and of beauty in companionship is another way of her saying: "I realize now how much I have lost with you, my husband, being gone." If we read the butterflies as a metaphor for her and her husband then she is saying that she and he are like paired butterflies except that they are not together. To see such pairs, then, "hurts" her because it reminds her how much she needs her husband. Notice, then, that this anger, and this complaint is based entirely on love. Only after her husband is absent does she realize the meaning of and the depth of her own love. In this letter/poem, then, she is communicating that love. To say "I grow older" is another way of saying, "I have grown wiser." She now understands the meaning of love. The last four lines of the poem, then, are more than just description. They are the inevitable result of the wisdom she has come to only now, in this fifth stanza.

The final four lines tell us that she is prepared to wait, that she will not give up on her husband, that if she feels angry she is by no means angry about or mistrustful of his love. In the end, the poem becomes a kind of meditative ode—a poem where one speaker in the course of the poem teaches herself a truth. It may only go as far as "Cho-fu-sa," and it may depend entirely on our knowledge as readers of what it means to be an eighth-century Chinese wife. Indeed, if that is the case, if it is true that her knowledge, her wisdom can only make sense if we know what it is like to be a Chinese sixteen-year-old wife in the eighth century then this poem as a translation from the Chinese of Li Po has, thanks to Pound, given us another culture and another time: it has become a masterpiece of translation itself.

Source: Jonathan N. Barron, in an essay for *Poetry for Students,* Gale Group, 2000.

Sources

Alexander, Michael, *The Poetic Achievement of Ezra Pound,* University of California Press, 1979, 247 p.

Eliot, T. S., "The Method of Pound," *The Athenaeum,* No. 4669, October 24, 1919, pp. 1065-66.

Kenner, Hugh, *The Pound Era,* Berkeley: California University Press, 1971.

O'Connor, William Van, *Ezra Pound,* ("University of Minnesota Pamphlets on American Writers" series, No. 26), University of Minnesota Press, 1963.

Pratt, William, "Ezra Pound and the Image," in *Ezra Pound: The London Years: 1908-1920,* edited by Philip Grover, AMS Press, 1978, pp. 15-30.

Rosenthal, M. L., and Sally M. Gall, "Ezra Pound I: The Early Sequences," in their *The Modern Poetic Sequence:*

"The Genius of Modern Poetry," Oxford University Press, 1983, pp. 184-203.

Ward, David E, "The Emperor's Clothes?" *Essays in Criticism,* January, 1968, pp. 68-73.

For Further Study

Chisholm, Lawrence W., *Fenollosa: The Far East and American Culture,* New Haven: Yale University Press, 1963.
   This book contains an interesting description of the influence of Oriental thought and art on many American artists and philosophers.

Froula, Christine, *A Guide to Ezra Pound's Selected Poems,* New York: New Directions, 1982.
   This helpful introduction to Pound includes comments on the wife's attitudes in the "The River Merchan't Wife."

Kenner, Hugh, *The Poetry of Ezra Pound,* Norfolk, CT: New Directions, 1951.
   This is one of the best sources for a clear introduction to Pound and his poetry.

Witemeyer, Hugh, *The Poetry of Ezra Pound, Forms and Renewal, 1908-1920,* Berkeley: University of California Press, 1969.
   The book discusses Pound's perspectives on Chinese poetry, discussing its similarity to Imagism.

Yip, Wai-lim, *Ezra Pound's Cathay,* Princeton, NJ: Princeton University Press, 1969.
   In this detailed study of *Cathay,* Yip examines three stages of the poems: the original, Fenollosa's English version, and Pound's translation.

The Seafarer

Anonymous

c. 450–c. 1100

"The Seafarer" was first discovered in the *Exeter Book,* a hand-copied manuscript containing the largest known collection of Old English poetry, which is kept at Exeter Cathedral, England. "The Seafarer" has its origins in the Old English period of English literature, 450-1100, a time when very few people knew how to read or write. Old English (the predecessor of modern English) is the name given to the Germanic tongues brought to England by the invading tribes who crossed the English channel from Northern Europe. Old English resembles German and Scandinavian languages, and one cannot read it without at least one year of intense study. Even in its translated form, "The Seafarer" provides an accurate portrait of the sense of stoic endurance, suffering, loneliness, and spiritual yearning so characteristic of Old English poetry. "The Seafarer" is divisible into two sections, the first elegiac and the second didactic. "The Seafarer" can be read as two poems on separate subjects or as one poem moving between two subjects. Moreover, the poem can be read as a dramatic monologue, the thoughts of one person, or as a dialogue between two people. The first section is a painfully personal description of the suffering and mysterious attractions of life at sea. In the second section, the speaker makes an abrupt shift to moral speculation about the fleeting nature of fame, fortune, and life itself, ending with an explicitly Christian view of God as wrathful and powerful. In this section, the speaker urges the reader to forget earthly accomplishments and anticipate God's

judgment in the afterlife. The poem addresses both pagan and Christian ideas about overcoming this sense of suffering and loneliness. For example, the speaker discusses being buried with treasure and winning glory in battle (pagan) and also fearing God's judgment in the afterlife (Christian). Moreover, "The Seafarer" can be thought of as an allegory discussing life as a journey and the human condition as that of exile from God on the sea of life. For comparison, read Samuel Taylor Coleridge's poem "The Rime of the Ancient Mariner." Whatever themes one finds in the poem, "The Seafarer" is a powerful account of a sensitive poet's interaction with his environment.

Poem Text

This tale is true, and mine. It tells
How the sea took me, swept me back
And forth in sorrow and fear and pain
Showed me suffering in a hundred ships,
In a thousand ports, and in me. It tells   5
Of smashing surf when I sweated in the cold
Of an anxious watch, perched in the bow
As it dashed under cliffs. My feet were cast
In icy bands, bound with frost,
With frozen chains, and hardship groaned   10
Around my heart. Hunger tore
At my sea-weary soul. No man sheltered
On the quiet fairness of earth can feel
How wretched I was, drifting through winter
On an ice-cold sea, whirled in sorrow,   15
Alone in a world blown clear of love,
Hung with icicles. The hailstorms flew.
The only sound was the roaring sea,
The freezing waves. The song of the swan
Might serve for pleasure, the cry of the sea-fowl,   20
The death-noise of birds instead of laughter,
The mewing of gulls instead of mead.
Storms beat on the rocky cliffs and were echoed
By icy-feathered terns and the eagle's screams;
No kinsman could offer comfort there,   25
To a soul left drowning in desolation.
     And who could believe, knowing but
The passion of cities, swelled proud with wine
And no taste of misfortune, how often, how
     wearily,
I put myself back on the paths of the sea.   30
Night would blacken; it would snow from the
     north;
Frost bound the earth and hail would fall,
The coldest seeds. And how my heart
Would begin to beat, knowing once more
The salt waves tossing and the towering sea!   35
The time for journeys would come and my soul
Called me eagerly out, sent me over
The horizon, seeking foreigners' homes.
     But there isn't a man on earth so proud,

          40

So born to greatness, so bold with his youth,
Grown so grave, or so graced by God,
That he feels no fear as the sails unfurl,
Wondering what Fate has willed and will do.
No harps ring in his heart, no rewards,
No passion for women, no worldly pleasures,   45
Nothing, only the ocean's heave;
But longing wraps itself around him.
Orchards blossom, the towns bloom,
Fields grow lovely as the world springs fresh,
And all these admonish that willing mind   50
Leaping to journeys, always set
In thoughts traveling on a quickening tide.
So summer's sentinel, the cuckoo, sings
In his murmuring voice, and our hearts mourn
As he urges. Who could understand,   55
In ignorant ease, what we others suffer
As the paths of exile stretch endlessly on?
And yet my heart wanders away,
My soul roams with the sea, the whales'
Home, wandering to the widest corners   60
Of the world, returning ravenous with desire,
Flying solitary, screaming, exciting me
To the open ocean, breaking oaths
On the curve of a wave.
     Thus the joys of God   65
Are fervent with life, where life itself
Fades quickly into the earth. The wealth
Of the world neither reaches to Heaven nor
     remains.
No man has ever faced the dawn
Certain which of Fate's three threats   70
Would fall: illness, or age, or an enemy's
Sword, snatching the life from his soul.
The praise the living pour on the dead
Flowers from reputation: plant
An earthly life of profit reaped   75
Even from hatred and rancor, of bravery
Flung in the devil's face, and death
Can only bring you earthly praise
And a song to celebrate a place
With the angels, life eternally blessed   80
In the hosts of Heaven.
     The days are gone
When the kingdoms of earth flourished in glory;
Now there are no rulers, no emperors,
No givers of gold, as once there were,   85
When wonderful things were worked among them
And they lived in lordly magnificence.
Those powers have vanished, those pleasures are
     dead.
The weakest survives and the world continues,
Kept spinning by toil. All glory is tarnished.   90
The world's honor ages and shrinks,
Bent like the men who mold it. Their faces
Blanch as time advances, their beards
Wither and they mourn the memory of friends.
The sons of princes, sown in the dust.   95
The soul stripped of its flesh knows nothing
Of sweetness or sour, feels no pain,
Bends neither its hand nor its brain. A brother
Opens his palms and pours down gold
On his kinsman's grave, strewing his coffin   100

With treasures intended for Heaven, but nothing
Golden shakes the wrath of God
For a soul overflowing with sin, and nothing
Hidden on earth rises to Heaven.
    We all fear God. He turns the earth,   105
He set it swinging firmly in space,
Gave life to the world and light to the sky.
Death leaps at the fools who forget their God.
He who lives humbly has angels from Heaven
To carry him courage and strength and belief.   110
A man must conquer pride, not kill it,
Be firm with his fellows, chaste for himself,
Treat all the world as the world deserves,
With love or with hate but never with harm,
Though an enemy seek to scorch him in hell,   115
Or set the flames of a funeral pyre
Under his lord. Fate is stronger
And God mightier than any man's mind.
Our thoughts should turn to where our home is,
Consider the ways of coming there,   120
Then strive for sure permission for us
To rise to that eternal joy,
That life born in the love of God
And the hope of Heaven. Praise the Holy
Grace of Him who honored us,   125
Eternal, unchanging creator of earth. Amen.

Poem Summary

Lines 1-5:

The elegiac, personal tone is established from the beginning. The speaker pleads to his audience about his honesty and his personal self-revelation to come. He tells of the limitless suffering, sorrow, and pain and his long experience in various ships and ports. The speaker never explains exactly why he is driven to take to the ocean.

Lines 6-11:

Here, the speaker conveys intense, concrete images of cold, anxiety, stormy seas, and rugged shorelines. The comparisons relating to imprisonment are many, combining to drag the speaker into his prolonged state of anguish. The adverse conditions affect both his physical body (his feet) and his spiritual sense of worth (his heart).

Lines 12-16:

The loneliness and isolation of the speaker's ocean wanderings are emphasized in these lines. The speaker highlights the opposition between the comfortable landlubber and the anguished, lonely, frozen mariner. Alone physically and without a sense of connection to the rest of the human race, the seafarer pushes on in his suffering.

Lines 17-19:

The speaker returns to depicting his adverse environment and the inclement weather conditions of hail, high waves, cold, and wind.

Lines 20-26:

The first of several catalogues, or lists of items using similar grammatical structures, appears in these lines; here the speaker invokes the names of four specific sea-birds that serve as his sole companions. The birds' plaintive cries only emphasize the distance from land and from other people. The speaker says that the swan's song might serve for pleasure, but in his case it will not. The swans, gulls, terns, and eagles only increase the mariner's sense of abandonment and illumine the lack of warm, human compassion in his stormy ocean wandering. The speaker metaphorically drowns in his loneliness.

Lines 27-30:

The speaker constructs another opposition, one between himself and the comfortable city dweller who puffs himself up with pride and drink. This city person cannot possibly know of the seafarer's suffering. The wilderness experience of the speaker cannot be translated for the sheltered urban inhabitant. The landlocked man cannot possibly understand the seafarer's motives; however, like all people, he will eventually be held accountable for his choice of lifestyle. This theme becomes predominant in the poem's second half.

Lines 31-38:

The speaker again describes the changes in weather. As day turns to night, and snow and hail rain down from black skies, the speaker says that he is once again drawn to his inexplicable wandering. The speaker cannot find words to say why he is magically pulled towards suffering and into foreign seaports. The phrase "seeking foreigners' homes" is a paradox, because, while he searches for the shelter of homes, the seafarer is isolated from the values represented by home: warmth, safety, compassion, friendship, and love.

Lines 39-43:

These lines introduce the central theme of the poem. The speaker displays his second catalogue, a list of earthy human virtues: pride, greatness, boldness, youth, seriousness, and grace. The speaker emphasizes that these virtues will all disappear, melting away in the presence of Fate. Even the person blessed with all these virtues feels fear at the onset of a journey on the sea. Thus, the speaker shows the possible allegorical reading that life itself is a journey on the raging sea; the seafarer may represent every person who must learn to rely on God's mercy and fear God's judgment.

Lines 44-46:

These lines continue the catalogue of worldly pleasures begun in line 39. The traveller on the stormy sea will never be comforted by harps, rewards, or the love of women, because he needs to wander and to face what Fate has in store for him. Readers should note that the concept of Fate, often described as a spinning wheel of fortune in Middle English poetry, is at odds with the Christian concept of divine providence or God's predestined plan.

Lines 47-57:

The speaker shifts away from deprivation and winter to fulfillment and summer. The imagery of orchards, flowers, and cities in bloom stands in stark contrast to that of icy winter winds and storms. The cuckoo, a bird of happiness and summer, contrasts with the earlier lists of winter ocean birds. The point is that these pleasant summer thoughts also bring the seafarer's wanderlust back again. The comfortable person mourns but does not understand the reason why he is called to abandon city life and search the frozen, stormy seas. Suffering and exile are not lessons well learned in good weather with city comforts; thus, the speaker implies that everyone must experience deprivation at sea to learn life's most important lesson—reliance on God.

Lines 58-64:

In this conclusion of the first major section, the seafarer says that his mind and heart constantly seek to roam the sea because that is acceptance of life itself. The paradox of the seafarer's excitement at beginning the journey shows his acceptance of suffering to come. Despite knowing of the isolation and deprivation, the speaker still is driven to resume his life at sea. Breaking his ties with humanity, the speaker expresses his thrill at returning to his tortuous wandering.

Lines 65-68:

The speaker announces the theme of the second section: that the joys of accepting God's will far exceed any form of wealth or earthly pleasure. Earthly wealth cannot reach heaven, nor can it tran-

Media Adaptations

- *Selected Readings in Old English,* read by Edward N. Irving, Jr., in 1996 for Brigham Young University's Chaucer Studios, contains "The Seafarer" among other poems in the original Old English. You can order this tape directly via the web at http://English.byu.edu/Chaucer. You can also download a sample of Old English poetry at the same web address with the suffix /oldeng.htm.

- Also out of BYU's Chaucer Studio comes another recording of Old English short poems along with riddles, made in 1990 by Rosamund Allen of the University of London under the title *Old English Elegies and Riddles.*

---

scend life. This section grows less personal and becomes mostly theological and didactic in nature.

Lines 69-72:

Describing three ways of death, the speaker says that no man is certain how life will end. The violent nature of Anglo-Saxon society is described by the possibility of death by an enemy's sword.

Lines 73-81:

The speaker writes that one wins a reputation through battle and bravery, that only earthly praise comes to warriors who take risks and perform great feats in battle. In this section, one imagines the creation of funeral fires, songs, and shrines in honor of the great warriors.

Lines 82-88:

The speaker says the days of glory and honor have passed. Another catalogue laments the lack of rulers, emperors, gold-givers, and lords. The power of the nobles and aristocrats has vanished; glory must be sought in other ways than through bravery in battle.

Lines 89-95:

The theme of lost glory is continued. The speaker uses the simile of faded glory being like old men who remember their former youth. The old men turn white, their beards grow thin, and they mourn the memory of departed companions. The sons of nobles who formerly fought to win glory in battle are now dust on the ground.

Lines 96-98:

The speaker focuses on the spiritual aspect of life after death and how the soul knows no earthly comforts; the soul removed from the body feels nothing and cares nothing for fame.

Lines 99-101:

The metaphor of a brother placing gold coins on his kinsman's coffin shows the uselessness of wealth and reputation to the dead. The speaker writes that all earthly wealth and fame are meaningless in the next world. God's anger against a sinful person cannot be reduced at any price; thus, the speaker urges all to heed the warning not to get taken in by wealth and fame.

Lines 102-107:

The speaker shifts to the final, concluding section of the poem, the most religious part of "The Seafarer." The speaker writes that all fear God because He created the earth and the heavens. God moves everything on earth and in the skies, according to the speaker.

Lines 108-116:

The speaker presents his final catalogue, a list of lessons or commandments to be learned by the humble person who fears his judgment day. According to the seafarer, each wise person must be humble, strong, courageous, chaste, firm with his friends, and never resort to violence even if enemies seek to burn and destroy him. The man who thinks about God will be comforted by angels.

Lines 117-124:

The speaker admonishes that God and Fate are more powerful than any person's will. According to to the seafarer, people should always consider God's purpose and think of their final resting place in heaven, their home. Here, the speaker talks of the joys, love, and hope that he feels await the faithful in heaven.

Lines 124-126:

The poem ends in a prayer of praise to God, the eternal creator of earth and its life. The traditional ending "Amen" raises the question about how, if at all, the concluding section connects or fails to connect with the more passionate, emotional

song of the forsaken seafarer adrift on the inhospitable waves in the first section.

Themes

Alienation and Loneliness

As a poetic genre, elegy generally portrays sorrow and longing for the better days of times past. To conjure up its theme of longing, "The Seafarer" immediately thrusts the reader deep into a world of exile, hardship, and loneliness. The speaker of the poem describes his feelings of alienation in terms of physical privation and suffering: "My feet were cast / In icy bands, bound with frost, / With frozen chains, and hardship groaned / Around my heart" (8b-11a). The cold that seizes his feet, immobilized in the hull of his open-aired ship while sailing across a wintry sea, corresponds to the anguish that clasps his mind. "Alone in a world blown clear of love," he listens to the cries of various birds whose calls take the place of human laughter, and he must sojourn with these feathered forces of nature without the warmth of the human bonds of kith and kin. For those whose cultural ideals exalt the fiercely solitary self-made individualist who struggles alone without help from family or friends, the poignancy of these lines may not be evident. Modern readers must remember that the Anglo-Saxon world was held together by a web of relationships of both family and fealty. Such a sense of isolation as the seafarer suffers in this poem was tantamount to a kind of psychic death for the people of that time. Because of his social separation, in fact, a *wr'ce,* that is, an "exile" or "wanderer" in Old English, was most vulnerable to the vicissitudes of Fate mentioned in this poem. Without the human web of close interrelationships, he was more likely to be stricken down by "illness, or age, or an enemy's / Sword" (71-72a).

Human Condition

Despite the seafarer's miserable seclusion while at sea, yet another inward longing propels him to return to the source of his sorrow. The human condition, universal in so many ways and perduring through time and across cultural differences, consists of a fragile balance between longing and loathing. How often have people found themselves in a "love-hate" relationship with a job or avocation or, even worse, with another person." Those who dwell in the safety of cities, well-fed and used to the pleasures of wine and song, cannot understand the "push-pull" the seafarer must endure. But the seafarer's equivocal position itself becomes a metaphor for the uncertainties and contradictions inherent within life itself: "Thus the joys of God / Are fervent with life, where life itself / Fades quickly into the earth. The wealth / Of the world neither reaches to Heaven nor remains" (65-69). These lines, so redolent of both sadness and resignation, find echoes throughout Western literature, whether of Christian *contemptu mundi* ("contempt of the world") or of existentialist angst before the absurd meaninglessness of life. The seafarer's response lies somewhere between these two opposing poles in the history of European thought. The Germanic heroic ideal of finding immortality in the living memory of one's people combines with the Christian goal of receiving a reward in the afterlife to give meaning to the seafarer's struggles in this world of pain, unfulfilled need, and unremitting sorrow.

Memory and Reminiscence

Yet a greater source of sadness for the seafarer lies in the disparity he sees between the present "fallen" world when compared to the glorious world of yore. The Germanic heroic era from the times of the great tribal migrations that ended the Western Roman Empire has been preserved in the literatures of the British Saxons, the Icelandic Norse, and the continental Germans who had remained in the older tribal areas of the Germanic peoples. These were the times of brave exploits that overwhelm and diminish any current glory: "Now there are no rulers, no emperors, / No givers of gold, as once there were, / When wonderful things were worked among them / And they lived in lordly magnificence. / Those powers have vanished, those pleasures are dead." (84-88). The contemporary world fares poorly in comparison: "The weakest survives and the world continues, / Kept spinning by toil. All glory is tarnished. / The world's honor ages and shrinks, / Bent like the men who mold it" (89-92). Like the Greeks before them, the Germanic peoples had a sense of the passing of a "Golden Age." One perhaps detects in the speaker's words a deeper longing for a wilder, more exhilarating time before the "civilization" brought by Christendom. Despite the poem's overt appeals to a Christian God, the memory of pagan heroism haunts "The Seafarer" with elegiac longing and explains why the speaker of the poem would seek out the pain and danger of seafaring as an alternative to the more settled life of the town. On the other hand, all the speaker's dissatisfaction with the

Topics for Further Study

- Given that many people have little idea of how those of former times viewed themselves or their cultural worlds, is it indeed possible for modern readers to relate to an art form and a cultural perspective that is so utterly foreign to postindustrial and postmodern reality? Should we even try to read "The Seafarer" from the original audience's point of view? If this seems impossible, then how should we read this poem? Can we read it any way we wish using reader's response?

- Since "The Seafarer" constitutes a form of lyric poetry called elegy—that is, a private reflection upon the tragic aspects of life's transitory nature—how is it similar or dissimilar to elegies from later periods of English literature, such as John Milton's "Lycidas" or Thomas Grey's "Elegy Written in a Country Churchyard"? Is there some quality that links all these poems together despite the vast differences that exist between them as to time and cultural perspective? If so, then what exactly in "The Seafarer" makes it elegiac?

- Even if we no longer share cultural memory with the writer of "The Seafarer," we do share at least some sense of the passing of the good old days? Everyone has some sort of precious memory of their own glory days toward which they feel a mixture of joy and regret. It could be adventures from the golden days of childhood or the swift passing away of childhood's good feelings. Break up into small groups and brainstorm your own elegies of sorrow for the passage of time and the disappearance of your own "Golden Age."

world as it is also reveals a genuine expression of Christian revulsion before the fleeting emptiness of life. The very ambiguity of the two themes truly sustain the poem's force as good literature in spite of cultural changes over the years.

Style

"The Seafarer" was probably first sung by a poet in the mead-halls of princes and kings, accompanied by the traditional instrument, the harp; thus the communal and oral nature of ancient poetry is reflected in the poem's structure.

Old English poetry has a special structure. In its original form, each line is divided symmetrically into two halves, one stressed and the other unstressed in its emphasis. To better appreciate what Old English looks like, here are the first two lines, untranslated, of "The Seafarer":

> Maeg ic be me selfum soth-gied wrecan,
> Sithas secgan hu ic geswinc-dagum

"The Seafarer" has two major parts, lines 1-64 (part 1) and lines 65-126 (part 2). Some scholars consider the poem a dramatic monologue by the same speaker moving between two subjects; others think the poem is a dialogue between a young, inexperienced sailor and an old, wise veteran of the sea giving advice about life's ultimate rewards. The poem has many repeated words and phrases that sound familiar, probably because they are borrowed from other sources such as the Psalms in the Bible. Missionaries from the Mediterranean and Ireland came to the native Celts in England during the 7th century; priests and monks may have transcribed old poetry and added their Christian views to a previously secular poem.

Old English poetry tends to use alliteration and rhythm. Another distinctive feature of Old English that is found in "The Seafarer" is kennings or compound words like "sea-fowl" or "whales' home." These compound words show how the speaker attempts to formulate new concepts in poetry working with a limited vocabulary. The many concrete, descriptive words show how part of an oral, traditional culture is preserved by the poets who sang these songs. The poem's vivid metaphors and images sharply portray the seafarer's tumultuous experience as he is tossed around in a boat on the wind-whipped ocean.

Historical Context

Without the interest of Church leaders and the patronage of West Saxon kings, modern readers would have no Old English literature to speak of. While the so-called Anglo-Saxon period of English history extends from 449 to 1066—from the beginning of the conquest of Britain by the Angles, Saxons, and Jutes, through the invasions and partial conquest of northern England by the Danish- and Norse-speaking Vikings, and until the defeat of the last Saxon King, Harold, by William the Conqueror—the literary period of the Old English peoples really only began after the conversion of these tribes to Christianity. Previous to this event, the literature of the migrating bands had been entirely oral. It consisted of ancient verse forms employing repeated stress patterns and alliteration, and it celebrated heroic figures of even earlier periods. But none of this oral literature could have survived the further invasions and cultural changes that later befell Britain if the tribes had not converted to Christianity and learned the art of letters. Furthermore, since the literate elite of the earlier part of this six-hundred-year period were almost entirely monks and other churchmen, without the abiding interest of ecclesiastical authorities in their ancestors' pagan roots, none of the poetry of the Angles and Saxons would have ever obtained to writing. Still, it was King Alfred (849-899) and his successors in Wessex who vigorously collected and preserved the literary heritage of their ancestors while extending the body of literature through translation and fresh composition.

"The Seafarer," an elegy and not a traditional Germanic epic (though an epic like *Beowulf* itself had elegiac sections), actually carries within itself evidence of a melding of cultures between Anglo-Saxons and the British. This merging points to a developing cultural synthesis between native and invader that was brought to an end by William's conquest with his French-speaking Viking retainers. The fact is that by the end of the Anglo-Saxon period, a body of English literature, an evolving amalgam of Germanic, Celtic, and Latin sources, was thriving with a growing readership, maturing in sophistication and complexity, and exploring new genres and themes. The Norman invasion cut off a process of development in English literature that would only begin again under entirely different cultural circumstances three hundred years later during the so-called "high" Middle Ages. Although modern readers are separated from the body of surviving Old English literature by the cultural watersheds of the Norman invasion, the Reformation and Renaissance, and the emergence of the present postmodern and post-Christian era, we must "stretch" our imaginations enough to try to appreciate this literature through the cultural lens of its original audience and understand it as a fascinat-

(Continued on page 188)

Compare & Contrast

- **600-100 BC:** Although Germanic peoples were first mentioned in writing some six hundred years before the common era, they did not "officially" burst into the Mediterranean world until the second century BC with the invasion of Italy by the Cimbri and the Teutons, who were finally routed by the Romans in 101 BC.

- **58-51 BC:** Caesar decides to invade Transalpine Gaul in 58 BC when protests by various Gallic tribes in loose confederation with Rome arise against the Suevi, a German tribe that had recently conquered territory in Gaul, and when he hears reports of a threatened invasion by the Helvetii, a Celtic tribe from the area that is now in Switzerland. Not only does he force the Helvetii to withdraw, but he also kills the Suevi's leader, Ariovistus, in Alsace after an arduous offensive. Over the course of the various campaigns that constitute the "Gallic Wars," Caesar has many occasions to meet and defeat various Germanic tribes, like the Usipites and Tencteri, that were then crossing the Rhine into Celtic territories. Caesar's consolidation of Roman power in Gaul stops Germanic migration into the area for a while.

- **AD 9:** Roman power in Gaul continues to grow after Caesar's adopted son, Augustus, settles his imperial claims at the end of the Roman Civil Wars and consolidates power. But in AD 9, Arminius (c. 17 BC-AD 21), a Cherusci tribal chieftain, leads a confederation of tribes in ambush and utterly destroys three legions under General Publius Quinctilius Varus in the Teutoburg Forest. Augustus wisely decides that the only defensible frontier for the Empire is at the Rhine River and breaks off further Roman incursions into German territory.

- **AD 167-175, 178-180:** Emperor Marcus Aurelius Pius, famous Stoic philosopher-king of the middle Roman Empire, begins a series of campaigns against the Marcomanni and other Germanic tribes allied with them along the Danube River in what is now known as Austria. Even though Marcus Aurelius hands on troubles along the Danubian frontier to his son and heir, Commodus, if he hadn't succeeded in defeating the Marcomanni, the Empire might well have ended much earlier than it does.

- **Third Century AD:** The Roman world collapses into a nearly fatal crisis chiefly due to the unbridgeable gap between the rich upper classes in the cities and the unemployed urban poor and barely civilized peasants. Also, the wars that began under Marcus Aurelius persist, and increased taxation steadily devours the prosperity of the Empire. To meet rising military expenses and to supply the ever-growing bureaucracy, emperors, like Caracalla (d. 217), devalue Roman money and precipitate an economic crisis from "runaway" inflation. Defenses along the Rhine and Danube also disintegrate further under tribal attack, and the provinces of the Eastern Empire are overrun by Iranians. Finally, the command and control of the army completely breaks down. Between the years 235 and 284 only one out of more than two dozen emperors escapes violent death.

- **Third Century AD:** The Goths, a Germanic people who probably migrated from southern Scandinavia sometime before the time of Christ, settle by the Third Century into territories near the Black Sea and stage occasional strikes into Roman territory. Those who inhabit an area in what is now the modern Ukraine come to be known as Ostrogoths, or the "East Goths," and those who occupy a region along the Danube are called Visigoths, or the "West Goths."

- **Third Century AD:** The Franks, also known as the Salians, Ripuarians, and Chatti, come to inhabit the lower and middle Rhine Valley. In time, the Franks start to breach the Roman borderland around Mainz but are eventually driven back by Emperor Probus.

- **284-305:** After much social, economic, and military disintegration, the Emperor Diocletian takes over the Empire and establishes total con-

(Continued on next page)

Compare & Contrast

trol over all aspects of Roman life. He adopts oriental court culture and protocols and transforms into an unending system the extraordinary measures adopted by the emperors of the third century to save the Roman state. Personal freedom is denied the peasantry, who then become tied to the soil of their birth. Artisans and higher civil servants are frozen into hereditary castes and taxed to the breaking point. Only rich landowners in fortified villas—a foreshadowing of medieval feudal lords—and the imperial bureaucracy predominate over the slowly collapsing social order.

- **Fourth Century AD:** Both the Ostrogoths and the Visigoths live peacefully near the Empire and trade with the Romans for luxury goods. They also adopt a heretical form of Christianity called Arianism, the belief that Christ was human and not divine.

- **306-337:** After having fought off numerous opponents, Constantine I successfully reorganizes the Roman Empire. He also decriminalizes Christianity and eventually converts to the emergent faith himself. He establishes a second capital at Byzantium and names it Constantinople after himself in 330. With two capitals as foci for the East and the West, he reorganizes the entire system of local government into prefectures, dioceses, and provinces under regional metropolitan control. Indeed, his reforms, though too late for the West, enable the Roman Empire to survive in the East until the year 1453. Still, Constantine's division of the Empire into two parts only becomes official in the year 395.

- **358:** Emperor Julian, later known as "the Apostate" because of his desire to return the Empire to paganism, grants the Salian Franks an area of land called Toxandria between the Meuse and the Scheldt rivers in exchange for Frankish military allegiance and support.

- **370:** The Ostrogoths are defeated by and forced into fealty with the Huns.

- **378-418:** With further pressure from the Huns pushing both Gothic tribes across the Roman frontier, the Visigoths in 378 defeat the Eastern Romans of Byzantium at Adrianople. Repudiating an alliance they had forged with the Byzantines after their victory, the Visigoths turn to the West and sack Rome in 410 under their king Alaric I and then continue migrating and marauding until 418, when they settle in Aquitaine in southwestern France.

- **Fifth Century AD:** The Ripuarian Franks and the Chatti, cousins to the Salian Franks, had also struck across the frontier of middle Rhine during the first quarter of the fifth century. As a result of the invasion of Gaul by the Huns, a band of Ripuarians takes over Cologne.

- **406:** The Vandals, another Arian Christian tribe that had originally migrated into what is now Hungary, also suffer attacks under Huns from the East. They eventually push across the frontiers of the Roman Empire in December 406, when they cross the Rhine into Gaul.

- **429-439:** Having pushed on into Spain by 409, the Vandals under their new ruler Gaiseric (ruling from 429 to 477) use Spain as a launchpad for their invasion of North Africa, leaving the Iberian peninsula for others to conquer.

- **449-1066:** From the times of the first incursions by Hengist and Horsa until the death of Harold II at Hastings, the so-called Anglo-Saxon period of British history presents an integral continuum of steady social evolution. The whole pattern of early Anglo-Saxon society first centers on families, clans, and tribes and depends upon a class of warriors bound together in a filial system of reciprocity called a *comitatus* in Latin. Scholars believe this same system predominated for all Germanic peoples. The regional and tribal leader (*ealdormann* or *eorl*) counted on both military support and undying loyalty from his *thegns* ("thanes," that is, armed retainers), who in return presumed their leader would provide them with an organized defense and luxurious bequests for their services to him. From the seventh until the eleventh century this tribal system

Compare & Contrast

evolves incrementally because of extending filiation into larger and larger kingdoms, most significantly the East Anglian kingdom of Mercia, the North Anglian kingdom of Northumbria, and the West Saxon kingdom of Wessex. But by 959, all of England is rather loosely filiated and united under the kings of Wessex, the greatest of whom was Alfred the Great (849-899). However, this West-Saxon lineage of kings is halted for a generation in 1016 when the Danish king Canute succeeds in conquering and holding England, thus crowning more than two centuries of sporadic Viking penetrations and seizures in England. Nevertheless, two Anglo-Saxon kings, Saint Edward the Confessor and Harold II, do return to reign again, but only for 24 years (1042-66) before the conquest of England by the Norman William I ends Anglo-Saxon cultural and political hegemony.

- **455:** Having consolidated power over the western Mediterranean, Gaiseric successfully invades and sacks Rome in 455. Because of this act of utter destructiveness, the name "Vandal" has come to signify anyone who barbarically and wantonly destroys property.

- **461-81:** After the Merovingians—one of the smaller bands into which the Salian Franks were divided, named after its chieftain Merovech—extended Salian domination to the south, perhaps as far as the Somme River, Childeric I (d. 481), Merovech's son, continues to support the Romans until the death of the Roman Emperor Majorian in 461. He then leads an uprising against Aegidius, the Roman governor in northern Gaul. Aegidius, however, prevails in the struggle and exiles Childeric across the Rhine among the Thuringian tribe. Nevertheless, Childeric returns after a few years and defeats the Romans with the help of some Saxon allies. In the end, Syagrius, Aegidius's son and successor, is able to keep Childeric from moving his people south of the Somme, but in the meantime another Salian tribal chieftain has taken control of Liege.

- **476:** Odoacer (or "Odovacar"), a member of either the Sciri or the Rugian tribe born around 433, deposes and replaces the child emperor, Romulus Augustulus, on August 28, 476, thus finishing off the already dying Western Roman Empire. In time, Odoacer also conquers Sicily and Dalmatia, menacing the possessions of the Eastern Roman Emperor, Zeno.

- **481-511:** Clovis, Childeric's son, converts to Roman Catholicism and in time conquers most of Gaul to unify the Franks under his Merovingian dynasty.

- **488-493:** Zeno, Emperor of the East, sponsors the Ostrogothic king Theodoric against Odoacer. Theodoric overruns Italy and assassinates Odoacer at a banquet on March 15, 493, a week after Odoacer had yielded up power to him.

- **493-553:** The Ostrogothic king Theodoric rules over all of Italy from 493 to 526. But when Theodoric's daughter, Amalasuntha, is murdered by her husband and co-ruler, Theodahad, in 535, the Byzantines themselves invade the kingdom to reestablish their influence over the area. By 553 the Byzantines and the Lombards, another Germanic tribe, have divided Italy between themselves.

- **507-08:** The last vestige of Visigothic presence in Aquitaine is driven out by Clovis, Merovingian King of the Franks. Over the years, however, Visigothic interests had already moved southward into Spain.

- **511-561:** Upon Clovis' death, his kingdom is split up, according to Frankish custom, among his four sons: Theodoric (d. 534), Chlodomer (d. 524), Childebert I (d. 558), and Chlotar I (d. 561), who make their respective capitals at Metz, Orleans, Paris, and Soissons. After a bloody forty years of struggle, Chlotar is finally able to reunite the Merovingian holdings by the time of his death.

- **533-534:** After Gaiseric's death, his descendants have problems safeguarding their borders. In

Compare & Contrast

533 the Byzantine general Belisarius attacks the strongholds of the Vandals and in turn reduces their kingdom in North Africa to absolute ruins by 534.

- **561-613:** Upon Chlotar's death, the Frankish kingdom is again divided among his four sons. This time, two of his sons, Sigibert I (d. 575) of Austrasia and Chilperic I (d. 584) of Neustria, begin a struggle for ultimate control over all Frankish lands that will last well beyond their respective deaths.

- **585-711:** By 585 the Visigoths have extended and consolidated their control over the Pyrenees to Spain. Visigothic power in Spain then basically goes unchallenged (except for exchanges with the Byzantines in the seventh century) until the Muslim invasion of 711, when they are utterly dispossessed of power.

- **629-639:** In the long run, Chilperic's family prevails in its struggle for Frankish supremacy, and Chilperic's grandson, Dagobert I, becomes king of all the Franks, the last Merovingian king of any significance. After Dagobert's death, the kings of the Merovingian dynasty become captives of various magnate families.

- **Seventh Century:** The Carolingians, a family of Ripuarian Franks that eventually took its name from Charles Martel, the grandfather of Charlemagne, had their origins in the union of the family of Arnulf, Bishop of Metz, with that of Pepin of Landen (d. 640), hereditary mayor of the palace in Austrasia, during the early Seventh Century. As mayors of the palace, the Carolingians are in fact the actual rulers of Frankish territories under the later Merovingian kings. Even though an attempt at taking away the crown fails in the mid-seventh century, family fortunes improve over the next hundred years.

- **845:** Having successfully mounted numerous short raids upon cities and villages around the North Sea from the late Eighth Century, Viking raiders adopt a new tactic. Instead of mounting short forays in spring and summer only to spend the winter back home, now larger bands begin to encamp on small islands at the mouths of major rivers. This tactic furnishes them with year-round bases near their quarry. Viking chiefs then combine to form larger armies in order to take advantage of fissures among the Anglo-Saxons and Franks and thereby extract larger and larger duties from Frankish and Anglo-Saxon kings.

- **878:** Danish Vikings control large parts of eastern and northern England in a region that comes to be known as the "Danelaw."

- **911:** A Viking leader named Rollo receives lands at the estuary of the Seine River from the Carolingian king, Charles III, for his pledge to defend the riverine approaches to Paris from the attacks of other Viking bands. This marks the beginning of what is to become the Duchy of Normandy.

- **Tenth Century:** During the same period, Gotlandic and Swedish Vikings, traveling down the Volga River, begin making contact with traders from the Muslim Empire, who pay them in silver for their trade goods. The Dnepr River takes them to the Black Sea and Constantinople, seat of the Byzantine Empire, where they form an elite guard in service to the Byzantine Emperor. According to Russian accounts, these so-called "Varangians" eventually raise up the first ruling house over the Rus or East Slavs under their leader Rurik in Kiev.

- **987:** Carolingian rule comes to an end in what is now called France after having already ceased in what is now Germany in 911.

- **Tenth through Eleventh Centuries:** The Normans, Danish Vikings who had settled in northern France under the Norwegian chieftain Rollo and his descendants, continue their activities in true Viking style, despite their conversion to Christianity, by raiding northward toward Flanders. Rollo's son, William Longsword (d. 942), becomes the true engineer of Norman triumph, however, by centralizing and enlarging the Duchy. Although disturbed by internal violence,

Compare & Contrast

particularly under Duke Robert I (reigning 1027-35) and during the minority of his son, Duke William II (later William the Conqueror), the state created by these early Norman rulers depends upon strong ducal authority and evolve administrative and feudal combinations to maintain it.

733-751: From 719 until his death, Charles Martel (c. 688-742), illegitimate son of Pepin of Heristal (d. 714), boosts the Carolingian family's fortunes even further by turning back a Muslim force at Tours in 733 and then completing his subjugation of southern France. Charles's son Pepin the Short finally deposes Childeric III, the last of the Merovingian monarchs, and with support from the Pope becomes king of all the Franks in 751.

- **768-771:** At his death, Pepin the Short, Charles's son, leaves joint rulership of the Carolingian domains to his two sons, Carloman and Charles (later known as Charlemagne). Carloman's death in 771 makes Charles sole ruler.

- **771-814:** During his long rule, Charlemagne not only doubles the Frankish kingdom by conquests in Germany, Italy, and Spain, but also succeeds in bringing about a renaissance in the arts and sciences of that time. In 800 he is crowned Emperor of the West by the Pope of Rome.

- **793:** Viking—whose name is eventually given to various North Germanic tribal groups and derives from the Old Norse verb *vika,* "to go off"—land on foreign shores for the first time and destroy the by-then-ancient Celtic monastery of Lindisfarne in Northumbria. This action establishes a pattern of marauding piracy that will persist for two more centuries.

- **804:** Moving in across northern Germany just south of the "Danevirke"—a defensive barrier built by the Danes under a powerful local king in Schleswig, during their 39-year war with the continental Saxons—the Franks under Charlemagne begin to note in their annals the disturbing presence of barbaric peoples farther to the north of their Empire.

- **840-843:** Louis I, Charlemagne's sole heir, inherits from his father both the Empire and its continuing problems: Viking intrusions, Muslim assaults, and a grasping nobility. In typical Frankish fashion, Louis then leaves his Empire to the joint rulership of his three surviving sons, Lothair I, Louis the German, and Charles II (Charles the Bald). After Louis's death in 840, however, the civil wars that had already begun during his reign continue and eventually lead to the division of the empire into three kingdoms under the Treaty of Verdun in 843.

- **1060-1091:** Robert Guiscard, one of the many sons of Tancred of Hauteville, a Norman noble who had taken on allegiance with the Lombards against the Byzantine Empire in southern Italy, establishes himself as an independent ruler in Calabria and Apulia. Between 1060 and 1091 he and his brother, Roger I, undertake the conquest of Sicily from the Muslims.

- **1066:** Not to be outdone by the sons of Tancred, Duke William II becomes King William I of England when he and his retainers defeat the West Saxon King Harold II in the Battle of Hastings. He moves rapidly to establish a centralized monarchy in England on the Norman pattern.

- **1087:** William dies, leaving a strong kingdom to his sons, William II and Henry I.

- **1102-1204:** Abrogating his father's will, Henry I invades and subdues the Duchy of Normandy under his control. Although William the Conqueror had left Normandy to his eldest son, Duke Robert II (c. 1054-1134), the Duchy will not return to French control until 1204.

- **1139:** Roger II succeeds in transforming earlier Norman conquests into the kingdom of Sicily, which serves as a foundation for further Norman extension into North Africa and Dalmatia during the later twelfth century.

- **1154:** Ending a prolonged struggle for power between William's descendants, Henry II, son to Matilda, William's daughter, finally van-

Compare & Contrast

quishes his cousin, Stephen, William's nephew. In doing so, he inaugurates the Angevin dynasty's control over England.

- **Twentieth Century:** The history of Western European peoples has ever been one of continual invasion and migration from early times until now. The presence of Germanic peoples all over the globe stands as evidence of the pervasiveness of this migration. The European colonization of the world since the sixteenth century is just a dimension of Germanic tribal migrations from ancient times.

- **Twentieth Century:** Descendants of the Romanized and Latin-speaking Gauls of the former Roman province of "Gallia" are still called after the name of their erstwhile conquerors, the "French" ("Frankish"). French culture itself represents a centuries-long melding of Celtic, Germanic, and Roman influences.

- **Twentieth Century:** Despite its long Moorish occupation, Spain still shows traces of its Visigothic past in both language and culture.

- **Today:** Despite the addition of French to its linguistic and cultural mix, Modern English still represents a compromise between a variety of competing dialects. Like French and Spanish, it has become a world language of millions of speakers.

---

ing intermingling of pagan and Christian elements that conjoined Mediterranean, Celtic, and Germanic cultures into a surprising new aggregate.

The first Germanic people in Britain were hired by a British king named Vortigern as mercenaries to defend the Romanized Britons against their more barbaric cousins, the Caledonian Picts, to the north in what is now called Scotland. These hired guns were promised land in return for protection. Even though they were unlettered and uncivilized, Hengist and Horsa, the leaders of these expeditionary forces, quickly ascertained the social and military situation of the demilitarized Celts who had ceased from being warlike after nearly four hundred years of Roman rule. These early Anglian settlers sent swift word across the North Sea to their relatives, the Saxons, Angles, and Jutes, to migrate over to these fresh lands which lay ready for seizure. The invaders quickly and easily gained a foothold in Britain and began pushing back the native Celts towards modern Wales and Cornwall in Great Britain and Brittany in northwestern France.

Ironically, however, the military conquest by the Angles and Saxons of the Celtic homeland began the cultural and spiritual conquest of these Germanic pagans by the Celtic Christians. The Irish Church, founded by St. Patrick (390-460), himself a Romano-Briton, took on the task of evangelizing the new invaders. Early Irish monastic foundations in Lindisfarne and other sites spread not only a new faith but the cultural remnants of Rome's Mediterranean civilization to the unlettered rulers. One by one, the "kings" of the Germanic "kin" saw the cultural advantages of embracing the new religion. Still, the coming of St. Augustine (who died in 607), an envoy sent by Pope St. Gregory the Great to extend the power of the Roman Church into northern Europe, sped up the Christianization process. The Roman and Celtic clergy, representing very different liturgical and theological traditions, finally made peace and common cause at the Synod of Whitby in 664.

The epic *Beowulf* provides us a wonderful glimpse into early Germanic cultural life. In one scene, a "scop" takes up a chanted narrative of past and present exploits in the "mead-hall," where warrior retainers sit drunk but attentive to the singer-poet's measured recitation. Once Christianization was complete, however, the work of the secular scop as entertainer and tribal historian was at first supplemented and eventually taken over by the monastic scribe, who not only committed earlier poems to writing but also composed works of his own. One such work, "The Seafarer," definitely represents a movement beyond the traditional epic form, however. In many respects, "The Seafarer" echoes themes that abound in Welsh verse: longing for times past, sympathetic responses to the speaker's lament in the voices of birds, and so forth. Perhaps composed in the seventh century at the Mercian borderland between Anglian intruder and native Briton in the west Midlands, "The Seafarer" embodies the blending of pagan and Christian, Germanic and Celtic traditions that was the cultural promise of those times.

But more than this process of gradual cultural coalescence ended with the coming of the Normans. The entire social fabric that had existed among lord, retainer, and serf changed irrevocably as French-speaking usurpers took the place of paternalistic clan leaders. The death of the Anglo-Saxon cultural nexus meant the real birth of Feudalism in England.

Critical Overview

Most of the commentary on "The Seafarer" centers around the Christian messages and rhetoric in the second half of the poem and tries to argue whether a submerged paganism may be found beneath the Christian ideas. Some critics believe the second half of the poem was added later by a Christian scribe who found or heard an earlier Germanic or Celtic narrative poem. Critics are also interested in deciding how many speakers are present in the poem. Dorothy Whitelock argues in *Early Cultures in North-West Europe* that the poem should be read as a monologue. Whitelock posits that the speaker is a religious person who deliberately chose a life of wandering as a means of taming his senses in preparation for the joys and rewards of the afterlife. Whitelock demonstrates the prevalence of such views in Anglo-Saxon literature and writes that the seafarer would see no contradiction between his ascetic life being tossed on icy waves and his abstract yearning for God in the second half. I. L. Gordon in *The Review of English Studies* agrees, suggesting that despite apparent structural discrepancies and transitions, the poem should be accepted as the work of one person. The poem's tension between dramatic and moralistic tendencies is part of the poet's exploration of the theme of suffering, transience, and isolation. However, Gordon believes it is the elegiac background of the poem—not the Christian message—that gives "The Seafarer" its real uniqueness.

W. A. Davenport in *Papers on Language and Literature* argues that the modern reader is most attracted to the personal voice of suffering and the sympathetic evocation of pain in the first part. Davenport believes that the voice of "a distant poet speaking directly across the centuries about passion and longing" contradicts the second half and its impersonal, religious views. Thus the poem must be read as imperfect and corrupted by the later additions. The modern reader cannot accept both parts as the work of one poet; readers end up seeing it as the expression of two minds, therefore as an antithetical and ironic poem. C. L. Wrenn in *A Study of Old English Literature* also focuses on the poem as a dialogue of inner voices depicting the Anglo-Saxon love of the sea and its alternate pains and turmoil. Wrenn describes "The Seafarer" as the most poetic of all Old English elegies; perhaps this is why several modern poets such as Ezra Pound have translated it. Wrenn believes the poem's catalogue of various ways of death (line 71) must have been borrowed from a Latin tradition. Also, "The Seafarer"'s idea of penance, pilgrimage, and deliberate exile from ties with human society is especially Irish in its nature, perhaps inherited by the Anglo-Saxon poet from the influence of Irish Christianity.

Criticism

Michael Lake

Michael Lake, a published poet who holds an M.A. in English from Eastern Illinois University, currently teaches English in a Denver area community college. In the following essay, Lake examines the manner in which language informs "The Seafarer."

If every artistic act is ultimately a social act, then poems as verbal artifacts cannot be removed from their social milieu, the totality of ambient conditions and circumstances existing among poet and audience at the time of the poems' creation and reception. In other words, poems as socially and temporally conditioned expressions of meaning can only be decoded from within psycho-social and intellectual perspectives of the era in which they were written and first read. But if this is so, we may well ask whether any poem like "The Seafarer" could ever be understood on its own merits by a modern reader without a full critical and historical commentary supplying any defect in information that reader might have. Is it then possible for modern

What Do I Read Next?

- Those who are not only interested in Old English literature but also charmed by Burton Raffel's masterful translation should pick up Signet's 1999 reprint of Raffel's *Beowulf.* Considerably longer than "The Seafarer" elegy, this epic narrates the exploits of some of the great heroes of the Germanic tribal past.

- Hard-core enthusiasts of Old English literature and Burton Raffel will also want to read *Poems and Prose from the Old English,* translated and edited by Burton Raffel with the editorial assistance of Alexandra Hennessey Olsen in Yale University Press's 1998 reissue of an entirely restructured and expanded version of Raffel's out-of-print classic. In fact, this edition includes the very translation of "The Seafarer" used here in *Poetry for Students* along with prose works by King Alfred the Great and other great prose stylists, lay and monastic, with more elegies, heroic poems, religious verse, and wisdom poetry.

- Just to round out one's knowledge of the literature of the Old English period, any interested student should read Stanley B. Greenfield's *Critical History of Old English Literature,* published by New York University Press in 1965. Greenfield does an excellent job of providing in-depth analysis of the entire Old English corpus using modern translations only. Translations from Raffel's *Poems and Prose from the Old English* are especially featured in Greenfield's study.

---

readers to engage "The Seafarer" as they would any other poem from any other era using a kind of reader's response to help craft its meaning for themselves? Perhaps this dichotomy is false. Maybe the fact that artistic acts are social acts also means that modern readers actually constitute an extension of the original poem's audience. However, the problem is not just how modern readers can join that audience but how the structure of the poem itself conveys its meaning to readers who

sometimes must eavesdrop as a class of cultural and temporal tourists.

In the case of "The Seafarer", the first consideration is that of language. Unless readers invest a lot of time studying Old English, they cannot read the poem in its original form because the divergence between the Englishes of the poem's writer and today's readers actually constitutes two different languages. Readers must then depend upon the skills of translators to render the poem's actual meaning, if not its prosodic music. The problem with this compromise, however, is that the original poem depends upon structural relationships that only exist within the original language. Replicating such verbal effects in translation is nigh unto impossible because of the different syntactical dynamics that exist in the original and the receiving languages. Still, despite these difficulties, one can yet discern rhetorical and poetic features that structure the meaning of the poem even in translation. Realizing that what the poem means really resides in how the poem works as a vehicle of meaning, readers can approach interpreting "The Seafarer" confident of understanding and appreciating a poem whose cultural as well as linguistic particularities are so unlike their own.

Adopting a realistic, matter-of-fact approach towards discovering meaning within the poem's rhetorical structure prevents readers from falling into further false dichotomies, like asking whether "The Seafarer" should be read literally or allegorically. Accepting the inherent ambiguity of the poem without a specific need to resolve all thematic disparities allows readers to reconcile the interrelated themes of isolation, loneliness, human and divine comfort, the desire for earthly and heavenly glory, and the ultimate emptiness of all earthly endeavors within the poem's inherent metaphysical presumptions about the nature of reality.

First, it must be said that out of all the cultural threads woven together in this poem, the pagan, both Germanic and Celtic, the heroic, the elegiac, the lay, and the Christian, the Christian thread holds the whole together. The poet who wrote "The Seafarer" (most likely a monk) brought together all the cultural riches at his disposal at the time to craft an ultimately Christian poem. This poem uses image, metaphor, irony, and allusion to craft its tale, just as any modern poem would, but it also employs a specifically medieval device: a moral. The moral of the poem can only be approached from within polar opposition. For, after all, the moral of the poem is that all opposites find resolution in God, the ultimate reality.

At its very beginning, the poem presents its first polar opposition: the deprivations of a life at sea with all its heavy cares versus the carefree life on the land. However, there is at the same time another polarity balancing the speaker's physical against his spiritual suffering: that which tears at the flesh as opposed to that which afflicts the soul. On both planes of opposition, though, the poem proceeds from generalities to specifics to draw its descriptive contrasts. It is clear from the beginning that the speaker's pain is both physical and psychic insofar as the sea "swept me back / And forth in sorrow and fear and pain" (2b-3). External and internal suffering are then set in a balance, so to speak. On the one side, we have a crystal image of the speaker's physical situation "when [he] sweated in the cold / Of an anxious watch, perched in the bow / As it dashed under cliffs" (6b-8a) with his "feet … cast / In icy bands, bound with frost, / With frozen chains" (8b-10a). And on the other we glimpse the speaker's interior condition given how the sea has "[s]howed me suffering" (4a) (that is, given him "*bitre breostceare*" or "bitter breast-care"), how "hardship groaned / Around my heart (10b-11a), and how "Hunger tore / At my sea-weary soul" (11b-12a). Taken together, the two opposites present an interesting duality: on one side we have a cold image of the frost acting as a fetter, and on the other, we have a rather "hot" image of care clasping the heart. In both his inner and outer dimensions, then, the speaker does not share the reality of those who enjoy the comfort of the land: "No man sheltered / On the quiet fairness of earth can feel / How wretched I was" (12b-14a).

The next few lines reinforce the poem's initial polarity and provide more concrete images of the speaker's inner and outer circumstances. With the concrete experience of a year at sea, the speaker knows full well the "paths of the exile" (15) ("*wraeccan lastum*" in Old English) far from the erstwhile comforts afforded by the communion of "friendly kinsmen" (16) ("*winemae gum*" in the original text). Unfortunately, here is where Raffel's text may fall down in relation to the original, because he has translated "*wraecca,*" the wretch banished into exile far from the protection of the tribe, as one "wretched" and "whirled in sorrow," and the comforts of the kinsmen are lost in "a world blown clear of love." But the concrete images of being berimed, "[h]ung with icicles," while "hailstorms flew" in showers about him carries forth the feeling of the original and reinforces the isolation and enclosure of the opening lines. Where Raffel's translation really fails is in setting up in the reader's

> *At its very beginning, the poem presents its first polar opposition: the deprivations of a life at sea with all its heavy cares versus the carefree life on the land.*

mind the full significance of a dichotomy yet to be fully explored: the polarity between the isolated "exile" far from the support system of the "kin," and the pagan and earthly joys and protections afforded by the "*duguth,*" the fighting band and extended family of any member of Anglo-Saxon society. In fact, the word only occurs twice in the poem, once properly translated as "host" (as in "heavenly host") in line 81a and another time incorrectly translated as "powers" in line 88. The opposition between the existential isolation of the "*wraecca*" and the communal life within a "*duguth,*" however, is fulcrum that moves the whole of "*The Seafarer*" to its ultimately Christian conclusion.

Hearing naught but the "roaring sea," the seafarer-exile evokes the life on land within a "*duguth*" by imagining the "song of the swan," the "cry of the sea-fowl," and the "croaking of birds" to take the place of human "laughter," and the "mewing of gulls" to replace the joys of the mead-hall where the warrior band (or "*duguth*") would gather to socialize and "recreate." Yet the fantasy fails because the bird voices that had feigned comfort are replaced with shrieks that drive home the seafarer-exile's utter loneliness, where "[no] kinsman could offer comfort there, / To a soul left drowning in desolation" (25-26). Basically, the "sea versus land" dichotomy has been expanded to include the "exile ("*wraecca*") bereft of '*duguth*'" polarity as well. All of these images serve to extend themes already established, however, by providing a new set of implied contrasts but with tactile and auditory stimuli embellishing an already developed aural style. Still, the images contrast with one another without an expressed relationship between them.

Nevertheless, even as the poem progresses toward a more detailed, concrete, and individualized expression of the speaker's existential experience, the imagery tends to "flatten out" a bit into a repetitive remonstration that those who live in "cities" ("*in burgum*") have no idea "how wearily / I put myself back on the paths of the sea" (29b-30). Still, notice how a new polarity is conjured here between the "passion of cities, swelled proud with wine" and the seafarer-exile's resigned return to the "paths of the sea" ("*brimlade*" in the original). This contrast actually sets up a later dichotomy between ascetic determination and earthly recklessness.

The real significance of the passage is that it leads to a reversal of the conditions first described in the poem. Indeed, one could say that a climax and a thematic shift change the direction of the whole poem here. Instead of on the sea, the frost and hail now fall on the land and bind the land fast, not the speaker's feet, and the speaker's "heart," instead of suffering with care, begins "to beat, knowing once more / The salt waves tossing and the towering sea!" (34-35). Though some may say that the shift is sudden and unexpected, the fact is that such an opinion assumes that the poem fails to eliminate the polarities between sea-exile-woe and land-*duguth*-weal or that the poem has failed to clarify the distinction between the internal and external states of the speaker. Lines 31-33a provide a bridge from one set of polar opposites to another, a transformed set of contraries that actually reverse the order of the earlier polar hierarchy so that the life on the sea appears as a new higher good as opposed to that on land. The only way this sudden shift makes sense, however, is from within the subsuming perspective of the whole poem. And this perspective is that life anywhere outside of God's presence is bound to be hardship and suffering. As far as the speaker is now concerned at this point of the poem, "the mind's desire urges … the spirit to travel" (a perhaps more literal rendition of lines 36-37 than Raffel's).

The fact is that the poet calls forth images and then qualifies his view of them while still keeping alive in the reader's mind the evanescent effects of the original images already so graphically depicted. Even though this may cause confusion for some, it bespeaks a kind of stylistical sophistication to others. While reaffirming the contrast between the *duguth*-lifestyle on the land with the seafaring life at sea, the speaker brings up God for the first time in the next passage (39-46). In this mix, God cannot be ignored by anyone on the sea, where no one knows "what Fate has willed and will do" (43). This may not be so for landlubbers, because the same polarity already mentioned shows up again at this

point of the poem. The ascetic seafaring life now contrasts with a looser and more frivolous life on the land, where "harps ring in [one's] heart" (44) and "passion for women" and "worldly pleasure" (45) play off against "the ocean's heave" (46). As stated above, the dichotomies remain in opposition to each other, but the contrariety between the elements has shifted. The privations of the sea are now a type for moral and spiritual purgation that sets seafaring at a higher moral order than the safe life within the "*duguth*." Still, the skill of the poet as rhetorician prevents him from pressing home his point just yet. He merely evokes an order of discontent that perhaps transcends the sufferings laid out earlier in the poem: "*ac a hafath longunge se the on lagu fundath*," that is, "but ever hath longing he who sets out to sea" (Raffel has "But longing wraps itself around him"). It is as yet unclear whether this "longing" is for the carnal life of the settled land or for something higher.

Nonetheless, the fresh fullness of life burgeoning on earth in the spring is perhaps at least one part of the speaker's "longing." The change of spring in the air also spells the beginning of other sea journeys for "that willing mind / Leaping to journeys, always set / In thoughts traveling on a quickening tide" (50b-52). The fact that the mind is now "willing" or "eager" ("*fusne*" in the Old English) to make its sea journey bespeaks a literal "sea-change" in the speaker's attitudes towards the seagoing life. And again, nature provides some response to the speaker's interior condition with the mournful cries of the springtime cuckoo, "summer's sentinel." Where the calls of the hatchling cuckoo may signify the fructification of the earth by nature to some, it may here bring about a polar opposite response. Here it reminds the speaker of the coming of "death's sentinel," the sea journey itself. As the speaker redundantly repeats, "Who could understand, / In ignorant ease, what we others suffer / As the paths of exile stretch endlessly on?" Perhaps only the cuckoo knows and answers with an equivocal call of invitation and warning.

The "push-pull" of the cuckoo's cry truly reflects the speaker's inner state of mind, in which his "heart wanders away" and his "soul roams with the sea," "returning ravenous with desire." The speaker's "soul" now flies "solitary, screaming, exciting me / To the open ocean, breaking oaths / On the curve of a wave" (62-64). These are a far cry from his earlier states of mind towards seafaring. The only explanation for this change of view can be found in the next section of the poem: all "the joys of God / Are fervent with life, where life itself / Fades quickly into the earth" (65-67). Only the "joys of God" are "fervent with life" while life itself is ephemeral. At last, the reason for the puzzling shift in perspective in lines 31-33a has become clearer. Life on the earth itself, whether with one's kinsmen or alone on the sea, is itself "empty" and "vain." Even the greatest strivings one can endure will only earn feeble praise, whether from earthly supporters or even heavenly hosts. The only surety in life is death, and only God can give death meaning. Despite making the thematic shift more understandable, the poet as yet has still not succeeded in closing the structure of his hierarchy of goods upon the transcendent *sine qua non* that holds his opposing polarities in order.

Before getting to that, the poet shifts the poem's outlook yet again with a hefty section of elegiac reflection from 82 to 104 in Raffel's translation. One can't really call this section a "lament" as such because of the healthy dose of Christian transience that underpins its *Weltanschauung*. A lament, properly speaking, would resound with despair, not with acquiescence. Here the vanity of life on earth is almost rattled off like a shopping list of "things to expect if you're alive." There isn't any whining or mourning about it all, really, just the cold, hard facts that all things put together fall apart. Those scholars who have labored long at fashioning this section as some kind of pagan elegy (Celtic or Germanic) fail to see the poet's examples of indictments of the tribal "*duguth*" to escape loss and privation. The loss of heroic times says more about the nature of time itself than whether or not pagan times were being missed in this passage. Notice how the passing of glory is attended with the giving of gold in this passage, much as with any pagan burial custom, "but nothing / Golden shakes the wrath of God / For a soul overflowing with sin, and nothing / Hidden on earth rises to Heaven."

In this last section of the poem, all the conflicting polarities finally find resolution. The hierarchy of conflicting goods ultimately rises up to the top, for God alone is the unchanging good, and losing the joy of His presence is the ultimate evil. Rather than being fools who "forget," we should remember that "God [is] mightier than any man's mind" and our "thoughts should turn to where our home is." At last it is clear that neither being a "wretched" exile nor being "*duguth*" member can solve these deeper existential issues in themselves. To set sail into harrowing circumstances or to stay in the safety of the tribal band is all one when

viewed from a transcendental point of view. All of life is a transitory journey, a brief sojourning before death takes all, good or bad. The "moral" of this medieval poem is that whatever we do, we should "[c]onsider the ways of coming there, / Then strive for sure permission for us / To rise to that eternal joy, / That life born in the love of God / And the hope of Heaven" (120-124). Otherwise, we merely suffer the pains of our exile without salvation ever finding us.

Source: Michael Lake, in an essay for *Poetry for Students*, Gale Group, 2000.

Bruce Meyer

Bruce Meyer is the director of the creative writing program at the University of Toronto. He has taught at several Canadian universities and is the author of three collections of poetry. In the following essay, Meyer contends that "The Seafarer" describes a harsh, lonely, and fallen world that one must navigate through to reach one's true home in heaven.

The world that is presented in many Anglo-Saxon poems, such as "The Seafarer," is a cold, cruel place. It is a world that has only one redeeming feature—God's grace—and even that is mitigated by an overwhelming sense of entropy that pervades everything. As is the case in another notable Anglo-Saxon poem, "The Wanderer," the civilized world is perceived as something that has passed from immediate view and remains only a faint memory, a series of ruins that suggest that the past was greater than the present. For the poetic personas of this world, there is a profound sense of living in a diminished universe, of a place less great than the past. What this sense of diminishment evokes is a deep sense of insecurity and rootlessness in the present, a notable absence of order, and a grave sense of grief that is reflected, organically, in the inhospitableness of nature. In short, the world we encounter in many Anglo-Saxon poems is the realm of the elegy. Nature has fallen and taken the survivors with it.

In "The Seafarer," "The days are gone / When kingdoms of earth flourished in glory." The Anglo-Saxon mind located itself in a time and place that offered few creature comforts; it perceived its place in the continuum as having come after the great events of history and in the wake of the Roman Empire and its splendor. Like the vacuum we encounter in a more modern rendering of the same theme, Allen Tate's "Ode to the Confederate Dead," the world presents a meager offering of pos-

> *In other words, as Thomas Gray put it, 'The paths of glory lead but to the grave.' The great elegiac question then arises: what is the purpose of life, and to this the poem answers to 'fear God.'"*

sibilities, and the future is a stark, if not totally bleak, prospect. Life can only be filled with a restlessness because the absence of greatness is so tremendously encountered. The world of the Anglo-Saxon poem is place of ruins, a cold, "darkling plain" (to borrow the phrase from Matthew Arnold's "Dover Beach") where the persona wanders homelessly from one place to the next, all the time feeling the bite and sting of a fallen Nature. One always has the feeling when reading Anglo-Saxon poetry that the world is locked in a perpetual winter, and in the chronology of English poetry, we really do not encounter a convincing thematic springtime until Geoffrey Chaucer returns from Italy in 1370 with the iambic line under his belt and the first inklings of the Renaissance Italian mind dancing fancifully on the road to Canterbury.

In the case of "The Seafarer," there is an Aeneas-like drive in the persona toward that "ever-retreating horizon," a restlessness that can perceive a better world where "Orchards blossom" and "towns bloom" but which is driven by an inward anxiety where "longing wraps around him" and his "heart wanders away." In this world, Nature is not man's respite, as it will become centuries later during the early Romantic era, but an animate, almost Ovidian setting where the elements work against human intention. The voice of "The Seafarer" explains in the second line that his life, "This tale" of "mine," is about "How the sea took me, swept me back / And forth in sorrow and fear and pain / Showed me suffering in a hundred ships, / In a thousand ports, and in me." The sea, a handy surrogate for Nature in these opening lines, takes the form of a nemesis in much the same way that Po-

seidon was the nemesis of Odysseus in *The Odyssey*. But unlike the very pointed intentions of the Greek gods who diced with so many fates in the vast scope of the Homeric universe, there is a blitheness to Anglo-Saxon nature, an ethos of misery for which Man, in the Christian context, is ultimately to blame. This is the realm of fallen Nature, where Man's free will, the very force that drives the seafarer anxiously from port to port, becomes his tormentor. The individual, in this context, is very much alone. He must bear, almost as an Everyman, the weight of a fallen world. Lament it as he may, there is no respite. The lot of the individual is so universal and so shared as the common destiny of humanity that there is no room for solace among shipmates, and everyone, ultimately, is a loner.

What is curious about Anglo-Saxon poetic personas is their capacity to pursue loneliness. The persona of "The Seafarer" finds some brief consolation in "the song of the swan" that "might serve for pleasure, the cry of the sea-fowl, / The croaking of birds instead of laughter, / The mewing of gulls instead of mead" or "The passion of cities swelled proud with wine / And no taste of misfortune." Yet he continually trudges back, "wearily, "on the paths of the sea." What calls him back "eagerly" is his "soul." The suggestion here is that the world is a place without peace or repose, that pleasure and comfort are illusions because they too, like the glories of the past, quickly fade from sight. One is reminded of the Latin maxim *sic transit gloria mundi* (so passes the glory of the world) as a kind of operative axiom behind the Seafarer's psychology. On the one hand, the Seafarer needs to tell his story and relate his hardships in a world that is far from accommodating, while on the other he feels an obligation, in the Boethian sense, to perceive the wonder of Nature as God's work and to offer, accordingly, the correct response of praise, even if he must struggle to praise God through a litany of meteorological misery.

The key to understanding "The Seafarer" lies in the relationship between its form and its content. As a poem, it is a complex set of paradoxes. On one hand, it complains about how awful it is to live in Nature, while on the other hand it offers praises and thanks to God for a world "fervent with life, where life itself / Fades quickly into the earth." There is not much to celebrate here, yet that is how the poem ends. The poem is a mixture of forms: a prayer to the glories of God with an Amen tucked neatly at the end; a narrative that tells of a life of hardship, suffering and anxiety; and an elegy that acknowledges a loss or imbalance in Nature and grieves over the perceived absence. As a prayer to God, the poem asks for God's grace to see the seafarer through his constant journeys and travails and presents a thankful praise to God who "Gave life to the world and light to the sky." The poem is also narrative that recounts with a balance of almost epic objectivity and personal involvement the harshness of the world and the difficulties of moving through a nature that, although of God's making, is not "user friendly" to the average mortal. But it is as an elegy that the poem speaks loudest. The reader is not quite sure what has been lost in Nature or what has made conditions so lamentable, but he is aware that "The praise the living pour on the dead / Flowers from reputation: plant / An earthly life of profit reaped / Even from hatred and rancor, of bravery / Flung in the devil's face, and death / Can only bring you earthly praise / And a song to celebrate a place / With the angels ..." In other words, as Thomas Gray put it, "The paths of glory lead but to the grave."

The great elegiac question then arises: what is the purpose of life, and to this the poem answers to "fear God." "Death," he notes, "leaps at the fools who forget their God. / He who lives humbly has angels from Heaven / To carry him courage and strength and belief." The relationship between God and the fallen, miserable world of the poem is that of an exemplum and an argument. The world is an example of God's handiwork, yet it has fallen because of human weakness. The Seafarer warns, "Treat all the world as the world deserves / With love or with hate but never with harm" because "Fate is stronger / And God mightier than any man's mind." In essence, the world's misery is a contrasting example to God's goodness and capabilities. The hardships, the pain, and the sufferings are set before Man to remind him of the glories of Heaven, because Heaven is "where our home is." To be an outcast in the world is only a paltry issue; to be an outcast from God is a pretty serious consequence. The allegory here is that humankind is meant to "navigate" the world in order to find that true home that always seems to be retreating on the horizon—a home called Heaven. The Seafarer notes, "To rise to that eternal joy, / That life born in the love of God / And the hope of Heaven" is the goal that lies beyond the hardship, the port at the end of the storm. In effect, the entire world, all of Nature is a cruel, unforgiving sea, but the good soul, the navigator, has his sights set on his destination. If the soul is restless, it is so because, like Odysseus, it is anxious to get home.

Source: Bruce Meyer, in an essay for *Poetry for Students,* Gale Group, 2000.

Sources

Davenport, W. A., "The Modern Reader and the Old English Seafarer," in *Papers on Language and Literature,* Vol. 10, No. 3, Summer, 1974, pp. 227-40.

Dyas, Dee, "Land and Sea in the Pilgrim Life: The 'Seafarer' and the Old English 'Exodus,'" *English Language Notes,* Vol. 35, No. 2, Dec., 1997, pp. 1-10.

Gordon, I. L., "Traditional Themes in 'The Wanderer' and 'The Seafarer,'" in *The Review of English Studies,* Vol. V, No. 17, pp. 1-13.

Greenfield, Stanley B., "The Formulaic Expression of the Theme of 'Exile' in Anglo-Saxon Poetry," *Essential Articles for the Study of Old English Poetry,* edited by Jess B. Bessinger, Jr., and Stanley J. Kahrl, Hamden, CT: Archon Books, 1968, pp. 458-514.

————, *The Interpretation of Old English Poems,* London: Routledge & Kegan Paul, 1972.

Irving, Edward B., "Image and Meaning in the Elegies," *Old English Poetry: Fifteen Essays,* edited by Robert P. Creed, Providence: Brown University Press, 1967, pp. 153-66.

Isaacs, Neil D., *Structural Principles in Old English Poetry,* Knoxville: The University of Tennessee Press, 1968.

Klein, W. F., "Purpose and Poetics of 'The Wanderer' and 'The Seafarer,'" *Anglo-Saxon Poetry: Essays in Appreciation for John C. McGalliard,* edited by Lewis E. Nicholson and Dolores Warwick Frese, Notre Dame: University of Notre Dame Press, 1975, pp. 208-23.

Partridge, A. C., *A Companion to Old and Middle English Studies,* Totowa, NJ: Barnes & Noble Books, 1982.

Pope, John C., "Dramatic Voices in 'The Wanderer' and 'The Seafarer,'" *Essential Articles for the Study of Old English Poetry,* edited by Jess B. Bessinger, Jr., and Stanley J. Kahrl, Hamden, CT: Archon Books, 1968, pp. 533-70.

Raw, Barbara C., *The Art and Background of Old English Poetry,* New York: St. Martin's Press, 1978.

Robinson, Fred C., "'The Might of the North': Pound's Anglo-Saxon Studies and 'The Seafarer,'" *Yale Review,* Vol. 71, winter 1982, pp. 199-224.

Stanley, E. G., "Old English Poetic Diction and the Interpretation of 'The Wanderer', 'The Seafarer', and 'The Penitent's Prayer,'" *Essential Articles for the Study of Old English Poetry,* edited by Jess B. Bessinger, Jr., and Stanley J. Kahrl, Hamden, CT: Archon Books, 1968, pp. 458-514.

Wardale, E. E., *Chapters on Old English Literature,* New York: Russell & Russell Inc., 1965.

Whitelock, Dorothy, "The Interpretation of the Seafarer," in *Early Cultures of North-West Europe,* H. M. Chadwick Memorial Studies, 1950, pp. 261-72.

Woolf, Rosemary, "'The Wanderer', 'The Seafarer', and the Genre of Planctus," *Anglo-Saxon Poetry: Essays in Appreciation,* edited by Lewis E. Nicholson and Dolores Warwick

Frese, Notre Dame, IN: University of Notre Dame Press, 1975, pp. 192-207.

Wrenn, C. L., "Lyric, Elegy, and Miscellaneous Minor Poems," in his *A Study of Old English Literature,* New York: Norton, 1967, pp. 139-60.

For Further Study

Crossley-Holland, Kevin, *The Anglo-Saxon World,* Woodbridge, Suffolk: Boydell Press, 1982.

    Six hundred years of Anglo-Saxon history and culture have been anthologized in this convenient volume. Poetry (both epic and lyric), history, sermons, and other prose works are masterfully anthologized in this rich volume. For comparison's sake, students can even read a different translation of "The Seafarer".

Lee, Alvin A., *The Guest-Hall of Eden: Four Essays on the Design of Old English Poetry,* New Haven: Yale University Press, 1972, pp. 125-70.

    Although Lee's four essays together constitute a thorough examination of form and meaning in Old English verse, the essay on these particular pages really illuminates the lyric elegiac tradition within the body of Old English poetry. It is excellent reading for those who want to go beyond an elementary understanding of the poetry of that time.

Pound, Ezra, " 'The Seafarer': From the Anglo-Saxon," *Personae,* New York: New Directions, 1950, pp. 64-66.

    Although Raffel's translation is in some ways culturally more faithful to the original "Seafarer," Pound's translation, made when he was quite young, is in terms of Anglo-Saxon prosody more nearly correct a translation because it provides the full flavor of the original poem's verbal music.

Sonnet 29

William Shakespeare
1609

In this sonnet by William Shakespeare first published in 1609, the speaker's extreme anguish concerning his "state" piques his audience's curiosity, which is further heightened by the repetition of this word in lines 2, 10, and 14. Is he "outcast" because of his physical, mental, or emotional condition? his fortune or social rank? his rejection from a lover, or from society? his sexual orientation? It is tempting to read Shakespeare's own life into "Sonnet 29" and consider his sometime unhappiness with his life in the theater, or his alleged bisexuality; but one must always bear in mind that the sonnets have never proven to be autobiographical. Though the cause of the speaker's pain remains a mystery, his cure is revealed: his religious devotion to another mortal, not a higher being such as God, transports him to Edenic bliss.

Author Biography

Shakespeare was born in Stratford-upon-Avon on or about April 23, 1564. His father was a merchant who devoted himself to public service, attaining the highest of Stratford's municipal positions—that of bailiff and justice of the peace—by 1568. Biographers have surmised that the elder Shakespeare's social standing and relative prosperity at this time would have enabled his son to attend the finest local grammar school, the King's New School, where he would have received an out-

William Shakespeare

standing classical education under the direction of highly regarded masters. There is no evidence that Shakespeare attended university. In 1582, at the age of eighteen, he married Ann Hathaway of Stratford, a woman eight years his senior. Their first child, Susanna, was born six months later, followed by twins, Hamnet and Judith, in 1585. These early years of Shakespeare's adult life are not well documented; some time after the birth of his twins, he joined a professional acting company and made his way to London, where his first plays, the three parts of the *Henry VI* history cycle, were presented between 1589 and 1591. The first reference to Shakespeare in the London literary world dates from 1592, when dramatist Robert Greene alluded to him as "an upstart crow." Shakespeare further established himself as a professional actor and playwright when he joined the Lord Chamberlain's Men, an acting company formed in 1594 under the patronage of Henry Carey, Lord Hunsdon. The members of this company included the renowned tragedian Richard Burbage and the famous "clown" Will Kempe, who was one of the most popular actors of his time. This group began performing at the playhouse known simply as the Theatre and at the Cross Keys Inn, moving to the Swan Theatre on Bankside in 1596 when municipal authorities banned the public presentation of plays within the limits of the city of London. Three years later

Shakespeare and other members of the company financed the building of the Globe Theatre, the most famous of all Elizabethan playhouses. By then the foremost London company, the Lord Chamberlain's Men also performed at court on numerous occasions, their success largely due to the fact that Shakespeare wrote for no other company.

In 1603 King James I granted the group a royal patent, and the company's name was altered to reflect the king's direct patronage. Records indicate that the King's Men remained the most favored acting company in the Jacobean era, averaging a dozen performances at court each year during the period. In addition to public performances at the Globe Theatre, the King's Men played at the private Blackfriars Theatre; many of Shakespeare's late plays were first staged at Blackfriars, where the intimate setting facilitated Shakespeare's use of increasingly sophisticated stage techniques. The playwright profited handsomely from his long career in the theater and invested in real estate, purchasing properties in both Stratford and London. As early as 1596 he had attained sufficient status to be granted a coat of arms and the accompanying right to call himself a gentleman. By 1610, with his fortune made and his reputation as the leading English dramatist unchallenged, Shakespeare appears to have retired to Stratford, though business interests brought him to London on occasion. He died on April 23, 1616, and was buried in the chancel of Trinity Church in Stratford.

Poem Text

When, in disgrace with Fortune and men's eyes,
I all alone beweep my outcast state,
And trouble deaf heaven with my bootless cries,
And look upon myself, and curse my fate,

Wishing me like to one more rich in hope,   5
Featured like him, like him with friends possessed,
Desiring this man's art and that man's scope,
With what I most enjoy contented least;

Yet in these thoughts myself almost despising
Haply I think on thee: and then my state,   10
Like to the Lark at break of day arising
From sullen earth, sings hymns at Heaven's gate;

For thy sweet love rememb'red such wealth brings
That then I scorn to change my state with Kings.

Poem Summary

Line 1:

The opening word "when" qualifies the whole poem, and sets up "Sonnet 29" as an "if-then" statement. The speaker may not be out of luck or the public's favor at the moment, at all. However, the strong emotions exhibited in the following lines suggest that these feelings of isolation and despair are not unfamiliar to him; indeed, by line 9, he seems to gain a certain satisfaction from wallowing in his self-pity.

Line 2:

The repetition of the word "state" in lines 2, 10, and 14 indicates its significance in the poem. But its many levels of meaning prevent the reader from understanding the cause of the speaker's rejection: "state" may signify a condition, a state of mind, an estate or a person's status. However, the adjective "outcast" does possess a religious connotation (as in "outcast from Eden") that is evident again in the sonnet's last three lines.

Lines 3-4:

The speaker's skyward wails receive no reply either from nature or from God. Angered and feeling abandoned, the speaker resorts to bitter sarcasm (when he facetiously remarks that he can "trouble" heaven) and swearing ("cursed my fate").

Line 5:

The second quatrain serves as the speaker's wish list for ways in which he might alter his "state." Despite these lines, his condition remains almost as ambiguous as ever. For example, someone "rich in hope" might be a more hopeful person; alternately, it might be someone who has prospects of wealth.

Lines 6-7:

The speaker continues to name the types of people he wishes to be like but proceeds to use descriptions with obscure or multiple meanings. Not only does "featured" have several definitions ("handsome" or "formed", to name two), but it refers to three possible types: those who are "rich in hope", those "with friends possessed," and perhaps those indicated by the speaker's pointed finger as he recites the first half of line 6. The speaker's admiration of someone's "art" may refer to his knowledge, abilities, or skills as a lover; a man's "scope" may be his freedom or his range of understanding.

Line 8:

This paradox is Shakespeare's version of the cliche "the grass is always greener on the other side": whatever the speaker possesses or formerly

Media Adaptations

- *William Shakespeare: A Poet for All Time.* Videocassette. The Master Poets Collection, Volume 2. Malibu, CA: Monterey Home Video. 1998.

- *William Shakespeare, his Life and Times.* Videocassette. Salt Lake City, UT: Bonneville Worldwide Entertainment. 1998.

- *William Shakespeare, Poet and Dramatist, 1564-1616.* Videocassette. West Long Branch, NJ: White Star. 1993.

- *The Complete Sonnets of William Shakespeare, Cassette 1: Sonnets 1-78.* Audiocassette. Camp Hill, PA: Book-of-the-Month Records. 1982.

- Martin, Philip. *Shakespeare, The Sonnets.* Audiocassette. Sydney: ABC Radio. 1980.

- *The Complete Sonnets of William Shakespeare, with "A Lover's Complaint" and Selected Songs.* Two audiocassettes. West Hollywood, CA: Cove Audio. 1996.

- Vendler, Helen. *Shakespeare's Sonnets: Helen Vendler Reads.* Audio disc. Cambridge, MA: Bellknap Press of Harvard University Press. 1997.

took pleasure in is now no longer a source of pride or amusement.

Lines 9-11:

After the speaker approaches his deepest depths of self-loathing in line 9, he experiences a moment of transcendence and a remarkable change of heart. By happy chance, his thoughts turn to his beloved; his spirits soar like a lark, a bird known to fly straight up in the air as it sings its morning song. The speaker's comparison of his state to a lark's ascending flight stands out as the only figure of speech in "Sonnet 29," just as this solitary songbird is a noticeable silhouette in the morning sky—and as the speaker had been set apart from the rest of humanity. The bird's rising motion represents the dawn of a new day, a revival of spirits, and perhaps even a step up in rank; its song fills the silence of the heavens and adds joy and life to what had been a dark, depressing poem. It seems appropriate that "lark" is also a verb, meaning "to play or frolic."

Line 12:

Earth is described as "sullen" for several reasons: because of the dull color of its soil, the sluggishness of its motion, and the general melancholy of its inhabitants. The mood is very different for those who have risen above it—as the lark literally has and the speaker has figuratively. The bird singing praises to the heavens is equated with the speaker glorifying his own earthly divinity.

Lines 13-14:

The "wealth" that is brought by memories of the speaker's loved one has several possible meanings, supported by the language of the previous lines. Monetary wealth does not connect well with the idea of love, though it would help a person who had fallen out of luck with material "Fortune" (line 1). A wealth of friends, talents, or opportunities were wished for in lines 5 through 8 and are all valid interpretations. But a strong possibility also lies with the connection of wealth and religion. The speaker has been saved through his worship of a very different "King" (line 14) than Christ; perhaps his final state is so heavenly that he would rather be surrounded by memories of his beloved than in any heavenly kingdom.

The speaker's "state" has moved dramatically from that of miserable hopelessness to pure elation. Though he still stands separate from humankind, he now does so by choice.

Themes

Alienation and Loneliness

Added to the misfortunes that the speaker of this poem faces is also the pain of knowing that he is facing his trials alone. Society tends to distance itself from sufferers; as the old adage puts it, "Laugh and the world laughs with you; cry and you cry alone." "Sonnet 29" starts by briefly identifying the source of the problem as "disgrace with Fortune" before settling in to examine the social ramifications of bad luck and the alienation that it causes. The remainder of the first stanza concerns itself with the speaker's feeling of isolation, a feel-

ing that forces him to withdraw into himself, mostly in anger: he weeps, cries to heaven, and curses fate. The speaker is alone, or so he says, because everyone else thinks badly of him. The next stanza, though, brings up the opposite side of the equation: it is the speaker's own dark thoughts that are forcing him to distance himself from others. He is jealous, listing the things that others have that he wishes were his own. By its placement in this poem, following the first mention of his isolation, there is a strong suggestion that it is the jealousy he feels, not his bad luck alone, that is at the root of his isolation. The second stanza is presented as an explanation for the speaker's loneliness, while no such explanation is offered for his bad fortune. The list of things that he envies of others progresses from the shallow to the more serious. He first mentions jealousy toward those who have more money, which is a trait that even the very wealthy may have. In line 6 the poem becomes a bit more specific about what this writer thinks others have that he himself is lacking, specifically good looks and plenty of friends. The third line of this stanza strikes modern readers as a little puzzling or amusing, since the past four hundred years have established Shakespeare as a supreme master of his art, unsurpassed in the scope of his understanding of human nature. The second stanza ends with a line that presents the speaker's problem as being ultimately one of internal attitude, not external fate: the same things that would satisfy him at other times, he says, just don't work for him any more. Ironically, the bad mood that he has projected to the outside world, forcing his withdrawal from society, is also broken by a force outside himself: in contrast with the expanding shame that alienates the speaker from most people, one relationship is so strong in itself that it alone can overcome the speaker's intense loneliness.

Doubt and Ambiguity

"Sonnet 29," like most of Shakespeare's sonnets, was written from a very close and personal perspective in regard to the circumstances of the author's life. In many poems, the speaker is a character made up by the author to present his or her ideas (even when the character has much in common with the author), but it is generally recognized by scholars that Shakespeare wrote his sonnets about events that were occurring in his life and the world around him. In doing this, Shakespeare took on a very difficult task, one that took courage and artistic integrity: capturing his own words and ideas even when he might not have been sure what he was thinking. The mood that prevails throughout "Sonnet 29" is one of insecurity, of feeling that, whatever life has to offer, the poet would not have the resources to deal with it. The poet describes himself as an outcast, but it is not the world that has cast him out: he has cast himself out with his shame, "myself almost despising" (line 9). Unsure about himself, about whether he is a victim of fate and other people or a small, insignificant person who deserves to be mistreated, he eventually finds his doubts erased by the thoughts of another, whom he loves. The metaphor of the lark rising from the earth, up to heaven, is such a strong and bold visual image (especially in a poem that does not use very much imagery) that readers cannot help but feel that the poet has resolved any and all doubts he may have had and come to a new position of self-certainty. The arrival of this new attitude and the dawn of the new day both merge at the end of the poem to indicate a mood of hope and forward motion.

Wealth

The "wealth" that is mentioned in this poem's final couplet is, of course, not material wealth. The word is instead used metaphorically, to imply the sort of accumulated value that has no physical basis. The word comes at the end of a pattern of expressions used throughout this poem to refer to matters of luck and attitude, a pattern that makes use of words one usually associates with money. Fortune, in the first line, refers to good luck and positive well-being, but it can just as easily be used to indicate material wealth; likewise the use of the word "rich" in "rich in hope" (line 5) is more than just a clever turn of a phrase but also part of the overall pattern. Financial wealth is a useful metaphor in this poem because it gives a physical presence to the issues of self-worth and comparison that Shakespeare explores here. This is a poem of measurement, that compares one's "scope" with that of others and balances what is most liked against what is least comforting. Fair or not, the standard that the social world often uses for comparison is material wealth.

Although it is not specific in the poem, a relationship is suggested here between wealth and social standing. In the first stanza, the speaker's problem is defined as his being an outcast, and by the poem's end he feels greater than a king—that is, above the peak of the social structure. A subtle transference takes place within the final couplet, which starts by using the "wealth" symbolism that is established throughout the poem and then, con-

Topics for Further Study

- Imagine yourself being an outcast, at a social low, rejected. Write a poem explaining what it would be like.

- Read Shakespeare's *Othello* and compare the character of Othello to the speaker of this poem. Write Othello's response to this speaker, defending his own jealousy and anger.

- Is this poem's speaker living in the past? Do you think this person should be more concerned with the world around him or her?

- A few years after he wrote this poem, Shakespeare achieved tremendous artistic and financial success. Find out about some other famous person who has been close to despair before their fame, and report on the person who helped them persevere.

necting the fact that kings possess money with their elevated social esteem, converts the "wealth" of line 13 into the sense of social well-being that the speaker has lacked at the beginning.

Style

The sonnet (from the Italian "sonnetto", or "little song") owes much of its long-standing popularity to the Italian poet Petrarch. By the mid-sixteenth century, this fixed poetic form was adopted by the English, who borrowed the fourteen-line pattern and many of Petrarch's literary conventions. English writers did, however, alter the rhyme scheme to allow for more variety in rhyming words: while the lines of an Italian sonnet might rhyme *abba, abba, cdc, dcd,* an English or Shakespearean sonnet rhyme pattern might be *abab, cdcd, efef, gg.*

In all but three of Shakespeare's 154 sonnets ("Sonnet 99," "Sonnet 126," and "Sonnet 145"), the first three groups of four lines each are known as quatrains, and the last two lines are recognized as a couplet. The three breaks between the quatrains and the couplet serve as convenient places where the writer's train of thought can take a different direction. In "Sonnet 29," a dramatic change in the writer's mind-set takes place in the beginning of the third quatrain, marked by the word "yet". The final couplet, which often contradicts or modifies the poem's argument, here confirms the writer's new mood as of line 10. Shakespeare's most unusual use of this poem's rhyme scheme is his repetition of "state" at the ends of lines 2 and 10. He may have wanted to draw attention to the word's many definitions, especially since he repeats it again in line 14; perhaps he was subtly connecting his "fate" (line 4) with "Heaven's gate" (line 12) through rhyme.

"Sonnet 29" is written in iambic pentameter. Iambic meter, the most familiar rhythm in the English language, is simply the succession of alternately stressed syllables; an iamb, a type of poetic foot, is a group of two syllables in which the first is unstressed and the second is stressed. The use of "penta" (meaning "five") before "meter" means that there are five iambs per line.

Stresses embody meanings; both variety and emphasis are added to lines in which the regular rhythm is broken. In this emotionally wrought poem, the often disrupted iambic meter symbolizes the speaker's own lack of composure and control. For example, the first poetic feet in lines 5, 6, and 10 are not iambic, but dactylic: "wishing me", "featured like", and "haply I" are all feet comprised of one stressed and two unstressed syllables. Other interruptions in the meter include "deaf heaven" (line 3) and "sings hymns" (line 12), which stand out not only because of their two successive stresses (known as spondees), but their assonance. "Men's eyes" (line 1), "I all" (line 2), "sweet love" (line 13), and "such wealth brings" (line 13), all break the sonnet's regular meter with two or more consecutive accented syllables; the writer thus calls attention to his sense of isolation and his regard for the poem's recipient.

Historical Context

The Reign of Elizabeth

This poem was written during the reign of Queen Elizabeth I of England. It was an exciting time of growth and prosperity for the country. Elizabeth was the daughter of King Henry VIII (1491-

1547) and his second wife, Anne Boleyn. Henry had six wives over the course of his lifetime, forcing him to separate England from the Roman Catholic church in order to follow his desire to divorce freely. After Henry's death in 1547, he was followed by Elizabeth's half-brother Edward, who was then only ten years old. Edward was king briefly until he died of tuberculosis in 1553. Because of a bill that one of his dukes, John Dudley, had him sign when he was dying, succession to the crown fell to Lady Jane Gray, who was Dudley's daughter-in-law. She reigned for four days until Mary I, another of Henry's children, was able to restore control of the crown to the Tudor dynasty. Elizabeth supported Mary, who was her half-sister, but Mary did not trust her because Elizabeth was a Protestant (Mary was a devout Catholic). Mary had Elizabeth locked up in the Tower of London in 1554. Elizabeth became queen in 1558 when Mary I died. There were plots against Elizabeth, but none were powerful enough to remove her from the crown. The Catholics wanted her cousin, Mary, Queen of Scots, to be queen, so she had Mary imprisoned; when she had Mary executed in 1587, Spain, which was a predominantly Catholic country, attacked England, hoping to defeat Protestantism and to take control from Elizabeth. Unexpectedly, with some luck and well-planned maneuvers, the British navy was able to defeat the Spanish Armada, and so Britain began to rise to the status of a world power. After years of struggle for the crown of England, the court settled down with one monarch who went on to rule for 45 years. Shakespeare, who was born in 1564, had spent his whole life under the reign of Queen Elizabeth at the time that his sonnets were written.

The Plague

During Elizabeth's reign England experienced a population explosion. By 1558 the population was four times what it had been a hundred and fifty years earlier. Between Shakespeare's birth in 1564 and his death in 1616, the number of people in Britain grew by another fifty percent. One reason was England's ascension to world power status, bringing immigrants from other countries. Another reason was the relative stability brought by Elizabeth's reign after hundreds of years of fighting between Catholics and Protestants for control of the country. One result of this huge sudden growth was overcrowding in the cities, especially London. The crowded conditions created poor sanitary conditions that provided a breeding ground for disease. Between 1538 and 1640, numerous epidemics

Compare & Contrast

- **1609:** England is on the rise to its eventual position as the dominant world power, having been considered a third-rate backwater as recently as 1558, when Elizabeth I ascended to the throne.

  Today: Having suffered great physical and financial losses during the two World Wars in the twentieth century, England is still an important member of the European community but is not considered one of the superpowers that influence world affairs.

- **1609:** The first newspapers with regular press schedules appear in Lower Saxony and Strasbourg.

  Today: With the advent of electric media, especially the internet, many doubt that print newspapers will survive for long into the twenty-first century.

- **1609:** Jamestown, the first permanent European settlement in what is now America, is nearly destroyed, having been founded two years earlier

by English gentlemen who were unprepared for breaking new soil. During the "Starving Time" of 1609-1610, residents were driven by hunger to cannibalism, raiding graves and victimizing one another.

  Today: Many Americans' understanding of colonial times is limited to the romanticized story of eleven-year-old Powhatan princess Pocahontas saving the life of Captain John Smith.

- **1609:** The most populous nation in Europe is France, with 16 million inhabitants. England has only 4.5 to 5 million. China has a population of roughly 120 million.

  Today: The latest population figures show France having 54.3 million people, just over three times what it is in 1609. China and England, though, have increased 900 percent since Shakespeare's time: England's population is 46 million, and China has a population of 1.2 billion.

---

swept across the country, especially the highly communicable bubonic plague. One key factor was the inability to keep the afflicted isolated from the healthy population under such conditions. Another contributing factor was the fact that rodents and the fleas that infest them are both capable of carrying the bubonic plague bacterium *Yersinia pestis*. Rats and mice thrive in crowded areas, where food and waste are not properly disposed of, and it was poor areas that were generally the most crowded. More poor areas were created by the rampant inflation that resulted from the population boom, opening up conditions for even quicker spread of the disease. In 1592 and 1593, the health authorities of London ordered the theaters to remain closed in an effort to slow the spread of the plague at public gatherings. It is believed that Shakespeare, whose career as an actor and dramatist was stalled by the theater closings, wrote his sonnets during this time of unemployment.

Critical Overview

Human love can be transcendent, and may even afford one a glimpse of "Heaven's gate": these themes have often been the focus of the discussions of "Sonnet 29," one of the sonnets in Shakespeare's sequence addressed to a young man. "Sonnet 29" says that God disappoints and the young man redeems, notes Paul Ramsey in *The Fickle Glass: A Study of Shakespeare's Sonnets*. He goes on to discuss the idea of love as an alternate religion, and the unearthly rewards of worshipping another mortal. David Weiser also reads "Sonnet 29" as a proclamation of love's saving grace, but with a twist: devotion to another can rescue someone from a preoccupation with oneself. "Irony pervades this sonnet, deriving from its basic contrast between love and self-love," he continues in his book *Mind in Character: Shakespeare's Speakers in the Sonnets*.

Figures of speech are often central to Shakespeare's sonnets, making "Sonnet 29" unusual in its support of a single metaphor. But the simile of the lark that appears in line 12 has been recognized as especially effective and powerful because of its dramatic isolation. In his article for the *Durham University Journal*, David Thatcher engages in an in-depth discussion of the lark's importance to the speaker, as well as to the poem.

Criticism

David Kelly

David Kelly teaches courses in poetry and drama at College of Lake County and Oakton Community College, in Illinois. In the following essay, Kelly examines Shakespeare's "Sonnet 29" in terms of the dramatic techniques that it uses.

It seems that a sonnet, by itself, is a paltry thing, hardly worth the attention of serious critics. Those who have read the current criticism on Shakespeare know that little is written about any one poem alone, that the group of them are often addressed together. There are good reasons for this. Shakespeare appears to have written them all in a close period of time (unlike the lifetime output of a more active poet), so that they can be studied as a group. Also, they are much more personal than sonnets of the sixteenth century, offering critics a clearer view of how writers thought of life's relation to poetry at that time. Finally, they are the work of the greatest playwright who ever lived, and so critics use the sonnets as a tool to dig for information on the dramatist more often than they appreciate the sonnets for themselves.

Rather than face the difficulty in addressing oneself to a single sonnet by Shakespeare, many literary critics open up their field of inquiry to that broader unit we know as "the sonnet sequence"—looking for patterns. In the case of the Shakespearean sonnets, we know only that there is a finite quantity, 154. After that, the best form that they make when put together is open to debate. Some are addressed to a younger friend or patron; some to the Dark Lady who is referred to as the mistress of the poems' speaker; some focus their attention on a rival poet. The identities of these people, their actual relationships to Shakespeare, and just what these relationships tell us about poetic inspiration are debated endlessly.

Looking at "Sonnet 29," which begins "When, in disgrace with Fortune and men's eyes," a reader's first response might be, "What was Shakespeare feeling so depressed about?" The question assumes, though, that he actually was feeling depressed and humiliated at the time of writing, even though that is specifically contrary to what the poem says. The first word, "when" is the qualifier, telling us that the emotions discussed in the following sixteen lines were not necessarily happening at the time of writing, but that they are emotions that came up every now and again. What Shakespeare is telling us is that he does know these feelings. The only thing we know regarding *when* he feels like this is that he experienced this hopelessness at some time during his relationship with the "thee" who is first mentioned in line 10. Historians place this sonnet within the series addressed to Shakespeare's younger friend and patron, and that understanding could open the door to a good deal of intellectual labor about social relations in the sixteenth and seventeenth centuries. But this sonnet seems to stand quite well without any knowledge of who Shakespeare meant by "thee." "Thee" could be one's girlfriend or boyfriend, spouse, or trusted confidant. For now, one can leave aside the question of what incidents Shakespeare was talking about and appreciate the poem on its own terms.

The players in Shakespeare's small drama of "Sonnet 29" are long gone, but we still have the drama itself. A judgment that is pretty universally accepted is that Shakespeare was a better playwright than a poet. Saying it this way makes it sound as if there was something wrong with his poetry, but the actual sum and substance is that he was such an astounding dramatist that there would be little he, or anyone, could do that would meet the level of skill in his plays. It seems plausible to suggest that it is Shakespeare's dramatic talent, not necessarily his poetic talent, that must shine through from the center of everything he did. "Sonnet 29," at first look, does not seem to be any more dramatic than it is autobiographical, but even in the tightly controlled sonnet form, Shakespeare's dramatic talent shows itself clearly.

One of the most important elements in creating the "soul" of a drama is dramatic tension. The most telling way to show that this poem is a drama at heart is to examine the tension of its central question. In recent times, the word "tension" is most often used to indicate having too much to do at once, and being exhausted and beleaguered by the constant demands that pull at you. We think of be-

What Do I Read Next?

- A. L. Rowse, one of the great critics of English literature of recent times, scrutinized each of the 154 sonnets for *Shakespeare's Sonnets: The Problems Solved,* published in 1973 by Harper & Rowe. Each sonnet is presented with limited notes, giving readers enough to see the story behind the poems without becoming bogged down with theory.

- A. L. Rowse is also the author of one of the most thoroughly-researched and readable biographies of the poet, *Shakespeare the Man.* The second edition was published in 1988 by St. Martin's Press.

- One of the most interesting projects related to Shakespeare's sonnets in recent years is *Love's Fire: Seven New Plays Inspired by Seven Shakespearean Sonnets,* published in 1998 by William Morrow & Co. Playwrights who have works in this collection include Eric Bogosian, Wendy Wasserstein, and Ntozake Shange.

- English playwright and poet Ben Jonson was the closest thing to a peer that Shakespeare had. The two knew each other as friends, and early in his career Shakespeare appeared as an actor in one of Jonson's plays. Readers can look at another great talent of Shakespeare's time by reading *The Complete Poems of Ben Jonson,* published in 1988 by Penguin Classics.

- There are two basic types of sonnets. The English sonnet is often called the Shakespearean sonnet after its most skilled practitioner. Similarly, the Italian sonnet is also regularly referred to as the Petrarchan sonnet after Petrarch, the fourteenth-century Italian poet who perfected the form. His sonnets can be found in *Petrarch: The Canzoniere, or Rerum Vulgarium Fragmenta,* translated by Mark Musa and introduced by Barbara Manfredi and published by the Indiana University Press in 1999.

- Oscar Wilde was a brilliant playwright (*The Importance of Being Earnest*) and novelist (*The Picture of Dorian Gray*). In 1899 he set his attention to discerning the truth of the identity of the person mentioned on the dedication page of the first publication of Shakespeare's sonnets, which resulted in the essay "The Portrait of Mr. W. H." That essay, reading like a mystery novel, is an impressive piece of work, and it contains ample scholarly details about Shakespeare's life, although modern scholars point out that the dedication to "Mr. W. H." was probably from the book's publisher, Thomas Thorpe; the dedication page is even signed "T. T." Whether it is accurate or not does not diminish the fun of reading Wilde's nearly-100-page essay and following his search for the ancient mystery.

- Several critics have speculated that the rival who is sometimes referred to in Shakespeare's sonnets was Christopher Marlowe, the English poet and playwright who died in 1593, as the sonnets were being written. The work of Marlowe's most often read today is his play *Dr. Faustus,* which was published after his death. His long poem "Hero and Leander" is thought to be a response to Shakespeare's own "Venus and Adonis."

---

ing tense as a nervous condition that shows itself, often, through anger. This is one meaning, but one that has drifted away from the word's core. "Tension" essentially means that something or someone is being pulled in opposite directions with fairly equal force (if one side pulled with much greater strength, the tension wouldn't last long).

In drama, tension is used to keep the audience engaged in the story that is unfolding. The audience keeps up with what is being presented, wondering which side will eventually pull with greater force: good or evil? hope or despair? jealousy or faith? A tense dramatic situation could entail someone trying to snip the right wire to disable a bomb with a few seconds left, but often the powers pulling against each other are more subtle than that. In "Sonnet 29," the dramatic tension lies between the speaker of the poem and his society; between

> *The poem reaches a climax with the ninth line, with the speaker almost despising himself—this is the high point of the poem's tension, where the forces pulling in opposite directions have stretched him as far as they can."*

self-worth and low-esteem; between the present and the world that one can access through memory. This all adds up to a dispute between humanity and Fortune. Fortune may be luck, it may be earned by talent, it may be the will of God (as indicated by deaf heaven ignoring the speaker's plight), but whatever it is, it is telling this person that he is not worth much. The force pulling away from Fortune throughout the sonnet is implied rather than stated—that the poem's speaker is trying to believe in the value of his own life.

The drama builds throughout the poem. The first stanza shows the speaker's self-worth under attack. The second has him floundering around, trying to regain his self-esteem with wishes and anger, doing whatever it takes to consider himself a worthy human. The poem reaches a climax with the ninth line, with the speaker *almost* despising himself—this is the high point of the poem's tension, where the forces pulling in opposite directions have stretched him as far as they can. Something has to give. In the tenth line, there is relief: the thought of that special other person comes flooding into the speaker's mind. The struggle between two conflicting ideas had been closely balanced up to this point, but once he has added the influx of self-worth that comes from this "sweet love remembered," the competition is not even close.

If "Sonnet 29" is a drama, then who are the characters involved? This is where the biographical approach to the entire sonnet sequence would make the most sense, as literary analysts try to piece together the personalities of the speaker and "thee." Theories abound about the financial difficulties that Shakespeare faced, about the Dark Lady who was his mistress, about who his patron was. As Rosalie L. Colie explained it in an essay called "Criticism and Analysis of Craft: The Sonnets," critics tend to read the entire sonnet sequence as one continuing drama. Reading the sonnet as part of the sonnet sequence may yield a richer interpretation than can be derived from a single poem, but it is likely to raise discrepancies that confuse issues further. For instance, most readers of "Sonnet 29" assume that its speaker is addressing the object of his romantic affection. Most critics, on the other hand, identify the subject of the poem as a man younger than Shakespeare with whom the poet had a financial relationship and a close friendship, but no romance. Which view is correct? Perhaps it is sufficient to know, just as the sonnet says, that the memory of this love (whatever the personal relationship) has the power to affect the outcome of the speaker's inner turmoil.

Finally, one should be able to find a dramatic situation, if this poem actually is a drama. Dramas have scenes: they involve characters in a place where they can voice their emotions. It is not enough to have an inner life. That inner life must be put in a place where it can be played out for the entire audience to understand and appreciate. This is where the sonnet form does the least service to Shakespeare's talent as a dramatist. In "Sonnet 29," one person is talking and the other is silent. Readers are not given a setting—there is no particular place where we could best imagine this person speaking his mind. In modern theater, innovative companies mount productions that are unspecific about where they take place, giving only a vacant stage representing some unreal terrain. Silent characters also are not that uncommon, but, on stage, there is interaction between the characters. But in this sonnet that interaction can be claimed only with a great deal of imagination. Perhaps one could say that the act of remembering is a form of interaction between the poem's speaker and "thee," but actually the memory is self-contained: the other person could be long gone from this world, and the speaker could still conjure him or her up in memory. One character goes through changes before our eyes, but the dramatic qualities of this sonnet collapse when we start to look for interaction between two characters.

William Shakespeare is often recognized as the greatest dramatist who ever lived. This talent for drama can be seen in the dramatic qualities of the sonnet: its dramatic tension and the characters of Shakespeare and of his former love. However, the drama of the sonnet falters in regard to dramatic situation and interaction between characters because one character appears only in the memory of the other.

Source: David Kelly, in an essay for *Poetry for Students,* Gale Group, 2000.

Bruce Meyer

Bruce Meyer is the director of the creative writing program at the University of Toronto. He has taught at several Canadian universities and is the author of three collections of poetry. In the following essay, Meyer interprets "Sonnet 29" as a rhetorical demonstration of "how one reasons one's way around circumstance."

In the narrative of Shakespeare's sonnets, "Sonnet 29" falls among the phase (sonnets 1-129) where the voice of the older poet, the voice of experience and good counsel, fights off challenges for a young man's affections from another poet and from a dark lady. In this schema, "Sonnet 29" falls at a low, melancholy point in the apparent narrative. It is a complaint, in the true Renaissance style, where the persona dwells on a sense of loss—in this context, the possible loss of favor in the eyes of the young man. The poem begins with the famous line, "When in disgrace with Fortune and men's eyes," as if the voice is reconnoitering his situation and finding that his stock is at an all-time low. What seems to pervade "Sonnet 29" is, however, a comic structure, a fall from and a return to favor and hope, and a sense of how one recovers from a type of "fall" from grace.

The word "Fortune," capitalized in the first line of the poem is set in the line as a personification. This "Fortune" is the classical "fortuna"—the idea of a force in the universe that controls the destiny of an individual. In classical literature, particularly Boethius's *A Consolation of Philosophy,* 'Fortune' is the antagonist who acts against reason and 'Philosophy.' Fortune, in the Sophoclean sense, is the predetermined pattern of an individual's life that cannot be avoided—it is the destiny of an individual, the narrative of a life, that must inevitably come to pass. In the Renaissance sense of the word as explained by Niccolo Machiavelli, fortune is the raw material of ability and circumstance that life presents to an individual. Machiavelli suggests, in his treatise on the nature of political leadership, *The Prince,* that an individual can overcome the negative powers of fortune or destiny by exercising what he calls "virtu" or the power of intelligence over circumstance. Shakespeare's "Sonnet 29" is a poem about how one reasons one's way around circumstance. The poem is

> *The form itself, the sonnet, is a rhetorical rather than a lyrical structure, and although it offers lyric elements such as the rhyming couplet at the conclusion or the balanced meter, its chief value is as an argumentative structure, a means of working one's way toward reason in any situation."*

not only a matter of counting one's blessings but of finding them. Like Boethius in the opening of *A Consolation of Philosophy,* the persona of "Sonnet 29" is woeful and announces that when he is "in disgrace" "I all alone beweep my outcast state." His plaintive cries fall on "deaf Heaven." God, as the poem suggests, does not tolerate complaints. The persona's cries are "bootless," or useless. The word "bootless," however, also suggests that the persona is thinking out loud without really having a firm foundation for his musings—a no-no in the world of Renaissance thought, where the Virgilian precept of approaching life with strong, emotionally detached, and objective reasoning was still the order of the day. Like Boethius in *A Consolation of Philosophy,* the persona of this poem must find his way to solace through the power of thought and through the banishment of emotions where he might feel sorry for himself. In the Renaissance perspective, feeling sorry for oneself and reason are incompatible. Suffice to say, cursing one's "fate" and "Wishing me like to one more rich in hope" or envying "this man's art, and that man's scope" may serve the need to air one's complaints but can do little to see one toward the kind of resolution that a sonnet must afford: the solution to the problem at hand.

Shakespeare's use of the sonnet form, especially in "Sonnet 29," allows him to air a complaint in poetry (in Boethius, Dame Philosophy sends the Muses packing in the first several pages because, as she reasons, poetry does nothing but lock one into one's problems) while at the same time reasoning the poet to demonstrate the possibilities and the complexities in the process of reason. The sonnet, unlike the lyric, cannot stand still either emotionally or rhetorically. It presents a problem in the opening octave and then determines to answer it in the sestet by what is often a one-hundred-and-eighty degree turn of reasoning between lines 8 and 9. This turn of reasoning, the volta, especially in "Sonnet 29," shifts the poem from being simply a litany of woes and self-indulgent "bemoaning" and into an examination of the cause and effect relationship behind the poem, to the point where the sonnet can almost be considered an early form of psychotherapy. The voice asks, "what is wrong" and then probes for the answer.

For the persona of "Sonnet 29," all is not lost. He realizes that even in his deepest moment of self-loathing, "in these thoughts myself almost despising," there is a glimmer of hope. The shift from woe to consolation demands that every issue under consideration be examined from the opposite perspective—a trait that Boethius spells out quite clearly. The emotions rarely allow one the privilege of seeing the other side of an argument; yet the persona of "Sonnet 29" rises out of his emotional distress in line 9, a tall order in that the volta demands considerable strength of intellect and a kind of hopeful dispassion that sees light in darkness and possibility in despair.

He announces in line 10, "Haply I think on thee," which suggests that the persona's lot is not as bad as he had thought because he has the young man's friendship. This is more than just a matter of considering the opposite idea as a matter of "thinking" one's way through the argumentative process of the sonnet: it is a miracle of images. "Like to the lark at break of day arising / From sullen earth, sings hymns at heaven's gate," the poet likens his friendship with the young man. The Platonic idea of friendship, what Jonathan Swift perceives as the great virtue in the Houyhnmms in Book IV of *Gulliver's Travels,* is, perhaps the highest possible ideal one can seek to attain. Friendship, in the classical sense, is something that is more continuous than love. It survives the momentary passage of passions, it advises and counsels, and it stands the test of time. It is more than power and more than wealth. Friendship, for the persona of "Sonnet 29," is "wealth" that is counted only in the spirit, and the memory of it brings him to the recognition that it is worth more than any amount of momentary recompense. "I scorn to

change my state with kings," he notes. What should be remembered is that in the center of Dante's Hell are those who betrayed friendship, Brutus and Judas.

What "Sonnet 29" proves is not only the value of friendship but the undeniable worth of reason. The form itself, the sonnet, is a rhetorical rather than a lyrical structure, and although it offers lyric elements such as the rhyming couplet at the conclusion or the balanced meter, its chief value is as an argumentative structure, a means of working one's way toward reason in any situation. The Renaissance mind pursued balance and proportion in all things, and the sonnet is a balanced way of looking not only at emotional problems but through them. In this process of pursuing balance, the tools are not only reason but imagination and memory.

The image of the lark ascending at daybreak to sing "hymns at heaven's gate," is not merely a flight of fancy but the realization that memory and the imagination are the repositories of hope, wherein the true value of the more lasting aspects of one's existence—friendship, truth, faith—are there to shore up one's defenses against a world bound up in entropy and emotional tides, if only one is able to reason his or her way to it.

Source: Bruce Meyer, in an essay for *Poetry for Students,* Gale Group, 2000.

Alice Van Wart

Alice Van Wart teaches literature and writing in the Department of Continuing Education at the University of Toronto. She has published two books of poetry and has written articles on modern and contemporary literature. In the following essay, Van Wart discusses the content of the poem in relation to its structure.

One of the most popular of the fixed poetic forms in English literature is the sonnet. Attributed to the Italian poet Petrarch in the fourteenth century, the sonnet is still used by many contemporary writers. The appeal of the sonnet lies in its two-part structure, which easily lends itself to the dynamics of much human emotional experience and to the intellectual mode of human sensibility for argument based on complication and resolution.

In the last decade of the sixteenth century, sonnet writing became highly fashionable following the publication of Sir Philip Sydney's sonnet sequence *Astrophel and Stella,* published in 1591. Sonnet sequences were widely read and admired at this time, circulated about the court, and read among friends and writers. Shakespeare took up this trend, adapting his considerable talent to the prevailing literary mode while writing for the theater. He specifically followed the form of the sonnet as adopted from the Italian into English by the Earl of Surrey and Sir Thomas Wyatt.

Bound by the conventions of the sonnet, Shakespeare used the form to explore the same themes as early Latin, Italian, and French verse. He treated the themes of the transient nature of youth and physical beauty, the fallibility of love, and the nature of friendship. Even the dominating conceit of Shakespeare's sequence—the poet's claim that his poems will confer immortality on his subject—is one that goes back to Ovid and Petrarch. In Shakespeare's hands, however, the full potentiality of the sonnet form emerged, earning for it the poet's name.

The Petrarchan and Shakespearean sonnet are similar in that they both present and then solve a problem. The Petrarchan sonnet does it through an octave which presents a problem and a sestet which provides the resolution. A different rhyme scheme and thus a different convention of logical and rhetorical organization determines the differences between the two sonnet forms. In the Petrarchan sonnet the problem is solved by reasoned perception or a meditative process. The Shakespearean sonnet maintains the basic two-part structure of conflict and resolution, now presented in fourteen lines of three quatrains and a concluding rhyming couplet. Each quatrain presents a further aspect of a problem, conflict, or idea. The resolution occurs in the last two of a rhyming couplet, achieved through logical cleverness that summarizes or ties together what has been expressed in the three quatrains. The rhyme scheme, subject to variation, is *abab, cdcd, efef, gg* in iambic pentameter.

The sonnet sequence is a gathering together of a number of sonnets to present a narrative or examine a larger theme. Shakespeare's sequence, like Sydney's, was intended as a series of love poems to celebrate the poet's affections for a young male friend. The poems were collected and published as a sequence in 1609, though initially they were private poems meant for a small circle of writers and friends, not for publication.

There are 154 sonnets in the sequence. Some scholars speculate these are ones that remain from a longer work, thus accounting for the sonnet's problems in chronology, thematic development, and connections between individual poems. Other scholars speculate that not all the poems in the sequence were written by Shakespeare himself, thus accounting for the uneven nature of the sequence. In fact, many puzzles surrounding the sequence still exist. Particularly intriguing is the ongoing attempt

> *The shift in the poem from the conflict presented in the first two quatrains begins in the third quatrain, pivoting in the first line of the third quatrain with the conjunctive adverb 'yet.'*

to identify the young man with the initials W. H., to whom the sequence is addressed and dedicated, along with the mysterious so-called dark woman who intrudes into the relationship between the younger man and the poet.

The story that unfolds within the sequence is that of a love triangle. It begins with the relationship between the speaker of the poems and a young man he admires and comes to love. Their relationship, however, is impeded by their differences in age, wealth, and rank. The poet is older and more established than his friend, while the young man is from an influential and wealthy family. The relationship is also threatened by the shadow of a dark and sensual woman, referred to by critics as "the dark lady" and presumed to be the poet's mistress.

Whoever the young man was, his image dominates the sequence, and whoever the mysterious woman may have been, we can see from the details in the sequence that she created a conflict for the poet between his profound affection for his friend and the sexual attraction that drew him to this woman. In the later sonnets of the sequence, the poet is thrown into misery and anguish when this woman betrays him by seducing the young man.

Aside from these few details about the circumstances of the complicated triangle within the poems, the sequence tells us little about the personal life of the poet. What it does show, however, is something of the nature of the man behind the words, a man who occasionally seems to be on the edge of emotional and physical exhaustion, even disillusionment, a man who is not always happy with his craft or the theater, and a man who sometimes distrusts the very gift he believes will confer immortality on his subject. Yet it also shows a man who perseveres because he remains engaged in the world and fascinated by the people and events around him, an involvement that enables him to rise above any personal setback and pain.

The sonnets in the sequence up to "Sonnet 127" (when the dark lady makes her appearance) celebrate the poet's love and affection for the young man. "Sonnet 29" specifically shows the importance of this friendship to the older man during a particularly low point in the poet's life. The poet is at odds with himself and the world around him, almost on the point of despair, and disliking himself for his self-pity. In the first quatrain the poet expresses his sense of personal failure. In the second he adds to this sense of failure by comparing himself to the young man he loves and the young man's friends. Beside their accomplishments his own bring him little contentment. In the third quatrain the thought of his friend reminds him of his friend and the love the young man gives to the poet's life. Immediately the nature of his thoughts changes and his spirits rise. In the final couplet, the poet concludes his reflection by acknowledging that the very existence of the young man's love makes all other accomplishments unimportant and his life far richer than any others—so rich, in fact, he would not change it for any other.

A surface paraphrase of the poem ignores the complexity of the intellectual process within the poem, particularly the quick turns of thought expressed in the poem's progression of logic and in the meaning of its diction. Each of the poem's quatrains advances the poet's complaint. In the first line of the first quatrain the poet expresses his sense of failure as "in disgrace with fortune and men's eyes." He feels he has failed in the eyes of others and therefore believes himself to be an outcast. The word "fortune" suggests both material wealth and the events or circumstances of the poet's life. He curses his "outcast state": "And trouble deaf heaven with my bootless cries, and look upon myself, and curse my fate." Fate in this sense is the situation into which the circumstances of his life have placed him.

In the second quatrain he further adds to his sense of failure by comparing himself to others "more rich in hope." Hope suggests a more optimistic nature and possibility in the future, both of which the poet feels he lacks. He wishes he were "featured like him," or as handsome as some others, and also like others "with friends possessed." "Him" is possibly the young man himself who is surrounded by friends. The poet further wishes he had what some others have by "desiring this man's

art and that man's scope." "Art" suggests both specific talent and objects of art such as paintings and fine artifacts, while "scope" points to opportunity and intelligence or the extent or range of one's understanding. In the final line he compares what others have to what he "most enjoys," which presumably is his talent with words but with which, paradoxically, he says he is "contented least." Though the poet writes because he wants to, it does not bring him the kind of satisfaction he believes the other qualities bring others.

In the final quatrain the poet acknowledges the self-pitying nature of his complaints and admits to disliking himself for them with his admission "in these thoughts myself almost despising." Fortunately, by recalling the presence of the young man in his life ("Haply I think on thee), the very nature of his thoughts changes. The poet expresses his turn of thought in the sweeping image of "the lark" who at break of day arises from "sullen earth" to sing hymns "at heaven's gate." Though the poet does not define the love between the young man and himself as spiritual, the very thought of his friend's love elevates the poet's "state," a state he compares to the lark. With the thought of his friend, the poet's spirits soar beyond his gloomy thoughts.

The shift in the poem from the conflict presented in the first two quatrains begins in the third quatrain, pivoting in the first line of the third quatrain with the conjunctive adverb "yet." Although the poet has almost given in to despising himself, the thought of the young man turns his thoughts in another direction and brings the poem to its final shift—the resolution of the concluding couplet: "For thy sweet love remember'd such wealth brings / That then I scorn to change my state with kings."

The resolution turns on the first word of the couplet "for" and exploits the double meaning of "wealth" and "state." In the first line of the sonnet the poet finds himself "in disgrace with fortune." Here "fortune" is associated with the material wealth and success of the material world, a "state" the poet has not achieved and because of which he believes himself to be a failure and an outcast. Yet the recollection of the young man's love reminds the poet of a different kind of richness, a wealth that has nothing to do with what a person owns, or how a person looks, or the way a person thinks, but with the special qualities of their relationship. Because of the poet's recollection of "thy sweet love," he now "scorns" to change his state with the "state of kings."

"State" is both a condition in the outer world and an inner state. The young man's love gives the poet something far more meaningful than anything in the material world. Like the image of the lark rising above "sullen earth" to sing at "heaven's gate," the poet now makes his own wealth known to the world in his poem. The poem will immortalize this love by lasting long after anything in the mutable material world. With this knowledge the poet is able to resolve his previous complaints, and he now scorns "to change my state with kings." In the logical progression of the poet's thoughts, the poet realizes he is far wealthier than any king.

The expression of the poet's affection for the younger man perfectly fulfills the logical and rhetorical structure. It presents its conflict in the twelve lines of the three qutrains and resolves it in the rhyming couplet. The enduring value of this sonnet rests, however, not so much in the argument it presents, which is merely a play in logic, but in the integrity of the rhetorical strategy and its perfect fusion of content and form.

Source: Alice Van Wart, in an essay for *Poetry for Students,* Gale Group, 2000.

Sources

Andrews, John F., ed., *William Shakespeare: His World, His Work, His Influence,* New York: Charles Scribner's Sons, 1985.

Colei, Rosalie L., "Criticism and the Analysis of Craft: The Sonnets," in *William Shakespeare's Sonnets,* edited by Harold Bloom, Philadelphia: Chelsea House Publishers, 1987, pp. 47-74.

Fox, Levi, *The Shakespeare Handbook,* Boston: G.K. Hall & Co., 1987.

Fussell, Paul, *Poetic Meter and Poetic Form,* New York: McGraw-Hill, 1979.

Quennell, Peter, *Shakespeare: The Poet and His Background,* London: Penguin Books, Ltd., 1969.

Ramsey, Paul. *The Fickle Glass: A Study of Shakespeare's Sonnets,* AMS Press, 1979, pp. 152-153.

Thatcher, David, "What a Lark: The Undoing of Sonnet 29." *Durham University Journal,* January, 1994, pp. 59-66.

Weiser, David K, *Mind in Character: Shakespeare's Speaker in the Sonnets,* University of Missouri Press, 1987, pp. 33-40.

For Further Study

Booth, Stephen, *An Essay on Shakespeare's Sonnets,* New Haven, CT: Yale University Press, 1969.

> Booth's academic study of the structure of the sonnets considers minute details that most readers disregard, such as chapters on "Rhetorical Patterns," "Phonetic Structure," etc. This is a difficult but useful work.

Greene, Thomas M., "Pitiful Thrivers: Failed Husbandry in Shakespeare's Sonnets," in *Modern Critical Interpretations: William Shakespeare's Sonnets,* edited by Harold Bloom, New York: Chelsea House Publishers, 1987, pp. 75-92.

> Greene examines a sense of inadequacy that shows throughout Shakespeare's poetry.

Ramsey, Paul, *The Fickle Glass: A Study of Shakespeare's Sonnets,* New York: AMS Press, 1979.

> Ramsey's scholarly work is careful and thoughtful, but it might be a little complex for some readers.

Shakespeare, William, *The Riddle of Shakespeare's Sonnets,* New York: Basic Book Publishers, 1962.

> Six notable critics—Northrop Frye, Edward Hubler, Leslie Fiedler, Stephen Spender, R. P. Blackmur, and Oscar Wilde—look for clues about Shakespeare's life and personality in his sonnets, coming to a surprisingly wide range of conclusions.

Smith, D. Nichol, ed., *Eighteenth Century Essays on Shakespeare,* London: University of Oxford Press, 1963.

> The essays in this book were written roughly one hundred to one hundred and fifty years after the poet's death. It is interesting to note how seldom critics of the 1700s, including Alexander Pope and Samuel Johnson, paid attention to Shakespeare's poetry, concentrating instead on his dramas.

Wait, R. J. C., *The Background to Shakespeare's Sonnets,* New York: Schocken Books, 1972.

> This source offers a good, intelligible mix of historical information and biographical information about Shakespeare.

Weiser, David K., *Mind in Character: Shakespeare's Speaker in the Sonnets,* Columbia, MO: University of Missouri Press, 1987.

> While many analyses identify the speaker of the sonnets with the author himself, Weiser's book meticulously dissects what we know from the poems and establishes a separate character used in the poems.

Wilson, Katharine M., "Shakespeare's Sonnets Imitate and Satirize Earlier Sonnets," in *Readings on the Sonnets,* San Diego, CA: Greenhaven Press, 1997, pp. 148-158.

> The examination of "Sonnet 29" here begins, "That this is parody we could not doubt." Wilson gives a spirited and intelligent argument with examples for her approach to Shakespeare's work.

Starlight

Philip Levine
1979

"Starlight" first appeared in the journal *Inquirey* and was reprinted in *Ashes: Poems New and Old* in 1979, a collection that won both the National Book Critics Circle Award and the American Book Award. This short 31-line poem, written in free verse, opens the second half of the book. Like the book's first and last poems, "Starlight" marks an attempt by the poet to come to terms with memories of his father. As the title of the collection itself implies, the primary subject of *Ashes* is loss. Like much of Levine's work, "Starlight" is a confessional poem, describing an experience from the poet's past. The narrator recounts a brief discussion from his childhood between himself and his father about happiness. Though the meaning of the experience was not clear to the narrator as a child, it is as an adult. The speaker obviously has grown emotionally and now has perspective on his past. He empathizes with his father, which makes sense when we understand that although Levine writes the poem from the viewpoint of an adult remembering himself as a child, the real change in the poem happens to the father. It is worth noting that Levine himself has three sons and may well be thinking of his own current relationship with them. Exploring ideas of innocence and experience, the poem suggests that regardless of how tired one may be, emotionally, psychologically, or physically, it is always possible to renew oneself through the experience of another, especially if that other person is a child. Levine presents his poem as a comment on the human condition, rather than merely an adult's memory of a childhood experience.

Author Biography

The second of three children—first of identical twins—Philip Levine was born in 1928. His parents, Harry Levine and Esther Gertrude Priscol were Russian-Jewish immigrants who had met in Detroit, the city of Philip's birth. He grew up among that city's working class, and although he received a B.A. in 1950 and an M.A. in 1955 from Wayne State University, he was no stranger to manual labor. Levine worked in a number of Detroit's automobile factories while earning his degrees. His experiences during this time helped to solidify the allegiances he already felt to the working poor and manifested themselves in his poetry which damned greedy capitalists as frequently as it praised the "lowly" wage-earner.

Levine's own desire to be a writer was in large part formed by the hardscrabble working world in which he grew up. Though he admired and paid homage to the working-class heroes of Detroit's factories, he himself desired a different life. Levine took an M.F.A. in creative writing in 1957 from the University of Iowa and won a Stanford University Jones Fellowship in poetry shortly thereafter. In 1958 he became a full-time faculty member at Fresno State College. By 1979 when "Starlight" appeared in *Ashes,* Levine had established his reputation as one of America's leading poets, having published a number of well-received poetry collections and having been awarded fellowships from the National Endowment for the Arts and the Guggenheim Foundation. He had also fathered three sons of his own, and poems about his sons, his father, and other family members pepper his collections.

Like "Starlight," many of these poems are narratives. Levine sees his task as poet to tell stories as well as he can. He claims that a successful poem is one in which the words become transparent and the reader is immersed in the world being described. One of the United States's most decorated poets, Philip Levine lives in Fresno, California and New York City, and teaches at New York University.

Philip Levine

Poem Text

My father stands in the warm evening
on the porch of my first house.
I am four years old and growing tired.
I see his head among the stars,
the glow of his cigarette, redder   5
than the summer moon riding
low over the old neighborhood. We

are alone, and he asks me if I am happy.
"Are you happy?" I cannot answer
I do not really understand the word,   10
and the voice, my father's voice, is not
his voice, but somehow thick and choked,
a voice I have not heard before, but
heard often since. He bends and passes
a thumb beneath each of my eyes.   15
The cigarette is gone, but I can small
the tiredness that hangs on his breath.
He has found nothing, and he smiles
and holds my head with both his hands.
Then he lifts me to his shoulder,   20
and now I too am there among the stars,
as tall as he. Are you happy? I say.
He nods in answer, Yes! oh yes! oh yes!
And in that new voice he says nothing,
holding my head tight against his head,   25
his eyes closed up against the starlight,
as though those tiny blinking eyes
of light might find a tall, gaunt child
holding his child against the promises
of autumn, until the boy slept   30
never to waken in that world again.

Poem Summary

Title:

Titles of poems can be deceptive. Their relationship to the writing they name is as varied as the writing itself. They can function to sum up a par-

Media Adaptations

- *Atlantic Unbound* provides links to text and RealAudio versions of six Levine poems, as well as an interview with Levine by Wen Stephenson. http://www.theatlantic.com/unbound/poetry/levine.htm

- National Public Radio's 1996 Fresh Air interview with Levine can be heard at http://whyy.org/freshair/BOFA/BOFA961115.html

- The Internet Poetry Archive's Philip Levine site: http://sunsite.unc.edu/ipa/levine/

ticular theme of the poem by providing an image which embodies that theme, or they might simply be named after a character or event in the poem. "Starlight" prepares us for a poem which involves revelation, as the image of light traditionally symbolizes insight or the achievement of wisdom.

Lines 1-3:

These first lines identify the speaker's point of view as an adult looking back on his childhood. The "warm evening" and the fact that the speaker's father is standing "on the porch of my first house" create a domestic scene and invite readers to see the same things that the speaker sees. The third line echoes both the world weariness felt by the father in the poem and that of the speaker himself. The line also tips us off that the memory might be more of an imagined event rather than an actual one. How many people can remember with such detail events that happened when they were four years old?

Lines 4-9:

The younger version of the speaker looks up at his father. That he sees his head "among the stars" is both literal and symbolic. From the perspective of looking up at someone much taller than himself, the child could literally see stars in back of his father's head. This image also captures the awe a young child feels for his father. By comparing the glow from his father's cigarette to the summer moon, the speaker conflates the romantic image of the moon, with the prosaic image of a cigarette, presenting an almost noirish scene of father and son. The moon, and all the romance and otherworldliness it represents, is close enough to touch, helping to create a dreamlike atmosphere. The phrase "the old neighborhood" underscores the nostalgic quality of the memory. Telling readers that the two are alone, a detail easily inferred, highlights the intimacy between the two. The father's question, an odd one to a four year old, and the child's inability to answer it, tells us more about the father than the boy, and our expectations are geared to learn more about the father.

Lines 10-15:

These lines remind us that the poem is a description of a memory. They have an almost incantatory effect. The speaker remembers himself not understanding the word "happy," and focuses on his father's voice, which he describes as "thick and choked." We understand that the father is very emotional, on the verge of tears, and that the speaker remembers seeing his father this way "often since" this episode, which highlights the significance of the event, for both father and son. The act of passing his thumb beneath his child's eyes implies that the father is looking for something in his son, a different way of seeing, perhaps. This physical gesture further develops the intimacy between the two. The father might also be reenacting a ritual the two have when the son gets tired, such as looking for sand from the sandman, a character from fairytales and folktales who sprinkles sand in children's eyes to put them to sleep. Or the father might be looking for tears.

Lines 16-23:

Images of residue mark these lines: the spent cigarette, the father's breath and weariness, the speaker's memory of the experience. Out of this residue, these "ashes," the father renews himself by bonding with his son, holding his head and lifting him to his shoulders. He has seen something in his son which allows him to see something in himself. Implied is a sense of recognition by the father that his question to his son has more to do with himself rather than his son. When the father lifts the boy to his shoulders the boy is now where he saw his father at the beginning of the poem, "among the stars." As a (symbolic) peer, he now asks his father the same question he was just asked, and the father responds affirmatively, enthusiastically.

Lines 23-31:

These lines complete the father's emotional epiphany. He no longer speaks with a tired voice but with a "new" one, one that says "nothing," telling us that true happiness is beyond language. Holding his son's head to his own is the only language he needs. As in the beginning of the poem, the father's head is among the stars, only this time his eyes are closed, suggesting that his newly acquired vision is internal. The image of starlight ("those tiny blinking eyes") underscore the theme of renewal and its universality as well, and because the stars "might find" (i.e., witness) the father holding his child, they can be seen as a symbolically religious presence or consciousness. The father is now a child, albeit a "gaunt" one, which might represent both the father's physical appearance and his thin emotional life, and the child is sleeping, to wake, presumably, to an adult world. "The promises / of autumn" is an ambiguous phrase. Literally, it suggests the coming season, but it could also suggest the time of life for the father, in which case "holding the child against [those] … promises" could be read as ironic.

Themes

Change and Transformation

"Starlight" suggests that world-weary and emotionally exhausted adults can be inspired to keep going by the very promise of future generations. Such adults literally come to live their own lives through the lives of their children. Their children, and particularly the hope children hold for the future, provide meaning for their lives. In some ways this theme echoes the myth of the Phoenix. According to the Roman poet, Ovid, the Phoenix is a bird which lives for 500 years, at the end of which it builds itself a nest and dies. Out of its own body, a new Phoenix is born which also lives 500 years, and the cycle repeats itself. Like the Phoenix, the father in "Starlight" is reborn. Through his own son, he becomes a child again. He is renewed by his love for his son, and his son's love for him. The speaker, too, experiences renewal through his own memory of his childhood experience. We can infer that the speaker had probably reached a point of exhaustion in his own life, an exhaustion which led him to remember how his own father had made it through this same point. The final image of the sleeping boy underscores the cyclical and universal theme of change and transformation, as it suggests the child's own move into the adult world.

Topics for Further Study

- Brainstorm some memories of your own of incidents when you felt particularly close to a parent or family member. In a descriptive essay try to capture as much detail of the incident as possible, and explain why you think the memory has remained with you.

- Interview five middle-aged males who are childless about what motivates them in their daily lives, and interview five middle-aged fathers. In an essay, compare and contrast the answers. What conclusions can you draw from them?

- Think hard about your earliest memory that involved other people and then write down in as much detail as possible everything about that memory. Then ask the people who are a part of that memory if they have the same memory of the incident. Discuss what this exercise tells you about the reliability of your own memory, and what it tells you about why you remember some events and not others.

Innocence and Experience: The Human Condition

The movement from innocence to experience is integral to the human condition and continues to be represented in coming of age novels and other forms of literature. In the eighteenth century William Blake popularized the very phrase in his collection of poems, *Songs of Innocence and Experience*. In "Starlight" the speaker narrates his own movement from innocence to experience by detailing an incident from his past in which as a child he learns about the difficulties of adulthood. Though he may not have been conscious at the time of the incident that he was learning this, the speaker narrates the situation as such. Thus the incident becomes a watershed in the speaker's own story of his life. The narrator explores the relationship among time, memory, and consciousness in the poem's final image. We can take that image to mean that, quite literally the boy never awoke to "that world again" because the moment was gone. We can also take the image to mean that the distance in the narrator's life between that moment and his current telling of the story has been considerably shortened. Once he entered the world of experience, time itself sped up. He is telling this story in order to remind himself that renewal is possible, that entry into the adult world of experience, though it is also entry into the world of knowledge, does not necessarily mean that all hope is lost.

Language and Meaning

"Starlight" asks if language creates the human world or reflects it. That the child did not even know what the word "happy" means tells us that his world, for him, was still largely one undivided by adult categories and language. That his father not only knows the word but uses it as a gauge for meaning in his own and his child's life shows us the relationship between language and experience. Specifically, it shows us that entering the world of language means entering a world which is able to be differentiated, categorized, and measured. Language, in effect, constructs that world. It provides ways of seeing it, understanding it, and interpreting it. Acquiring language means acquiring self awareness and ways of consciously thinking about our own relation to things and people around us. The speaker's very recounting (or creating) of the event, which may or may not be mythical, also suggests the speaker's own paradoxical relation to language: although language is the "thing" which creates and names our world, it is (or can be) also our undoing.

Style

"Starlight" is a free verse poem, almost artless in its construction. The tone is conversational, as if the speaker is recounting the memory at an intimate gathering of friends. This tone is fitting for the anecdotal quality of the poem. Although Levine does not use much rhyme in this poem, he does use repetition, and light use of synaesthesia to give the memory a dreamlike character. Apposition, a grammatical construction in which a noun or a noun phrase is placed with another as an explanatory equivalent, is a form of repetition which Levine uses in the following lines:

> and the voice, my father's voice, is not
>
> his voice, but somehow thick and choked,

a voice I have not heard before, but

heard often since….

These lines thicken the description of the father's voice and readers have to slow down to digest them, just as the child in the poem has to slow down because he cannot understand the word "happy."

Contributing to the dreamlike quality of the memory is the quietly surreal imagery, as found in the lines, "The cigarette is gone, but I can smell / the tiredness that hangs on his breath." Describing one sense in terms of another or using one type of stimulation to evoke the sensation of another is known as synaesthesia and was a favorite technique of both the surrealists of the early twentieth century and some poets of the late twentieth-century, Levine among them, who at various points in their careers have been named "neo-surrealists." These poets include Mark Strand, James Wright, Robert Bly, Diane Wakowski, and others.

Historical Context

Levine wrote "Starlight" in the 1970s when he himself was close to fifty years old, much older, in fact, than the age of his own father in the poem. But there is nothing necessarily historically specific about "Starlight." The poem may or may not relate an actual experience or memory. It may be just a mythical anecdote meant to evoke an idea of fatherhood, or a point about reasons human beings find for continuing in their lives in the face of emotional or spiritual exhaustion. This type of poem—often short, anecdotal, first person, frequently confessional, vaguely surreal—was in vogue during the 70's in the United States. Some critics have called the poems resulting from this formula "McPoems," a pejorative designation used to underscore the seeming simplicity of their composition. Critics largely blamed university creative writing workshops and in particular M.F.A. programs for helping to produce so much of this type of writing. Levine himself taught in such a program for years, first at California State University at Fresno, and then at New York University.

The idea of "voice" became increasingly important in American poetry of the 1970's, and according to some critics underscored the growing proliferation and popularity of the poetry reading, the return to narrative poetry, and the emergence of the importance of personality in poetry. Voice-

Compare & Contrast

- **1977:** David Berkowitz, also known as the "Son of Sam" and the .44 caliber killer, receives life imprisonment for six murders he committed before his arrest in August.

  1999: Spike Lee makes a movie, *Summer of Sam,* about the summer of 1977 in New York City and the fearful grip that Berkowitz had on the City.

- **1978:** Earthquakes rock Greece, Japan, Mexico, Iran, and Central Europe.

  1999: A massive earthquake rocks Turkey. More than 12,000 people die.

- **1977:** George Lucas's film *Star Wars* is released and breaks all box-office records.

  1999: The prequel to the Star Wars Trilogy, *The Phantom Menace,* is released. Calling it a "cultural holiday," many companies give their workers the day off on the day the movie opens.

- **1979:** The American public's fear of a nuclear meltdown increases after an accident at Pennsylvania's Three Mile Island Nuclear plant.

  Today: Largely because of the American public's continuing distrust of nuclear power, the number of nuclear reactors working in the U.S. today is 104, down from 112 in 1990.

- **1978:** The world's first test-tube baby, Louise Brown, is born in Britain.

  Today: After having successfully cloned a sheep, scientists are now exploring ways to clone human beings.

based poetry frequently focused on the authenticity of individual experiences, and the degree to which the poem succeeded rested on the degree to which those experiences were believed. The diversity of experience, then, underwrote the explosion of poetry during the last twenty years by groups previously underrepresented. One can now easily find anthologies and single-authored collections of self-described lesbian poetry, Czechoslovak-American poetry, Native-American poetry, Sado-Masochistic poetry, etc. More than merely thematic groupings, these books rely on the very identity of the authors to establish the category under which the poems are published.

The weariness his father feels in the poem could very well be the weariness of work, a common theme in Levine's poetry. Levine's father emigrated to the United States from Russia and worked in Detroit his whole life, and Levine himself worked in the city's automobile factories while attending university at Wayne State in Detroit. Many of his poems describe the struggle of blue collar urban workers to survive while keeping their families intact. When Levine wrote "Starlight" in the late 70's, the face of labor in America was dramatically changing. In 1977 more than two thirds of Americans worked in service industries. Technology, particularly computer technology, made information-based industries such as health, finance, government, and communications, more efficient, and lucrative, and many young professionals flocked to them. These young urban professionals, called "yuppies," were voracious consumers of technology as well, buying videocassette recorders and cameras, personal computers, answering machines, and the like. Ironically, Many of these young professionals had been a part of the rebellious youth culture of the 60's and early 70's which had eschewed excessive material consumption and spoke out against the intrusion of big business into our lives.

Critical Overview

Ashes: Poems Old and New, the collection of poems in which "Starlight" appeared, received, along with *7 Years from Somewhere,* the National Book Critics Circle Award and the American Book Award in 1979 and 1980, and was widely hailed as Levine's best book to date. Reviewing *Ashes* in *Soho Weekly News,* Rochelle Ratner writes that

"The remnants of his working-class childhood carry through an identification with the workers, the oppressed, he meets now, as if in a romanticized attempt to call back his childhood." Commenting on Levine's "great compassion and tenderness," Ralph Mills points out that poems about the poet's father frame the book, and claims that Levine "frequently views himself under various forms as dying and being reborn within the compass of an individual lifetime." Such a volatile view of the self intrigues many critics, who, like William Matthews, see in Levine's intensely emotional poems "a sense of time different than that of most lyric poetry." Commenting on "Starlight," Matthews writes "How rapidly Levine can move, the way our inner lives move, from truculence to tenderness, and back, and back and forth." He manages those movements both when writing about his family and writing about others for whom he feels empathy. In a New York Times Book Review article, Herbert Leibowitz says that in *Ashes* "Levine has returned again and again in his poems to the lives of factory workers trapped by poverty and the drudgery of the assembly line, which breaks the body and scars the spirit." Levine also has his detractors, many of them criticizing his seemingly artless style. A representative detractor is Helen Vendler, who writes: "Often Levine seems to me simply a memoir-writer in prose who chops up his reminiscent paragraphs into short lines." Vendler also attacks Levine's realistic bent, saying that, "He believes, as a poet, only in what he can see and touch."

Criticism

Jonathan N. Barron

Jonathan N. Barron is associate professor of English at the University of Southern Mississippi. The author of numerous articles, he has edited several books of essays on poetry and is editor of The Robert Frost Review. *In the following essay, Barron shows how "Starlight" explores the complex emotion that is happiness and, in so doing, risks being too sentimental and nostalgic. Barron judges the poem successful because of the way it uses the techniques of an early twentieth-century free-verse poetic movement called Imagism.*

In her textbook *Poems Poets Poetry: An Introduction and Anthology* (1997), Helen Vendler, professor of poetry at Harvard, singles out one distinctive element common to the best poetry everywhere. She tells her readers that good poetry "manages to avoid cliche." What Vendler means is that good poetry is determined to combat both the language of cliche as well as the attitudes, sentiments, and thoughts that have also become cliche. Poetry, in short, is that which is surprising, fresh, new, and unusual both in terms of the language and words used and in terms of the ideas, attitudes, feelings, and thoughts expressed by those words.

One of the most persistent set of cliches that Vendler has in mind takes the name "sentimentality." The sentimental poem, as a type of poetry, has only one goal: to provoke the reader to some intense, already familiar, easily recognizable emotion. Rather than upset the reader with uncomfortable, surprising, even dangerous thoughts and so provoke frightening emotions, the sentimental poem wishes to comfort the reader by reminding her or him that other people too have the same problems. Sentimental poetry, then, depends on cliche. At their best such poems want to comfort and ease the reader; at their worst, they merely provoke an emotion for no other purpose than entertainment and "cheap thrills." Not surprisingly, then, a poetry whose goal is to produce an emotion in the reader and render in familiar language easily recognizable emotions often makes use of the language of cliche: long familiar images and metaphors that provoke no surprise whatsoever.

Such sentimental poetry is today as popular and widespread as ever. One finds it in nearly every greeting card, and in the works of such "best-selling" poets as Susan Polis Schutz. In the first decade of the twentieth-century, such poetry was equally present and even more popular. Its popularity eventually provoked a group of Modernist poets, particularly T. S. Eliot and Ezra Pound, to establish a counter-poetics, a movement dedicated to nothing less than the eradication of sentimentality from all "good" poetry. Henceforth, they argued, one would determine a poem's value by virtue of its ability to war against sentimental themes and language. For the most part, the past 90 years have endorsed this anti-sentimental standard. Today, in fact, one usually measures the artistic value of a poem by assessing its anti-sentimental themes and language.

Given this general disdain for sentimentalism in poetry, Philip Levine's poetry is particularly intriguing. As the contemporary American poet Dave Smith once said of Levine's work: he "risks the maudlin, the sentimental, the banal." Rather than go to war against sentimentality, in other words, Philip Levine actively courts it. He welcomes it into his poetry, and takes the risk that those schooled in the anti-sentimental attitudes of Modernist poetry might well condemn him for it. In fact, the occasion for Dave Smith's praise was his review of *Seven Years from Somewhere* (1979), the collection that contains, among other fine poems, "Starlight."

What makes "Starlight" so interesting is that it plays the sentimental, even maudlin theme of the love of a child for his father and of a father for his son against the flat, anti-sentimental language and techniques of Modernist Imagism. Imagism was the name given to the first specific, self-declared Anglo-American poetic movement devoting itself to anti-sentimentalism. Announced to the literary community in 1913 in a now famous manifesto printed in *Poetry* magazine (a magazine still flourishing today), Imagism called on poets to turn their attention to the precise, concrete visible image rendered in poetry. Rather than focus on meter, and the music of language created by a traditional metrical system, the Imagists argued instead for a free-verse line, a rhythm built out of breath units: as Ezra Pound phrased it: "compose in the sequence of the musical phrase not in the sequence of the metronome." This new free-verse music would help eradicate what Pound referred to as the sticky "cream puffs" of an all too lush and all too musical sentimental poetry. Sixty-six years later, one can measure the success of Imagism merely by reading poems like Levine's "Starlight," which tell their story entirely through a set of precisely rendered visible images in mostly free-verse lines. In its 31 lines, "Starlight" paints an extremely visible vignette of a summer evening between a tired working class father and his four year old son. So precisely drawn is the scene that we see it as if the words themselves did not matter.

This attention to the image, to what we see, is a particular point of pride for the craftsman Levine. In a much cited comment from an interview he gave in the poetry journal *Parnassus*, Levine went so far as to say that in his "ideal poem … no words are noticed. You look through them." In this comment, made in 1978 when he was composing the poems of the volume containing "Starlight," Levine explains that his goal in crafting his work is to make the reader see the characters, the scene, the event rather than the words that portray the event. This goal is common to the Imagist tradition of using free-verse lines to render descriptions with exactitude.

With this in mind, then, look again at the first seven lines of "Starlight." Combined they account

What Do I Read Next?

- *Don't Ask,* a collection of interviews with Levine, was published by the University of Michigan Press in 1981. These interviews are at times enlightening, funny, troubling, and annoying. Levine talks about the inspiration behind many of his poems, about his politics, and about his childhood in Detroit, Michigan.

- Perhaps Levine's best-known book, *They Feed They Lion* was published in 1972. The poems in this collection waver between celebration and despair, showing Levine to be adept at crafting art from the most disparate of experiences. Included in this collection are some of Levine's most popular poems about the working class of Detroit, Michigan.

- For an historical look at how Levine's poetry has been received, read Christopher Buckley's collection of criticism and reviews on Levine's poetry, *On the Poetry of Philip Levine: Stranger to Nothing,* published in 1991 by the University of Michigan Press.

- Levine's 1994 collection of essays, *The Bread of Time: Toward an Autobiography,* is a collection of disparate essays about poetry, work, and the author's family life in Detroit. These essays are helpful in understanding Levine's thinking about poetics and poetry.

for three and a half sentences. Also, each line breaks when the image concludes. In other words, the rule of thumb for the rhythm of the line breaks is a visual one: new image, new line. This rule, too, is in keeping with Imagist tradition. And, like the Imagist poetry of the 1910s, it is virtually impossible to paraphrase the poem without at once reciting it. The images are rendered so exactly that to say what they reveal is quite literally to repeat the poem word for word. Nonetheless, what are the images that stand out in these seven lines? A man standing on the porch of a house, the speaker's father; the speaker himself as a sleepy four year old;

> *A little four-year-old, already so young, loses his innocence as, through a moment of happiness, he discovers the reality of his father's life of pain, a reality his father wishes to hide, and protect him from, a reality the stars blinkingly acknowledge."*

the glowing tip of a cigarette; and the red moon of late summer.

Ironically, these images, in conjunction with the title, create exactly the kind of atmosphere, mood, and thematic message that Imagism was designed to eradicate once and for all from poetry. For in these opening lines, Levine establishes what the poet Dave Smith rightly refers to as a nearly "maudlin" connection between father and son in the glowing dusk of summer. The emotional core of the poem is as familiar as the filial relationship. There is no surprise here in terms of what the poem is saying. Rather, the surprise comes from how the poem says it. Rather than resort to poetic cliche about a "blood red moon" or the "dying embers of summer," Levine merely depicts the "glow of his cigarette." If readers are reminded of such cliches they will do well to note that they do not come from the poem's language.

As an anti-sentimental counter to his sentimental theme, his decidedly flat descriptive language has also gotten Levine into much trouble. Such prose-like, "unpoetic" language is regularly cited as poor poetry because it asks readers to attend to character and story detail (classic issues for prose) rather than to the words themselves (the classic concern of poetry). For nearly twenty years now, critics have condemned Levine as much for ignoring the music of language in poetry as for being too sentimental in his themes. Those who attack his diction—his language use—claim that in any given poem he has merely chopped up a good story into arbitrary lines. This criticism, however,

ignores or, worse, is blind to Levine's heritage in Imagism. For, as already indicated, there is nothing arbitrary about his line breaks. But, more importantly, the prose-like language is poetically, stylistically necessary because it acts as an antidote, a counter, to the sentimental themes Levine's poetry so often address.

In "Starlight," for example, Levine presses the sentimental expression of love between father and son so far that he sends the poetic theme into the even more sickly sweet land of nostalgia. Already risking the loss of respect from readers trained in anti-sentimentality, Levine, through the verb tense and other clues, pushes this poem's story over the edge of a certain kind of respectability when he makes it clear that this is a nostalgic memory and not just a "you are there" anecdote. In the poem, it is clear that the speaker, the child, is now himself a grown man, possibly much older in the telling of the poem than even his father was in the scene depicted. In other words, not only does Levine take the risk of writing a sentimental poem but he also locates the sentiment in nostalgia: a double-dare, and a major risk for a poet as much today as in 1979.

The risk pays off, and the poem is a triumph of art and wisdom. It is the highest expression of what poetry does best. What makes a poem like "Starlight," then, both a triumph and an example of great technical skill? Simply stated, by line 13, the poem takes a dramatic turn so that it does surprise, and does, paradoxically, war against the cliche sentiments it appears in the first 12 lines to endorse. The opening lines of the poem make one think that this will be another example of a poem saying little more than "those were the good old days" and "gee, how I miss my dad." While those feelings are no doubt powerful and true, in poetry they can too often become merely banal tricks that do little more than the poetic equivalent of a bad vaudeville performer saying "let me make you cry by merely tapping into feelings you yourself have long had." Levine, however, only seems to resort to these tricks. By the eighth line, just as the poem has traveled into the twin realms of sentiment and nostalgia, he reverses our expectations and calls into question the easy emotion he made possible with his stark images of moon, cigarette, father, son, porch. By line eight, the poem's sentimentality itself is called into question.

When the father asks the son if he is happy, he is, by extension, calling into question the very purpose of the poem. Is the poem just an exercise in nostalgic memory? Is it just a magic act designed to make the poet and his audience feel better? Or, instead, is the poem questioning the very heart of sentimentalism itself, the very idea of "happiness"?

In this question, in other words, the father speaks from his own sad life experience recognizing that his four year old son's future will yield not more joy but only the grim reality of future pain. In the telling of the poem, that four year old, himself an older man, realizes how right his father was about that future pain and, also, how wrong. At the time, when he was four, he did not understand this very complicated adult emotion called "happiness": few, if any, four year olds could or even should. But rather than meditate poetically on that adult emotion, Levine, instead, continues the father-son tale by reporting to us the gesture his father makes after asking his son if he is happy. After the father presses his fingers into his son's face, after the son smells the "cigarettes and sadness," a single line offers what amounts to a very mysterious conclusion. So mysterious is this line that it could very well have concluded the poem: "He has found nothing, and he smiles." Had the poem ended here, the images in conjunction with the precise, flat language would have established an ironic dance between nostalgia and pain, sentiment and wisdom. As it is written, however, the line comes a little more than half way into the poem. And its placement has the effect of reversing the anti-sentimental direction of the poem that had begun in line eight. For this weird smile, we are told, comes from finding nothing in his son's expression. What happens next is both unexpectedly exuberant and wonderfully strange.

The smile brings us back into the sentimental terrain Levine has been both courting and challenging:

Then he lifts me on his shoulder,
and now I too am there among the stars,
as tall as he. Are you happy? I say.
He nods in answer, Yes! oh yes! oh yes!

Here, the father, seeing in his son's future a grim destiny of more of the same hard luck he has had in his own life, finds a way to combat such pessimism by putting his son on his shoulder. To combat the future he foresees, the father celebrates their life together now, this evening, on the porch. When the son asks his father the same question, "are you happy?" he may not have any idea of the full implications, the sadness latent in that question. But what this scene tells us is that, in answer to his father's question, right now the son is happy. And so too is the father. Are the words, "Yes! oh yes! oh yes!" actually spoken? Notice they have no

quotation marks. I believe these words are what the father's gesture, his nodding head, imply: they are not what he says. The fact that his joy is implied but not actually spoken explains the concluding sentence of the poem: a sentence consisting of the final eight lines.

In this conclusion, Levine speaks for his father, and for himself now that he is an older man. In these final lines, he explains what the entire scene on the porch must have meant to his father then and to himself now.

And in that new voice, he says nothing,
holding my head tight against his head,
his eyes closed up against the starlight,
as though those tiny blinking eyes
of light might find a tall, gaunt child
holding his child against the promises
of autumn, until the boy slept
never to waken in that world again.

First, notice that the father actually says "nothing." This is the second time that "nothing" resonates with deep meaning in this poem. This time, as with its first usage, the word refers to the fact that the father's joy, and sheer pleasure in this moment with his son are beyond words. In the end, poetry itself takes us to that realm beyond words. The final sentence, these eight lines, is in fact a beautiful and precise image. The father holds his son's head and together they look at the stars. Notice, though, that Levine changes the perspective at precisely this point.

Just as he brings father and son together in a moment of pure joy, he changes the scene entirely and gives us the stars' view of it. Referring to the starlight as "tiny blinking eyes" Levine tells us that what, looking down, these stars must have seen was two children. The father, no matter how old, is still just a child to the stars' billion year history. When returned to his innocent state as a child—a child of nature—the father becomes far more understandable. His sadness has to do with protection. The father hopes to be able to protect his child from "the promises / of autumn," from the certainty of a fall from innocence and the inevitable process of death and dying. The tragic fact of the poem, however, is that while happiness is discovered here, the son also, from that moment on, lost his own innocence, his own ignorance as to the complexity of this strange thing called "happiness."

In the end, then, Levine's tender poem of a father and a son, chock full of potentially smarmy sentimental images like hugs, stars, and moonlight, becomes a powerfully wise work of art. A little four-year-old, already so young, loses his innocence as, through a moment of happiness, he discovers the reality of his father's life of pain, a reality his father wishes to hide, and protect him from, a reality the stars blinkingly acknowledge.

Source: Jonathan N. Barron, in an essay for *Poetry for Students,* Gale Group, 2000.

Pamela Steed Hill

Pamela Steed Hill is the author of a collection of poetry, In Praise of Motels, *and has had poems published in more than 90 journals and magazines. She is an associate editor for* University Communications *at Ohio State University. In the following essay, Hill points how this poem quickly takes us from a summer scene of peaceful tranquility between father and son to one of desperation and fear, forcing a turning point in the boy's young life and leaving his father clinging to a world he knows must end.*

Reading Philip Levine's "Starlight" is somewhat like reading an entry from the poet's diary, had he been keeping one at the age of four. Much of Levine's poetry is autobiographical, and many of his poems address the loss of his father when he was a young boy and the subsequent anger, grief, sorrow, and sense of abandonment. "Starlight" is a "father" poem that occurs before the parent dies, and, therefore, no mention of the traumatic event actually appears in the poem. The child's thoughts are revealed through the voice of the now-grown man who may allude to his father's eminent death only in the last line. But we understand throughout that a heaviness pervades the scene described in the poem, and even if we have not read enough of Philip Levine's work or do not know about the actual death of his father, we still sense that "Starlight" portrays an ill-fated moment marking a child's entrance into the real world—a world full mostly of hardship, brutality, and sadness.

The poem is a relatively short one, written in free verse and told in the present tense. By using the present tense, Levine provides us greater immediacy to what is going on in the child's mind as well as on the porch where he and his father stand "in the warm evening." The poet's simple description and clear language take us directly to the setting: it is nighttime, and a tired four-year-old boy is outside with his father looking up at the stars. But what the child sees when he looks up is father's "head among the stars, / the glow of his cigarette, redder / than the summer moon riding / low over the old neighborhood." (The "old neighborhood" is in Detroit, where Levine grew up and

which would become the source of inspiration for many of his "working class" poems.) The scene seems peaceful at this point—a father and son enjoy a quiet summer evening beneath the stars. Serenity is short-lived, however, for the father soon brings up a subject that both confuses and, ironically, saddens the boy: the question of happiness.

Line 9 is a turning point in the poem, moving the speaker and his subject from a setting of contentment to one of uncertainty. Very often the question, "Are you happy?" makes the person being asked uneasy at best and in some cases defensive and cynical. It's a difficult question to give a blanket "yes" or "no" answer to because so many factors play into what being happy really means. Levine tells us that even a four-year-old knows that. The boy's thought on the matter is simply, "I cannot answer," and so he doesn't. Eventually, in line 22, he will offer a response that only turns the question around to the father: "Are you happy? I say." In between lines 9 and 22, though, we learn more about the relationship between the father and son and more about the pending gloom that hangs over them and that ultimately will separate them for good.

The speaker tells us that he does not understand the word "happy" and, more importantly, that his father's voice in asking it "… is not / his voice, but somehow thick and choked, / a voice I have not heard before, but / heard often since." This indicates that he now looks back on that night as a discovery of sorts—not one of enjoyment, but one that introduces the child to his father's fears and his father's sorrow. The parent does not ask the boy if he's happy in a cheerful voice and a lighthearted manner, but rather he speaks as though he is fighting back tears. Until then, the child had not heard (or, at least, had not noticed) distress and suffering in his father's voice, but the adult speaker has by now heard it countless times. We have to assume that since his father would die a year after this poem takes place, the "thick and choked" voice that the narrator keeps hearing is not only his father's. Rather, it is a collective "human" voice, including his own that permeates human existence and exposes our pain and sorrow. By hearing it in a parent's voice, children are thrust into the real world where the comfort and security they've always known are suddenly no longer steadfast.

After asking his son if he's happy and getting no immediate response, the father "… bends and passes / a thumb beneath each of my eyes." In other words, he is checking to see if the boy is shedding tears, and the father is glad to learn that he is not: "He has found nothing, and he smiles / and holds my head with both his hands." Perhaps it is this demonstration of pure innocence and naivete in his son—the boy doesn't "know enough" to be sad that allows the father to answer the question of happiness in a fairly exuberant way: "Yes! oh yes! oh yes!" But it is still a forced exuberance, spoken to try to convince not only his son but himself that he really is happy. Now holding the boy in his arms, their heads pressed together, the father "says nothing" and yet he says nothing "in that new voice." Since the son has heard it once, he knows it is there within his father, and he will never erase the memory of it even during times of silence.

By the end of the poem, the scene has changed from one of peaceful serenity to one of a desperate man clinging to his son with "his eyes closed up against" the same starlight that he had been merely gazing upon earlier. Something has altered the father's mood and, therefore, the young son's, and it is most likely the fact that the boy cannot answer whether he is happy. The father understands the irrelevance of even trying to answer for he knows that the warmth of summer will give way to the chill of autumn ("… holding his child against the promises / of autumn …"), that young, innocent boys will become hardened, sorrowful men, and that there is nothing he can do to stop either. The speaker believes his father saw himself as a child as well as the boy he held in his arms—or at least "a tall, gaunt child" who would like to escape back into a safe, secure fantasy world and to keep his son there with him. He would like to keep the boy asleep because he knows that when he wakes, it will never be "in that world again."

We may look at the last line of the poem as an allusion to Levine's father's pending death because we know that the loss had a profound effect on the poet. It did indeed force him into a new world and forever strip him of the feeling of security he had when his father was living. Of course, given the benefit of hindsight, we know what will happen to the boy in the poem even though he is completely unaware of it at the time. This is most often the case in Levine's work—he speaks with the voice of one who knows although his subject may not be so wary. In *Kayak,* critic Mark Jarman states that "One of the powerful, unifying factors is that in all the poems [in the collection called *1933*], Levine's voice, even when remembering his perceptions as a child, is that of an adult, an adult who has not only not forgotten what it is like to be a child, but how at five years old … one is becoming an adult: the process is one of loss, in this book intensified by the loss of a father…."

> … 'Starlight' portrays an ill-fated moment marking a child's entrance into the real world—a world full mostly of hardship, brutality, and sadness."

"Starlight" has not been singled out by critics nearly as often as Levine's more popular, highly anthologized works such as "They Feed They Lion," "Not This Pig," and "Animals Are Passing from Our Lives." This poem appears in the 1979 collection entitled *Ashes,* which contains 13 poems from an earlier book as well as 19 new ones, including "Starlight." The poem has been compared, however, to those in Levine's 1974 publication of *1933,* a book dealing nearly entirely with the loss of his father and so named because it was the year he passed away. While some of the father poems denote feelings of anger and abandonment, especially the early ones, just as many soften into compassion and a quiet sadness on the part of their narrator. In an *Ohio Review* article, poet and critic William Matthews contrasts the endings of "Starlight" and a poem called "Father," also contained in *Ashes.* The latter poem's last four lines are: "I find you / in these tears, few, / useless and here at last. / Don't come back." There is a striking difference between the sentiment portrayed here and that found in "Starlight." Matthews points out "How rapidly Levine can move, the way our inner lives move, from truculence to tenderness, and back, and back and forth." And in a *Margins* article, critic Christopher Buckley states that some of the father poems end "on an emotional tone of solitude, abandonment, personal anguish, but there is no anger or defiance at the world. Levine is not angry with his father for his absence but rather offers us a vision of a father we can cherish with him."

Throughout his career, Philip Levine has paid poetic homage to the world's downtrodden—the poor, the victims of racism, those persecuted by politics and wars. Though the poet would probably claim a personal happiness with his wife and children and now grandchildren, he does not shy away from displaying his contempt for the world that most of us live in, a world of hard work, low pay, and often violence born of frustration and resentment. Levine contends that all "normal" people come to that inevitable realization at some point in their lives, sometimes by way of a traumatic event. For him, we may obviously assume it was the death of his father, and yet a poem like "Starlight" indicates another possibility. Perhaps even before the father's death, the young boy was hurled into the harsh realities of a grown-up world on a peaceful summer night when he first heard something unsettling, something mournful, in his parent's voice. Although he could not know that a year later his father would be dead, he did somehow realize that his world was changing and that "happiness" was not likely to follow him into the new one.

Source: Pamela Steed Hill, in an essay for *Poetry for Students,* Gale Group, 2000.

Chris Semansky

Chris Semansky's most recent collection of poems, Blindsided, *published by 26 Books of Portland, Oregon, has been nominated for an Oregon Book Award. In the following essay, Semansky explores thematic issues of emotional survival in three of Philip Levine's "father" poems in his collection,* Ashes: Poems New and Old.

Philip Levine has written a number of poems describing his attempts to come to grips with his father's memory. In *Ashes,* his 1979 award-winning collection of poems, Levine begins both sections with poems about his father and also ends the book with a poem about him. Together, these poems provide a complex portrait of a man looking for ways to behave in the world, for ways to survive the crush of time.

The opening poem, "Father," describes a nightmarish industrial landscape in which a son searches for his father, both as a child and later as an adult.

> The long lines of diesels
> groan towards evening
> carrying off the breath
> of the living.
> The face of your house
> is black,
> it is your face, black
> and fire bombed
> in the first street wars,
> a black tooth planted in the earth
> of Michigan
> and bearing nothing,
> and the earth is black,
> sick on used oils.

The imagery of war and apocalypse is fitting for a poem about loss, and more so when we understand that Levine's father, a Russian Jew, fought with the British during World War I, and later emigrated to Detroit, Michigan, a heavily industrialized working-class city of automobile factories. The image of the poet as a loss-stricken child permeates Levine's poems, as does the movement between personal and public representations of self, his and others. In "Father" the speaker moves between the past and the present to show how managing grief makes us who we are. Levine's father died when he was a young boy and, presumably, it is his absence that he describes when he writes

> I waited
> at windows the rain streaked
> and no one told me.

It is only later as an adult, and in the act of writing about his father, that he achieves any resolution to his grief.

> I found you whole
> toward the autumn of my 43rd year
> in this chair beside
> a mason jar of dried zinnias
> and I turned away.
> I find you
> in these tears, few,
> useless and here at last.
> Don't come back.

The starkness and seeming anger towards his father in this poem is tempered by his sentimental memories in both "Starlight" and "Lost and Found," the book's last poem. More anecdotal and conventionally realistic than "Father," "Starlight," a story with a moral, borders on the sappy in its treatment of the father and son relationship. In this poem the father learns from the son, just as the speaker of the poem learns from his own father, albeit years after his father has died. Presumably, the speaker has reached a point in his life that the father in the poem had also reached in his. But instead of being renewed by his own children, the speaker is renewed through a memory of his father. This type of renewal is based not on innocence, as is the father's in the poem, but on the very knowledge that experience brings. The speaker, as father *and* son, has learned how to incorporate the loss of his own father into his life and how to draw emotional sustenance from his memory in order to keep going. The concluding image of the poem, like many of Levine's conclusions, is ambiguous enough to rescue the poem from syrupy emotionality. After finding joy in the company and love of his four-year-old boy, the father proclaims his happiness:

And in that new voice says nothing,
holding my head tight against his head,
his eyes closed up against the starlight,
as though those tiny blinking eyes
of light mind find a tall, gaunt child
holding his child against the promises
of autumn, until the boy slept
never to waken in that world again.

The child's implied and symbolic entry into the adult world of language marks the end of innocence. His father, trying to gauge the meaning of his own life learns that "happiness" resides not in the self but in relation to others, in this case his own family. The lesson the boy, who becomes a poet, learns is that language lies, but it is all that we have. What ostensibly begins as a poem about the emotional life of the poet's father turns out to be a poem about the poet's own emotional life, about his ability to salvage meaning from the past and to use it as ballast for and in the future. Read this way, the "promises / of autumn" becomes ironic, if we take "autumn" to mean the late-middle part of one's life. The gesture of holding his boy "against" these "promises" is actually a gesture of protecting the boy from all he does not know, but will discover as he grows up. Like much of Levine's poetry, however, "Starlight" exists somewhere between confession and myth. Very few of us have the capacity to remember with such detail events from our lives when we were four years old. More likely the poem sprang from an impulse to put his volatile emotional life into narrative form.

In the book's final poem, appropriately titled "Lost and Found," the search for his father that the poet starts somewhat angrily in the opening poem, concludes. Back in the land of symbolic mythology, the poem presents "a boy lost in a huge city, / a boy in search of someone / lost and not returning …" There is no mistaking that this boy is a version of the poet's self. Gone are the realistic details tying the past to place, as in "Starlight's" domestic scene of the speaker's childhood house. Those details are replaced by the more abstract and symbolic language of a quiet spirituality. The speaker makes peace with the memory of his father, not through recounting an incident of childhood bonding, but through the realization that his loss is a universal one, part of the cycle of death and birth common to human experience.

… I have
come home from being lost,
home to a name I could accept,
a face that saw all I saw
and broke in a dark room against

> *What ostensibly begins as a poem about the emotional life of the poet's father turns out to be a poem about the poet's own emotional life, about his ability to salvage meaning from the past and to use it as ballast for and in the future."*

a wall that heard all my secrets
and gave nothing back. Now he
is home, the one I searched for.

The found father is as much a recognition of how the father has lived on *inside* the son as it is an acceptance of representative memories. Because the speaker-son has been able to embrace the father in himself, he has also been able to accept the fact that the dead always live on. He has now learned to give them their due.

The day is here, and it will last
forever or until the sun fails
and the birds are once again
hidden and moaning, but for now
the lost are found. The sun
has cleared the trees, the wind
risen, and we, father and child
hand in hand, the living and
the dead, are entering the world.

This final image is one of reunion and recovery. Based in the universal and public realm of nature, it is free of the pettiness of personal loss, the "little deaths" that mar all of our individual lives. By locating the context of his loss (and recovery) in the natural world, the speaker recognizes that his own pain is part of life's process, and that he is not alone in it. Making peace with his father, the poet has finally made peace with himself.

Source: Chris Semansky, in an essay for *Poetry for Students,* Gale Group, 2000.

Alice Van Wart

Alice Van Wart teaches literature and writing in the Department of Continuing Education at the

> *The poet's description of his father's actions as he remembers them on that night are immediate and physical, as if there were occurring in the present moment.*"

University of Toronto. She has published two books of poetry and has written articles on modern and contemporary literature. In the following essay, Van Wart explains how Levine "uses a complex dual perspective" to look back upon an event from his childhood.

Philip Levine has written 17 books of poetry, studied with John Berryman and Yvor Winters, held a fellowship in poetry at Stanford University, won numerous prizes including the Pulitzer and the National Book award, and earned his living as a college professor from the late 1950s to his retirement. Yet his roots remain firmly in his pre-academic and literary life. Born in 1928 into a lower middle-class Jewish family, Levine worked as a manual laborer in Detroit where he formed a strong identification with the men and women he met as an industrial worker. His work often depicts the bleak, dirty industrial cityscape of his childhood.

Levine's poetry presents a wide range of themes, particularly about the contemporary experiences of the common man and about those people who have left their hometowns for work in industrial cities such as Detroit, where they find themselves out of place and isolated. His poems provide an honest exploration of human life and its complexity, conveying a wide range of emotions from pity to condemnation, anger, awe, and lamentation. He often forces the reader to confront the unendurable and the horror that humankind has created. Writing in *Contemporary American Poetry,* A. Polin Jr. noted that Levine's poetry offers a "seemingly contradictory range of emotional, moral, and often profoundly religious responses to the horror and the beauty in the word around him."

Levine is a master of both poetic form and voice. One of his gifts lies in telling stories in dramatic and narrative voices. More recently Levine has returned to his past for his subject matter, employing free verse, a narrative style, and the use a colloquial language to present his proletarian, often autobiographical subjects. "Starlight" is such a poem. Written in free verse it deals with an incident in his childhood that integrally links the past to the present and its theme to its technique.

In "Starlight" Levine's uses free verse, a colloquial voice, and loose rhythms to create a narrative style, while he employs image and enjambment, the running together of the sense and syntax of one line with the next, to convey the complexity of the poet's private meditation as he watches his father on his porch smoking a cigarette. While watching his father, he remembers another time on a summer's evening when he was a child. Recalling the incident from the past, the poet creates a dual perspective that shows his growing awareness of the connection between the past and present and between father and son.

Levine begins his poem informally. He watches his father smoke "on the porch of my first house." The house, we assume, is the poet's house. However, in the third line the poet announces: "I am four years old and growing tired." The jump back in time suggests the house could also be the poet's first house as a child. The ambiguity between present and past time continues in line four when the poet says, "I see his head among the stars, the glow of his cigarette." The reference to the image of the "glow of his cigarette, redder / than the summer moon" is also ambiguous as to whether the poet is referring to his father in the present moment or in the past. The enjambment between lines five and six clarifies the ambiguity by linking past and present time. The enjambment of lines six and seven moves the time into the past by clarifying that the moon is "riding / low over the old neighborhood."

The use of the present tense to relate the past event creates a sense of immediacy, collapsing past time with the present as the poet relates the incident that marked the end of his childhood. Standing alone with his father under the light of the summer stars the poet's father unexpectedly asks his child, "Are you happy?" The child is confused by the question, saying, "I cannot answer / I do not really understand the word." His confusion is further enhanced by his father's voice, which the poet says "is not his voice, but somehow thick and choked." The child's response, however, merges into the adult's when the poet says, it was "a voice I have not heard before, but / heard often sense." The sound in the father's voice is new to the child, but the adult knows it well.

The poet's description of his father's actions as he remembers them on that night are immediate and physical, as if there were occurring in the present moment. He tells us his father "bends and passes a thumb beneath each of my eyes," and then "he smiles and holds my head with both his hands" before he "lifts me to his shoulders." Here Levine's use of kinetic diction creates both the physical sense of the moment and a sense of the child's feelings as he is lifted onto his father's shoulders. At the same time the poet conveys his feelings as he recalls the event. He remembers being aware that "the cigarette [was] gone" and that he could "smell / the tiredness that hangs on his breath."

While Levine creates the child's response to his father's physical presence as the father "lifts him to his shoulder," he also shows the more specific awareness of the adult looking back. In line eighteen when the poet says, "he has found nothing," he is referring both to his father's touch beneath his eyes, where there is nothing to find, and to a more general fact about his father's life. The adult suggests a larger loss on the part of his father, something in his life he never found. The grown son is aware of something about his father he could not have known as a child.

On his father's shoulder the child finds himself "among the stars." The repetition of this image from line four again colapses past and present time. In line four the child sees his father's head "among the stars"; in line twenty-one sitting on his shoulder, he says, "and now I too am among the stars / as tall as he." The poet's description of the child feeling "as tall as he" goes beyond the child's awareness and suggests the father and the child are now on an equal footing.

Feeling as tall as his father the child asks his father the same question his father has just asked him. He asks him if he is happy. His father's response is "to nod[s] vigorously, "Yes! oh yes!" The child is aware that in "that new voice he says nothing." The "new" voice is the voice the child has just heard his father use, which sounds "thick and choked." The child is not able to understand his father's emotions at the moment, only that he had held his "head tight against his head / his eyes closed up against the starlight."

The poet's description of his father closing his eyes "as though those tiny blinking eyes / might find a tall, gaunt child / holding his child against the promises of autumn," returns the poet to the

present moment and the reader to his adult consciousness. The poet now understands his father's gesture. He expresses this awareness in his association of autumn with maturity and the relinquishing of power. He realizes his father had wanted to hold on to his child and his childhood a little longer. He had wanted to keep him for a while longer from becoming the "tall gaunt child / holding his child." "The tall gaunt child" is the poet, who is now a a father, himself. Because he too is a father he understands what he could not have known as a child, the night his father held him under the starlight, the night he now sees as the end of his childhood.

Only in retrospect is the poet able to understand the significance of the night. Having fallen asleep on his father's shoulders, the poet says he was "never to waken in that world again." The night was the beginning of his awareness of his father as a fallible being, someone outside himself, capable of intense feeling, perhaps not so god-like as he had believed. It is an understated moment: the adult sees his father, the man smoking on the porch, as he is, aware at the same time that he is now the father.

Despite its surface simplicity "Starlight" uses a complex dual perspective to show the poet's empathetic understanding of an event from his childhood. The poem's lack of formal artifice, its colloquial voice, and the use of image and enjambment convey an alternating sense of past and present and the merging of the two times in the consciousness of the narrator as he silently meditates on the nature of fatherhood and the connection between past and present.

Source: Alice Van Wart, in an essay for *Poetry for Students*, Gale Group, 2000.

Sources

Bedient, Calvin, An Interview with Philip Levine, in *Parnassus*, Vol. 6, No. 2, 1978, pp. 40–51.

Buckley, Christopher, "The Extension of Method in Philip Levine's *1933*," *Margins*, September 10, 1975, pp. 62-63, 194.

Buckley, Christopher, ed., *On the Poetry of Philip Levine: Stranger to Nothing*, Ann Arbor: University of MIchigan Press, 1991.

Horowitz, David A., Peter N. Carroll, and David D. Lee, eds., *On the Edge: A New History of 20th-century America*, Los Angeles, West Publishing Co., 1990.

Jarman, Mark, "The Eye Filled with Salt," *Kayak*, Vol. 38, 1975, pp. 63-66.

Levine, Philip, *Ashes: Poems New and Old,* New York: Atheneum, 1979.

———, *The Bread of Time: Toward an Autobiography,* New York: Knopf, 1994.

———, *Don't Ask,* Ann Arbor: University of Michigan Press, 1981.

———, *1933,* New York: Antheneum, 1974.

———, *7 Years from Somewhere,* New York: Atheneum, 1979.

Malkoff, Karl, *Escape from the Self: A Study in Contemporary American Poetry and Poetics,* New York: Columbia University Press, 1977.

Matthews, William, "Wagoner, Hugo, and Levine," *Ohio Review,* Vol. 26, 1981, pp. 126-37.

Meyers, Jack, and David Wojahn, eds. *A Profile of Twentieth-Century American Poetry,* Carbondale, IL: Southern Illinois University Press, 1991.

Smith, David, "The Second Self: Some Recent American Poetry," in *American Poetry Review,* Vol. 8, No. 6, November-December, 1979, pp. 33–37.

Vendler, Helen, *Poems Poets Poetry: An Introduction and Anthology,* Boston: Bedford Books of St. Martin's Press, 1997.

For Further Study

Cowan, Nelson, ed., *The Development of Memory in Childhood,* Psychology Press, 1998.

Cowan edits a collection of essays detailing theories of childhood memory and why some events are remembered and others not.

Dillard, Annie, *An American Childhood,* New York: HarperCollins, 1998.

This memoir of Annie Dillard's childhood details her endless fascination with language and new experiences.

Klein, Art, *Dad and Son: A Memoir About Reclaiming Fatherhood and Manhood,* Champion Press, 1996.

This memoir is a close look at how the author found meaning in his life through fatherhood after he is stricken with a debilitating disease.

Levis, Larry, *Elegy,* Pittsburgh, University of Pittsburgh Press, 1997.

Larry Levis, who died suddenly in 1996 of a heart attack, was an outstanding poet, and a student and colleague of Philip Levine. Levine, who edited this posthumous manuscript, writes that Levis's "early death is a staggering loss for our poetry, but what he left is a major achievement that will enrich our lives for as long as poetry matters."

Linton, Bruce, *Finding Time For Fatherhood: The Important Considerations Men Face When They Become Parents,* Fathers' Forum Press, 1998.

Linton's essays are thoughtful and fascinating in their variety, ranging from revisiting the Oedipus myth, to looking at the men's movement, to examining the role food and meals play in the family, to discussing sex and fatherhood.

To a Sad Daughter

Michael Ondaatje
1984

"To a Sad Daughter" appears in Michael Ondaatje's 11th collection of poetry, *Secular Love,* published in 1984. In "Coming Through: A Review of *Secular Love,*" critic Sam Solecki comments that the poems in this book read "more like the chapters of a novel than parts of a collection." "To a Sad Daughter," however, can easily be pulled from the rest and enjoyed alone, for it encompasses a theme common in many of our lives and presents it in a striking, not-so-common way: a father's love for his daughter and his longing to guide her "into the wild world" (line 64) gently, but with eyes wide open.

While there have been countless father-daughter poems written over the decades, not many include hockey goalies, purple moods, and *Creatures From the Black Lagoon.* Ondaatje's poetry is rich in all forms of human experience, and his use of everyday language and everyday events to define that experience makes his work both compelling and accessible. "To a Sad Daughter" is written while the speaker sits at his daughter's bedroom desk when she is not present. At one point, he refers to the poem as his "first lecture" to the 16-year-old, but it is a lecture full of love and wonderment and admitted anxiety, not anger and rebuke.

While the title identifies the daughter as melancholy or grieving, she is not actually present in the work, and so we must consider the word "sad" as only an interpretation of the father's. After reading the poem, we may also consider that the doleful adjective is really a reflection of the speaker's own

Michael Ondaatje

emotion and that he too experiences the apprehension, blue funk, and growing pains that his adolescent daughter does.

Author Biography

Michael Ondaatje was born in Colombo, Ceylon (now Sri Lanka), in 1943. Located off the southern tip of India and sometimes called India's "teardrop" because of its shape, this small island has been home to much conflict between various religious, ethnic, and political factions. Ondaatje's family was a member of Ceylon's wealthy colonial society who distanced themselves as much as possible from the civil strife but often created their own combat in the form of drunkenness and raucous parties. His mother performed part-time as a radical dancer, and his father was an alcoholic tea and rubber plantation superintendent. Eventually, his mother had enough of the father's drinking and outrageous behavior—he reportedly liked to board trains and run the aisles waving a gun and spouting "revolutionary" slogans—and the couple divorced. When Michael was 11, he moved to London with his mother, and, at 19, he moved to Canada, began his college career, and has lived and worked there ever since.

Ondaatje's writing career also began when he moved to Canada, and he has produced an abundant amount of work in various genres since then: to date, 13 poetry collections, four novels, numerous screen plays, and dozens of critical articles for literary journals. While his literature and criticism have long been respected and admired by scholars, teachers, fellow writers, and avid readers in general, Ondaatje did not make his debut into worldwide "popular" culture until 1997, when the major motion picture film adaptation of his 1992 novel *The English Patient* won an Academy Award for Best Picture.

Ondaatje's work has never shied away from being factual in the sense that he writes about real people and real occurrences in his life. Critics over the years have treated his "family" poems as autobiography with a creative bent, and "To a Sad Daughter" is presumably one of them. His novel/autobiography, *Running in the Family* (1982), is a sometimes funny, sometimes shocking discourse on his life and family in Ceylon, and we must consider how much the turmoil of his early years affected his responses to the growth of his own children. While all fathers with sixteen-year-old daughters may suffer the distress that goes along with the role, Ondaatje seems to include a particular urgency in his message and his advice to his daughter. Perhaps his strained relations with and eventual separation from his own father added a dimension of fervor and immediacy in expressing feelings for his child, or perhaps it was simply that she was growing up in a world much different from the one he knew as a young boy, and his desire both to protect her and to set her free was at times overwhelming.

Michael Ondaatje received his bachelor's degree in 1965 from the University of Toronto and his master's in 1967 from Queen's University in Kingston, Ontario. Although he never pursued a doctorate, he has taught in the English Department of Glendon College, York University in Toronto since 1971.

Poem Text

All night long the hockey pictures
gaze down at you sleeping in your tracksuit.
Belligerent goalies are your ideal.
Threats of being traded
cuts and wounds   5
—all this pleases you.
O My god! you say at breakfast
reading the sports page over the Alpen

as another player breaks his ankle
or assaults the coach.   10

When I thought of daughters
I wasn't expecting this
but I like this more.
I like all your faults
even your purple moods   15
when you retreat from everyone
to sit in bed under a quilt.
And when I say 'like'
I mean of course 'love'
but that embarrasses you.   20
You who feel superior to black and white movies
(coaxed for hours to see *Casablanca*
though you were moved
by *Creature from the Black Lagoon*.

One day I'll come swimming   25
beside your ship or someone will
and if you hear the siren
listen to it. For if you close your ears
only nothing happens. you will never change.

I don't care if you risk   30
your life to angry goalies
creatures with webbed feet
You can enter their caves and castles
their glass laboratories. Just
don't be fooled by anyone but yourself.   35

This is the first lecture I've given you.
You're 'sweet sixteen' you said.
I'd rather be your closest friend
than your father. I'm not good at advice
you know that, but ride   40
the ceremonies
until they grow dark.

Sometimes you are so busy
discovering your friends
I ache with a loss   45
—but that is greed
And sometimes I've gone
into *my* purple world
and lost you.

One afternoon I stepped   50
into your room. You were sitting
at the desk where I now write this.
Forsythia outside the window
and sun spilled over you
like a thick yellow miracle   55
as if another planet
was coaxing you out of the house
—all those possible worlds!—
and you, meanwhile, busy with mathematics.

I cannot look at forsythia now   60
without loss, or joy for you.
You step delicately
into the wild world
and your real prize will be

                                                    65

the frantic search.
Want everything. If you break
break going out not in.
How you live your life I don't care
but I'll sell my arms for you,
hold your secrets forever.   70

If I speak of death
which you fear now, greatly,
it is without answers.
except that each
one we know is   75
in our blood.
don't recall graves.
Memory is permanent
Remember the afternoon's
yellow suburban annunciation.   80
Your goalie
in his frightening mask
dreams perhaps
of gentleness.

Poem Summary

Lines 1–11:

The first stanza of "To a Sad Daughter" provides a snapshot of the girl who is the subject of this poem. If we did not know the title, our first assumption may be that the speaker is describing his *son* who is a typical sports enthusiast. Knowing the name of the piece, however, we are intrigued by the description of the bedroom that belongs to a girl and by her behavior at the breakfast table. She has not only selected sports figures as her idols, but she has chosen players from a very violent, rough, and highly male-dominated sport: "Belligerent goalies are your ideal." She has posted pictures, probably from sports magazines, of hockey players on the walls of her bedroom where most young girls may hang photos of popular singers or handsome movie stars. She does not sleep in a pretty gown or in typical girls' pajamas, but in a tracksuit. Perhaps most revealing in the description of the daughter is that "Threats ... / cuts and wounds" *please* her. These are words not commonly thought to describe pleasant circumstances for anyone, especially a young female, but, nonetheless, the subject here is attracted to the bloodshed, bruises, and ruthlessness of the sport of hockey. The only hint of "girlishness" that appears in this first stanza is in line 8 where we see her italicized reaction to a sports page article: "*O my god!*" she exclaims, and it is easy to imagine the scene as a father watches his wide-eyed daughter hold a newspaper over her bowl of cereal ("Alpen") and spout out her alarmist remark about a broken ankle or fight between

Media Adaptations

- An audio cassette of *The English Patient* is available from Random House (Audio) in an abridged edition. The tape is narrated by Michael Ondaatje and the reader is Michael York.

- Two cassettes containing Michael Ondaatje reading his entire *Running in the Family* is available from Random House (Audio). The tapes run a total of three hours.

player and coach. Obviously, in the sport of hockey, neither of these incidents is even unusual, much less alarming, but Ondaatje is careful to let us know there is still a bit of innocence and "silliness" beneath the otherwise tough exterior of his little girl.

Lines 12-25:

The second stanza discloses more of the daughter's vulnerable, softer side and also provides insight into the father's personal assessment of his female child: "When I thought of daughters/ I wasn't expecting this/ but I like this more." He also confesses that he likes her "purple moods" when she demonstrates a typical teenager's aloofness and reclusiveness, probably stalking off to her room "to sit in bed under a quilt" with a *nobody understands me* attitude. Ondaatje admits that he uses the word "like" only in deference to his daughter's embarrassment over hearing a parent talk about love, although *love* is precisely what he feels for her. We also see the girl's youthful disposition in her scoffing at things old-fashioned, as she feels "superior to black and white movies." In the last three lines of the stanza, the poet returns to the image of a daughter with prevalent tomboy features, telling us that she had to be "coaxed for hours to see *Casablanca,*" a romantic love story that many women, as well as men, have watched over and over, but that she was "moved / by *Creatures from the Black Lagoon,*" an old horror movie featuring a web-footed lizard-like creature who rises from

murky waters and terrorizes everyone in its path—not typically a "girl's" movie.

Lines 26-36:

The third stanza gives us a first look at the father's main concerns involving his daughter's future. Some parents may find his advice unthinkable and even dangerous, but Ondaatje delivers such a compelling rationale that we cannot help but understand he has the girl's best interest in mind. In the first five lines, the poet uses striking mythological imagery to make his "cautionary" point, although we may see it as "reverse" caution, since he urges her to do exactly the opposite of what many fathers would advise. In mythological tales, sirens were sea nymphs whose sweet singing lured unsuspecting sailors to their island. The catch was that the island was surrounded by craggy rocks, and the mariners met their fate when their ships were destroyed by the hidden danger. Eventually, some sailors learned to cover their ears and pass the seductive singing without falling victim to it, but many failed. In this poem, the father tells his daughter, "One day I'll come swimming/ beside your ship or someone will / and if you hear the siren / listen to it." This may sound like astonishing advice—a father telling his daughter to follow a path to sure destruction, but he offers his reasons in the next lines: "For if you close your ears / only nothing happens. You will never change." Here, the poet indicates that "change" is vital to growth and to living a fulfilling life. He would rather his daughter take risks and discover what the world has to offer than to hide away in a protective shell where "nothing happens" but the same experiences, the same thoughts, the same beliefs. He refers back to hockey and to the old horror movie in saying, "I don't care if you risk / your life to angry goalies / creatures with webbed feet." He then goes on to reiterate his point that he'd rather his daughter go out into the world and learn from her own mistakes than be led by the opinions and actions of others: "You can enter their caves and castles/ their glass laboratories. Just / don't be fooled by anyone but yourself."

Lines 37-50:

In the fourth and fifth stanzas the father declares that his poem is "the first lecture" he has given his daughter who is "'sweet sixteen,'" and he also reveals a confession about his relationship with her: "I'd rather be your closest friend / than your father." Lines 44-46 tell us why: "Sometimes you are so busy / discovering your friends / I ache with a loss." Most parents go through a time of "losing" their children to friends who seemingly become more important to the young people, and with whom they prefer to share their most private thoughts. The father also confesses he is "not good at advice," but he asks his daughter to bear with him while he performs his paternal duties ("… but ride/ the ceremonies"), and he asks for her patience only until those duties fade with age and no longer shed light on her future: "until they grow dark." As a final confession, the father states that he too has bad moods and retreats into his own "purple world" where feeling the loss of his daughter is his own fault.

Lines 51-60:

The sixth stanza captures beautifully a single moment in time—one that is now only a memory for the father and that the daughter does not even know occurred. The father remembers stepping into the girl's room, probably just in the doorway long enough to see her busy doing homework while sunlight and shrubs with bright yellow blooms cast a "thick yellow miracle" over her. Although his daughter is oblivious to the significance of the moment ("and you, meanwhile, busy with mathematics"), the father imagines the golden glow surrounding her as "another planet / … coaxing you out of the house." Referring back to his notion that there is so much of life and so many opportunities out there for his daughter, he exclaims "all those possible worlds!" and we sense both excitement and resignation in his remark.

Lines 61-71:

The seventh stanza is a reaffirmation of Ondaatje's advice to his daughter which he so fervently conveyed in the third stanza. He begins by conceding that he cannot think of the other worldly yellow light he envisioned luring the girl away from him without feeling both pain and joy. He has already claimed to want her to explore all the options the future holds for her, but he also must face the sadness it will bring him when she leaves home for good. Because she is still innocent and naive in many ways and unaware of all the world's dangers, he sees her "… step delicately / into the wild world." Lines 65-66 present an intriguing comment on what the father hopes his daughter discovers *out there*, and it is not any one thing in particular. Rather, it is the search itself that will be most fulfilling for her to experience, that will be "the real prize." She should "want everything," not just one thing or another, for that would leave her short of discovering the countless opportunities (as well as misfortunes) that real living has to offer. He then reiterates his provocative advice: "If you break/ break going out not in." By this, he means that it is better to try something and fail than not to try it at all. If his daughter is going to "break," he would rather it be after she has already attempted an opportunity instead of before she has ever tried to get "in." Lines 69-70 present an interesting juxtaposition of emotions, first depicting a seeming nonchalance, and then describing love so strong that it is the ultimate in selflessness. The father claims, "How you live your life I don't care," and then quickly announces his willingness to sacrifice for her no matter what path she chooses: "but I'll sell my arms for you / hold your secrets forever."

Lines 72-85:

In the final stanza, the poet makes first mention of death, and he offers his advice regarding it in a much more somber and gentler manner than that regarding life. He acknowledges that the young girl fears death and admits that he cannot really explain or understand it himself—he is "without answers," except for one. What he does know is that each time someone we know dies, we die a little bit ourselves, for "each / one we know is / in our blood." Accepting that, the father cautions his daughter not to dwell on the deaths of loved ones, not to "recall graves" because if she does, that is all she will remember about them: "Memory is permanent." Instead, he encourages her to "Remember the afternoon's / yellow suburban annunciation." In other words, he wants her to share his anticipation and wonderment at all the possible worlds calling her, the worlds he imagined when he came upon her in her room with the sunlight pouring over her in the backdrop of yellow flowers outside the window. The father obviously clings to this memory because it is one of both peacefulness and possibility, both tranquility and hope. He ends the poem on his own note of hopefulness, telling his daughter that even her tough, frightening goalie "dreams perhaps / of gentleness." By saying this, he puts all his other, less "typical," advice in perspective. He wants his daughter not to be afraid to explore and take chances and not to back down from the challenges or hardships of a full life; but he also wants her to understand that beneath even the roughest, coldest exteriors, we may find a longing to be tender and kind.

Themes

"To a Sad Daughter" attempts to define the realm of emotions that persists on a daily basis within a

Topics for Further Study

- Pretend you are the parent of a daughter turning sixteen and you want to give her something special for her birthday. You decide to write her a letter as a "gift" of advice for her future. What would your letter say?

- Consider the encouragement to "Want everything" and write an essay on how children who take this advice seriously will lead their adult lives.

- Your hometown is trying to raise funds for a professional women's hockey team. Write a letter to the newspaper editor thoroughly explaining your feelings for or against the new team.

- Write a poem that begins with the lines: When I thought of having sons/ this isn't what I thought.

---

man raising a daughter. The poet describes his role as both father and friend, protector and motivator, and as the one who would like to hold on to his little girl forever but who must open the door "into the wild world" and essentially push her through it.

Reality and Ambiguity

Michael Ondaatje is widely accepted as a writer of reality, but how he defines reality is a recurring theme within his work. Most often, the world he describes is chaotic, and the typical human response to it is panic. But at the center of the chaos, and, therefore, the center of the panic, lies a good reason for both: ambiguity. Very little is clear-cut in this poet's world. Even his daughter turned out to be not what he was "expecting," but rather something he likes even more. Her own life is full of turmoil and uncertainty, easily attributed to the fact that she's a teenager, but, even so, she is not the "usual" adolescent girl. We can simply list the images that portray her qualities, her emotions, her likes and dislikes to note a type of self-inflicted chaos: belligerent goalies, threats, cuts and wounds, purple moods, horror movie creatures, and the caves and castles in which they live. On the

other hand, we also see her in a "retreat" mode, sitting quietly "in bed under a quilt," and we catch her in an innocent moment when she is engrossed in schoolwork within a sun-filled room, a positive and peaceful scene. Ondaatje's poetry reflects a cryptic reality, both puzzling and exhilarating, and it sometimes results in a variety of descriptions of one entity in a single poem. In "To a Sad Daughter," he uses three different adjectives to describe the world: "purple" (line 49), "possible" (line 59), and "wild" (line 64). Note how each of these descriptors carries a different connotation, with "purple" implying a gloomy or melancholy world, "possible" offering hope, opportunity, and excitement, and "wild" indicating an untamed or dangerous world. While seeming to be contradictory, each description is true, or real, in its own right; therefore, the only *one* word that can accurately define the world, or reality, in general, is "ambiguous."

Taking Risks

One of the most daring aspects of Ondaatje's "To a Sad Daughter" is his encouraging the girl to take risks in her life—to listen to the "siren," "want everything," and to "break going out not in." The father tells his daughter to live frantically in order to live fully, for taking chances is much better than leading a reserved, protected life in which "nothing happens." Perhaps this advice is only a reflection of how the father lives his own life or how he *wishes* he lived it, and he wants the same, or more, for his child. Imagery is a key in depicting the fervor of the father's intentions, and in several of Ondaatje's poems, water imagery is that key. Water is both frightening and calming, and in this piece we have the two working together. "One day I'll come swimming/ beside your ship ..." depicts a peaceful scene, or at least one in which there is no hint of pending trouble. In the next line, however, the poet alludes to shipwrecks and death, the result of deception, and, despite the new imagery, he presents the deadly waters as inviting and worth tempting. Here again there is a note of panic in the desire to experience real life, a desire that overrides what many may view as common sense. The father in this poem would have us believe that common sense leads only to boredom and a wasted life.

Unselfish Love

Even those who read "To a Sad Daughter" and feel uneasy, or even angry, with the advice the father gives the girl cannot deny the evidence proclaiming the poet's intense love for her. He loves even her faults, though he uses the word "like" to keep from embarrassing her; he would rather be her friend than her father during this stage of life because her friends are closer to her; he feels both loss and joy when he thinks of "all those possible worlds" awaiting her; and he would "sell" his arms for her, make any sacrifice to show his love. Ironically, it is this unselfish love that underpins the father's desperate attempt to thrust his daughter headlong into the real world. He wants her to have the most complete life possible, even if it means risking it "to angry goalies / creatures with webbed feet." And although he experiences the natural pangs of all parents whose children grow up and venture out on their own, he does not even consider standing in her way or offering advice that may thwart her curiosity and daring spirit. He asks only that she does not limit herself and declares his support no matter what.

Style

"To a Sad Daughter" is an 85-line poem with eight stanzas written in free verse. While Ondaatje does not rely on any overt poetic devices here, a close look does reveal considerable use of alliteration, as well as a strategy fairly common and always remarkable in this poet's work—his ability to sharply define a message with brief, surprising statements.

Many of the lines in "To a Sad Daughter" are quite prosy, detracting from the assonance and consonance that would otherwise be more prevalent. We find, however, a good flow of sound in such instances as the repetition of the "p" in "... reading the sports page over the Alpen/ as another player ..."; the repetition of the "ah" sound in "When I thought of daughters / I wasn't ..."; the various uses of "s" in "... I'll come swimming / beside your ship or someone will / and if you hear the siren / listen ..."; the "s" sound again in "You were sitting / at the desk where I now write this / Forsythia outside the window / and sun spilled over you ..."; and even the near-rhyme at the end of the poem with the use of "mask" and "perhaps." What keeps the alliteration in this poem from seeming forced and unnatural is that it is cloaked within casual verbiage, giving the words more of a prose cadence than a poetic one. In a 1984 interview with Ondaatje, Sam Solecki asked the poet about his recently published *Secular Love,* and Ondaatje had this to say about its form: "I wanted to call my new book of poems ... 'a novel.' I structured it like one. For me, its structure and plot are novelistic." Even

so, "To a Sad Daughter" contains just enough of the elements of poetry to prevent it from sounding like a paragraph broken into short lines.

While these short lines, however, do string together into complete sentences throughout the poem, Ondaatje includes an element of surprise by shifting suddenly to abrupt short phrases that startle us both with their message and their exactness. For example, the first two "sentences" of the third stanza, read as such, are followed by a four-word statement that suddenly rings of doom: One day, I'll come swimming beside your ship, or someone will, and if you hear the siren, listen to it. For if you close your ears, only nothing happens. *You will never change.* In the seventh stanza, an even more poignant message appears in only two words, preceded by a longer sentence: You step delicately into the wild world and the real prize will be the frantic search. *Want everything.* Critic George Bowering, in his article "Ondaatje Learning to Do," claims that "the poet shows us a sure comprehension of what a line is, not just a length, not only a syntactic unit, but a necessary step in knowing and surprise." In the final stanza, the poet employs his "knowing and surprise" once again in advising his daughter about death: If I speak of death, which you fear now, greatly, it is without answers, except that each one we know is in our blood. *Don't recall graves.* This mixture of lengthy and brief lines in the poem is an appealing addition to an already intriguing work.

Historical Context

Time and place are not essential in Michael Ondaatje's "To a Sad Daughter." The message, or the advice, passed down from father to daughter is the central issue, and it could occur anywhere at any time. It is unlikely, however, that a man would offer such liberal advice to his little girl in years prior to the second half of the twentieth century, and so we may assume the time frame is "contemporary." The only confirmation of that in the poem is the reference to items and events that were not prevalent or not available earlier, tracksuits and the National Hockey League, for instance. We also know that the poem takes place when color motion pictures have been common for many years since the 16-year-old feels "superior" to black and white movies. As for place, we may assume that the father and daughter live somewhere in the "north" since hockey is the sport of choice, although we

Compare & Contrast

- **1982:** A Supreme Court decision in *Mississippi University for Women v. Hogan* finds that an all-female state supported nursing school that denied admission to a male is unconstitutional.

  1997-98: The Virginia Military Institute is ordered by the U.S. Supreme Court to accept women into its program after its all-male policy was found unconstitutional.

- **1981:** In what was called a "fairy tale" match, Prince Charles of England marries Lady Diana Spencer while millions watched on TV.

  1996: Prince Charles and Princess Diana divorce; Diana is killed in a car crash one year later.

- **1978:** The world's first test-tube baby is born in London to mom Lesley Brown.

  1997: Scottish geneticists announce the successful cloning of a sheep and name her Dolly.

---

now have professional ice hockey teams located in cities in the southern United States. Another clue is the mention of the cereal "Alpen," a popular breakfast food in northern Europe and Canada, though not a household name in America. Our best sense of setting for this poem stems simply from knowing that Ondaatje writes mainly from real-life experiences and that his "family" poems are primarily creative nonfiction. Given that, "To a Sad Daughter" probably takes place in Ontario, Canada, sometime during the early 1980s.

The decade of the 1980s is sometimes looked back on as culturally benign. The disco craze and flashy fashions of the 1970s gave way to a more bland mixture of "new-wave" music and power-chord rock as well as the "grunge" look of loose-fitting jeans, sweatshirts, and flannel shirts. But more was going on than some of the decade's admittedly "me-first" generation recognized. Perhaps an anonymous author who has posted a Web page entitled "Children of the Eighties" captures best both the spirit and the lack of spirit that made up this often-thought mundane, self-indulgent period of time: "We are the children of the Eighties…. We collected Garbage Pail Kids and Cabbage Patch Kids … and He-Man action figures and [I] thought She-Ra looked just a little bit like I would when I was a woman…. In the Eighties, nothing was wrong. Did you know the president was shot? … Did you see the Challenger explode or feed the homeless man? We forgot Vietnam and watched Tiananman's Square on CNN and bought pieces of the Berlin Wall at the store."

This was the world in which Michael Ondaatje was raising his daughter. Wars still raged across the world, there was plenty of violence happening in the streets at home, crack cocaine was invented, assassination attempts were not uncommon on the nightly news, and the general public reaction to it all was less than remarkable. While the murders of John and Robert Kennedy and Martin Luther King Jr. in the 1960s outraged people and sent them pouring into the streets in protest and in grief, the attempts to kill President Ronald Reagan and Pope John Paul II, both in 1981, elicited only cursory, often cynical, responses from millions of people around the world. Also in the early 80s, AIDS began to be recognized as an epidemic, but most people brushed the deadly disease off as a plague on homosexuals and something that could not touch their own "straight" lives. The father in "To a Sad Daughter" surely knows that his child will face more than "angry goalies" and "creatures with webbed feet" when she grows up and leaves home, and he wants her to be prepared to face everything—including war, drugs, and disease—with her eyes wide open. In light of the "wild" and dangerous society she will become a part of, he wants her not only to accept the challenges of it, but also to look deep inside it, to search out whatever good she may find hidden beneath the chaos. He wants her to understand that even a "goalie / in his frightening mask / dreams perhaps / of gentleness."

Also evident in the historical context of this poem is that it presents a subject—a girl who can, and does, take her freedom and her self-confidence for granted. She does not appear to have any concerns over or struggles with "liberation" because she does not know what it's like *not* to be liberated. She has no qualms about pursuing interests typically sought by boys and men, and if she prefers reading the sports page over the society section and would rather watch horror films instead of love stories, so be it. She is growing up in a decade when many young girls do not give second thought to crossing the gender barrier, and she is being brought up in a home where her aspirations are apparently respected. The father does not attempt to turn his daughter into a "little lady," but rather eggs on her free spirit by encouraging her to "want everything." In the 1980s, many people did indeed want everything, and some, as it turned out, got more than they bargained for.

Critical Overview

Secular Love has not been the subject of an abundance of critique over the years, but, in general, Ondaatje's poetry has been highly acclaimed. One of the poet's most faithful reviewers has been critic Sam Solecki who, in his article "Nets and Chaos: the Poetry of Michael Ondaatje," says that in Ondaatje's work "the fundamental or essential nature of experience is consistently being described and examined. The entire thrust of his vision is directed at compelling the reader to reperceive reality...." We can see this theory at work in "To a Sad Daughter" in the way the speaker keeps describing and examining his own responses to his daughter's actions. He feels joy, he feels loss, and he seems to feel nearly everything in between. Although he is sometimes compared to Robert Lowell, John Berryman, or even Anne Sexton because of his tendency to write from real-life experiences, Ondaatje cannot really be called a "confessional" poet. As Solecki points out, " ... he's rarely interested in enacting or describing his darkest and most problematic emotions and situations: the voice is too laconic, the tone too detached, and the attitude to the self is ironic, even self-mocking."

Since Ondaatje has been such a prolific writer in various fields, he has encountered a wide-circuit of critics. By far, most have dealt with his novels, in particular *The English Patient*. In her book, *Michael Ondaatje: Word, Image, Imagination*, Leslie Mundwiler sums up the critics of his poetry with, "All of [them], it seems, have wanted to account for the imaginative force of his work, if only

in passing.... Still, because the imagery is what makes so much of the poetry work, ... reviewers and critics must at least suggest the extraordinary moments that are there in the reading even while trying out the standard 'litcrit' labels." Regardless of the genre, however, Ondaatje's work is respected and admired, especially for its candor, its unusual imagery, and its ability to make us confront realities we may otherwise shun.

Criticism

Bruce Meyer

Bruce Meyer is the director of the creative writing program at the University of Toronto. He has taught at several Canadian universities and is the author of three collections of poetry. In the following essay, Meyer interprets Ondaatje's poem as a story of two lives and two universes separated by protective masks, and he evaluates how the distance between these two universes is bridged through Ondaatje's use of color imagery.

Michael Ondaatje's "To a Sad Daughter" is a poem about the way that surfaces mask much deeper emotions. The recurring theme of the hockey goalie, those caged athletes who don the personas of highly decorated masks not only to protect themselves but to make a statement about their own identities to the shooters from the opposing teams, act almost as mouthpieces—personas in the sense of classical drama—through which a father can speak lovingly to a teenaged daughter. In the process of attempting to bridge two very disparate worlds, Ondaatje manages to show how close, yet how far apart they really are. The distance that exists between the father and his daughter is the paradoxical distance of closeness that emerges in the most intense relationships. These are not merely two ships that pass in the night, to quote the rock star Ian Hunter, but two lives that live in parallel, almost similar universes.

The similarity between the two universes, the one of the father and the one of the daughter, can be fixed in Ondaatje's use of color imagery. Purple and yellow, the traditional colors of rebirth, Easter and the self-sacrifice associated with springtime mythopoeia, are used as markers by the poet to pinpoint the proximity of two separate beings within the same environment. The father notes, "I like all your faults / Even your purple moods / when you retreat from everyone," an idea that links the

What Do I Read Next?

- By the time Michael Ondaatje published his collection of poems called *Rat Jelly* in 1973, he had already developed a reputation as a writer unafraid of taking chances with both descriptive language and subject matter. This book carries on that bent with what may be the precursor to some of the subjects in *Secular Love* in poems that deal with living with a wife who has been married before and in being the son of a temperamental, alcoholic father.

- In addition to novels, plays, and collections of poems, Ondaatje has also published book-length poems, or epics, one in 1970 called *The Collected Works of Billy the Kid*. This well-received publication explores the history of the young gunslinger in both fact and fiction, told primarily from Billy's point of view. Ondaatje provides interesting, colorful twists to the typical "Billy the Kid" story.

- Because Michael Ondaatje relies so heavily on real-life accounts and personal relationships as inspiration for his work, it is worth having a better understanding of "where he's coming from"—literally. *Sri Lanka: Ethnic Fraticide and the Dismantling of Democracy,* written by Stanley Jeyaraja Tambiah and published in 1991, details the events leading up to and the continued fighting between the two most prominent political factions in Sri Lanka, the Sinhalese and the Tamils. The struggles are religious, cultural, and political in nature, and this book does a good job examining the reasons for so many deaths in this small island nation.

- The daughter in Ondaatje's poem makes icons of hockey players, but we are not sure whether she has any inclinations to play the sport herself. Many women have, and *Too Many Men on the Ice: Women's Hockey in North America* (Joanna Avery, Glynis Peters, Julie Anne Stevens; 1998) explores the history of women's hockey in the U.S. and Canada, including the 1998 Olympic gold medal for the U.S. team in Nagano. Although there has been little recognition of, and even less support for, women playing this "man's" sport, there were actually female college teams as early as the 1920s.

- While much has been written on mother-daughter and father-son bonds, not too much literature has appeared on the opposite relationship—sat least not much in a "positive" vein. In 1998, editors Dewitt Henry and James Alan McPherson put together a collection of essays highlighting the ties between fathers and daughters in *Fathering Daughters: Reflections by Men.* This book is filled with touching and intriguing, not always happy, accounts by fathers who reveal some of their most personal, provocative feelings about their female children. From one man's refusal to "baby talk" with his infant to another's worrying about his daughter's political consciousness to a third recounting a vacation he took with a daughter dying of leukemia—this is a sensitive collection of work on parenting girls and young women from the father's point of view.

- Sirens may appear in only one line of "To a Sad Daughter," but the impact of its meaning is crucial to the poem. Meri Franco-Lao discusses the history and celebration of the allure of sirens and mermaids over 3000 years of art and literature in her *Sirens: Symbols of Seduction,* published in 1997. With a mixture of text, photos, and illustrations, Franco-Lao depicts the ongoing love affair between some of the world's greatest writers, artists, and poets and the mythological creatures who almost enticed Ulysses to an early demise with their sweet, bewitching songs.

color purple to the hormone driven mood swings of the teenaged daughter. The similarities between the two, an association of the familial cliche 'like father, like daughter,' is echoed in the father's own statement, "And sometimes I've gone / into *my* purple world / and lost you." What seems to come between them is not merely the generation gap, but their own inner universes and complex range of passions that dwell there. What Ondaatje seems to be suggesting is that true intimacy is based on an acknowledgment of distances where the individuals co-exist not only in their shared world but in parallel universes of private lives that neither can fully comprehend or hope to penetrate. In the end, the most private experience of all, that of one's own death, is something that presents the ultimate distance between them—a vacuum that is filled by the in-rush of fear: "If I speak of death / which you fear now, greatly, / it is without answers, / except that each / one we know is / in our blood." The distance between the two individuals, perhaps, is not as great as one would think in that they share the same fates, the same destinies as well as the same DNA patterns. In this light, the color purple takes on the appearance of a mourning cloak, a sense of inescapable finality where the father cannot hope to protect the daughter from the destiny that her physiology has imposed on her from the moment of her conception. Such a recognition makes the father's pleas that "I'll sell my arms for you" even more touching, though just as fruitless.

The color yellow, however, offers a balancing perspective to the issues of mortality and isolation that are suggested by the color purple. The blooming yellow forsythia outside the daughter's window as the father writes the poem at her desk is a signal of rebirth, of the continuance of life and of the way in which the cycles of existence repeat and replicate themselves. The final stanza of the poem asks the daughter to "Remember the afternoon's / yellow suburban annunciation," the color that he comes to associate not with their private, inner lives but with the moment at which he passes fatherly advice to his daughter. "This is the first lecture I've given you," he notes and the moment of their contact is illuminated and commemorated by the brightness of all the associations that the color yellow carries with it. It suggests an illuminating gesture where one individual reaches out to another to bridge a noticeable gap, and he underscores this dash of brightness with a statement that leaves some hope that the gap itself can be bridged: "I'd rather be your closest friend / than your father." What Ondaatje seems to be suggesting is that fa-

> *Living, he seems to understand, is a whole series of 'yellow miracles' where the discovery of life, either in bushes outside a window or in moments of shared experience, far outweigh the inner, purple gloom of private moments of despair."*

milial relations impose boundaries and strictures on individuals that, for the sake of issues such as authority and even parental love, are hard to breach or bridge with moments of understanding.

The difficulty of the bridging process, aside from the color symbolism that Ondaatje has constructed, is that it leads to the need to warn or at least advise. The father wishes to share his knowledge of the world with his daughter, but without appearing preachy or pompous. He is sensitive to her need to discover her own individuality on her own terms—even through the interest in hockey which he has difficulty understanding—but his urgency to give advice, at moments, overcomes his need to exercise reserve out of a sense of respect for her own individuality. "Just / don't be fooled by anyone but yourself," he proffers as he realizes "You step delicately / into the wild world / and your real prize will be / the frantic search." Life itself, he says, is the prize. The experiences that she will have will far outstrip any advice he can give, and he realizes that his own wisdom is a very limited matter: "I'm not good at advice / you know that, but ride / the ceremonies / until they grow dark." Living, he seems to understand, is a whole series of "yellow miracles" where the discovery of life, either in bushes outside a window or in moments of shared experience, far outweigh the inner, purple gloom of private moments of despair.

For Ondaatje, the process of communication is a means of understanding what goes on behind the masks, whether those masks are the gauzes on the face of a dying Hungarian spy in his novel *The Eng-*

lish Patient, the mask of bravado worn by William Bonney in *The Collected Works of Billy the Kid* or the protect gear donned by the daughter's heroes in "To a Sad Daughter." By laying bare the truths that one must speak, even if those truths are hard to comprehend or can only be reached through a labyrinth of metaphors, the process of communication is the avenue by which even the fiercest specters in the world become "gentle." The poem ends with the lines "Your goalie / in his frightening mask / dreams perhaps / of gentleness." For Ondaatje, the root of all human experience lies in that sense of gentleness that is there for all if only one takes the time and effort to find the articulate means of reaching it.

Source: Bruce Meyer, in an essay for *Poetry for Students,* Gale Group, 2000.

Alice Van Wart

Alice Van Wart teaches literature and writing in the Department of Continuing Education at the University of Toronto. She has published two books of poetry and has written articles on modern and contemporary literature. In the following essay, Van Wart describes how Ondaatje employs an atypical, plain style in order to amplify his subject.

One of Canada's most popular and one of its best writers, Michael Ondaatje, came to Canada by way of Ceylon and England before immigrating to Canada in 1962. Perhaps his early experiences in such diverse cultures account for the predominating trends in his work of a wide and general range of themes. As a successful writer of both poetry and prose, Ondaatje was the first Canadian writer to win the prestigious Booker Prize for his novel *The English Patient* (1992), which was subsequently made into a film of the same name and nominated for an Oscar.

The primary strength in his writing is the adaptation of technique to theme; in each new work he employs a technique that accurately corresponds to its theme. In his extended poem *The Collected Works of Billy the Kid,* for instance, he employs both poetry and prose to suggest the two sides of the legendary Billy the Kid. In *Coming Through Slaughter* he uses a variety of techniques and blends poetry with prose to create a form that suggests the improvisational nature of the music associated with his protagonist the legendary jazz musician Buddy Bolden. In each of his different works structure and characterization suit his subject.

Critics of Ondaatje's work point to his love of film as having a strong influence on his writing,

particularly the techniques used in film to create its sense of immediacy. Ondaatje uses documents, photographs, first person accounts, interviews, historical records, and blurs the boundaries between poetry and prose and fact and fiction in his work in an attempt to record the immediacy of experience, or the processes of recollecting experience. In this respect he forces the reader to reperceive reality, to assume an unusual angle of vision from which reality appears to be absurd, inchoate, dynamic, ambiguous, even surreal. Even the ordinary and the domestic take on overtones of the exotic and the extravagant as he retrieves and reshapes information from history, personal account, myth, and legend to suit his needs.

Pointing out these general features of Ondaatje's work shows just how atypical is his poem "To a Sad Daughter." Gone is the exotic image, the lyrical language, and the experimental structure. Instead we have one of a handful of his poems written in a casual, plain style. This style, however, is intentional, working once again to correspond to and amplify his subject. "To a Sad Daughter" is written in the form of a letter to his daughter. The very simplicity of its language and its form is appropriate to the poem's intentions. In this poem/letter Ondaatje creates the same familiar sense of immediacy found in his other work as he struggles to put into words what he wishes to say to a daughter who is growing away from him. The emotional power of the poem rests in the emotional context of the poem as the poet attempts to bridge a gulf between them by offering some fatherly advice and asking for her friendship. As he composes his poem/letter to her the poet conveys both the subtleties of their relationship and his feelings.

The poem moves progressively through eight verses and contains what can be thought of as three parts composed of appeal, apology, and advice. The poem's title informs us that this poem/letter was written during one of his daughter's withdrawals, what he calls her "purple moods." He begins his letter by using gentle humor. His tone is slightly ironic as he pictures her sleeping in her "track suit" under the gaze of "hockey players." He acknowledges "Belligerent goalies are your ideal / threats of being traded / cuts and wounds." He seems baffled by her "ideal" found in the masculine world of violence, threats, aggression, and injury. He is amused at his daughter's response of "O my god" as she reads "the sports page over the Alpen."

In the second stanza the irony is confirmed when the poet admits to her, "When I thought of daughters / I wasn't expecting this." The discrepancy between what he imagined and what she is like suggests he was comparing her to another ideal, that of the stereotype of a girl more concerned with fashion than sports. Having acknowledged his mistake he quickly assures, "but I like this more. / I like all your faults/ even your purple moods / when you retreat from everyone / to sit in bed under a quilt." The lines suggest that the poet has said something, which may have unwittingly hurt his daughter's feelings, perhaps even the reason for her withdrawal. Possibly he made a remark about her tomboyish nature. Whatever has transpired there is a rift between them, which has motivated him to write this letter/poem to her. It is clear the poet is stepping cautiously, appeasing and reassuring her. He back steps and qualifies his use of his word "like," by telling her matter of factly, "And when I say 'like' / I mean of course 'love' / but that embarrasses you." Though she may be old enough to be embarrassed by the word love, the poet points out to her that she is not too old to be moved by certain sentimental films like Creature from the Black Lagoon. There is an edge of annoyance in the poet's voice when he recalls her outright dismissal of black and white movies ("You who feel superior to black and white movies," even Casablanca, though he had coaxed her to see it.

In the third stanza the poet shifts his tact and appeals to her from a different point of view arriving indirectly to the point he wants to make: "One day I'll come swimming / beside your ship or someone will / and if you hear the siren / listen to it." The shift to poetic language and the clumsy metaphor (in the hands of a poet who skillfully works with metaphor) ironically points to an unwillingness on his part to get to the point. His intention is to explain his reason for pushing her to watch a film in which she has no interest: "If you hear the siren / listen to it." The "siren" is an allusion to the mythical creatures, who sang such beautiful songs sailors lost their lives by being shipwrecked when they tried to find their source. The poet is suggesting she open herself to new experiences, rather than turn away from them. Even though there may be danger in hearing the sirens, if she "closes" her ears "only nothing happens" and she "will never change."

In the next line the poet's tone shifts again as he returns to prosaic language, using images from her world of reference to make his point clear: "I don't care if you risk / your life to angry goalies," or "creatures with webbed feet. / You can enter their caves and castles / their glass laboratories." The poet's ambiguous words in the last line of the

> *Ondaatje's poem to his sad daughter is in fact a love letter that is at different time wistful, challenging, didactic, and gentle."*

stanza: "Just don't be fooled by anyone but yourself," imply it is better to make your own mistakes by trying new experiences.

In the fourth stanza the poet shifts his direction again. He offers an apology realizing what he has said may sound too didactic and alienate her further: "This is the first lecture I've given you." He admits he is not always good at giving advice and appeals to her understanding: "I'm not good at advice / You know that." Remembering that his daughter had reminded him of her age, "'sweet sixteen'," he now steps outside of the role of father he tells her it would be easier to talk to her if she were a friend and not a daughter: "I'd rather be your closest friend / than your father." He justifies his ineptness in the role of father by saying he is better at "rid[ing] the ceremonies / until they grow dark." The switch to metaphor suggests again his own awareness of the difficulty of his position. He is aware it is easier to observe the formalities of his role as a father, even though they may be inappropriate at this stage of her life.

In the fifth short stanza the situation between father and daughter clarifies. The poet puts ceremony aside and frankly tells his daughter what is bothering him. "You are so busy / discovering your friends / I ache with loss." The poet understands it is entirely normal for a sixteen year old to want to spend her time with her friends, but he also realizes she is growing away from him. He knows it is "greed" on his part to continue to want her to be the child. In an attempt to breech their differences he acknowledges that he, too, is guilty for the space between them, that he sometimes draws away from her by going into his own "purple world" and "lost" her. The poet's "purple world" is equivalent to his daughter's "purple moods" in the first stanza, a trait they both share, though in his case it also suggests periods of time he has withdrawn into his writing.

The use of the word "purple" intentionally shows his awareness of the emotional alienating effects of withdrawal.

In the sixth stanza the poet recalls a particular poignant moment, a day he had stepped into her room while she was "busy with mathematics." For the poet the moment resonated with meaning and he expresses it, as a poet would, through metaphor. He recalls her sitting at her desk, the desk he "now writes this," with "the forsythia outside the window" and the sun spilling over her "like a thick yellow miracle." The forsythia is a harbinger of spring and suggestive of new life; the miracle is the fact of his daughter's life. The poet saw the bright yellow of the sun and forsythia pulling her like "another planet" and "coaxing" her "out of the house," though she was oblivious "busy with mathematics." For the poet the moment represented his awareness of that fact that his daughter is growing away from him into her own life, "all those possible worlds!" He sees all the possibilities before her. Recalling the moment leads the poet to sentimental hyperbole as he writes: "I cannot look at forsythia now / without loss or joy of you."

At this point the poet steps back again into the role of father offering her further advice, this time from his own experience. He resorts again to figurative language to make his point by telling her that she will "step delicately into the wild world" where her "real prize will be / the frantic search." For the poet the "frantic search" is what drives a person on to find something, yet he knows now that the search itself is more important than the "prize" itself. There is a certain irony in the comment from a father who has won his fair share of prizes for his writing. Having won prizes, however, he knows the real value is not in the prize but in the process of creating. He tells her to "want everything" in the journey. The poet reiterates what he has told her in stanza three, which is quite simply to open herself to all experiences. Only in this way will she grow and change.

The poet is aware of the danger in his advice. By telling her to "want everything," he knows there are times she will be disappointed and times she will fail. The syntax in the line "Want everything. If you break / break going out not in" connects wanting everything to the risk of pain and possible breakdown; yet he would rather that she take the risk and live her life to its fullest. The suggestion recalls his previous allusion to the siren and his advice, "if you hear the siren / listen to it." Rather than withdrawing and avoiding risk for fear of failure, he advises her to take risks suggesting it is bet-

ter to fail than withdraw and suffer a different form of failure and pain in the form of loneliness and isolation. Having offered his advice the poet once again steps back and qualifies his comments. "How you live your life I don't care." No matter how she chooses to live her life he will always love her and be her friend: "I'll sell my arms for you / hold your secrets forever."

In the final stanza the poet's mood becomes solemn as he addresses his final point. He returns to the role of father this time to put her fears at ease on a subject that has been troubling her. He begins almost apologetically, as if he were reluctant to bring the subject up: "If I speak of death / which you fear now, greatly / it is without answers." His advice is honest; there are no answers to something that is a fact of each person's life. He offers no philosophical or spiritual consolations. Instead he tells her "each / one we know is / in our blood." He suggests that she take consolation in the fact that only the physical state ends in death, not the connection to another, which lives one. He tells her not to "recall graves" but to remember life instead. He reminds her of the power of memory, which is "permanent," and points to his own memory of her, "the afternoon's / yellow suburban annunciation." The memory is of the afternoon he saw her surrounded by forsythia with the sun shining on her. The moment is etched forever in his mind and has taken on a symbolic significance as the moment he knew he was losing her. In the final lines he reminds her of the importance of keeping her gaze on the living, "your goalie / in his frightening mask" and to look to the future and whatever surprises it may bring, her goalie, for instance, who "dreams perhaps of gentleness."

Ondaatje's poem to his sad daughter is in fact a love letter that is at different time wistful, challenging, didactic, and gentle. It addresses a changing relationship between a father and the daughter as the father comes to terms with her move towards adulthood and independence. It is a moving tribute that shows his own weaknesses and insecurity as he maneuvers between his role of father and what he hopes will be a growing friendship. It is a testament to the power of love.

Source: Alice Van Wart, in an essay for *Poetry for Students,* Gale Group, 2000.

Sources

Bowering, George, "Ondaatje Learning to Do" in *Spider Blues: Essays on Michael Ondaatje,* edited by Sam Solecki, Montreal, Canada: Vehicule Press, 1985, pp. 61-69.

Mundwiler, Leslie, *Michael Ondaatje: Word, Image, Imagination,* Vancouver: Talonbooks, 1984.

Ondaatje, Michael, *Secular Love,* New York: W.W. Norton & Co., 1984.

Solecki, Sam, "Coming Through: A Review of *Secular Love,*" *The Canadian Forum,* 745, January 1985, pp.32-36.

Solecki, Sam, "Nets and Chaos: The Poetry of Michael Ondaatje" in *Spider Blues: Essays on Michael Ondaatje,* edited by Sam Solecki, Montreal: Vehicule Press, 1985, pp. 93-109.

Solecki, Sam, "An Interview with Michael Ondaatje (1984)" in *Spider Blues: Essays on Michael Ondaatje,* edited by Sam Solecki, Montreal: Vehicule Press, 1985, pp. 321-32

World Wide Web site, Amazon Books at www.amazon.com

World Wide Web site, The History Channel at www.historychannel.com.

For Further Study

Davey, Frank, *From Here to There: A Guide to English Canadian Literature since 1960,* Erin, Ontario: Porcepic, 1974.

Davey presents a very colorful review of Ondaatje's poetry, claiming his poems "reverberate with exotic violence," and contain "a strong photographic element." He calls the poet's work "superbly tense, multicolor, explosive, [and] macabre."

Marshall, Tom, *Harsh and Lovely Land: The Major Canadian Poets and the Making of a Canadian Tradition,* Vancouver: Univ. of British Columbia Press, 1979.

This book offers a good overall look at Canadian literature, both past and at the time of publication. It is interesting to read about Ondaatje's work among his Canadian contemporaries, and he is cited as one of those poet-novelists who "seek to depict in fiction rather than in epic verse a world of primal psychic conflict, a dark underground of the soul."

Ondaatje, Michael, *Running in the Family,* New York: W.W. Nortron & Co., 1982.

Considering the real-life experiences examined in "To a Sad Daughter," it is beneficial and enlightening to read the poet's own creative autobiography dealing with the lives of his father and mother in Ceylon (Sri Lanka). This book tells the tale of broken engagements, drunken suicide attempts, and of parties where wealthy revelers tango in the jungle.

Vancouver Lights

Earle Birney
1942

"Vancouver Lights" appears in Birney's first collection of poems, *David and Other Poems,* most of which Birney wrote shortly after World War II began in 1939. The collection launched Birney's career as a poet and the book received the Governor General's Award for Poetry in 1942, the most prestigious award given for poetry in Canada. Birney read the poem on a CBC radio program on Canadian poetry in early February 1943. Consisting of five stanzas which utilize a kind of visual prosody, the poem is a lyric meditation on humanity's frailty, and on the possibility of faith in humanity's future. In that sense it is similar to Matthew Arnold's "Dover Beach." However, "Vancouver Lights" is a much more difficult poem, to read and to understand. Birney's grammatical inversions, frequently abstract allusions, and at times impossible to grasp associations require multiple readings before meaning coheres. Although the poem suggests despair born of World War II, Birney's pessimism goes deeper, implying a cosmic hopelessness which has no remedy. Using thick descriptions of nature and humanity (figured as the lights from the city of Vancouver, British Columbia) colliding and overlapping, the speaker presents humanity as a small and insignificant part of the universe which has only itself to blame for its self-destructive behavior. The poem makes generous use of Greek mythology to underscore the idea that World War II is only the latest manifestation of humanity's impulse to destroy itself, that what history teaches us is that we make the same mistakes over and over

again. At the end of the poem, the speaker questions whether humanity has the capacity to change its course.

Author Biography

The only child of farmers Will Birney and Martha Robertson, Earle Birney was born May 13, 1904, in Calgary, located in the foothills of Alberta, when it was a part of the Northwest Territories. Birney spent much of his childhood hiking and camping, and learning first hand about the natural world in the Kootenay Valley of eastern British Columbia. These experiences served him well when he later worked as an axeman and a rodman on survey crews. In 1922 Birney enrolled at the University of British Columbia, first intending to be a chemical engineer, and then a geologist, but wound up taking a degree in English. Birney's political awakening came shortly afterwards, while he was a graduate student at the University of Toronto. In Toronto, Birney steeped himself in political philosophy, particularly the writings of Marx and Trotsky, and by the time he graduated was a self-proclaimed socialist. He practiced his new found political ideals while in London on a Royal Society Fellowship, working for the Independent Labour Party. In Europe, Birney met Trotsky and had a few run-ins with the Nazi Party in Berlin, being arrested once for not saluting during a Nazi rally. When World II broke out Birney enlisted with the Canadian Army and was posted overseas, serving for three years as a personnel specialist in Belgium, England, and Holland before returning home in 1945. Birney wrote some of his most well-known poems during this time. Upon his return he was offered a full professorship at the University of British Columbia. His experience in the war provided him with material for novels, plays, television scripts, and essays, as well as poems. *Turvey,* perhaps his best prose work, is a darkly comic work set in World War II whose main character is a personnel officer like Birney himself. Birney was a tireless promoter both of his own writing and of Canadian literature, traveling the world to give readings and lectures. Critics consider Birney to be one of the first true Canadian modernists. His collaboration with musicians and film makers, and his attempts at sound poetry, concrete poetry, and other forms of visual prosody mark him as a writer who always tried to expand the horizons of his field, looking for news ways of poetic expression. When Earle Birney died in 1995 he left behind him one

Earle Birney

of the most significant and diverse collections of Canadian writing to date.

Poem Text

About me the night moonless wimples the
    mountains
wraps ocean land air and mounting
sucks at the stars The city throbbing below
webs the sable peninsula The golden
strands overleap the seajet by bridge and buoy   5
vault the shears of the inlet climb the woods
toward me falter and halt Across to the firefly
haze of a ship on the gulf's erased horizon
roll the lambent spokes of a lighthouse

Through the feckless years we have come to the   10
    time
when to look on this quilt of lamps is a troubling
    delight
Welling from Europe's bog through Africa's
    flowing
and Asia drowning the lonely lumes on the oceans
tiding up over Halifax now to this winking
outpost comes flooding the primal ink   15

On this mountain's brutish forehead with terror of
    space
I stir of the changeless night and the stark ranges
of nothing pulsing down from beyond and between

the fragile planets We are a spark beleaguered
by darkness this twinkle we make in a corner of   20
        emptiness
how shall we utter our fear that the black
        Experimentress
will never in the range of her microscope find it?
        Our Phoebus
himself is a bubble that dires on Her slide while
        the Nubian
wears for an evening's whim a necklace of nebulae

Yet we must speak we the unique glowworms   25
Out of the waters and rocks of our little world
we conjured these flames hooped these sparks
by our will From blankness and cold we fashioned
        stars
to our size and signalled Aldebaran
This must we say whoever may be to hear us   30
if murk devour and none weave again in gossamer:

    These rays were ours
we made and unmade them Not the shudder of
        continents
doused us the moon's passion nor crash of comets
In the fathomless heat of our dwarfdom our   35
        dream's combustion
we contrived the power the blast that snuffed us
No one bound Prometheus Himself he chained
and consumed his own bright liver O stranger
Plutonian descendant or beast in the stretching
        night-
there was light   40

Poem Summary

Stanza 1:

The poem opens with the speaker describing the landscape surrounding him. The "moonless" night has an almost omnivorous quality, as it "wimples," "wraps," and "sucks" everything around it. Birney uses the word "wimple" to show the way the darkness creates what looks like folds or ripples around the mountain. The city itself "webs" the peninsula, suggesting its spider-like qualities. This buried metaphor is taken up again at the end of the fourth stanza. The lights of the city, which itself is described as "throbbing," are as active as the night is hungry, as they "overleap," "vault," and "climb" towards the speaker. In the distance, the speaker sees a lighthouse, from which light emanates like "lambent spokes." The overwhelming sense we have from the description is one of humanity and nature overlapping, with light serving both as both agent and effect of that overlapping. The speaker locates himself in an almost dreamlike world which we feel could change at any time. As is typical in lyric poems, the speaker will use his surroundings as backdrop and metaphor for the ideas upon which he will meditate.

Stanza 2:

The vague, dreamy setting described in the first stanza prepares us for the statements made in the second. Birney moves from an "I" to a "we," emphasizing that his descriptions are meant to speak for all of humanity, not just himself. He characterizes history as "feckless," meaning that it has been purposeless and meandering. But he also finds hope in humanity when he says that to look on it (figured as the city of Vancouver, itself figured as a "quilt of lamps") "is a troubling delight." This last phrase is an oxymoron, that is, it joins two terms which are contraries. The "bog" of Europe refers to the chaos of conflicts engulfing that continent during the onset of World War II, when Birney wrote the poem. The city's lights, paradoxically, drown the ocean's waves. Birney plays on images of lightness and darkness throughout the poem, suggesting a war between hope and meaninglessness that humanity has waged and continues to wage. The final few lines in the stanza are ominous, as humanity, first represented by the city of Halifax, Nova Scotia, on Canada's east coast, and then Vancouver, "this winking / outpost," located on the country's west coast, is on the brink of being overwhelmed by the ocean's dark waters, "the primal ink".

Stanza 3:

The mountain Birney refers to in the first line is Grouse Mountain, from whose high ridge one can look down upon Vancouver. By using the adjective "brutish" to describe the mountain's ridge, Birney echoes Thomas Hobbes's well-known statement that human life is "nasty, short, and brutish." He now considers humanity in light of the universe, and sees human beings as "a spark beleaguered / by darkness." The sinister "black Experimentress" is that darkness. Not even the sun god, Phoebus, can penetrate her black emptiness for very long. For all of his brightness he amounts to nothing more than "a bubble that dries on Her [microscope's] slide." The stars themselves (the "necklace of nebulae" the Nubian wears) are only an "evening's whim," to be extinguished in time themselves. Images of despair punctuate this stanza ("terror of space," "stark ranges / of nothing," "corner of emptiness"), underlining the speaker's own sense of foreboding.

Stanza 4:

Against all of this darkness and emptiness, against all the meaninglessness that the speaker cat-

Media Adaptations

- The National Film Board of Canada produced a film in 1981 titled *Earle Birney: Portrait of a Poet.*

- High Barnet of Toronto has sound recordings of Birney reading his poems.

- C.B.C. Learning Systems of Toronto has produced a cassette by Birney called *The Creative Writer.*

- A font of information about Earle Birney can be found on this website dedicated to him: http://www.cariboo.bc.ca/ae/E_BIRNEY/Home.htm

- *Bushed,* with words by Earle Birney and music by Nancy Telfer, can be purchased from Waterloo Music of Waterloo, Ontario.

- The Ontario Institute for Studies in Education has produced a number of Birney poetry readings on tape.

- In 1966 the Canadian Broadcasting System produced an audiocassette of Birney reading his poems.

- In 1994 the National Film Board of Canada produced a short animated film of Earle Birney's expressive interpretation of "Trawna Tuh Belvul," a poem by Knayjim Psifik. This film is an adventure aboard a train. The characters on the train, their stories, and the evocative blend of rail sounds, original music, and Earle Birney's reading of the poem all contribute to a memorable experience of the journey from Toronto to Belleville, Ontario.

- The University of Toronto sponsors a Canadian Poetry website, with useful and informative links to Canadian poetry journals and information on Canadian poets including Earle Birney: http://www.library.utoronto.ca/canpoetry/

---

alogues, he nevertheless insists that "we must speak." Describing humanity as "unique glow-worms," he claims that we have created the world "by our will." But not even Aldebaran (the red star which is the eye of the constellation Taurus, Birney's own astrological sign) which humanity has created by our sheer act of naming, will survive time. Speaking out for the voiceless has been a traditional role of poets, and one that Birney takes on in this poem to both describe the past and to sound a warning for the future. The last image of the stanza completes the weaving metaphor introduced in the first stanza.

Stanza 5:

In Greek mythology Prometheus was one of the Titans, a family of gods who roamed the earth before the creation of man. He and his brother were entrusted with providing man with animals and the means for preserving and taking care of them. With the intention of helping man, Prometheus gave him the gift of fire (which he stole) from heaven. Jupiter then created woman and sent her to Prometheus to punish him for stealing the fire. The woman, Pan-dora, was given a jar, or in some versions of the story a box, and forbidden to open it. She disobeyed orders and opened the box, releasing plagues of the mind and body upon humanity. The only thing which did not escape was hope, which lay at the bottom. Prometheus was punished by Zeus, who had him chained to a boulder, where an eagle pecked at his liver until he was eventually freed by Hercules. Contrary to Percy Bysshe Shelley's "Prometheus Unbound," in which humanity is described as having the capacity to perfect itself, Birney's Prometheus is responsible for his own suffering, and it is not clear that he will be rescued. Pluto is the god of the underworld and for Birney represents humanity's darker impulses, its drive towards self destruction.

Themes

Nature

Birney's description of the relationship between nature and culture in "Vancouver Lights" is a metaphor for humanity's relationship to the universe

Topics for Further Study

- Existentialism, a philosophy which holds that humanity is essentially alone in the universe and that individuals choose their own destinies, was a popular idea in the mid-twentieth century. After researching existentialist thinking, write an essay exploring how "Vancouver Lights" can be seen as an example of this philosophy. Use lines or phrases from the poem to support your claims.

- Find a place of high altitude which affords a view of your city or town and go there on a moonless night. Write a short descriptive essay on your observations, paying particular attention to how the city lights change how you see what surrounds them.

- After researching the history and causes of World War II, write a speculative essay proposing how you think the war could have been avoided.

and to history. In the first stanza the speaker, his vision "guided" by the moonless night, sees lights from the city "overleapping the seajet" and "vault[ing] the shears of the inlet," metaphorically suggesting that human beings have overrun nature, that human-made things such as cities dramatically affect the ways in which we see and interact with the natural world. But nature also overruns culture, as in the second stanza when the ocean, metaphorically described as "the primal ink," threatens to engulf cities. Birney both underlines Nature's indifference to human concerns *and* figures Nature as a malleable substance which can be molded by human will. His description of the "mountain's brutish forehead" and night that "black Experimentress," which threatens to swallow all of human existence, shows a view of a natural world that does not need human beings. However, when he claims that "out of the water and rocks of our little world / we conjured these flames," Nature is presented as less threatening and a substance with which humanity can do as it desires. Birney also seems to imply that distinguishing between what is human-made and what is natural has become

more difficult, giving rise to a greater sense of dislocation in human beings. This sense of "lostness" is reinforced in the many images of emptiness and space, and the description of history as "feckless years." The universe itself, the poem seems to say, is like history. Both are governed by whim and chance and circumstances beyond humanity's control. We attempt to control the randomness by controlling and colonizing the wilderness, but this also will prove impossible.

Meaning of Life

"Vancouver Lights" asks not what kind of meaning human life has, but if it has *any*. Writing like a prototypical existentialist, Birney appears to conclude that humanity is responsible for making its own meaning, and it will be responsible for negating that meaning. Birney underscores the randomness of human existence when he refers to history as "feckless," and he emphasizes that emptiness is at the root of life in his figure of the "black Experimentress," an all encompassing darkness that continually threatens to blot out humanity itself. For Birney, humanity "is a spark beleaguered / by darkness," but that darkness is as much inside as outside ourselves. Birney's insistence that humanity is responsible for its own condition is a familiar existential refrain, one popularized by writers such as Jean Paul Sartre, Albert Camus and others during the mid-twentieth century. In existential thought, existence precedes essence. There is no predetermined self or a destiny that human beings float toward. Rather, we create our own essence by the choices that we make: "we conjured these flames hooped these sparks / by our will From blankness and cold we fashioned stars / to our size ..." When we are told that "No one bound Prometheus," we are being told that he created his own circumstances by the choice he made in stealing fire from the Titans and befriending man. Birney uses Greek mythology—a system of stories which came about to explain natural phenomena and give meaning to existence—to undercut the influence of such stories, and to highlight the notion that there are no forces which create us, only we who create ourselves.

Style

"Vancouver Lights" is a meditative-descriptive lyric. In five irregular stanzas, Birney uses a kind of visual prosody to map the poem and to embody the poem's subjects. His inter- and intra-sentence spacings makes for a kind of staccato reading experience: we read the poem in the same way that the light and darkness Birney describes appear to him. Similarly, his enjambed lines emphasize the overlapping of the natural and the human worlds.

The poem's descriptive elements utilize concrete imagery and symbolic metaphors to depict a turbulent sea and busy, chaotic city. The active verbs—"wimples," "wraps," "sucks," "webs," "vault," "climb," "falter," "halt"—used to describe the light and darkness in the first stanza echo the ebb and flow of the sea described in the second stanza. Light and darkness themselves symbolize the flow of time and the alternating currents of hope and despair throughout human history. Many of the metaphors employ visual images. For example, "this quilt of lamps" in the second stanza refers to the lights of Vancouver that Birney sees from the "mountain's brutish forehead," as does "this winking / outpost." By referring to humanity as "unique glowworms," Birney captures both the ephemeral quality of human life as well as its animal nature.

The poem's didactic elements are embodied in Birney's use of characters from Greek mythology. Just as the ancients used myths to make sense of their own world, so too does Birney use them to make sense of his. Birney's use of myth is two-fold: on one hand he alludes to these characters and stories to emphasize the theme of creation; on the other hand he comments on the myths to highlight their function *as* stories. As long as we have history, Birney suggests, we cannot *not* have stories. But if we have them let's tell the truth about ourselves.

The poem's highly stylized diction and grammatical inversions also undergird the serious, grave tone of the poem and add to the image of the speaker as an oracle of sorts. At times phrases and metaphors veer towards melodrama and hyperbole, as when in the final stanza the speaker locates humanity's relative unimportance "In the fathomless heat of our dwarfdom ..."

Towards the end of his life Earle Birney chose to call his writings not poems, but "makings" and "alphabeings." He did so that readers might approach them without so many of the (potentially) debilitating expectations sometimes brought to poetry. According to Peter Aichinger in his book *Earle Birney,* Birney eschewed the label "poet," choosing instead to refer to himself and other Canadian writers as "men of letters" or "men of images."

Historical Context

The Treaty of Versailles, which had officially ended World War I, crippled Germany's economy, guaranteeing the country a future of social turmoil which only added to the insecurity the German people already felt. In 1933, The National Socialist German Workers Party exploited this sentiment and took power, installing Adolf Hitler as its leader. With much of the German population supporting him, Hitler spent the next six years re-building the German military while invading and occupying nearby countries such as Czechoslovakia and Austria. Exhausted from the first world war, European countries did little or nothing to confront Hitler, practicing appeasement and negotiation instead of militarily confronting Hitler's army.

When Birney wrote "Vancouver Lights" in 1941 he was already at the end of a decade-long experiment in extreme politics. As World War II approached, Birney become more and more disenchanted with organized revolution and finally managed to distance himself from it. He took up poetry writing in earnest shortly afterward. In a 1939 interview he says that "I was writing because I felt, dammit, I wanted to say this kind of thing, I wanted to do this kind of thing, or see if I could do it, for a long time, and now I see the war closing around me and I'm either going to go to jail [for his political work] or I'm going to go overseas, and don't know who's going to survive or what. In 1939 as soon as war's declared, I began writing poems" (quoted in Davey).

Canada had the spent the 21 years from the close of World War I until the beginning of World War II fighting for autonomy from Great Britain, which they finally achieved in 1931 when Britain passed the Statute of Westminster, a law which gave Canada the right to form its own foreign policy. But Canada's ties to the United Kingdom were hard to break, and they joined England in declaring war on Germany September 10, 1939. This was just nine days after Germany had sent troops and tank divisions into Poland, marking the beginning of the war, and just one week after Britain itself had declared war on Germany. Birney enlisted in 1941, serving as a personnel specialist with the Canadian army in Canada, Britain, and various locations in Northwest Europe, attaining the rank of major before he was sent home in 1945. In 1941 shortly before he enlisted, the Royal Canadian Navy, the Canadian Merchant Navy, and the Royal Canadian Air Force were all fighting to help keep the sea lanes of the North Atlantic free of enemy warships. Halifax, Nova Scotia, which Birney names as a threatened city in the second stanza, was a major port from which Canada shipped goods and troops to the United Kingdom. The Royal Cana-

Compare & Contrast

- **1941:** Adolf Hitler becomes Commander-in-Chief of the German army.

  Today: Right-wing military groups and neo-Nazis are gaining in popularity in Germany once again.

- **1941:** German writer Bertolt Brecht's play about the absurdity of war, *Mother Courage,* is staged for the first time, foregrounding the relationships between capitalism and war.

  1991: President George Bush sends American troops to the Persian Gulf to fight against Iraqi troops who have invaded Kuwait, claiming that it is in America's political as well as economic interest.

- **1943:** Joe Louis knocks out Buddy Baer to retain the world heavyweight boxing championship. Boxing's popularity is soaring.

  Today: Boxing's heavyweight division is in chaos, and many of its former stars are considered to be jokes by the public. Former champion George Foreman continues to fight, though he is approaching fifty years old, and former champ Mike Tyson continues to make a spectacle of his life both inside and out of the boxing ring.

- **1942:** Albert Camus publishes *The Stranger,* which becomes a classic text for understanding existentialism.

  Today: Theories of Existentialism are a staple of literature and philosophy classes in higher education in the West.

- **1951:** Mid-century census records Canada's population as 14 million.

  Today: Canada's population stands at thirty million.

---

dian Navy's chief responsibility during the war was escort work for cargo ships. It was dangerous work and many sailors died, as much from exposure and accidents in the treacherous Atlantic waters as from enemy fire. All told, Canada lost more than 40,000 men and women in World War II, no small number for a country its size. The war affected Canadians both economically and psychologically. On the one hand, employment soared and women entered the workforce in large numbers, taking jobs traditionally performed by men. By 1944 more than 400,000 women were working in the service sector while almost that many worked in manufacturing. On the other hand, there were shortages of basic foodstuffs and goods, and luxury items were hard to come by.

Critical Overview

Birney began writing poetry in earnest after the outbreak of World War II. In a burst of creative energy he wrote many of the poems that would be included in *David and Other Poems,* his first collection. "Vancouver Lights" was one of these. Peter Aichinger writes that it is "one of the few poems Birney ever wrote that expresses any sort of pride or satisfaction in the human race and its accomplishments." Aichinger believes that the poem "suggests the cyclical pattern in the affairs of men, of grand achievement followed by wretched disaster. It is an expression of pride in man's ability to raise a Camelot at the same time that it acknowledges the probable victory of the forces of darkness in man's spirit." Frank Davey in *Earle Birney* sees "Vancouver Lights" as an indicator of Birney's own movement away from Trotskyism and towards a sense of himself as a poet. Davey writes that "Throughout the thirties he [Birney] had seen himself 'as a scholar, critic, Marxist, potential novelist,' but not as a poet." Birney biographer Cameron Elspeth considers the poem a statement of Birney's inherent distrust of humanity's capacity to do good. Elspeth writes in *Earle Birney: A Life* that "['Vancouver Lights'] is suffused with self-disgust, stark terror and a suspicion that man is headed for self-destruction as he pollutes and destroys the planet." David Stouck agrees with this view, but elaborates on it, observing that according to Birney, humanity's capacity for violence and malevolence is mirrored by nature as well. Stouck writes in *Major Canadian Authors* that for Birney "Nature is beautiful but frightening .... [although] nature's malevolence exists primarily in the mind of the human observer." In a letter to critic Dorothy Livesay and quoted in Elspeth's biography, Birney himself says about the poem that "What I want to say, though I grant I may not have said it, is something much more complicated and tenuous—that man has now reached a stage in his development in which for the first time he has created the conditions for his own destruction."

Criticism

Bruce Meyer

Bruce Meyer is the director of the creative writing program at the University of Toronto. He has taught at several Canadian universities and is the author of three collections of poetry. In the following essay, Meyer suggests that Birney's poem represents humankind as a Prometheus who is responsible for both his own success and his own failure. The failure threatens to destroy the whole race, but there is a faint hope for ultimate survival.

The late Canadian literary critic, Northrop Frye, used to tell a story about Earle Birney's poem "Vancouver Lights" and the events of one single winter evening that helped Frye, at least spiritually, through the darkest days of World War II. Just before Christmas in 1941, the prospects for Canada and Great Britain looked dim. Earlier in the month, the garrison at Hong Kong had fallen—taking with it a third of the Canadian Army, many of them University of Toronto students. The United States Pacific fleet had been mauled at Pearl Harbor. England lay devastated during the worst days of the Blitz and its gradually dwindling air force was a thin line of dogged determination that lay between the British Empire and Nazi domination. The overwhelming drain on manpower, from both the call to arms and the call to factory work had depleted the enrollment at the University of Toronto to the point where the university was about to close its doors and submit to the veil of darkness that lay across the free world.

On that winter night shortly before Christmas in 1941, Frye gathered at Earle Birney's apartment on Hazelton Avenue along with a group of other Canadian poets that included the Canadian poet-

What Do I Read Next?

- Frank Davey's *Earle Birney* provides a solid and succinct introduction to the life and writings of the Canadian poet.

- In 1967 M. L. Rosenthal published *The New Poets: American and British Poetry Since World War II*. This critical study describes many of the movements and individuals who have helped define landscape of poetry written in the English-speaking world in the last half of the twentieth century.

- David Stouck's *Major Canadian Authors*, published in 1984, provides a comprehensive introduction to the life and works of seventeen Canadian authors from the nineteenth and twentieth centuries. Stouck locates the work of these writers in the context of both regional and world literature.

- *Out of the Shadows: Canada in the Second World War*, a 1995 study by William A. B. Douglas and Brereton Greenhous, explores the contributions and sacrifices of Canada during World War II.

- *Existentialism: From Dostoevsky to Sartre*, published in 1988 and edited by Walter Kaufmann, provides a strong introduction to some of the more prominent existentialist thinkers throughout history.

laureate E. J. Pratt, and younger voices such as Roy Daniels and A. J. M. Smith. Binrey was about to leave academic life for a tour of duty in the Canadian Army (the events of which would form the basis for his comic novel, *Turvey*). Pratt opened the evening by reading his poem, "The Truant," a fantasy/satire which tells the story of how a little "three by six" foot man stands up to a huge deistic entity called "the Great Panjandrum." Daniels and Smith chimed in with their new wartime poems. Birney then followed with a poem he had written while out West to visit friends in his home city of Vancouver the previous summer.

"Vancouver Lights" was based on an actual experience that Birney had while climbing a mountain above the west coast metropolis. It was night time and, as Birney stared from the mountaintop down onto the city below, district by district of the city suddenly went black—the first of many wartime black outs. As Birney often later recalled during my many lunches with the poet, it "was as if I was witnessing the end of the world from the point-of-view of God in Heaven." Birney speculated on the annihilation of the free world and what would cause, in the words of Winston Churchill, "the lights to go out" not only "all over Europe" but around the world. At the same time, Birney was struck by the idea that even in the face of total darkness and a bleak future there still exists "a will to light and life."

It was the final line of "Vancouver Lights," that profound statement "there was light," that so moved Northrop Frye. Perhaps the light had gone out of the world for the perceivable future, but the memory of it continued to exist, and that alone was signal enough of why the university should remain open and why Canada and the free world should be dedicated to the cause at hand. Like the defiant Prometheus who was bound and chained to the mountain side, Birney perceived the very heroic, yet ultimately responsible position of mankind for the sad state of affairs the world had become in the winter of 1941. For Frye, that paradox, the possibility of the world seeing its way clear of Fascism and mass destruction, was a signal of hope, albeit a faint one, that gave him the reassurance that the free world would endure.

Some of that hope resides in the position of the persona in "Vancouver Lights." The voice is one of an individual who finds himself lost and awed by both the splendor and the horror of the world around him. The poem begins with the phrase, "About me the night moonless wimples the mountains" as if the darkness is enveloping everything. The word "wimples" is also unique in that it signals a sense of almost cloistered withdrawal on the part of the world from the aspects of light, a humbling gesture that covers even "the mountains." That same darkness, however, is more than a habit donned to mask the glory of earth—it is a force that "sucks at the stars," as if to drain the very life force from the heart of the universe. The city below, still "throbbing" is treated almost as an amulet or jeweled talisman, a signal of vitality, beauty and elegance in an otherwise empty cosmos. The lamps of the city streets "webs the sable peninsula" (a reference to the fact that Vancouver is composed of five major peninsulas that jut into the Georgia Strait like five hands

reaching into the sea). The diction and cadence of Birney's descriptions of the geographic interaction between the sea and the land are very reminiscent of the descriptions utilized by E. J. Pratt in many of his sea poems such as "Silences."

In fact, Birney makes a subtle tribute to Pratt's poetry in his use of the words "seajet," "buoy," and "shears," and in the cadence of the three lines in stanza one that deal with the city's venue. Also evident in the opening stanza is Birney's love of Anglo-Saxon poetry (he was, by academic profession a medievalist, and many of his poems, such as "Anglo-Saxon Street" are written in parody of Anglo-Saxon poetry). The use of alliteration in "by bridge and buoy" underscores this very elemental "Englishness" and aligns the world of "Vancouver Lights", at least in an allusory sense, to the cold, cruel world that is depicted in such early English poems as "The Wanderer" or "The Seafarer." The resulting staccato rhythm of the poem's sonics is further enhanced by the 'breaks' or 'rests' within the lines where the addition of spaces creates a series of halting pauses, breathing spots, where a tentativeness enters the voice. Birney recorded this poem many times (the last recording with the percussion group Nexus shortly before his final illness) and it is evident from listening to these recordings that the pauses were intended to punctuate with silence the rhythms of the lines and, in a very Black Mountain fashion (in later editions of the poem Birney removed his punctuation) to serve as points of grammatical organization. As is the case with Anglo-Saxon masterpieces, "Vancouver Lights" is intended to be an oral poem, a voice sounding in the darkness and taking up Wilfred Owen's claim that "the purpose of poetry is to warn."

The opening stanza concludes with a brief description of the lighthouse: "Across [to] the firefly / haze of a ship on the gulf's erased horizon." What the first stanza of poem establishes is the tension between what is and all that might vanquish it. The language, for its energy and beauty of description, flirts with an overwhelmingly negative presence where the "horizon" is "erased" and the cloaking darkness that "wimples the mountains" is set to humble everything that is visible either to the eye or the spirit. The reader is told from the outset that this is a poem about fear, and about confronting the challenge of a world where possibilities are suddenly diminishing.

The second and third stanzas of the poem attempt to trace the sequence within the cause and effect relationship that underlies that moment in history. History, in this sense, is not perceived in the Nineteenth century idiom of "progress" but as a kind of 'spreading-out' or European culture to the point where the problems of European culture have become the problems of the world. The years, he says, have been "feckless" and the source for the problems is "Europe's bog." This description of Euro-cultural growth serves to make the world a small place where even the "outpost," that supposed safe haven on the very edge of the world is under the thumb of that darkness which emanated from the very heart of European culture. In this sense, Birney is presenting an indictment as well as an apology for his culture; the bad and the good seem so inextricably intertwined that only a 'Promethean' effort of distinction can separate them. In the world of "Vancouver Lights," eschatology is a gray area; and while one is attempting to sort it out, the "primal ink" of spiritual and political darkness continues to flow. One is reminded of C. Day Lewis's famous lines on the eve of the Second World War that mankind was confronted with the dilemma of "defending the bad against the worse." Politically speaking, "Vancouver Lights" shares that same sense of ambivalence, a distrust of the verities of the world which the century had called into question. Birney was, during the Thirties, a committed Communist and spent almost a year and a half living with Leon Trotsky and his family in Mexico. His sense of political cynicism feeds into the poem in the subtle distrust of culture and in the tone of ambivalence in the poem's delineation of good and evil. In this sense, "Vancouver Lights" is not a typical wartime poem. It does not offer a "rah-rah" take on events or a political "cause." Instead, the persona takes the position of the epic observer, the voice that is both elevated and objective. The point-of-view is not of someone on one side or another in the war, but that of a besieged humanity. "We are the spark beleaguered," he announces. The darkness that the persona faces is "the changeless night" where the end result of human suffering is the ultimate negation of death where the "black Experimentress," perhaps fate but certainly nothingness, stares back at the observer and leaves him with an acute sense of littleness and Kierkegaardian angst. Even the sun, that eternal source of light (associated since Classical times with Phoebus Apollo, the god of light and learning) is but a "bubble" on the side of the "Experimentress," and the endless night, "the Nubian" dwarfs the tiny sparks of possibility in the cosmos by wearing the stars as a "necklace of Nebulae."

What remains for mankind among all these shards of light and dying sparks, is the determina-

tion to articulate itself into existence. "Yet we must speak" is a declaration that there is a divine spark in mankind, an animate and life-affirming force, that cannot be snuffed out. Just as Prometheus stole the gift of fire from the gods, so mankind is driven [by] the scintillation, the energy, to confirm and reconfirm "our will." What mankind has made, beyond culture, beyond politics and beyond civilization, is an on-going pact with himself to exist: "we conjured these flames." What is important regardless "if the murk devour and none weave again in gossamer" is that mankind has sent a signal to the cosmos that "there was light" and that "these rays were ours," as if the dimming lights of the city were affirmations of the marvel of humanity and footprints left on a dark beach even as the tide comes in. In a statement that would be sounded by the likes of William Faulkner in his Nobel speech, Birney sees mankind as the master of its own fate, where the decision to exist or to cease rests solely in its own will: "No one bound Prometheus Himself he chained / and consumed his own bright liver." Many critics of Birney's have pointed out that the phrase "the blast that snuffed us" is eerily prophetic and foreshadows the coming of the atomic bomb and the nuclear age. What Birney did acknowledge is that he feared that mankind was on the verge of annihilating itself and that he sought to produce a poem that would warn while offering the choice between existence and destruction.

The final line, "there was light," reverberates with the tone of ambivalence that is carried throughout the poem. There was light. Will there be light again? What does the light say and to whom? As much as the final statement is a conclusion, it is not a conclusion—it is the presentation of a future thesis; yet it is the open-endedness of the statement that offers a sense of hope. It was this sense of hope that Northrop Frye acknowledged that night in Birney's apartment on Hazelton Avenue. What Frye saw was not the fear in the persona's words, but the presence of possibilities past, present and future, that even if the light should go out of the world, there had been enough of it, particle traces floating through the universe, to suggest that what was here was meaningful, alive and worth preserving.

Source: Bruce Meyer, in an essay for *Poetry for Students,* Gale Group, 2000.

Chris Semansky

Chris Semansky's poetry, essays, and stories appear regularly in literary magazines and journals. In the following essay, Semansky explores

"

Figuring human beings as worms and insects (spiders weave gossamer webs) makes sense in that both create worlds out of themselves, the former reproducing itself, the latter spinning its own abode. But they are also sub-human species and hence underscore humanity's own insignificance in relation to the universe and history itself."

how Birney uses the imagery of light and darkness in "Vancouver Lights" to question and comment on the meaning of human existence.

For most of his life Earle Birney was a relentless traveler and seeker of new experiences, concerned as much with the processes of becoming as he was with the work of being. Raised on the outskirts of the Canadian wilderness, Birney was also acutely attuned to nature and its processes. His best poems embrace both his passion for exploration of life's meaning and his experience with the natural world. "Vancouver Lights," included in *David and Other Poems,* his first collection, is one such poem. In it, Birney uses light and darkness in their various and varied forms as its central metaphoric images, allowing him to meditate on the relationships between insight and vision, between how we see the physical world and what sense we make of it. Birney's typographic use of space itself also underscores the poem's preoccupation with seeing.

We are introduced to light and darkness in the first stanza. Darkness is the province of space and has the capacity to alter the natural world for the speaker. The night "wraps ocean land air" and "sucks at the stars." Birney takes up the impersonal but ominously omnivorous quality of darkness later in the poem but here it serves as the backdrop which

enables the speaker to see light as well. For without the darkness, the speaker would be unable to witness "The city throbbing below." In this stanza it is light which, underscoring the poems mythic theme of good versus evil, fights against the darkness. The speaker sees "strands" of it which "falter and halt," and through a "firefly / haze" spies the "lambent spokes of a lighthouse." The thinness and attenuated nature of the light he describes is apropos for what they signify: humanity's striving in the dark for meaning. This striving occurs, as Birney tells us in the second stanza, "Through the feckless years," underscoring the inherent futility of human effort. The light in this stanza similarly has a temporal quality to it. The city's lights are described as a "quilt of lamps" (lamps are lighted and go out) and the city itself as a "winking / outpost." Darkness is the constant, Birney implies, the backdrop of time and existence itself, the natural state to which all things and beings eventually revert. Again, he figures darkness as a consuming force, this time in the guise of the oceans, which threaten civilization, as represented by the Canadian city of Halifax, located in Nova Scotia on the country's east coast. The "primal ink," another form of darkness, here represents the world's many wars and conflicts at this time. Its "flooding" highlights the ways in which these wars are spilling and threatening to spill over onto every continent. In his 1971 work *Earle Birney,* Richard Robillard writes that "This section suggests the question: Can we, having lived through careless, thoughtless, spiritless years, read the message of the 'primal ink'? The great irony is, of course, that there is little whiteness or brightness to set off the message: the ink floods almost the whole page."

Birney emphasizes the constancy of the dark in the third stanza where—in its incarnation as night—he describes it as "changeless," yet "pulsing," a kind of symbolic blood in which even planets are shown to be "fragile," presumably because they too will succumb to time. In this "atmosphere" Birney locates humanity as "a spark beleaguered / by darkness." The paradox *and* the irony is that the very thing which gives birth to the light is responsible for its death. The symbol of light representing deity and life and darkness representing evil and death is universal. In this vein the speaker's question—"how shall we utter our fear that the black Experimentress / will never in the range of her microscope find it?"—can also be read as an implicit death wish, for to be found surely means to be devoured, blotted out. Even Phoebus Apollo, the Sun God, does not stand a chance against darkness; he is merely "a bubble that dries on Her slide." Calling darkness an "Experimentress" also underscores an intentionality behind it, a force which is merely playing, "experimenting," and that humanity falls within the scope of the potential subjects on which she experiments. Birney's biographer Elspeth Cameron believed that after Birney lost faith in Trotsky, who epitomized for him the "visionary male leader," "What was left was the principle of female power represented not by humanist vision but by scientific investigation."

The encroaching darkness is no reason, however, for humanity not to try, not to voice its place in the darkness. In the fourth stanza, the speaker, building on his own identity as a representative spokesman for humanity, insists on this, suggesting even that language itself, in the form of speech, is a form of salvation, of hope.

> Yet we must speak we the unique glowworms
> Out of the waters and rocks of our little world
> we conjured these flames hooped these sparks
> by our will From blankness and cold we fashioned
>   stars
> to our size and signalled Aldebaran
> This must we say whoever may be to hear us
> if murk devour and none weave again in gossamer:
>
> These rays were ours
> we made and unmade them Not the shudder of
>   continents
> doused us the moon's passion nor crash of comets
> In the fathomless heat of our dwarfdom our
>   dream's combustion
> we contrived the power the blast that snuffed us
> No one bound Prometheus Himself he chained
> and consumed his own bright liver O stranger
> Plutonian descendant or beast in the stretching
>   night-
> there was light

Describing humanity as "unique glowworms" is apt, as the poem returns again and again to the claim that humanity has created itself, and so is responsible for its own condition. Figuring human beings as worms and insects (spiders weave gossamer webs) makes sense in that both create worlds out of themselves, the former reproducing itself, the latter spinning its own abode. But they are also sub-human species and hence underscore humanity's own insignificance in relation to the universe and history itself.

Humanity contains both the forces of light and the forces of darkness, Birney suggests. We can either choose to live or choose to destroy ourselves: "We contrived the power the blast that snuffed us", he says. The "black Experimentress" did not incite man to make war; it was "Not the shudder of con-

tinents / ... the moon's passion nor crash of comets", but man himself who makes and unmakes his own light. In *Major Canadian Authors* David Stouck observes that "Humankind's capacity to create light ... is threatened by a primal instinct for violence and destruction." If indeed these forces are built into human beings, as the poem implies, then the speaker's insistence that humanity has created its own mess because it chose to is a contradiction at best, disingenuous at worse. The lines make more sense if we see it as a contradiction. In this way Birney's probing examination of humanity's drive to both destroy and save itself is echoed in the poem's own logic, something of which the writer may or may not be aware. As if to emphasize the (apparently) irresolvable nature of the conflict, the poem juxtaposes Pluto and Prometheus in the last stanza, again foregrounding the mythic battle between light and darkness, this time in the figures of the god of fire and the god of the underworld. The poem ends with an image of light, echoing the light of Genesis at the beginning of the world. The prophetic tone of these last lines in particular and of the entire poem in general, position the speaker as a kind of demi-god who has also has the power to create and destroy the world through his words.

Source: Chris Semansky, in an essay for *Poetry for Students*, Gale Group, 2000.

Sources

Aichinger, Peter, *Earle Birney,* Boston: Twayne Publishers, 1979.

Atwood, Margaret, *Survival: A Thematic Guide to Canadian Literature,* Toronto: Anansi, 1972.

Birney, Earle, *The Collected Poems of Earle Birney,* Toronto: McClelland and Stewart, 1975.

———, *David and Other Poems,* Toronto: Ryerson, 1942.

Cameron, Elspeth, *Earle Birney: A Life,* Toronto: Viking, 1994.

Davey, Frank, *Earle Birney,* Toronto: Copp Clark Publishing Co., 1971.

Nesbitt, Bruce, ed., *Earle Birney,* Toronto: McGraw-Hill Ryerson, 1974.

New, W. H., ed, *Dictionary of Literary Biography,* Volume 88: *Canadian Writers, 1920-1959,* Detroit: Gale Research, 1989, pp. 14-29.

Robillard, Richard, *Earle Birney,* Toronto: McClelland and Stewart Limited, 1971.

Pacey, Desmond, *Creative Writing in Canada,* Toronto: Ryerson, 1952.

Stouck, David, *Major Canadian Authors,* Lincoln: University of Nebraska Press, 1984.

Woodcock, George, *The World of Canadian Writing,* Seattle: University of Washington Press, 1980.

For Further Study

Atwood, Margaret, *Survival: A Thematic Guide to Canadian Literature,* Toronto: Anansi, 1972.

> For those interested in the history and themes of Canadian literature, this is a must read. Novelist and poet Margaret Atwood provides not only an idiosyncratic thematic overview of Canadian literature but also her own polemics and manifestos on literature and the literary life.

Birney, Earle, *David and Other Poems,* Toronto: Ryerson, 1942.

> Birney's first collection of poetry is also his best known and most widely praised. The collection contains "David," one of the most anthologized poems in Canadian literature, as well as "Vancouver Lights" and others. Most of the themes and many of the poetic techniques that Birney would develop throughout his career can be found here.

Cameron, Elspeth, *Earle Birney: A Life,* Toronto: Viking, 1994.

> Elspeth has written the definitive biography of Earle Birney. She uses Birney's volumnuous correspondence, notes, and his published and unpublished writing to construct a fascinating portrait of a complex and complicated literary figure. Cameron pays particular attention to the intersections between Birney's volatile emotional life and his productive professional life as political activist, poet, novelist, critic, and teacher.

Why I Am Not a Painter

Frank O'Hara's "Why I Am Not a Painter" was first published in 1957 in the *Evergreen Review.* Having a reputation for publishing some of the more adventurous works of the day, *Evergreen Review* was a fitting venue for O'Hara. Going against the predominant "neo-Symbolist" poetry of the time—a poetry in the tradition of T. S. Eliot, which critic Paul Carroll characterized in his *The Poem in Its Skin* as "civilized, verbally excellent, ironic, cerebral"—O'Hara's work is usually conversational and casual in tone. "Why I Am Not a Painter," in fact, like many of O'Hara's poems, reads as if O'Hara had simply improvised it off the top of his head.

Considered by many critics to be one of O'Hara's greatest poems, "Why I Am Not a Painter" reflects upon the creative process by comparing the writing of O'Hara's poem "Oranges: 12 Pastorals" with the painting of "SARDINES," a canvas by O'Hara's friend, the painter Mike Goldberg. Told in the first person from O'Hara's point of view, "Why I Am Not a Painter" is a narrative poem in which we see O'Hara dropping in on Goldberg who, at the moment, is starting his painting. After describing the process Goldberg goes through in order to complete "SARDINES," O'Hara reflects upon the process he himself goes through in order to write "ORANGES."

Both "ORANGES" and "SARDINES" have what appear to be unusual starting points, with O'Hara initiating the poetic process by thinking about the color orange, and Goldberg beginning his

Frank O'Hara

1957

painting by brushing the word "SARDINES" on his canvas. In the end, however, neither of the finished works contains a trace of what originally inspired them: O'Hara's poem never mentions "orange" and Goldberg's painting no longer has the word "SAR-DINES" in it.

During the course of "Why I Am Not a Painter," O'Hara does not mention the title of either the poem or the painting he is discussing. He saves that until the end when he reveals that, despite the disappearance within each work of the original source of inspiration, the finished poem and painting are titled, respectively, "ORANGES" and "SARDINES."

Critic Marjorie Perloff, writing in her *Frank O'Hara: Poet among Painters,* describes "Why I Am Not a Painter" as "a profound jest" in answer to the question of why O'Hara—who was heavily involved with the art world and who eventually became a curator at the Museum of Modern Art in New York—was not himself a painter. Indeed, on a certain level the poem *is* a joke. Yet, as critics such as Perloff have noted, the humor and levity one finds in O'Hara's poetry does not make his work any less profound.

Frank O'Hara

Author Biography

Born on June 27, 1926, in Baltimore, Maryland, Francis Russell O'Hara was the first of Katherine Broderick O'Hara and Russell J. O'Hara's three children. In 1927, the family moved to Massachusetts, where Frank O'Hara grew up and attended St. John's High School in Worcester, and studied piano at the New England Conservatory. From 1944 to 1946, O'Hara served in the U.S. Navy as a sonarman on the destroyer USS *Nicholas.* Upon completing his military service, O'Hara attended Harvard College to study music before changing his major to English. Here, O'Hara met fellow poet John Ashbery who, with O'Hara, Kenneth Koch, and James Schuyler, founded what would later be dubbed the "New York School" of poets.

After receiving a master's degree in 1951 from the University of Michigan at Ann Arbor, O'Hara moved to New York City. There, he soon found a job at the front desk of the Museum of Modern Art. In 1952, O'Hara's first book of poems, *A City Winter, and Other Poems,* was published. In addition to writing poetry, O'Hara actively pursued his interest in visual arts, participating in panel discussions at The Club of the New York Painters, and

meeting artists such as Jackson Pollock, Willem de Kooning, and Helen Frankenthaler. After leaving the Museum of Modern Art in 1953 to become an associate editor at *Art News,* O'Hara returned to the museum in 1955. Over the years O'Hara's responsibilities at the museum grew, and he found himself writing his numerous poems during lunch or other breaks in his busy schedule—hence the title of his 1964 collection, *Lunch Poems,* published by City Lights Books.

In 1965, O'Hara was appointed Associate Curator at the museum. As his duties in the art world expanded, his poetic output decreased. Nevertheless—despite his work with the museum and his continued work in music as well as theater—he always considered poetry his primary calling. O'Hara died on July 25, 1966, one day after being struck by a beach buggy on Fire Island in New York. He was forty years old.

Poem Text

I am not a painter, I am a poet.
Why? I think I would rather be
a painter, but I am not. Well,

for instance, Mike Goldberg
is starting a painting. I drop in.   5
"Sit down and have a drink" he

says. I drink; we drink. I look
up. "You have SARDINES in it."
"Yes, it needed something there."
"Oh." I go and the days go by   10
and I drop in again. The painting
is going on, and I go, and the days
go by. I drop in. The painting is
finished. "Where's SARDINES?"
All that's left is just   15
letters, "It was too much," Mike says.

But me? One day I am thinking of
a color: orange. I write a line
about orange. Pretty soon it is a
whole page of words, not lines.   20
Then another page. There should be
so much more, not of orange, of
words, of how terrible orange is
and life. Days go by. It is even in
prose, I am a real poet. My poem   25
is finished and I haven't mentioned
orange yet. It's twelve poems, I call
it ORANGES. And one day in a gallery
I see Mike's painting, called SARDINES.

Poem Summary

Lines 1-3:

O'Hara begins the poem with a simple statement of fact. Answering the implied question of the
poem's title, O'Hara notes that he is not a painter
for what, to him, is a very obvious reason: he is a
poet. Still, the question begs a more elaborate answer, and O'Hara admits, "I think I would rather
be / a painter, but I am not." (At the time, "abstract
expressionist" painters, such as Jackson Pollock,
had gained an enormous amount of attention in the
popular press, so it was inevitable that O'Hara,
what with his own involvement in the art world,
would be asked why he himself had not become a
painter.) The third line of the poem then ends with
the word "Well," with the remainder of the sentence continuing on the next line after a stanza
break.

At first, this sudden ending of the line may
seem arbitrary, but allowing the word "Well" to
dangle here serves a purpose. First, by keeping it
close to the sentence, "I think I would rather be /
a painter, but I am not," the word "Well" hints at
how O'Hara feels about the fact that he is not a
painter. Here, "Well" could just as easily be "oh
well," which is to say that not being a painter is
not something that upsets O'Hara to any great degree—certainly, O'Hara does not consider his being a poet a liability. Placed at the end of this line,

"Well" serves the dual purpose of providing commentary on O'Hara's situation, and of initiating the
more precise explanation that continues after the
stanza break.

Lines 4-9:

In this next stanza, O'Hara narrates an account
of the creation of a painting by his friend, Mike
Goldberg. O'Hara does not present a cliched image of the artist as a tortured individual slaving over
a painting, but rather a portrait of the artist as a
calm working man.

As Goldberg begins his painting, O'Hara
comes to visit. With O'Hara saying, "I drop in,"
one should note that this is an informal situation:
O'Hara and Goldberg are on equal footing, and his
unscheduled visit is neither an imposition nor an
inconvenience. Goldberg takes a break from his
work and offers O'Hara a drink. With the words,
"I drink; we drink," O'Hara starts to delineate the
similarities between his friend, the painter, and
himself, the poet: just as the painter drinks, he too
drinks. What one immediately sees here is that art
and everyday life go together.

O'Hara then casually looks up at the painting
and makes the simplest of comments: "You have
SARDINES in it." (Putting an actual word in his
painting, Goldberg is, in a way, borrowing from the
poet's territory.) Goldberg's reply, "Yes, it needed
something there," is equally simple and direct.
Their discussion of the painting is devoid of any
self-conscious analysis or direction, which implies
that the painting is being created in a similar
fashion.

Lines 10-16:

The word, "Oh," which begins the following
line does not indicate surprise on O'Hara's part.
O'Hara, needing no further explanation of what
Goldberg is attempting to do with his painting, is
simply closing this brief dialogue between himself
and his friend. O'Hara then shows how life continues without anything remarkable going on. "And
the days go by," he writes, and when he drops in
a second time Goldberg is still working on the
painting. Again, O'Hara writes, "and the days go
by." Using the same phrase over and over again,
O'Hara simulates the passage of time.

When O'Hara drops in a third time he finds
that the painting is finished. Seeing that Goldberg
has removed the word "SARDINES," leaving just
random letters with no "meaning" in them, O'Hara
asks, "Where's SARDINES?" This time O'Hara *is*

Media Adaptations

- *Three Voices: for Joan La Barbara,* released by New Albion Records in 1989, is a compact disc featuring a composition by Morton Feldman that sets O'Hara's poem "Wind" to music.

- *Four Songs,* published by E. C. Schirmer in 1986, is the musical score for a voice composition by Ned Rorem that sets O'Hara's poem "For Poulenc" to music. Another score is 1972's *Three Airs for Frank O'Hara's Angel,* which was published by Edition Salabert. This composition by Lukas Foss features the O'Hara poems "Three Airs" and "Four Little Elegies."

- *Lost, Lost, Lost* is a film diary by experimental filmmaker Jonas Mekas. This lengthy video, which was released in 1995 by Recycled Video, includes scenes dealing with Mekas's friendships with O'Hara and other New York poets like Allen Ginsberg and LeRoi Jones (Amiri Baraka).

- *Frank O'Hara Second Edition,* released by American Poetry Archive in 1978, features outtakes from the 1966 NET series *USA: Poetry* and shows Frank O'Hara reading and discussing his work with filmmaker Al Leslie.

- *Disconnected: The Dial-a-Poem Poets,* a 1974 long-playing record from Giornio Poetry Systems, includes readings by O'Hara among many other poets.

---

surprised. Goldberg answers, "It was too much," indicating that he arrived at the finished work of art through a process of removal.

Lines 17-29:

Writing "But me?" at the opening of the final stanza, O'Hara sets forth to explain what he thinks is the difference between the process by which he creates a poem and the process by which Goldberg creates his painting. Where Goldberg starts by painting the word "SARDINES" on a canvas, O'Hara starts by thinking about the color orange.

Like Goldberg borrowing from the poet's territory by using a word, O'Hara is borrowing from the painter's territory by using a color. But rather than removing things from his work, like Goldberg, O'Hara keeps adding things. "Pretty soon," O'Hara writes, "it is a / whole page of words, not lines. / Then another page." To further clarify the difference between the poem and the painting, O'Hara notes that what he is adding are "words, not lines." At this point the poem comes to a climax with a battle of sorts between the language of a poem and the lines of a painting. Also of note here is the struggle of the poet to express in words what the painter can express by the simple use of a color.

As O'Hara continues with the poem, he finds that what he wants to add is far removed from his original idea: "There should be / so much more, not of orange, of / words, of how terrible orange is / and life." O'Hara lets the closing of this sentence, "and life," begin another line. Again, this is not an arbitrary ending of a line. Here, O'Hara is employing what Perloff calls a "floating modifier"—namely, "word groups that point two ways." The words, "and life," are connected to the concept "of how terrible orange is." But they also reflect upon the words that directly follow it, providing a transition to yet another repetition of the phrase, "Days go by."

In repeating this phrase, which is used twice in the first stanza where the process of painting is described, O'Hara is subtly setting up the closing revelation of the poem in which O'Hara realizes that there are more similarities than differences in the way he and Goldberg work. As with Goldberg, it takes a number of days to complete his work. Furthermore, when the poem is finished, O'Hara finds that it does not even mention "orange," his starting point—just as Goldberg's finished painting no longer contains the word "SARDINES," which was his starting point.

In the lines, "It is even in / prose, I am a real poet," O'Hara, after temporarily struggling with the apparent limitations of words, is reaffirming the power of words and the art of poetry. Although he says that his work is "in prose," he is not saying that his work is not a poem—it most certainly *is* a poem, a poem that has taken the form of prose. In addition to this, O'Hara is also implying that he can't help but be a poet.

Finally, even though O'Hara never mentions orange in his poem, he nevertheless decides to call it "ORANGES." Then, upon seeing Goldberg's painting in a gallery, O'Hara finds that Goldberg has done the same thing, calling his SARDINE-less painting "SARDINES." In other words, O'Hara, though he never actually uses orange in his poem, still needs the painterly concept of color; and likewise, Goldberg, though he has no words in his painting, still needs the poetic tool of language to provide entry to his art. Thus the poet and the painter, despite their different approaches, are equals in the overall world of the arts.

Themes

Art and Experience

In comparing the painting of Mike Goldberg's "SARDINES" with the writing of the poem "OR-ANGES," "Why I Am Not a Painter" presents the creation of both poetry and painting as processes that are rooted in normal, everyday experience. Certainly, there is nothing extraordinary about O'Hara idly dropping in on Goldberg as he works on his painting "SARDINES." Nor is there anything remarkable in Goldberg interrupting his work to have a drink with his friend. But what one senses beneath the surface is that O'Hara's visit, far from being an imposition, is in fact welcomed as a possible source of inspiration. Unlike the clichéd image of the temperamental artist working in solitude, Goldberg is more like a gracious host at a cocktail party, welcoming his guest and whatever ideas and conversation he may bring with him.

O'Hara begins work on the poem "OR-ANGES" with a similarly casual attitude: "One day I am thinking / of a color: orange." As in the section dealing with Goldberg's painting, the phrase "days go by" is used to denote the mundane passage of time. Like Goldberg's work as a painter, O'Hara's work as a poet is rooted in the normal—and often uneventful—passage of time.

The creation of art, as O'Hara sees it, does not involve an esoteric process that cannot bear interruption. The creative process, rather than being some undertaking that is disconnected from normal life, follows the rhythms of everyday experience. Furthermore, the mundane passage of time is not an obstacle to creativity. O'Hara, in fact, finds inspiration, beauty, and art in familiar experience. Neither the common orange nor the prosaic sardine is unworthy of artistic presentation.

Language and Meaning

Another important theme addressed in "Why I Am Not a Painter" is the relationship between language and the actual objects or qualities it attempts

Topics for Further Study

- Explain what happens when you take the lyrics from a popular song and attempt to read them as you would a poem. In other words, how do a song's lyrics depend upon its music to give its words weight and meaning?

- Green is considered to be a color that relaxes people while orange is believed to have the opposite effect. Report on some of the theories of the psychological effects of color.

- Explain the speaker's reasons for why he is not a painter.

- Write a poem and paint a picture. Describe the differences between the two artistic expressions.

to describe. Language, the poem seems to say, is inescapable in any attempt to describe the world. Even someone working in a visual medium, like Mike Goldberg, cannot completely avoid the influence of language in the way he looks at the world. Goldberg first adds the word "SARDINES" to his painting because "it needed something there." This shows how, ironically, language has inspired a work of visual art. As the painting progresses, Goldberg removes the actual word, leaving just random letters in what can be seen as an attempt to remove any specific meaning from language and transform it into something purely visual. Yet in the end his attempt fails, as he feels compelled to title the painting "SARDINES." Even though the actual word has vanished from the painting, it is that word that has informed the vision he presents in his painting.

While O'Hara thus argues for the necessity of language, he is nevertheless aware of its limitations. Beginning the poem that will eventually be titled "ORANGES" by thinking of the color orange, O'Hara uses words to try to describe what that color means to him, how it affects him, and how it fits into the world at large. Soon, O'Hara finds himself writing page after page "of words, not lines. / Then another page. There should be / so much more." Here, O'Hara is struggling with language, trying to reach some sort of description and definition of orange and finding that language can only go so far toward this end.

What O'Hara offers us here may seem paradoxical: language (in this case the word "SARDINES") somehow gives birth to a painting, while something visual (the color orange) gives birth to page upon page of words. But what O'Hara is saying here is simply that, for people with the ability to use language, the word and what that word denotes are inseparable. Language is such an integral part of our thought processes that we cannot see anything, be it a specific object or a general attribute like color, without referring back to language.

Identity

O'Hara had worked on and off at the Museum of Modern Art since 1952 and counted many of the famous painters of the day among his friends. With O'Hara being so closely involved with the world of visual art, it was inevitable that he would be questioned as to why he himself was not a painter, especially at a time when painters from the "New York School"—as opposed to poets from the "New York School"—had gained a great amount of attention in the media. Implied, of course, is the question of whether O'Hara might not be somewhat envious of the attention his painter friends were receiving while he, as a poet, was not publicly celebrated to quite the same degree.

For an artist without a clear sense of identity, these would be bothersome questions. But for O'Hara these questions are merely foolish. One will note the tone implicit in the lines, "I think I would rather be / a painter, but I am not. Well." Although it may not be apparent at first, "Why I Am Not a Painter" shows how the fact that O'Hara is not a painter bothers other people much more than it bothers him. Thus, in saying, "I think I would rather be / a painter," O'Hara is most likely being facetious.

Regarding identity, O'Hara is implicitly responding to critics and other readers who are not secure with the idea of O'Hara as poet—people who may not believe that O'Hara's writing, with its odd, conversational style, actually *is* poetry. In "Why I Am Not a Painter," O'Hara asserts his identity as a poet with bravado, noting that "ORANGES," the poem he is working on, "is even in / prose, I am a real poet." In other words, O'Hara is so confident in his skills as a poet that he does not even need to write his poems in conventional verse.

O'Hara's strong sense of identity, addressed obliquely in "Why I Am Not a Painter," can be seen very clearly in his brief essay, "Personism: A Manifesto," where he writes, "But how can you really care if anybody gets it, or gets what it means.... Too many poets act like a middle-aged mother trying to get her kids to eat too much cooked meat.... I don't give a damn whether they eat or not." Here, one sees that O'Hara is that rare person in possession of true confidence, a confidence that does not compel him to prove himself to anyone. And although O'Hara may on occasion take the time to explain what he does, it's an explanation he offers only grudgingly.

Style

"Why I Am Not a Painter" is written in free verse and divided into an introductory stanza of three lines, followed by two stanzas of thirteen lines each. While free verse, which has no regular meter or line length, has been the most common form of twentieth-century poetry, what made this poem—and O'Hara's work in general—stand out in the 1950s is the degree of freedom with which O'Hara wrote his poetry. As it was, O'Hara disliked many of the most common poetic qualities and techniques.

In "Personism: A Manifesto," O'Hara went so far as to say, "I don't even like rhythm, assonance, all that stuff. You just go on your nerve." This does not mean O'Hara did not use rhythm; he just preferred the rhythm of natural conversation. Thus, within "Why I Am Not a Painter," O'Hara presents what can be laid out as actual dialogue; but, in keeping with O'Hara's preferences, it is one of the least "poetic" instances of dialogue one will ever encounter in a poem:

"You have SARDINES in it."

"Yes, it needed something there."

"Oh."

This is, indeed, a far cry from the poetic exchanges one sees, for example, in a Shakespearean play. (Not surprisingly, O'Hara was not a great fan of William Shakespeare, preferring the less "poetic" work of some of Shakespeare's contemporaries instead.)

Despite the predominantly "free" quality of his poetry, O'Hara (especially in his earlier work) usually adhered to some sort of formal structure. As noted previously, "Why I Am Not a Painter" is di-

Compare & Contrast

- **1957:** American avant-garde filmmaker Stan Brakhage releases his film *Anticipation of the Night.* Attempting to portray the world as it would look to an infant who has yet to develop the ability to organize his impressions, the film has no narrative content and presents a continual flow of shadows and colors.

- **1961:** Jazz saxophonist Ornette Coleman releases his recording of *Free Jazz.* Featuring the Jackson Pollock painting *White Light* on its album cover, *Free Jazz* dispenses with many of the traditional melodic and harmonic conventions of jazz in order to allow the musicians to improvise without constraint.

- **1965:** Folksinger Bob Dylan is booed at the Newport Folk Festival for playing an electric guitar, an instrument that was frowned upon by traditional folk music fans.

- **1973:** Thomas Pynchon's novel *Gravity's Rainbow* wins the National Book Award. Complex as well as comic, the novel uses a variety of styles and draws upon everything from science to popular culture to explore a wide range of human experience.

- **1986:** The Green Mill bar in Chicago holds its first "poetry slams." A contest in which poets compete against each other (reading poems that are then rated by appointed judges), the poetry slam soon gains widespread popularity.

- **1999:** New York City Mayor Rudolph Giuliani attempts to halt funding to the Brooklyn Museum of Art after the opening of its controversial *Sensation* exhibit.

vided into three stanzas, each of which serves a rather logical purpose. Here, the first stanza presents the basic premise of the poem, and is followed by a stanza where O'Hara discusses the art of painting. In the final stanza, O'Hara brings everything together, discussing his own art (poetry), and then connecting it to Goldberg's work in the visual arts. In this stanza O'Hara also manages to bring the poem to a climax, and then leads it to a proper conclusion.

By the time one has finished reading "Why I Am Not a Painter," one will have experienced some of the same things one would experience by reading a well-crafted story—even though at first glance the poem may seem chaotic and arbitrary, even sloppy. However, this is the quality that is at the heart of O'Hara's poetry: taking common, everyday (and sometimes even ugly) elements, and turning them into a thing of beauty.

Historical Context

The 1950s, the period during which O'Hara first began to develop his poetry, often has been portrayed as an era when "normality" or convention ruled the day. And, when contrasted with the more obvious turbulence of the 1960s, the 1950s certainly did seem like a peaceful, uneventful era. As seen in popular situation comedies of the time, such as *I Love Lucy* and *Leave It to Beaver,* one might think the 1950s were a time when social problems did not exist. More likely, it was a time when social problems were often not addressed. Dwight David Eisenhower, who was the president of the United States for most of the 1950s, was socially and economically conservative. The social reforms that did come about during the Eisenhower years usually resulted from the efforts of the Supreme Court led by Chief Justice Earl Warren. One of the major decisions of the Warren Court, for example, involved the 1954 case of *Brown v. the Board of Education,* which ruled that racial segregation in public schools was unconstitutional. Of course, the United States still had a long way to go as far as the rights of minorities were concerned.

On occasion one will see explicit references in O'Hara's poetry to some of the more troubling aspects of the time. "Personal Poem," written in 1959, mentions that African-American jazz trumpeter

"Miles Davis was clubbed 12 / times last night outside BIRDLAND by a cop." More often, O'Hara's
references are less specific, as in "Why I Am Not
a Painter," when he writes "of how terrible orange
is / and life." O'Hara, who was gay, had himself
experienced some of the problems of minorities and
other people in the 1950s who were considered
"different."

That the problems O'Hara and others experienced led to rebellion in one form or another isn't
surprising. The 1950s, so conservative in many aspects, was actually a time that was rife for rebellion in the arts. (This was, after all, the era when
rock 'n' roll music first came to prominence.) In
the world of jazz, pianists such as Thelonius Monk
and Cecil Taylor were venturing into new territory,
creating sounds that stretched the boundaries of that
musical genre. Painters like the aforementioned
Jackson Pollock rebelled against simple representation in art and strove to display action and movement in their paintings. Likewise, in the realm of
literature, O'Hara's work stood out as something
incomparably new.

Dubbed "the last avant-garde" by writer David
Lehman, O'Hara and the New York School of poets were writing poems that were decidedly different from most of the work being published at the
time. O'Hara, for instance, resented what he saw
as the institutionalization of poetry. O'Hara would
be witty where a more traditional poet would be
solemn, ironic where another poet would be mor-
alizing. O'Hara's poetry takes what on the surface
looks mundane and holds it up to the light to show
that it has its own patterns, its own beauty, and its
own depth. Like the era of the 1950s, O'Hara's poetry may at first seem light on the surface, but lying underneath that are serious issues that O'Hara
deals with in his own unique and—some would say,
inimitable—style.

Critical Overview

Just as the reputation of Robert Lowell, long considered one of the foremost American poets of the
century, has fallen somewhat, O'Hara's reputation
has risen. At first O'Hara wasn't taken all that seriously. As Marjorie Perloff notes in her *Frank
O'Hara: Poet Among Painters,* O'Hara was first
seen as "a coterie figure—adored by his New York
School friends and acolytes, especially by the
painters whose work he exhibited and wrote about,
but otherwise regarded (when regarded at all) as a
charming minor poet."

In fact, the first really insightful criticism on
O'Hara's work did not appear until 1968, two years
after his death, when Paul Carroll's critical survey
of some of the younger poets of the day, *The Poem
in Its Skin,* appeared. Carroll writes that, "No one
could have guessed ten years ago that the poems
of Frank O'Hara would be among the most seminal influences on the work of the youngest generation of American poets now in their 20s." Perloff
goes on to report that, at a 1996 conference on the
poetry of the 1950s, "there were more papers
(eleven in all) on O'Hara than on any other single
poet, and his name cropped up repeatedly in the
various keynote addresses on larger topics."

Among O'Hara's large body of work, "Why I
Am Not a Painter" is one of his most popular poems. Commenting on this poem, David Lehman
writes in *The Last Avant-Garde* that it "made poetry seem as natural as breathing, as casual as the
American idiom, and so imbued with metropolitan
irony and bohemian glamour as to be irresistible."
The engaging irony and the attractiveness of the
artistic life, as presented through the work of
O'Hara, were never in question. But it was a long
time before critics saw that these qualities, in addition to being entertaining, were worthy of serious study.

Criticism

David Caplan

*David Caplan is a doctoral candidate at the
University of Virginia, writing a dissertation on
contemporary poetry and poetic form. In the following essay, he considers how O'Hara's poem relates to other poems about paintings and questions
the relationship it establishes with the reader.*

Frank O'Hara's "Why I Am Not a Painter"
continues a long and distinguished line of ekphrasis poetry. From the Greek word for "description,"
this category includes poems that describe other
works of art. This tradition dates to classical an-
tiquity; the most famous articulation of its guiding
principle remains Horace's dictum, "ut pictora poe-
sis": "as a painting, so a poem." As this comparison suggests, this position stresses a basic similarity between poetry and painting. They are "sister
arts" which inspire each other.

A host of modern poets have composed works
under these guiding assumptions. O'Hara's friend,
John Ashbery, wrote one of the most widely admired poems of this kind. The title poem of a col-

What Do I Read Next?

- Published in 1988, *A Certain Slant of Sunlight* is a collection of poems Ted Berrigan originally wrote on postcards. Some of these poems are actually collaborations with other poets and artists who would take a postcard and write a line or even draw on them. Berrigan would then take these postcards and use them as a starting point for his own work. Berrigan, like a great number of poets who came to prominence in the 1960s, was highly influenced by the work of O'Hara.

- The Unbearables are a loose-knit collective of writers and artists from New York City whose predilection for extreme parody (combined with a subtle sense of irony) makes them stand out among contemporary literary movements. *Unbearables*, published in 1995, is a collection of stories, poems, and graphics by the Unbearables collective, which includes poets such as Ron Kolm and Hal Sirowitz, fiction writers like Carl Watson, Bart Plantenga, and Jose Padua, and the artists David Sandlin and Michael Randall.

- O'Hara's *Lunch Poems* was first published in 1964 and has since gone through numerous printings. This slim volume collects some of the poems O'Hara wrote during his lunch breaks, hence the title of the book. Included here is "The Day Lady Died," which, like "Why I Am Not a Painter," is considered one of O'Hara's greatest poems.

- *In Memory of My Feelings: Frank O'Hara and American Art* (1999) by Russell Ferguson concentrates on O'Hara's involvement in the art world. Included here are reproductions of work by some of the artists O'Hara promoted as a curator at the Museum of Modern Art.

- Frederick Exley's *A Fan's Notes* (1968) is a fictionalized memoir in which Exley recounts his life from his college days up until the time when he attempts to write his first book—a book that will eventually become *A Fan's Notes*. Exley—a fan of professional football who did not associate with many writers or artists—provides an interesting contrast to the more Bohemian view of a writer's life.

---

lection that won the 1975 Pulitzer Prize, National Book Award, and National Book Critics Circle Award, "Self-Portrait in a Convex Mirror" meditates upon the Italian Renaissance painter Parmigianino's "Self Portrait in a Convex Mirror":

> The soul has to stay where it is,
> Even though restless, hearing raindrops at the pane,
> The sighing of autumn leaves thrashed by the
>   wind,
> Longing to be free, outside, but it must stay
> Posing in this place. It must move
> As little as possible. This is what the
> portrait says.

This exemplary passage suggests the most common tactic of ekphrasis. The poem analyzes a painting in order to draw some truth from it. "This is what the portrait says," Ashbery writes, and even though the self-portrait he witnesses appears in "a convex mirror," it mirrors his own experiences.

A friend of many visual artists and a professional curator, Frank O'Hara possessed great expertise about painting and the commercial art world. His numerous poems on these subjects include "Joseph Cornell" and "Ode to William de Kooning," and he also collaborated with the artists Jasper Johns, Norman Bluhm, and Larry Rivers. In "Why I Am Not a Painter," O'Hara tries a different approach from Ashbery's in "Self Portrait in a Convex Mirror." The poem quickly demonstrates one of these differences: unlike Ashbery, O'Hara describes the process of composition, not a finished painting. The poem starts with the start of a painting:

> I am not a painter, I am a poet.
> Why? I think I would rather be
> a painter, but I am not. Well,
> for instance, Mike Goldberg
> is starting a painting. I drop in.

Part of what is distinctive about O'Hara's poems is their chatty casualness. The speaker doesn't "visit" his friend; instead, "I drop in." On the rare occasions that poems use phrases elevated enough for expository prose, it undercuts their potential pretensions. The speaker declares, "[F]or instance, Mike Goldberg / is starting a poem"—but not before opening the sentence with a less-than-authoritative interjection, "Well."

This technique underscores O'Hara's stance of taking a potentially serious subject less than seriously. Listen to how flatly the speaker describes his interaction with Mike Goldberg, "'Sit down and have a drink,'" he / says. I drink; we drink. I look up." This scene is far from an august meeting of great minds ready to discourse on the subject of painting, life, and poetry. As always skeptical of any great claims for art, O'Hara describes the creative process in very prosaic terms. Two friends talk about what they are doing, although they barely know themselves: "'Where's SARDINES?'/ All that's left is just / letters, 'It was too much,' Mike says."

O'Hara's similar determination to keep "too much" out of his art, though, leaves the reader wondering exactly what he includes. Describing his composition process, the speaker exclaims:

> There should be
> so much more, not of orange, of
> words, of how terrible orange is
> and life. Days go by. It is even in
> prose, I am a real poet.

This crescendo of language rises to the height of an epiphany, but its culminating boast seems more ironic than sincere. The statement raises a host of questions. If the speaker is "a real poet," what does that mean? If the artistic process is this accidental, what separates "real" art from "fake"? In the poem's own terms, O'Hara finds these questions to be "too much"; declining to answer them, he again reveals an interest in poetic process—that is, in how artists make art—not in exposition—in how he might explain his own poetry.

Even when read ironically, the declaration, "I am a real poet," though, contains more than a hint of authorial arrogance. In the best critical study of Frank O'Hara's work, *Frank O'Hara: Poet Among Painters,* Marjorie Perloff, a leading scholar of twentieth-century poetry, calls "Why I Am Not a Painter" "a profound jest. If someone asks a stupid question, O'Hara implies, he deserves a stupid answer … O'Hara is a poet not a painter for no better reason that is what he is." Perloff's general point

is very convincing, as the poem's sly humor archly deflects a kind of clueless interrogator's implied question. But is the question, "Why are you a poet, not a painter?" really that "stupid"? One hesitates to say that it is not, as, according to both the poem and its most sympathetic reader, to do so would be to mark oneself as hopelessly naive.

From Alexander Pope's satirical couplets to Ezra Pound's sneers at bourgeois respectability, poets have scoffed at, derided, and mocked the general public's philistine assumptions about art and culture. Indeed, the modern age almost defines such disdain as a necessary (but not sufficient) condition for poetic creativity. Yet, even though there are many reasons to think that "real" and "fake" are not the most sophisticated terms to apply to poetry, one also might recoil at how much energy O'Hara's poem exerts in turning his answer into a "jest." The poem ultimately tells the reader that poetry and painting are interconnected artistic acts and that temperament decides an individual's suitability to one or the other. But is this point "profound"? Lacking the generosity of O'Hara's other poems or even their more biting derision of worthier objects, "Why I Am Not a Painter" wins a pyrrhic victory over an easy opponent.

Source: David Caplan, in an essay for *Poetry for Students,* Gale Group, 2000.

Aviya Kushner

Aviya Kushner, the poetry editor for Neworld Renaissance Magazine, *earned an M.A. in creative writing from Boston University. In the following essay, Kushner discusses O'Hara's interest in painting and its enormous influence on his life and writing as well as his desire to be perceived as what he truly was: a poet. She also compares the process of O'Hara writing a poem to Mike Goldberg creating a painting, as portrayed in "Why I Am Not a Painter."*

Lunch hour. That is when O'Hara wrote many of his poems, while on break from his job as a curator at the Museum of Modern Art. His famous volume, *Lunch Poems,* includes descriptions of coffee with "a little sour cream in it," bare-chested construction workers downing a sandwich, and women walking over subway grates as the afternoon wind blows their skirts up over their knees. These mid-day moments fit in with O'Hara's mesmerizing poetry of moments, snippets of life that, when read together, form a rich and fascinating chronicle of a man and his city—New York.

According to many of his friends, O'Hara never worked at becoming a famous poet. He worked at getting to know art, and he worked at living a full life. Although he had a circle of writer friends like John Ashbery and Kenneth Koch, O'Hara spent much of his time surrounded by painters. Many of his poems refer to painters or painting movements, and his work is deeply visual. As Marjorie Perloff, author of the biography *Frank O'Hara: A Poet among Painters* has observed, O'Hara wrote for the eye, not the ear. His lines are exciting to look at. They can be long and sensual, like a brushstroke, or perky and staccato, like music notes.

O'Hara originally wanted to be a concert pianist, and his knowledge of and interest in composers like Erik Satie, Sergei Rachmaninoff, and Arnold Schoenberg can be seen in his work. Perloff's observation of O'Hara as an "eye" poet may explain all of the punctuation in O'Hara's poetry, which create numerous built-in pauses. The musical background naturally influences the sound, and O'Hara himself used to call writing "playing the typewriter," which of course alludes to playing the keys of a piano. While O'Hara was not known as a good reader of his own work, his poems are interesting to read aloud, and they sound playful and conversational. This can be misleading, because, as Perloff has observed, O'Hara was among the most learned and best-read poets of his day. While his poems may have been scribbled during lunch or written on the Staten Island Ferry on the way to a reading, they are also steeped in tradition and deeply aware of the concerns of visual art, music, and literature.

"Why I Am Not a Painter" is one of O'Hara's most famous poems. It may have been the answer to a question O'Hara was frequently asked, as a curator of modern art and friend of many painters. It is written in O'Hara's trademark off-the-cuff, casual tone, but it hints at how O'Hara achieves that casual tone.

Like many of O'Hara's poems, "Why I Am Not a Painter" mentions individual people. Another O'Hara poem, "The Day Lady Died" is an homage to Billie Holliday. "Lana Turner Has Collapsed" is about Lana Turner. Other poems are about his lovers, friends, and muses. He is the king of name-dropping. And yet, despite all the interest in fame and persons of fame, he himself was not interested in fame. This casual attitude and love of poetry for poetry's sake seems crucial to understanding this poem about not only painting, but poetry. Here is

> *While his poems may have been scribbled during lunch or written on the Staten Island Ferry on the way to a reading, they are also steeped in tradition and deeply aware of the concerns of visual art, music, and literature."*

Floating Bear magazine editor Diana di Prima's account of how she found O'Hara's poems:

> I would go over to Frank O'Hara's house pretty often. He used to keep a typewriter on the table in the kitchen, and he would type away, make poems all the time, when company was there and when it wasn't, when he was eating, all kinds of times. There would be an unfinished poem in his typewriter and he would do a few lines on it now and again, and he kept losing all these poems. They would wind up all over the house.... The poems would get into everything and I would come over and go through, like, his dresser drawers. There would be poems in with the towels, and I'd say, "Oh, hey, I like this one," and he'd say, "OK, take it." Very often it would be the only copy. My guess is that huge collected Frank O'Hara has only about one-third of his actual work."

"Why I Am Not a Painter" begins very simply, with an opening line that doubles as a manifesto. The first line says it all: "I am not a painter, I am a poet." That sounds pretty authoritative, but in the second line, O'Hara starts to explain:

> Why? I think I would rather be
> a painter, but I am not. Well,

O'Hara admits that he likes painters and paintings. But he was careful to state that he is not a painter, but a poet. The "well," hanging seductively at the end of the brief opening stanza, begins the explanation. Now O'Hara will really explain the real reason why he is not a painter—because he is a poet. And he proceeds to prove that he looks at the world as a poet does. Clarity departs after those first few lines, as people and thoughts start dropping in:

> for instance, Mike Goldberg
> is starting a painting. I drop in.

"Sit down and have a drink" he
says. I drink; we drink. I look
up. "You have SARDINES in it."
"Yes, it needed something there."
"Oh."

O'Hara drops in as Mike Goldberg starts a painting. Of course, as Goldberg begins to put his painting together, O'Hara is actually beginning to compose a poem. O'Hara mentions Mike Goldberg by name, just as the name "Lana Turner" functions as a building-block for his other poem.

The plot of the poem is "I drink; we drink." On the surface, Goldberg and O'Hara are simply drinking, but beneath, Goldberg is painting and O'Hara is writing a poem. O'Hara comments on Goldberg's work—"You have SARDINES in it." Goldberg answers that "it needed something there," and O'Hara, the professional curator, plays naive friend. "Oh," he says.

Then there is a blur, depicted by O'Hara as simply the days going by. Life is lived:

I go and the days go by
and I drop in again. The painting
is going on, and I go, and the days
go by. I drop in. The painting is
finished. "Where's SARDINES?"
All that's left is just
letters, "It was too much," Mike says.

Already, "needed something" and "too much" refer to a painter's interest in proportion. O'Hara has stated that he is not a painter. Naturally, then, he has different concerns.

But me? One day I am thinking of
a color: orange. I write a line
about orange. Pretty soon it is a
whole page of words, not lines.
Then another page. There should be
so much more, not of orange, of
words, how terrible orange is
and life.

"There should be / so much more"—that is the difference, for O'Hara. He wants there to be "so much more," and Goldberg is concerned that there was "too much." For O'Hara, a thought about a color becomes a line, then a page, then several pages, then a rumination on "terrible", and of course, life itself. The narrative continues:

Days go by. It is even in
prose, I am a real poet. My poem
is finished and I haven't even mentioned
orange yet. It's twelve poems, I call
it ORANGES.

Life continues, and the moments pile up. O'Hara finishes the poem, he finishes twelve poems. He has not mentioned the color orange yet,

but the reader gets the feeling he has mentioned all kinds of other things. He is writing about life, about the "days" that "go by." He manages to make fun of himself, as he always does. "It is even in / prose, I am a real poet."

The whole poem is composed of the simplest of words, and a dictionary is definitely not needed here. O'Hara is explaining how he writes without the slightest touch of artifice. The last two lines go back to the original question of why he is not a painter, returning to the painter Mike Goldberg and his SARDINES painting:

And one day in a gallery
I see Mike's painting, called SARDINES.

So Goldberg and O'Hara work similarly after all. Goldberg's painting, one can surmise, has nothing to do with sardines, except for the letters that form it. Abstract Expressionism was at its height, and O'Hara's description is probably right on target. However, O'Hara's poem series, titled "Oranges," probably has nothing to do with oranges. Yet while Goldberg tried to get the excess out, O'Hara aims to cram the excess in.

This is a very playful, somewhat sarcastic poem. It can be read as a stupid answer to a stupid question. But it also provides a priceless window into the mind of a poet, and it begins to explain why O'Hara lived his life as a poet among painters. The paintings stimulated him, and painters helped him both become a poet and continue as one.

Source: Aviya Kushner, in an essay for *Poetry for Students*, Gale Group, 2000.

Morton D. Rich

Morton D. Rich is an associate professor of English at Montclair State University who teaches a variety of courses in writing and contemporary literature. He is guest editor of the Spring 1999 issue of Inquiry: Critical Thinking Across the Disciplines, *an issue dedicated to autobiography and critical thinking. In the following essay, Rich describes "Why I Am Not a Painter" as O'Hara's definition of a poet and his or her art and discusses how the poem portrays the differences between the work of a poet and a painter.*

The voice and personality of the poet, O'Hara himself, are strongly present in "Why I Am Not a Painter." He does not hide behind a persona or create a character to act in his poetic drama. It is O'Hara presenting incidents and thoughts of his daily life. They are, of course, selected thoughts and incidents, not just anything that came to his mind. The poem may sound like a journal entry, but it is not; it is a shaped statement about what a poet is and does, what a poem is, and obliquely, a statement about what poetry should be and how poetry should be read. It can be read as an example of O'Hara's manifesto about composition he called "Personism":

> Personism has nothing to with philosophy, it's all about art ... one of its minimal aspects is to address itself to one person ... thus evoking overtones of love ... It puts the poem squarely between the poet and the person ... The poem is at last between two persons instead of two pages.

First, what is the plain sense of the poem? The speaker says what he is not and what he is in the first line. All doubt, we are told, is removed because the poet has asserted his position. However, he knows that the reader will ask why, so he asks first and then answers. The writer and his writing are in control here and the reader must follow or stop reading the poem. "I think I would rather be / a painter, but I am not." Do we believe him? Should we? He moves into an example: "Well, / for instance, Mike Goldberg / is starting a painting." While "for instance" is usually used as an informal logical connector, logic is absent here. But the poem is conversational, and strict logic does not apply to conversation. The rules of thought used here are those of everyday life, not those of academia. "Well," as used at the end of line 3, is without content; it is used to get the poem and the reader from one stanza to the next. Should we care that Mike Goldberg is starting a painting? Apparently, since the work of the painter is likely to be compared to the work of the poet and the promise of the title must be kept. Since O'Hara knew many painters, Mike Goldberg, Willem de Kooning, and Jackson Pollock among them, what he writes about the connection between poetry and painting is important for the reader to understand.

The poem continues: the poet drops in on the painter, he drinks, they drink, and the poet looks up and notes that "SARDINES" is in the painting, but is it a word, or an image? The answer may be provided later in the poem. What is the rationale for including it? As the painter says, "it needed something there." This is what abstract painters do—include what they feel is needed. The stanza continues with seemingly nonchalant statements about the days and the painting going on, and when the painting is finished, the poet asks "Where's SARDINES?" and observes "All that's left is just / letters." We are left to wonder what this means and given but little help by the painter's answer,

> *The poem may sound like a journal entry, but it is not; it is a shaped statement about what a poet is and does, what a poem is, and obliquely, a statement about what poetry should be and how poetry should be read."*

"it was too much." Too much of what? We would need to see the painting in progress to know.

The second long stanza switches back to the poet answering the reader's implied question: "But me?" Now the poet-painter comparison is developed. What does this poet do? He thinks of

> a color: orange. I write a line
> about orange. Pretty soon it is a
> whole page of words, not lines.
> Then another page. There should be
> so much more, not of orange, of
> words, of how terrible orange is
> and life.

He writes for days, twelve poems, "and I haven't mentioned / orange yet." Nevertheless, he calls it "ORANGES," just as Mike's painting, sans sardines, is called "SARDINES."

In "Why I Am Not a Painter" O'Hara takes a stand similar to that of Emily Dickinson in her number 505 from *The Complete Poems of Emily Dickinson:*

> I would not paint—a picture—
> I'd rather be the One
> Its bright impossibility
> To dwell—delicious—on—

The painter and the poet work in different media and while the poet can appreciate the work of the painter, he or she must work in words, however tempting the other medium might be. O'Hara dabbled in painting, but found it too time consuming and less immediate than writing.

After O'Hara writes "ORANGES," he sees Mike's painting in a gallery. Including that occasion in his poem is equivalent to Dickinson's "To dwell—delicious—on—".

O'Hara's biographer, Brad Gooch, writes in *City Poet: The Life and Times of Frank O'Hara* that "Why I Am Not a Painter" begins "with his usual deferential salute to painters," and goes on to say that it "remained one of the self-doubting poet's favorites. Writing to Goldberg once to complain of writer's block, O'Hara added, 'In the midst of the sh—— a little flame glows and it spells SAR-DINES.'" For O'Hara, Goldberg's painting was a light in the darkness of writer's block.

Critic Alan Feldman suggests in his work *Frank O'Hara* that the need to follow the demands of the work, painting or poem, drives the artist:

> Mike begins with a word and ends up with a design; O'Hara begins with a color and ends up with a poem. The work creates itself according to its own serendipitous will. (The poem seems to "drop in" on O'Hara in the same casual way that O'Hara drops in on Mike Goldberg.) … The work seems to complete itself, and all the artist can or wants to explain about it is when and how it got done, but not its logic or formal structure.

However, there is organization in the poem, if not a structure in the sense that a sonnet or villanelle has structure. As critic Marjorie Perloff observes in *Frank O'Hara: Poet among Painters* repetition is "the rhetorical device governing the poem." ("I drink; we drink"; "I go and the days go by"; "I drop in … I drop in again"). Perloff reads the poem as

> a profound jest. If someone asks a stupid question, O'Hara implies, he deserves a stupid answer. For in fact, Frank's art turns out to be just like Mike's. If Mike's painting finally contains no sardines, so Frank's "Oranges" never mentions the word "orange" … O'Hara is a poet not a painter for no better reason than that is what he is … the poem is also saying that poetry and painting are part of the same spectrum, that in the final analysis SARDINES and ORANGES are one.

But are they? Goldberg's abstract paintings contain some recognizable images and seemingly random selections of words that require full suspension of disbelief or training in the appreciation of abstract art to understand them, whereas "Why I Am Not a Painter" contains statements that follow and flow from each other. If it were presented as paragraphs, it might be even easier to follow:

> I am not a painter, I am a poet. Why? I think I would rather be a painter, but I am not. Well, for instance, Mike Goldberg is starting a painting. I drop in. "Sit down and have a drink" he says. I drink; we drink. I look up. "You have SARDINES in it." "Yes, it needed something there." "Oh." I go and the days go by and I drop in again. The painting is going on, and I go, and the days go by. I drop in. The painting is

finished. "Where's SARDINES?" All that's left is just letters, "it was too much," Mike says.

> But me? One day I am thinking of a color: orange. I write a line about orange. Pretty soon it is a whole page of words, not lines. Then another page. There should be so much more, not of orange, of words, of how terrible orange is and life. Days go by. It is even in prose, I am a real poet. My poem is finished and I haven't mentioned orange yet. It's twelve poems, I call it ORANGES. And one day in a gallery I see Mike's painting, called SARDINES.

What has been lost and what gained by paragraphing the poem? Obviously it no longer looks like a poem, so the reader's expectations are different. And because of the absence of lines with breaks it must be read with a different pace and different emphasis on words and pauses marked by punctuation rather than line breaks. But is a poem simply words set down in lines of verse? Certainly not. Poems are traditionally made of images, sounds, meter, movement, and form. Line breaks are meaningful in good poems, not arbitrary, as they appear to be in O'Hara's poem.

But is it fair to apply the criteria of traditional criticism to a poem that does not fit a known mold? Or can a poet join with other poets to create something new? O'Hara moved in a group of innovating writers known as the New York Poets, including Kenneth Koch and John Ashbery, and knew many abstract painters, among them Jackson Pollock, from whom they drew inspiration. O'Hara writes a new kind of poetry, of daily experience, of immediacy, and he writes in the frenetic America of the 1950s and 1960s. His style reflects his response to contemporary life, not his response to earlier literary works, so readers must allow new criteria, based on innovative poetry, to emerge. Literature evolves, it is not static. However, some attention must be paid to what discerning readers have appreciated in earlier poetry, unless the poet hopes to nurture a new kind of reader. Has O'Hara succeeded in doing this? In the future, will he be read in other than school anthologies or only as a curiosity in the history of modern poetry?

Source: Morton D. Rich, in an essay for *Poetry for Students,* Gale Group, 2000.

Sources

Allen, Donald, ed., *The Collected Poems of Frank O'Hara,* New York: Knopf, 1971.

Ashbery, John, *Selected Poems,* New York: Penguin, 1985.

Carroll, Paul, *The Poem in Its Skin,* New York: Follett Publishing Company, 1968.

Feldman, Alan, *Frank O'Hara,* Boston: Twayne, 1979.

Gooch, Brad, *City Poet: The Life and Times of Frank O'Hara,* New York: Knopf, 1993.

Johnson, Thomas H., ed., *The Complete Poems of Emily Dickinson,* Boston: Little, Brown, 1960.

Lehman, David, *The Last Avant-Garde,* New York: Doubleday, 1998.

O'Hara, Frank, *The Collected Poems of Frank O'Hara,* first paperback printing, edited by Donald Allen, Berkeley: University of California Press, 1995.

Perloff, Marjorie, *Frank O'Hara: Poet among Painters,* New York: George Braziller, 1977, Chicago: The University of Chicago Press, 1997.

Race, William H., "Ekphrasis" in *The New Princeton Encyclopedia of Poetry and Poetics,* edited by Alex Preminger and T.V.F. Brogan, Princeton: Princeton University Press, 1993, pp. 320-321.

For Further Study

Berkson, Bill and LeSuer, Joe, eds., *Homage to Frank O'Hara,* Berkeley: Creative Arts Book Company, 1980.
   This was first published as issue 11/12 of the journal *Big Sky* in 1978, and collects various remembrances of O'Hara by a wide variety of writers and painters. As such, it makes for a nice companion volume to Gooch's biography.

Stern, Jane and Michael, *Encyclopedia of Pop Culture,* HarperPerennial, a division of Harper Collins Publishers, 1992.
   This book contains essays on various elements of popular American culture going back to the 1940s. Easy to read, it nonetheless provides some critical perspectives on America's recent past.

Glossary of Literary Terms

A

Abstract: Used as a noun, the term refers to a short summary or outline of a longer work. As an adjective applied to writing or literary works, abstract refers to words or phrases that name things not knowable through the five senses.

Accent: The emphasis or stress placed on a syllable in poetry. Traditional poetry commonly uses patterns of accented and unaccented syllables (known as feet) that create distinct rhythms. Much modern poetry uses less formal arrangements that create a sense of freedom and spontaneity.

Aestheticism: A literary and artistic movement of the nineteenth century. Followers of the movement believed that art should not be mixed with social, political, or moral teaching. The statement "art for art's sake" is a good summary of aestheticism. The movement had its roots in France, but it gained widespread importance in England in the last half of the nineteenth century, where it helped change the Victorian practice of including moral lessons in literature.

Affective Fallacy: An error in judging the merits or faults of a work of literature. The "error" results from stressing the importance of the work's effect upon the reader—that is, how it makes a reader "feel" emotionally, what it does as a literary work—instead of stressing its inner qualities as a created object, or what it "is."

Age of Johnson: The period in English literature between 1750 and 1798, named after the most prominent literary figure of the age, Samuel Johnson. Works written during this time are noted for their emphasis on "sensibility," or emotional quality. These works formed a transition between the rational works of the Age of Reason, or Neoclassical period, and the emphasis on individual feelings and responses of the Romantic period.

Age of Reason: See *Neoclassicism*

Age of Sensibility: See *Age of Johnson*

Agrarians: A group of Southern American writers of the 1930s and 1940s who fostered an economic and cultural program for the South based on agriculture, in opposition to the industrial society of the North. The term can refer to any group that promotes the value of farm life and agricultural society.

Alexandrine Meter: See *Meter*

Allegory: A narrative technique in which characters representing things or abstract ideas are used to convey a message or teach a lesson. Allegory is typically used to teach moral, ethical, or religious lessons but is sometimes used for satiric or political purposes.

Alliteration: A poetic device where the first consonant sounds or any vowel sounds in words or syllables are repeated.

Allusion: A reference to a familiar literary or historical person or event, used to make an idea more easily understood.

Amerind Literature: The writing and oral traditions of Native Americans. Native American literature was originally passed on by word of mouth, so it consisted largely of stories and events that were easily memorized. Amerind prose is often rhythmic like poetry because it was recited to the beat of a ceremonial drum.

Analogy: A comparison of two things made to explain something unfamiliar through its similarities to something familiar, or to prove one point based on the acceptedness of another. Similes and metaphors are types of analogies.

Anapest: See *Foot*

Angry Young Men: A group of British writers of the 1950s whose work expressed bitterness and disillusionment with society. Common to their work is an anti-hero who rebels against a corrupt social order and strives for personal integrity.

Anthropomorphism: The presentation of animals or objects in human shape or with human characteristics. The term is derived from the Greek word for "human form."

Antimasque: See *Masque*

Antithesis: The antithesis of something is its direct opposite. In literature, the use of antithesis as a figure of speech results in two statements that show a contrast through the balancing of two opposite ideas. Technically, it is the second portion of the statement that is defined as the "antithesis"; the first portion is the "thesis."

Apocrypha: Writings tentatively attributed to an author but not proven or universally accepted to be their works. The term was originally applied to certain books of the Bible that were not considered inspired and so were not included in the "sacred canon."

Apollonian and Dionysian: The two impulses believed to guide authors of dramatic tragedy. The Apollonian impulse is named after Apollo, the Greek god of light and beauty and the symbol of intellectual order. The Dionysian impulse is named after Dionysus, the Greek god of wine and the symbol of the unrestrained forces of nature. The Apollonian impulse is to create a rational, harmonious world, while the Dionysian is to express the irrational forces of personality.

Apostrophe: A statement, question, or request addressed to an inanimate object or concept or to a nonexistent or absent person.

Archetype: The word archetype is commonly used to describe an original pattern or model from which all other things of the same kind are made. This term was introduced to literary criticism from the

psychology of Carl Jung. It expresses Jung's theory that behind every person's "unconscious," or repressed memories of the past, lies the "collective unconscious" of the human race: memories of the countless typical experiences of our ancestors. These memories are said to prompt illogical associations that trigger powerful emotions in the reader. Often, the emotional process is primitive, even primordial. Archetypes are the literary images that grow out of the "collective unconscious." They appear in literature as incidents and plots that repeat basic patterns of life. They may also appear as stereotyped characters.

Argument: The argument of a work is the author's subject matter or principal idea.

Art for Art's Sake: See *Aestheticism*

Assonance: The repetition of similar vowel sounds in poetry.

Audience: The people for whom a piece of literature is written. Authors usually write with a certain audience in mind, for example, children, members of a religious or ethnic group, or colleagues in a professional field. The term "audience" also applies to the people who gather to see or hear any performance, including plays, poetry readings, speeches, and concerts.

Automatic Writing: Writing carried out without a preconceived plan in an effort to capture every random thought. Authors who engage in automatic writing typically do not revise their work, preferring instead to preserve the revealed truth and beauty of spontaneous expression.

Avant-garde: A French term meaning "vanguard." It is used in literary criticism to describe new writing that rejects traditional approaches to literature in favor of innovations in style or content.

B

Ballad: A short poem that tells a simple story and has a repeated refrain. Ballads were originally intended to be sung. Early ballads, known as folk ballads, were passed down through generations, so their authors are often unknown. Later ballads composed by known authors are called literary ballads.

Baroque: A term used in literary criticism to describe literature that is complex or ornate in style or diction. Baroque works typically express tension, anxiety, and violent emotion. The term "Baroque Age" designates a period in Western European literature beginning in the late sixteenth century and ending about one hundred years later.

Works of this period often mirror the qualities of works more generally associated with the label "baroque" and sometimes feature elaborate conceits.

Baroque Age: See *Baroque*

Baroque Period: See *Baroque*

Beat Generation: See *Beat Movement*

Beat Movement: A period featuring a group of American poets and novelists of the 1950s and 1960s—including Jack Kerouac, Allen Ginsberg, Gregory Corso, William S. Burroughs, and Lawrence Ferlinghetti—who rejected established social and literary values. Using such techniques as stream of consciousness writing and jazz-influenced free verse and focusing on unusual or abnormal states of mind—generated by religious ecstasy or the use of drugs—the Beat writers aimed to create works that were unconventional in both form and subject matter.

Beat Poets: See *Beat Movement*

Beats, The: See *Beat Movement*

Belles-lettres: A French term meaning "fine letters" or "beautiful writing." It is often used as a synonym for literature, typically referring to imaginative and artistic rather than scientific or expository writing. Current usage sometimes restricts the meaning to light or humorous writing and appreciative essays about literature.

Black Aesthetic Movement: A period of artistic and literary development among African Americans in the 1960s and early 1970s. This was the first major African-American artistic movement since the Harlem Renaissance and was closely paralleled by the civil rights and black power movements. The black aesthetic writers attempted to produce works of art that would be meaningful to the black masses. Key figures in black aesthetics included one of its founders, poet and playwright Amiri Baraka, formerly known as LeRoi Jones; poet and essayist Haki R. Madhubuti, formerly Don L. Lee; poet and playwright Sonia Sanchez; and dramatist Ed Bullins.

Black Arts Movement: See *Black Aesthetic Movement*

Black Comedy: See *Black Humor*

Black Humor: Writing that places grotesque elements side by side with humorous ones in an attempt to shock the reader, forcing him or her to laugh at the horrifying reality of a disordered world.

Black Mountain School: Black Mountain College and three of its instructors—Robert Creeley, Robert Duncan, and Charles Olson— were all influential in projective verse, so poets working in projective verse are now referred to as members of the Black Mountain school.

Blank Verse: Loosely, any unrhymed poetry, but more generally, unrhymed iambic pentameter verse (composed of lines of five two-syllable feet with the first syllable accented, the second unaccented). Blank verse has been used by poets since the Renaissance for its flexibility and its graceful, dignified tone.

Bloomsbury Group: A group of English writers, artists, and intellectuals who held informal artistic and philosophical discussions in Bloomsbury, a district of London, from around 1907 to the early 1930s. The Bloomsbury Group held no uniform philosophical beliefs but did commonly express an aversion to moral prudery and a desire for greater social tolerance.

Bon Mot: A French term meaning "good word." A *bon mot* is a witty remark or clever observation.

Breath Verse: See *Projective Verse*

Burlesque: Any literary work that uses exaggeration to make its subject appear ridiculous, either by treating a trivial subject with profound seriousness or by treating a dignified subject frivolously. The word "burlesque" may also be used as an adjective, as in "burlesque show," to mean "striptease act."

C

Cadence: The natural rhythm of language caused by the alternation of accented and unaccented syllables. Much modern poetry—notably free verse—deliberately manipulates cadence to create complex rhythmic effects.

Caesura: A pause in a line of poetry, usually occurring near the middle. It typically corresponds to a break in the natural rhythm or sense of the line but is sometimes shifted to create special meanings or rhythmic effects.

Canzone: A short Italian or Provencal lyric poem, commonly about love and often set to music. The *canzone* has no set form but typically contains five or six stanzas made up of seven to twenty lines of eleven syllables each. A shorter, five- to ten-line "envoy," or concluding stanza, completes the poem.

Carpe Diem: A Latin term meaning "seize the day." This is a traditional theme of poetry, especially lyrics. A *carpe diem* poem advises the reader or the person it addresses to live for today and enjoy the pleasures of the moment.

Catharsis: The release or purging of unwanted emotions—specifically fear and pity—brought about by exposure to art. The term was first used by the Greek philosopher Aristotle in his *Poetics* to refer to the desired effect of tragedy on spectators.

Celtic Renaissance: A period of Irish literary and cultural history at the end of the nineteenth century. Followers of the movement aimed to create a romantic vision of Celtic myth and legend. The most significant works of the Celtic Renaissance typically present a dreamy, unreal world, usually in reaction against the reality of contemporary problems.

Celtic Twilight: See *Celtic Renaissance*

Character: Broadly speaking, a person in a literary work. The actions of characters are what constitute the plot of a story, novel, or poem. There are numerous types of characters, ranging from simple, stereotypical figures to intricate, multifaceted ones. In the techniques of anthropomorphism and personification, animals—and even places or things—can assume aspects of character. "Characterization" is the process by which an author creates vivid, believable characters in a work of art. This may be done in a variety of ways, including (1) direct description of the character by the narrator; (2) the direct presentation of the speech, thoughts, or actions of the character; and (3) the responses of other characters to the character. The term "character" also refers to a form originated by the ancient Greek writer Theophrastus that later became popular in the seventeenth and eighteenth centuries. It is a short essay or sketch of a person who prominently displays a specific attribute or quality, such as miserliness or ambition.

Characterization: See *Character*

Classical: In its strictest definition in literary criticism, classicism refers to works of ancient Greek or Roman literature. The term may also be used to describe a literary work of recognized importance (a "classic") from any time period or literature that exhibits the traits of classicism.

Classicism: A term used in literary criticism to describe critical doctrines that have their roots in ancient Greek and Roman literature, philosophy, and art. Works associated with classicism typically exhibit restraint on the part of the author, unity of design and purpose, clarity, simplicity, logical organization, and respect for tradition.

Colloquialism: A word, phrase, or form of pronunciation that is acceptable in casual conversation but not in formal, written communication. It is considered more acceptable than slang.

Complaint: A lyric poem, popular in the Renaissance, in which the speaker expresses sorrow about his or her condition. Typically, the speaker's sadness is caused by an unresponsive lover, but some complaints cite other sources of unhappiness, such as poverty or fate.

Conceit: A clever and fanciful metaphor, usually expressed through elaborate and extended comparison, that presents a striking parallel between two seemingly dissimilar things—for example, elaborately comparing a beautiful woman to an object like a garden or the sun. The conceit was a popular device throughout the Elizabethan Age and Baroque Age and was the principal technique of the seventeenth-century English metaphysical poets. This usage of the word conceit is unrelated to the best-known definition of conceit as an arrogant attitude or behavior.

Concrete: Concrete is the opposite of abstract, and refers to a thing that actually exists or a description that allows the reader to experience an object or concept with the senses.

Concrete Poetry: Poetry in which visual elements play a large part in the poetic effect. Punctuation marks, letters, or words are arranged on a page to form a visual design: a cross, for example, or a bumblebee.

Confessional Poetry: A form of poetry in which the poet reveals very personal, intimate, sometimes shocking information about himself or herself.

Connotation: The impression that a word gives beyond its defined meaning. Connotations may be universally understood or may be significant only to a certain group.

Consonance: Consonance occurs in poetry when words appearing at the ends of two or more verses have similar final consonant sounds but have final vowel sounds that differ, as with "stuff" and "off."

Convention: Any widely accepted literary device, style, or form.

Corrido: A Mexican ballad.

Couplet: Two lines of poetry with the same rhyme and meter, often expressing a complete and self-contained thought.

Criticism: The systematic study and evaluation of literary works, usually based on a specific method or set of principles. An important part of literary studies since ancient times, the practice of criticism has given rise to numerous theories, methods, and "schools," sometimes producing conflicting, even contradictory, interpretations of literature in general as well as of individual works. Even such basic issues as what constitutes a poem or a novel have been the subject of much criticism over the centuries.

D

Dactyl: See *Foot*

Dadaism: A protest movement in art and literature founded by Tristan Tzara in 1916. Followers of the movement expressed their outrage at the destruction brought about by World War I by revolting against numerous forms of social convention. The Dadaists presented works marked by calculated madness and flamboyant nonsense. They stressed total freedom of expression, commonly through primitive displays of emotion and illogical, often senseless, poetry. The movement ended shortly after the war, when it was replaced by surrealism.

Decadent: See *Decadents*

Decadents: The followers of a nineteenth-century literary movement that had its beginnings in French aestheticism. Decadent literature displays a fascination with perverse and morbid states; a search for novelty and sensation—the "new thrill"; a preoccupation with mysticism; and a belief in the senselessness of human existence. The movement is closely associated with the doctrine Art for Art's Sake. The term "decadence" is sometimes used to denote a decline in the quality of art or literature following a period of greatness.

Deconstruction: A method of literary criticism developed by Jacques Derrida and characterized by multiple conflicting interpretations of a given work. Deconstructionists consider the impact of the language of a work and suggest that the true meaning of the work is not necessarily the meaning that the author intended.

Deduction: The process of reaching a conclusion through reasoning from general premises to a specific premise.

Denotation: The definition of a word, apart from the impressions or feelings it creates in the reader.

Diction: The selection and arrangement of words in a literary work. Either or both may vary depending on the desired effect. There are four general types of diction: "formal," used in scholarly or lofty writing; "informal," used in relaxed but educated conversation; "colloquial," used in everyday speech; and "slang," containing newly coined words and other terms not accepted in formal usage.

Didactic: A term used to describe works of literature that aim to teach some moral, religious, political, or practical lesson. Although didactic elements are often found in artistically pleasing works, the term "didactic" usually refers to literature in which the message is more important than the form. The term may also be used to criticize a work that the critic finds "overly didactic," that is, heavy-handed in its delivery of a lesson.

Dimeter: See *Meter*

Dionysian: See *Apollonian and Dionysian*

Discordia concours: A Latin phrase meaning "discord in harmony." The term was coined by the eighteenth-century English writer Samuel Johnson to describe "a combination of dissimilar images or discovery of occult resemblances in things apparently unlike." Johnson created the expression by reversing a phrase by the Latin poet Horace.

Dissonance: A combination of harsh or jarring sounds, especially in poetry. Although such combinations may be accidental, poets sometimes intentionally make them to achieve particular effects. Dissonance is also sometimes used to refer to close but not identical rhymes. When this is the case, the word functions as a synonym for consonance.

Double Entendre: A corruption of a French phrase meaning "double meaning." The term is used to indicate a word or phrase that is deliberately ambiguous, especially when one of the meanings is risque or improper.

Draft: Any preliminary version of a written work. An author may write dozens of drafts which are revised to form the final work, or he or she may write only one, with few or no revisions.

Dramatic Monologue: See *Monologue*

Dramatic Poetry: Any lyric work that employs elements of drama such as dialogue, conflict, or characterization, but excluding works that are intended for stage presentation.

Dream Allegory: See *Dream Vision*

Dream Vision: A literary convention, chiefly of the Middle Ages. In a dream vision a story is presented as a literal dream of the narrator. This device was commonly used to teach moral and religious lessons.

E

Eclogue: In classical literature, a poem featuring rural themes and structured as a dialogue among shepherds. Eclogues often took specific poetic forms, such as elegies or love poems. Some were written as the soliloquy of a shepherd. In later centuries, "eclogue" came to refer to any poem that was in the pastoral tradition or that had a dialogue or monologue structure.

Edwardian: Describes cultural conventions identified with the period of the reign of Edward VII of England (1901-1910). Writers of the Edwardian Age typically displayed a strong reaction against the propriety and conservatism of the Victorian Age. Their work often exhibits distrust of authority in religion, politics, and art and expresses strong doubts about the soundness of conventional values.

Edwardian Age: See *Edwardian*

Electra Complex: A daughter's amorous obsession with her father.

Elegy: A lyric poem that laments the death of a person or the eventual death of all people. In a conventional elegy, set in a classical world, the poet and subject are spoken of as shepherds. In modern criticism, the word elegy is often used to refer to a poem that is melancholy or mournfully contemplative.

Elizabethan Age: A period of great economic growth, religious controversy, and nationalism closely associated with the reign of Elizabeth I of England (1558-1603). The Elizabethan Age is considered a part of the general renaissance—that is, the flowering of arts and literature—that took place in Europe during the fourteenth through sixteenth centuries. The era is considered the golden age of English literature. The most important dramas in English and a great deal of lyric poetry were produced during this period, and modern English criticism began around this time.

Empathy: A sense of shared experience, including emotional and physical feelings, with someone or something other than oneself. Empathy is often used to describe the response of a reader to a literary character.

English Sonnet: See *Sonnet*

Enjambment: The running over of the sense and structure of a line of verse or a couplet into the following verse or couplet.

Enlightenment, The: An eighteenth-century philosophical movement. It began in France but had a wide impact throughout Europe and America. Thinkers of the Enlightenment valued reason and believed that both the individual and society could achieve a state of perfection. Corresponding to this essentially humanist vision was a resistance to religious authority.

Epic: A long narrative poem about the adventures of a hero of great historic or legendary importance. The setting is vast and the action is often given cosmic significance through the intervention of supernatural forces such as gods, angels, or demons. Epics are typically written in a classical style of grand simplicity with elaborate metaphors and allusions that enhance the symbolic importance of a hero's adventures.

Epic Simile: See *Homeric Simile*

Epigram: A saying that makes the speaker's point quickly and concisely.

Epilogue: A concluding statement or section of a literary work. In dramas, particularly those of the seventeenth and eighteenth centuries, the epilogue is a closing speech, often in verse, delivered by an actor at the end of a play and spoken directly to the audience.

Epiphany: A sudden revelation of truth inspired by a seemingly trivial incident.

Epitaph: An inscription on a tomb or tombstone, or a verse written on the occasion of a person's death. Epitaphs may be serious or humorous.

Epithalamion: A song or poem written to honor and commemorate a marriage ceremony.

Epithalamium: See *Epithalamion*

Epithet: A word or phrase, often disparaging or abusive, that expresses a character trait of someone or something.

Erziehungsroman: See *Bildungsroman*

Essay: A prose composition with a focused subject of discussion. The term was coined by Michel de Montaigne to describe his 1580 collection of brief, informal reflections on himself and on various topics relating to human nature. An essay can also be a long, systematic discourse.

Existentialism: A predominantly twentieth-century philosophy concerned with the nature and perception of human existence. There are two major strains of existentialist thought: atheistic and Christian. Followers of atheistic existentialism believe that the individual is alone in a godless universe and that the basic human condition is one of suffering and loneliness. Nevertheless, because there are no fixed values, individuals can create their own characters—indeed, they can shape themselves—through the exercise of free will. The atheistic strain culminates in and is popularly associated with the works of Jean-Paul Sartre. The Christian existentialists, on the other hand, believe that only in God may people find freedom from life's anguish. The two strains hold certain beliefs in common: that existence cannot be fully understood or described through empirical effort; that anguish is a universal element of life; that individuals must bear responsibility for their actions; and that there is no common standard of behavior or perception for religious and ethical matters.

Expatriates: See *Expatriatism*

Expatriatism: The practice of leaving one's country to live for an extended period in another country.

Exposition: Writing intended to explain the nature of an idea, thing, or theme. Expository writing is often combined with description, narration, or argument. In dramatic writing, the exposition is the introductory material which presents the characters, setting, and tone of the play.

Expressionism: An indistinct literary term, originally used to describe an early twentieth-century school of German painting. The term applies to almost any mode of unconventional, highly subjective writing that distorts reality in some way.

Extended Monologue: See *Monologue*

F

Feet: See *Foot*

Feminine Rhyme: See *Rhyme*

Fiction: Any story that is the product of imagination rather than a documentation of fact. Characters and events in such narratives may be based in real life but their ultimate form and configuration is a creation of the author.

Figurative Language: A technique in writing in which the author temporarily interrupts the order, construction, or meaning of the writing for a particular effect. This interruption takes the form of one or more figures of speech such as hyperbole, irony, or simile. Figurative language is the opposite of literal language, in which every word is truthful, accurate, and free of exaggeration or embellishment.

Figures of Speech: Writing that differs from customary conventions for construction, meaning, order, or significance for the purpose of a special meaning or effect. There are two major types of figures of speech: rhetorical figures, which do not make changes in the meaning of the words, and tropes, which do.

Fin de siecle: A French term meaning "end of the century." The term is used to denote the last decade of the nineteenth century, a transition period when writers and other artists abandoned old conventions and looked for new techniques and objectives.

First Person: See *Point of View*

Folk Ballad: See *Ballad*

Folklore: Traditions and myths preserved in a culture or group of people. Typically, these are passed on by word of mouth in various forms—such as legends, songs, and proverbs—or preserved in customs and ceremonies. This term was first used by W. J. Thoms in 1846.

Folktale: A story originating in oral tradition. Folktales fall into a variety of categories, including legends, ghost stories, fairy tales, fables, and anecdotes based on historical figures and events.

Foot: The smallest unit of rhythm in a line of poetry. In English-language poetry, a foot is typically one accented syllable combined with one or two unaccented syllables.

Form: The pattern or construction of a work which identifies its genre and distinguishes it from other genres.

Formalism: In literary criticism, the belief that literature should follow prescribed rules of construction, such as those that govern the sonnet form.

Fourteener Meter: See *Meter*

Free Verse: Poetry that lacks regular metrical and rhyme patterns but that tries to capture the cadences of everyday speech. The form allows a poet to exploit a variety of rhythmical effects within a single poem.

Futurism: A flamboyant literary and artistic movement that developed in France, Italy, and Russia from 1908 through the 1920s. Futurist theater and poetry abandoned traditional literary forms. In their place, followers of the movement attempted to achieve total freedom of expression through bizarre imagery and deformed or newly invented words. The Futurists were self-consciously modern artists who attempted to incorporate the appearances and sounds of modern life into their work.

G

Genre: A category of literary work. In critical theory, genre may refer to both the content of a given work—tragedy, comedy, pastoral—and to its form, such as poetry, novel, or drama.

Genteel Tradition: A term coined by critic George Santayana to describe the literary practice of certain late nineteenth-century American writers, especially New Englanders. Followers of the Genteel

Tradition emphasized conventionality in social, religious, moral, and literary standards.

Georgian Age: See *Georgian Poets*

Georgian Period: See *Georgian Poets*

Georgian Poets: A loose grouping of English poets during the years 1912-1922. The Georgians reacted against certain literary schools and practices, especially Victorian wordiness, turn-of-the-century aestheticism, and contemporary urban realism. In their place, the Georgians embraced the nineteenth-century poetic practices of William Wordsworth and the other Lake Poets.

Georgic: A poem about farming and the farmer's way of life, named from Virgil's *Georgics*.

Gilded Age: A period in American history during the 1870s characterized by political corruption and materialism. A number of important novels of social and political criticism were written during this time.

Gothic: See *Gothicism*

Gothicism: In literary criticism, works characterized by a taste for the medieval or morbidly attractive. A gothic novel prominently features elements of horror, the supernatural, gloom, and violence: clanking chains, terror, charnel houses, ghosts, medieval castles, and mysteriously slamming doors. The term "gothic novel" is also applied to novels that lack elements of the traditional Gothic setting but that create a similar atmosphere of terror or dread.

Graveyard School: A group of eighteenth-century English poets who wrote long, picturesque meditations on death. Their works were designed to cause the reader to ponder immortality.

Great Chain of Being: The belief that all things and creatures in nature are organized in a hierarchy from inanimate objects at the bottom to God at the top. This system of belief was popular in the seventeenth and eighteenth centuries.

Grotesque: In literary criticism, the subject matter of a work or a style of expression characterized by exaggeration, deformity, freakishness, and disorder. The grotesque often includes an element of comic absurdity.

H

Haiku: The shortest form of Japanese poetry, constructed in three lines of five, seven, and five syllables respectively. The message of a *haiku* poem usually centers on some aspect of spirituality and provokes an emotional response in the reader.

Half Rhyme: See *Consonance*

Harlem Renaissance: The Harlem Renaissance of the 1920s is generally considered the first significant movement of black writers and artists in the United States. During this period, new and established black writers published more fiction and poetry than ever before, the first influential black literary journals were established, and black authors and artists received their first widespread recognition and serious critical appraisal. Among the major writers associated with this period are Claude McKay, Jean Toomer, Countee Cullen, Langston Hughes, Arna Bontemps, Nella Larsen, and Zora Neale Hurston.

Hellenism: Imitation of ancient Greek thought or styles. Also, an approach to life that focuses on the growth and development of the intellect. "Hellenism" is sometimes used to refer to the belief that reason can be applied to examine all human experience.

Heptameter: See *Meter*

Hero/Heroine: The principal sympathetic character (male or female) in a literary work. Heroes and heroines typically exhibit admirable traits: idealism, courage, and integrity, for example.

Heroic Couplet: A rhyming couplet written in iambic pentameter (a verse with five iambic feet).

Heroic Line: The meter and length of a line of verse in epic or heroic poetry. This varies by language and time period.

Heroine: See *Hero/Heroine*

Hexameter: See *Meter*

Historical Criticism: The study of a work based on its impact on the world of the time period in which it was written.

Hokku: See *Haiku*

Holocaust: See *Holocaust Literature*

Holocaust Literature: Literature influenced by or written about the Holocaust of World War II. Such literature includes true stories of survival in concentration camps, escape, and life after the war, as well as fictional works and poetry.

Homeric Simile: An elaborate, detailed comparison written as a simile many lines in length.

Horatian Satire: See *Satire*

Humanism: A philosophy that places faith in the dignity of humankind and rejects the medieval perception of the individual as a weak, fallen creature. "Humanists" typically believe in the perfectibility of human nature and view reason and education as the means to that end.

Humors: Mentions of the humors refer to the ancient Greek theory that a person's health and personality were determined by the balance of four basic fluids in the body: blood, phlegm, yellow bile, and black bile. A dominance of any fluid would cause extremes in behavior. An excess of blood created a sanguine person who was joyful, aggressive, and passionate; a phlegmatic person was shy, fearful, and sluggish; too much yellow bile led to a choleric temperament characterized by impatience, anger, bitterness, and stubbornness; and excessive black bile created melancholy, a state of laziness, gluttony, and lack of motivation.

Humours: See *Humors*

Hyperbole: In literary criticism, deliberate exaggeration used to achieve an effect.

I

Iamb: See *Foot*

Idiom: A word construction or verbal expression closely associated with a given language.

Image: A concrete representation of an object or sensory experience. Typically, such a representation helps evoke the feelings associated with the object or experience itself. Images are either "literal" or "figurative." Literal images are especially concrete and involve little or no extension of the obvious meaning of the words used to express them. Figurative images do not follow the literal meaning of the words exactly. Images in literature are usually visual, but the term "image" can also refer to the representation of any sensory experience.

Imagery: The array of images in a literary work. Also, figurative language.

Imagism: An English and American poetry movement that flourished between 1908 and 1917. The Imagists used precise, clearly presented images in their works. They also used common, everyday speech and aimed for conciseness, concrete imagery, and the creation of new rhythms.

In medias res: A Latin term meaning "in the middle of things." It refers to the technique of beginning a story at its midpoint and then using various flashback devices to reveal previous action.

Induction: The process of reaching a conclusion by reasoning from specific premises to form a general premise. Also, an introductory portion of a work of literature, especially a play.

Intentional Fallacy: The belief that judgments of a literary work based solely on an author's stated or implied intentions are false and misleading. Critics who believe in the concept of the intentional fallacy typically argue that the work itself is sufficient matter for interpretation, even though they may concede that an author's statement of purpose can be useful.

Interior Monologue: A narrative technique in which characters' thoughts are revealed in a way that appears to be uncontrolled by the author. The interior monologue typically aims to reveal the inner self of a character. It portrays emotional experiences as they occur at both a conscious and unconscious level. Images are often used to represent sensations or emotions.

Internal Rhyme: Rhyme that occurs within a single line of verse.

Irish Literary Renaissance: A late nineteenth- and early twentieth-century movement in Irish literature. Members of the movement aimed to reduce the influence of British culture in Ireland and create an Irish national literature.

Irony: In literary criticism, the effect of language in which the intended meaning is the opposite of what is stated.

Italian Sonnet: See *Sonnet*

J

Jacobean Age: The period of the reign of James I of England (1603-1625). The early literature of this period reflected the worldview of the Elizabethan Age, but a darker, more cynical attitude steadily grew in the art and literature of the Jacobean Age. This was an important time for English drama and poetry.

Jargon: Language that is used or understood only by a select group of people. Jargon may refer to terminology used in a certain profession, such as computer jargon, or it may refer to any nonsensical language that is not understood by most people.

Journalism: Writing intended for publication in a newspaper or magazine, or for broadcast on a radio or television program featuring news, sports, entertainment, or other timely material.

K

Knickerbocker Group: A somewhat indistinct group of New York writers of the first half of the nineteenth century. Members of the group were linked only by location and a common theme: New York life.

Kunstlerroman: See *Bildungsroman*

L

Lais: See *Lay*

Lake Poets: See *Lake School*

Lake School: These poets all lived in the Lake District of England at the turn of the nineteenth century. As a group, they followed no single "school" of thought or literary practice, although their works were uniformly disparaged by the *Edinburgh Review*.

Lay: A song or simple narrative poem. The form originated in medieval France. Early French *lais* were often based on the Celtic legends and other tales sung by Breton minstrels—thus the name of the "Breton lay." In fourteenth-century England, the term "lay" was used to describe short narratives written in imitation of the Breton lays.

Leitmotiv: See *Motif*

Literal Language: An author uses literal language when he or she writes without exaggerating or embellishing the subject matter and without any tools of figurative language.

Literary Ballad: See *Ballad*

Literature: Literature is broadly defined as any written or spoken material, but the term most often refers to creative works.

Lost Generation: A term first used by Gertrude Stein to describe the post-World War I generation of American writers: men and women haunted by a sense of betrayal and emptiness brought about by the destructiveness of the war.

Lyric Poetry: A poem expressing the subjective feelings and personal emotions of the poet. Such poetry is melodic, since it was originally accompanied by a lyre in recitals. Most Western poetry in the twentieth century may be classified as lyrical.

M

Mannerism: Exaggerated, artificial adherence to a literary manner or style. Also, a popular style of the visual arts of late sixteenth-century Europe that was marked by elongation of the human form and by intentional spatial distortion. Literary works that are self-consciously high-toned and artistic are often said to be "mannered."

Masculine Rhyme: See *Rhyme*

Measure: The foot, verse, or time sequence used in a literary work, especially a poem. Measure is often used somewhat incorrectly as a synonym for meter.

Metaphor: A figure of speech that expresses an idea through the image of another object. Metaphors suggest the essence of the first object by identifying it with certain qualities of the second object.

Metaphysical Conceit: See *Conceit*

Metaphysical Poetry: The body of poetry produced by a group of seventeenth-century English writers called the "Metaphysical Poets." The group includes John Donne and Andrew Marvell. The Metaphysical Poets made use of everyday speech, intellectual analysis, and unique imagery. They aimed to portray the ordinary conflicts and contradictions of life. Their poems often took the form of an argument, and many of them emphasize physical and religious love as well as the fleeting nature of life. Elaborate conceits are typical in metaphysical poetry.

Metaphysical Poets: See *Metaphysical Poetry*

Meter: In literary criticism, the repetition of sound patterns that creates a rhythm in poetry. The patterns are based on the number of syllables and the presence and absence of accents. The unit of rhythm in a line is called a foot. Types of meter are classified according to the number of feet in a line. These are the standard English lines: Monometer, one foot; Dimeter, two feet; Trimeter, three feet; Tetrameter, four feet; Pentameter, five feet; Hexameter, six feet (also called the Alexandrine); Heptameter, seven feet (also called the "Fourteener" when the feet are iambic).

Modernism: Modern literary practices. Also, the principles of a literary school that lasted from roughly the beginning of the twentieth century until the end of World War II. Modernism is defined by its rejection of the literary conventions of the nineteenth century and by its opposition to conventional morality, taste, traditions, and economic values.

Monologue: A composition, written or oral, by a single individual. More specifically, a speech given by a single individual in a drama or other public entertainment. It has no set length, although it is usually several or more lines long.

Monometer: See *Meter*

Mood: The prevailing emotions of a work or of the author in his or her creation of the work. The mood of a work is not always what might be expected based on its subject matter.

Motif: A theme, character type, image, metaphor, or other verbal element that recurs throughout a single work of literature or occurs in a number of different works over a period of time.

Motiv: See *Motif*

Muckrakers: An early twentieth-century group of American writers. Typically, their works exposed the wrongdoings of big business and government in the United States.

Muses: Nine Greek mythological goddesses, the daughters of Zeus and Mnemosyne (Memory). Each muse patronized a specific area of the liberal arts and sciences. Calliope presided over epic poetry, Clio over history, Erato over love poetry, Euterpe over music or lyric poetry, Melpomene over tragedy, Polyhymnia over hymns to the gods, Terpsichore over dance, Thalia over comedy, and Urania over astronomy. Poets and writers traditionally made appeals to the Muses for inspiration in their work.

Myth: An anonymous tale emerging from the traditional beliefs of a culture or social unit. Myths use supernatural explanations for natural phenomena. They may also explain cosmic issues like creation and death. Collections of myths, known as mythologies, are common to all cultures and nations, but the best-known myths belong to the Norse, Roman, and Greek mythologies.

N

Narration: The telling of a series of events, real or invented. A narration may be either a simple narrative, in which the events are recounted chronologically, or a narrative with a plot, in which the account is given in a style reflecting the author's artistic concept of the story. Narration is sometimes used as a synonym for "storyline."

Narrative: A verse or prose accounting of an event or sequence of events, real or invented. The term is also used as an adjective in the sense "method of narration." For example, in literary criticism, the expression "narrative technique" usually refers to the way the author structures and presents his or her story.

Narrative Poetry: A nondramatic poem in which the author tells a story. Such poems may be of any length or level of complexity.

Narrator: The teller of a story. The narrator may be the author or a character in the story through whom the author speaks.

Naturalism: A literary movement of the late nineteenth and early twentieth centuries. The movement's major theorist, French novelist Emile Zola, envisioned a type of fiction that would examine human life with the objectivity of scientific inquiry. The Naturalists typically viewed human beings as either the products of "biological determinism," ruled by hereditary instincts and engaged in an endless struggle for survival, or as the products of "socioeconomic determinism," ruled by social and economic forces beyond their control. In their works, the Naturalists generally ignored the highest levels of society and focused on degradation: poverty, alcoholism, prostitution, insanity, and disease.

Negritude: A literary movement based on the concept of a shared cultural bond on the part of black Africans, wherever they may be in the world. It traces its origins to the former French colonies of Africa and the Caribbean. Negritude poets, novelists, and essayists generally stress four points in their writings: One, black alienation from traditional African culture can lead to feelings of inferiority. Two, European colonialism and Western education should be resisted. Three, black Africans should seek to affirm and define their own identity. Four, African culture can and should be reclaimed. Many Negritude writers also claim that blacks can make unique contributions to the world, based on a heightened appreciation of nature, rhythm, and human emotions—aspects of life they say are not so highly valued in the materialistic and rationalistic West.

Negro Renaissance: See *Harlem Renaissance*

Neoclassical Period: See *Neoclassicism*

Neoclassicism: In literary criticism, this term refers to the revival of the attitudes and styles of expression of classical literature. It is generally used to describe a period in European history beginning in the late seventeenth century and lasting until about 1800. In its purest form, Neoclassicism marked a return to order, proportion, restraint, logic, accuracy, and decorum. In England, where Neoclassicism perhaps was most popular, it reflected the influence of seventeenth-century French writers, especially dramatists. Neoclassical writers typically reacted against the intensity and enthusiasm of the Renaissance period. They wrote works that appealed to the intellect, using elevated language and classical literary forms such as satire and the ode. Neoclassical works were often governed by the classical goal of instruction.

Neoclassicists: See *Neoclassicism*

New Criticism: A movement in literary criticism, dating from the late 1920s, that stressed close textual analysis in the interpretation of works of literature. The New Critics saw little merit in historical and biographical analysis. Rather, they aimed to examine the text alone, free from the question of how external events—biographical or otherwise—may have helped shape it.

New Journalism: A type of writing in which the journalist presents factual information in a form usually used in fiction. New journalism emphasizes description, narration, and character development to bring readers closer to the human element of the story, and is often used in personality profiles and in-depth feature articles. It is not compatible with "straight" or "hard" newswriting, which is generally composed in a brief, fact-based style.

New Journalists: See *New Journalism*

New Negro Movement: See *Harlem Renaissance*

Noble Savage: The idea that primitive man is noble and good but becomes evil and corrupted as he becomes civilized. The concept of the noble savage originated in the Renaissance period but is more closely identified with such later writers as Jean-Jacques Rousseau and Aphra Behn.

O

Objective Correlative: An outward set of objects, a situation, or a chain of events corresponding to an inward experience and evoking this experience in the reader. The term frequently appears in modern criticism in discussions of authors' intended effects on the emotional responses of readers.

Objectivity: A quality in writing characterized by the absence of the author's opinion or feeling about the subject matter. Objectivity is an important factor in criticism.

Occasional Verse: poetry written on the occasion of a significant historical or personal event. *Vers de societe* is sometimes called occasional verse although it is of a less serious nature.

Octave: A poem or stanza composed of eight lines. The term octave most often represents the first eight lines of a Petrarchan sonnet.

Ode: Name given to an extended lyric poem characterized by exalted emotion and dignified style. An ode usually concerns a single, serious theme. Most odes, but not all, are addressed to an object or individual. Odes are distinguished from other lyric poetic forms by their complex rhythmic and stanzaic patterns.

Oedipus Complex: A son's amorous obsession with his mother. The phrase is derived from the story of the ancient Theban hero Oedipus, who un-

knowingly killed his father and married his mother.

Omniscience: See *Point of View*

Onomatopoeia: The use of words whose sounds express or suggest their meaning. In its simplest sense, onomatopoeia may be represented by words that mimic the sounds they denote such as "hiss" or "meow." At a more subtle level, the pattern and rhythm of sounds and rhymes of a line or poem may be onomatopoeic.

Oral Tradition: See *Oral Transmission*

Oral Transmission: A process by which songs, ballads, folklore, and other material are transmitted by word of mouth. The tradition of oral transmission predates the written record systems of literate society. Oral transmission preserves material sometimes over generations, although often with variations. Memory plays a large part in the recitation and preservation of orally transmitted material.

Ottava Rima: An eight-line stanza of poetry composed in iambic pentameter (a five-foot line in which each foot consists of an unaccented syllable followed by an accented syllable), following the abababcc rhyme scheme.

Oxymoron: A phrase combining two contradictory terms. Oxymorons may be intentional or unintentional.

P

Pantheism: The idea that all things are both a manifestation or revelation of God and a part of God at the same time. Pantheism was a common attitude in the early societies of Egypt, India, and Greece—the term derives from the Greek *pan* meaning "all" and *theos* meaning "deity." It later became a significant part of the Christian faith.

Parable: A story intended to teach a moral lesson or answer an ethical question.

Paradox: A statement that appears illogical or contradictory at first, but may actually point to an underlying truth.

Parallelism: A method of comparison of two ideas in which each is developed in the same grammatical structure.

Parnassianism: A mid nineteenth-century movement in French literature. Followers of the movement stressed adherence to well-defined artistic forms as a reaction against the often chaotic expression of the artist's ego that dominated the work of the Romantics. The Parnassians also rejected the moral, ethical, and social themes exhibited in the works of French Romantics such as Victor Hugo. The aesthetic doctrines of the Parnassians strongly influenced the later symbolist and decadent movements.

Parody: In literary criticism, this term refers to an imitation of a serious literary work or the signature style of a particular author in a ridiculous manner. A typical parody adopts the style of the original and applies it to an inappropriate subject for humorous effect. Parody is a form of satire and could be considered the literary equivalent of a caricature or cartoon.

Pastoral: A term derived from the Latin word "pastor," meaning shepherd. A pastoral is a literary composition on a rural theme. The conventions of the pastoral were originated by the third-century Greek poet Theocritus, who wrote about the experiences, love affairs, and pastimes of Sicilian shepherds. In a pastoral, characters and language of a courtly nature are often placed in a simple setting. The term pastoral is also used to classify dramas, elegies, and lyrics that exhibit the use of country settings and shepherd characters.

Pathetic Fallacy: A term coined by English critic John Ruskin to identify writing that falsely endows nonhuman things with human intentions and feelings, such as "angry clouds" and "sad trees."

Pen Name: See *Pseudonym*

Pentameter: See *Meter*

***Persona*:** A Latin term meaning "mask." *Personae* are the characters in a fictional work of literature. The *persona* generally functions as a mask through which the author tells a story in a voice other than his or her own. A *persona* is usually either a character in a story who acts as a narrator or an "implied author," a voice created by the author to act as the narrator for himself or herself.

***Personae*:** See *Persona*

Personal Point of View: See *Point of View*

Personification: A figure of speech that gives human qualities to abstract ideas, animals, and inanimate objects.

Petrarchan Sonnet: See *Sonnet*

Phenomenology: A method of literary criticism based on the belief that things have no existence outside of human consciousness or awareness. Proponents of this theory believe that art is a process that takes place in the mind of the observer as he or she contemplates an object rather than a quality of the object itself.

Plagiarism: Claiming another person's written material as one's own. Plagiarism can take the form of direct, word-for-word copying or the theft of the substance or idea of the work.

Platonic Criticism: A form of criticism that stresses an artistic work's usefulness as an agent of social engineering rather than any quality or value of the work itself.

Platonism: The embracing of the doctrines of the philosopher Plato, popular among the poets of the Renaissance and the Romantic period. Platonism is more flexible than Aristotelian Criticism and places more emphasis on the supernatural and unknown aspects of life.

Plot: In literary criticism, this term refers to the pattern of events in a narrative or drama. In its simplest sense, the plot guides the author in composing the work and helps the reader follow the work. Typically, plots exhibit causality and unity and have a beginning, a middle, and an end. Sometimes, however, a plot may consist of a series of disconnected events, in which case it is known as an "episodic plot."

Poem: In its broadest sense, a composition utilizing rhyme, meter, concrete detail, and expressive language to create a literary experience with emotional and aesthetic appeal.

Poet: An author who writes poetry or verse. The term is also used to refer to an artist or writer who has an exceptional gift for expression, imagination, and energy in the making of art in any form.

Poete maudit: A term derived from Paul Verlaine's *Les poetes maudits* (*The Accursed Poets*), a collection of essays on the French symbolist writers Stephane Mallarme, Arthur Rimbaud, and Tristan Corbiere. In the sense intended by Verlaine, the poet is "accursed" for choosing to explore extremes of human experience outside of middle-class society.

Poetic Fallacy: See *Pathetic Fallacy*

Poetic Justice: An outcome in a literary work, not necessarily a poem, in which the good are rewarded and the evil are punished, especially in ways that particularly fit their virtues or crimes.

Poetic License: Distortions of fact and literary convention made by a writer—not always a poet—for the sake of the effect gained. Poetic license is closely related to the concept of "artistic freedom."

Poetics: This term has two closely related meanings. It denotes (1) an aesthetic theory in literary criticism about the essence of poetry or (2) rules prescribing the proper methods, content, style, or diction of poetry. The term poetics may also refer to theories about literature in general, not just poetry.

Poetry: In its broadest sense, writing that aims to present ideas and evoke an emotional experience in the reader through the use of meter, imagery, connotative and concrete words, and a carefully constructed structure based on rhythmic patterns. Poetry typically relies on words and expressions that have several layers of meaning. It also makes use of the effects of regular rhythm on the ear and may make a strong appeal to the senses through the use of imagery.

Point of View: The narrative perspective from which a literary work is presented to the reader. There are four traditional points of view. The "third person omniscient" gives the reader a "godlike" perspective, unrestricted by time or place, from which to see actions and look into the minds of characters. This allows the author to comment openly on characters and events in the work. The "third person" point of view presents the events of the story from outside of any single character's perception, much like the omniscient point of view, but the reader must understand the action as it takes place and without any special insight into characters' minds or motivations. The "first person" or "personal" point of view relates events as they are perceived by a single character. The main character "tells" the story and may offer opinions about the action and characters which differ from those of the author. Much less common than omniscient, third person, and first person is the "second person" point of view, wherein the author tells the story as if it is happening to the reader.

Polemic: A work in which the author takes a stand on a controversial subject, such as abortion or religion. Such works are often extremely argumentative or provocative.

Pornography: Writing intended to provoke feelings of lust in the reader. Such works are often condemned by critics and teachers, but those which can be shown to have literary value are viewed less harshly.

Post-Aesthetic Movement: An artistic response made by African Americans to the black aesthetic movement of the 1960s and early '70s. Writers since that time have adopted a somewhat different tone in their work, with less emphasis placed on the disparity between black and white in the United States. In the words of post-aesthetic authors such as Toni Morrison, John Edgar Wideman, and Kristin Hunter, African Americans are portrayed as

looking inward for answers to their own questions, rather than always looking to the outside world.

Postmodernism: Writing from the 1960s forward characterized by experimentation and continuing to apply some of the fundamentals of modernism, which included existentialism and alienation. Postmodernists have gone a step further in the rejection of tradition begun with the modernists by also rejecting traditional forms, preferring the anti-novel over the novel and the anti-hero over the hero.

Pre-Raphaelites: A circle of writers and artists in mid nineteenth-century England. Valuing the pre-Renaissance artistic qualities of religious symbolism, lavish pictorialism, and natural sensuousness, the Pre-Raphaelites cultivated a sense of mystery and melancholy that influenced later writers associated with the Symbolist and Decadent movements.

Primitivism: The belief that primitive peoples were nobler and less flawed than civilized peoples because they had not been subjected to the tainting influence of society.

Projective Verse: A form of free verse in which the poet's breathing pattern determines the lines of the poem. Poets who advocate projective verse are against all formal structures in writing, including meter and form.

Prologue: An introductory section of a literary work. It often contains information establishing the situation of the characters or presents information about the setting, time period, or action. In drama, the prologue is spoken by a chorus or by one of the principal characters.

Prose: A literary medium that attempts to mirror the language of everyday speech. It is distinguished from poetry by its use of unmetered, unrhymed language consisting of logically related sentences. Prose is usually grouped into paragraphs that form a cohesive whole such as an essay or a novel.

Prosopopoeia: See *Personification*

Protagonist: The central character of a story who serves as a focus for its themes and incidents and as the principal rationale for its development. The protagonist is sometimes referred to in discussions of modern literature as the hero or anti-hero.

Proverb: A brief, sage saying that expresses a truth about life in a striking manner.

Pseudonym: A name assumed by a writer, most often intended to prevent his or her identification as the author of a work. Two or more authors may work together under one pseudonym, or an author may use a different name for each genre he or she publishes in. Some publishing companies maintain "house pseudonyms," under which any number of authors may write installations in a series. Some authors also choose a pseudonym over their real names the way an actor may use a stage name.

Pun: A play on words that have similar sounds but different meanings.

Pure Poetry: poetry written without instructional intent or moral purpose that aims only to please a reader by its imagery or musical flow. The term pure poetry is used as the antonym of the term "didacticism."

Q

Quatrain: A four-line stanza of a poem or an entire poem consisting of four lines.

R

Realism: A nineteenth-century European literary movement that sought to portray familiar characters, situations, and settings in a realistic manner. This was done primarily by using an objective narrative point of view and through the buildup of accurate detail. The standard for success of any realistic work depends on how faithfully it transfers common experience into fictional forms. The realistic method may be altered or extended, as in stream of consciousness writing, to record highly subjective experience.

Refrain: A phrase repeated at intervals throughout a poem. A refrain may appear at the end of each stanza or at less regular intervals. It may be altered slightly at each appearance.

Renaissance: The period in European history that marked the end of the Middle Ages. It began in Italy in the late fourteenth century. In broad terms, it is usually seen as spanning the fourteenth, fifteenth, and sixteenth centuries, although it did not reach Great Britain, for example, until the 1480s or so. The Renaissance saw an awakening in almost every sphere of human activity, especially science, philosophy, and the arts. The period is best defined by the emergence of a general philosophy that emphasized the importance of the intellect, the individual, and world affairs. It contrasts strongly with the medieval worldview, characterized by the dominant concerns of faith, the social collective, and spiritual salvation.

Repartee: Conversation featuring snappy retorts and witticisms.

Restoration: See *Restoration Age*

Restoration Age: A period in English literature beginning with the crowning of Charles II in 1660 and running to about 1700. The era, which was characterized by a reaction against Puritanism, was the first great age of the comedy of manners. The finest literature of the era is typically witty and urbane, and often lewd.

Rhetoric: In literary criticism, this term denotes the art of ethical persuasion. In its strictest sense, rhetoric adheres to various principles developed since classical times for arranging facts and ideas in a clear, persuasive, appealing manner. The term is also used to refer to effective prose in general and theories of or methods for composing effective prose.

Rhetorical Question: A question intended to provoke thought, but not an expressed answer, in the reader. It is most commonly used in oratory and other persuasive genres.

Rhyme: When used as a noun in literary criticism, this term generally refers to a poem in which words sound identical or very similar and appear in parallel positions in two or more lines. Rhymes are classified into different types according to where they fall in a line or stanza or according to the degree of similarity they exhibit in their spellings and sounds. Some major types of rhyme are "masculine" rhyme, "feminine" rhyme, and "triple" rhyme. In a masculine rhyme, the rhyming sound falls in a single accented syllable, as with "heat" and "eat." Feminine rhyme is a rhyme of two syllables, one stressed and one unstressed, as with "merry" and "tarry." Triple rhyme matches the sound of the accented syllable and the two unaccented syllables that follow: "narrative" and "declarative."

Rhyme Royal: A stanza of seven lines composed in iambic pentameter and rhymed *ababbcc*. The name is said to be a tribute to King James I of Scotland, who made much use of the form in his poetry.

Rhyme Scheme: See *Rhyme*

Rhythm: A regular pattern of sound, time intervals, or events occurring in writing, most often and most discernably in poetry. Regular, reliable rhythm is known to be soothing to humans, while interrupted, unpredictable, or rapidly changing rhythm is disturbing. These effects are known to authors, who use them to produce a desired reaction in the reader.

Rococo: A style of European architecture that flourished in the eighteenth century, especially in

France. The most notable features of *rococo* are its extensive use of ornamentation and its themes of lightness, gaiety, and intimacy. In literary criticism, the term is often used disparagingly to refer to a decadent or over-ornamental style.

Romance:

Romantic Age: See *Romanticism*

Romanticism: This term has two widely accepted meanings. In historical criticism, it refers to a European intellectual and artistic movement of the late eighteenth and early nineteenth centuries that sought greater freedom of personal expression than that allowed by the strict rules of literary form and logic of the eighteenth-century neoclassicists. The Romantics preferred emotional and imaginative expression to rational analysis. They considered the individual to be at the center of all experience and so placed him or her at the center of their art. The Romantics believed that the creative imagination reveals nobler truths—unique feelings and attitudes—than those that could be discovered by logic or by scientific examination. Both the natural world and the state of childhood were important sources for revelations of "eternal truths." "Romanticism" is also used as a general term to refer to a type of sensibility found in all periods of literary history and usually considered to be in opposition to the principles of classicism. In this sense, Romanticism signifies any work or philosophy in which the exotic or dreamlike figure strongly, or that is devoted to individualistic expression, self-analysis, or a pursuit of a higher realm of knowledge than can be discovered by human reason.

Romantics: See *Romanticism*

Russian Symbolism: A Russian poetic movement, derived from French symbolism, that flourished between 1894 and 1910. While some Russian Symbolists continued in the French tradition, stressing aestheticism and the importance of suggestion above didactic intent, others saw their craft as a form of mystical worship, and themselves as mediators between the supernatural and the mundane.

S

Satire: A work that uses ridicule, humor, and wit to criticize and provoke change in human nature and institutions. There are two major types of satire: "formal" or "direct" satire speaks directly to the reader or to a character in the work; "indirect" satire relies upon the ridiculous behavior of its characters to make its point. Formal satire is further divided into two manners: the "Horatian," which

ridicules gently, and the "Juvenalian," which derides its subjects harshly and bitterly.

Scansion: The analysis or "scanning" of a poem to determine its meter and often its rhyme scheme. The most common system of scansion uses accents (slanted lines drawn above syllables) to show stressed syllables, breves (curved lines drawn above syllables) to show unstressed syllables, and vertical lines to separate each foot.

Second Person: See *Point of View*

Semiotics: The study of how literary forms and conventions affect the meaning of language.

Sestet: Any six-line poem or stanza.

Setting: The time, place, and culture in which the action of a narrative takes place. The elements of setting may include geographic location, characters' physical and mental environments, prevailing cultural attitudes, or the historical time in which the action takes place.

Shakespearean Sonnet: See *Sonnet*

Signifying Monkey: A popular trickster figure in black folklore, with hundreds of tales about this character documented since the 19th century.

Simile: A comparison, usually using "like" or "as", of two essentially dissimilar things, as in "coffee as cold as ice" or "He sounded like a broken record."

Slang: A type of informal verbal communication that is generally unacceptable for formal writing. Slang words and phrases are often colorful exaggerations used to emphasize the speaker's point; they may also be shortened versions of an often-used word or phrase.

Slant Rhyme: See *Consonance*

Slave Narrative: Autobiographical accounts of American slave life as told by escaped slaves. These works first appeared during the abolition movement of the 1830s through the 1850s.

Social Realism: See *Socialist Realism*

Socialist Realism: The Socialist Realism school of literary theory was proposed by Maxim Gorky and established as a dogma by the first Soviet Congress of Writers. It demanded adherence to a communist worldview in works of literature. Its doctrines required an objective viewpoint comprehensible to the working classes and themes of social struggle featuring strong proletarian heroes.

Soliloquy: A monologue in a drama used to give the audience information and to develop the speaker's character. It is typically a projection of the speaker's innermost thoughts. Usually delivered while the speaker is alone on stage, a soliloquy is intended to present an illusion of unspoken reflection.

Sonnet: A fourteen-line poem, usually composed in iambic pentameter, employing one of several rhyme schemes. There are three major types of sonnets, upon which all other variations of the form are based: the "Petrarchan" or "Italian" sonnet, the "Shakespearean" or "English" sonnet, and the "Spenserian" sonnet. A Petrarchan sonnet consists of an octave rhymed *abbaabba* and a "sestet" rhymed either *cdecde, cdccdc,* or *cdedce.* The octave poses a question or problem, relates a narrative, or puts forth a proposition; the sestet presents a solution to the problem, comments upon the narrative, or applies the proposition put forth in the octave. The Shakespearean sonnet is divided into three quatrains and a couplet rhymed *abab cdcd efef gg.* The couplet provides an epigrammatic comment on the narrative or problem put forth in the quatrains. The Spenserian sonnet uses three quatrains and a couplet like the Shakespearean, but links their three rhyme schemes in this way: *abab bcbc cdcd ee.* The Spenserian sonnet develops its theme in two parts like the Petrarchan, its final six lines resolving a problem, analyzing a narrative, or applying a proposition put forth in its first eight lines.

Spenserian Sonnet: See *Sonnet*

Spenserian Stanza: A nine-line stanza having eight verses in iambic pentameter, its ninth verse in iambic hexameter, and the rhyme scheme abab-bcbcc.

Spondee: In poetry meter, a foot consisting of two long or stressed syllables occurring together. This form is quite rare in English verse, and is usually composed of two monosyllabic words.

Sprung Rhythm: Versification using a specific number of accented syllables per line but disregarding the number of unaccented syllables that fall in each line, producing an irregular rhythm in the poem.

Stanza: A subdivision of a poem consisting of lines grouped together, often in recurring patterns of rhyme, line length, and meter. Stanzas may also serve as units of thought in a poem much like paragraphs in prose.

Stereotype: A stereotype was originally the name for a duplication made during the printing process; this led to its modern definition as a person or thing that is (or is assumed to be) the same as all others of its type.

Stream of Consciousness: A narrative technique for rendering the inward experience of a character. This technique is designed to give the impression of an ever-changing series of thoughts, emotions, images, and memories in the spontaneous and seemingly illogical order that they occur in life.

Structuralism: A twentieth-century movement in literary criticism that examines how literary texts arrive at their meanings, rather than the meanings themselves. There are two major types of structuralist analysis: one examines the way patterns of linguistic structures unify a specific text and emphasize certain elements of that text, and the other interprets the way literary forms and conventions affect the meaning of language itself.

Structure: The form taken by a piece of literature. The structure may be made obvious for ease of understanding, as in nonfiction works, or may be obscured for artistic purposes, as in some poetry or seemingly "unstructured" prose.

Sturm und Drang: A German term meaning "storm and stress." It refers to a German literary movement of the 1770s and 1780s that reacted against the order and rationalism of the enlightenment, focusing instead on the intense experience of extraordinary individuals.

Style: A writer's distinctive manner of arranging words to suit his or her ideas and purpose in writing. The unique imprint of the author's personality upon his or her writing, style is the product of an author's way of arranging ideas and his or her use of diction, different sentence structures, rhythm, figures of speech, rhetorical principles, and other elements of composition.

Subject: The person, event, or theme at the center of a work of literature. A work may have one or more subjects of each type, with shorter works tending to have fewer and longer works tending to have more.

Subjectivity: Writing that expresses the author's personal feelings about his subject, and which may or may not include factual information about the subject.

Surrealism: A term introduced to criticism by Guillaume Apollinaire and later adopted by Andre Breton. It refers to a French literary and artistic movement founded in the 1920s. The Surrealists sought to express unconscious thoughts and feelings in their works. The best-known technique used for achieving this aim was automatic writing—transcriptions of spontaneous outpourings from the unconscious. The Surrealists proposed to unify the contrary levels of conscious and unconscious, dream and reality, objectivity and subjectivity into a new level of "super-realism."

Suspense: A literary device in which the author maintains the audience's attention through the buildup of events, the outcome of which will soon be revealed.

Syllogism: A method of presenting a logical argument. In its most basic form, the syllogism consists of a major premise, a minor premise, and a conclusion.

Symbol: Something that suggests or stands for something else without losing its original identity. In literature, symbols combine their literal meaning with the suggestion of an abstract concept. Literary symbols are of two types: those that carry complex associations of meaning no matter what their contexts, and those that derive their suggestive meaning from their functions in specific literary works.

Symbolism: This term has two widely accepted meanings. In historical criticism, it denotes an early modernist literary movement initiated in France during the nineteenth century that reacted against the prevailing standards of realism. Writers in this movement aimed to evoke, indirectly and symbolically, an order of being beyond the material world of the five senses. Poetic expression of personal emotion figured strongly in the movement, typically by means of a private set of symbols uniquely identifiable with the individual poet. The principal aim of the Symbolists was to express in words the highly complex feelings that grew out of everyday contact with the world. In a broader sense, the term "symbolism" refers to the use of one object to represent another.

Symbolist: See *Symbolism*

Symbolist Movement: See *Symbolism*

Sympathetic Fallacy: See *Affective Fallacy*

T

Tanka: A form of Japanese poetry similar to *haiku*. A *tanka* is five lines long, with the lines containing five, seven, five, seven, and seven syllables respectively.

Terza Rima: A three-line stanza form in poetry in which the rhymes are made on the last word of each line in the following manner: the first and third lines of the first stanza, then the second line of the first stanza and the first and third lines of the second stanza, and so on with the middle line of any

stanza rhyming with the first and third lines of the following stanza.

Tetrameter: See *Meter*

Textual Criticism: A branch of literary criticism that seeks to establish the authoritative text of a literary work. Textual critics typically compare all known manuscripts or printings of a single work in order to assess the meanings of differences and revisions. This procedure allows them to arrive at a definitive version that (supposedly) corresponds to the author's original intention.

Theme: The main point of a work of literature. The term is used interchangeably with thesis.

Thesis: A thesis is both an essay and the point argued in the essay. Thesis novels and thesis plays share the quality of containing a thesis which is supported through the action of the story.

Third Person: See *Point of View*

Tone: The author's attitude toward his or her audience may be deduced from the tone of the work. A formal tone may create distance or convey politeness, while an informal tone may encourage a friendly, intimate, or intrusive feeling in the reader. The author's attitude toward his or her subject matter may also be deduced from the tone of the words he or she uses in discussing it.

Tragedy: A drama in prose or poetry about a noble, courageous hero of excellent character who, because of some tragic character flaw or *hamartia*, brings ruin upon him- or herself. Tragedy treats its subjects in a dignified and serious manner, using poetic language to help evoke pity and fear and bring about catharsis, a purging of these emotions. The tragic form was practiced extensively by the ancient Greeks. In the Middle Ages, when classical works were virtually unknown, tragedy came to denote any works about the fall of persons from exalted to low conditions due to any reason: fate, vice, weakness, etc. According to the classical definition of tragedy, such works present the "pathetic"—that which evokes pity—rather than the tragic. The classical form of tragedy was revived in the sixteenth century; it flourished especially on the Elizabethan stage. In modern times, dramatists have attempted to adapt the form to the needs of modern society by drawing their heroes from the ranks of ordinary men and women and defining the nobility of these heroes in terms of spirit rather than exalted social standing.

Tragic Flaw: In a tragedy, the quality within the hero or heroine which leads to his or her downfall.

Transcendentalism: An American philosophical and religious movement, based in New England from around 1835 until the Civil War. Transcendentalism was a form of American romanticism that had its roots abroad in the works of Thomas Carlyle, Samuel Coleridge, and Johann Wolfgang von Goethe. The Transcendentalists stressed the importance of intuition and subjective experience in communication with God. They rejected religious dogma and texts in favor of mysticism and scientific naturalism. They pursued truths that lie beyond the "colorless" realms perceived by reason and the senses and were active social reformers in public education, women's rights, and the abolition of slavery.

Trickster: A character or figure common in Native American and African literature who uses his ingenuity to defeat enemies and escape difficult situations. Tricksters are most often animals, such as the spider, hare, or coyote, although they may take the form of humans as well.

Trimeter: See *Meter*

Triple Rhyme: See *Rhyme*

Trochee: See *Foot*

U

Understatement: See *Irony*

Unities: Strict rules of dramatic structure, formulated by Italian and French critics of the Renaissance and based loosely on the principles of drama discussed by Aristotle in his *Poetics*. Foremost among these rules were the three unities of action, time, and place that compelled a dramatist to: (1) construct a single plot with a beginning, middle, and end that details the causal relationships of action and character; (2) restrict the action to the events of a single day; and (3) limit the scene to a single place or city. The unities were observed faithfully by continental European writers until the Romantic Age, but they were never regularly observed in English drama. Modern dramatists are typically more concerned with a unity of impression or emotional effect than with any of the classical unities.

Urban Realism: A branch of realist writing that attempts to accurately reflect the often harsh facts of modern urban existence.

Utopia: A fictional perfect place, such as "paradise" or "heaven."

Utopian: See *Utopia*

Utopianism: See *Utopia*

V

Verisimilitude: Literally, the appearance of truth. In literary criticism, the term refers to aspects of a work of literature that seem true to the reader.

Vers de societe: See *Occasional Verse*

Vers libre: See *Free Verse*

Verse: A line of metered language, a line of a poem, or any work written in verse.

Versification: The writing of verse. Versification may also refer to the meter, rhyme, and other mechanical components of a poem.

Victorian: Refers broadly to the reign of Queen Victoria of England (1837-1901) and to anything with qualities typical of that era. For example, the qualities of smug narrowmindedness, bourgeois materialism, faith in social progress, and priggish morality are often considered Victorian. This stereotype is contradicted by such dramatic intellectual developments as the theories of Charles Darwin, Karl Marx, and Sigmund Freud (which stirred strong debates in England) and the critical attitudes of serious Victorian writers like Charles Dickens and George Eliot. In literature, the Victorian Period was the great age of the English novel, and the latter part of the era saw the rise of movements such as decadence and symbolism.

Victorian Age: See *Victorian*

Victorian Period: See *Victorian*

W

Weltanschauung: A German term referring to a person's worldview or philosophy.

Weltschmerz: A German term meaning "world pain." It describes a sense of anguish about the nature of existence, usually associated with a melancholy, pessimistic attitude.

Z

Zarzuela: A type of Spanish operetta.

Zeitgeist: A German term meaning "spirit of the time." It refers to the moral and intellectual trends of a given era.

Cumulative Author/Title Index

Cumulative
Nationality/Ethnicity Index

Cumulative Nationality/Ethnicity Index

Subject/Theme Index

Subject/Theme Index